PENTAGON'S

SOUTH ASIA DEFENCE AND STRATEGIC YEAR BOOK

2013

The view expressed in the various articles are those of the authors.

The boundaries of India, the alignment of the Line of Control, the Actual Ground Position Line and the Line of Actual Control shown in the maps and illustrations in this book are neither authentic nor correct and are only representational.

Acknowledgments

- The data for the Country Reports has been obtained from the US Library of Congress website, CIA handbook website and UNO website, besides other sources.
- The data for the Military Balance has been obtained from the International Institute of Strategic Studies, US Department of Defense Annual Reports, and Center for Strategic and International Studies, besides other sources.
- The report on Terrorism has been obtained from the South Asia Terrorism portal website.

PENTAGON'S

SOUTH ASIA DEFENCE AND STRATEGIC YEAR BOOK

2013

Editor

Col Harjeet Singh (Retd)

PENTAGON PRESS

Published by
PENTAGON PRESS
206 Peacock Lane, Shahpur Jat
New Delhi-110049 (India)
Phones:+91-11 6470 6243, 2649 1568
Fax:+91-11-26490600
email: rajan@pentagonpress.in
www. pentagonpress.in

Printed at Aegean Offset Printers, Greater Noida

Cataloging in Publication Data--DK
Courtesy: D.K. Agencies (P) Ltd. <docinfo@dkagencies.com>

Pentagon's South Asia Defence and Strategic Year Book, 2013 /
editor, Harjeet Singh.
p. cm.
Includes bibliographical references.
ISBN 9788182747128

1. South Asia—Defenses—Periodicals. 2. National security—South Asia—Periodicals. 3. South Asian cooperation—Periodicals. I. Harjeet Singh.

DDC 355.033054 23

एयर चीफ मार्शल एन ए के ब्राउन
प वि से मे अ वि से मे वा मे एडीसी
Air Chief Marshal N A K Browne
PVSM AVSM VM ADC

Tel : (011) Off : 23012517
Res : 23017300
Fax : 23018853

Email : hawkeye@bol.net.in

वायु सेना मुख्यालय
नई दिल्ली-110106
Air Headquarters
New Delhi - 110 106

FOREWORD

South Asia is at cusp of history. Home to some of the fastest growing economics of the world, this region today is witnessing fierce resource competition amongst its major players. The ever increasing threat of terrorism, transnational as well as home grown, has added another worrying dimension to the already delicate security situation. Needless to say, world's geostrategic attention today has shifted to the Asia-Pacific region. Going by the current geopolitical trends, the Asian region will continue to occupy a pre-eminent place in the global strategic consciousness.

The South Asia region – one of the most culturally diverse regions in the world, is transforming the economic conditions of its people and playing a significant role in the development of human civilisation. If the present trends in GDP growth continue, then in the next two decades China is likely to be the largest economy in the world, US the second largest and India the third largest economy. However, if South Asian countries were to develop an integrated economy, then South Asia could become the second largest economy in the world after China. Given the geographic proximity and economic complementarities between South Asia on the one hand and China on the other, this region therefore, has the potential to become the greatest economic powerhouse in human history.

Geopolitics is not just relevant in the military-strategic sphere only. The Afghan endgame is inspiring several tracks in the geopolitics of the region – the US "Pivot to Asia" being the latest initiative in this regard. Today Asia is an important determinant of global outcomes in a wide variety of matters ranging from the environment issues on one hand to nuclear proliferation on the other. Nuclearisation, particularly in the Asian Context projects some very peculiar dynamics. It is difficult to say whether this has contributed to strategic stability or instability in the region

Regional organisations in every continent are becoming stronger. While each will follow its own version of economic and political integration, security related issues have acquired new transnational dimensions and these have to be dealt with quite differently from traditional security concerns. While sovereignty and territorial integrity remain the foundation of the international system, India envisages a region where stability and cooperation prevail. In addition, there is a need to ensure maritime security for all nations and a collective ability to deal with non-traditional security threats. Apart from the 90% of global commerce in goods and 65% of world oil supplies that are carried by sea, today 95% of internet traffic today is carried by undersea cables. Over a hundred thousand ships pass through the sea lanes near India each year. India had a stark reminder of threats from the sea when, on 26/11 terrorists came from Karachi by sea to attack Mumbai. The criticality of the sea lanes need no reminding of the importance of the oceans and of the common interest of littoral and other major powers in keeping them open and free. And yet most of the debate among strategists on this issue is phrased solely in adversarial terms, as a zero sum game.

A change is required in the policy paradigm of nation states: from competition to cooperation, from the production of new weapons as emblems of state power to the nurturing of a new sensibility that can sustain life on earth. We need to create an atmosphere of greater inter-governmental coordination to contain the transnational network of terrorist, arms proliferation and religion radicalisation. We also need to build new structures that can cope with new dimensions of security such as the power of non state actors. These structures must be inclusive, networked and flexible enough to avoid the inadequacies of existing international organizations to counter the nature of the threats that we face. This is a historic moment for the people of South Asia to recognize that they have a new tryst with destiny. They are affirming that their security and wellbeing lies not in inter-state conflict but in peace and cooperation.

In this endeavour, publications like the "South Asia Defence & Strategic Year Book" are doing a yeoman service in bringing such issues to the forefront with clarity, comprehensiveness and candour. This facilitates changing of mindsets and thereby the contours of relationships within the region, and the world. My sincere compliments to the editorial team for this meticulous effort.

Jai Hind !

Air Chief Marshal
Chief of the Air Staff

01 Jan 13

CONTENTS

COUNTRY STUDIES

MILITARY BALANCE

TERRORISM

FEATURES

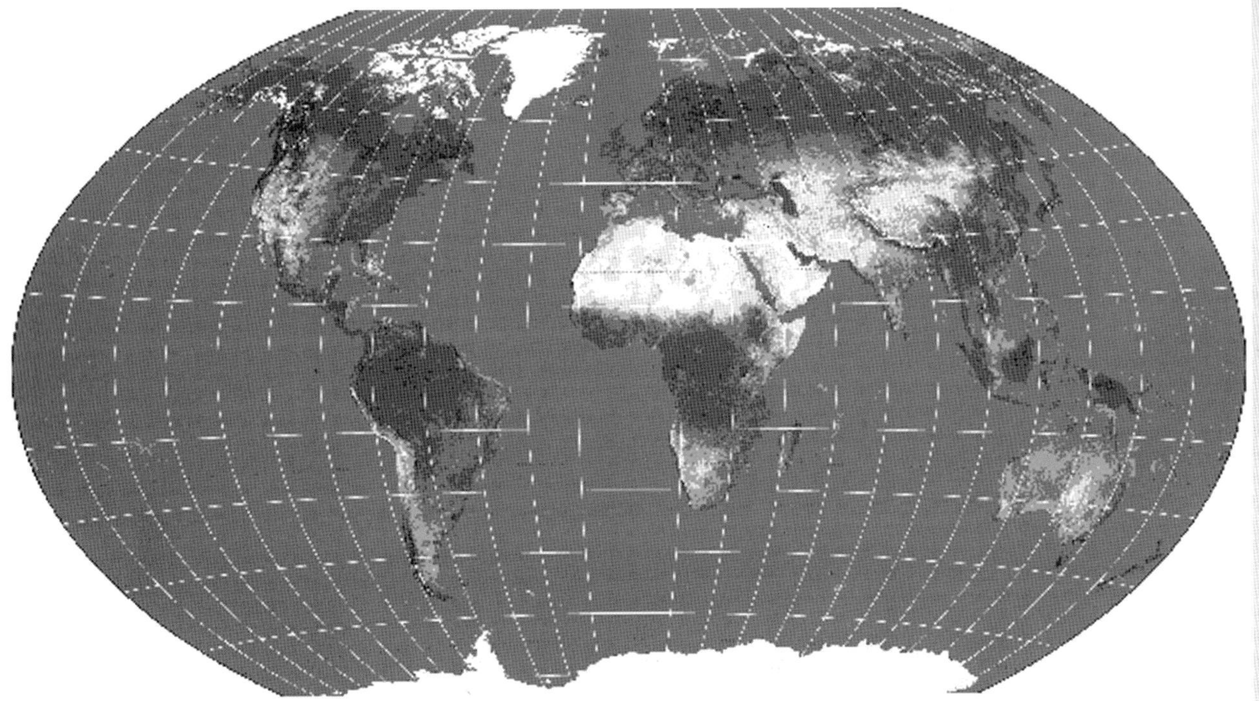

PERSPECTIVE ON SOUTH ASIA

"All things are subject to interpretation; whichever interpretation prevails at a given time is a function of power and not truth."

—Friedrich Nietzsche

Overview

World security is becoming more dynamic, complex and transnational, with intensified and increasing flows of information, people, capital and goods. States continue to be the dominant security actors, but there is a growing importance of non- and quasi-state actors in shaping the global and regional security scene. The security governance system—the institutions, agreements and processes to manage the challenges of global and regional security, armaments and disarmament—is under mounting pressure. Many organisations that promote peace and security find it increasingly difficult to generate the political will and financial resources that are required to meet their mandates or to establish needed governance mechanisms. In light of these challenges, the world is likely to face a difficult period of growing uncertainty and fragility, and a diffusion of risks and threats.

Commentators on the international security situation frequently remark on the continued expansion of the role and impact of 'new powers' at global and regional levels. The global and regional security governance institutions need to accelerate the equitable integration of these powers. Such steps could include an expansion in the permanent membership of the UN Security Council and a more active security-related role for the Group of 20 (G20) major economies.

South Asia is traditionally defined as the region ensconced between Afghanistan and Bangladesh. Poverty, corruption, lack of governance, as well as social and regional apartheid still drive the political discourse of the region. The fact that the countries of the region have strained relations with each other accentuates the lack of trust and sense of despair. South Asia has changed and so has the basis of US and other big powers' relations with it. The currents of change, spawned by globalisation, the region's nuclearisation, resurgence of China and the emerging shift in the balance of power in Asia, the rise of religious extremism and war on terrorism, have been flowing in varying directions presenting new threats, challenges and opportunities.

The past year has witnessed dramatic developments within South Asia and the region's evolving relations with the US, China, Russia, Japan, Iran, the Middle East and the Central Asia. Pakistan, both as a partner and a potential target , in the war against religious extremism and terrorism, has become a major foreign policy challenge for the US and is likely to occupy an important place in the national security and foreign of America for some time. The region also compels attention because of great strategic and economic opportunities especially in India with its projection of military power, marked economic and technological achievement and potential, its democratic structure, and its aspirations for big power status and a plausible balancer of China. Also requiring mention is the manner in which the US and its energy deficient allies, Europe and Japan, are coordinating their policies to promote regional peace and stability in South Asia and pursuing a policy of benign encirclement of China and containment of Russia by courting countries on their periphery.

The regional diatribe notwithstanding, South Asia has experienced extreme external pressures due to the west-sponsored war on terror. For the last three decades, the region has seen external forces in military expeditions to further their interests in Afghanistan—Soviet and American. This has enabled Pakistan to spread its terror module to ensure control of a pliant Afghanistan regime once the Americans depart, i.e. if they do. India finds its interests in Afghanistan severely degraded because of Pakistan's intransigence.

With each passing day, Pakistan is becoming an even more crucial player in world affairs. Home of the world's second largest Muslim population, epicentre of the global jihad, location of perhaps the planet's most dangerous borderlands, and armed with nuclear weapons, this South Asian nation will go a long way toward determining what the world looks like a decade from now.

The countries of the region have to take a call on the larger picture—sail or sink together or be fragmented and status quoists propelling the region towards greater darkness.

Afghanistan

After more than a decade of war, the United States and its NATO partners plan to withdraw most of their military forces from Afghanistan by the end of 2014. Although coalition forces succeeded in their mission to oust al Qaeda, the Taliban remains a resilient fighting force. Elements of the Afghan government are perceived to be corrupt, undermining US efforts to develop it into a credible agency for governance. These challenges raise questions about the feasibility of US and NATO plans to drawdown their forces while preserving the hard-fought gains of the last decade. Over the next two years coalition forces will seek to prevent a Taliban resurgence and strengthen Afghan security forces, while partnering with an imperfect civilian government. Constitutional term limits prevent Karzai from running again, and no clear frontrunner has emerged.

Western publics have grown weary of the war—a trend exacerbated by the recent rise of insider, or "green-on- blue," attacks on ISAF forces by their Afghan counterparts. The war's cost, both human and financial, weighs on coalition nations. More than 2,000 Americans have been killed and more than 17,500 wounded in 11 years of war. Approximately 70 percent have died since the surge began in 2009. According to a 2012 study by the Centre for Strategic and International Studies, the war's costs total nearly $650 billion - $198 billion of which will be spent in 2012 and 2013.

Despite the campaign against them by the International Security Assistance Force (ISAF) and the progressively strengthening Afghan National Security Forces (ANSF), as well as the growing popular resentment and resistance, the Taliban have, nevertheless, gained steadily in strength and intensity of operations since 2006, when they restored their campaigns with Pakistan's visible (though vociferously denied) support. The statistics of the casualties (killed) in Afghanistan are at the Table below. There is some evidence, however, of a slowdown and a significant challenge to their dominance in wide areas of the country over the past months.

Years	*ANA*	*ANP*	*ISAF*	*Civilian*	*Militant*	*Total*
2007	278	688	232	1523	4500	7221
2008	259	724	295	2118	5000	8396
2009	292	639	521	2412	4610	8474
2010	821	1292	711	2777	5225	10826
2011	511	569	566	3021	4275	8942
2012	188	245	382	1463	2539	4817
Total*	2349	4157	2707	13314	26149	48676

Source: *Institute for Conflict Management*, *Data till 18 November 2012.

China Rising

The Chinese challenge to US primacy and the liberal democratic order is far more potent than that of the previous contenders. China is a multi-dimensional (economic, military, scientific and technological) superpower. Just as no great power goes quietly, no great power arrives quietly. Rising powers are never status-quo powers. Whenever opportunity presents itself, they flex their muscles and test influence. New players don't play by the old rules. They seek to recast their region in their image. In times of power transitions, rising powers seek to remake existing international systems. China remains a non-status-quo power—in terms of territory, status and influence. Like other great powers in the past, China is also laying down new markers, drawing new lines in the land, water, sand and snow all around its periphery. Increased assertiveness signals transition from Deng Xiaoping's strategic directive of "hiding capabilities to bide our time, and never taking the lead" to "seizing opportunities, taking the lead and showing off capabilities to shape others' choices in China's favour."

Power shifts have already created pressure for the reform of global institutions in which China, India and other emerging economies are not fully represented: the World Bank and the IMF and the UN Security Council. The exclusive G-7 has given way to the G-20. There has been a proliferation of regional and global organisations in sync with the re-configuration of power: APEC, ARF, APT, BRICS, IBSA, EAS, and ADMM+8.

China's size, historical grievances, level of development, and nationalist aspirations dictate that Beijing only plays by Western rules when those are to its advantage. Chinese strategic writings indicate a preference for a uni-polar Asia with China at the centre of regional order and a multi-polar world. Naturally, this makes it hard for China to accept any externally imposed barriers to its growth. Beijing's policies on climate change, nuclear non-proliferation, world trade and UN Security Council reform are a sign of times to come. In commenting on the failure of the Copenhagen climate negotiations, the Chinese Ambassador for Climate Change, Yu Qingtai, drew the ominous lesson that "the developed countries need to make up their minds whether they want to pursue confrontation or co-operation with China."

The financial aid and bailouts that China can offer to recession-hit countries surpass those of existing international financial institutions. China has shown willingness to use its growing financial influence in international institutions such as the ADB and the IMF to wield veto power over rescue packages for countries that do not comply with its political demands—especially over issues such as Tibet and Taiwan. However, discord between "China and the rest" could still make the West prevail. China is a polarizing rising power. Among regional countries, China will continue to arouse unease because of its size, history, proximity, power, unresolved territorial/ maritime disputes, and more importantly, because memories of the tributary state system have not dimmed. The United States will, therefore, remain the balancer of choice for most countries on China's periphery and elsewhere.

In particular, the Sino-Indian relationship will be marked by a "positional" rivalry in multilateral forums—a concern over their relative positions in the regional and global hierarchy. With the notable exception of environment and some trade issues, there are not many issues of collaboration and cooperation between China and India. In fact, far from mitigating their power competition, regional and international organisations will become the new arenas of Sino-Indian rivalry for maximizing relative power and for gaining advantage and influence.

China, the rising giant, has deepened its political and economic engagement with the countries of South Asia, which is about the least integrated part of the world. Neighbours supply just 0.5% of India's imports, and consume less than 4% of its exports. India and Pakistan, mutually antagonistic, account for a fifth of all living humans, yet their bilateral trade is miniscule, at less than $3 billion a year.

Chinese diplomatic and economic footprint has expanded to an extent where it is reportedly being handed over Gilgit-Baltistan by Pakistan on a lease for 50 years. Constitutionally and legally, Pakistan-Occupied Kashmir and Gilgit-Baltistan are still being claimed by New Delhi. And this claim has been recognised by the international community. Pakistan's military chief Ashfaq Parvez Kayani said, in June 2012, that the two countries are starting a strategic programme—the Pakistan-China Strategic Programme for Gilgit-Baltistan. Eventually it will enable China to have more military presence in the region. China does understand that having control over Gilgit-Baltistan is important to safeguard its economic and military interests in east Turkistan and Tibet, besides having more access to the Persian Gulf and Afghanistan. Depending on the choices made by the countries, this may be a zero sum game adding fuel to the now emerging cold war between US and China in the region.

China announced that its annual military expenditure will exceed $100 billion for the first time in 2012. At 670.274 billion yuan ($106.39 billion), the 2012 budget is up 11.2% on last year's $92 billion. It represents another year of double digit growth for China's military spending. It dwarfs India's 2012 spending, reported to be around $36 billion and has led some commentators to suggest it could heighten friction in the region. Of further concern is the allegation that this figure only represents about half of China's true spending on defence since the Chinese budget does not include modernisation, dual-use technologies, R&D aspects and export-import numbers. Western estimates say the actual figure should be at least double, although Indian estimates place the budget at $150 billion rather than the Pentagon's $220 billion figure. China is not just buying more defence equipment; it is also in the process of creating an entire defence industrial base. Over the longer term, this will challenge the West both in terms of innovation and exports.

Bangladesh

More than 160 million people—greater than the population of Russia—populate Bangladesh's sea-level, semi-aquatic landscape. While the northern part of the country is prone to drought, the flatlands of southern Bangladesh are threatened by rising sea levels, which deplete soil with the addition of salt. In other words, the country is squeezed by water problems from both directions. What's more, the country's rough terrain has hindered both internal economic development and trade. That could change if China, India, and Myanmar open trade routes through Bangladesh. Geography has been a curse to Bangladesh, threatened as it is by both drought and rising sea levels. But geography could become a blessing in an era that might see routes and pipelines operating in many directions, organically connecting the Indian subcontinent with Tibet and China.

Foreign Policy Magazine Failed States Index 2012

Rank	*Total*	*Country*	*Demographic Pressures*	*Refugees/ DPs*	*Group Grievances*	*Human Flight*	*Uneven Development*	*Economic Decline*	*Delegitimisation of the State*	*Public Services*	*Human Rights*	*Security Apparatus*	*Factionalized Elites*	*External Intervention*
6	106.0	Afghanistan	8.9	9.0	9.4	7.4	8.1	7.7	9.5	8.5	8.5	9.7	9.4	10.0
13	101.6	Pakistan	8.5	9.0	9.6	7.2	8.2	7.2	.3	7.0	8.6	9.3	9.1	9.4
21	96.2	Myanmar	7.9	8.2	8.7	5.7	8.7	7.6	9.4	8.4	8.6	7.5	8.6	6.9
27	93.0	Nepal	7.7	7.7	9.0	5.6	8.4	7.6	8.0	7.4	8.2	7.5	8.2	7.4
29	92.2	Bangladesh	8.0	6.8	8.9	7.8	8.1	7.4	8.2	7.8	6.8	7.6	8.9	5.9
29	92.2	Sri Lanka	7.1	8.7	9.1	7.1	8.1	5.6	8.1	5.8	8.7	8.2	9.2	6.5
59	82.4	Bhutan	6.7	6.6	7.6	6.5	7.8	6.6	6.3	6.6	7.3	5.9	7.5	7.0
76	78.3	China												
78	78.0	India												

Trade Ties—India and Pakistan

New thinking argues that the peaceful resolution of Kashmir can go hand in hand with trade normalisation between India and Pakistan. However, most people subscribe to the traditional view that Indo-Pak relations cannot be normalised unless the core issue of Kashmir is settled. The idea of according Most-Favoured Nation in trade ties between the two countries is thus held hostage to history. It needs to be appreciated that no single issue should be allowed to impede progress in other areas of cooperation between India and Pakistan.

In the face of massive economic challenges, a burgeoning population, energy and water shortages, and huge and growing numbers of unemployed workers, especially youth, Pakistan needs to look for ways to move itself out of the economic hole into which it has fallen. Greater trade with India offers an immediate and rich possibility of economic growth for both Pakistan and India. Recent meetings between the commerce ministers of both countries in New Delhi appear to have yielded some good intentions to increase trade from its current level of $2 billion a year to $6 billion, still well below what many scholars estimate to be the potential.

The size of Pakistan's domestic market is only $180 billion (GDP). Currently, its share of global trade is only 0.14 percent. Even a 0.5 percent share in the global export market implies that its exports could rise from the current $25 billion to $60 billion, creating millions of jobs. Trade between India and Pakistan could increase threefold if Pakistan followed India's example and accorded India Most Favored Nation (MFN) status, and both countries imposed a maximum tariff rate of 50 percent.

MFN status is no special preference to India. It is a normal trading relationship Pakistan enjoys with the rest of the world. Pakistani industry and exports will improve by MFN-inspired competitiveness. Obsession with nuclear power borders on insanity. Confrontation is no longer the exclusive licence to patriotism. The paradigm of a national security state must give way to the imperative of a national welfare state, which is not possible without normal trading with India.

Table: India-Pakistan Trade (US $ Millions)

Year	Pakistan's Exports to India	India's Exports to Pakistan	Trade Flows
2004–05	288	547	835
2005–06	293	802	1,095
2006–07	343	1,235	1,578
2007–08	255	1,701	1,956
2008–09	320	1,914	2,234

Source: Federal Bureau of Statistics, Pakistan; Reserve Bank of India.

According to the Board of Investment in Pakistan, the FDI was US$485 million during 2001-02, after which there was a steady increase for the next six years. The FDI peaked during 2007-08, reaching US$5409 million. Since then, there has been a steady decline to the current 2011-12 level. In a nutshell, if the peak during 2007-08 is to be taken as a benchmark between 2001 and 2012, there was an increase by 10-15 per cent till 2007-08, and then a steady 89 per cent decline till 2011-12.

Foreign Direct Investment in Pakistan since 2001 (in US$ million)

2001-02:	485
2004-05:	1,524
2006-07:	5139.60
2007-08:	5,409.80
2008-09:	3,719.90
2009-10:	2,150.80
2010-11:	1,739.40
2011-12:	595.1 (Up to April 2012)

Source: Board of Investment.

Table: India's Major Trading Partners 2009–10 (Percentage % Share)

Country	Exports	Country	Imports
USA	10.9	China	15.0
UAE	13.4	UAE	11.4
Japan	9.2	Switzerland	8.6
Germany	7.1	S. Arabia	7.1
UK	6.4	USA	7.0
Singapore	2.2		
Total (US $ Billions)	178	Total (US $ Billions)	287

Source: Department of Commerce, India.

Table: Pakistan's Major Trading Partners 2009–10 (Percentage % Share)

Country	Exports	Country	Imports
USA	17.4	UAE	14.5
UAE	8.9	Saudi Arabia	9.7
Afghanistan	8.1	Kuwait	6.9
UK	4.9	Malaysia	5.0
Germany	4.3	USA	4.6
Hong Kong	2.2	Japan	4.4
		Germany	3.4
		UK	1.7
Total (US $ Billions)	19.3	Total(US $ Billions)	34.7

Source: Federal Bureau of Statistics, Government of Pakistan

Security in South Asia

The 1990's saw the international security debate expand radically. Concepts such as 'human security' and 'non-traditional security' became part of the discussions. By the early 2000's, it was no longer considered illogical to argue for the meaning of security to go beyond state stability and regime survival, and refer also to the safety and well-being of individuals and communities from a range of threats. Yet in South Asia, these discussions were few and far between. This remains the case even today.

It is not surprising then, that there is very little by way of a solid academic or policy-oriented understanding of the issues which prevent South Asians from living lives free from fear and want—two essential components of security as enshrined in the UN Charter and highlighted in particular by human security proponents. Perhaps a little ironic, since South Asia is home to the world's largest concentration of the poor and hungry. Already, it faces colossal resource constrains in the face of growing populations, diminishing arable land, increasing water scarcity and high vulnerability to climate change. The latter in particular poses a critical threat to agriculture, rural livelihoods and coastal urban population centres in the region. Socio-economic inequalities together with ethnic and religious cleavages threaten to add further complexity to these circumstances. Finally, these dynamics also impinge significantly on concerns around political instability and violence in a region where most countries have weak governance institutions, lacking adequate capacity and often riddled with corruption.

Opening up the study of security in the region to include these issue areas reveals that the state is not the only (and in some cases even the primary) security actor in South Asia. It helps unearth a previously unnoticed, sub-state layer of security governance and related practices led by non-state actors (NSAs). These include including non-governmental organisations (NGOs), civil society groups and networks, epistemic communities (i.e. knowledge-based communities of experts) and media organisations.

Security continues to be viewed in limited terms in South Asia. For hundreds of millions of South Asians, daily life is a ruthless battle. It involves being assaulted brutally by insecurities arising from socio-economic, political, environmental and even military threats to their lives and livelihoods. Despite this, at the national level, South Asian countries remain stuck to a simplistic and narrow view of what security means, i.e. the safety of the state (or regime) from military threats.

It is a view which stands fundamentally challenged in the globalised, post Cold War world. The case for a wider understanding of security is now well-established, and in many countries, regional institutions and international organisations, academic and policy debates are informed in this way.

For South Asia, the narrow approach to security is unhelpful in at least two ways. One, it makes it very difficult for a more people-oriented, holistic and inclusive understanding of security to emerge, despite it being highly relevant to the needs of South Asians. When thinking of security, policymakers continue to be driven by the limited, state-centric approach. Likewise, security analysts continue to look to the state when seeking expressions of insecurity, while ignoring other similar expressions at the sub-state level.

Five million illegal immigrants are residing in Pakistan in different parts of the country due to local and regional disturbances. Approximately two million were Bangladeshis, 2.5 million were Afghans, and 0.5 million other nationals, including Africans, Iranians, Iraqis and Myanmarese, who had been living in the country for more than three decades.

Managing South Asia's Himalayan Rivers

The great Himalayan rivers of South Asia, particularly the Ganges and Brahmaputra, have been the subject of decades of discussion between governments of the region. These rivers have contributed, through flood and drought, to the uncertainty and impoverishment of the lives of the largest concentration of poor people anywhere in the world. Their chances for prosperity can be increased by harnessing the potential of these rivers for irrigation and power, by controlling their perils (such as floods), and managing them in the face of increasing threats from climate change.

Various climatic and social changes have transformed the context for cooperation over the Himalayan rivers. The conventional wisdom was that these waterways had stable futures, that social interaction with the rivers was guided by the demands of agrarian economies and that trans-boundary negotiations could be approached through traditional diplomacy. At the beginning of the 21st century, these three assumptions have changed. Glacial melt and climate change have undermined the assumption that these rivers hold a stable future. The rapid growth of industrial economies in India and China will change the predominant social demands on the rivers from those of agrarian societies to those of industrial ones, and will insert China as a possible major player in the discussion.

While in the 1990s, several international agreements, particularly between India and Nepal, established important precedents for cooperation over water, the potential for reduced conflict and greatly improved regional development has only partly been realised. There is a lack of an institutional framework for overall evaluation and facilitating implementation. More recently, a wave of hydroelectric projects in the Himalayan valleys of India, Pakistan and Nepal has raised concerns. Foreign capital, including from China, adds to the complexity of the situation. China's own hydroelectric projects on the Tsangpo-Brahmaputra have potentially important implications for Bangladesh and India.

One possible path to best manage the rivers would be a new regulatory body that encompasses all the nations with stakes in the Himalayan rivers. This body would incorporate a mix of expertise and interests—including a panel of technical experts, experienced diplomats from each country and representatives of key interest groups. A new water regulatory institution could serve as a knowledge clearing house and source of technical information for a range of water issues. It could also monitor the health of river basins, the progress of various projects and adherence to international agreements.

From India's perspective, China's presence in such a body would unavoidably change the strategic balance of South Asian river discussions, reducing India's bargaining power or ability to act relatively unilaterally as a result of its dominant position in South Asia. Yet China's ability to drastically affect water supplies throughout South Asia, particularly as the impacts of climate change become more severe, means that its inclusion is necessary and potentially valuable to all parties. The participation of both Chinese and Indians in the International Centre for Integrated Mountain Development (ICIMOD), including senior politicians and technical experts, indicates that cooperation between the two giants in this sphere is feasible. A new basis for Himalayan cooperation would make possible new water and environmental management initiatives, both small and large scale.

The history of managing the Mekong basin, from the control of colonial powers to a Mekong River Commission that does not include major upstream nations (China and Myanmar), indicates some of the problems with traditional nationalist approaches to multilateral cooperation, as well as the limitations of investment-oriented multilateral institutions. There is no ideal or easy solution and the success of any institution depends on the specifics of design and implementation. The importance and urgency of the problem requires some institutional innovation, and design and implementation can only occur once the idea has been firmly placed on the agenda of policy makers in the countries at risk from future water shortages and crises.

China and India as Strategic Partners

Before the arrival of the British East India Company in the late 18th century, the sub-continent's share in world manufacturing was 24.5 percent in 1750 (32.8 percent for China). But by the time the British had finished with India, the sub-continent's share had fallen to 1.7 percent (in 1900) and that of the British increased from 1.9 percent (in 1750) to 22.9 percent (in 1880).

The transfer of wealth from Hindustan to Great Britain is defined by the bald figures below, which hide tens of millions of deaths in famines, destruction of India's industry and massive transfer of wealth following the onset of colonialism.

Table: Relative Shares of World Manufacturing Output 1750-1900

	1750	*1800*	*1830*	*1860*	*1880*	*1900*
(Europe as a whole)	23.2	28.1	34.2	53.2	61.3	62.0
United Kingdom	1.9	4.3	9.5	19.9	22.9	18.5
Habsburg Empire	2.9	3.2	3.2	4.2	4.4	4.7
France	4.0	4.2	5.2	7.9	7.8	6.8
German States/Germany	2.9	3.5	3.5	4.9	8.5	13.2
Italian States/Italy	2.4	2.5	2.3	2.5	2.5	2.5
Russia	5.0	5.6	5.6	7.0	7.6	8.8
United States	0.1	0.8	2.4	7.2	14.7	23.6
Japan	3.8	3.5	2.8	2.6	2.4	2.4
Third World	73.0	67.7	60.5	36.6	20.9	11.0
China	32.8	33.3	29.8	19.7	12.5	6.2
Indian subcontinent	24.5	19.7	17.6	8.6	2.8	1.7

Source: Paul Kennedy; The Rise and Fall of the Great Powers: Economic Change and Military Conflict from 1500 to 2000 (London: Fontana Press, 1989)

It is becoming quite obvious that the balance of global economic power is moving away from developed countries to developing countries. China has overtaken Germany to become the largest exporting country, and has surpassed Japan to become the second-largest economy in the world. China and India are projected to be the two fastest-growing economies of the world over the next several decades.

The economic rise of China and India, though it lags behind, is accompanied by a roughly commensurate rise in their political and military weight. Although they confront many problems at home encouraging overwhelming preoccupation with domestic political affairs, the growing relative power of these emerging economies has enhanced the potential of military strategic competition.

Economics is driving India and China closer together. China became India's largest trading partner in 2008, and India–China trade hit US$60 billion this year. The leaders have set a target of US$100 billion of two-way trade by 2015. China and India are also pursuing similar energy strategies via state firms and in developing economies.

Challenges in Myanmar

Myanmar's road to democracy is proving hard. President Thein Sein has declared the changes irreversible and worked to build a durable partnership with the opposition. While the process remains incomplete, political prisoners have been released, blacklists trimmed, freedom of assembly laws implemented, and media censorship abolished. The promising narrative of the recent past in Myanmar has, however, been marred by the ethnic violence facing the country's young hybrid civilian-military government. Violence between the Arakanese (or Rakhine) and Rohingya communities erupted again in October, leaving at least 56 dead. In June, scores were killed and more than 70,000, mostly Rohingya, were left homeless in another bloody spasm in Arakan state. Many remain without shelter today, living in the most basic of refugee camps. A ceasefire in Kachin State remains elusive. Political leaders have conflicting views about how power should be shared under the constitution after the 2015 election.

The bloodshed has polarized Myanmar. Some people from the ethnic Bamar (or Burman) nationality, which shares a Buddhist faith with the Arakanese, accuse the Muslim Rohingya of being recent illegal immigrants from nearby Bangladesh. They contend that the Rohingya, most of who do not have Burmese citizenship, should be deported. The Bangladeshi government also refuses most members of the 800,000-strong community citizenship. The Arakanese feel that the Rohingya are waging a kind of fertility war by procreating more prolifically than the local Buddhist population. The United Nations has labelled the Rohingya one of the world's most oppressed minorities.

President Thein Sein has stated that the Rohingya are not Burmese nationals. Earlier, he prevented the Organisation of the Islamic Conference from opening up offices in Burma, after Buddhist clerics protested the Muslim body's proposed entry into the country. Even Burma's democracy icon Aung San Suu Kyi has tended to shy away publicly from the ethnic issue.

Kyaukphyu, on an island off the Arakan coast, is the starting point of the controversial Shwe energy pipeline project that will feed China. The project has angered Arakan locals because much of the state is without electricity, even though rich natural-gas reserves are located just offshore. A special economic zone is being planned for Kyaukphyu, which will include a deep-sea port for ships from the Middle East to disgorge oil and send it by land to China, thereby allowing Beijing to avoid the pirate-plagued Malacca Strait. Much of current overseas investment in the area comes from South Korea, China and India.

Rich in timber, hydropower, natural gas, diamonds, and even uranium, Myanmar has suffered from decades of economic stasis under repressive military rule. But if the country can continue to open up politically, as it has done over the past year, it could in turn fashion itself into a crucial throughway connecting China with the Bay of Bengal. At the moment, China relies heavily on the Strait of Malacca, a roundabout route farther south, to ship exports out from the South China Sea, while oil and natural gas from the Middle East reach China only after travelling across the Indian Ocean and through the strait. China and India are both developing offshore natural gas fields and building ports in the region; if these two economic superpowers are permitted to build pipelines across Myanmar, the newly resurgent country could unite the subcontinent with East Asia, allowing a real Indo-Pacific region to take hold.

Comparisons have been drawn between Afghanistan and Myanmar as two challenging vectors of India's neighbourhood policy. Crafting policy toward countries in transition is always challenging. It must be remembered that over 2 million Indians were summarily told to leave that country by the Rangoon authorities in the 1950s and the ministry of external affairs in South Block kept a unit till the end of seventies tasked with coordinating the rehabilitation of 'Burmese refugees.'

The British who were Burma's 'saviours' in World War II had the experience of being overnight eased out once their job was accomplished. The sudden decision by Nay Pyi Taw last year to suspend work on the country's biggest hydroelectric project financed by China Power Investment Corporation shows Beijing's experience is no different, either. This despite China being Myanmar's biggest investor, with Chinese companies having pledged more than $14 billion investment in Myanmar's 2010-2011 fiscal year, taking the total investment pledges to $20 billion.

Myanmar is a highly nationalistic country, which has a highly focused mind with a steely resolve. The political transformation in Myanmar—transition to democracy as well as national reconciliation—is essentially an indigenous effort. The dexterity with which Aung San Suu Kyi, leader of the opposition in Myanmar, has shown that she is neither a pushover nor a recalcitrant opponent of the regime shows how there is going to be a 'Myanmarese way' out of military authoritarianism. Myanmar is unlikely to make any major policy shift toward China or India following its reengagement with the west.

Climate Change

Global efforts have been slow on climate change, despite active efforts by those supporting the United Nations Framework Convention on Climate Change to forge an international consensus to limit greenhouse gas emissions. At the same time, global emissions continue to rise, and have increased by more than 3 percent since 2011. The frequency of extremely hot events (such as the droughts which inflicted the US and Russia in 2012) has risen by a factor of around 50 by comparison to the decades before 1980. Forty years ago, extreme summer heat typically affected between 0.1 and 0.2% of the globe. Today it scorches some 10%. This is where we stand with just 0.8 degrees of global warming and a 30% loss of summer sea ice. The consequences of global warming can be clearly seen in the Arctic. In 2012 the summer melting of sea ice in the Arctic reached a record high, which may further accelerate future global warming, since shrinking ice sheets reflect less solar heat.

Climate change threatens to harm South Asia in several ways, including large-scale flooding affecting coastal communities, and more severe and sustained droughts affecting the heartland. More severe and frequent hurricanes and other storms are also likely. Thus food prices are rising. Even so, this is not one of the worst global harvests in years. It's one of the best. World grain production in 2011 was the highest on record; this year's crop is just 2.6% smaller. The problem is that, thanks to the combination of a rising population and the diversion of grain into animal feed and biofuels, a new record must be set every year. Though 2012's is the third biggest global harvest in history (after 2011 and 2008), this is also a year of food deficit, in which consumption was some 28 million tonnes more grain than farmers produced. If 2013's harvest does not establish a new world record, the poor are in serious trouble.

The question of how climate change might alter food production is significant. It is also extremely hard to resolve. The problem is that there are so many factors involved. Broadly, the consensus is that climate change will hurt farmers in the tropics and help farmers in temperate countries. Papers published foresee hard times for farmers in South Asia, where yields will rise just as developing countries become less able to feed themselves. Climate change is likely to be devastating for many of the world's poor. If farmers in developing countries can't compete, both their income and their food security will decline, and the number of permanently malnourished people could rise. Farmers will find it difficult to adapt to extreme events, especially if those events are different every year. Perhaps there is no normal any more.

State of Armed Conflict

An armed conflict is a contested incompatibility which concerns government and/or territory where the use of armed force between two parties, of which at least one is the government of a state, results in at least 25 battle-related deaths.

The world is presently at an evolutionary low in violence. State-on-state conflict is far less likely than it has been in the past. The problem is that other kinds of conflict, other kinds of violence, are exponentially more likely as technology spreads, as the information age allows organisations and individuals, middle-weight nations, if you will, to have capabilities that heretofore were the purview of major nation-states. So it's a paradox; large conflict is less likely but the chance of violence and those using violence for ideological and other purposes is exponentially greater.

The new report from the Human Security Report Project at Simon Fraser University argues that long-term trends are reducing the risks of both international and civil wars. The Report, which is funded by the governments of Canada, Norway, Sweden, Switzerland and the United Kingdom also examines recent developments that suggest the world is becoming a more dangerous place. These include the following:

- Four of the world's five deadliest conflicts—in Iraq, Afghanistan, Pakistan, and Somalia—involve Islamist insurgents.
- Over a quarter of the conflicts that started between 2004 and 2008 have been associated with Islamist political violence.
- In the post-Cold War period a greater percentage of the world's countries have been involved in wars than at any time since the end of World War II.
- Armed conflict numbers increased by 25 percent from 2003 to 2008 after declining for more than ten years.
- Inter-communal and other conflicts that do not involve a government increased by more than 100 percent from 2007 to 2008.
- The impact of the global economic crisis on developing countries risks generating political instability and increasing the risk of war.
- Wars have become "intractable"—i.e., more difficult to bring to an end.

Left-Wing Extremism in India

Prime Minister's Manmohan Singh's speech at the annual conference of Directors General and Inspectors General of Police, on 8 September 2012, provided a sweeping overview of existing internal security challenges in India and raised six critical issues:

- The ethnic violence in Assam and its resultant fallout.
- The Maoist threat and its changing trajectory.
- The evolving challenge in J&K.
- Threat from coastal areas.
- Terrorism in the hinterland.
- Cyber security.

The use of bulk messages and social networking sites to mobilise groups and spread the message of hate became an issue of national debate as a result of violence in Assam and its resultant impact across the country. The seriousness of the threat led the government to initially limit bulk SMS to five and thereafter to 20 per day. A number of Twitter and Facebook accounts as well as blogs were also frozen as a result, leading to protests. After dwelling on the challenges, the Prime Minister dealt with measures that were required to address some of these:

- The need to develop capability within the police force to "effectively track" people's sentiments and "inter community tensions", which is based on the analysis that local forces did not have the ability to read the situation as it developed;
- "Identification of potential trouble makers" as a basis for effective pre-emption, which reinforced the core policing duty of providing preventive security through focused measures aimed at early neutralisation of trouble makers (such measures have been practiced in J&K, especially after the experience of 2010 street protests);
- The need to employ influential segments of the local population to assist in positively

influencing polarised communities, which reinforced community policing as an important element of internal security;
- The need to build upon traditional strengths of the police in terms of grassroots intelligence, which came up as a timely reminder, given the criticality of time specific actions; and
- The development of soft skills, thereby incorporating some of these aspects along with traditional policing activities.

As regards the threat of Left Wing Extremism (LWE), reports indicate the development of an indigenous capability to "fabricate hardware", and the additional military capacity it is likely to provide. Another aspect was the ability of Maoists to mobilise people against the government and security forces in the immediate aftermath of operations, on the basis of alleged human rights violations. This highlights the vital aspect of ensuring minimum collateral damage, even as operational effectiveness is achieved. Respecting human rights and achieving operational success are very much complementary and not contrarian objectives.

The Taliban and Pakistan

Pakistan's seemingly uncontrollable slide into a sectarian nightmare appears to have gained further momentum. The militant Deobandi Islamists have now launched a clear campaign to cow down sources of potent social and political resistance such as the Muttahida Qaumi Movement (MQM). What is very worrying is that the Army is clearly abandoning its earlier pretence of readiness to take the Islamic zealots head on and sections of the establishment seem more willing now to be just silent accomplices.

Pakistan has to choose between a Pakistan in Jinnah's vision or a Talibanised state. The Taliban spokesman in Karachi, Umar Farooq, a former Jamaat-e-Islami functionary, declared "We are a group of Islamic warriors fighting against infidels" and that "Karachi is our base and we will target anyone our leader Hakimullah Mehsud tells us to". TTP's surrogate body of madrassas in Karachi, Wifaqul Madaris, has on its part warned MQM, whose cadres are predominantly Barelvi, to desist from prying into the functioning and affairs of its affiliates. Many MQM cadres had been alleging that an overwhelming number of inmates of these madrassas were Pashtun and Afghans and some of them were being trained in the handling IEDs of inside the seminaries. Karachi is an ethnic tinderbox and sectarianism makes it even more explosive. The Taliban threat in Karachi cannot be minimized.

There appears to be an unholy nexus of the Pakistan Army with Islamic radicals. Some retired Generals have entered into secret deals with Taliban factions to either secure the release of captured Pakistani servicemen or for preventing Army units from being targeted. Apparently, these deals have been cemented by transferring large amounts of money to Taliban commanders. In other instances, the spirit of camaraderie between the two sides emerges under the influence of GHQ's propensity to treat Taliban factions—the Good Taliban"—as its 'strategic assets'. Apparently, it is Hamid Gul who controls the GHQ's mind-set, even though Kayani is the commander in uniform. The assassination of Major General Faisal Alvi of the SSG in Islamabad (November 2008) occurred after he had written to General Kayani against two of his senior generals for their complicity with the Taliban and their conspiracy to have him sacked for his refusal to play along. Many Pakistani observers had pointed out that the weapons used in Alvi's assassination and the clinical manner of the attack suggested it to be an inside job by sections of the Army rather than a terrorist attack by Taliban or their local supporters. In separate statements Jamiat-ul Ulema-e-Islam's Maulana Fazl-ur Rehman and Jamaat-e-Islami's Munawwar Hassan have warned the Army against going after the Taliban in North Waziristan.

The Pakistan Army is the only national institution that retains its cohesiveness and, therefore, it is expected to protect Pakistan from internal and external threats. Any hopes of Pakistan pulling out of the present sectarian crisis require the Army to not only keep the Islamic zealots under check, but also to support and protect the winds of moderation. However, the Pakistan Army appears neither willing to play this role, nor seems to have confidence in its own capabilities. This is a new phenomenon in Pakistan and does not augur well for the country's fight against Islamic sectarianism and radicalism and for upholding moderation.

ISSUES

IMPACT OF DRONES ON AIR OPERATIONS AND THEIR FUTURE RELEVANCE

Air Marshal R.S. Bedi, Former Director General, Defence Planning Staff, India

Introduction

Human conflict is singularly responsible for new inventions. In order to meet the newly emerging challenges, man has gone in for more and more lethal discoveries. The desire to dominate an adversary has been a paramount factor in this race. Most military inventions have come about from this singular urge. Drones or Unmanned Aerial Vehicles (UAVs) or Remotely Piloted Vehicles (RPVs) have, likewise, appeared in a similar fashion to meet ever changing contingencies and peculiarities of modern day warfighting techniques. Over a period, these have evolved from mere radio controlled toys to remotely controlled deadly instruments of war.

Starting with initial functions like surveillance, reconnaissance and electronic intelligence, drones have gradually evolved into highly precise and destructive armed vehicles today. Besides, drone operations have the advantage of precluding own casualties, for the operators sit miles away from the scene of action. US drones operating over Afghanistan and Pakistan are being flown from 7,000 kilometres away from Nevada in continental America and beam back hundreds of hours of live videos of militants going about their daily routines. They are observed closely for days and their behaviour analysed. They are oblivious of what is going on till they are struck. These drone operations are in fact akin to aerial sniper missions and are tantamount to asymmetric tele-warfare with serious implications for the future.

This one factor may have far reaching implications on the nature of future air warfare. The sole aim of the armed forces has always been to have weapons that maximise enemy losses without much damage or injury to itself. This significant technological innovation in air power will, in all likelihood, alter the very course of air warfare in the coming years. There are sufficient indications from the ongoing R&D and concept studies as to how the drones, in the not too distant future, would be tasked to undertake almost all types of air operations including ground attack and air defence functions. The fighters would perhaps be left with air combat role only.

Evolution of Drones

The western powers, particularly the US, have been innovating and developing this technological marvel for decades now. The cold war estrangement between the superpowers and the recent wars in Iraq, Afghanistan and other hot spots all over the world has given an impetus to R&D in this field. Cutting edge technology in solid state electronics coupled with continued emphasis on miniaturisation has helped the designers to pack maximum electronic pay load in a vehicle of this type.

Today, these vehicles come in all sizes, varying from a few kilograms to almost an equivalent of an aircraft.

They are capable of flying at high subsonic speeds and at altitudes of 12 kilometres plus. Portable hand-launched Micro UAVs that can provide information about the enemy in immediate vicinity are also in use presently. The US has been using mini-drones in Afghanistan which weigh even less than six pounds. They are dubbed as "Flying Shot Guns" and given to the soldiers battling the Taliban militants close to the border with Pakistan. These are used by the soldiers for pinpoint accuracy for eliminating a militant without any collateral damage. These drones can be carried in a backpack and used in the battlefield to preclude calling for an air strike. These small drones however do not carry heavy explosive charge as compared to their more lethal predecessors like Predator and Reaper etc. The backpack drones have led to more decision making autonomy at the lower levels which may have its own implications.

There are varieties of UAVs that carry more sensors and can operate over long distances; some are however limited by ground to air communication constraints. Heavier UAVs can carry a wide range of on-board equipment and sensors. These UAVs use satellite links.[1] These links can manage long distance high bandwidth data or video information acquired by on-board sensors. For the purpose of command and control and dissemination of data, these drones also carry line of sight communication equipment. UAVs like the US Predator, Reaper and Pathfinder etc. belong to this class and are capable of being armed for precision delivery of onboard weapons. These vehicles are very effective against both stationary as well as moving targets. These are ideal for hunter killer role. Notwithstanding this, a certain degree of collateral damage is implicit in these attacks as has been seen in drone operations in Pakistan and elsewhere.

These drones are also susceptible to jamming and interception. That is what has led to stealth technology and digital links being worked upon on future drones to make them less prone to enemy action. It is imperative that the communication links for control of UAV flights as well as for down loading of information which is in the form of data imagery or video is secure and reliable. That is why the analogue FM is being replaced with digital links. Services will have to ensure adequate coordination amongst them for spectrum and frequency management when employing UAVs of varying capabilities in restricted air space.

The US, despite having a number of advanced combat capable UAVs, continues to work on still more capable such platforms for future needs. UAVs are fast proliferating worldwide, for both military as well as civil application. Drones are being used for anti-drug missions in South America, keeping watch over ships in pirate-infested seas and for patrolling US-Mexican border. It was also reported that the UK was at one time considering employing UAVs for protecting the Olympic Games against terrorist threat. Almost every advance country has a variety of UAVs, capable of performing devious roles.

The capability to carry weapon loads and deliver with precision is however not universally available as yet. A number of advance countries including a number of third world countries are currently engaged in developing their own unmanned vehicles to meet their specific needs. Realising the importance of the role likely to be played by the unmanned vehicles in future air warfare, most countries like India, Pakistan , China, Japan, Brazil, Australia, Iran, Israel, France, Italy, Argentina, UK, Russia and of course the US have all gone in for their indigenous programmes in a big way. Some countries like Brazil, Pakistan, China and Israel etc. have a long list of UAVs in use with a fairly large number in different stages of development.

India's DRDO also has ambitious plans for developing unmanned vehicles including with stealth technology. Independent unmanned surveillance air vehicle (IUSAV) is a precursor to the unmanned combat air vehicle concept. A number of other projects are on the shelf. Amongst the more near term projects is Rustom-2 which is capable of flying up to 35,000 ft height, with 24 hours endurance and 350 kg pay load. If all goes well, it could fructify by the year 2016.[2] The DRDO chief further stated that this vehicle, though initially designed for surveillance, could evolve into an armed platform. He also claimed that a solar powered high altitude unmanned vehicle is also on the agenda. However, he stated that India was looking for partnership in some of these projects.

The South Asian scenario with China, Pakistan and India all working feverishly on UAV projects does not augur well. New technologies are being evolved to meet the emerging challenges in this field. Armed, stealth and electronic warfare capable UAVs will alter the very scenario of air warfare in coming decades.

---

[1] Lt Gen Harbhajan Singh; "Communication to and from UAVs", *USI Journal* Jan- Mar 2012.

[2] Mr. Saraswat, Chief of India's DRDO, mentioned this in an interview with Aviation Week and Technology magazine on 4 June 2012.

Strategy as a Weapon

Armed drones like many other military technologies such as tanks; aircraft etc. are here to stay as an important instrument of modern warfare. As warfare becomes more and more technologically innovative, the drones become increasingly more meaningful. The Americans have taken the lead in developing and employing drones for a multitude of roles. However, no clear-cut strategy has so far been evolved as to how to employ drones as weapons of war. Can they be incorporated in a broader strategic frame work? Have drones been effective in providing support to other forces in some ways? As is known, the drones have so far been mostly operating in stand-alone mode only. Real analytical studies have not yet been carried out on the strategic effect of the US drone campaign. Since the Americans are employing drones extensively in various theatres of wars, both overt and covert and mostly against individuals or groups of people, they have become the cause of substantial political as well as social blowback in the form of anti-Americanism as seen in Pakistan.

The drones were first used as a weapon of war by the Americans in the late 1990s when unmanned and unarmed aircrafts were employed in Afghanistan to track the Al Qaeda.[3] It was after 9/11 that then President George W. Bush ordered US drones equipped with missiles to kill Al Qaeda leaders first in Afghanistan and later in Yemen and Pakistan. When he realised that Pakistan was not sincere enough in curbing the war against terrorism, he went on the offensive. Bush first authorised a targeted killing on 17 September 2001. Starting with less than a dozen drone attacks during 2004-2007, Washington went on to attack 35 times in the rugged northwest region of Pakistan during the last year of the Bush Presidency in 2008. Later, President Obama took up the cudgels and went on the offensive in a big way.[4] Based on the published data, both domestic and international, the number of US strikes as on July 2012 is tabulated below:

2004	*2005*	*2006*	*2007*	*2008*	*2009*	*2010*	*2011*	*2012*
1	1	3	5	35	53	117	64	28

Of the total 307 strikes recorded till now, 297 took place between 2008 and 2012. Since 2006 (data for 2004 and 2005 not available) 2,354 Al Qaeda and Taliban leaders including their followers have been killed. 138 civilians have also been killed so far.

President Obama's desire to pull out from Afghanistan by 2014 and in the interim reduce American casualties led him to intensify the drone attacks. These attacks have continued with similar ferocity ever since. US frustration over Pakistan's refusal to crack down on militants who continue to cross over to Afghanistan from their safe havens in Pakistan has forced the Obama Administration to intensify drone strikes. The US has also realised that drone strikes have been quite successful in eliminating the militants on the CIA hit list.

The US has used drones in Pakistan, Afghanistan, Yemen, Somalia, Iraq and Libya with amazing effectiveness. Thousands of people have been killed by CIA drone attacks in these countries. The US policy of killing by remote control drones has been in practice since well over a decade now. US have also been using UAVs in Columbia, Iran, Haiti, Mexico, North Korea, Philippines and Turkey for the purpose of surveillance.

The US requires a network of air bases for comprehensive UAV operations across the globe. These bases house the drones, mostly Predators, Reapers and Sentinels with explicit support of host nations. They are used for takeoff, landing, weapon loading and technical maintenance.[5] For obvious reasons, these bases remain unidentified. However, from the published information it seems these bases are scattered over all the continents. At any given time, three dozen armed unmanned UAVs fly over Afghanistan and Iraq. They linger over there all day and all night and when one lands, another replaces it. They guard soldiers on patrol, spy on Al Qaeda, and strike at the insurgents massing at night. The coalition countries too are using their drones in Afghanistan.

The drones play a very important role in Pakistan and Afghanistan. The terrain is very difficult and it is often almost impossible to access the hideouts and sanctuaries created by Al Qaida as well as the Haqqani clans. They conduct their operations with impunity. The drones have proved very effective in reconnaissance and striking these hideouts. The drones have emerged single most effective weapon in the hands of the Americans in taking on the Taliban leadership selectively. As the force reduction takes place with 2014 approaching, the use of drones in all likelihood would increase.

---

[3] "Washington's Phantom War" by Peter Berger and Kathenne in *"Foreign Affairs"*, July\August, 2011.

[4] "Charting data for US air strikes in Pakistan 2004-2012". By Bill Roggio and Alexander Mayer in *"The Long War Journal"*. (Last updated on 1 September 2012) This page is updated regularly to cater for recurring data.

[5] "Where the Drones are" by Micah Zenko and Emma Welch in *"Foreign Policy"*, 29 May 2012

The casualty figures, including that of civilians, vary vastly from source to source. However, as per the 'Bureau of investigation Journalism', the drone attacks in Pakistan have killed between 2,464 and 3,145 of which 482 to 830 have been civilians. As per another data, between 2004 when the US started the drone operations in Pakistan and July 2012, a total of 305 strikes have taken place, of which 295 occurred since January 2008. A total of 2,335 leaders of Taliban, Al Qaida and extremists and 138 civilians were killed since 2006. Yet another study brings out altogether different figures. A total of 311 drone strikes were carried out in Pakistan between 2004 and July 2012 which resulted in total deaths varying between 1,879 and 2,887. Of this, the militant's death varies between 1,586 and 2,416.[6]

According to another study, the US drone attacks have had no great effect on the Taliban's ability to mount operations in Pakistan and Afghanistan or to deter potential recruits. Majority of those killed belonged to low level cadre and fighters together with a small number of civilians. However, a precedence having been set, the use of drones will soon become an established practice with most armed forces the world over.

A word about comparative flight safety would be in order here. As per the Congressional budget office, initial mishap rate of 28 incidents per 100,000 flying hours has now been brought down to 7.6 per 100,000 flying hours through enhanced pilot training and improved Predator technology. However, when compared with fighter aircraft, say for example the F-15 mishap rate of 2.56 in 2011, it is still far above. However, the lower per unit cost of a drone offsets the lower crash rate vis-a-vis the higher unit cost of the fighter aircraft is another way of looking at it. Overall, drones present a slight cost advantage over manned aircraft.

Drone attacks Vs Air Strikes

In case of Pakistan, both the US drones and Pakistan Air Force have attacked targets in north and South Waziristan. Little over three hundred drone attacks have taken place since 2004 which has resulted in weakening of their organisational structure as a result of elimination of some leaders. Air Chief Marshal (Retd) Rao Suleiman of the Pakistan Air Force made a startling observation in his address in a conference of Air Chiefs in Dubai, in November 2011, that the PAF flew 5,000 strike sorties dropping 11,600 bombs on 4,600 targets in Pakistan troubled areas since May 2008.[7]

It was necessary to carry out a comparative and an objective analysis of drone attacks and air raids by the PAF in tribal areas in order to assess the effectiveness of each weapon system. Both the print and electronic media have overstated the estimates of drone attack casualties in the absence of authentic and realistic assessment, because access to tribal areas was highly restricted to outsiders. He quoted locals as having said that PAF and artillery firing had done far more damage than the much demonised drones. They bombed the civilian population indiscriminately, killing thousands of them and turning their houses in rubble. But nobody in Pakistan dare speak about it.

US Hegemony and World Opinion

The drones are being employed freely, particularly by the US and some other nations with total disregard to violation of sovereignty, territorial integrity and legality of such operations. Yet there is very little explicit criticism of these operations by international forums or even human rights organisations.

A Poll was conducted recently by the Pew Research Centre to ascertain global views on the use of drones by the US. 62 percent of the Americans approved of it, though it is a substantial reduction from 83 percent polled by the Washington Post a few months earlier. An overwhelming majority of seventeen out of twenty countries opposed the use of drones by the US. 75 to 90 percent citizens of these countries, except the UK with mere 47 percent, opposed it. Amazingly, despite marked opposition by the citizens, the leadership of these countries had supported the US drone strikes. Not only that, they also hesitate to raise the issue in international forums where the US human rights record could be debated. Surprisingly, most nations are simply silent on the issue despite the Americans drone attacks taking place in an ever increasing number of countries.

The biggest mystery is Pakistan who despite being attacked by US drones day in and day out has not reacted against the US offensive seriously. The first drone attack took place during President Musharraf's time which killed many innocent children. Except for public posturing, it has not resorted to any of the available options to prevent the Americans from doing so. The fact that these drones operate from Shamsi base in Baluchistan only suggests that the

---

[6] "The Year of the Drone " by Peter Burger and Kathenne, *"New America Foundation"* 24 February 2012

[7] Mohammad Zubai, *Daily Times*, 4 June 2012

powers that be are perhaps complicit in this decision.[8] Islamabad is understood to have approved drone strikes against the Al-Qaida and the Taliban in the past.

Actually speaking, it is a myth that the Pakistani government opposes drone attacks. The military and the ruling government have long offered support for the drone strike programme, opposition from the members of Parliament and the opposition parties notwithstanding. Gen. Kayani is known to have asked for more strikes in the past. Not only that, even the human intelligence support has always been forthcoming from within Pakistan. It is learnt that in the FATA region many welcome these drone attacks. But with mutual relations literally nose-diving lately, the government has become increasingly critical. Now the government insists that the drone strikes are notified in advance. After the Salala episode where a number of Pakistani soldiers were killed by a US drone attack, the government wanted an increased role in the decision making process in these strikes.

Drones, like any other aerial platforms, are susceptible to air interception and destruction. Surprisingly, Pakistan has not resorted to this also despite all the noise about its sovereignty being violated by the US. Nor for that matter has it lodged any formal complaint with the United Nations in this regard. This matter came up in June 2012 in a Peshawar court where it was contended that despite a resolution having been passed in the parliament against CIA-led drone attacks, the government has done nothing to implement it. The Ministry of Defence however denied any secret agreement with the US. After Pakistan ordered the CIA to vacate the Shamsi base consequent to their faceoff, the drones still continued to strike from across the border in Afghanistan with impunity.

Legal Aspects and Ethics

Drone attacks raise serious legal and ethical questions. These silent killers from the air are potentially cruel and are in fact tantamount to assassination of unsuspecting victims. Israel is most closely associated with targeted assassinations of its enemies in recent decades because of the existential threat it continues to face. The march of technology has obviously outpaced the existing laws, conventions and institutions, requiring a new set of regulations and acceptability.

Does the Obama Administration's policy of decapitating attacks on Al Qaida and other similar extremist organisations make the US any safer? There are different viewpoints. Critics of US say that the policy of selective killing of leadership is counterproductive, as these are bound to inflame the victim organisations. There are others who say that such killings are illegal and immoral. But there are some who view these attacks as highly productive and the only way to neutralise the extremists and terrorism.[9] Two recent studies done this year highlight the fact that the drone attacks are indeed effective in diminishing and demoralising the Al Qaida and other militant groups and therefore the Obama Administration should maintain the offensive.

During a recent conference in Islamabad, UN Human Rights Chief, Ms, Navi Pillai said that drone attacks raise serious questions about compliance with international law. She questioned the very legality of such operations since they kill innocent civilians. When drone attacks are conducted outside the military chain of command, it is not easy to comply with international law. Drone attacks violate human rights as they lead to civilian casualties. These civilians are not combatants nor are they direct participants in the hostilities. She emphasised that the UN Chief Ban ki-moon had urged states to be more transparent about the circumstances in which drones are used and take precautions to ensure that the drone attacks comply with international law. She even went on to stress the importance of investigation and compensation to the victims. It may be mentioned here that even the US Civil Liberty Union expressed concern that "US drone killings have not complied with international law requirements mandating protection of civilians". The US however describes these drone attacks as self defence. Pakistan denies having agreed to any drone attacks on its territory after the so-called reconciliation. Drone attacks it feels are counterproductive and only help radicalise people. Pakistan sees them as predatory and against the law but has done little to prevent it. As usual, Pakistan is playing a duplicitous game.

Earlier, the US had criticised the Israelis for such extra-judicial killings but now when it comes to it, it finds an alibi in self-defence in the war against Al-Qaida. These attacks are taking place all over without any declaration of war, as also without the consent of the victim country's government. Really speaking, it's an ultimate asymmetric warfare which is tantamount to summary executions.

---

[8] Quazi and Jillani ,*The Diplomat Blog*, 9 June 2012

[9] Studies published by Harvard Kennedy School, Belfer Centre's Journal, and *International Security*

These attacks have all the potential of being recognised as war crimes by international lawyers in the not too distant future. These attacks are in fact terrorising the people and breeding terrorism further instead of wiping it out as the US tends to think. Such unilateral attacks by the US are setting a wrong precedence for the future. A number of countries would soon have armed drones. What position would the US take if these countries decide to employ them in similar fashion? The Chinese, Iranians and the Russians all have their problems with the separatists, so does India for that matter.

Interestingly, the UN Charter provides a subtle opening for the type of drone offensive the US has been indulging in. As per Article 51, a state "has the inherent right of individual or collective self defence", until the UN Security Council takes action. Article 51 applies if the targeted state agrees to the use of force in its territory by another nation, or the targeted state or a group operating within its territory was responsible for an act of aggression against the targeting state. Only one of these conditions must be satisfied to justify a unilateral extra-territorial use of force by a UN member.

In the case of Pakistan, Yemen and Somalia, both conditions seemed to have been satisfied. All three countries seemed to have consented explicitly or otherwise to the US operating drones within their territories. It may be emphasised that all these countries are "safe havens" for groups that that have launched violent attacks against the US or its interests. The US has not invoked Article 51 so far, but it operates within the bounds of this article only. Legally therefore US drone attacks cannot be challenged.

Future Trends

The US is investing heavily in developing future drones, capable of performing a multitude of roles, including combat air patrol over specific VAs and VPs. In fact, the US is buying more UAVs than manned aircrafts. The USAF is training more UAV pilots than the fighters and the bombers put together. The air force now has more than 1,300 drone pilots and it needs still more. Pentagon has projected that the US air force would need more than 2000 drone pilots by 2015.[10] There are more than 13 bases across the US besides an equally large number spread over various continents from where the US conducts its global operations with the help of drones.

The future UAVs, some in concept stage and others being developed are likely to be used in almost all types of air operations. Employment of helicopters as new types of drones for logistics purposes, as is being experimented currently in Afghanistan, will add new dimensions to future air operations. Wars afford rare opportunities for proving new concepts, designs and weapons.[11] The Americans have been flying two unmanned helicopters in Afghanistan since December 2011 on experimental combat missions for delivering goods to Marine outposts. K-MAX helicopters built by Kaman, an aerospace firm, and modified for autonomous flights with the help of Lockheed Martin as a joint venture have been flying in Afghanistan and delivering under-slung loads for some time now. Unlike the fixed wing drones which are remotely piloted, K-MAXs fly autonomously as programmed, using GPS to navigate.

The US is not the only one in this race for dominance of the skies by drones. A number of European and the Asian countries are all investing heavily in next generation UAVs.[12] A few examples as highlighted below illustrate this point.

(a) Northrop Grumman is developing X-47B for the US navy for carrier operations. Flight tests are to begin next year. It can fly up to 420 mph speed over a range of 2400 miles.

(b) Boeing's *Phantom Ray* is presently in the development stage. Its maiden flight took place on 27 April 2011. It can fly up to 614 mph speed.

(c) General Atomics' *Predator* is incredible and was the first ever UAV to be weaponised. It has been used extensively in Iraq and Afghanistan. It can remain airborne for 20 hours at a stretch. It is being developed further.

(d) BAE is developing UK's *Tarani*. Its ground tests have been completed and flight trials are up coming. This drone is likely to have inter-continental capabilities.

(e) EADS' *Cassidian Barracuda* is a joint German and Spain venture. It is a ground attack drone. Although, its maiden flight took place in 2006, development has been impeded due to some unforeseen circumstances.

(f) Mikoyan *Skat* is a Russian concept drone under development, to be used against enemy

---

[10] "Joy Stick War" by Elisabeth Bumiller in the *New York Times*; reproduced in *Indian Express*, 31 July 2012

[11] "Robocopter Arrives" *The Economist* Newspaper Ltd. (reproduced in *Indian Express* , 19 September 2012)

[12] *Business Insider*, Military and Defence Walter Hickey, 6 June 2012

air defence as well as ground attack. However, its development has been discontinued for the time being.

(g) Lockheed Martin *RQ-170* was developed for the purpose of covert surveillance by the Americans but it suffered a setback when Iran captured one after putting it down.[13]

It is estimated that about $ 81.3 billion is likely to be spent globally on unmanned aircraft R&D, procurement and services in the next ten years. The global market will grow despite worldwide budget constraints. The current global market is estimated to be $ 11 billion with the US share being $ 4.5 bn. During the last five years, the US unmanned aircraft market has experienced a double digit growth. As of now, the US accounts for two thirds of the market. Wars in Iraq, Afghanistan and other Middle East have served as a catalyst.

Here also lies the answer to an old debate on whether the use of modern fighter aircraft worth millions of dollars with irreplaceable human life (aircrew) to just kill a tank or few vehicles or troops on the ground is worth its while. With the ground defence environment becoming extremely hostile, risking a pilot and aircraft worth millions, particularly in close air support role is becoming questionable. And therein lies the importance of UAVs.

Conclusion

The manned vs. unmanned aircraft debate is already raging. Both have their advantages and disadvantages depending upon the type of role and the environment for which they get tasked. There is however no doubt that the unmanned aircrafts are here to stay, though they may take years if not the decades to develop further as a vehicle and still longer as a weapon system. Unmanned vehicle utility would be fully realised only when it progresses beyond stand-alone mode capability to wider employability. At present only a few countries have drones with weapon capability; others are still on the fringes.

[13] "Unmanned aircraft market growing" by Marcus Weisgerber, in "*Defence News*" 8 August 2012

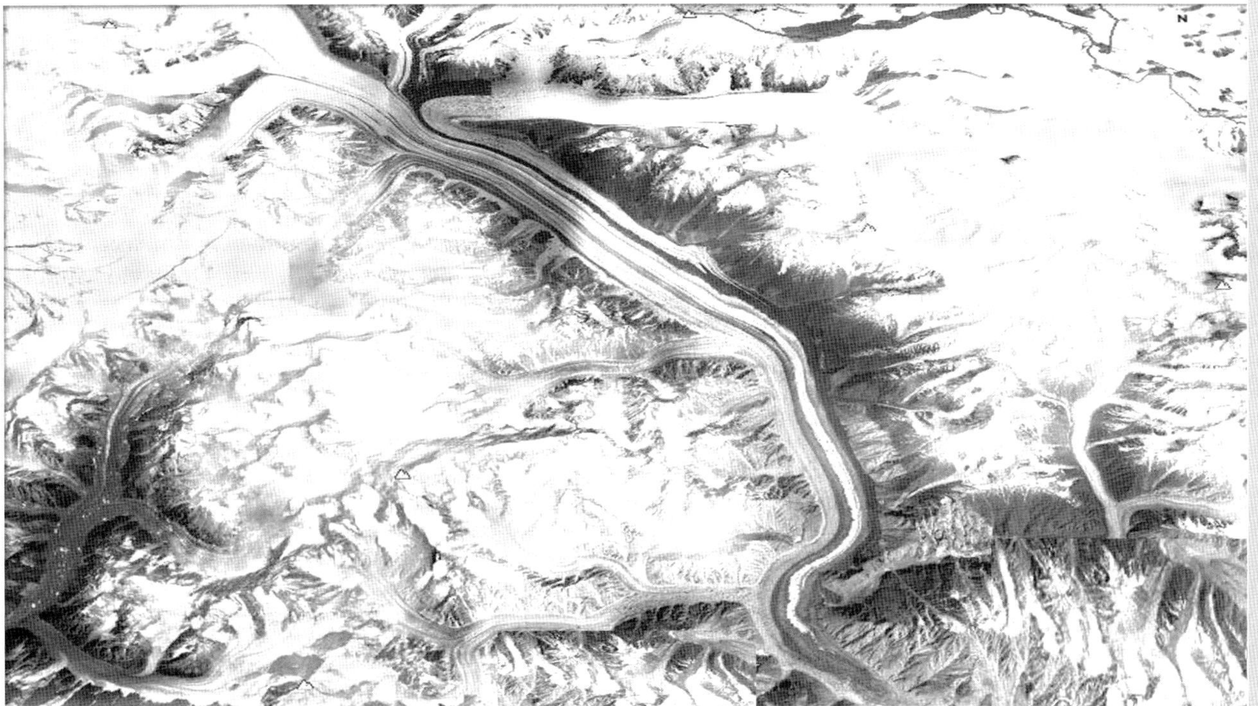

THE SIACHEN IMBROGLIO: A WAY FORWARD

Brian Cloughley, Author and Defence Analyst

Most animals are territorial in nature and mankind is no exception, with occupation of ground being regarded as imperative for human survival. It is therefore not surprising that discord is frequent between individuals, tribes and nations concerning claims to terrain that may appear to offer economic or social benefit. Nationalism, religion and greed are potent determinants of war, but in many instances of conflict the root cause has been and will continue to be the conviction that control must be effected over stretches of land (or water) that might be wholly irrelevant to the well-being and development of inhabitants—if any—or to those of the wider population. Such disputes can exercise lethal attraction for those in a position to direct that military action be taken to establish territorial ascendancy and can lead to wider and disastrous conflict. There seems to be no limit to man's appetite for confrontation, even when it is apparent that muscular bluster almost always leads to the catastrophe of war.

It can be contended that in some circumstances there may be little alternative to a military 'solution' to bilateral topographic disagreement. But even were this an acceptable postulation it is clear that negotiation has the merit of avoiding destruction, slaughter and adverse economic consequences. There are problems in agreeing to engage in discussions, however, not the least of which is reluctance of leaders to embrace moderation, because that can involve unpopularity and even loss of power. These are the ultimate disaster for politicians and to be avoided at almost any cost, even if that involves the sacrifice of numerous lives and creation of lasting hatred. To combat commonsense consideration pointing to a practical peaceful resolution that might incur voter displeasure, the fall-back position is to beat the drum of inflammatory chauvinism. Not for nothing did Dr Johnson describe patriotism as 'the last refuge of a scoundrel.'

In spite of resistance to dialogue, some territorial disputes have been settled by peaceful means, and one outstanding illustration of the paramountcy of negotiation over the lure of war is the Rann of Kutch agreement of 1968. There had been a series of minor clashes between Indian and Pakistani forces in that region in early 1965 before the outbreak of general war in August, and *Global Security* records that:

> It was only on 8 April 1965, when the Indian forces attacked a Pakistan outpost at Ding in an endeavour to complete a military takeover of the territory to present Pakistan with a fait accompli, that the Pakistan forces went into action for the first time, and it was on 19 April 1965 after watching India's actions in the Rann of Kutch for three and a half months that Pakistan forces went into the disputed territory.[1]

A cease-fire was arranged through diplomacy, as recorded in the British Parliament's *Hansard* of 30 June 1965, when the Prime Minister, Mr Wilson, said he was:

---

[1] *Global Security*, 'Rann of Kutch 1965'. http://www.globalsecurity.org/military/world/war/rann-of-kutch.htm

happy to inform the House that the Indian and Pakistan Governments have announced the signature of an agreement for a cease-fire and the restoration of the status quo in the Rann of Kutch as at 1st January, 1965, and on the arrangements for the determination and demarcation of the border in that area . . . I am glad to say that both President Ayub and [Prime Minister] Mr Shastri made it clear to me that when the agreement was completed they would at once instruct their troops to withdraw from their present advanced positions along the Indo-Pakistan border in the confidence that this would also contribute to the reduction of the present tension between the two countries. The whole House, will, I am sure, wish to welcome this settlement and I would like to take the opportunity to pay tribute to the wisdom and statesmanship of President Ayub and Mr. Shastri.[2]

Wilson was premature in his congratulations, because at the very time of his speech President Ayub's plan for military infiltration of the Kashmir Valley was well-advanced, but for the moment a conflict had been avoided through the good offices of the Commonwealth. It was apparent that skilfully exercised third-party diplomacy had been effective. Further mediation was successful in subsequent resolution of the dispute, which went to UN arbitration. The findings and award of the UN Tribunal concerning the Rann of Kutch were pronounced on 19 February 1968, and ever since have been scrupulously adhered to by both countries in a gratifying example of mature acceptance of wise and impartial international adjudication.[3]

Perhaps similar success could be achieved concerning the Siachen imbroglio.

***

As with the Rann of Kutch, the Siachen area is devoid of economic or strategic value. It is barren, unattractive, and a magnet that attracts misdirected national fervour in both India and Pakistan. (Recommended books on the subject are by Lieutenant General VR Raghavan, a defence intellectual and former Director General Military Operations in Delhi, and Myra MacDonald of Reuters.[4]) So far as the Indian stance is concerned, there is illuminating impartial commentary in a cable of 22 November 2006 from the US Embassy in New Delhi, in which the Ambassador, Dr David Mulford, summarised that India had:

> come 'very close' to an agreement on the Siachen issue in 1989, and again (less so) in 1993. Each time the Prime Minister of the day was forced to back out by India's defence establishment, the Congress Party hard line, and opposition leaders. The Indian Army is resistant to giving up this territory under any condition for a variety of reasons—strategic advantage over China, internal Army corruption,* distrust of Pakistan, and a desire to keep hold of advantageous territory that thousands of Indian soldiers have died protecting. Ultimately, the greatest positive in the talks was that the Indian side was able to meet with their Pakistani counterparts and conclude cordially this round of the composite dialogue. While there is no agreed date for an Indian Prime Ministerial visit to Pakistan and formal dates for Foreign Minister level talks are still being firmed up, the most important CBM is that the talks continue, with the Singh government clearly committed to the broader goal of rapprochement with Pakistan.[5]

The Singh government's efforts to establish trust and progress in bilateral relations with Pakistan have been steady and positive, and Dr Singh seems genuinely concerned about the Siachen stalemate. In June 2005 he was the first prime minister to visit the glacier, where he told troops that "Now the time has come and we should try to convert this battlefield into a peace mountain,"[6] This is a laudable aim, but, as with so many other public expressions of concern, has not been followed by firm direction to achieve 'an environment of peace.' Dr Singh is no humbug, but perhaps there was more sincerity than resolve in his pronouncement.

There can be no martial solution to the Siachen disagreement, and it does not make sense to maintain military deployments that result in nothing but suffering, death, and economic depletion in countries that should be concentrating on improving the lives of their ever-growing populations.

---

[2] *HC Deb 30 June 1965 vol 715 cc622-4.* http://hansard.millbanksystems.com/commons/1965/jun/30/rann-of-kutch-cease-fire. The exertions and expertise of the British High Commissioners in New Delhi and Islamabad and the integrity, discretion and professionalism of their Indian and Pakistani interlocutors have never been formally recognised.

[3] The deliberations of the *Indo-Pakistan Western Boundary Case Tribunal* run to 579 pages of fascinating detail, and can be accessed at http://untreaty.un.org/cod/riaa/cases/vol_XVII/1-576.pdf

[4] *Siachen: Conflict Without End.* Lt Gen V.R. Raghavan, Viking India 2002; and *Heights of Madness: One Woman's Journey in Pursuit of a Secret War.* Myra Macdonald Rupa India 2007.

* This observation is not understood by the author. There was no question of army corruption.

[5] Wikileaks. http://www.cablegatesearch.net/cable.php?id=06NEWDELHI7954

[6] *The Tribune*, Chandigarh, 12 June 2005. http://www.tribuneindia.com/2005/20050613/main1.htm. Also *India Today*, 4 May 2012. 'Blood Politics on Siachen'; by Gaurav Aawant and Shiv Aroor: http://indiatoday .intoday.in/story/demilitarisation-of-siachen-glacier-indian-army-pakistan/1/187337.html

The posture of Nawaz Sharif, a former prime minister of Pakistan, and again a would-be national leader, cannot be taken seriously because his comments on Siachen have been aimed at obtaining publicity rather than proposing practical measures for resolution, which he had ample time to attempt during his five years in power in the 1990s. In April 2012, following the massive avalanche that killed 129 soldiers and 11 civilians, he was reported as saying that "once Pakistan took [the] initiative to pull back troops from Siachen, India would also follow suit,"[7] but changed his mind after President Asif Zardari stated that "We cannot unilaterally withdraw troops from Siachen. If India withdraws its troops we will be ready to take similar step,"[8] which was also political fanfare to disguise the fact that his party had hardly had Siachen to the forefront of its agenda since it formed a coalition government in 2008.

Attempts over the years to solve the Siachen problem have foundered on political rocks that are quite as hostile as the jagged crags of the north. Well-intentioned realists have had their sensible solutions destroyed by shady malignancy, and thousands of soldiers have died because leaders, for all their publicity-oriented displays of concern and compassion, have ignored the fact that their avoidance of decision has cost thousands of lives and left countless families in despairing bereavement. Typical of this insouciant callousness was Zardari's pronouncement in April 2012 that "India is suffering more losses in Siachen than Pakistan,"[9] which is neither true nor justifies occupation of a swathe of totally useless territory.

***

Describing the beginnings of the confrontation, in *A History of the Pakistan Army* I wrote that:

> An Indian force advanced from Ladakh to the northern end of the Siachen Glacier in the spring of 1984, there having been a lodgement the previous year. New Delhi could have made a reasonable case in international law for a claim on the region, but chose to use force rather than negotiation. Its agreement at Simla, 'That the two countries are resolved to settle their differences by peaceful means' was apparently annulled by contemporary considerations whose urgency and essentiality has never been satisfactorily explained. [In the same fashion as Pakistan's illegal foray in the Kargil Sector of the Line of Control in 1999.] India's claim was based on the fact that the Line of Control ended, as agreed by representatives of India and Pakistan, at Grid Reference NJ980420, there being no further delineation in any direction. India came to consider, eleven years after agreeing with Pakistan about the Line of Control, that because there was no formal accord governing the barren lands between the end of the Line and the Karakoram Pass, the area should belong to India. No attempt was made to enter the contiguous Aksai Chin area occupied by China.

Of some consequence in the Indian position—had it been decided to follow diplomacy rather than take military action—would have been the fact that Pakistan and China concluded an agreement on 2 March 1963 concerning demarcation of territory between Xinjiang Province and Pakistan-controlled Kashmir, a sensible arrangement to which India took exception at the time. It could be argued with some reason that Pakistan and China had no right to apportion territory to each other (1,350 square miles to Pakistan; 2,050 to China) while some of it was, possibly, in dispute with a third party. A case could have been made for adjudication by the International Court of Justice, or even by an independent body of assessors, but India, since the decision of the tribunal concerning the Rann of Kutch in 1968, has resisted mediation or 'good offices' intended to defuse tension in the subcontinent.

I further noted that:

> Casualties in the icy wastes mounted as the years went by. There was no possibility of a military solution. Neither side could advance beyond the areas they held. There was stalemate until mid-1989, when a breakthrough took place. Or seemed to take place. An excited journalist (well, as excited as that phlegmatic race can be) contacted the author [in Islamabad] on 17 June and said he had just sent a piece to the effect that the Indian and Pakistani foreign secretaries (respectively Mr SK Singh and Mr Humayun Khan) had agreed that troops would be withdrawn to the positions occupied at the time of the Simla Accord. The journalist said it was a final agreement that was, obviously, authorised by the two governments and only needed the armies to implement it forthwith. A major occurrence in the subcontinent, he said; at last an indication that the countries seemed to be serious about rapprochement and working for peace; there might even be a new era of trust and co-operation. (He was quite enthusiastic, for a journalist.) The BBC reported that the foreign secretaries:

[7] *The News*, 20 April 2012. http://www.thenews.com.pk/Todays-News-13-14051-Nawaz-reiterates-Siachen-withdrawal-call

[8] *The Nation*, 20 April 2012. http://www.nation.com.pk/pakistan-news-newspaper-daily-english-online/ national/20-Apr-2012/zardari-rules-out-unilateral-troops-withdrawal-from-siachen

[9] Ibid.

> had been meeting for two days and their discussions set the seal on the earlier meetings ... between the defence secretaries. At a joint news conference Mr Khan announced that both sides have now decided to withdraw to the positions that they held at the time of the Simla Accord.
>
> A corresponding report was broadcast in Urdu on government-controlled All India Radio. It seemed, even to the most sceptical observers in Islamabad and New Delhi, that at long last senior representatives of the countries were not only sitting down and talking about matters of substance, but were authorised to take decisions that would smooth the way for further confidence-building measures. Wrong.
>
> A 'clarification' was issued by the Indian Ministry of External Affairs. The 'chronology of events', said a spokesman, had been 'muddled and confused'. He went on to state that, 'The Indian foreign secretary had endorsed the Pakistani foreign secretary's observations on their talks, whereas the report has made out as if he had endorsed the Pakistan foreign secretary's remarks on the defence secretaries' talks.' Which statement was, of course, not muddled or confusing. The Indian government denied 'that Pakistan and India had reached an agreement on this [Siachen] issue'. The foreign correspondents in Islamabad shrugged their collective shoulders. 'What,' asked one of them, rhetorically, 'can you expect of a bunch of people like that?'
>
> If there has been one occasion, a single identifiable point, a precise moment in the history of the subcontinent at which India and Pakistan might have been placed on the road to establishment of reasonable relations, it was that day in June 1989. An agreement such as the one that was reached and then denied would have saved hundreds of soldiers' lives and cost nothing in national pride. The strategic positions of the countries would not have altered one jot. The accord would have proved to the world that bilateralism actually worked (a real winner for Indian objectives concerning Kashmir), and terminated an unjustifiable drain on national budgets (India's much more than Pakistan's). But it was not to be.

It was a depressing situation, and subsequent meetings were also unproductive in spite of optimism that the countries were anxious to reach agreement. In August 2004 the *Indian Express* recorded that:

> The second time both sides came within breathing distance of an agreement was during the 6th India-Pakistan meeting in New Delhi in November 1992. NN Vohra and Salim Abbas Jilani were the two Defence Secretaries and quickly reached agreement, along the lines of the 1989 paper. Both at first agreed to 8-figure grid maps about locations, including base camps, then brought it down to 4-figure references, then to "nearest" positions—all because of objections by Pak High Commissioner to India, Riaz Khokhar, currently Pak Foreign Secretary. Both delegations even agreed to sign maps.
>
> Jilani and Vohra, who had by now become friends, agreed over a game of golf that given the hawkishness on both sides, this was about the last time they could pull something off like this. That night, when Prime Minister PV Narasimha Rao called Foreign Secretary JN Dixit, DGMO General VR Raghavan and Vohra to a meeting, they assumed it was to finalise the agreement. A hand-written brief had, in fact, even been signed by Rao. Instead, Rao is believed to have hemmed and hawed. I haven't even spoken to the leader of the Opposition about this, he began, why don't we postpone this for a couple of months? Afraid of the gathering storm over the Babri Masjid—it was pulled down a month later—Rao couldn't bring himself to act. Once again and despite much labour, an agreement on Siachen was aborted.[10] [It is notable that Mr Dixit does not describe the meeting in his memoirs,[11] in which there is no mention of the word 'Siachen' which may be an indication of the level of attention given to the problem by the Ministry of Foreign Affairs.]

The story of Siachen negotiations is disheartening because rational accords were rejected by people whose motives were as confused as their horizons were limited. The only positive development was agreement for a cease-fire in 2003, which has saved at least some lives, but until the avalanche in April 2012 there was little media interest in the confrontation.

Other post-avalanche public comment by politicians in Islamabad included that of the Interior Minister, Rehman Malik, who declared that "every inch of the country is sacred" which may have given him personal satisfaction but added nothing whatever to the furthering of tranquillity in the sub-continent. The avalanche may have focused politicians on the Siachen imbroglio, but still they seem incapable of steeling their spines and making decisions that would end a futile confrontation and contribute to building much-needed bilateral confidence.

***

[10] *Indian Express*, 5 August 2004, 'The Blood-stained Glacier'. http://www.indianexpress.com/oldStory/52397

[11] *My South Block Years*, JN Dixit, UBSPD Delhi, 1996.

The concept of impartial mediation appears to be anathema to many political leaders and media commentators around the world. It seems they are nervous about ultra-nationalist populists gaining propaganda advantage by portraying moderation and sanity as weakness. As observed by US Ambassador Mulford in Delhi in 2006, "Any Siachen compromise would give the BJP a political cudgel to wield against the UPA government. BJP and Hindutva firebrands would spin any deal, including the creation of a DMZ [demilitarised zone], as being a territorial concession."[12]

But independent arbitration has been effective in the past—and has saved countless lives as well as contributing to bilateral confidence-building. The Rann of Kutch accord has worked well, and another example of success of externally-managed 'good offices' in the sub-continent is the Indus Waters Treaty, an outstanding illustration of the beneficial effects of applying commonsense and flexibility to a sensitive bilateral problem. Involvement of the World Bank and subsequent mediation by an independent adjudicator have not in the smallest way diminished the credibility, sovereignty or national ethos of either India or Pakistan. In accordance with the 1960 *Indus Waters Treaty between the Government of India, the Government of Pakistan and the International Bank for Reconstruction and Development*, in February 2012 the Permanent Court of Arbitration was called upon in the dispute about a dam on India's Neelum River (because its waters flow into Pakistan via the Jhelum), and a panel of distinguished jurists from Germany, Slovakia, Sweden, Switzerland, the UK and the US was appointed to rule on the matter. Irrespective of some resistance in India and Pakistan the matter should be resolved rationally, provided both governments keep their nerve. In spite of this, it appears difficult for ultra-nationalists to accept that when bilateral agreement cannot be reached by national governments, then the best way forward is to seek independent assistance and abide by the findings of impartial international mediators.

It is notable that the Rann of Kutch ruling was greatly in favour of India, with Pakistan being awarded a mere 780 square kilometres of the claimed 9,100. According to *Global Security*, the award "was reluctantly accepted by Pakistan, but bitterly resented in India,"[13] but there appears to have been no disagreement with the summation that "The Rann of Kutch Arbitration was extremely successful in resolving a territorial dispute between two nations with a history of conflict. Throughout the proceedings, the parties cooperated with each other and with the Tribunal. Neither side questioned the authority of the Tribunal, and both sides worked together to implement the decision."[14] Negotiations were predicated on the UN Charter which states that "The parties to any dispute, the continuance of which is likely to endanger the maintenance of international peace and security, shall, first of all, seek a solution by negotiation, enquiry, mediation, conciliation, arbitration, judicial settlement, resort to regional agencies or arrangements, or other peaceful means of their own choice."[15]

***

Neither India nor Pakistan has formally attempted to amend the terms of the 1972 Shimla Agreement in which two main declarations are that

- the principles and purposes of the Charter of the United Nations shall govern the relations between the two countries; and
- the two countries are resolved to settle their differences by peaceful means through bilateral negotiations *or by any other peaceful means mutually agreed upon between them* [emphasis added]. Pending the final settlement of any of the problems between the two countries, neither side shall unilaterally alter the situation and both shall prevent the organisation, assistance or encouragement of any acts detrimental to the maintenance of peace and harmonious relations.

In India, however, there have been attempts to accentuate 'bilateral negotiations' in order to make it appear that such arrangements must exclude involvement of outside parties, but although this cannot be so, given endorsement of the UN Charter and the Simla Accord by both countries, it did not prevent the Ministry of External Affairs from issuing a statement in 2009 to the effect that the:

> Government of India is committed to resolving all outstanding issues with Pakistan *through a peaceful bilateral dialogue in accordance with the Simla Agreement* [emphasis added]. A third country role cannot be envisaged nor is it necessary.[16]

[12] Wikileaks. US Embassy Cable 64523. http://dawn.com/2011/06/02/2006-us-assessment-of-indian-position-on-siachen/

[13] *Global Security*, 'Rann of Kutch 1965'. http://www.globalsecurity.org/military/world/war/rann-of-kutch.htm

[14] *Fordham Law Review* Volume 67, Issue 6, 1 January 1999: 'The Use of Arbitration To Settle Territorial Disputes', by Carla S. Copeland. http://ir.lawnet.fordham.edu/cgi/viewcontent.cgi?article=3585&context=flr

[15] UN Charter June 1945, Article 33 (1).

[16] *Outlook India*, 18 November 2009. 'A Third Country Role Cannot be Envisaged, Nor is it Necessary'. http://outlookindia.com/article.aspx?262929. Also CNN World, 18 November 2009. http://articles.cnn.com/ 2009-11-18/world/india.pakistan.talks_1_india-and-pakistan-simla-agreement-countries-claim?_s=PM:WORLD

Given Simla's *or by any other peaceful means mutually agreed upon between them,* this was sailing close to the wind of misrepresentation, and the stance was made even clearer by Defence Minister AK Antony, when he stated that:

> "We are not in favour of involvement of any third country in talks between India and Pakistan. India's basic policy is that we don't want any interference from any country in our bilateral relations with Pakistan. We don't believe in third party mediation."[17]

Mr Antony did not elaborate on his reasons for refusal to countenance mediation, which is defined as "a form of conflict management in which a third party assists two or more contending parties to find a solution without resorting to force."[18] It is strange indeed that anyone can object to a process specifically designed to avoid bloodshed at no cost whatever to the disputants. It must be apparent to even rigid minds that peace is preferable to war and that to ensure freedom from strife is a main duty of a country's leaders. Mediation does not require capitulation. Acceptance of independent judgement is not declaration of weakness, and the parties involved could with profit bear in mind Pandit Nehru's appeal to "Let us be a little humble; let us think that the truth may not perhaps be entirely with us."

Referees, umpires, judges and arbitrators are vital instruments in human affairs who seek the equitable and civilised conduct of sport, justice, commercial affairs and industrial relations. They are appointed and accepted throughout the world as highly-trained experts in their fields and disciplines without whom the conduct of impartial adjudication in almost all aspects of the lives of mankind would be impossible.

If a bilateral problem has proved impossible to solve for almost thirty years, there is a case for the parties involved to agree on and employ other than purely national means to attempt to resolve it, but the barriers against compromise appear substantial—and not only political in nature. US Ambassador Mulford recorded in 2006 that:

> Former Indian Ambassador Parthasarthy, who personally dissuaded Rajiv Gandhi from making a similar deal on Siachen in 1989, said this concession [Pakistan's agreement to demarcate points on the map] does not satisfy India's underlying concern —that points be agreed to in advance so the Pakistani Army would be unable to simply march back in to the area and take the high peaks around the Siachen glacier that India currently controls. He said if Pakistan agreed to demarcate points on a map, this would still fall short of agreeing to an Agreed Ground Position Line (AGPL), because it would not amount to an extension of the Line of Control (LOC) or even a cease fire line (as the LOC area was called before 1972). Ambassador Parthasarthy further remarked that he had discussed the issue with senior Congress Party members, who have significant sway over Sonia Gandhi and Congress Party politics, and there is "no way in hell" that they would allow India to withdraw under disadvantageous conditions. He added that the "Prime Minister won't get away with what he is trying to do."[19]

This intriguing insight into the mindset and influence of an unelected public official is complemented by the US ambassador's reflections about the military stance on the Siachen question, as Dr Mulford observed that:

> Army Chief JJ Singh appears on the front page of the 'Indian Express' seemingly fortnightly to tell readers the Army cannot support a withdrawal from Siachen. Given India's high degree of civilian control over the armed forces, it is improbable that General Singh could repeatedly make such statements without MoD civilians giving at least tacit approval. Whether or not this is the case, a Siachen deal is improbable while his—and the Army's—opposition continues to circulate publicly.

The Tribune, Chandigarh, which carries notably high-grade defence reporting, noted in May 2012, in the context of the following month's bilateral talks on the problem, that the Indian army's contentions are:

- Siachen is its high-value strategic asset;
- Any diplomatic misstep would help Pakistan and China;
- A firm no to the proposal unless Islamabad agrees to Actual Ground Position Line (AGPL) on the glacier;
- Indian Army is at the strategic heights. Once vacated, these would become vulnerable; and

---

[17] *Times of India*, 24 February 2010. http://articles.timesofindia.indiatimes.com/2010-02-24/india/28135714 _1_indo-pak-ties-talks-between-foreign-secretary-india-and-pakistan

[18] *Journal of Conflict Resolution*: 'Understanding Success and Failure in International Mediation,' Marieke Kleiboer, University of Leiden, http://www.jstor.org/discover/10.2307/174357?uid=3738016&uid=2129&uid= 2&uid=70&uid=4&sid =47699055562937

[19] Wikileaks. US Embassy Cable 68738. 22 November 2006. Difficulty of resolving Siachen Dispute. http://www.cablegatesearch.net/cable.php? id=06NEWDELHI7954

- Pakistan, it is feared, might repeat Kargil-type misadventure.[20]

(*India Today* carried a similarly well-sourced analysis titled 'Blood Politics on Siachen' which rehearsed like points but was stirringly sub-titled 'Siachen Demilitarisation: Could PM gift away to Pakistan what Army has won?'[21])

In September 2012 the Army Chief, General Bikram Singh, referred to the region as "strategically important," and declared "we must continue to hold it always ... and we have expressed our concern to the government. It's now for the government to decide."[22]

These are intriguing reasons for maintaining a position of non-negotiation. First of all, Siachen is of no strategic value. Even were it to be occupied by China, as is the Aksai Chin region to the east (37,244 square kilometres or 14,380 sq miles; about the same size as Switzerland, India's State of Kerala or the US State of Indiana), there would be no adverse economic or military impact on India. But China does not want Siachen. Its leaders are too pragmatic and far-sighted to commit thousands of troops to an area totally without value. The PRC took over Aksai Chin because it wanted to build a road from the western province of Xinjiang to Tibet, but Siachen offers Beijing nothing.

Refusal of further negotiation if there is no agreement to determine the 'Actual Ground Position Line' is emplacement of a needless barrier. As reported by the *Times of India* in May 2012, "Indian officials involved in the Siachen negotiations stressed that there was no change in India's position. India wants both countries to authenticate their current positions on the AGPL. This would establish the respective positions of the two armies. This is necessary because of a prevalent trust deficit on both sides."[23] But the exact position of every bunker is known to each side and their maps of each other's defended localities are most detailed. It would be simple to recognize formally what is already common knowledge. In summary: there is no problem, because when both sides withdraw and the area is declared a demilitarised zone nobody will care about the location of former positions, because they will all have been destroyed. There is no question of either party having a territorial claim in law as a result of having occupied parts of the territory.

The statement that "Indian Army is at the strategic heights. Once vacated, these would become vulnerable" is irrelevant, because following formal agreement to withdraw and refrain from reoccupation, the emplacement of ground detection sensors and regular patrols by neutral observers, together with employment of remote surveillance systems, would ensure that the demilitarised zone would cease to be 'vulnerable' to both countries. Even if Pakistan were to "repeat Kargil-type misadventure', it is not clear how continuation of the Siachen confrontation could influence any such foray in its favour. It is understandable that India and Pakistan are wary of each other's intentions along the Line of Control and the Siachen region, but a policy of delineation, demilitarisation and independent verification would ensure that there could be no undetectable movement of troops in the region.

The uncompromising announcement by Mr Antony in August 2012 that "The area of Siachen glacier is an integral part of India,"[24] was not helpful, and his statement that "A total of 846 armed forces personnel have made supreme sacrifices on the Siachen glaciers since 1984"[25] highlighted the price successive governments have been prepared to pay for national pride.

There are strong feelings on both sides concerning the Siachen imbroglio, and, given the political conditions applying in both countries, bilateral negotiations have little chance of success. But if there is no resolution, the pointless dispute will continue to fester, and soldiers will continue to die for the sake of injudicious nationalism and paltry political advantage.

A Suggested Solution

The attractions of placing the Siachen question in the hands of independent adjudicators are many. The

[20] *The Tribune*, 26 May 2012. 'Army cautions on concessions on Siachen.' http://www.tribuneindia.com/ 2012/20120527/main4.htm

[21] *India Today*, 5 May 2012. http://indiatoday.intoday.in/story/siachen-glacier-demilitarisation-indian-army-pakistan/1/187356.html

[22] *The Tribune*, Chandigarh, 19 September 2012. 'Chinese Troops in POK: Army Chief'. http://www.tribuneindia.com/2012/20120920/main3.htm

[23] *Times of India*, 5 May 2012. 'Siachen thaw? Pak stokes Line of Control fire.' http://articles.timesofindia. indiatimes.com/2012-05-05/pakistan/31586227_1_agpl-saltoro-ridge-siachen

[24] *Hindustan Times*, 13 August 2012: http://www.hindustantimes.com/Punjab/Chandigarh/PoK-an-integral-part-of-India-Antony/SP-Article1-913085.aspx

[25] *Business Standard*, 28 August 2012: http://business-standard.com/india/news/846-indian-soldiers-have-died-in-siachen-since-1984/484677/

advantage of neutral mediation is that passions are not involved, except perhaps in presentation of cases by each side. To quote from a wise statesman of yesteryear, "Arbitration means simply this—that no individual or nation is a judge in its own cause; and if you want a fair and impartial judgment you must go to somebody who is wholly unconnected with the transaction."[26] This principle was endorsed by none other than Prime Minister Pandit Nehru in speeches to the United Nations and in particular his observations in 1960 when he stated that "The role of the United Nations is a mediatory one: to reconcile and to help in the proper functioning of the Central Government [of the Congo] . . . We are convinced that these questions cannot be dealt with on a bilateral basis, or even by a group of countries. They are of immediate and vital concern to the entire world."[27]

It would be a major step forward for India and Pakistan and indeed for the world if the prime ministers of these countries were to declare simultaneously that the Siachen region was to be demilitarised as soon as practicable. The armies would be given ten weeks in June-August in which to withdraw troops and equipment and destroy fortifications and other installations. A UN mission of 60 international military officers (forty to be available at any one time for verification tasks) would form and undergo briefings and acclimatisation for six weeks and then deploy. Concurrent with their training there would be construction of the HQ of the Mission in neutral ground as close as possible to Grid Reference NJ980420, from which AS350 B3 high altitude helicopters would operate. The duty of the mission would be to observe the region and verify that no forces or facilities remained. (A major challenge would be cleansing the region of the vast amount of waste material that has accumulated in the almost 30 years of occupation: difficult and costly but far from impossible.)

On withdrawal of the parties' troops the region would be demilitarised and, as observed by defence expert Gurmeet Kanwal, this "will not only act as a huge military-to-military confidence-building measure, but will also test the Pakistan Army's sincerity and will be an opportunity for that army to prove that it has actually had a change of heart at the strategic level in wanting peace with India. It is a low-risk option to test whether the Pakistan Army can be trusted, and India must not lose the opportunity to do so. However, India must draw up a demilitarisation agreement that takes care of all political and military apprehensions and make it clear to the Pakistan leadership that no military violation will be tolerated."[28] Brigadier Kanwal does not advocate third party involvement, but his summation of the advantages of demilitarisation is succinct and there is no doubt the initiative is practicable.

Following the exit of military forces, one environmentalist proposes that Siachen be declared an ecologically-protected area which will "not only demilitarised but also will have a regular monitoring team of ecologists, meteorologist and other experts."[29] And this composition would be infinitely preferable, in the longer term, to having a UN military mission. Most importantly, the region could be properly delineated by an international commission.

***

A solution to the Siachen Imbroglio will take goodwill, commonsense, and appreciation that proposals for solely bilateral deliberations would be subject to determined delaying tactics. To reiterate what US Ambassador Mulford wrote from Delhi in 2006 "Any Siachen compromise would give the BJP a political cudgel to wield against the UPA government. BJP and Hindutva firebrands would spin any deal, including the creation of a DMZ, as being a territorial concession," and there is no reason to believe that ultra-nationalists on the Pakistan side would be any less partisan.

As observed by Mr Nehru: "in ages long past, a great son of India, the Buddha, said that the only real victory is one in which all are equally victorious and there is defeat for no one. In the world today, that is the only practical victory. Any other way will lead to disaster."[30]

The best way ahead to avoid disaster and achieve lasting peace, establishment of trust, and the end of an entirely unproductive military confrontation is third party mediation, which could be speedily agreed by the countries' leaders. Nobel prizes have been awarded for less.

[26] Earl of Derby 1871: Debate on the Treaty of Washington. HL Deb 12 June 1971 vol 206 cc1823-901. http://hansard.millbanksystems.com/lords/1871/jun/12/motion-for-an-address#3V0206p0_18710612_HOL_10

[27] Speeches by Pandit Nehru at the UN General Assembly: http://www.scribd.com/doc/33371739/PANDIT-NEHRU-Speeches-at-the-United-Nations-General-Assembly

[28] *The Tribune*, Chandigarh, 1 June 2012. Gurmeet Kanwal: 'Siachen Demilitarisation'. http://www.tribuneindia.com/2012/20120601/edit.htm#4. This is one of the most perceptive analyses of the problem in recent times.

[29] Dr. Seeme Mallick, Assistant Professor, Department of Management Sciences, COMSATS Institute of Information Technology, Islamabad. Contact with author. Professor Mallick helped draft Pakistan's National Climate Change Policy.

[30] As Note 26.

TRANSITION AND DRAWDOWN IN AFGHANISTAN: PREPAREDNESS FOR 2014

*Shanthie Mariet D'Souza, Research Fellow, Institute of South Asian Studies, National University of Singapore**

Introduction

A decade after the military intervention that dislodged the Taliban-Al Qaeda combine in Afghanistan, peace and stability remains elusive. There is no consensus in Western capitals on what constitutes the 'end-state' in Afghanistan. The Western public's frustration with a long-drawn war has coalesced with the global economic slowdown, the Euro crisis and the pressures of electoral campaign politics—thereby complicating the efforts for the long-term stabilisation of Afghanistan. As the momentum towards the drawdown gathers and the western countries are in a rush to exit, there are concerns of reversal of gains made in the last decade of international intervention. This paper is a stock taking exercise of the transition *(inteqal)* process and levels of preparedness among the Afghans to take matter into their own hands in key sectors - security, political, peace processes, governance and economic development.

The Af-Pak Strategy, Surge & Exit

The United States (US) President Barack Obama, in emphasising on a renewed focus and allocating more resources to the 'good war' in Afghanistan, announced a troop surge in his speech at West Point on 1 December 2009. Along with the surge, he also set a date- end of 2014 - for drawdown of forces from the war torn country. The declaration had twin impacts. Within the US, it provided some clarity to his domestic constituency. It assuaged the concerns of the civilian team, led by Vice-President Joe Biden who had opposed the requests of the military commanders (General Stanley McChrystal and General David Petraeus) in Afghanistan for deploying additional troops for a population-centric counter-insurgency (COIN) campaign. At the same time, inside Afghanistan, Obama's declaration sent a different message. It evoked concerns among the Afghans. It also fed into the propaganda of the Taliban-led insurgency.[1]

* The views expressed in this paper are those of the author and do not necessarily reflect those of ISAS. The author's views and findings are based on her extensive interactions, discussions and interviews with serving and former ministers, potential presidential contenders, political leaders, government officials, security personnel, media, academia, members of think tanks, international organisations, non-governmental organisations, civil society and women's groups, entrepreneurs and locals during field visits to Afghanistan in May-June 2007, October 2010, March 2011, May-June 2011, October 2011, January-February 2012 and June-July 2012.

[1] The present-day Taliban-led insurgency is an agglomeration of various anti-government elements and armed opposition forces which include followers of Afghan warlord Gulbuddin Hekmatyar's radical group Hizb-i-Islami, the Haqqani network, Al Qaeda and its affiliates, anti government elements, religious clerics, power brokers, narcotic traffickers, bandits, smugglers, unemployed youth, tribal fighters in the Pakistan-Afghanistan border region. Discussions with government and security officials in Kabul, June-July 2012.

While the 2010 troop surge achieved notable security gains on the ground, analysts argue that such gains are reversible and almost un-sustainable by the Afghan National Security Forces (ANSF) alone. According to the drawdown plan, the additional 33,000 troops have been withdrawn in September 2012 leaving behind 68,000 US troops in the country. As the debate on the usefulness of the surge continues,[2] the US-Afghan Strategic Partnership Agreement signed on 1 May 2012 has ensured a minimal troop presence for limited counter-terrorism, train and assist missions in the post-2014 period.[3]

While the security situation is said to have improved in south-western Afghanistan, eastern Afghanistan, primarily the provinces of Paktika, Paktia, and Khost (known as the P2K region), bordering Pakistan's Federally Administered Tribal Areas (FATA), and area of operations of the Haqqani Network, remain deeply insurgency infested. The campaign of violence by the insurgents has been lethal and continues to sap the nascent institutions of the Afghan state. By employing asymmetric tactics with increasing use of improvised explosive devices (IEDs) and suicide bombers, the insurgents have managed to keep the levels of troop deaths high. High-profile attacks on symbolic targets like the Intercontinental Hotel (June 2011), British Council (August 2011), the American Embassy (September 2011), Kabul Star Hotel (April 2012), Qargah (June 2012) and Camp Bastion (September 2012) demonstrate their deep strike capability and intent to garner instant and worldwide media attention through such manoeuvres.

The Taliban have indeed adopted tactics of violent retribution and intimidation of the population, targeting those deemed to be associated with, or sympathetic to, the government. This strategy witnessed rampant killing and abduction of government officials, aid workers, and teachers, religious and tribal leaders. Systematic targeting and elimination of power brokers, government officials and police chiefs in 2011 led to leadership crises and raised the spectre of civil war in the north. Likewise, elimination of key government officials and power brokers in the South, led to a power vacuum in the Pashtun areas. The Taliban have established shadow governments in areas where the writ of the Afghan government was limited or non-existent.

Much of the insurgent strength is derived from the sense of safety the insurgents are accorded across the Durand Line, within Pakistan. Taliban recruits and enjoys safe havens in that country. The Pentagon's April 2012 report to Congress on Security and Stability in Afghanistan stated that "The Taliban-led insurgency and its Al Qaeda affiliates still operate with impunity from sanctuaries in Pakistan. The insurgency's safe havens in Pakistan, as well as the limited capacity of the Afghan Government, remain the biggest risks to the process of turning security gains into a durable and sustainable Afghanistan." The heightened tensions between Pakistan and the US over the assassination of Osama bin Laden by American Special Forces in Abbottabad in May 2011, the subsequent accidental killing of 28 Pakistani security forces during a NATO air raid in Salala in November 2011 and increase in drone strikes inside Pakistani territory, have added complexities and limited the scope of the United States counter-terrorism cooperation with Pakistan.

Security Sector and Preparedness of the ANSF

At the 2010 Lisbon Summit, NATO provided a road map to transfer security responsibility to the Afghans. The first tranche of provinces, districts, and municipalities, which has 25 per cent of Afghanistan's population, was handed over to the Afghans in July 2011. The second and third tranches were announced in November 2011 and March 2012 respectively. While the second tranche put the Afghans in the lead for providing security for more than 50 per cent of the country's population[4], with the beginning of the third tranche, 75 per cent of the Afghan population will be living in areas where the ANSF have lead security responsibility.[5] In conformity with the decisions arrived at the May 2012 Chicago Summit, full transition in all parts of Afghanistan will begin by mid-2013.

[2] Rajiv Chandrasekaran, 'The Afghan Surge Is Over: So did it work?' Foreign Policy, 25 September 2012, http://www.foreignpolicy.com/articles/2012/09/25/the_afghan_surge_is_over?page=full. Accessed on 26 September 2012; Frances Z. Brown, Taking stock of the surge - from the bottom up, The Af-Pak Channel, Foreign Policy, 26 September 2012. http://afpak.foreignpolicy.com/posts/2012/09/26/taking_stock_of_the_surge_from_the_bottom_up. Accessed on 27 September 2012.

[3] Shanthie Mariet D'Souza, Is the US–Afghan Strategic Partnership in doldrums?, ISAS Brief No. 231, 23 March 2012, http://www.isas.nus.edu.sg/Attachments/PublisherAttachment/ISAS_Brief_232_-__Is_the_US_Afghan_Strategic_Partnership_in_Doldrums_1_23032012144409.pdf. Accessed on 275 September 2012.

[4] Statement by NATO Secretary General on Afghan Transition Announcement, North Atlantic Treaty Organisation, 27 November 2011, http://www.nato.int/cps/en/SID-656CC458-77FAA000/natolive/news_81068.htm. Accessed on 20 April 2012.

[5] Louisa Brooke-Holland and Claire Taylor, *Afghanistan: The Timetable for Security Transition*, Briefing Paper, British House of Commons, 9 July 2012, www.parliament.uk/briefing-papers/SN05851.pdf. Accessed on 9 August 2012.

The natural corollary of the ANSF taking charge of the security of Afghanistan is a change in NATO mission—from combat to an advisory role. The shift to a 'train and assist' mode has further compounded the complexities and brought into sharp focus the levels of preparedness of the Afghan forces for independent action. The contours of post-2014 security assistance to Afghanistan will be mentoring, training, and funding the ANSF. Although numerically, both the Afghan National Army (ANA) the Afghan National Police (ANP) is impressive, with 194,466 troops and 149,642 policemen[6] respectively, widespread reservations have been expressed on their capacities. Will the ANSF—the product of a rushed, under-resourced and frequently revamped recruitment and training procedure, be able to deliver, remains a critical question. While the US and NATO and the Afghan security officials[7] are willing to underline the latter's ascending capacities, such views have been viewed with considerable scepticism among non-governmental, civil society and women groups in Afghanistan.

The impressive performance of the ANSF during some of the high-profile and well co-ordinated insurgent attacks has been cited as evidence of its growing strength and capabilities. Analysts insist that they have come of age and are no longer the 'rag tag' men in uniform they used to be. At the same time, concerns still exist on the ANSF capability to gather adequate intelligence on countering the planning and execution of well-coordinated multiple sieges, an insurgent tactic that has gained predominance.

The ANA has been primarily employed to augment the international forces' COIN campaign. In 2011, over 90 per cent of ISAF operations were conducted in conjunction with the ANA, an increase from 62 per cent of such operations in spring and summer of 2008. However, this projected conjunction could actually be a misnomer. According to a recent US Department of Defence report in 2012, only 13 out of the 156 Afghan Army battalions are classified as 'independent with advisers' and only 74 are seen as 'effective with advisers'. In effect, there is very little to indicate that the ANA will be able to act autonomously over large swathes of the countryside in the next two or three years. Especially remote in the coming years is the possibility of transferring responsibility for the protection of the provinces bordering Pakistan to the Afghan army.[8]

Alongside the questions of capacities, maintaining a huge security force establishment is a financial impossibility for the resource-starved Afghan government. The total strength of the ANSF in October 2011 reached 306,903 (170,781 soldiers and 136,122 policemen). By October 2012, it was supposed to reach 352,000 personnel (195,000 ANA and 157,000 ANP) and would remain at that level till 2017. The government in Kabul is bound to face the most formidable challenge of mentoring the forces and finding continuous funding for such a huge project. It was after much deliberation, that the US and its allies at the Chicago summit envisaged a working target of 228,500 with an estimated annual budget of $4.1 billion.[9]

The greater worry, however, lies in the scenario of acceleration of training impinging on the quality of the forces. Analysts suggest that the ANSF is already 'unmanageable' and hence, the term 'expansion' is nothing but a paradox.[10] While observers perceive some success in terms of raising a capable and independent ANA, serious concerns have been expressed about the capabilities of the ANP and the convoluted attempts in establishing the rule of law. Analysts point out that while the ANA is seen as a relative success vis-a-vis the ANP, the chronic deficiencies and problems of funding, equipment, training, desertion, ethnic balancing and infiltration cannot be overlooked.[11]

---

[6] Report on Progress Towards Security and Stability in Afghanistan: United States Plan for Sustaining the Afghanistan National Security Forces, US Department of Defence, April 2012, p.4, http://www.defense.gov/pubs/pdfs/Report_Final_SecDef_04_27_12.pdf. Accessed on 1 May 2012.

[7] Discussions with General Sheer Mohammad Karimi, Chief of Staff, Afghan National Army, Kabul, 27 June 2012; Gen Azimi, Spokesperson, ANA, Kabul, 26 June 2012; ISAF officials, Kabul, 25 June 2012.. The contrasting views of the prevailing security condition and preparedness of ANSF was evident during discussions with civil society groups, NGO's and locals in Afghanistan.

[8] Gilles Dorronsoro, Afghanistan: The Impossible Transition, The Carnegie Papers, South Asia, Carnegie endowment for International Peace, June 2011, http://www.carnegieendowment.org/files/impossible_transition.pdf. Accessed on 20 May 2012.

[9] Chicago Summit Declaration on Afghanistan issued by the Heads of State and the Government of Afghanistan and Nations contributing to the NATO-led International Security Assistance Force (ISAF), 21 May 2012, http://www.nato.int/cps/en/natolive/official_texts_87595.htm. Accessed on 23 May 2012.

[10] Thomas Johnson and Matthew Dupee, 'Transition to Nowhere: The Limits of "Afghanisation"', Foreign Policy, 22 March 2011, http://afpak.foreignpolicy.com/posts/2011/03/22/transition_to_nowhere_the_limits_ of_afghanisation. Accessed on 5 April 2011.

[11] Author's discussions with academia, members of think tanks and non-governmental organisations, civil society and women's groups in Kabul, June-July 2012.

There are additional concerns of creating a 'hyper-militarised' state.[12] The feasibility of building a large army without addressing larger issues of civil-military relations has been questioned, particularly when the government in Kabul is perceived to be weak. The lingering concerns of ethnic balancing and representation combined with the challenges of building a national army on merit remain. Despite major efforts by the NATO Training Mission in Afghanistan (NTM-A) in recent years, the development of the institutional capacity of the ANSF will take years. The ANSF's quality, its professional and institutional capability and its capacity to function in an unstable and conflict-ridden environment are bound to be tested in the coming years.[13]

The rising incidence of 'green on blue attacks', i.e. rogue soldiers and police turning their weapons on their ISAF mentors, remains a serious concern. In 2011, 35 NATO soldiers and trainers were killed in 21 incidents of such 'green on blue' attacks by the Afghan soldiers. In the first half of 2012, there have been 32 such incidents, killing 40. In addition to problems associated with inadequate vetting mechanisms and background checks due to the rush to recruit, the increased number of attacks has led to a 'trust deficit' between the Afghan soldiers and their mentors leading to scaling down of the NATO's training and mentoring assistance.[14]

Political Sector Reform

While most of the debate on transition has veered towards the security sector, meaningful discussion on the transition in the political sector, particularly when the year of handover of responsibility coincides with the 2014 presidential elections in Afghanistan, seems to be missing. Analysts posit that 'placing sole responsibility for Afghanistan's future stability on the ANSF without making progress in creating a stronger political consensus among Afghanistan's diverse factions, both armed and unarmed, is a high-risk gamble'.[15]

Over the past decade, the highly centralised executive form of political system has been constantly challenged, both by the insurgent campaign to discredit the present political system and also by challenges from within the system. The constant bickering between the President and Parliament, deteriorating security, poor governance and the near-absence of rule of law have sparked debates inside and outside Afghanistan for the need for wide-ranging political sector reforms. The magnitude of the problem and simmering discontent has led observers to forewarn: 'If in 2001 the West was afraid that the absence of a strong centralised government in Kabul would prompt Afghanistan's dissolution, by 2011 the West has come to fear that a dysfunctional centralised government could cause this same outcome.'[16]

In addition to the existing challenges in the political sector, the complexity of holding elections in the year of handover of authority is daunting. Analysts point out, 'The Afghan presidential election slated for 2014 is an uninspiring prospect given the sky-high levels of corruption, nepotism, and patronage that beleaguers the Afghan political system. To make things worse, President Hamid Karzai has suggested holding the elections in 2013 to avoid an overlap with the planned end of NATO's combat mission. And there is still no functional plan in place for a smooth transfer of political power to a post-Karzai government.'[17] In the absence of large scale political sector and electoral reforms, the danger of a repeat of previous instances of electoral malpractices at a crucial time of transition is cause for widespread concern.[18]

---

[12] Julian Glover, 'Few politicians say it, but most think it: our Afghan war is a disaster', The Guardian, 11 April 2011, www.guardian.co.uk/commentisfree/2011/apr/11/afghanistan-strategy-failed. Accessed on 11 April 2011.

[13] Ali A. Jalali, 'The Challenges and Prospects of Transition in Afghanistan' in Shanthie Mariet D'Souza (ed.) Afghanistan in Transition: Beyond 2014? (New Delhi: Pentagon Press, 2012).

[14] Greg Jaffe and Kevin Sieff, Training suspended for new Afghan recruits, The Washington Post, 2 September 2012, http://www.washingtonpost.com/world/asia_pacific/training-suspended-for-new-afghan-recruits/2012/09/01/adc4ed1c-f398-11e1-b74c-84ed55e0300b_story.html. Accessed on 3 September 2012.

[15] Caroline Wadhams, Colin Cookman & Brian Katulis, Afghanistan Transition: Elevating the Diplomatic Components of the Transition Strategy at the Chicago NATO Summit and Beyond, Center for American Progress, 17 May 2012, http://www.americanprogress.org/issues/2012/05/afghanistan_transition.html. Accessed on 20 May 2012.

[16] Thomas Barfield, 'Afghanistan's Ethnic Puzzle: Decentralising Power before the US Withdrawal', Foreign Affairs (September/ October 2011).

[17] Javid Ahmad, 'Election 2014: Afghanistan's chance to get it right?', Foreign Policy, 10 May 2012, http://afpak.foreignpolicy.com/posts/2012/05/10/election_2014_afghanistans_chance_to_get_it_right. Accessed on 20 May 2012.

[18] Authors' discussion with various political leaders and potential presidential contenders mainly from the National Coalition and National Front – Ahmed Zia Massoud, Ahmed Wali Massoud, Dr. Abdullah, Amrullah Saleh, Fawzia Koofi, Kabul, June-July 2012.

Peace Talks, Reconciliation and Reintegration

The ambiguity of the peace processes, reconciliation, reintegration, and secret negotiations with the insurgents has complicated the search for a 'political solution' to end the long war in Afghanistan. As individual countries are involved in unilateral and parallel efforts of negotiations, setting up office and contacts outside Afghanistan, this has further reinforced the notion that the West is willing to cut a deal with the insurgents and leave.

The indigenous peace-building efforts like the High Peace Council (HPC) and the Afghan Peace and Reintegration Programme (APRP)[19] appear to be a casualty in the process, of both the insurgent onslaught[20] and the international community's strategy of omission. Even with the long-standing focus on negotiation with the high-ranking Taliban leaders, it is unclear if the international community has moved beyond a phase of opportunistic negotiation, i.e. negotiating with whosoever is available and willing rather than with insurgents of consequence and insurgents enjoying the sanction of top leaders in the insurgent hierarchy. It is still not clear whether the process involves the Taliban leadership based in Quetta (Quetta Shura Taliban). Or, is it simply trying to rope in people who have grown irrelevant to the insurgent movement, sometimes even getting duped by impostors who pose as interlocutors or representatives of the Taliban.

While the lack of credible information on the identity of the interlocutors is a lesser problem, several critical hurdles remain for the parties involved to make any significant headway. The most important is the demand of the US that it would retain bases within Afghanistan beyond 2014. President Karzai has down played the talk of a permanent presence of US troops, stating that it would be an impediment for negotiations with the Taliban who demand complete withdrawal of foreign forces as a precondition for talks. Some moves were made to release imprisoned Taliban commanders from the detention centre at Guantanamo Bay, the failure to do so prompted the Taliban to suspend the peace talks in March 2012. Efforts, however, continued to keep the fledgling negotiation process going, both by the US and its allies.

Lack of a Pakistani endorsement, rooted in the country's fear of being sidelined from the end-game in Afghanistan, has also played spoiler. In 2009, the prospect of negotiation with the Taliban made some progress through a Taliban commander Mullah Baradar, second-in-command to Mullah Omar, the leader of the Taliban. However, the Pakistani establishment stepped in and arrested Baradar in early 2010, derailing the entire process. The control of the Pakistani military and intelligence on their 'strategic assets'—the Taliban leadership - would make any meaningful Afghan-led reconciliation process an arduous task.

Aid, Economic Development and Regional Cooperation

Most of the discourse on transition has focused on the numerical strength of the troops that would be adequate to maintain the country's security. Civilian capacity building, economic opportunities, trade, transit and investment that would change the discourse of Afghanistan from being an aid-dependent 'rentier state' to a self-sustaining economy, thereby bringing in long-term stability, has received comparatively less attention.

At a time of dwindling international financial assistance to Afghanistan, concerns abound on sustaining its economy and revenue beyond 2014. Contrary to the Afghan government's November 2011 estimate, it requires US$120 billion (at the rate of US$10 billion per year) in aid in the post-2014 period, through 2025.[21] At the Tokyo summit in July 2012, the international community promised to give US$16 billion through 2015 to build its economy and make necessary reforms. Such dwindling financial aid is construed as a natural corollary of the declining interest of the West in Afghanistan. Over the coming years, Afghanistan will have to compensate for such shrinkage of external support. The full impact of the shrinkage on Afghanistan's economic growth, fiscal sustainability and service delivery will probably not be felt until after 2014.

---

[19] For more details on the HPC and APRP, see Mohammad Masoom Stanekzai, 'Peace, Reconciliation and Reintegration in Afghanistan: Challenges and Milestones Facing Peace Talks, Transition and Stability in the Region' in Shanthie Mariet D'Souza (ed.) Afghanistan in Transition: Beyond 2014? (New Delhi: Pentagon Press, 2012).

[20] The killing of the HPC chief Burhanuddin Rabbani in September 2011 by a Taliban 'peace emissary' was a major setback for the peace process. On 14 April 2012, Salahuddin Rabbani, the son of slain Burhanuddin Rabbani was chosen to lead the HPC. The next day, Taliban carried out multiple siege attacks, showing complete disdain towards the peace process.

[21] *Towards a Self-Sustaining Afghanistan, An Economic Transition Strategy*, Speech of President Hamid Karzai, Bonn Conference, 30 November 2011. Government of the Islamic Republic of Afghanistan, and dated November 29, 2011.

Afghanistan's tragedy lies in the fact that time and again its internal contradictions have got trapped in the external power agenda. With the intensification of the search for the 'end-game', a regional consensus[22] by forging greater cooperation is seen as a way out of the imbroglio. One way of building a cooperative regional architecture is through greater trade, transit and investment opportunities, including energy pipelines. The Istanbul Conference for Afghanistan: Security and Cooperation in the Heart of Asia, held on 2 November 2011, provided a new agenda for regional cooperation, by placing Afghanistan at its centre and engaging the 'Heart of Asia' countries in sincere and result-oriented cooperation for a peaceful and stable Afghanistan, as well as a secure and prosperous region as a whole. The emphasis for the first time on a regionally owned process led by Afghanistan, with support and collaboration from its near and extended neighbours, would make this effort 'sustainable and irreversible' in the long term.[23]

Not all is lost in Afghanistan. As Afghanistan traverses a difficult course of transition, there is an immediate need to unify efforts and bridge the perception gap between the Afghans and the international community, to build on the gains and address the immediate areas of concern. In the decade-long international involvement, a unified effort of putting Afghans in the lead for rebuilding their state and society remains the missing link in the long term stabilisation efforts. It is critical to rectify this trajectory and set realistic timetables on drawdown based on conditions on the ground. The gains made thus far are substantial but remain fragile. Unless critical efforts are made to shore up the state's institutions and capacities before the drawdown date of 2014, peace and stability in Afghanistan would remain a distant dream.

[22] Haroun Mir, 'Is Regional Consensus on Afghanistan Possible?' in Shanthie Mariet D'Souza (ed.) Afghanistan in Transition: Beyond 2014? (New Delhi: Pentagon Press, 2012).

[23] Author's interview with Javed Ludin, Deputy Foreign Minister, Government of Afghanistan, Kabul, 30 June 2012.

INDIA-CHINA RELATIONS

Mohan Guruswamy, Chairman, Centre for Policy Alternatives, New Delhi

The inexorable growth of China's GDP has now taken it past Japan and it now takes aim at surpassing that of the USA ($14 trillion), whose economy is at present more than two and a half times bigger than that of China. It took China a little less than a decade to make a similar leap to overtake Japan. But then Japan has hardly been growing from 1995 and its GDP has been roller coasting between $4-5 trillion. If the growth of economies were a horserace, this would be akin to passing a fast starter who has slowed down to a trot. Overtaking the USA will still take time and some effort as that country has begun posting some smart growth after the gargantuan Obama stimulus package pump primed, not just the US economy but also the world's economy, and particularly of countries like China which have a symbiotic economic relationship with it. Despite this Chinese GDP is expected to surpass that of the USA before 2030 when it will about $20 trillion.

China's growth in past three decades is the miracle story of our times. To replicate it might be a tall order for a country like India, which matches it in size and potential, but not yet in political and national will. But GDP alone does not make a nation wealthy. China's current per capita income keeps it in the company of countries like Algeria and Albania. Even in 2050 when the Chinese GDP will be much bigger than that of the US, its per capita income will still be less than a fifth of the American per capita. If India keeps growing at the rate of about 9%, its GDP will surpass that of China by 2045 and if India's population peaks in 2050 at 1.6 billion, then in all likelihood, a decade or so later, so will its per capita income, now about one-third of China's.

But what does this imply for the world's power structure? True the world's economic fulcrum will shift to Asia. But when you get down to the basics, power is more a relation of the money available with a government than its GDP. This simply means the larger the revenues, the greater the power at the disposal of a government. The US today has a Tax/GDP ratio of about 35, while that of China is less than half that. The ability to raise revenues is linked to the per capita income, income inequality and tax compliance. Given this, the ability of countries like India and China to squeeze more out of their people and squeeze greater effort is limited. So we shouldn't be counting our chickens before the eggs hatch. Nevertheless, it is being confidently predicted that the top three places in global GDP rankings will be held by the USA, China and India, with the other major economies and powers like Brazil, Germany, Japan, Russia and UK straggling well behind in GDP terms.

Geography and recent history have made the India-China relationship a difficult one. It is one in which the USA will find ample space and opportunity to inveigle itself to its advantage. This is a made to order situation for strategists and leaders in the three countries to ply their trade with plenty of worst-case scenarios. It would seem that India and China are destined to live out the foreseeable future as rivals, if not adversaries. But rivals need not be enemies and neighbours need not get fratricidal. If there are two large and rising powers in a region, rivalry is inevitable. France and Germany or Brazil and Argentina come readily to mind. A hundred and fifty years ago France and Britain were bitter adversaries. The rise of Teutonic nationalism and of Nazism united the two countries against a common enemy. The "end of history" with the triumph of liberal democracy has largely blunted Franco-German rivalry by entwining them economically, while the advent of the European Union has made the borders seamless. The ratification of the Treaty of Tlatelolco of 1967 by Argentina in 1994, making all of Latin America and the Caribbean a nuclear free zone, has more or less eliminated any vestigial military fears Argentina and Brazil may have had. On the other hand go to a Brazil-Argentina soccer match or to a France-England rugby game and you will wonder if things have changed at all? Rivalries, it seems, are forever!

The situation between India and China is not very different. Nationalism arrived in both countries at about the same time in the early 1900's with the advent of Sun Yat Sen in China and MK Gandhi in India. This was after centuries of foreign rule over the Han and Hindu ethnic majorities. After decades of turbulence both countries emerged as "free nations" with entirely different systems in the waning 1940's. Mao Zedong and Jawaharlal Nehru were leaders with entirely different personalities and world views. Mao's ruthless instincts were honed as the leader of the Communists in a bloody civil war. On the other side Nehru's were finessed under the tutelage of Mahatma Gandhi into that of a somewhat naïve and dreamy idealist. The isolation of the two countries that the British had so assiduously nurtured by supporting an independent Tibet was rudely shattered by its annexation by China in 1951. This and the handing over of Xinjiang by the then USSR to the new PRC made the Han and the Hindu neighbours for the first time in history.

Since 1954 the legacy of a disputed border has flared up into a bitter row. Both countries are guilty of misinterpreting history to further their claims. India's claim of the barren and windswept Aksai Chin plateau rests on an arbitrary extension of the border in 1939 to the present claim line first suggested by WH Johnson in 1865. Johnson was a discontented official of the Survey of India who made his fortune by vastly extending the Kashmir Maharaja's domain on the map. The 1939 extension was done to create a buffer between Xinjiang, which had turned into a Soviet protectorate, and British India.

On the other side in China the obsequious courtiers of the Qing (Manchu) dynasty were not averse to some cartographic conquests of their own. Ge Jianxiong, a well respected history professor at China's prestigious Fudan University, has written that "the notions of Greater China were based entirely on one-sided views of Qing court records that were written for the courts self-aggrandizement." Ge has also written criticizing those who feel that the more they exaggerate the territory the more "patriotic" they are. The present Dalai Lama lent weight to this by formally staking a claim over Tawang to the newly independent India in 1947. Such is the stuff that wars are made of and the two countries are in a military face-off since 1962.

To be fair to the Chinese, they have at several times offered a package deal of settling by foregoing each other's un-historic and unsubstantiated claims in Ladakh and Arunachal Pradesh. India's leadership has balked at this lest it be accused by the opposition of the day of selling out. Only in recent days a new wisdom seemed to creeping into South Block, but the Chinese have suddenly turned recalcitrant. They now seem to suggest that the package deal is no longer on offer?

That Sino-Indian relations are strained is to state the obvious. Ironically enough they have been on a slow downslide ever since the 2006 visit of Hu Jintao which was intended to showcase the upswing in the relations between both the countries. It began when the Chinese Ambassador to India, Sun Yuxi, made a rather indiscreet and untimely comment to a TV news channel that the status of Arunachal Pradesh was still an unresolved issue between the two countries. Whether Sun Yuxi made this comment as mere restatement of the old Chinese claims for the record or to deliberately stir the pot can be debated. Sun Yuxi had told me that he did not intend it to stir things up and that a partly American-owned Indian TV channel repeatedly and deliberately played it up to blight the improving ties between the two nations. Sun Yuxi also, quite significantly, added that while he might have been indiscreet his statement won him a great deal of support from many groups in China who maintain a hard-line view about India and its increased chumminess with Washington. The leadership of the PLA is most certainly among these forces. He also hinted that the Chinese Foreign Ministry was more inclined towards a softer line over India.

This line generally favours an extension of the Deng Xiaoping offer to Rajiv Gandhi in 1988 to settle the border dispute on an 'as is where' is basis. The increasingly beleaguered Rajiv Gandhi felt that he did not or could not expend the political capital on a deal to essentially forego claims on Aksai Chin for an alignment along the disputed McMahon Line. The two leaders then agreed to keep the issue frozen for settlement at some future time. (See *"India China Relations: The Border Issue and Beyond"* by Mohan Guruswamy and Zorawar Daulet Singh for a detailed discussion on this).

Following this and the visits of Narasimha Rao and Atal Behari Vajpayee, it was generally accepted in India that the Chinese claim on Arunachal Pradesh was now in the past and that only the issue of actually defining the lines of control in Ladakh and aligning the border along an agreed McMahon Line remained. Vajpayee even formally recognized that Tibet was an integral part of China in exchange for a similar recognition of Sikkim as a part of India. Every Chinese General Secretary since Zhao Ziyang too has visited India. The relations seemed to be vastly improved. The result of the Sun Yuxi statement was that what had become a mere border alignment issue was once again transformed into a territorial issue. In the recent days the situation has been vitiated by a series of stories in the Indian media, many of them false, suggesting fresh troubles on the border.

As if the border row wasn't enough to heat up relations, other issues too have cropped up. The question of the Dalai Lama's continued residence has emerged as the waters of distrust began receding. China's inability to deal with increased Tibetan resistance to its policies of assimilation also makes it angrily point a finger at India. India has been very correct in restraining the Tibetan government-in-exile and strained sinews in a China-like manner to allow the Olympic torch pass through New Delhi unhindered. When in India the Dalai Lama is restricted to just performing his ecclesiastical duties which include a large Indian flock adhering to the Tibetan school of Mahayana Buddhism. The Chinese have now taken umbrage over his visit to the ancient monastery at Tawang. This is his fifth visit to Tawang. So the obvious question is why now?

The global economic crisis has exacerbated problems within its rapidly growing economy. With US markets rapidly shrinking, China needs to find markets elsewhere to sustain its export-led growth model. The rapidly growing Sino-Indian trade is increasingly unbalanced in China's favour, mostly due to an undervalued Yuan is yet another festering issue. China derives much of its export prowess due to its undervalued Yuan and exploitative practices in the work place. The economic profligacy of the USA and China's somewhat naïve hoarding of trillions of dollars as reserves makes it the USA's co-equal in causing the global economic mayhem. There is no sign that China has derived lessons from this and will take a more positive attitude to reconstruct global economic order.

China still does not seem to have grasped the essential reality of its trade relationship with the USA. Many American economists have taken to describing it as akin to that of a dope peddler and drug addict. China supplies cheap goods to the USA and then proceeds to invest its trade surplus in US securities, which in turn fuels more American consumption. This gives China the two digit GDP growth rates it has got addicted to, and the Americans the high standards of living they have got addicted to. The way out of the current crisis is only when the US starts to curb its appetite for overseas goods and overseas adventures like in Iraq and Afghanistan, and China gets used to more realistic and manageable growth rates, in which case the revaluation of the Yuan becomes a mandatory obligation. The problem is that the Chinese consider any such suggestion as a criticism of their wise policies that made them a world player! Sensible opinion from India and elsewhere will only keep pointing out to this as the key destabilizer of global economic order.

India-China trade is burgeoning and is now headed to pass $60 billion by the end of 2011. The trade balance favours the Chinese to the extent of $12 billion. The irony of this is that even this relatively small amount of money will end up as a part of China's US securities portfolios, thereby feeding the consumption frenzy in the US even more. Clearly a way has to be found out of this situation as well. China's suggestion that the Renminbi also becomes a world reserve currency finds few takers in India. One will not be too surprised if this too is taken as a sign of India's essential anti-China orientation? On the other hand the Chinese may not be reckoning that India might prefer a more market oriented Rupee-Renminbi trade arrangement to keep the books balanced and business orderly? The bridge needs to be crossed soon. But it is still not seen to be on the agendas of the two leaderships.

In the recent years there has been much speculation about the emerging rivalry between India and China. A good deal of this owes to the fact that India too has joined China in the high GDP growth club. While Chinese reforms which began in the mid-1970's gave it an edge, India's reforms which began in the early 1990's have begun to show signs of having taken root. Since the turn of the century India has been posting annual growths of close to 8%. Given its more favourable demographic profile India's GDP is predicted to soon grow at a faster rate than China's. If these projections are realized, in another quarter of a century India's GDP will not only overtake that of the USA, but will hover pretty close to that of China. While this should not be a cause of friction, it actually does cause some. Higher GDP's means bigger military budgets. With bigger budgets both nations will inevitably sense greater threats. The unsolved border issue then assumes a critical dimension.

Then there are smaller irritations which crop almost every other month. For instance, the misuse of business visas by Chinese construction and other companies to bring in what is now estimated to be 58,000 workers into India is another one. Latest in the series of provocations is the issue of visas on a separate sheet of paper to Indian residents of J&K and Arunachal Pradesh to highlight their disputed status. Prior to this China has objected to the Asian Development Bank's loan for a hydel project on the Siang river in Arunachal. Compounding these is the rather dubious role played by China during the Vienna conference to ratify the IAEA's exemption for India from the stringent provisions instituted after India's 1974 nuclear test. China has also opposed the expansion of the UN Security Council's permanent membership and by extension India's entry into it.

India has always been concerned about the China-Pakistan axis against it. In the recent days several new publications and books have exposed how extensively China assisted in the development of Pakistan's nuclear programme and its missiles. It is believed that not only did the Chinese give Pakistan the design for its weapons, but also allowed it to test it in its test grounds in Lop Nor, Xinjiang in early 1993. Documents seized from Pakistan's rogue nuclear scientist, AQ Khan, revealed that the Chinese actually gifted Pakistan 50kgs of fissile Uranium to build its first lot of nuclear bombs. Since Pakistan's nuclear programme is entirely India-centric this is quite revealing about Chinese hostility towards India. New Delhi is even more concerned about this aspect of China's behaviour, particularly since it too faces an Islamic *jihad* in Xinjiang. This co-operation endures despite well known concerns about the safety of Pakistan's nuclear weapons? The Chinese however insist that this was in the past and China is now committed to improving ties with India. But the proof of the pudding is in the eating and China, despite its much vaunted policy culinary abilities, has not yet put it out on the table!

Now we must consider another relationship, for long disdained by economists and social scientists - growth and size of population. GDP has a directly relationship with the size of nation's population and its demographic profile. If a population is suitably educated, vocationally skilled and in good health, particularly it's productive age cohort of between 18 - 60 years, then the size of this productive age cohort will determine GDP growth. At this moment of time, China has the world's largest productive age cohort. But by 2050 India's productive age cohort will be a couple of hundred million more than that of China's. That is because populations too rise and wane as families get smaller and death rates overtake birth rates. By 2050, many of today's major economies will be showing deep declines in population. Japan, Russia and most of Western Europe will lose huge numbers. Russian population will decline by as much as 40-50 million or a third of what it is now. As China's population starts flattening its dependency ratio—that is the number of people, young and old, who need to be supported by the families or society - will start rising. China's dependency ratio will be 64 as opposed to India's 48. So there is some hope after all for us, if our leaders don't mess it up?

Finally, let me leave you with this. In village of Lokur in Dharwad district of Karnataka, India's biggest joint family, the Narsingannavar's, live on a 200-acre estate. The Narsingannavar family now numbers 188 persons of all ages. The family estimates its annual consumption expenditure to be over Rs.14 lakhs annually. Their collective property is worth over Rs.20 crores. This should make them among the more wealthy families in India. But the Narsingannavar family still has to live frugally eating millet *rotis* and locally-grown vegetables. They get new sets of clothes once a year. But since the family has over one hundred voters, no *gram panchayat* can be elected without their support and this gives it much clout even in the district. China's story, as is India's, is much like this. The coats may be frayed at the elbows but when they walk, talk, smile or snarl, the world will take note.

INTERNAL CONFLICTS AND REGIONAL SECURITY IN SOUTH ASIA

Arshi Saleem Hashmi, National Defence University, Islamabad

Introduction

Most problems the South Asian states are facing today stem from their complex internal dynamics with external factors impacting, exasperating and garbling the situation. Cold war security kinetics focused primarily on Indo-Pakistan relations, Sino–India relations and nuclear proliferation. But post-9/11 the geopolitical situation has brought some very significant changes, mainly because of the extra-regional powers, particularly the US and the direct alliance of Pakistan with the US on the war against terror. Since South Asia is, unfortunately, the flash point for the Global War on Terror, despite its linkages in the Arab world with particular reference to Al-Qaeda, post-9/11 global politics have altered the internal dynamics within the societies and the states in the forefront of the war on terror, such as Pakistan. Due to the war in Afghanistan, it has had to suffer political consequences domestically, as well as economic costs.

With huge diversity in culture, religion, language and civilisation in South Asia, the region is also one of the most populated in the world as approximately one quarter of the world's population resides here. Along with inter-state tensions especially with two nuclear states, Pakistan and India, intra-state conflicts have devastating effects in the region. South Asia has witnessed some very serious inter and intra-state conflicts causing political and economic environment negatively. The region remains at the mercy of international powers politics disturbing domestic and external policies. In general the security of South Asia greatly depends upon the stable and progressive internal environment of the states.

In South Asia intra-state conflicts have amplified in the last few decades. Whether there are communal riots in India, sectarian and ethnic violence in Pakistan, rift between monarchy and the communist party in Nepal, rivalry and conflict between the main political parties in Bangladesh or the power struggle in Afghanistan after Soviet withdrawal, South Asia faces regional security threats because of internal crisis and conflicts of the states. Being one of the most ethnically, culturally and linguistically diverse regions, it has witnessed many inter-state and intra-state conflicts and war which have disturbed the overall security of the region.

Within states, the ethnic and religious composition of the population is also very diverse. Apart from a large number of ethnic and religious minorities in a state, there are also significant cross-border connections between ethnic and religious communities in the different states. The state boundaries cannot control or enclose ethnically and religiously harmonised regions.[1]

[1] Dahal, S H, Gazdar, H, Keethaponcalan S.I. & Murth, P. (2003). *Internal Conflict and Regional Security in South Asia: Approaches, Perspectives and Policies.* UNIDIR, United Nations Institute for Disarmament Research, Geneva.

Main argument

Any security analysis of South Asia would give us a gloomy picture depicting all the ingredients for serious catastrophe. Governance problems, deteriorating security and economic meltdown in most of the countries are making the region vulnerable to a serious stability crisis. Apart from regional concerns and lack of mistrust, domestic conflicts are not restricted within national boundaries, and often these internal issues lead to external conflicts. Foreign policy priorities often clash with any agreement on collaborative security arrangement in the region. Despite the obstacles, the common traditional and non-traditional security issues in South Asia require serious attention and willingness to think beyond state interest to regional interest. The region undoubtedly suffers from several constraints; nevertheless, forces of change and hope are also working at the civil society level, people's movement against violent conflict within and outside the framework of state is slowly and surely moving in the direction of cooperative framework. The challenge, however, is to sustain that momentum.

Profile of South Asian states

Besides ethnic, religious and linguistic diversity, there is great political diversity in the South Asian region. The political systems in this region have produced many forms of government, based on the internal dynamics of each state. This region has seen democracy, socialism, martial law and monarchy.[2] Presently Pakistan, Bangladesh, India, Maldives, Nepal and Sri Lanka are democracies, Bhutan is a monarchy and Afghanistan is under a US-led Afghan government. All these eight countries have different religious and ideological foundations. Bangladesh, India, Maldives and Sri Lanka, are formally secular, although a particular religious majority rule the state in each case. Pakistan is a declared Islamic republic and Nepal used to be a Hindu state. Many countries in this region were British colonies before becoming independent. Since independence, the focus has been unfortunately more on security rather than human development. South Asia currently spends around USD 15 billion annually on the military, which reduces the budget for human development.[3]

Corruption, international political and economic environment, ineffective and disorganised state institutions, and growing militarisation is fast affecting the development of the region.[4] Political instability in the states is one of the major causes for slow development and an increasingly deteriorating economic condition in the region as a whole which is not very promising. With the exception of India's growing economic progress, the political instability in the region does not provide a healthy environment for markets to flourish. Even India is criticized for not really pursuing a policy of economic development which can reach its poor and improve its infrastructure.

Major Internal Conflicts in South Asian States

The intra-state conflict dynamics in the region are multifarious. It is also true that most of the internal conflicts in the region are caused by the unsettled inter-state conflicts. Intra-state conflicts have long been hampering real progress in the region. The security dynamics of South Asia is very unstable as two of the world nuclear power are neighbours and have fought three wars yet the causes for trouble are not resolved. Due to constant inter and intra-state conflicts, the influx of refugees and internally displaced people cause problems especially between Pakistan and Afghanistan, and India and Bangladesh. Insurgency, sectarian and communal violence, political instability and politically-instigated violence is also high in this region. The situation has affected the very fabric of the society, hence hindering social, economic and political development of the region. The growing trend of separatist movements and insurgencies in the region has disrupted the internal and external environment of the states.

Conflict is normally discussed and estimated through its impact on the civilian population as they are the main victims. Civilians suffer in terms of human rights violations, displacement, war crimes and economic sufferings. Life afterwards is unstable, as poverty increases and economic and social condition is unimaginable and communal violence further deteriorates the human sufferings.[5] The conflict in this region can be categorised as political, economic and socio-cultural. Class and caste-based violence has also deeply affected the social system in the region.

Afghanistan

The present internal conflict in Afghanistan can be traced back to post-Soviet withdrawal, the Taliban regime and 9/11. Afghanistan is under a constant

[2] Nepali, R K. (2009); *Democracy in South Asia*, International Institute for Democracy and Electoral Assistance; Stockholm, Sweden

[3] Ibid

[4] Ibid

[5] Dahal, S H, Gazdar, H, Keethaponcalan S.I. & Murth, P. (2003).*Internal Conflict and Regional Security in South Asia: Approaches, Perspectives and Policies*.

wave of some of the worst conflicts after King Zahir Shah was deposed in early 70's. The Soviet invasion of Afghanistan led to disturbances not only in Afghanistan but Pakistan, as an immediate neighbour, had to bear the brunt. After the Soviet withdrawal, Afghanistan was already going through a serious legitimacy crisis of the forces fighting for the control of the country. The post-9/11 geopolitical situation brought Afghanistan once again to the forefront of world politics. The Taliban's approval of Osama bin Laden's stay in Afghanistan was enough to provoke the international community to attack and remove the Taliban regime. More than a decade has passed since 9/11 and the USA, with NATO and ISAF, are fighting inside Afghanistan, sadly without success. Resultantly, the war on terror has disrupted the security of the entire region. The internal conflict in Afghanistan is yet another dimension of the problem. Warlords and extremists groups are all fighting for power and do not approve the present government or any future political dispensation in the country. The clash of interests between the neighbouring countries vis-à-vis Afghanistan has proved to disastrous for the country as well as the region.

Bangladesh

Since the inception of Bangladesh in 1971, it has experienced some serious internal crises, primarily due to political reasons. Besides political instability that crops up time and again in the country, Bangladesh also faces challenges from extreme Islamist groups which have been time and again disrupting the peace.

The extreme rivalry between the two main political parties, Bangladesh Nationalist Party (BNP) and the Bangladesh Awami League (AL) have contributed more in disrupting the political process than strengthening it. The struggle for power has pushed both the parties towards violence.[6] Since 2002, Bangladesh experienced high level of terrorist's activities including bomb blasts, perhaps in reaction to the hunt down of the terrorist organisations post-9/11. The Jama'atul Mujahideen Bangladesh (JMB) is one of the extremist Islamist organisations responsible for the most number of terrorist incidents and blasts. In 2007, the military in Bangladesh carried out a massive operation against the JMB which resulted in the execution of many seniors leaders. After the military operation, the country returned back to normalcy and the democratically-elected government of Awami League party came to power in late 2008.[7]

Bangladesh has also experienced ethnic conflict in its tribal areas that led to not only violence but displacement of a great number of people. The Chittagong Hill Track (CHT) is a diverse region, comprising of almost 13 different ethnic groups and they differ in religion, customs and tradition from the rest of Bangladesh. Through military intervention by the Bangladeshi Army, the government tried to control the area. It is argued that in order to change the demographic composition of the area, the government tried to move Bengalis to CHT. This migration process created serious political tensions in the region. It also led to the creation of the militant wing of Parbattya Chattagram Jana Sanghati Samity (PCJSS). For around three decades, the government and the tribes have confronted each other violently in the CHT. Thousand of local and ethnic Bengalis got displaced due to the conflict and many human rights abuses were reported. The civil war ended through a peace accord between the Government and tribal leaders. This accord gave more autonomy to the CHT locals and the military presence was also reduced. Thousands of families are still displaced.[8]

India

India with its huge territory and rising economy faces serious internal conflicts, separatist movements, terrorists' incidents and the Maoists Naxalite movement, to name a few, besides a rising rich-poor gap. These have increased violence, internal conflict and instability in the country. Separatist movements in India have been active, especially in Assam, Manipur, Nagaland and Tripura. The violence and conception of a separate homeland began in 1979 and the United Liberation Front of Assam (ULFA) was formed to separate Assam as an independent state. The ULFA armed insurgency has caused much trouble. The government tried to initiate indirect negotiations but they were not very successful. Apart from this, another separatist movement from the Bodo tribe in Assam, started in the 1980's, was countered by the government. It was settled through negotiations by fulfilling few demands of the Bodo tribe. Another separatist movement emerged in Manipur after the formation of United National Liberation Front (UNLF) in the 1960's.[9]

---

[6] Ibid

[7] Iyer L. (2009). *The Bloody Millennium: Internal Conflict in South Asia.* Harvard Business School Paper prepared for the World Bank Report on the Lagging Regions of South Asia

[8] Dahal, S H, Gazdar, H, Keethaponcalan, S.I. & Murth, P. (2003). *Internal Conflict and Regional Security in South Asia: Approaches, Perspectives and Policies.*

[9] Iyer L. (2009). *The Bloody Millennium: Internal Conflict in South Asia.*

One of the very troubling internal conflicts is the Naxalite movement. It has caused serious security issues for the Indian government. It is also known as the Maoist-Naxalite movement, because it is inspired by communism and it can be also understood as communist revolutionary terrorism.

Prime Minister Manmohan Singh highlighting the seriousness of the issue commented, "they are the single biggest internal security challenge ever faced by our country."[10] Taking its name from a worker uprising in the tea gardens in the north Bengal countryside, near Naxalbari in 1967, the Naxalite movement has become synonymous with communist revolutionary terrorism.[11] Apart from these conflicts, the Kashmir issue which is still unresolved after more than six long decades is source of instability with both inter and intra-state dimensions. Though India is cited as a positive example of sustaining democratic system since its inception, the inability of the successive governments to find a permanent solution to disparity and ethnic tensions is a major cause of concern.

Nepal

Like the entire South Asian region Nepal possess a wide range of cultural, ethnic, religious and linguistic groups. Still Hinduism has a great influence on overall structure of the Nepali society. This region is also highly dominated by caste system, feudalism and Nepali language, so one can say that there is an inherent system of suppression and domination in Nepal for centuries.[12] The conflict was related to power struggle in the state, as the Maoists rebels wanted to replace the monarchy with a communist state.

For more than a decade, Nepal witnessed the Maoist insurgency. This 'People's War' was instigated by the Communist Party of Nepal (Maoist) to change the social system in the country. The 1990 People's Movement *(Jana Andolan I)* brought democracy in the state and the King ceded his powers and became a constitutional monarch. The idea was that democracy would change the social order and bring relief to the poor, but nothing happened. The Maoists then decided to adopt a revolutionary armed struggle to replace the corrupt and inept government. In the late 1990's a radical movement headed by the Maoists spread. They very rapidly expanded all over the country with arms to start guerrilla warfare against the government.[13] In September 2001, the conflict escalated as the government declared a state of emergency and declared Maoists as a terrorist group.[14] The Royal Nepal army launched operations against the Maoists insurgents. This episode witnessed some of the worst human rights abuses and violations from both Maoists and the government side. The nature of internal crisis in Nepal stems from not one source but factors including caste and gender discrimination, feudalistic suppression, lack of political representation and decision making, education system, economic inequality and exploitation are few of the main causes for the prolonged armed conflict.[15] The Maoists managed to control a major part of the country in 2005 and signed peace agreements with main political parties in 2006. A sharp decline in the conflicts was observed, as elections were held to form a new constitutional assembly and the monarchy was completely abolished in 2008.[16]

Pakistan

Since its inception, many internal conflicts have caused instability in Pakistan, but not to the extent that could threaten its survival despite its very vulnerable situation. Sectarian issues and political instability have remained one of the main problems of Pakistani polity. Besides three major wars with India, it is now fighting another long war for more than a decade against violent extremism inside the country and terrorism in the Pak-Afghan border area. One of the major upsets to the country was the separation of East-Pakistan in 1971. Neither has the internal situation of the country remained at peace, nor the political environment. During the Soviet invasion of Afghanistan, Pakistan became a frontline state which led to internal chaos, religious radicalisation and easy access to arms creating an intolerant society. The war has shattered the socio-political infrastructure and security has collapsed. Fighting the battle of survival on both internal and external fronts, Pakistan is dealing with the menace

[10] ThottamJ & Dantewada (2010). India's Scourge. *Time Magazine*, November 1 http://www.time.com/time/magazine/article/0,9171,2026792,00.html#ixzz29UkTLtWP

[11] Ray, R. (1992). *The Naxalites and their ideology*, Oxford University Press

[12] Shakya, A. (2009). *Social Impact of Armed Conflict in Nepal: Cause and Impact*. http://www.internal-displacement.org/8025708F004CE90B/(httpDocuments)/BA26441B80B500C5C1257677004DC85F/$file/Social+Impact+of+Armed++Conflict+in+Nepal+by+Anjana+Shakya.pdf

[13] Ibid

[14] Iyer L. (2009). *The Bloody Millennium: Internal Conflict in South Asia.*

[15] Shakya, A. (2009)

[16] Iyer L. (2009)

of TTP (Tehrik-e-Taliban Pakistan) which is responsible for suicide killings all over the country, calling for its own brand of Islam and believing in Talibanisation of the country; and on the external front with the Al-Qaeda-Taliban foreign terrorists. Pakistan's tribal belt has become a battlefield with regular confrontations between the Pakistani army and the terrorists along with the US-targeted drone strikes in the Waziristan area.

Disturbance in Baluchistan is a great concern to Pakistan which is making the country even more vulnerable. Though the separatist movement does not have much credibility amongst the majority of the Baluchs, discontentment and frustration due to bad governance needs to be dealt with if a long term peace and integrity of the borders is to be ensured. Nawab Akbar Bugti's death in the military action led to an escalation of the conflict. But the conflict cannot be categorised as an ethnic conflict only, as it has a sectarian dimension as well, Brutal killings of the Shi'ite Hazara in Baluchistan are causing a rift between the communities. Pakistan's economic centre, Karachi is struggling with internal chaos despite the fact that major representatives of the Sindhis and Urdu-speaking community have their parties (Pakistan People's Party- PPP and Mutahid Qaumi Movement—MQM) in power. The Pushtun community has also managed to have its representatives in the provincial assembly on the platform of Awami National Party-ANP and is striving for its space in the city politics. The city is going through worst kind of violent conflict and the daily death toll is at an average of 10 human lives as cited in daily newspapers and local TV channels. The crisis is more political rather than ethnic or religious. The political power struggle, and claim over certain areas lead to the killing of party members of all three parties which are part of the government.

Sri Lanka

Sri Lanka has witnessed the worst kind of violent conflict in the region. The Tamil separatist movement became a violent conflict because of the discriminatory policies of the majority government in power. The guerrilla group, Liberation Tigers of Tamil Eelam (LTTE) was formed and waged an armed struggle against the state for a separate homeland for the Tamil community. The LTTE fought one of the most sophisticated and organised insurgencies in the world. The LTTE were a highly trained and aggravated group and one of the most terrifying in the world. They extensively used suicide bombing to achieve their goals and eliminating important political figures.[17] In 2002, the government signed a cease fire accord; as a result violence was decreased. In 2005, the LTTE split in two factions and there was a sharp increase in violence. In 2006, the Sri Lankan army commenced an all-out operation against the LTTE. The army took a hold of the Eastern province which resulted in the decline in the violence. The LTTE then raided Colombo with aerial bombing and suicide attacks.[18] The Sri Lankan army continued the massive military operation resulting in major success after nearly three decades. Though there are serious accusations of human rights violation by the Sri Lankan army against the Tamil population during the operation, the three decades of violent armed conflict has come to an end. A lot on the political front is yet to be determined as a long lasting peace can only be ensured when the ethnic and religious minorities feel secure and well-represented politically in the society.

Intra and Inter- state Armed Conflicts: Trends

Observing the pattern of the internal conflicts it can be seen in two ways. The first type of internal conflict is against the state or a civil war. The separatist movements and terrorists activities against government in organised form have sharply increase during the last decade. The second type includes the ethnic conflict or people-to-people conflict. This may include localised land conflicts, religious and ethnic riots, homicides or other crimes.[19] State-to-state conflict has seen a decline in the region while intra-state conflicts have taken a rise. There are several factors and sources responsible for this.

According to the SIPRI Yearbook of 2002, inter-state wars and conflicts get global attention, but intra-state conflicts have a more severe affect on the region. Pakistan and India fought three wars and casualties in those wars can easily be surpassed by the number of fatalities from internal conflicts during the same period.[20]

The last decade has seen inter-state wars and conflicts decreasing in the region while an increasing trend in insurgency, terrorist incidents and separatist

[17] Ibid

[18] South Asia Terrorism Portal. *Sri Lanka Assessment*. (2008) http://satp.org/satporgtp/countries/shrilanka/index.html

[19] Varshney, A. (2002), *Ethnic Conflict and Civic Life: Hindus and Muslims in India*. Yale University Press

[20] SIPRI Yearbook (2002).*Armaments, Disarmament and International Security*, New York: Oxford University Press.

movements is on the rise. Almost all the South Asian countries are or have been through chaotic situations within their boundaries with the exception of Bhutan. The Maldives has recently experienced a serious political crisis. The conflicts in Afghanistan and Pakistan are linked, because of the current war on terror. The presence of US forces in Afghanistan has augmented violence in both the countries and has caused instability and serious security concerns in the region. RAND-MIPT Terrorism Incident Database and Global Terrorism Database (GTD) shows that post-2001 incidents of terrorist violence in Pakistan, Afghanistan, Nepal, Sri Lanka and India have made the states and the region vulnerable to serious crisis.[21]

Regionalisation of Local Conflict: Politics, Ideology and Economics

Local terrorism and insurgency in South Asian states is no more restricted within national boundaries. This has in fact led to the regionalisation of conflicts. An International Peace Academy seminar report states, "Regional conflict formations are interconnected wars among adjacent countries that are mutually reinforcing and therefore typically protracted. They are characterised by complex political, economic, social, and military trans-border linkages. Regional conflict formations are distinct from interstate and intrastate wars, and thus also require new strategies for intervention by the international community."[22]

It is important to understand that inter-state conflicts and intra-state conflicts with multiple parties are different from conflicts that are interconnected and have roots or linkages beyond the region. It cannot be reduced to situations where there is simply a "spillover" effect from one conflict to another. "Rather, regional conflict formations are typically characterized by fundamental, interconnected networking and processes within a region: institutional weaknesses of one or more states, regional security competition, a parallel and transnational informal economy, trans-border social networks, illegal trafficking and trade, natural resource exploitation, militarisation and arms transfers, and trans border armed groups".[23]

This grave situation demands a serious regional arrangement which means a lot of effort on trust building. The interconnectedness of the issues having roots in one country and impact on another cannot be left alone. The individual approach to deal with the common conflicts has led to more complications.

Political and Security Implications on the Region

The increased internal conflicts in the region have affected both the political and security spheres in the region. The constant wave of conflict has grave repercussions on the affected communities and the multifaceted problems give rise to new conflicts hence the cycle continues. The economic condition of the region has direct implications on the security, as poverty has been identified as one of the major factors to stand against a government or regime. This has been a valid argument that poor countries and unstable societies are at a greater risk of internal conflicts.[24] Incidents of internal conflict have become increasingly concentrated in economically lagging regions after 2001.[25] Conflict anywhere in the world is unavoidable, but it's more prevalent in societies which are diverse in culture and ethnicities and there exists great economic discrepancies.[26]

The security implications of conflict in the region are no longer restricted to South Asian states. Insurgencies nowadays have become large scale and global because of their linkages, transnational support, easy flow of weapons and hidden political connections. The present day militancy, which has become transnational, has affected almost all the South Asian states.[27] Sometimes due to the internal conflicts in a country, the political process faces serious setbacks, in the shape of derailing of democracy and military rule. The regional diversity also causes internal conflicts as explained in the examples of the aforementioned South Asian states.

Human Cost of Conflict

Being the most populated region in the world, development and progress is not very encouraging. There is poverty, lack of education and awareness, lack of basic facilities for life and human rights abuses

[21] Iyer L. (2009). *The Bloody Millennium: Internal Conflict in South Asia.*

[22] Cater, C. (2003). *The Regionalization of Conflict and Intervention.* IPA Seminar Report, International Peace Academy. New York.pg 1

[23] Ibid, pg 2

[24] Collier, Paul, Elliott, Hegre.H, Hoeffler. A, Reynold-Querol. M, Sambanis. N. (2003). *Breaking the Conflict Trap: Civil War and Development Policy.* Oxford University Press.

[25] Iyer L. (2009).

[26] Dahal, S H, Gazdar, H, Keethaponcalan S.I. & Murth, P. (2003). *Internal Conflict and Regional Security in South Asia: Approaches, Perspectives and Policies.*

[27] Nepali, R K. (2009).*Democracy in South Asia.*

are very much visible. There are many regions facing conflicts across the globe, but South Asia is submerged in serious internal conflicts and terrorism. According to Ghani and Iyer, "after Iraq, South Asia is the second most violent place on earth."[28] There is no doubt that South Asia is a violent place, as in 2007 alone, there were 3,607 incidents of terrorist violence which claimed 4,737 lives. This represents a quarter of all terrorist attacks worldwide, second only to Iraq.[29] Due to the war on terror, Afghanistan and Pakistan have gained global attention. Some parts of India, Sri Lanka and Nepal have seen extended conflicts, mainly the separatist movements and insurgencies. The effects and cost of the conflicts can be seen in shape of human misery, destruction of infrastructure and social cohesion, and large-scale homicide.[30]

Internal conflicts are more deadly than the inter-state conflicts, as they gain less attention and suffer more human rights violations and they are more long-running. Internal conflicts have resulted in three times as many deaths as wars between states since World War II.[31] Due to economic, social and political vulnerability, conflicts recur mainly because of inappropriate and short-term measures to end the conflicts. Human rights violations and worsening condition after the de-escalation of the conflict helps in the renewal of the clashes.[32]

According to the *SIPRI Yearbook 2002*, the combine number of deaths of three wars (1949, 1965, and 1971) between India and Pakistan were around 20,000 combatants. The casualties from the internal conflict during the same period can very easily surpass the figure of the inter-state wars between the two countries. The deaths of the internal conflicts from 1999-2001 are more than 20,000. If we see the number of casualties in the last 50 years from internal conflicts within Sri Lanka only, more than 60,000 people and in India more than 23,000.[33] There is an increase in the internally displaced people and refugees, who migrate to other parts of the country due to security reasons, causing social problems.

Major Obstacle to Peace in South Asia

The conflicts and clashes in South Asia are generally caused by growing inequalities, caste and class system, ethnic and religious intolerance. Government policies and reforms have not brought any significant result. Elite representation in the politics of each country negatively affects the democratic process, a common obstacle across this region. Along with this, with an increasing trend in globalisation, trans-national mechanisms have flourished, which have created troubles for the governments and law enforcement agencies internationalizing the local conflicts.

Growing inequalities within the states have given rise to separatist movements calling for access to resources belonging to "their" land. The socio-economic class differences and identity politics is also another cause of unrest. Foreign interventions in the state affairs and proxy wars for varied reasons have increased internal instability and increased regional insecurity. Last but not the least, mutual distrust and lack of collective approach to own and protect the region is an important impediment to peace in South Asia.

The Way Forward

The regional organisation SAARC has failed in resolving the regional conflicts. The states should develop confidence and trust and mutual sharing of information to establish a regime of peace in the region.

Joint efforts can reduce terrorism and conflicts both inter-state and intra-state. Regional cooperation is very important and necessary in defeating insurgencies. SAARC should redefine its role and play its part in building peace in the region. The intra-state conflicts should be addressed in the light of all inequalities. The growing economic discrepancies and discriminations should be addressed and countered through reform and justice. Conflict prevention mechanism to deal with the root causes of the civil unrest, interstate interference and violent approach for rights should be developed.

Afghanistan is the key issue in any discourse on the future of present day South Asia for prompting internal and external tensions within and outside the countries in the region. Though regional involvement in Afghanistan was criticized by some of the neighbours but it is also argued at the same time that it might also work in preventing India, Iran and Pakistan from

---

[28] Ghani,E &Iyer, L. (2010).*Conflict and development*. http://www.voxeu.org/article/conflict-and-development-lessons-south-asia

[29] National Counterterrorism Center. (2008) .*2007 Report on Terrorism.* http://www.fbi.gov/statsservices/publications/terror_07.pdf

[30] Ghani, E & Iyer, L. (2010)

[31] James, F & Laitin, D. (2003). "Ethnicity, Insurgency, and Civil War." *American Political Science Review.* 97:75-90.

[32] Dahal, S H, Gazdar, H, Keethaponcalan S.I. & Murth, P. (2003). *Internal Conflict and Regional Security in South Asia: Approaches, Perspectives and Policies.*

[33] SIPRI Yearbook (2002). *Armaments, Disarmament and International Security.*

fighting proxy wars in Afghanistan which has been the major cause of direct or indirect interference.

India and Iran have huge economic projects in Afghanistan that demand security and stability. The US facilitated efforts to let India directly engage in Afghanistan economically, which has actually long-lasting implications. Afghanistan, which is no more struggling with the confusion whether it is South Asian or Central Asian state, is now crucial in how South Asia moves forward as an economic bloc. A troubled Afghanistan would not be desirable as it would continue to create problems for stability hence shifting the focus of the countries in the region from economic to a hard core security approach. Pakistan is still struggling with the idea of giving up its long-lost goal of having a friendly government in Kabul. In the present circumstances, when Pakistan is fighting many wars internally as well as on its borders with Afghanistan, the best bet would be to become a part of the collective effort to combat extremism and terrorism and then enjoy the benefit of economic prosperity by focusing on mutual economic interests rather than continuing with the policy of confrontation. An accommodative policy, based on peaceful coexistence, is the only option left with Pakistan.[34]

As for India's role in the region, Raghav Sharma writes, that "there is a serious need to deal with the concerns Pakistan has about India's role in the crisis. Should India place its boots on the ground? To what extent can India continue to expand its diplomatic and economic profile in Afghanistan without an appropriate security apparatus in place? The emerging political and military situation makes it imperative for India to evolve a clear policy, to establish a meaningful presence in the region and realize some of its larger interest."[35]

Any long term solution to the complex web of conflicts requires a one-point agenda, i.e. ensuring economic development and good governance. Unfortunately, South Asian countries have yet to devise a mature outlook towards their priorities, unlike other regions (EU, ASEAN). South Asian states still believe in looking outwards for the reasons of their problems. It is all the more important that they start looking inward, do some introspection and identify wrong policies that have led to an atmosphere of distrust and suspicion towards each other. Once that bottleneck is removed, the collective efforts to build a secure, economically stable South Asia would not be hard to achieve.

---

[34] Arshi Saleem Hashmi, "Growing Vulnerability of South Asian States to Extremism and Terrorism: Redefining the Discourse", *Focus on Regional Issues*, Institute of Regional Studies, Vol XXVII, No 1, August 2009

[35] Raghav Sharma, "India and Afghanistan: Charting the Future," *IPCS Special Report # 69*, New Delhi India, available at <http://www.ipcs.org/ publications_special_details.php?recNo=242&pT=4>

EMERGING GEOPOLITICAL DYNAMICS OF AFGHANISTAN AND ITS IMPACT ON INDIA

*Prof. Nirmala Joshi, Director, India Central Asia Foundation, New Delhi and Maj Gen (Retd) BK Sharma, United Service Institution of India, New Delhi**

Introduction

Developments in Afghanistan have drawn and continue to draw the attention of policy makers, diplomats, academia, analysts and observers. As the drawdown date (end of 2014) for the withdrawal of US-led North Atlantic Treaty Organisation (NATO) forces is away by just over two years, debates and discussions in India have been initiated on the future of Afghanistan. Between now and the end of 2014 two important developments are crucial and would have a bearing on the Emerging scenario in the region. One is the US Presidential elections and the future of American strategy in Afghanistan and the region. The second is the forthcoming Presidential elections in Afghanistan followed by the Parliamentary one. The moot question is; who would succeed Hamid Karzai? Linked with the election would be the status of the reconciliation process on which Karzai has staked a lot. As of now this process has led nowhere. Intertwined with the issue of reconciliation would be the nature, strength and the leadership question in the on-going insurgency, particularly that of the Taliban.

Today, insurgency and terrorism is the biggest source of instability in Afghanistan, Pakistan and the region. Of greater importance is how strong the underpinnings of the insurgency and their *jihadi* mindset are. These are highly insidious forces and pose a grave danger to free and secular societies. With access to global communication and mobility, and advanced technology, these forces have acquired immense lethal power. It remains to be seen how strong these forces would be in the years to come. The eleven years "war on terror" has certainly weakened the insurgency but it has neither been defeated completely nor their terrorist infrastructure dismantled. In all probability, the insurgency in the years to come would remain alive.

These developments of the past two decades did impact on Indian security. When the Taliban was at the helm of affairs in Afghanistan, insurgency in the Indian state of Jammu and Kashmir (J&K) escalated manifold, and India lost all contact with its traditional ally. After the defeat of the Taliban in 2001 India was able to restore its ruptured ties with Afghanistan. When Karzai became the first democratically-elected President of Afghanistan, it was easy for India to

*The authors acknowledge the comments by Brig (Retd) S.S. Pabla, former Vice-Chancellor, Manipal University, Jaipur and Brig (Retd) S. Mishra, Vice Chancellor, Manipal University, Sikkim.

re-connect with Afghanistan. At stake for India are its deep and abiding interests, not only in Afghanistan but in the Central Asian region as well. Hence in the Indian perspective a stable, independent and an open Afghanistan is essential, and would be able to meet the challenge of non-traditional threats such as religious extremism, international terrorism, narco-trafficking, smuggling of small weapons and criminal activity. The India-Afghanistan Strategic Partnership Agreement of 4 October 2011 symbolizes the computability of these interests leading to a multi-dimensional relationship.

Emerging Afghan Scenario

In the recent past, attempts at forecasting the future Afghan scenarios have been made. They range from the break-up of the country along ethnic lines—a possibility that appears remote at present, to take care of Afghanistan by the inflexible and hardcore Taliban elements, which also appears unlikely at present. Another scenario often mentioned is the outbreak of a civil war as it happened in 1989.

Nevertheless, on the basis of the emerging trends, tentative projections can be made. The post-2014 scenario would be a mixed one; having both certainties and uncertainties. Such an assumption is based on the growing strategic significance of Afghanistan for the regional as well as external powers. What is certain is the phased withdrawal of NATO troops by the end of 2014. Perhaps the US and its allies realize that overstaying in Afghanistan with active combat activity will not lead them to their great goal of a democratic, stable and an independent Afghanistan. President Barack Obama aptly said at a Press Conference in Chicago in May 2012:

> "We have been there ten years and I think no matter how much good we are doing and how outstanding our troops and our civilians and diplomats are doing on the ground, ten years in a country that's very different, that's a strain not only on our folks, but also on that country, which is at a point is going to be very sensitive about its own sovereignty".[1]

It is also hoped that the Afghan National Security Force (ANSF) and the Afghan National Police (ANP) could emerge as a capable force able to protect its citizens and the sovereignty and integrity of the country.

It is also amply clear that the military presence of International Security Assistance Force (ISAF) would continue beyond 2014. During her visit to Kabul, in July 2012, Secretary of State Hilary Clinton reiterated that Washington did envision keeping American troops in Afghanistan, where they would also be on hand to provide the kind of air power and surveillance capabilities needed to give Afghan forces an edge over the Taliban.[2] At the same time the US declared Afghanistan a major non-NATO ally. Indeed a significant development. It is expected that approximately anything between 23,000 to 70,000 troops would stay back. At the Chicago summit, however it was made clear that the ISAF would shift its focus primarily from a combat to a support role in all parts of the country, that is training, advice and assist the ANSF till it could independently confront the challenge of insurgency. President Hamid Karzai requested, at the Lisbon Summit in 2010, that Afghanistan would need the support and assistance from the US and its allies beyond 2014. He felt that the ANSF and ANP may not be ready to handle this task independently. The same argument was made at the Chicago Summit in May 2012.

The core interest hence forward would be in reconstruction activity with emphasis on capacity building in the security forces in particular, and in education and healthcare among other areas. The international community has pledged financial assistance to Afghanistan beyond 2014. This process was taken further at the Tokyo conference of July 2012, where Members have pledged aid worth US$ 16 billion spread over four years. The decade would be known as the "transformational decade". From the foregoing it is evident that Western interests in Afghanistan had not waned. This interest lies in the strategic significance of Afghanistan for all the stake holders.

The prime interest of the US and its allies is that Afghanistan in future should not emerge as an epicentre of terrorism, threatening democratic and open societies as had happened in 2001. An equally vital concern is that the nuclear weapons of Pakistan should not fall in the wrong hands. The commitment of Western countries to this objective is evident from the Strategic Partnership Agreements signed by the US, France, Germany, Australia with Afghanistan.

Apart from enduring security interests of all the stake holders in meeting the challenge of non-traditional threats, an additional dimension that is gathering momentum is the strategic significance of Afghanistan. The US and its allies would continue their presence even after 2014 by focusing on reconstruction activity in economic and political

---

[1] President Barack Obama's Press Conference at the Chicago summit of the North Atlantic Treaty Organization; May 2012.

[2] *Indian Express*, 8 July 2012

sphere. China is also making its presence in Afghanistan. It has made investment in the Ayinak copper mines and is prospecting for gas in the Amu Darya basin. In this context it is involved in infrastructure activities. China has constructed its road access to northern Afghanistan via the Kulma pass in Tajikistan and then into the country. Similar activity in northern Pakistan is underway to lift the Afghan copper. Indian involvement in Afghanistan is substantial and will be discussed later in the article. Iran is focusing on rail and road connectivity with western Afghanistan. The three Central Asian States —Tajikistan, Turkmenistan and Uzbekistan may not have presence in economic terms, but share their ethnic affinity with northern Afghanistan. Pakistan's role is crucial and, by now, the kind of role it is playing in Afghanistan is well recognised.

The underpinnings of this growing strategic significance of Afghanistan are the abundant natural resources of the country. The economic potential of Afghanistan especially its natural resources—natural gas, copper, iron ore and vital minerals are drawing world attention. As mentioned, China has invested over US$ 3 billion in the mining sector and is conducting exploration for natural gas in the Amu Darya basin. At the political level, Afghanistan was given the status of an Observer state in the Shanghai Co-operation Organisation (SCO) summit meeting at Tashkent in June 2012. China's leading role in the SCO is well recognised. What lends further significance to Afghan natural resources is its geographical proximity to Central Asia, which is equally rich in natural resources and energy resources—oil, natural gas and hydro carbons, uranium, gold, hydel power and aluminium. Since the nineties Central Asia has been caught in the vortex of international politics, with nations vying with each other to secure, if not control the energy resources.

It must be mentioned that both Afghanistan and the Central Asian States (CAS) are landlocked. Hence it was the construction of energy pipelines and transport corridors that became a tool in the hands of countries trying to access Central Asian energy, in particular. In view of their landlocked status, Afghanistan and the CAS belong to the same geopolitical space. Western multinationals have a large presence in the extractive industries. Their flagship the Baku-Tbilisi-Ceyhan (BTC) pipeline, bypassing Russia, has become operational. Chinese engagement with the CAS is extensive and substantive encompassing energy pipelines, infrastructural activities and economic interaction. Turkey and Iran are also involved in Central Asia in various sectors. With focus on reconstruction this competition has expanded into Afghanistan as well. However, for the present this competition between external powers and the regional states is benign and has not reached a conflictual level. However, many analysts and observers perceive this competition as a replay of the nineteenth century great game for the control of Afghanistan. A debatable point indeed! But what is certain is that the natural resources of the region would be the central focus of the involved countries.

A related factor is the question of overcoming the landlocked status of Afghanistan and the Central Asian region. The success of the reconstruction strategy would to a large extent depend on Afghanistan gaining an opening to the outside world. One of the most relevant ideas is the concept of "Greater Central Asia" that seeks to connect Central Asia with South Asia through Afghanistan. It aims to recreate the past ancient trade when Afghanistan was the hub of trade and transit routes; routes from China, the Indian subcontinent, Persia, Central Asia and the Caspian region criss-crossed its territory. Today, this idea is being revived as sea commerce is getting congested and the danger of piracy makes the sea lanes risky. Hence Afghanistan's emergence as a land bridge to Eurasia and beyond would be highly beneficial to all the countries in the region. The Istanbul Conference on Afghanistan "Security and Cooperation in the Heart of Asia" held in November 2011 mentioned the importance of Afghanistan as a land bridge in its final Declaration. The subsequent Bonn Conference of December 2011 highlighted the urgent need for economic development of Afghanistan. The Asian Development Bank (ADB) has been deeply involved in projects relating to transport corridors and energy pipelines. Recently the US initiated the New Silk Road strategy, while the Chinese have launched their worn initiative on the Silk Road.

However, for Afghanistan to emerge as the land bridge to Eurasia and beyond a lot of investments would be required for infrastructure activities; such as upgrading and modernising the existing roads, and building new ones. It is also necessary to bring about uniformity in rules, regulations and procedures for the smooth running of this transport corridor. This would in turn facilitate greater involvement of countries in the Afghan reconstruction effort. The benefit of Afghanistan as a hub of transport corridors was succinctly brought out by Ashley Tellis, an American scholar, who wrote:

> "The expansion of transportation corridors in and around Afghanistan thus permits all the regional states to benefit from the rapidly expanding

> Chinese and Indian economies by becoming either new sources of raw material exports to these states or new markets for their goods or even by simply enjoying transit fees for commodities passing in any direction through their territories..."[3]

The concept of 'greater Central Asia' would also benefit the CAS who are keen for an opening in the southern direction in order to connect with India, South East Asia and Africa. However, a great deal would depend on the collaborative approach of all the stake holders in Afghan stability and economy upliftment.

Consequently, closely linked with Afghanistan's emergence as a land-bridge is the kind of co-operation regional countries would extend. Collective efforts are also essential to keep in check the insurgency and the Taliban. It can be said with modest certainty that the insurgents would interfere in transport corridors. In this context the Northern Distribution Network located in Central Asia is a target for the insurgents.

However, despite recognising the urgent need for regional cooperation, most of the countries have adopted a bilateral approach instead of a cooperative one. For instance, Iran would like the coalition forces to withdraw. Though it is opposed to the Taliban and its insurgency, Pakistan considers certain terrorist groups and organisations such as the Haqqani network, Lashkar-e-Toiba, Hezb-i-Islami and Jamat-ud Dawa as strategic assets, unlike most countries who perceive them as challenges to their integrity. Indian and US interests converge considerably, whereas for China its strategic support to Pakistan is more important. India feels the lack of a suitable regional or international forum that brings together all major stakeholders in this endeavour. India feels that regional players should be involved in support for any future reconciliation process and that any regional approach should have a strong economic underpinning.[4]

Another factor that would shape the dynamics of Afghanistan and the region is the level and nature of threat posed by the Taliban. Would the insurgency remain strong and what kind of leadership would come forward? There is wide apprehension among the stake holders that the insurgents would be quick in adapting to the changed scenario of post-2014 in which there is a strong possibility that the Taliban would interfere. Such interference could take the shape of disrupting the supply lines both from the Pakistan side and with the Northern Distribution Network that passes through Central Asia. What is certain is that insurgency would remain alive and in all probability heighten the sense of vulnerability of the CAS and Tajikistan in particular.

Indian Interests

In view of the changing nature of Afghan dynamics, it is important to understand the impact it would have on Indian interests.

Traditionally India and Afghanistan have had close historical, cultural and economic ties dating back to antiquity. India's ancient trade route to the West passed through Afghanistan. After India gained independence 1947, adherence to non-alignment and secularism cemented the existing friendly ties between the two countries. In the last decade of the twentieth century these ties of friendship had come under considerable strain and in the Taliban period the relationship verged on animosity. India's interest lay in seeing that Afghanistan did not emerge as a centre for religious extremism and terrorism. In official thinking "Indian concerns vis-à-vis the Taliban originate from their close links with Pakistan, with their fundamentalist disposition and the known involvement of Afghan mercenaries in the Jammu and Kashmir militancy".[5] Indian concerns for its security were not unfounded for the evolving scenario in India's neighbourhood had started deteriorating. India found that many of the extremist and terrorist groups and organisations that had sprung up during the ten year war with the Soviet Union were neither disarmed nor their infrastructure dismantled. These extremist groups were well trained, well armed and had a safe haven in the borderlands between Afghanistan and Pakistan, and in POK.

A historic development that occurred simultaneously was the break-up of the Soviet Union in 1991 and the unexpected independence of the five CAS. In the unfolding situation, Indian apprehension was that the newly emergent CAS who had always adhered to a secular, liberal and modern outlook were highly vulnerable to non-traditional threats. Developments in Afghanistan could cast their shadow in Central Asia. The activities of Pakistan and Saudi Arabia who were freely distributing copies of the Koran and providing financial support to build mosques showed that Indian concerns were not baseless. What added to Indian concerns was the beginning of the Tajik war

[3] Ashley Tellis and Anoop Mukarji eds. *Is a Regional Strategy Viable in Afghanistan*? Carnegie Endowment Washington, DC p. 97

[4] Gautam Mukhopadhyaya, *"India"* in Ashley Tellis and Anoop Mukharji, ibid

[5] Ministry of Defence, Government of India *Annual Report 2000-2001*

in September 1992. The Tajik Opposition fled to Afghanistan where they received full support in terms of training, equipment and safe havens. The Tajik civil war fuelled the spectre of Central Asia breaking up and idea of "Greater Afghanistan" gained momentum. However, with the end of the civil war the idea lost shine. The Tajik civil war, perceived as an ideological war between secular and religious forces, was to a large extent a power struggle. One of the main opposition parties in the civil war, the Islamic Renaissance Party of Tajikistan, joined the coalition government in 1997. A factor aggravating Indian concerns, however, was the huge stockpile of weapons in the region and their easy accessibility to extremist groups.

In the evolving situation in India's neighbourhood, its prime concern was that Pakistan would seek to acquire "strategic depth" vis-à-vis India by bringing the CAS within the Islamic fold. Pakistan's quest was to create a vast strategic integrated region, oriented towards a religious order and comprising Afghanistan and the CAS. From the Indian strategic perspective Afghanistan and the CAS are perceived as one geopolitical unit. Hence the CAS are considered as part of India's extended/strategic neighbourhood. The notion of strategic depth had to be countered by focusing on building strong independent and secular states in the region. The moderate Islam that had flourished in the region had to be sustained and strengthened. India welcomed and supported the Central Asian leaders when they emphatically declared their intention to build a liberal, secular and a modern polity. A typical example is the speech of President Askar Akayev of Kyrgyzstan during his visit to India, in March 1992. At the banquet speech he said "Kyrgyzstan is looking to India as an example, as it sets about restructuring its economy and socio-political order. We categorically reject extremism of any kind. Let it be neither extremism of communist type nor of religious fanatics".[6] Similar views were expressed by other Central Asian leaders.

India backed the western initiative of Operation Enduring Freedom (OEF) launched in October 2001. OEF aimed at defeating the Taliban by military action. India also extended full support to the effort at reconstructing Afghanistan. The turn of the century also saw the broadening of Indian strategies on security matters. While the core of India's strategic interests lay in its periphery, its own rising international profile and a desire to play a role in Asia led it to look beyond the South Asian region. In this context the "strategic defence dialogue has assumed a significant role in the defence partnership between India and a number of countries leading to greater joint partnership towards preparations for a globally coordinated initiative to fight against the menace of terrorism, proliferation, trafficking, piracy and nefarious activities of non state actors".[7]

Apart from security and strategic considerations, economic interests in the region have also begun to figure prominently in Indian thinking. Indian involvement in Afghanistan's reconstruction effort is substantial. Some of the projects undertaken by India are construction of the Zaranj-Delaram Road from the border of Afghanistan-Iran to the Garland Highway, completion of the Salma Dam power project in Herat province, and sustained efforts in capacity building activity in numerous areas. In Central Asia, the Indian policy is highly pro-active in the security, defence, economic and cultural spheres. The Strategic Partnership Agreements with Kazakhstan (2009), Uzbekistan (2011) and Tajikistan (2012) reflect the mutually beneficial relationship that has evolved over the years. Indian activity in the region can be further energised, if it is able to connect with Afghanistan and the CAS in a reliable way.

India has been keen to revive its ancient trade and transit route that passed through Afghanistan and the links with Central Asia constituted an important segment of this route. Historically, the trade route was the lifeline of the region and the source of its prosperity. The possibility of re-establishing the trade route holds immense promise in today's context as well. For India, the prospect of linking Central Asia with South Asia would provide it an opportunity to intensify its engagement with both Afghanistan and the CAS. Emergence of Afghanistan as a trade and transit hub is supported by India, and is a point that is often emphasised in Indian policy makers' statements. To cite an example, former Foreign Secretary Nirupama Rao said:

> "... India was to utilize its development programme in Afghanistan to (deny such ideologies space to grow) help Afghanistan stabilize and emerge as an economic hub linking South and Central Asia through a network of trade and transit linkages that would benefit the people of the entire region".[8]

Afghanistan was and is the key for India to reach out

---

[6] *Indian Express*, 18 March 1992

[7] Ministry of Defence, Government of India, *Annual Report*, 2005-2006, p 6

[8] *"Reaching out to Afghanistan"*, Ministry of External Affairs, Government of India, www.meaindia.nic.in/mystart.php?Id=8400(Accessed on 6 December 2010).

to Central Asia and beyond. There are two options for India to reach out to Afghanistan; one is through Iran and the second via Pakistan. The route via Iran is an important transport link and it is operational, but needs revitalising. The route via Pakistan is perhaps the best option, but appears difficult at present because of the troubled India-Pakistan relations. Part of the explanation is that Pakistan would like to emerge as the only country to offer this landlocked region an opening in the southern direction. Pakistan's approach is exclusive and seeks to exclude India from this transport corridor. The agreement between Afghanistan-Pakistan on an overland transit corridor is a hopeful development. According to the Agreement, Afghan goods are permitted to transit through Pakistan up to the Indian border, but Indian goods bound for Afghanistan and beyond are not allowed. Perhaps, in due course, the logic of economic benefits may make two-way traffic of goods a reality.

Energy is another vital area where Afghanistan's role as a transit corridor is crucial. Turkmenistan and Kazakhstan are richly endowed with energy resources—oil, natural gas and hydrocarbons. An Asian Development Bank (ADB) supported energy project the Turkmenistan-Afghanistan-Pakistan-India (TAPI) pipeline has been under discussion for many years. If the project has not taken off, it is because of uncertain conditions in Afghanistan and Pakistan. TAPI is a natural gas pipeline project and Turkmen natural gas from its Daulatabad gas field would be fed into it. However, TAPI is likely to go on board in the near future. Once TAPI becomes operational, it is plausible that Kazakhstan could also be associated with it and other projects are likely to come up. Fur Turkmenistan and Kazakhstan such a possibility would activate the southern vector of their foreign policies, including energy policy. Importantly, it would help them to diversify their markets. At the same time India could access Central Asian energy resources.

The emergence of Afghanistan as the hub of transport, trade and energy corridors would not only dispel the centuries-old notion of perceiving Afghanistan as a "buffer" or "an intermediate zone", but would instead lead to a network of corridors criss-crossing the area and weave the countries into interdependence. Such underpinnings of economic interdependence would lead to the stability of Afghanistan. Similar views are expressed by Afghan author Ahmad Qassem who opines that "... the objective of regional co-operation is to transfer Afghanistan into an inter-regional transit link and forge strong economic this with neighbouring countries so as to affect economic prosperity in Afghanistan and create a stake for the neighbouring countries in Afghanistan's stability".[9] Two aspects are, however, crucial to stabilize Afghanistan; one is security of the country; and second, acceleration of reconstruction efforts which are an integral part of the stabilisation strategy evolved by the international community. Both are onerous tasks requiring a collective and collaborative approach.

Concluding Observations

The evolving dynamics in Afghanistan will impact on Indian interests. Since the last decade India has built strong and overriding security and economic interests both in Afghanistan and Central Asia. Between now and 2014 there are imponderables and challenges for India, which can be best met in a collective and a collaborative way. At stake are not only peace and stability in the region, but an insidious ideological threat that has the potential to strike at the basis of democratic, open and secular polities. Economic prosperity and well-being of the people of the region could act as a catalyst for peace and stability. Regional cooperation is the best way forward. Sustained effort on the part of India is required to work out common approaches at the political and diplomatic level. What is required is generation of the necessary political will.

[9] Ahmad Shayeq Qassem, *Afghanistan's Political Stability: A Dream Unrealized* (Ashgate, London, 2009) p 151

TIBET AND THE GREAT POWERS [1950]

R.S.Kalha, former Secretary, Ministry of External Affairs, New Delhi

When Chinese troops entered Tibet in 1950 the question uppermost in the minds of most observers was whether Tibet was an independent country or was it an appendage of China. This question becomes important for—if Tibet was an independent country then certainly the Chinese intervention must be classified as an invasion. If, on the other hand, Tibet was but an appendage of China, in whatever form—whether an autonomous region or whether China exercised suzerainty—then the right of China to restore its administrative rule cannot be faulted. The Chinese intervention in Tibet, in 1950, in that case cannot be classified as an invasion of an independent country.

In modern times all Chinese governments have steadfastly held on to the belief that Tibet has always been a part of China. This has not always been so. China first occupied Lhasa in 1720, but did not displace the local government of the Dalai Lama. For the next two hundred years Chinese authority was intermittent and at times non-existent. In 1792 a Chinese army helped the Tibetans expel a Nepalese invasion and such help was welcomed by the Tibetans. The 1876 Anglo-Chinese Convention was the first international document in which Tibet figured. The Manchu general Chao Erfang occupied Lhasa in 1908-1910; the first Chinese army to occupy Lhasa against the wishes of the Tibetans. However at the fall of the Manchu Empire, the Chinese garrison at Lhasa had to surrender and in 1912 was finally repatriated to China via India.

Sun Yatsen, 'the father of the Chinese revolution,' called for the establishment of a strong Chinese state that would expel the Japanese from Manchuria, the Russians from Mongolia and the British from Tibet. The Republican President Yuan Shihkai went even further and issued an edict on 21 April 1912 declaring Tibet to be 'a province' of China, on an equal footing with all other Chinese provinces. Even at a time when the central government in China was weak and Tibet outside its control, China never surrendered the belief, or the right, that Tibet was a part of China. Whether China was the 'suzerain' power or otherwise, it has tenaciously maintained that Tibet has always been a part of the larger Chinese family. Throughout this period China resisted all efforts by outside powers to recognize Tibet as anything other than 'autonomous'. At best China was only willing to concede that Tibet was but an 'autonomous province' of China.

The KMT government of Chiang Kaishek [Jiang Jieshi] was as adamant as any other regime in China that Tibet was a part of China; in fact a Chinese province. For example, this is what the British told the US State Department on the meeting between Foreign Secretary, Antony Eden, and the KMT Chinese Foreign Minister, TV Soong, on Tibet:

> *893.24/1594*—The British Embassy to the Department of State
>
> AIDE-MEMOIRE
>
> On the 15 March 1943, Mr. Eden had a conversation in Washington with Dr. TV Soong during the

> course of which the latter raised the question of Tibet. Dr. Soong said that Mr. Eden would doubtless be aware of the fact that the Government of China *had always regarded Tibet as a part of the Republic* [emphasis added].

The expansion of the Chinese state to incorporate Tibet has always had great prestige value in China itself. In addition, the Chinese were aware of the immense influence that successive Dalai Lama's have exercised over the Mongols and other peoples inhabiting Inner Asia and this, in turn, has added to Tibet's political value. For the Chinese, ownership of the Tibetan landmass was crucial and a strategic necessity for without Tibet the essential unity of the 'new' China could never be realized. The Chinese considered Tibet as a bulwark against outside powers that might wish to use Tibet to mount incursions from south of the Himalayas to destabilize the Chinese state. The population of non-Han minorities in China is about 100 million, but crucially they occupy almost half the land area! In other words, although Han Chinese constitutes nearly 90% of the population, yet they occupy only less than half the land! It was not surprising therefore that China claimed and insisted that Tibet was a Chinese province; whose land mass is about 25% the size of Western Europe.

The Chinese Communists were not too far behind either. As far back as 1922, when the Communist Party held its Second National Congress, the manifesto of the CCP listed amongst the principal aims, 'achievement of a genuine republic by the liberation of Mongolia, *Tibet* and Sinkiang.'[1] Mao on the other hand, in July 1936, spoke of a Chinese 'Federation' of which Outer Mongolia, *Tibet* and Sinkiang would be autonomous constituent parts.[2] Later, in 1949, Mao was to change his views when he noted that 'although Tibet's population is small, its international position is extremely important and we must occupy it'.[3]

Nevertheless on attaining power the new Communist government of China gave the concept of a 'Chinese Federation' a wide berth and reverted to the concept of a strong central government. There appear to be two fundamental reasons for this. The new Communist government was determined to eliminate all foreign influence and any vestige of China's earlier humiliations at the hands of foreigners. A part of the restoration of national dignity *involved restoring full sovereignty over all the areas that were previously considered 'Chinese'* [emphasis added]. Restoring Tibet to the larger Chinese family thus had deep nationalistic as well as great symbolic value. Secondly, the Chinese leadership was conscious of the fact that Tibet, a religious theocracy, was inclined towards independence and was deeply influenced by Britain and India. For China, the possibility that countries hostile to it would continue to play a role in Tibet from where they could threaten the Chinese provinces of Sinkiang, Qinghai and Yunnan was clearly an unacceptable risk. China wished to maintain stability on its south-western front, as it faced military encirclement and an economic embargo imposed by the US, following the victory of the Communists in China and the outbreak of hostilities in Korea.

Reflecting Mao's thinking, it came as no great surprise when the new Chinese government emphatically stated that it would brook no interference in Tibet. It rudely emphasized to India that:

> Tibet is an integral part of Chinese territory. The problem of Tibet is entirely the domestic problem of China. The Chinese People's Liberation Army must enter Tibet, liberate the Tibetan people and defend the frontiers of China.[4]

Thus for China an independent Tibet never existed. It was considered a part of China.

From the very beginning of British rule in India, Britain was not prepared to accept the responsibility of taking over and governing a huge territory such as Tibet. Britain was never interested in recognizing an 'independent' Tibet, or even declaring Tibet as a British protectorate. Britain realized that there were no economic advantages to be gained in Tibet. The British knew that to fortify and garrison the north-east frontier of India on the same lines as the north-west frontier would be financially ruinous. As Sir Charles Bell remarked, 'it was recognized on our side *from the first* that this would have developed too heavy a burden upon us, the responsibility of protecting the distant and difficult expanses of Tibet' [emphasis added].[5] Additionally, it would have meant that Britain would have had to police an additional frontier of about 2,000 miles, enclosing an area of almost 500,000 square miles. No one in the

---

1 C Brandt, B Schwartz, JK Fairbank; *A Documentary History of Chinese Communism* [Cambridge, Massachusetts, 1950], p. 64.
2 Edgar Snow; *Red Star Over China*, p. 444.
3 Heping Jiefang Xizang [*The Peaceful Liberation of Tibet*], p. 47. See also M Taylor Fravel; *Strong Borders, Secure Nation*, p. 72.
4 Note from the Foreign Ministry of the People's Republic of China dated 10 November 1950.
5 Sir Charles Bell; *Tibet, Past and Present*, p. 247.

British establishment, not even the most ardent imperialist, was ready for such a venture. At the same time, Tibet could not be left in a vacuum for other powers to exploit, for it was strategically located just north of Britain's Indian empire. What Britain wanted was to politically sterilize and sanitize Tibet. Taking up arms for the cause of an independent Tibet was never a British option.

On the other hand, British strategists knew that China of the 19th Century was a weak, ineffective, struggling country beset with internal dissension and in no position to check British inroads into and ambitions in Tibet. Although, under the Anglo-Russian Convention of 1907, both Russia and Britain had come to an agreement over Tibet, Britain still remained highly suspicious of Imperial Russia. By promoting the concept of China as the suzerain power in Tibet, Britain hoped to achieve both its aims without bearing any additional financial costs. This way Russia would be kept out of Tibet and as China was too weak to exert anything but nominal influence, Britain could play the role it desired of being the dominant power in Tibet. British policy towards Tibet at that time was designed to ensure that Tibet constituted a buffer against perceived Russian ambitions in Central Asia. No thought was given to the fact that Britain might need Tibet as a buffer [???/ *huan zhong guo*] between its Indian Empire and Chinese ambitions. Therefore, throughout this early period it was Britain that was the principal proponent of establishing Chinese *'suzerainty'* over Tibet. As Curzon was to put it, 'we regard the so-called *suzerainty* of China over Tibet as a constitutional fiction—a political affectation which has only been maintained because of its *convenience* [emphasis added] to both parties'.[6]

In the British concept Chinese *suzerainty* over Tibet did not mean total Chinese control over Tibet. It did not mean that Tibet was a province of China, nor did it mean that Tibet, apart from exercising complete internal autonomy, could not conduct relations with other countries independent of China. To allow full Chinese control or even influence over Tibetan policy would mean, in fact, giving a veto to the Chinese. This was something that the British were not prepared to concede. The linkage between full Tibetan autonomy and allowing China to claim *suzerainty* over Tibet was firmly established in the British mind. The two concepts were always stressed together.

However the question of China's legal position as regards Tibet remained unresolved. At this point in time the British were convinced that the only first rate power that could threaten its Indian Empire was Russia[7], although British apprehensions over Chinese ambitions remained. These were the main reasons why Britain attempted to come to terms with China and Tibet at the Simla Conference, in 1914.

In terms of British diplomacy the Simla Agreement was a spectacular success. They had prevailed over China to recognize the participation of Britain, China and Tibet *on an equal footing, each with plenipotentiary powers*. They secured a boundary agreement between India and Tibet [The McMahon Line], eliminated any Chinese influence near the north-east regions of India and yet prevailed upon the Tibetans to save Chinese 'face' by acknowledging Chinese 'suzerainty' over Tibet. The Simla Agreement, although signed by the Chinese plenipotentiary Ivan Chen, was subsequently not ratified by the Chinese government but that was for altogether different reasons. The Chinese government sole objection to the Agreement related to the proposed boundary between Tibet and China! It is a moot point, but had the First World War not commenced so soon after the conclusion of the Simla Agreement; British diplomacy would have prevailed upon the Chinese government to ratify the Agreement. In any case, the differences between the Tibetans and the Chinese over their boundary alignment were not of such magnitude that it would have prevented the British from prevailing. After the conclusion of the First World War it was a different ball game altogether for the British were now fatally weakened by the horrendous losses in manpower and economic strength that they had suffered. The baton of the main superpower in the western world had passed from the British to the United States. The Chinese were conscious of this fact.

Nevertheless, British policy in the inter-war period was firmly established. While nominally acknowledging Chinese *suzerainty*, they felt free to conduct relations with Tibet as they perceived in their best interests. It was a simple, pragmatic, but an opportunist policy. In this way the British hoped not to offend other western powers suspicious of British aims in Tibet. The British did however make some efforts to get China to ratify the Simla Agreement. On 21 August 1921 Curzon, now Foreign Secretary and a former Viceroy of India, informed the Chinese Minister thus:

> In view of the commitments of HMG to the Tibetan government arising out of the tri-partite negotiations of 1914, and in view of the fact that

[6] File No. L/PS/7/151; *Curzon to Hamilton* [No 182] dated 8 January 1903.

[7] *The Hardinge Papers*; Memo by Viceroy Lord Hardinge dated 1 February 1911.

> the Chinese government accepted, with the exception of the boundary clause, the draft Convention of 1914, HMG do not feel justified, failing a resumption of negotiations in the immediate future, in withholding any longer their recognition of the status of Tibet as an autonomous State under the suzerainty of China, and intend on dealing on this basis with Tibet in future.[8]

It was pure British bluff for they were in no position to force the issue. The Chinese prevaricated, made the excuse of pretending to be busy with the forthcoming Washington conference [1922] and let the British proposal lie. Conscious of the fact that its bargaining position was weak, as its strength did not match its responsibilities, Britain did not force the issue. For Britain its own interests were above and by far more important than those of India and in a sense this immobilized her efforts. This can also be seen in the consistent British refusal to supply arms to Tibet, in adequate quantities, even though they were obligated to do so under promises made to the Tibetans during the Simla negotiations. In any case, after the First World War, the British realized that in the near future they would have to grant India self-government and to that extent British enthusiasm to push China for clarity over Tibet's status considerably lessened. The zeal exhibited earlier by British officials noticeably declined and, as the movement for Indian independence gathered steam and since no imminent security threat appeared over the horizon, issues pertaining to Tibet were pushed into limbo.

The Chinese were, of course, not in any position to challenge the British decision. In 1943, even at the height of the Second World War, when the Americans queried the British on their position on Tibet, the British in line with their stated policy were very explicit. A memorandum from the British Embassy in Washington to the State Department clarified British policy as under:

> Ever since the abortive 1913 Convention, the attitude of the government of India has been that they wished to secure agreement between China and Tibet and were willing to advise the Tibetan government to admit formal Chinese suzerainty, although such an admission would in no sense constitute Tibet a province of China. The government of India has always held that Tibet is a separate country in full with other powers. The relationship between China and Tibet is not a matter which can be unilaterally decided by China, but one on which Tibet is entitled to negotiate, and on which she can, if necessary, count on the diplomatic support of the British government along the lines shown above.[9]

The principal British objective was to ensure that its trade and commercial interests in China were not harmed. To facilitate such a policy the British were apt to disclaim any interest in territorial aggrandizement of China including Tibet. Britain's efforts were largely devoted to ensuring the territorial integrity of China, for if Britain engineered to slice Tibet away from China what would prevent other great powers from similarly slicing away Chinese territory? The British envoy to China, Sir John Jordan, reminded his own government that 'Britain's gigantic trade throughout China was hostage against any strong anti-Chinese policy' that might be contemplated by the British.[10] The British were fully aware that they needed to balance their strategic interests in the Tibet region with expected commercial gain in China and, therefore, they were not inclined to needle Chinese sentiments unnecessarily. Thus it was the considered opinion in Britain that the dismemberment of China would be disastrous for British trade. In 1898, the House of Commons passed a resolution declaring that 'it is of vital importance for British commerce and influence that the independence of Chinese territory be maintained'. That being so, how could Britain 'detach' Tibet from China and bring it completely into the British-Indian political orbit or even encourage its independence?

Just prior to the end of the Second World War, there seems to have been a subtle shift in British opinion. Perhaps aware that they would soon have to leave India, the British were not keen to continue their involvement with Tibet. They now began to look at a suitable time and opportunity to disentangle themselves from Tibetan affairs. Understandably, Britain now felt that the lead role should be played by the new Indian government. In a remarkably prescient note this is what the India Office in London said:

> China is bound to absorb Tibet after the war, if not before, and we can do nothing to prevent it. In the event of India gaining its independence we shall be unable to help Tibet further and therefore it is poor service to the Tibetans to encourage them against the Chinese now....it is our desire to maintain the Tibetan buffer for as long as we are responsible for India's foreign relations....the development of modern warfare have rendered out

---

[8] File No. FO 371/35/55

[9] Letter No. 803.24/1594 from British Embassy, Washington to State Department dated 19 April 1943.

[10] Public Relations Office; [*Jordan Papers*] Jordan to Langley, 13 November 1912.

> of date the policy of buffer state.....Chinese suzerainty over Tibet is very deep-rooted in history and even if the Tibetans refuse to acknowledge it now, they might quite possibly do so...[11]

Therefore, it came as no surprise that when Britain finally departed from India, it largely abandoned its interests in Tibet. The US Embassy in London, on 26 August 1947, confirmed to the State Department in Washington such a change in attitude and policy and the lack of interest in Tibet on the part of Britain. The US Embassy in London informed Washington as follows:

> The UK no longer has an abiding interest in the future of Tibet since British control was withdrawn from India.[12]

From this point on, Britain's commercial and political interests in China became the pivot on which British policy was formulated. Thus, not unsurprisingly, in 1948 Britain refused to give visas on Tibetan passports to a Tibetan delegation travelling to Britain. Two years later, the British Ambassador to the UN advised the Home government that 'what we want to do is to create a situation which does not oblige us in practice to do anything about the Communist invasion of Tibet'.[13] Later speaking first at the UN, the British Ambassador obfuscated the issue by informing his colleagues that after half a century of 'intimate' relations, HMG felt that the status of Tibet 'was unclear' and suggested that the Tibetan appeal be postponed!

But what was the policy on the status of Tibet that Soviet Russia was following? Had the policy followed by Imperial Russia changed after the Communists took over in Moscow? Imperial Russia had in an agreement with the British in 1907 recognized Chinese *suzerainty* over Tibet. On the conclusion of the Second World War, Mao timed his visit to Moscow in 1949 [December 1949/January 1950] to enable him to participate in Stalin's seventieth birthday celebrations. Mao gave Stalin a signed photograph of himself with the inscription, 'to our leader Comrade Stalin from Mao Zedung'. Elated at such flattery, the Soviet leader was quite emphatic that Tibet was a part of China. An exchange of views on Tibet, in a meeting on 22 January 1950 in Moscow, between Mao and Stalin aptly highlights the Soviet Russian view:

> Mao Zedong: I would like to note that the air regiment that you sent to China was very helpful. They transported 10 thousand people. Let me thank you, comrade Stalin, for the help and ask you to allow it to stay a little longer, so it could help transport provisions to [CCP CC member and commander of the PLA's Second Field Army] Liu Bocheng's troops, currently preparing for an attack on Tibet.
>
> Stalin: It's good that you are preparing to attack. The Tibetans need to be subdued. As for the air regiment, we shall talk this over with the military personnel and give you an answer.[14]

Stalin also advised flooding Tibet and other border areas with Han Chinese. Two years later, on 3 September 1952, when Zhou sought Soviet help in subduing the Tibetans, Stalin once again emphasized that:

> Tibet is a part of China. There must be Chinese troops deployed in Tibet.[15]

Not unsurprisingly, therefore, when the Tibetan appeal came before the UN in November 1950, the Soviet delegate categorically stated that 'Tibet was an inalienable part of China and its affairs were the exclusive concern of the Chinese government.' Not only did Soviet Russia fully support the Chinese, but went a step further when Pravda, on 30 May 1951, accused Britain of 'unlawfully' taking Bhutan and Sikkim from Tibet in 1890! In other words, Pravda, undoubtedly reflecting the Kremlin's views, did not even recognize independent India's relations with Sikkim and Bhutan. Moscow welcomed the 17-Point Agreement, of 23 May 1951, between Tibet; and China and Pravda, of 29 May 1951, and gave wide coverage to statements of Mao and Zhu De. Later, Moscow also helped in the construction of an airfield in Lhasa and Soviet pilots flew test flights to Lhasa.[16]

On the other hand the other major power that had influence over events in Tibet and China was the United States. From early twentieth century, the US has consistently held the view that it was in US interest to 'preserve the territorial and administrative integrity' of China. The US accordingly informed major European powers of this policy.[17] A little later Secretary Hay reiterated the same policy, once again, to US Ambassadors abroad in a circular Telegram on 13 January 1905. He clarified that:

---

11 FO 371/35755 [7 May 1943].

12 Telegram No. 1841 from US Embassy, London to Department of State, Washington.

13 Tsering Shakya; *Dragon in the Land of Snows*, p. 55

14 Cold War International History Project [CWIHP] 1995-96

15 Ibid.

16 Davidenko; *Soviet Russia and Tibet*, p. 390

17 Secretary of State Hay/Letters to European Powers dated 3 July 1900

the US has repeatedly made its position well known of its broad policy of maintaining the integrity of China.

So pleased were the Chinese with the US position that, on 5 July 1905, the then Emperor of China expressed to the US President, 'China's *great obligation for proclaiming to the whole world that China's territorial integrity must be maintained*'. The American Minister in Peking, W.W. Rockhill, in 1908, even went to the extent of making statements that 'the Lama [the Dalai Lama] was a vassal prince' and that he must 'bow to his sovereign's command'! The broad parameters of this view continued to be US policy throughout this period.

In line with this thinking and policy, the US has consistently held the view that Tibet was under Chinese '*suzerainty*.' The US State Department reaffirmed its views to the British Embassy in Washington in 1943. It stated that:

> 'With regard to the position of Tibet in Asia, the British Government has been so good as to give an account of its historical attitude. For its part, the Government of the United States has borne in mind the fact that the Chinese Government has long claimed suzerainty over Tibet and that the Chinese constitution lists Tibet among areas constituting the territory of the Republic of China. This Government has at no time raised a question regarding either of these claims. The Government of the United States does not believe that a useful purpose would be served by opening at this time a detailed discussion of the status of Tibet.[18]

The United States was also not prepared to cause any offence to the Chinese authorities by even remotely suggesting that Tibet was not a part of or independent of China. President Roosevelt was 'advised' by his Secretary of State, Hull, to be careful when addressing a letter to the Dalai Lama, so as not to hurt Chinese susceptibilities. Addressing a memo to the President this is what Secretary Hull said:

> *103.91802/687*—The Secretary of State to President Roosevelt
>
> WASHINGTON, July 3, 1942.
>
> Colonel William J. Donovan, Director of the Office of Strategic Services, is sending two members of his organization on a special and confidential mission to China via India and Tibet. It is believed that the work of the mission in Tibet would be greatly facilitated if you were to provide it with a letter of introduction to the Dalai Lama of Tibet. A draft of such letter is attached. The letter is addressed to the Dalai Lama in his capacity of religious leader of Tibet, rather than in his capacity of secular leader of Tibet, thus avoiding giving any possible offense to the Chinese Government which includes Tibet in the territory of the Republic of China.
>
> *Hull*

Letters from the US were always addressed to the Tibetan '*Foreign Affairs Bureau*' and not to the '*Tibetan Foreign Office*'! US Secretary of State Hull further confirmed the US point of view in a telegram to the US Ambassador to China [Gauss] when he clearly stated:

> As you are aware, the Chinese Government has long claimed *suzerainty* over Tibet, the Chinese constitution lists Tibet among areas constituting the territory of the Republic of China, and this Government has at no time raised question regarding either of these claims.[19]

From the US point of view it was essential that the territorial unity of China be maintained. For the US, China at that point in time, was a necessary strategic counter-weight to Japanese expansionism in Asia. As such, the US warned the Japanese that 'the US could not regard with indifference the assumption of political, military or economic domination over China by a foreign power [Japanese]'.[20] It is thus clear that it remained an axiom of US policy that it was not prepared to see the emergence of a single formidable power that could dominate the East Asian landscape. Even as late as 1945, the US indicated that it was willing to work with 'any other leadership' in China provided it contributed to achieving peace and stability in East Asia. This line of thinking is clearly reflected in the memorandum prepared by the Far Eastern Department of the US State Department.

> *71-1.93/4-2545*—Memorandum Prepared in the Office of Far Eastern Affairs
>
> WASHINGTON, April 18, 1945
>
> Our major objectives with respect to China are: effective joint prosecution of the war against Japan; and from a long-range standpoint, the establishment of a strong and united China as a necessary principal stabilizing factor in the Far East. However, with regard to our long-term objective and against the possible disintegration of the authority of the existing Government, it is our purpose to maintain a degree of flexibility to permit cooperation with any other leadership in China which may give greater promise of achieving unity and contributing to peace and security in East Asia. We are, meanwhile, assisting China, as a nation, to attain a position of recognized equality among the major powers.[*relevant portions*]

18 File No. 893.24/1594/Washington, 15 May 1943

19 File No. 893.24/1377H/Washington, 3 July 1941

20 File No. 793.94/570

The US conscious of its vital interests in Asia, in which China played a predominant part, was not prepared to push the line of Tibetan *suzerainty* beyond a point and certainly not towards independence. Tibet was never a core issue of interest of US foreign policy. At best the US was willing to exploit the situation for tactical purposes and utilize the developments to further its strategic interests.

After the defeat of the KMT forces in China, the Communists moved rapidly to consolidate their hold over the country. It was a foregone conclusion that the days of Tibetan quasi-independence would soon be over. It was imminent that Chinese forces would soon move to occupy Tibet. The US was deeply worried over the shape of events taking place in China. The collapse of the KMT regime and the rise of the Communists had a far reaching effect on US policy. If there was a time to change its attitude towards China in general, and Tibet in particular, it was now. While the US attitude towards the new Communist government stiffened, yet it was not prepared to re-consider its position towards Tibet, even if Chinese troops moved to occupy Tibet. A report from the National Security Council, on 25 August 1950, recommended that in the event of an attack by Chinese troops against Tibet, the US should *take political action, but was not expected to take military action* [emphasis added].[21]

The US was deeply worried that any attempt to detach Tibet from mainland China could have cascading consequences elsewhere. The Soviet Union had not as yet fully withdrawn its troops from Manchuria and the US was worried that the Soviets too might be tempted to detach Manchuria from China, just as the Japanese had done earlier. It would be recalled that the Soviets had successfully detached Outer Mongolia from China and formed the Mongolian People's Republic under its tutelage and had managed to obtain the acquiesce of this action from both the KMT and the Communist governments of China. Therefore, while the US strongly opposed the new Communist regime in China and even refused to recognize its existence, ensuring the maintenance of the territorial integrity of China remained uppermost in the minds of US policy strategists. The US thus operated at two levels. Strategically, it would do nothing to violate the territorial integrity of China, while tactically, it would lose few opportunities to embarrass the new Communist government.

A memorandum from the Department of State [Far East Department] dated 12 April 1949 *for internal circulation* spells out US policy succinctly. It says:

> The Department informed the Chinese Embassy [KMT] that this government has no intention of acting in a manner to call into question China's *de jure* sovereignty over Tibet....a decision to recognize Tibet involves a reconsideration not merely of our policy over Tibet but also of our policy towards China. A basic principle of our policy towards China has been respect for China's territorial integrity.... As a practical matter, Tibet's importance both ideologically and strategically is very limited....unless minerals are found in Tibet, the Army does not regard Tibet as of strategic significance.[22]

And to confirm this assessment, the then US Ambassador in India, Henderson, informed the State Department, on 12 April 1949, by Telegram No. 302 that:

> Present American economic interests in Tibet are of little importance. There is no information available regarding mineral resources of Tibet.

Nevertheless, the advantage of embarrassing the new Communist government of China was too good to be missed. The intervention of Chinese troops in Korea also played on the American mind. The intention of the US was not to help Tibet, but only as a cold war tactic to challenge the Chinese. The cause of Tibet *per se* was of secondary importance. The US was fighting Communism and not China and was mainly concerned in preventing the spread of Communism rather than providing serious or committed aid to Tibet. In practical terms, the US tried very hard to avoid any military confrontation with China over Tibet. Thus, as can be seen and as so eloquently put by the State Department, 'no third country' was prepared to recognize that Tibet was an independent state.

The major powers that could have played a decisive role in promoting Tibetan independence; Britain, India, the US and even Soviet Russia were all interested in maintaining good relations with China. Almost all were prepared to sacrifice whatever little interests that they had in Tibet for the sake of developing friendly relations with China. Clearly, the US support for the Tibetans was not out of some moral principle or sympathy, but because of its world-wide antipathy to Communism.

---

21 FRUS Vol. 1 [1950]

22 FRUS Vol. IX [1949]

Nehru explained the intricate workings and compulsions of great power politics in a similar vein to the Dalai Lama in 1959 in Mussoorie. Nehru informed him as follows:

> In America, there is no real sympathy for Tibet. Chiang Kai-shek has no sympathy.... They all want to exploit Tibet in their cold war with the Soviet Union.

Earlier Nehru wrote in a Note on 18 November 1950:

> It must be remembered that neither the UK nor the USA, nor indeed any other power, is particularly interested in Tibet or the future of that country. What they are interested in is embarrassing China.

Thus Nehru was spot on in his assessment when he told Parliament that, *'at no time did any country, any foreign country considers it [Tibet] independent'* [emphasis added].[23]

Although strictly speaking recognition is not a criterion for statehood, not a single major power desired an independent Tibet. No one wanted to antagonize China, even less so the rising power of modern China. There is no doubt that Tibet had achieved *de facto* independence in the inter-war years, but unfortunately failed to convert it to *de jure* independence. Herein lies the tragedy of Tibet.

---

[23] *Foreign Affairs Record* [August 1958] p. 145

INDIA'S MILITARY MODERNISATION: PLANS AND STRATEGIC UNDERPINNINGS

Gurmeet Kanwal, Defence Analyst and former Director, Centre for Land Warfare Studies, New Delhi

Preparing for a Two-Front Future War

Southern Asia is among the world's most unstable regions due to the ongoing war against the Al Qaeda and the Taliban in Afghanistan and on the Af-Pak border. In addition, growing fundamentalist terrorism, creeping Talibanisation in Pakistan, political instability in Bangladesh, Myanmar, Nepal and Sri Lanka, unrest in Tibet and Xingjian, narcotics trafficking and the proliferation of small arms and light weapons are also destabilising factors. Unresolved territorial and boundary disputes with China and Pakistan, over which the country has fought four wars, internal security challenges in Jammu and Kashmir, the north-eastern states and the rising tide of Maoist insurgency in the heartland, further vitiate India's strategic environment. China is engaged in the strategic encirclement of India through its nuclear and missile nexus with Pakistan, the sale of military hardware to Bangladesh, Nepal, Myanmar and Sri Lanka and its 'string of pearls' strategy to ring India with naval bases in the northern Indian Ocean region.

The prevailing strategic environment has forced India's armed forces to prepare for a 'two-front' future war while the army and other security forces are engaged in fighting an ongoing 'half-front' internal security war. Even though the probability of conventional conflict remains low due to steadily improving relations and military confidence building measures with China and Pakistan, its possibility cannot be completely ruled out. While the armed forces have drawn up elaborate plans for modernisation and qualitative upgradation of their capabilities for future combat, including the ability to secure the sea lanes of communication and project power in India's area of strategic interest, the pace of modernisation has been rather slow due to the lack of adequate funding support, delayed decision making and a low-tech defence industrial base.

India's defence budget is pegged at less than 2.0 per cent of the GDP at present and the bulk of the expenditure is on the 'revenue' account, that is pay and allowances, rations, fuel, oil and lubricants, ammunition and vehicles. Very little remains in the 'capital' account to be spent on modernisation. In the case of the army, it is as little as 20 to 25 per cent. According to Defence Minister A K Antony, "New procurements have commenced... but we are still lagging by 15 years." There is now increasing realisation that unless immediate measures are taken to speed up the pace of modernisation, the military gap with China, which is only a quantitative gap at present, will soon become a qualitative gap as well as the People's Liberation Army is modernising at a rapid rate. Also, the slender edge that the Indian armed forces enjoy over the Pakistan armed forces in conventional conflict is being eroded as Pakistan is spending considerably large sums of money on its military modernisation under the garb of fighting radical extremism. The positive news is that India is expected to procure defence equipment worth US$ 100 billion over the next two five-year plans, most of it ex-import. Simultaneously, efforts are being stepped up to enhance indigenous capabilities so as to reduce India's dependence on imports by an order of magnitude.

Army Modernisation: Enhancing Capabilities without Reducing Manpower

The Indian Army, with personnel strength of 1.1 million soldiers (6 regional commands, training command, 13 corps, 38 divisions), has kept the nation together through various crises, including four wars since independence, Pakistan's 'proxy war' in Jammu and Kashmir and insurgencies in many of the north-eastern states. It is a first-rate army with large-scale operational commitments on border management and in counter-insurgency operations and cannot afford to reduce its manpower numbers till these challenges are overcome. Many of the army's weapons and equipment are bordering on obsolescence and need to be replaced. The next step would be to move gradually towards acquiring network-centric capabilities for effects-based operations (EBOs) so as to optimise the army's full combat potential for defensive and offensive operations. The army is also preparing to join the navy and the air force in launching intervention operations in India's area of strategic interest when called upon to do so in future.

Lt Gen J P Singh (Retd), former Deputy Chief of the Army Staff (Planning and Systems), said in an interview with the CLAWS Journal, "The critical capabilities that are being enhanced to meet challenges across the spectrum include battlefield transparency, battlefield management systems, night-fighting capability, enhanced firepower, including terminally guided munitions, integrated manoeuvre capability to include self-propelled artillery, quick reaction surface-to-air missiles, the latest assault engineer equipment, tactical control systems, integral combat aviation support and network centricity." The army's mechanised forces are still mostly 'night blind'. Its artillery lacks towed and self-propelled 155mm howitzers for the plains and the mountains and has little capability by way multi-barrel rocket launchers and surface-to-surface missiles. Infantry battalions urgently need to acquire modern weapons and equipment for counter-insurgency and counter-terrorism operations for greater operational effectiveness and lower casualties.

Main battle tanks and infantry combat vehicles (ICVs) are the spearhead of India's conventional deterrence in the plains. Pakistan has acquired 320 T-80 UD tanks and is now inducting Al Khalid tanks that it has co-developed with China. The Indian armour fleet is also being modernised gradually. The indigenously developed Arjun MBT has entered serial production to equip two regiments. 310 T-90S MBTs have been imported from Russia and a contract has been signed for 347 additional T-90S tanks to be assembled in India. A programme has been launched to modernise the T-72 M1 Ajeya MBTs that have been the mainstay of the army's Strike Corps and its armoured divisions since the 1980s. The programme will upgrade the night fighting capabilities and fire control system of the tank. Approximately 1,700 T-72 M1s have been manufactured under license at the Heavy Vehicle Factory (HVF), Avadi. The BMP-1 and, to a lesser extent, the BMP-2 ICVs, which have been the mainstay of the mechanised infantry battalions for long, are now ageing and replacements need to be found soon. The new ICVs must be capable of employment for internal security duties and counter-insurgency operations in addition to their primary role in conventional conflict.

Despite the lessons learnt during the Kargil conflict of 1999, where artillery firepower had paved the way for victory, modernisation of the artillery continues to lag behind for one reason or another. Artillery modernisation plans include the acquisition of towed, wheeled and self-propelled 155mm guns and howitzers for the plains and the mountains through import as well as indigenous development. The artillery is also acquiring weapon locating radars, muzzle velocity measuring radars and meteorological sounding radars to achieve the capacity to launch effects-based operations (EBOs). The Corps of Army Air Defence is also faced with problems of obsolescence. The vintage L-70 40mm AD gun system, the four-barrelled ZSU-23-4 Schilka (SP) AD gun system, the SAM-6 (Kvadrat) and the SAM-8 OSA-AK, among others, need to be replaced by more responsive modern AD systems that are capable of defeating current and future threats. The indigenously developed medium range Akash surface-to-air missile has not yet been inducted into service. The acquisition of short-range and medium-range SAMs also needs to be speeded up.

The modernisation plans of India's cutting edge infantry battalions, aimed at enhancing their capability for surveillance and target acquisition at night and boosting their firepower for precise retaliation against infiltrating columns and terrorists holed up in built-up areas, are moving forward but at a slow pace. These include the acquisition of shoulder-fired missiles, hand-held battlefield surveillance radars (BFSRs), and hand-held thermal imaging devices (HHTIs) for observation at night. Protective gear also needs to be acquired to reduce casualties in war and counter-insurgency operations. Stand-alone infra-red, seismic and acoustic sensors need to be acquired in large numbers to enable infantrymen to dominate the Line of Control (LoC) with Pakistan and detect infiltration of Pakistan-sponsored terrorists. A system called F-INSAS (future infantry soldier as a system) is under development. One infantry division has been designated as a rapid reaction force for employment on land or in intervention operations. It will have one amphibious brigade and two air assault brigades.

Similarly, the operational capabilities of army aviation, engineers, signal communications, reconnaissance, surveillance and target acquisition (RSTA) branches need to be substantially enhanced so that the overall combat potential of the army can be improved by an order of magnitude. Modern strategic and tactical level command and control systems need to be acquired on priority for better synergies during conventional and sub-conventional conflict. Plans for the acquisition of a mobile corps-to-battalion Tactical Communications System (TCS) and a battalion-level Battlefield Management System (BMS) need to be hastened. Despite being the largest user of space, the army does not yet have a dedicated military satellite to bank on for its space surveillance needs. Cyberwar capabilities are also at a nascent stage.

Naval Modernisation: Major Fleet Expansion

The Navy's ambitious Maritime Capabilities Perspective Plan seeks to dominate the Indian Ocean Region by acquiring blue water operational capability while, simultaneously, effectively countering current and emerging threats closer to the coastline. There is a perceptible shift in emphasis from an increase in the number of platforms to the enhancement of capabilities. According to a report tabled in Parliament in the last week of April 2012 by the Standing Committee on Defence, the Navy's modernisation plan seeks to achieve the following objectives:

- Augment airborne maritime surveillance, strike, anti-submarine warfare (ASW) and air defence capability through induction of shore-based aircraft, integral helicopters, carrier-based aircraft, space-based assets and UAVs, along with suitable weapons and sensors.
- Develop ASW capability through induction of suitable platforms, weapons and sensors.
- Build adequate stand-off capability for sea-lift and expeditionary operations to achieve desired power projection force levels, influence events ashore and undertake military operations other than war (MOOTW).
- Induct assets and develop suitable infrastructure to augment forces available for low intensity maritime operations (LIMO), protection of off-shore assets and for coastal security.
- Induct force multipliers like satellite-based global communications, reconnaissance and network-enabled platforms to achieve battle-space dominance capability and perform network centric operations.
- Induct state-of-the-art equipment and specialised platforms for Special Forces to enhance niche capabilities to conduct maritime intervention operations.
- Develop support infrastructure in island territories to support the planned force levels as well as support infrastructure for ships/ submarines/aircraft at ports and airbases.

According to Admiral Arun Prakash (Retd), former Chief of Naval Staff, India's naval modernisation plans are designed to meet the following aims:

- Acquiring a capability for maritime domain awareness in the area of responsibility. This would include space-based surveillance, MR, AEW&C, and UAVs.
- Capability for expeditionary and joint warfare, supported by special operations.
- Acquiring reach and sustainability through long endurance, tankers, turn-around facilities in friendly foreign ports and longer intervals between maintenance cycles.
- Acquisition of modern capabilities in fields of tactical aviation, ASW, anti-air/anti-missile, land-attack, mine countermeasures and electronic warfare.
- Networking of ships, submarines and airborne platforms via satellite.
- Commitment to self-reliance and indigenisation, with the objective of harnessing national strengths in shipbuilding, engineering, electronics and IT.

The Indian Navy has two operational fleets, Eastern Naval Command and Western Naval Command. Both the fleets are proposed to be centred round an aircraft carrier each. Eventually, the navy hopes to graduate to three Carrier Battle Groups. At present the navy has only one aircraft carrier, the ageing INS

Viraat. The navy has been waiting for long for the INS Vikramaditya (Admiral Gorshkov) aircraft carrier, which is being refurbished in a Russian shipyard at exorbitant cost and is expected to be delivered in December 2012. Construction of an indigenous air defence ship is lagging behind schedule. INS Chakra, a nuclear-powered submarine leased from Russia, will join the fleet later in 2012. INS Arihant, the first of three to four SSBNs, is expected to become fully operational by about late-2014. Russian Nerpa class submarines have begun to be inducted; these will give a much needed fillip to the submarine fleet and considerably enhance sea denial capabilities. Three stealth frigates have only recently been added to the fleet. Amphibious landing capability has gone up considerably by the acquisition of INS Jalashva (ex-USS Trenton) and other landing ships.

The Indian Navy's modernisation plans, though much delayed, have now begun to pick up steam. Pointing out the navy's role as a key facilitator in promoting peace and stability in the Indian Ocean region, Defence Minister A. K. Antony said while commissioning a stealth frigate in July 2012 that the present operating environment of "our Navy dictates that we balance our resources with a strategy that is responsive across the full range of blue and brown water operations... The maintenance of a strong and credible navy and strengthening cooperation and friendship with other countries to promote regional and global stability is the need of the hour."

The navy plans to expand to a 150-ship fleet in the next 10 to 15 years. Fifty warships are under construction and 100 new vessels are in the acquisition pipeline. These include four landing platform docks, eight mine counter measure vessels, one floating dry dock, 16 coastal submarine vessels, one survey training ship, two deep submersible vessels, six submarines and seven new stealth frigates. The Navy is also engaged in setting up operational turnaround bases, forward operating bases and naval air enclaves with a view to enhancing India's surveillance efforts in the region. Plans for accretions to the naval aviation fleet are also progressing smoothly. Boeing 737 P8I maritime reconnaissance aircraft have begun to be inducted. Five additional Kamov Ka-31 AEW helicopters will be added to the existing fleet of 11 helicopters. The Indian Navy is on the cusp of acquiring the capabilities necessary to join India's strategic partners in safeguarding the sea lanes of communication in the northern Indian Ocean and ensuring unfettered freedom of the seas for trade and commerce.

Air Force Modernisation: Air Dominance and Force Projection

Air Chief Marshal N.A.K. Browne, the Chief of Air Staff, has said that till recently India's traditional strategic sphere lay between the Gulf of Aden and the Straits of Malacca; but, with India's global footprint expanding, the IAF should be ready to serve wherever India's future strategic interests lie. Clearly, the IAF is gearing up to provide the country with the strategic outreach that it needs as a growing regional power and to project power where necessary in order to defend the country's vital national interests. According to Air Vice Marshal Kapil Kak (Retd), a senior defence analyst, though vision-capability dilemma persists with regard to shaping India's strategic neighbourhood, forward movement is now visible. In his view, the modernisation plans of the IAF are aimed at achieving the following objectives:

- Air dominance/control of the air.
- Deterrence, by both denial and punishment.
- Long range offensive reach: Penetration, Precision, Persistence, and Parallelity—simultaneous tactical, operational and strategic-level operations.
- Strategic airlift capability for power projection through both hard and soft power (HADR—humanitarian assistance and disaster relief operations) and Diaspora evacuation.
- Build-up of capability for coercion.
- The acquisition of force enablers/multipliers and related combat support systems, including networking for tri-service command and control.
- Capability for conducting cyberspace and information operations.
- Indigenisation of future capabilities for design and development.

From a sanctioned strength of 39 squadrons, the Indian Air Force (IAF) is down to 34 squadrons at present due to decades of neglect, but plans to enhance its strength to 42 squadrons by 2022. The plans of the air force to acquire 126 multi-mission, medium-range combat aircraft, in order to maintain its edge over the regional air forces, are stuck in the procurement quagmire. The Mig-21 fleet has become obsolescent. Tejas, the indigenously designed Light Combat Aircraft (LCA), which is expected to replace the Mig-21, is still a few years away from becoming fully operational. India is developing a fifth-generation fighter with Russia and aims to fly it in 2015, as well as a fleet of 272 Sukhoi-30 MKI, half of which have already been built. AEW aircraft are being acquired from Israel as well being developed indigenously.

Six C-130J Super Hercules aircraft have been acquired for the Special Forces and six more are likely to be ordered. C-17 Globemaster heavy lift aircraft are also likely to be acquired shortly. A contract has been signed with a Swiss firm for 75 basic trainer aircraft Pilatus PC-7. Jet trainers continue to be deficient. In the rotary wing category, the indigenously manufactured Dhruva utility helicopter has entered service. The IAF is in the process of acquiring medium lift transport helicopters and attack helicopters. All three Services need a large number of light helicopters in the short term.

In order to beef up its offensive and defensive capabilities and operate all types of aircraft along the northern border with Pakistan and China, the IAF is making old advanced landing grounds (ALG) operational. Disused ALGs at Daulat Beg Oldie, Fukche and Nyoma, all in Ladakh, have been recently activated. The runway at Kargil is being extended to enable larger transport aircraft to operate. Similarly, existing but out-of-use ALGs in Arunachal Pradesh, close to the border with China, are also being activated. Other airbases are being upgraded in a phased manner with modern navigation equipment and runway aids. Flight safety measures are being stepped up. The IAF has initiated a project for the creation of Rapid Action Medical teams (RAMT) and their deployment along with 25-bed Tent Based Medical Shelters (TBMS) in the wake of natural calamities.

India's nuclear forces are also modernising at a steady pace. The Agni-I and Agni-II missiles are now fully operational. Immediate requirements include the Agni-III IRBM (5,000 km range) and nuclear-powered submarines with suitable ballistic missiles to acquire genuine second-strike capability. INS Arihant, India's first indigenously built SSBN, is likely to become fully operational by late-2014. While the emphasis is on mobile missile launchers, a small number of hardened silos are also being constructed. The armed forces do not have a truly integrated tri-Service C4I2SR system suitable for network-centric warfare, which will allow them to optimise their individual capabilities. However, plans have been made to develop such a system in the next five to 10 years. In fact, all new weapons and equipment acquisitions are now being planned on a tri-Service basis to ensure interoperability.

India's Quest for Strategic Outreach

In keeping with its growing power and responsibilities, India has been steadily enhancing its expeditionary and military intervention capabilities—even though no such directive appears to have been given to the armed forces. These growing capabilities have been amply demonstrated in recent times. During the 1991 Gulf War, India had airlifted 150,000 civilian workers who had been forced to leave Iraq, from the airfield at Amman, Jordan, over a period of 30 days. This was the largest airlift since the Berlin airlift at the end of World War II. During the South East Asian tsunami in 2004, the Indian armed forces were in the forefront of rescue and relief operations. Over 70 Indian Navy ships had set sail with rescue teams and relief material in less than 72 hours of the disaster even though the Indian population on the country's eastern seaboard had themselves suffered horrendous damage. Indian Navy ships on a goodwill visit to European countries during the Lebanon war in 2006 lifted and brought back 5,000 Indian civilian refugees.

From the ongoing modernisation plans, it is evident that India is preparing to join the world's major powers in terms of its ability to undertake out of area contingency operations. With the arrival of INS Jalashwa (exercise-USS Trenton), India's strategic sea-lift capability has been upgraded to lifting one infantry battalion at a time. India is planning to acquire more such ships. The SU-30 MKI long-range fighter-bombers with air-to-air refuelling capability, the C-130J Hercules Special Forces transport aircraft and the AWACS and maritime surveillance capabilities that India intends to build over the next five to 10 years, will give India considerable strategic outreach. However, India has consistently favoured military interventions only under a UN umbrella. Though that position is unlikely to change quickly, India is likely to join future coalitions of the willing even without UN approval when its vital national interests are threatened and need to be defended.

As a key player in Asia and a large democracy with which India has commonality of interests, the US is emerging as India's leading strategic partner. There is a broad national consensus on the contours of the emerging relationship with the US, particularly enhanced defence cooperation and civil nuclear energy cooperation. During his visit to New Delhi in June 2012, US Defence Secretary Leon Panetta had identified India as a 'linchpin' in the emerging US strategy in the Asia-Pacific region. While there was no reaction from the Indian government, it is clear to perceptive observers that these two large democracies need to work together militarily in order to main freedom of the seas in the Indian Ocean region and to ensure peace and stability in the Asia-Pacific region. Should China implode, or should China behave irresponsibly in asserting its territorial rights—as it is tending to do in the South China Sea—both India and the US will need strong strategic partners to face worst case scenarios effectively.

Mr Shiv Shankar Menon, India's National Security Advisor, said in a recent speech: "As a nation state India has consistently shown tactical caution and strategic initiative, sometimes simultaneously. But equally, initiative and risk taking must be strategic, not tactical, if we are to avoid the fate of becoming a rentier state." He went on to mention that India was cooperating extensively with other militaries to fight the menace of piracy off the Horn of Africa. Military cooperation of this type will increase in future as India adds to its intervention capabilities.

As it faces complex strategic scenarios and is located in an increasingly unstable neighbourhood, it is in India's interest to encourage a cooperative model of regional security and to work with all friendly countries towards that end. At the same time, India finds it pragmatic to hedge its bets just in case 'worst case' scenarios begin to unfold and threaten its economic development or territorial integrity. The increasing emphasis on maritime cooperation, particularly with the US, is part of India's continuing efforts to discharge its growing obligations and responsibilities as a regional power. India is now making concerted efforts to cooperate with all the major Asian powers to maintain peace and stability in the Indian Ocean and Asia-Pacific regions, but without aligning militarily with any one of them. Towards this end, besides traditional territorial defence—land, sea and air—the armed forces are working together to achieve joint warfare capabilities for intervention operations in India's area of strategic interest in keeping with the country's growing regional responsibilities as well as interests. In sum, a rising India will soon become a net contributor to security in the Indian Ocean region.

THE ARITHMETIC OF MAOISM, THE INDIAN STATE AND THE SOUTH ASIA CAULDRON

Maj Gen (Retd) JS Kataria, Defence Analyst

"You must be the change you want to see in the world"

—Mahatma Gandhi

The Indian State

Historical Perspective. India has a long history spanning centuries of subjugation by the Greeks, Afghans, Moguls and the Europeans - primarily by the British, till the country had its tryst with destiny and became independent in 1947. The foreigners exploited the internecine acrimony of the Princely States then ruling the country. There are innumerable sagas of individual bravery viz. Prithvi Raj Chauhan, Maharana Pratap, Shivaji, Maharaja Ranjit Singh and many more, but they lost to the foreign invaders not because they lacked in tenacity, tactics or strategy, but because of their infighting and internal intrigue. With the decline of the Princely States came the feudal lords/the Zamindars who were adept at exploiting their own subjects and caused unparalleled atrocities on the poor and downtrodden. The tribals and the lower castes were discriminated and suffered the most. At the same time, the arrival of the British and Christianity exposed Indians to education and the outside world that was going through political revolution. Predominant political movements of the period were Marxism- Leninism and later Maoism.

Impact of Historical Past. The British who adopted the policy of 'Divide and Rule' exploited the infighting amongst the Princely States and the feudal mindset of the big landlords to cement their rule in India. Except for those involved in the Gandhian movement, most of the Indian rulers/ feudal lords lived by the motto 'Self before the Nation'. The current system of governance, though democratic, has not disconnected from the feudal mind-set of the pre-independence era. Our political leaders have emerged as the 'new class of feudal lords'. In independent India corruption became rampant—exploitation of tribals, schedule castes/schedule tribes and the landless or poor farmers continues unabated. Their continued neglect, apathy by the rich and the political class made them rise against the State leading to the early Naxal movement and the rise of the current Maoists.

Hypothesis

It is hypothesised that antiquated policies, neglect of tribals/schedule castes, the rural poor, their exploitation by the new feudal lords of Independent India (politicians), apathy in implementation of reforms and inept understanding of insurgency/ terrorism by government agencies has led to the current rise of Maoists posing a serious challenge to the sovereign authority of India. The situation is further compounded by the lack of cooperation between the Centre and the States. The Maoists in India, Nepal and other Non-State Actors in the region portend ominous clouds of continued violence, if not handled with alacrity.

Philosophy and Origin of Maoism

Philosophy. The political theory of Marxism-Leninism promoted the creation and development of an International Communist Society through the dictatorship of the proletariat. It had gained currency in the early nineteenth Century in many countries—the prominent being Russia, a number of Eastern European States and a couple of Latin American States. In the aftermath of the Second World War, the world witnessed a strong upsurge of Marxism–Leninism. The People's Republic of China under Mao Zedong developed its own unique brand of Marxism–Leninism known as Maoism. According to Maoism, the agrarian peasantry formed the key revolutionary force, rather than the working class as enunciated by Lenin. This shift was primarily driven to meet the needs of the then Chinese Society which was mainly agrarian, as compared to Russia and the European States where industrialisation had already been ushered. The CPI (Maoist) has drawn its philosophy from the amalgam of Marxism-Leninism-Maoism to meet the perceived challenges in India.

Origin of Communism/Maoism in India

a) **Communism in India—Pre/Post Independence Period.** The roots of the Communist Party of India (CPI) can be traced back to 1920 (though contested by some).[1] In the 1920s and 1930s, the party remained splintered as it was banned by the British Government in India. The party openly participated in the independence movement after 1942, when it was formally recognised. After independence, the party remained in a state of flux between the 'right wing and the left wing' philosophy, leading to insurgencies in Andhra, Kerala, Telengana and Tripura which did not get much public support.[2] Later, the party contributed immensely to improve the conditions of textile workers that led to its emergence as the largest opposition party in the 1957 General Elections. Serious differences emerged within the party, during the 1962 Indo-China conflict. Some members took a stance that the war was a conflict between a 'socialist and a capitalist state'. This ideological clash between 'the left versus the right wing' led to the party's formal split in 1964 and emergence of the CPI and Communist Party of India (Marxist). It set the stage for the formation of the more radical wing that believed in armed struggle to seize power from the state, as done by Mao's Red Army.

b) **Birsa Munda Revolt.** Back in the heyday of the freedom movement, numerous bands of patriots operated from the jungles of Odisha, Bihar, Madhya Pradesh and the present day Jharkhand, and carried out guerrilla attacks on the British Colonial Government. The most popular tribal leader of that era who revolted against the British was Birsa Munda. He belonged to one of the lowest rungs of the tribal hierarchy i.e. the Ryots or the tenant farmers".[3] The primary cause of his revolt was the allocation of tribal land to the settlers (landlords/Zamindars) from Chota Nagpur, by the British Government, thereby depriving the real proprietors of the land. The landlords/Zamindars were under obligation to pay a certain amount of tax to the British Government. They in turn exploited the poor tillers who were forced to lead a life of penury. It could be argued that this sowed the first seeds of the present-day Maoist movement in the region.

c) **Post Independence—Failure of Land Reforms**. At the time of independence, the political leaders had promised abolition of Zamindari, "land to the tiller and growth with equity".[4] Despite abolition of the Zamindari System and inclusion of land reforms in the First Five Year Plan of independent India, all these remained lofty promises. The distribution of land remained a miniscule of the available land. The quantum of surplus land turned out to be far less than the estimation that had emerged in many independent national surveys. "Out of the total declared 73.5 lakh acres of surplus land, only 53.9 lakh acres have been distributed. Many of the poor/SC/ST continue to be landless and are without a roof on their head".[5] A lion's share of the land distribution came through the yeoman efforts of Acharya Vinoba Bhave, architect of the Bhoodan Movement. Corruption and nepotism amongst those in positions of influence became the major road block. The discontent-

---

1 http://en.wikipedia.org/wiki/Communist_Party_of_India
2 http://www.hindustantimes.com/News-Feed/NM2/History-of-Naxalism/Article1-6545.aspx
3 http://js2012.wordpress.com/why-jansatyagraha-2012/land-reforms-in-india/
4 http://js2012.wordpress.com/why-jansatyagraha-2012/land-reforms-in-india/
5 http://planningcommission.nic.in/plans/planrel/fiveyr/11th/11_v3/11th_vol3.pdf

ment amongst the rural masses, especially the schedule class and tribal population needed a spark to engulf the nation.

d) **Naxalbari Episode—the Ground Zero of Naxal Movement**. In early 1967, a tribal youth named Bimal Kissan from Naxalbari, a small village in Darjeeling District of West Bengal obtained a judicial intervention to plough his field. It was a legitimate attempt to break the feudal stronghold. While Bimal Kissan was in his field, the upper-caste landlord attacked him, denying him his lawful right in independent India. This act provided the spark to ignite the fire of vengeance and the emergence of an Ultra-Leftist Front under the leadership of Charu Mazumdar and Kanu Sanyal, which later came to be known as the Naxalites. The group retaliated by occupying the land forcibly. This unleashed anarchy and mayhem in the area leading to the death of many, including some police personnel. The state units of the CPI (M) in West Bengal, Bihar, Odisha, Andhra Pradesh, Tamil Nadu, Kerala and Uttar Pradesh supported the movement and it became a national-level uprising. In the beginning the movement was immensely popular. Many students from Delhi University, IITs and other institutions joined the fight for the rights of the poor tribals and farmers. With the dilution in principles and the raising of the slogan "Chinese Chairman is our Chairman", the Naxal Movement started waning and was temporarily suppressed. However, the main cause of the uprising remained unaddressed.

Assembly Constituencies in Darjeeling District

e) **Switch from Naxalism to Present Day Maoism.** The Naxalbari episode drew student support from across India and had an impact on the ideology of the Communist Movement in India. Questions were raised on the dogmatic adherence to Mao Zedong thoughts and belief that it formed the essence of Marxism- Leninism Philosophy. Khokan Mazumdar, the grand old veteran of the Communist Movement in India has stated that the single most important cause of the failure of the Naxalbari Movement was the slogan, "the Chinese chairman is our chairman'.[6] In the early phase of the Naxalbari Movement, there was a split between the two stalwarts, Charu Mazumdar and Kanu Sanyal, leading to the formation of the Communist Party of India CPI (M-L) and the Maoist Communist Centres (MCC)[7]. They went on to spread their wings in Bihar. Their aim was to launch a 'peasant armed struggle' to annex political power. Around the same time a guerrilla movement in Andhra Pradesh also appeared which was initially crushed by the application of force. It revived again in 1976, with a daring raid on village Tappalpur, in 1976, leading to the formation of the Peoples War Group (PWG). The activists of PWG when under pressure from the state would migrate to Odisha, Maharashtra, Bihar; giving birth to the infamous 'red corridor' of the Maoists. The merger of the MCC and PWG in 2004 led to the current rise of the Maoists in India- CPI (Maoist). The movement has engulfed more than one third of the nation's districts—the figures range from 168–200.

Inadequacies of the Modern Indian State

Socio-Economic Neglect. In the early 1980s, the then Prime Minister Indira Gandhi had sent a study team headed by the Member-Secretary of the Planning Commission to conduct field-level studies of the Naxal-affected areas in Bihar and Andhra Pradesh, and render recommendations both for the Centre and the States. The study team conclusively brought out

[6] More militarism less mass support: Naxalbari veterans- The Times of India, New Delhi, 08 Oct 2012.

[7] http://redbarricade.blogspot.in/2009/12/history-of-indian-communist-movement.html

that the socio-economic concerns of the weaker sections of the Naxal affected areas must be addressed meaningfully. Again, in May 2006, the Planning Commission appointed an expert committee headed by D Bandopadhya who was dealing with the Naxalites in West Bengal in the 1970s. The committee highlighted that the poor implementation of reforms and absence of empowerment of the local communities as the main cause of popular support to the Naxals. The report states that "we have two worlds of education, two worlds of health, and two worlds of housing."[8] Despite these reports the political system and the administrative machinery ignored the urgency to address the needs of the people.

Forest and the Tribals. Forest legislation in India dates back to 1865 and the process continued till the Indian Forest Act 1927 came into being during the British rule. The 1927 Act was deemed anti-tribal. After independence, the government nationalised the forests and the connected forest wood industry, in 1953, and revised the Indian Forest Act in 1982.[9] In 1980, the government also introduced the Indian Forest Conservation Act. amendments to which were made in 1988. An analysis of these legislations reveals that, though the intent was positive, their implementation was faulty and the powerful timber mafia lobby exploited this to the hilt. It not only resulted in dwindled forest cover but also made the tribals, whose livelihood depended on the minor forest produce, aliens in their own land. Even today, 80% of tribals/rural population of India depend on wood as the source of energy. During 1980-2000, numerous cases were registered against tribals for accessing minor forest produce. This became a major tribal grievance—a perfect recipe for the Naxalites to exploit.

Absence of Benefits from Economic Development. The beginning of the 21st century witnessed a slew of reforms unleashed to usher fast track development in India. The forest and mineral wealth were tapped but the fruits of economic developments hardly reached the poor, especially the tribals. In many cases they were deprived of their land and livelihood for development projects, without the requisite compensation. The period between 2002- 2005 witnessed a sudden spurt in Maoist activities in the country, majority of which are in areas dominated by tribals. The large scale disturbance caused to the tribals due to projects in Kalinga Nagar in Odisha, Polavaram in Andhra Pradesh and Narmada Valley project in Madhya Pradesh provided the ideal nesting ground to the Maoist.[10]

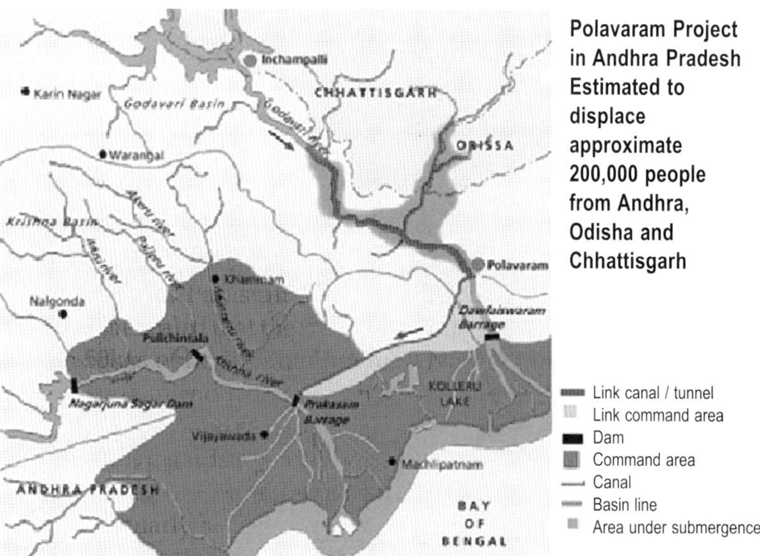

Polavaram Project in Andhra Pradesh Estimated to displace approximate 200,000 people from Andhra, Odisha and Chhattisgarh

Politicking. Political parties have known to hobnob with the Naxals/Maoists to gain advantage during elections. In Andhra Pradesh, every election in the past, except the 2009 election, was dominated by the Naxals. Politicians are known to pay protection money to such groups and hurl accusations on each

---

[8] Report on the working group of land relations for the formulation of Eleventh Five Year Plan, 31 July 2006.

[9] http://en.wikipedia.org/wiki/Forestry_in_India

[10] Chapter IV, Page 43, Report of the working group on land relations for formulation of the 11th Five Year Plan.

other.[11] In a similar situation, Mamata Banerjee, the then Railway Minister was allegedly hobnobbing with the Maoist's during a rally at Lalgarh. She had even called the killing of Maoist leader Azad, a murder. The incident had rocked Parliament.[12] The Maoists have been taking advantage of these situations to gain time and regroup/reorganise.

Maoist Strategy and Modus Operandi

Maoist Strategy. CPI (Maoist) has enunciated its strategy in the document, "Strategy and Tactics of the Indian Revolution".[13] Chapter 4 – titled, 'Two Stages of Revolution', defines that Stage-1 involves capture of power by armed struggle, which is possible only through the proletariat, largely the peasantry. The People's Revolutionary Army and the United Revolutionary Front with political committees (both covert and overt) at various levels are the two pillars of the revolution (Model 1 refers). The Politburo is at the top and is responsible for defining the strategy. Chapter 6 of the document defines the imperative need of seizure of power through the People's Army. It is deemed as the most important facet of the struggle. It is planned to be achieved in three strategic stages, as envisaged by Mao (Model 2 refers). Stage-2 of the revolution would be establishment of the Socialist State which can follow after Stage-1 is completed. It was pledged to develop cooperation between the Maoist Army Nepal and Communist Party of India (Maoist).

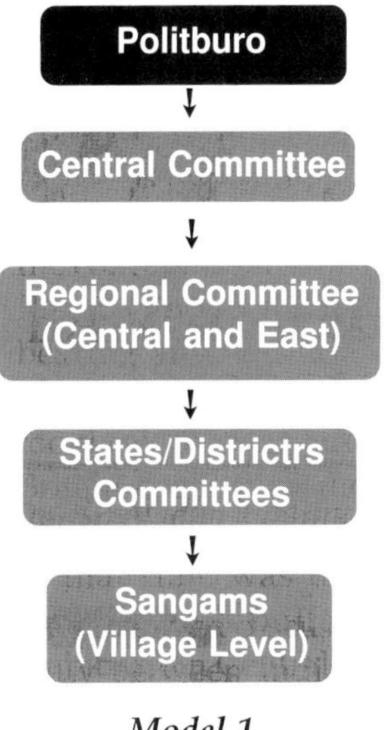

Model 1

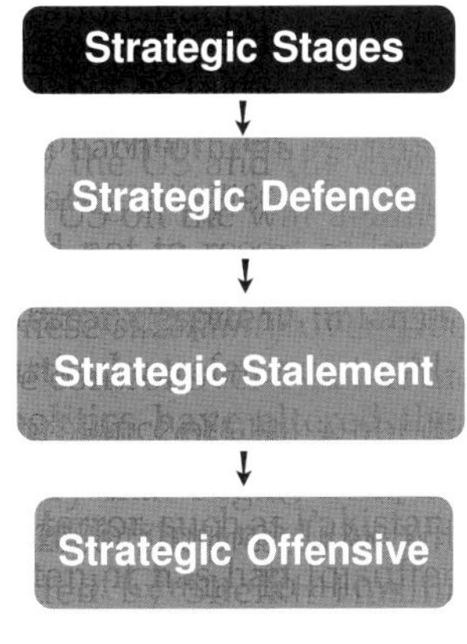

Model 2

Tactics. The Maoist tactics involve developing strong guerrilla bases in the thickly forested areas of Abujhmad and Dandakaranya—where it is difficult for the security forces to approach.[14] The rural areas around the bases were to act as catchment areas for recruitment. Progressively, the guerrilla bases were to be enlarged into Guerrilla Zones and then converted into 'Liberated Zones'. The People's Army was constituted into three tiers. The first tier consisted of the main force of platoons and companies. This force was to be equipped with the best available weapons, to form the teeth-arm of the CPI (Maoist). Local guerrilla squads/ popular militia constituted the second tier and the self defence squads formed the third tier.[15] The tactics involved attacking the police and their informers; targeting government's infrastructure such as railways, bridges, roads, schools and telecommunication centres.[16] The denial of development of mines is part of their tactics.

Modus Operandi. In consonance with the strategy and tactics of CPI (Maoist), guerrilla bases were established in the Dandakaranya/Abhujamad and the villages in the periphery of forests became part of the guerrilla zones. In the aftermath of the CPI (Maoist) initial success against the CRPF and the police, some of these areas came to be known as 'Liberated Zones'. The covert wing of Maoists functioned from the jungles/rural areas; held Lok Adalats (Kangaroo Courts) and passed on-spot judgments, including severing of limbs. These activities were designed to discredit the government machinery. Raids were conducted on police stations and banks to project ascendancy. A detailed network was established for collection of intelligence and information was shared on a 'need to know' basis, making tracking extremely difficult. It also kept the senior leadership insulated from the security forces. The Maoists deployed their part-time members of the United Revolutionary Wing (the political arm) for covertly functioning in both the rural/urban areas. Their task was to assist in propaganda, establish cells in urban areas and provide technology, logistics, communication and allied support to the People's Army to keep in pace with technology. The arrest of Kobad Ghandy, a CPI (Maoist) politburo member from New Delhi, is a case in point. Sensational media reports like abduction of politicians and government officials to facilitate release of their arrested comrades

[11] http://syedakbarindia.blogspot.in/2009/03/assembly-elections-2009-no-talk-of.html

[12] http://www.indianexpress.com/news/mamata-s-tears-for-maoist-azad-anger-oppn-why-is-the-pm-silent-/658820/

[13] http://www.satp.org/satporgtp/countries/india/maoist/documents/papers/strategy.htm#4

[14] http://www.aworldtowin.org/back_issues/2004-30/inside_MCC_Country.htm

[15] http://www.satp.org/satporgtp/countries/india/maoist/documents/papers/strategy.htm- Chapter VII of the Strategy and tactics of CPI(Maoist)

[16] http://news.bbc.co.uk/2/hi/8266550.stm, Sunil Raman BBC, New Delhi, Sep 2009.

are like oxygen to the Maoist movement. News of the attack on the Lakhisarai District police station, (in August 2010) in Bihar, in which seven policemen were killed and four were taken hostages is case in point.[17]

Application of IEDs (Improvised Explosive Devices). The Maoists have used IEDs in multiple ways to prevent the penetration of police and the Para-military forces into their strongholds, cause casualties and maintain ascendency of morale. The IEDs are often laid in connivance with corrupt contractors involved in road construction and local sympathizers. In the early part of the anti- Maoist operations, the Para-military forces launched into the area suffered heavy casualties from these IEDs which were often triggered by the Maoists in concert with their pre-planned ambushes. It is estimated that, since 2007, approximately 40-45 % casualties have occurred due to IED blasts.[18] It made the roads virtually inaccessible to vehicular movement and had an adverse impact on the anti- Maoist operations.

Source of Funding. All Non-State Actors are known to have an elaborate plan to fund their organisation. Available reports indicate that the CPI (Maoist) generates anywhere between Rs. 1000 to 2000 crores annually,[19] to fund and equip their organisation. The vast variation in the assessment is but natural since it depends upon unauthenticated reports and interrogation of apprehended Maoists. The Maoists resort to looting of banks and government treasuries, extortion of businessmen, industrialists, mining companies, big landlords and even some government officials and politicians. Illegal mining is another major source of Maoist financing. They even collect taxes from some middle class families but that forms a very small portion of their collection. The Maoists are also known to tax some of the forest produce viz. 'tendu leaves' etc. There is a nexus of corrupt politicians, businessmen and the Maoists. The money collected is used to procure weapons and other warlike material, provide logistic support, medical aid and payments to their cadre.

Government Response

Deep Slumber. The government's response to the Naxals/CPI (Maoist) challenge has been typical of the 'Blind Men of Hindustan'. In the past forty years, numerous committees constituted by the government repeatedly highlighted the inadequacies in the developmental works and land reforms in tribal/ backward areas. The reports were widely discussed without any concrete steps to ameliorate the conditions of the tribal/poor. Even in the aftermath

[17] http://indiatoday.intoday.in/story/lakhisarai-naxal-attack-bihar-govt-shifts-sp/1/111058.html

[18] http://www.thehindu.com/opinion/op-ed/article388033.ece

[19] http://business.rediff.com/slide-show/2010/may/21/slide-show-1-naxal-extortion-economy-worth-rs-2000-crore-a-year.htm

of the formation of CPI (Maoist) in 2004, the government's machinery was akin to a mammoth in deep slumber. The period from 2004 to 2010, witnessed numerous attacks on banks, railway lines/trains, police stations, destruction of schools and public infrastructure by the Maoists. Politicians and government officials were abducted from different locations and the government was coerced to meet the Maoists' demands. The Maoists started holding open courts and meetings with the local population[20] in their so-called 'Liberated Zones' to dispense justice. They claimed to be working for the amelioration of the poor which is highly questionable. The response of the government's machinery was slow and tardy and lacked coordination, despite early warning by the intelligence agencies.

Salwa Judum. *Salwa Judum*[21] (in Gondi language means 'Purification Hunt') was launched in 2006 in Chhattisgarh, as a people's movement to counter the Maoist oppression. The roots of *Salwa Judum* lie in the *'Jan Jagaran Abhyan'* of 1991 started by the local traders to fight the rising Naxal power in the area, when the government had turned a blind eye to their growing influence. The movement died when the leaders were forced to flee by the Naxals and seek police/Naxal protection. Initially, *Salwa Judum* witnessed unequivocal support from the state machinery that was struggling for an appropriate response to the growing power of the Maoists. The members of *Salwa Judum* were largely armed with medieval weapons, except a few who were given obsolete rifles by the state. To begin with, the state forces supported by the members of *Salwa Judum* carried out some successful operations against the Maoists but their tactics of burning villages and herding large number of people in camps was severely flawed. It led to large scale Human Rights violations and finally their operation were suspended under the directions of the Honourable Supreme Court.

Operation Green Hunt. In the aftermath of *'Salwa Judum'* came the much-fancied operation 'Green Hunt', launched in the latter part of 2009. It has continued thereafter under different code names. The operation was planned to be executed in the Red Corridor, covering Chhattisgarh, Jharkhand, Orissa, Maharashtra and Andhra. A 40,000 square kilometres of area of Abujhmad in Chhattisgarh, Bastar District was seen to be the 'key area' of the operation. The assessed application of troops as put up by various agencies has a large variation ranging from 20,000 to 75,000.[22] The forces involved were the Grey Hounds, BSF, ITBP, CRPF and the state police. A large portion of the troops were employed for securing the roads ('Road Opening Parties'- ROPs) which were known to be infested with IEDs and prone to ambush by the Maoists. The application of ROPs was imperative for the safe delivery of the force into the designated launch pads and for the follow up logistics support. Evidently, it was a large scale operation aimed to force the Maoist leaders and cadres to move out of their hideouts in the thickly forested areas, to facilitate their apprehension or annihilation. To execute this objective the security forces should have had a strong operational grid in place before the launch of 'Operation Green Hunt'. As reported the apprehended or killed Maoists were largely 'Sangam members', i.e. unarmed sympathizers. Such large-scale operations have often led to fatigue to the troops with very little contribution towards the pre-mediated objectives. The hardship caused to the local population and allegations of human rights violations, further add to the negative spin-offs.

Ineffective Coordination. In the early phase of anti-Maoist operations, absence of coordination between various agencies of the Centre and the States was starkly evident. It served to the benefit of the Maoists and proved to be a major drawback in the conduct of successful operations by the security forces, leading to the loss of many gallant personnel. The inadequacies in coordination came into the public domain when some of the states stoutly resisted the 'National Counter Terrorism Centre' by the Home Minister in 2012, an imperative need for coordination of collection and dissemination of intelligence. Even Kautilya in Volume X (Treaties of War) of the *Arthashastra* laid great emphasis on acquiring information about the adversary. After more than 2,300 years of Kautilya[23], the nation is still grappling

[20] http://newshopper.sulekha.com/maoists-injure-13-policemen-in-bengal_news_1228231.htm

[21] http://en.wikipedia.org/wiki/Salwa_Judum

[22] http://articles.timesofindia.indiatimes.com/keyword/operation-green-hunt and http://www.tehelka.com/story_main42.asp?filename=Ne031009coverstory.asp

[23] http://en.wikipedia.org/wiki/Chanakya

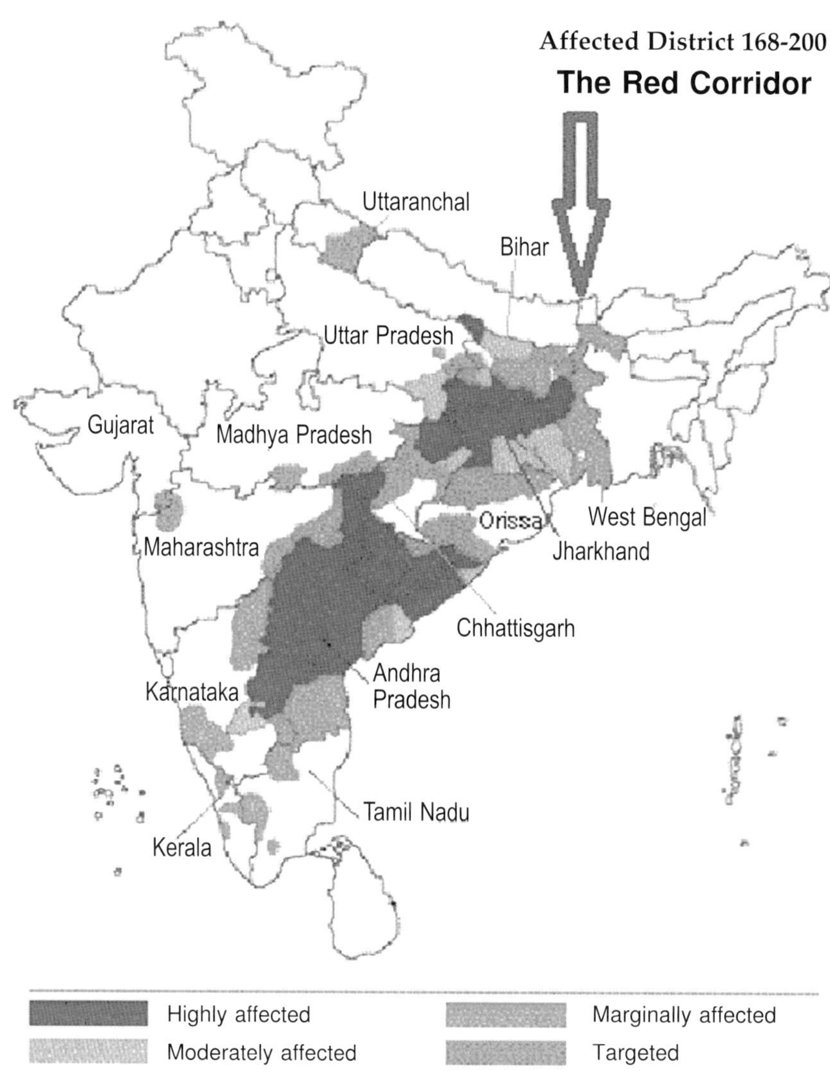

with the need to understand the importance of coordinated flow of intelligence in ensuring the security and safety of our nation. Are some of the Chief Ministers behaving like the princes of medieval India who played into the hands of the forces inimical to the integrity of the nation?

The Way Ahead

Strategy. As stated by Dr Manmohan Singh the Maoists are "the single biggest threat to the internal security of India" and has impacted more than one-third of the nation's districts. Clearly, it is a pan-India, socio-political problem with its roots deeply embedded in the lack of development and exploitation of the tribals and poor in the rural areas. Hence, the strategy should focus on ironing out the socio-political anomalies. There is a need for a fast pace development of the tribal and rural areas and ruthless implementation of land reforms to wean away the local support to the Maoists who are advocating a classless society. The recent report of the 'Union Road Transport and Highway Ministry' coming under criticism for executing only 25% of the planned projects, needs to be improved.[24] In the Eleventh Five Year Plan there is an allocation of Rs, 500 crores for the development of infrastructure in the Maoist affected areas. It should be taken on a war footing and all development projects should be executed with the active involvement of the three tiers of Panchayat Raj and not by the political-bureaucratic-contractors nexus. Transparency in the execution of development works supported by the application of 'minimum essential force' is the right remedy to this chronic disease, threatening the security and integrity of the nation.

Intelligence. Acquisition of real time intelligence and its speedy dissemination is pivotal in the execution of anti- insurgency/terrorist operations. In the recent past, be it 26/11 or the September 2012 exodus of people from the North-East due to doctored

[24] http://www.dailymail.co.uk/indiahome/indianews/article-2141985/Parliament-committee-picks-holes-governments-highway-plans.html

SMS/MMS; the intelligence apparatus of the country has failed to meet the emerging challenges. The lack of coordination, trust deficit and 'one up-man ship' between the multiple agencies operating both at the national and the state level continue to be our nemesis. There is a need to revamp the entire intelligence machinery in the country. The current system of RAW being responsible for the external intelligence and the Armed Forces (Army, Navy and Air Force) having their organic structure should be continued. The entire gamut of internal security, to include the charter and functioning of the IB, NTRO (which has been under flak from various quarters), the proposed National Counter Terrorist Centre and the futuristic need of technology needs to be studied by an expert panel on a time-bound schedule to invigorate this vital facet of national security.

Unified Command. The Unified Commands that are currently functioning in the states of Manipur, Assam and J&K are chaired by the respective Chief Ministers. The meetings are largely confined to the activities that have rolled over. There is hardly a discussion on the future plans, acquisition of time-bound intelligence and the facets that merit coordination to make the operations seamless. Since the anti-Maoists operations involve multiple states they merit a different approach. There is a need of a two-tier Unified Command; tier one at the Centre and the tier two at the States level. The periodicity of the meeting could be suitably defined. At the Centre, it should be chaired by the Home Minister/ the National Security Advisor with Director IB, RAW, appropriate representatives of the concerned ministries and the Chief Secretaries of the affected states along with the senior most official of the Security Forces as members. The second tier meetings should be chaired by the respective Chief Ministers. At the national level the meeting should aim at defining the strategy, broad policy guidelines, coordination and allocation of central resources based on the states' requirement. The meetings at the State level should focus on the planned operations, coordination, allocation of time-bound tasks and feedbacks, in sync with the policy guidelines defined by the Centre to facilitate seamless operations within the State and along the inter- state boundaries.

Application of Minimum Force. In a scenario where the problem is socio-political in nature and the Maoists have resorted to an armed struggle to capture power by active involvement of the masses, the application of force should be restricted to minimum essential to bring the affected area back under the control of the government. The application of force should be supported by projects aimed to 'Win the Heart and Minds' of the people. Any large-scale operation of the 'Green Hunt' kind often leads to human rights violations and facilitate the Maoists only.

Small Things—the Vital Link. It is a well known adage, 'if you take care of small things the big things take care of themselves'. In anti-Maoist operations, it is vital to prepare our forces to excel in sharp shooting and minor tactics to beat the Maoists in their own game. The troops should be trained to operate in small teams of six to eight personnel, be able to live in jungles for three to four days, seek encounters and annihilate the armed Maoists hiding in inaccessible areas. The small teams should be able to sneak in and out of their bases—'mobile grids' and those left in the bases should be able to defend themselves, without looking for any reinforcement over their shoulders. These kinds of operations would build morale ascendency over the Maoists, win over the local populace, usher development works and set the stage for removing the cancerous growth of the Maoists from the nation's underbelly.

Policy Imperatives. The abduction tactics of the Maoists, be it the case of Sukma or Koraput Collectors, the MLA from Odisha or the policemen from West Bengal found the government in a quandary. The abduction tactics of the Maoists has been in place for quite some time. Strategic analysts have been recommending an explicit policy spelling out the government's stance that there will be no exchange of Maoists/terrorists with the hostages. There is also the need for well-orchestrated hostage negotiation teams which could be activated at short notice, and release of NSG to carry out rescue missions, if essential. It is heartening to see that the government has recently put out a draft policy on 'Hostages' taking cognizance of the recommendations made by the strategic analysts. Similarly, a national level 'Surrender and Rehabilitation' policy factoring the lessons drawn from our past experiences is also an imperative need of the hour. The government would do well to bring critical draft policies into the public domain and seek views of the strategic analysts before these are given the final shape.

Media. In a democratic state, the media is a great source of building bridges but it needs to be understood by all those operating on behalf of the government that it is a double-edged weapon. For the Maoists/terrorists sensational news is like oxygen, essential for their survival and growth. Therefore the government's administrative machinery and the security forces have to learn to keep the media in the loop and ensure that information released is timely, factually correct and ordain well for the government.

The South Asia Cauldron

Socio- political Milieu. South Asia is home to one fifth of the world's population and is the most densely populated region in the world. It also has the dubious distinction of having more than 40% of its population living below the International Standard of $1.25 per day, second to the Sub-Sahara Region.[25] A demographic analysis of the region reveals that the region has more than 2,000 ethnic entities of which about 64% is Hindu, 33% Muslim, 2% Buddhist and 1% Christian. This has made the region fault-prone and the ideal ground for insurgents/terrorists activities.

The Cauldron. Currently, the region is considered the hub of terrorist activities, especially Pakistan and Afghanistan. In the last two decades the region has witnessed an exponential increase in terrorist groups in Pakistan of which many are hosted along with the elements of the state machinery. Sri Lanka had been waging its own battle against LTTE. The country has been able to eliminate LTTE by application of massive force, but there are dark clouds of human rights violations against Sri Lanka. In the first decade of the 21st century Nepal witnessed the Maoist Armed Revolution that led to the overthrow of the monarch. During the same period India also witnessed the formation of CPI (Maoists) and the Red Corridor linking to Nepal. The Maoists are known to have established links with the terrorist organisations in the North East of India, Myanmar, Bangladesh, Pakistan and even the remnant cells of LTTE. Here we see an intermingling of the proponents of Communist ideology, religious fundamentalists and other terrorist groups. This marriage of convenience is a new phenomenon that needs to be studied. The main causes of their emergence are the failure of the states to alleviate poverty, check corruption and improve governance.

Conclusion

India and South Asia are going through a period of transition. The economy of the region is growing at an unprecedented rate of 5-6% and more. There is an ever-widening gulf between the rich and the poor—'the haves and the have-nots'. Governance in the region is extremely poor with a large percentage of population living below the minimum international standards. According to the World Bank survey of 2009, the population bulge in South Asia and India between the ages of 0-14 years is 31.15% and 30.2%,[26] respectively. In consonance with the survey of 2011, the literacy rate in India is 74.04% but there is vast disparity between the gender literacy. It is the young adult who account for half of the unemployment as they lack the requisite skills despite a fair percentage of them being classified as literate. Due to the growing population there is a continuous shift taking place from rural to the urban areas. Literacy and skills developments are growing at an extremely sluggish pace. In the absence of good governance, genuine implementation of land reforms, the Forest Act and the labour reforms that impact the poor and the tribals, the growth of Maoists and their amalgamation with other fundamental Non-State Actors is a natural process. It needs to be addressed by the government, the administrative machinery and the corporate sector in tandem so that the impact of the economic reforms reaches the poor and the tribals to checkmate the Maoists and fundamental organisations. Last but not the least; peace will continue to elude South Asia till the border dispute between India and Pakistan is resolved.

"It is very easy to defeat someone, but it is very hard to win someone"

—Dr Abdul Kalam

[25] http://en.wikipedia.org/wiki/South_Asia

[26] http://search.worldbank.org/data?qterm=youth+bulge+india&language=EN&format=

TRANSBORDER SECURITY DEBATES AND THE ROLE OF BANGLADESH AND INDIA: CHALLENGES TO FORMULATE A SUSTAINABLE TRANSBORDER SECURITY PARADIGM

Iqbal Shailo, Carleton University, Ottawa, Canada

Introduction

The division of the Indian sub-continent took place after the Second World War, which quickly brought about many global changes—the most important transformation in world affairs being the end of the colonial era and the re-emergence of liberty and self-determination in the form of nation-states. The War collapsed Hitler's Third Reich, eased the emergence of individual nations in Europe and elsewhere, initiated a new system of inter-state integration in Europe and offered hope of political stability and some economic prosperity among nations.

The division of the subcontinent has wounded India and Pakistan. According to some Indian historians, the relationship between Hindus and Muslims began to deteriorate during the British colonial era. The division sowed the seeds of mistrust, jealousy and animosity between Hindus and Muslims, which ultimately led to an unprecedented bloodshed in the world history of ethnic and communal violence.[1] The triangular struggle between the Congress (led by Nehru and other political elites and the Congress was recognized mainly as the party of Hindus, though some Muslim elites joined the party along with thousands of their followers), the Muslim League (led by Jinnah of Pakistan and other political elites from East Bengal [Bangladesh] and India) and the British regime made it difficult to create a harmonious relationship amongst the stakeholders, as "between the Congress and the League there needed to be accommodation and mutual tolerance."[2] Until now, the following factors had been a source of hatred and mistrust between the two communities: the Two-Nations Theory, Radcliffe's boundary map for division (especially Bengal including Assam and Punjab), the fate of more than 565 small and large princely states including Jammu and Kashmir, the division of the inheritance, and the human displacement from both sides.

The legacy of partition turned the subcontinent into a chaotic zone, with conflicts resulting in war, riot, rape, arson, insurgency, political interference and communal instability. Both India and Pakistan became enemy to each other and after the independence the immediate crisis was the Kashmir issue that put both countries to stand face to face in conflict. Both countries tried to occupy the princely state of Kashmir of the region and it became the principal bone of territorial contention between India

[1] Chadda, Maya. 2007. "Debating Strategies for Disrupting Violence- Lessons from South Asia," in Linell E. Cady and Sheldon W. Simon, (eds.) *In Religion and Conflict in South and Southeast Asia: Disrupting Violence*, London Routledge: p.137

[2] Chapman, Graham P. 2003. *The Geopolitics of South Asia: From Early Empires to The Nuclear Age*, Second Edition, Ashgate: p.158

and Pakistan soon after the partition. India and Pakistan fought for the formal accession of Kashmir into their own territory. The war continued until 1949. "The UN resolution of 3 April 1948 called for the establishment of a neutral administration, and the holding of a plebiscite to determine whether the state should accede to Pakistan or India."[3] The part of the state occupied and now administered by Pakistan is known as Azad (Free) Kashmir with a population of more than 2.5 million while India's part includes over 8 million people. Relations between India and Pakistan worsened, eventually leading to two more wars over Kashmir in 1965 and 1999.

This paper is organized as follows: First, the introductory chapter discusses the division of the Subcontinent through a brief history of the hatred and mistrust that eventually led to wars between India and Pakistan for taking hold of Kashmir. Second, it focuses on the breakup of Pakistan into two territories (Bangladesh and Pakistan) that has given India an opportunity to dominate the South Asian region politically. Third, it demonstrates friendly relations between Bangladesh and India that could reinforce cooperation between them in solving bilateral conflicts. Fourth, it highlights the presidential visit by Barack Obama to reveal the close relationship between India and the USA, as well as India's emerging strength as one of the global political players in the world system. Fifth, it puts forward some proposals to construct trans-border security paradigm for the sub-continent in particular and the South Asian region in general.

Breakup of Pakistan, Regional Politics and the Changed Role of India

The breakup of Pakistan into two territories, Bangladesh and Pakistan, has provided India strengths to act as a regional power to dominate the South Asian region, politically and economically. The narrative of security in respect of India propels this fundamental concept that India's hegemonic behaviour has been dominating the region since 1980s. The period of the 1970s and 1980s was, as Malone described, one of intermittent realism exhibited by India towards its external approaches.[4]

Malone further notes that India's treaty with the Soviet Union in 1971; its military intervention in the Bangladesh war; its first nuclear test in 1974 and its occupation of Sikkim incorporating it into the Union are testimony to its realist approaches toward foreign affairs. In addition, India, as Pattanaik describes, closed the transit points between Nepal and India in 1988; carried out food bombing in Jaffna in 1986; sent the IPKE (Indian Peace Keeping Force) to Sri Lanka to help President Jayewardene in quelling the insurgency in the late 1980s; and intervened in the Maldives in 1988 at the request of it's the then president Gayoom.[5] Malone has rightly noted that:

> [T]his era dominated by Indira Gandhi was characterized by lip service to anti-imperialism, Third World solidarity, non-alignment abroad and secularism, democracy at home. However, in both spheres, there was a marked drift in practice toward power politics, in spite of which Mrs. Gandhi remains a tremendously popular, indeed iconic, figure within her own country, remembered more fondly by many Indians than the historically more remote Nehru and Gandhi, who are more admired than loved.[6]

New Delhi's strategic plans have long been a problem; the people of Bangladesh have mixed reactions about India's role in the region, especially with regard to Bangladesh. Some groups believe that during the colonial era, the rule of Hindu feudal lords was representative of domination and exploitation, therefore any relationship with India ideologically will turn into hegemonic by any means.[7] The contemporary major opposition party of Bangladesh claims that independence and sovereignty of the country are safe in BNP's (Bangladesh National Party) hand and not in the grip of the ruling party (i.e., AL) of the country that has a huge relation with India.[8]

Still both countries experience deep mistrust and suspicion. The degree of cooperation and collaboration between them varies from regime to regime and it depends on the political parties of both sides and the level of trust existing between each other. "Bangladeshi perceptions *vis-à-vis* India are based on historical baggage, deep-seated suspicion, reality of power gap, the communal dimension of partition, construction of an 'enemy image' through politically motivated media campaigns and highly nationalistic and sovereignty-sensitive elites that seek their

[3] Ibid., p.192

[4] Malone, David M. 2011. *Does the Elephant Dance? Contemporary Indian Foreign Policy*, Oxford University Press: p.50

[5] Pattanaik, Smruti S.2010. "India's Neighbuorhood Policy: Perceptions from Bangladesh" *Strategic Analysis*, Vol. 35 (1): p.71-87

[6] Malone, David M. 2011. *Does the Elephant Dance? Contemporary Indian Foreign Policy*, Oxford University Press:p.50

[7] Pattanaik, Smruti S.2010. "India's Neighbourhood Policy: Perceptions from Bangladesh" *Strategic Analysis*, Vol. 35 (1): p.71-87

[8] Hasan, Rashudin. 2008. "Country in Deep Crisis," *The Daily Star*, Bangladesh, December 13

political sustenance through non-cooperation."[9] These are the main issues that have been hovering over the relationship between Bangladesh and India for a long time.

Of late India has changed its political strategy and felt the necessity to forge a continued relationship with opposition parties of Bangladesh. It has understood that the present pro-Indian ruling government of Bangladesh is not enough to consolidate its friendship with Bangladesh to solve mutual disputes and the opposition parties are also an integral part to achieve bilateral cooperation, especially to address the issues like trans-border security, trade, transit, connectivity, various treaties and agreements. India invited the opposition leader of Bangladesh to discuss mutual issues of interest, and thus Begum Khaleda Zia, the chief of BNP (Bangladesh Nationalist Party) and opposition party in the present Parliament of Bangladesh, had been on a week-long visit to India staring from 28 October 2012. She met with President Pranab Mukherjee, Prime Minister Manmohan Singh, and other political elites of New Delhi and assured of her cooperation with India in all aspects, especially not to allow terrorists and separatists to use Bangladesh territory to orchestrate any terror attacks to harm India and its citizens.

BNP-Chairperson Khaleda also urged Prime Minister Dr. Manmohan Singh to implement the sharing of Teesta and other common river flowing treaties, consider stopping construction of the Tipaimukh dam as well as to allow more duty-free goods from Bangladesh. The dialogue of Begum Zia with the Foreign Minister of India, Salman Khurshid, got momentum when Zia told him that "connectivity between Bangladesh and India was "inevitable" and the same must be expanded to include China and South East Asia."[10] Her party opposed this connectivity and transit facility to India earlier and India has been facing a land-lock to connect with its northeastern states. "Khaleda welcomed the idea for a consortium including India, China and other countries undertaking the Sonadia deep-sea port of Bangladesh because of the huge amount of investment needed for it and said it would benefit Bangladesh, India, China and Thailand."[11]

Prime Minister Dr. Singh also invited former President H.M. Ershad, currently the chairman of Jatiya Party which is the third largest political party of Bangladesh in the Parliament, in August 2012, to discuss some mutual issues pertinent to the interest of both countries.

Security Debates and the Role of Bangladesh and India

The events of 9/11 have changed the security discourse at the national, regional and global scale. Concern over the insurgency and infiltration into the north-eastern territory and other hub cities of India has led the country to take serious steps towards curbing terrorism. The government of India has argued that the Pakistani intelligence service, the ISI, had been conducting terror activities through and across the Bangladesh border.[12] India's political elites were seriously concerned about trans-border terrorism, smuggling and human trafficking alleging that Bangladesh had been facilitating terror activities on India's soil while helping the insurgency in the north-eastern territory. Such allegations, among others, include: a) insurgent groups or so-called liberating forces operating in the north-eastern territory (seven sisters) of India use the soil of Bangladesh for anti-India activities. India even claimed that the Pakistani ISI (intelligence Service) used Bangladeshi operatives or middlemen/agents to assist the insurgents in launching terror activities in the north-eastern part of India; b) the existence of a flow of illegal immigration from Bangladesh, where individuals crossing the border swarm Indian cities to find employment and to become involved with illicit and anti-state activities; and c) the Indian Border Security Forces (BSF) alleges that the smuggling of cattle and contraband items was an everyday phenomenon across the border.

The governments of Bangladesh have long denied such allegations and refuse India's claims about aiding the insurgency and cross-border terrorism. In fact, Bangladesh has been working to fulfil the following demands to ensure a more peaceful relation between the two countries by way of: a) ensuring the demarcation of disputed border areas between Bangladesh and India by ratifying the historic Indira-

---

[9] Pattanaik, Smruti S. 2010. "India's Neighbourhood Policy: Perceptions from Bangladesh" *Strategic Analysis*, Vol. 35 (1): p.74

[10] Bhattacharya, Pallab. 2012. "Khaleda backs India-China consortium," *The Daily Star* (of Bangladesh), October 31

[11] Ibid.

[12] Jones, Reece. 2009. "Geopolitical boundary narratives, the global war on terror and border fencing in India," *Transactions*, The Institute of British Geographers: p. 295

Mujib Agreement of 1974; b) resolving maritime boundary disputes in the Bay of Bengal; c) refraining to erect the Tipaimukh dam in the upper streams of the Barak River; d) undertaking the necessary measures to ensure the free movement of enclave residents, especially the populations of Angarpota and Dohogram; e) stopping the push of Bengali-speaking Indians inside the border of Bangladesh; f) ceasing the flow of drugs and other addictive tablets/ pills, including phensidyl (a cough syrup used as a liquid drug for intoxication); g) rooting out the local illegal drug industry established across the border of India to supply hand-made drugs and other substances for Bangladeshi consumers; and h) stopping the killing of Bangladeshi citizens as well as the BSF's frequent intrusion into Bangladesh in violation of international border laws.

Bangladesh is maintaining a good relationship with India, and there exists a cultural and linguistic affinity between Bangladesh and the Indian state of West Bengal. For instance, they both speak the same language and share the same cultural heritage and traditions despite differing religious beliefs and faith. They eat the same foods, celebrate the same festivities including the Bengali New Year, and women wear the same *saris*. The province of Bengal was divided in 1947. In the late 1960s, the motto of the independence movement of Bangladesh was "Buddhist, Christians, Hindus and Muslim, we are all Bengali." The cultural and social bridge between the two wings of Bengal was so strong that the people of West Bengal resisted the construction of a fenced wall along the border of Bangladesh in the 1990s.[13]

The present pro-liberation government of Bangladesh has so far maintained a good relationship with India and its neighbouring states. To appease Delhi's wrath, and to demonstrate its cooperation with India, the present government has made a series of gestures: a) it arrested a number of influential ULFA and other north-eastern territory leaders, who had been hiding in Bangladesh for a couple of years, and handed them over to India while some remain in jail awaiting deportation. The Indian government takes this initiative as a positive one and has congratulated Bangladesh for its heroic action; b) it signed a US$ 1billion loan agreement with India in August 2010 to realize 14 projects, which include infrastructural development, river dredging, and the purchasing of energy from India. Despite criticism from opposition parties including the BNP (Bangladesh Nationalist Party), Prime Minister Sheikh Hasina has paid no attention to the political parties' demands to cancel the agreement. This loan is going to be used to build roads to provide India access to its troubled north-eastern territory through Bangladesh and in exchange Bangladesh will gain transit through India, Nepal and Bhutan; and c) Both Bangladesh and India have agreed to open the border to commence a border *haat* (transborder market/bazaar) on the Bangladesh and Meghalaya (India) frontier to increase cooperation between the people on both sides.

South Asian Geopolitics, Obama's 2010 *Diwali* Trip and India's Strength

US President Barak Obama's November-2010 *Diwali* trip to India reflects how the country has accumulated power both internally through rapid economic growth and externally through regimented military power and its innovative technology, IT development, and nuclear arms and weapons. The presidential visit focused on issues of trade and business but the president's gesture was an endorsement of India's candidature for a permanent seat on the UN Security Council. India's significant role in the geo-strategic and geo-political arena has echoed time and again, particularly across Asia.

Moreover, India's rise in the face of neighbouring China would give the US solace in knowing it has a good friend in south and south-east Asia. Obama's *Diwali* trip did not pressure India to sign any non-proliferation or nuclear treaties. He indicates that they rely on each other as economic and development partners. That said, the joint statement released in New Delhi talked about "a shared commitment to a world without nuclear weapons." The US expressed its support for India to be included in the Nuclear Suppliers Group (NSG), Missile Technology Control Regime (MTRC), the Australia Group (AG) and the Wassenaar Arrangement. This is a very positive step towards integrating India into the global political stage, but at the same time, President Obama pointed out India's "shyness" in criticizing the autocratic regimes, military juntas and human rights violations in the world such as those recorded in Myanmar. Despite some criticism from the left and Hindu fundamentalist groups about Obama (who managed to create 50,000 to 60,000 jobs in the US by launching bilateral business and technological treaties with India), the Singh government has shown its utmost willingness and cooperation to work with the Obama administration.

President Obama has described the Indo-US relationship as 'the defining partnership of the 21st century' which underscores how India has stepped

[13] Ibid., p.291

onto the political stage as one of the most powerful countries in the world. His recognition has added value to an increased role for India in the region to resolve bilateral and trilateral issues, allowing the country to exhibit its sincerity and responsibility in making South Asia a better region. In order to resolve present crisis for sake of India's growth, progress and development, Obama reiterated his call for India to improve diplomacy with Pakistan in a statement to the Parliament of India in New Delhi as well as in a town hall meeting with students in Mumbai in November 2010. A peaceful neighbourhood does not need policing and this is especially desired in the South Asian region to promote better growth and progress for one fifth of the world's population.

Security Threats: from Realism to Diplomacy

Despite ever-present threats to security and danger in the Sub-continent, what has remained an issue of debate is about what specifically is being threatened, by whom, from whom, and from where. Also up for debate are the ways in which Bangladesh, India and Pakistan perceive security, and how they protect themselves from each other's threats and dangers. The confusion lies between security, geography, identity and danger. Threats and dangers are concerned with 'sensitive geographical locations', the line of control (LOC), border posts, smuggling zones, issues surrounding the smuggling of guns, small arms ammunition, and narcotics as well as other substantial issues including human trafficking, trans-border terrorism, insurgency and infiltration, and these have remained central to public debates for decades.

The contemporary research agenda of security in South Asia has gradually shifted from a realist approach to soft diplomacy, and researchers are mainly concerned with Track II and Track III diplomacy (between people to people). Scholars of the sub-continent hold workshops, seminars and fora before the annual SAARC (South Asian Association for Regional Cooperation) summit in the region, where scholars, researchers and academics enthusiastically put forward proposals in an attempt to convince SAARC leaders that there are other significant issues yet to be addressed, such as environmental and social issues of the region. These soft diplomacies, however, are generally not well received by leaders at summits but scholars believe that one day the leaders will give more attention to their recommendations for the betterment of the region.

Construction of Transborder Security for the Sub-continent

My recent field research in New Delhi (India) and Dhaka (Bangladesh) helped me gain a textured perspective on the general conception of security in both India and Bangladesh. I conducted a series of interviews with a cross section of people in India, and my key question was: How do the people of India define security and perceive their own security and national security? It seems that most of them are concerned with the security of the individual in particular and society as a whole. They do not sense or predict a nuclear attack or a war by the two rivals, Pakistan and China. On the contrary, they worry about national and transnational insurgency/trans-border terrorism, which is becoming a recurring phenomenon in the Indian political and social scene.

On the other hand, the concept of security is different in Bangladesh. Interview data with respondents within representative sections of society suggest that security is based on emancipation i.e., alleviation of poverty, reducing illiteracy, freedom of speech, human rights, and accessing facilities like shelters, food and health. They are not afraid of India as a threat but they believe that India creates/would create some geopolitical environment to control or influence Bangladesh and its neighbours. They have cited, for example, some issues of mutual interest and emerging issues pertinent to sovereignty, security and survival—namely water sharing, land and border disputes, maritime boundary, floods, and embankments, deforestation, trade, migration, mobility and so on.

Pakistan defines security very narrowly, and has adopted a narrow vision of envisaging the possibility of security threats and attacks from its neighbour - India. This attitude is prevalent in public discourse, and has become an orthodox pattern of elite thinking in Pakistan. After the fall of the Taliban in Afghanistan, Pakistan has been constantly fighting on its north-western front to wipe out insurgency and some of the areas within Pakistan have turned into a breeding ground for terrorism. Now, the number one priority of the country is to disarm the Taliban and restore security across the country.

At first glance, the Sub-continent experience does not show any possibility of redefining the concept of security or security paradigm in South Asia. There is no doubt that each stakeholder of the region is determined to secure the sovereignty, safety and protection of its citizens. These three countries shared threat perceptions and the threat they are responding to, specifically India and Pakistan, was not only external but internal too. Both countries have their internal forces— "insiders" (Taliban and Jihadists in Pakistan; and the Naxalites, the communist insurgency and terrorists in India) that are active to destabilize peace and growth in both countries. For several decades, India viewed Pakistan as a major security threat and more dangerous to national security and regional order while Pakistan continues to believe that India plays a hegemonic role and does not cooperate for regional growth and stability.

The South Asian security perspectives might involve economic, environmental, militarily and societal sectors to reformulate the security paradigm bilaterally, trilaterally or regionally. I feel that the following can be accommodated to formulate any transborder security paradigm in the Sub-continent as well as for the South Asian region. They are as follows:

First, security can be redefined and reconstructed in terms of economic criteria. An economic globalizing dynamic is the main factor that brings countries, mostly neighbours, closer to each other which Barnet (1981) terms as a global interdependence. Since the inception of SAARC, South Asian countries have not shown any desire of signing a trade agreement. India has several bilateral trade agreements with Bhutan, Maldives, Nepal and Sri Lanka. But it has restricted some trade relations with Bangladesh and Pakistan by putting some barriers on cross-border movement of goods. The member-countries envisaged initiating a free trade zone (South Asian Free Trade Area [SAFTA]) within the regional boundaries. The acceleration of economic cooperation took place in 1991 with the establishment of a study on Trade, Manufactures and Services (TMS) for the region. In 1995, the council of ministers agreed to set up SAFTA and after a long negotiation it was signed on 6 January 2004 covering 1.6 billion people. The agreement came into force in 2006. After this agreement, SAARC members enjoy some facilities in customs revenues from India.

Second, the concept of security can be reformulated in respect of human security. While the concept of human security has earlier roots, its recent prominence comes from the 1994 *Human Development Report* of the United Nations Development Program (UNDP). The report has helped solidify the concept of human security, although recognition of people's security independent of state security is nothing new.[14] Hampson (2002) asserts that the concept of 'security' can be defined as the absence of threat to the core human values, including the most basic human values, the physical safety of the individual.[15] While writing in the context of Latin America, Jorge Nef (1991), a pioneering scholar, warns of the danger of human insecurity and urges maintenance of the economic, social and political well-being of the individual as the individual is the receiver rather than the state.[16] The idea of human security has become the central issue of the EU, United Nations and Group of Eight (G8). They have softened the realist security paradigm and (specifically the EU) paved the way for the inclusion of non-traditional security agenda since the early 1990s.[17] The United Nations Development Programme has fostered the term, human security. In respect of the Sub-continent, millions of people suffer from human security. Ethnic conflicts in India (Muslims, *Dalits*, tribal), Pakistan (the *Shiites*, the *Sunnis* and the *Ahmadiyas*) and Bangladesh (religious minorities and native [*adivasi*] people), poverty, lack of human rights, injustice and fair trial are significantly alarming and stand in the way of development and growth. Thus security should be considered in human aspects too.

Third, the environment is an important aspect of human security and any threats to human security includes environmental degradation. However, the environment as a security issue is not widely accepted and has not received enough attention either by the governments or the public in the South Asian region. Global warming, erosion, water scarcity, drought, floods, climatic hazards and other disasters can be a great issue for a regional workout on security. All low-lying states such as Bangladesh, Netherlands, Maldives and Egypt would be adversely affected by global warming and rises in sea level. But some states might benefit from global warming, for example those with extensive territory now under permafrost (Canada, Russia, Greenland). Bangladesh, India and Pakistan have also been facing environmental disasters and the root of disasters is regional not local. Indian waters often cause floods in Bangladesh and

[14] Axworthy, Lloyd. 2001. "Human Security and Global Governance: Putting People First," *Global Governance*, Vol. 7 (1): p.19

[15] Hampson, Fen Osler. 2002. *Madness in the Multitude*, Oxford University Press

[16] Nef, Jorge. 1991."Democratization, stability and Other Illusions: Militarism, Nationalism and Populism in the Political Evolution of Latin america with Special Reference to the Chilean Case", in Mark Dickensen and Stephen Randall (eds.), *Canada and Latin America: Issues to the year 2000 and Beyond*, The International Centre of the University of Calgary: p. 73-122

[17] Dosch, Jörn. 2003. "Changing Security cultures in Europe and Southeast Asia: Implications for inter-regionalism," *Asia Europe Journal*, Vol. 1:pp. 483-501

Pakistan and Bangladesh is dependent on upstream states including India to meet up its water crises.[18] The Farakka barrage built in India, on the Ganges, has made the northern part of Bangladesh a desert and people are gradually becoming climate refugees. Infrastructural development and economic growth in India entail huge dams, embankments and roads and highways throughout the country that affect the environment as well the local people's homes and farm land which eventually force them to live as internally displaced populations (IDPs). Thus any security pact taking environmental issues as a priority would reduce the negative effects in national life.

Fourth, the concept of security in the Sub-continent may include the issue of arms control and the theme of non-proliferation. The problem of nuclear non-proliferation has become an issue of anxiety in the region and antagonism and hostility between India and Pakistan might escalate to nuclear war, as some pundits suggest, at any time for any causes accidentally. Both parties are holding various initiatives, meetings and dialogues to reduce the risk of accidental use of nuclear weapons in the region. They have already signed a declaration in 1999 in Lahore in which the two countries agreed to take immediate steps for reducing the risk of accidental or unauthorized use of nuclear weapons.

Fifth, the Sub-continent can expand security in terms of societal aspects such as friendship and alliances with ethnic units/groups within the country. The ethnic conflicts that made the Sub-continent a disastrous zone might generate some brighter hope in the country. Instigating deep interactions between and among Hindus/Muslims/Sikhs/Dalits in India, the Sunnis and Shiites in Pakistan and Muslims/Hindus/tribals in Bangladesh would be the best option to keep the country and region more peaceful and stable. In addition, the Sub-continent can drive for more engagement in cultural aspects such as sports (cricket, soccer, and SAARC inter-state games), cultural programmes (musical programmes, dances, competition in literary programmes), and education and training (exchange of students, providing SAARC scholarships and cross-country tours).

[18] Chapman, Graham P. 2003. *The Geopolitics of South Asia: From Early Empires to The Nuclear Age*, Second Edition, Ashgate: p.241

STRATEGIC IMPLICATIONS OF GLOBAL WARMING ON TRADE

SK Sharma, Professor Emeritus, Energy Research Centre, Panjab University, Chandigarh, India

Introduction

Control of trade and resources is the goal of all powerful nations, as trade is central to economic growth of any country. Trade sanctions and concessions have been used as a major tool for world dominance.[1] There is a historical struggle for dominance in world trade. Wars have been fought to control trade since ancient times, as wars are extension of trade wars.[2] Wars develop, when two or more powerful nations deny each other equal trading rights and other resources. It may be said that control of markets was the main cause of wars in twentieth century.[3]

Historical Trade wars in South Asian subcontinent

Since Roman times, Asian spices had been prized in Europe. In the14th century India and China together controlled a major share of world trade due to their supremacy in spices, cotton and silk. Europe was an insignificant player in the Indian Ocean trade until 1500 AD. The major supply routes were through Egypt and the Byzantine/Ottoman Empire. Restrictions created in the trade due to heavy transit tax imposed by these empires resulted in the historic voyage of Vasco da Gama to Calicut in 1498 for discovering a new route to India. Subsequently, the Portuguese captured the shipping lanes in 1530AD to monopolize the spice trade. The Portuguese were followed by East India Companies of Dutch Republic and Great Britain around 1600 AD for trade in valuable Indian cotton and spices. To control this trade, European countries fought many wars. After the Anglo-Dutch war and due to weak governance in India, Great Britain conquered India and other countries in the region and monopolized the trade in cotton, spice, tea and other products.

Green Trade War

In recent times a new kind of threat is looming on the horizon in the form of green trade war, in which global warming concerns are being used as a smokescreen by the developed nations to create technical barriers to trade. Developed nations want to protect their economies and trade from the less-costly products from fast developing emerging economics such as the BRIC countries. Ground work for this new strategy was laid during the formulation of the Kyoto Protocol, which was skewed in favour of developed countries.

Developing countries were outmanoeuvred and could not understand the long-term designs of the

[1] Steven Schlosstein; *Trade War* (New York: Congdon & Weed, 1984) p. 9.

[2] William Appleman; *The Contours of American History* (New York: W.W. Norton, 1988) pp. 54, 66, 122-23, 128-29.

[3] World wars decide who controls world trade, The Institute for Economic Democracy; http://www.ied.info/articles/america-gains-economic-freedom/world-wars-decides-who-controls-world-trade,

developed countries. Selection of base year, clubbing of EU countries together for emission reduction, introduction of an Environmental Trading system between Annexure 1 countries, CDM, Hot air allocations and an additional allowance for sinks etc. were all loaded in favour of the developed countries. These concessions allowed them to meet a major portion of their carbon dioxide emission target without undertaking substantial green measures on the ground. The first salvo of the green war has already been fired by the European Union in the form of its recently-imposed aviation and shopping carbon tax. Different facets of this new emerging green trade war are articulated in the subsequent sections of this paper.

Global Warming

Catastrophic predictions of climate change, as a consequence of global warming, have drawn the attention of governments, corporates and the public at large for the past two decades. Major causes of global warming has been attributed to the significant addition of greenhouse gases such as carbon dioxide, methane, Nitrous oxide, Chlonflorocarbons and SF_6 to the atmosphere, as a result of extensive use of fossil fuels for energy, transport and other activities during the past 150 years. However, this excessive use of energy in the form of fossil fuels was also the prime mover for ushering the first industrial revolution in Europe and the subsequent exponential growth of the developed countries, which gave them a prime position in the international arena.

The first international initiative to discuss the issue of global warming was the Stockholm Declaration during the United Nations Conference on the Human Environment, adopted on 16 June 1972. A real framework for combating global warming, including the role of developed and developing countries was laid down in the Principles of Rio Declaration. In order to stabilize the emission of GHC and reduce global warming and reduce the impact of climate change, a number of international initiatives have been undertaken since creation of UNFCC in 1994 as shown in Figure 1.

Developing countries are home to one-fifth of the world population. People in these countries live in extreme poverty, from hunger and lack health care. They need an accelerated use of energy for development. To address this issue, the Rio Declaration recognized the principle of commons by differential responsibilities for global warming mitigation. The United Nations Framework Convention on Climate Change (UNFCCC) Treaty was signed in 1992 to cooperatively consider measures to limit average global temperature increase and resulting climate change. The UNFCCC also recognized the developmental needs of the under-developed countries and underlined the imperative for the members to "protect the climate system for the benefit of the recent and future generations of humankind on the basis of equity and accordance with their common but differentiated responsibilities and respective capabilities". It also recognized that economic development is essential for adopting measures to address climate change.

Figure 1: Major International Initiatives to combat Global Warming

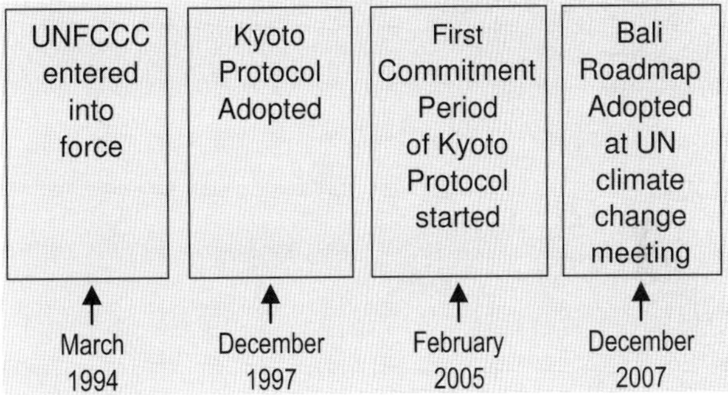

By 1995, it was recognized that the emission reduction measures envisaged to tackle climate change were inadequate and hence new negotiations were launched and the Kyoto Protocol was adopted in 1997. The protocol provided the framework for the most significant beginning of the stupendous efforts made by the international community to adequately address the issue of global warming with proper milestones. Under the Kyoto Protocol, industrialized countries (referenced as Annexure 1 Countries) committed to reduce greenhouse gas emissions by 5.2 percent from base year 1990 between 2009 and 2012. All Annexure 1 countries were given targets as per Annexure B. Developing countries were exempted from any emission cuts, keeping in view their developmental needs for providing basic amenities for their population and to fulfil the principle of common but differentiated responsibilities. The main aim of the Kyoto Protocol was to restrict the rise of global temperature to not more than two degrees Celsius than pre-industrial level and reduction in greenhouse gas emissions by 80 percent by 2050 from the 1990 level; so as to avoid devastating consequences of global warming.

Carbon Emission reduction by Developed Countries through Trade

Despite taking legally binding commitments to reduce their carbon emissions under the Kyoto Protocol, very few developed countries are making real progress on meeting their targets.[4] Developed countries have claimed that they have reduced their collective emissions by almost 2% between 1990 and 2008. A critical analysis of the record of carbon reduction by developed countries shows that the majority of their reductions in carbon emissions have been accomplished through various non-technical measures such as:

(i) Purchasing carbon credits under Clean Development Mechanism (CDM) from Non Annexure 1 countries.
(ii) EU Environment Trading System (ETS), which allows free allowance to industry, which results in reduced carbon trading prices.
(iii) Out-sourcing of carbon intensive products from Non Annexure1 countries , setting the base line as 1990, when their carbon emissions had already peaked.
(v) Bunching of EU countries, whereby they could transfer their excess or deficit between themselves.
(vi) Allocation of free carbon allowance (Hot air) to Former Soviet Union (FSU) states and its subsequent purchase by Annexure1 countries at low prices.

However, in spite of availing above mentioned major advantages, there is an increase of 7% in their carbon emission vis-à-vis their Kyoto Protocol commitment during 1990-2008, if the carbon embedded in imports of products is added to each country.[4] UK claims that its carbon emissions have reduced by 28 million tons during this period. However, when imports and exports are taken in to account, the domestic emissions in UK have increased by more than 100 million tons. European Union, a self professed champion of carbon emission reduction, claims a 6% cut in carbon emission reduction. When imports are factored in, it gets reduced to only 1%. US had promised a 7% cut under the Kyoto Protocol. However, it did not ratify the protocol and its carbon emissions within its borders increased by 17% between 1990 and 2008. In case exports and imports are taken in to account, its carbon emissions increased by 25%, during this period. Thus, it can be concluded that claims of emission reduction by developed countries is merely a paper exercise without any serious action on the ground.

Following in the footsteps of USA, Canada has already announced its withdrawal from the Kyoto Protocol under Article 27 of the protocol, which allows any country to withdraw three years after the protocol came into force. Some analysts claimed that Canada has taken this action as it could not benefit from the favourable provisions of the Kyoto Protocol due to their EU specific nature, as has been done by EU. Canadian officials claimed that to meet the Kyoto Protocol target of 6% cut in emissions by 2012 from 1990 level, Canada would have to purchase carbon emission permits (AAU's) worth $ 14 billion from other Annexure 1 countries.[5] Taking in to consideration such great economic liabilities for meeting the Kyoto Protocol targets, Canada, Japan and Russia have also refused to undertake addition cuts in greenhouse gas emissions after 2012, the terminal year of the first commitment period.

A study undertaken by Glen Peters from the Centre for International Climate and Environmental Research at Oslo,[6] states that, "our study shows for the first time that emissions from increased production of internationally-traded products have more than offset the emissions reductions achieved under the Kyoto Protocol." This study estimated that the net import of carbon was five times greater than emission reduction during 1990-2008.

Thus, it can be concluded that developed countries are, in fact, exporting emissions to the developing countries via trade in carbon-intensive products and purchasing them under CDM. It has been estimated that the net emission transfer via international trade from developing to developed countries increased from 0.4 Giga tons CO^2 in 1990 to 1.6 Giga tons CO^2 in 2008, which exceeds the emission reduction targets of Developed countries.[7] This shows how developed countries gained from the serious loopholes in the Kyoto Protocol, without taking any concrete measures themselves. They are creating hype about global warming for creating unnecessary hurdles in the development process of the developing countries.

On an international scale, it has been estimated that 25% of all carbon dioxide emissions from human activities are being exported or imported from one country to the other. Roughly 50 percent of traded emissions are associated with trade in commodities such as steel, cement, chemicals, pharmaceuticals and the remaining 50 percent is in finished/semi-finished products, such as motor vehicles, clothing, industrial machinery and equipment.

[4] Glen P. Peters and Edgar G. Hertwich, Nature Reports Climate Change vol.2, April 2008; www.nature.com/reports/climatechange.

[5] Peter Kent, *The Huffington Post*, Canada, 6 December 2012

[6] See Note 4 ante.

[7] Glen P. Peters, Jan C. Minx, Christopher L. Weber & et al: *Proceedings of the National Academy of Sciences* Vol: 108 Issue 2011, p.1

Table 1 shows that consumption emissions are significantly higher than the production emissions in most of the developed countries between 1990 and 2008.

Table 1: Percent Increase in Consumption Carbon Emission over Production Emission

Country	*Percent increase in Emission from Trade*
Germany	29
Japan	19
USA	13
France	43
Sweden	61
UK	34

Carbon Leakage and Technical Barriers to Trade (TBT)

The initial delight of developed countries in reducing their carbon emission and meeting the Kyoto protocol target at low cost through import of energy intensive commodities, without initiating any strong local action for decarbonisation of their economies has given way to a new concern of carbon leakage. Carbon leakage is the shifting of production in carbon intensive products to Non-Annexure 1 countries (Developing Countries which do not have carbon reduction targets under Kyoto protocol) having less stringent emission laws. This will result in developed countries losing market share, economic activity and investment to the developing countries. As a result, their economic development and growth will be impacted. The European Commission has classified 164 sectors at risk of leakage. These represent over three quarters of manufacturing emission. Cement, Aluminium and Steel were classified as most vulnerable industries. It has been estimated that by 2016, more than 10-15 percent of EU steel and clinker production will move to the developing countries, if a Euro 20 carbon tax per ton of carbon emission is imposed to reduce carbon emission from these sectors, so as to meet the carbon reduction targets as per Kyoto Protocol.

In order to arrest the carbon leakage, EU and other developed countries are contemplating various measures to stop this migration of production and other economic activities from developed to developing countries. These measures can be in the form of policy or technical barriers to trade.

Policy Measures against Developing Countries

The most potent measure being contemplated by the developed countries is to force developing countries to take legally binding commitments to reduce carbon emission in line with the developed countries. To meet the emission reduction targets, developing countries will have to put strict emission norms in their production processes or introduce policies such as carbon tax, cap-and-trade schemes so as to introduce equivalent carbon cost in the production of all traded goods. These measures will result in the increase in the cost of production of the energy-intensive commodities in the developing countries and put them at a disadvantage for export of their products to developed countries.

On 14 October 1999, the Secretariat of the World Trade Organization (WTO) issued a report on "Trade and Environment." This Report concluded that the data does not support the hypothesis that production is moving to countries with more lax environmental standards. Thus, it appears that there is a deliberate attempt by the developed countries to neutralize the cost advantage of the products from developing countries vis-à-vis developed countries, under the garb of eliminating the carbon leakage from developed countries. A proposal of EU and other developed countries to launch the new Durban Platform to enforce legally-binding carbon emission reduction by both developed and developing countries is a step in this direction. It is a calculated move put forward under the smoke screen of global warming, to force developing countries to introduce equivalent carbon cost in their products. This will shake the very foundations of the Principle of "common but differentiated responsibility", the bedrock of the Kyoto Protocol and UNFCC. The EU claims that with the signing of the Durban Platform, the Kyoto Protocol will be phased out and a new regime, by which all countries, including developing countries, will take legally binding commitments to reduce their carbon emissions. It will result in a quiet burial of the Kyoto Protocol. It will also result in putting an end to the Bali Action plan, started in the 13th COP in Bali, for extending the Kyoto Protocol. This is what developed countries desperately want.

India and China have voluntarily taken a commitment to reduce their Carbon Intensity by 25% and 40% respectively, on 2005, level by year 2020. This commitment will be in addition to the proposed burden of binding emission reduction commitments under the Durban Platform. These commitments will certainly derail the development process of these countries. Nearly 500 million people in India do not have access to electricity and 800 million people still use agricultural and animal residues for cooking. Biomass is the only source of energy available to rural households to meet 80% of their household energy requirements. On the other hand, 80% of the commercial energy is being used by the 25% population living in urban areas. Major sections of society in rural areas and urban slums are living in grave poverty and have a dismal Human Development Index (HDI). Energy is the major input for development and opening up of rural areas. Thus, accelerated energy use will be needed to uplift the major section of the population in the developing countries, who are suffering from extreme energy and economic poverty. Additional carbon reductions targets will severely impeded the development process and keep these nations in perpetual poverty.

Table 2: Energy Consumption and Carbon Emissions

Parameters	*India*	*OECD*	*World*
Energy Supply (Mtoe)	537.31	5,548	11,434
Energy Intensity (Kgoe/$PPP GDP)	0.16	0.20	0.32
Per Capita Electricity Consumption (kWh)	672	8365	2596
Per Capita CO_2 Emissions (Tonnes)	1.5	11.02	4.22

Table 2 shows that India's per capita electricity consumption and commercial energy supply are woefully low as compared to developed countries. On the other hand, its energy intensity and per capita carbon emissions is also very low. In view of this, additional carbon reduction target will severely erode the efforts of the country to uplift a large section of its society above the poverty line and provide them with gainful employment opportunities. It is the same story with other countries in South Asia and developing countries in other parts of the world.

Keeping the aforesaid in view, it is very important that developing countries should not fall in to the new trap of Durban Platform, which is being vigorously pursued by the developed countries. After making an unprecedented use of energy for their development during the last 150 years, developed countries want to thwart the progress of emerging developing countries, while continuing to maintain their own high-consumption pattern of living.

Technical Barrier to Trade

Another parallel strategy being pursued by developing countries is the introduction of border carbon tariff to neutralize the disadvantage that their domestic products may face vis-à-vis imports from developing countries. Justifying the introduction of climate tax, Presidents Sarkozy and Angela Merkel jointly wrote to the UN Secretary General that, "it would be unacceptable for the efforts of the most ambitious countries to be undermined by carbon emission released by lack of or insufficient action by other countries". Sarkozy stated that "we would not accept goods that fail to conform to our environmental standards", adding that "in future we will levy a climate tax at the European border." America went a step further by enacting the American Clean Energy and Security act (ACESA) 2007, 2009, with a view to establish a border carbon adjustment programme. The unilaterally imposition of civil aviation and shipping carbon tax by the EU is the first indication of the major onslaught being contemplated by developed countries for imposing a border carbon tax.

Technical Barriers to Trade Measures

Some of the measures being contemplated by developed countries to put environmental technical trade barrier on imported products from developing countries are:

- Cap and trade
- Carbon subsidies (purchasing of emission allowance)
- Reduced access to CDM projects in developing countries
- Border carbon adjustment Tax, which is a mechanism to compensate for economic distortions caused by regional climate policy differences
- Standards and labelling (Carbon Footprint)

The main targets of these measures are the BRICs countries, so as to force them to arrive at a new international collective agreement and elicit a binding commitment for mitigation of GHG, as stipulated in the Durban Platform. In addition, there is a proposal to reduce carbon credits being purchased currently by EU companies under CDM or joint implementation credit from 10% to 5%. The EU is also contemplating providing free emission allowance to their vulnerable industries, while forcing the exporting countries to purchase these so as to neutralize the competitive differential of India, China and other developing countries.

Under World Trade Organisation (WTO) rules, unilateral activities such as border carbon adjustment tax and other TBT are not legal. In order to circumvent WTO rules, a new strategy in the form of carbon footprint standards and labelling has been worked out by developed countries. The European Parliament, for example, has recently passed a resolution that calls for "the introduction of WTO compatible common standards and labelling schemes regarding the GHG implications of different products, including at the production and transport stages"; "a procedure to assess and label these ecological footprints and to develop software in order to enable businesses to calculate the quantity of GHG emitted from every production process"; and "the development of a scheme based on sound life-cycle data which includes finished goods, such as cars and electronic equipment" (European Parliament 2007).[8] However, EU's move to levy carbon tax is against Article 3.5 of the UNFCCC, which says that "measures taken to combat climate change, including unilateral ones, should not constitute a means of arbitrary or unjustifiable discrimination or a disguised restriction on international trade."

Carbon Footprint of Products

Carbon footprint measures the residual effect of manufacturing activities of organisations on global warming. 'Carbon footprint' is defined as the total amount of CO^2 and other greenhouse gases, emitted directly or indirectly over the full life cycle of a process or a product. It is expressed as grams equivalent of CO^2, which accounts for the different global warming effects of other greenhouse gases. The greenhouse gases considered for calculating carbon footprint are Carbon dioxide, Methane, Nitrous oxide, CFC_s (CF_4–C_6F_{14}) and SF_6. Grams equivalent of CO^2 of these different greenhouse gases is calculated by multiplying the emission factor with their 100-year Global Warming Potential, which is 1, 21, 310, 6,500-9,200 and 23,900 respectively. The data, which calculates carbon footprint is the bedrock of this whole concept, needs to be relevant, complete, consistent, transparent, and accurate. These conditions are hard to achieve and have been overlooked by most of the practitioners. As a result there is a chance for the manipulation of the results.

The carbon footprint issue has taken a central stage during the last couple of years at the international level, due to the interests of developed countries in primarily using it as a trade barrier.[9] A large number of industrial, private, government and Non government organisations have become involved in this activity.

Figure 2: Stages of Life Cycle (Cradle to Grave)

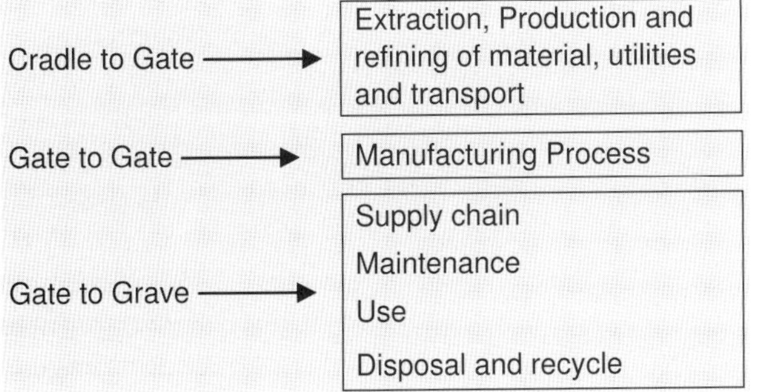

Adverse Impact of carbon footprint labels on Industry in South Asia Region

The new carbon footprint standard ISO 14067 being prepared by the ISO will have serious repercussions on industry in South Asia, as it will be used as a tool for border carbon adjustment tax. Carbon footprint of power, transport, raw material extraction and purification, warehousing, supply chain and disposal will be much higher in these countries as compared to developed countries due to lack of clean energy sources and other efficient infrastructure. For example, carbon dioxide, methane and nitrous oxide emissions of power in India are 990, 0.01664 and 0.01959 kg/MWh respectively, while the corresponding emission values of power in France are 0.083, 0.00395and 0.00093 kg/MWh respectively. As a result, France has a distinct advantage of 10 times in power emissions alone due to the difference in fuel mix used to produce power.

Similarly, in transportation sectors, emissions produced for transport of material from Delhi to Bombay is one and a half times that of USA for the same distance, due to quality of roads, vehicles and traffic bottlenecks. A similar situation exists in other South Asian countries. Keeping in view the cumulative effect of these parameters, the carbon footprint of the products manufactured in South Asia will be many times higher, as compared to the same products manufactured in developed countries. This will give developed countries a handle to create technical barriers to trade in form of carbon tax on the products having higher carbon footprint. Products will be taxed according to their embodied GHG emission as per carbon footprints. However, in the face of strong opposition against this carbon labelling measure from India, China and other developing countries, the ISO standard on carbon footprints is still in the process of finalisation.

If an ISO standard on carbon footprint comes in to force, it will be difficult to challenge the border adjustment tax, even under WTO framework, due to some ambiguous provisions. Large supply chains like Wall Mart and TESCO have already taken steps in this direction to outsource materials with lower carbon footprint, thereby putting the suppliers from developing countries at a disadvantage. The economy of South Asian countries will be extremely vulnerable to such restrictive measures, as the share of their total exports to the EU in the list of 164 leakage-sensitive items is very large.

[8] European Parliament, Trade and Climate Change Resolution T6-0576/2007

[9] Michelle Egan, *Business Strategy Review*, 2002, Volume 13 Issue 1, pp 51-64

Measures to Counter the Trade Restrictions

No developing country on its own can face the restrictive trade actions of the developed countries, due to their great economic might. Only a unified action by the developing countries can work. This has been demonstrated by the combined resistance of the developing countries articulated in the Moscow summit against civil aviation and shipping carbon tax. As a result, the EU has been forced to withhold these taxes. There is also need for vigilance during the multilateral negations so as to not allow the developed countries to get away with their own agenda by default. Developing countries should create their own consultative platforms, where all the global warming issues should be discussed and strategies formulated well in advance. South Asian countries should take a lead in this direction under SAARC. Due to lack of funds, many developing countries do not attend the meetings of ISO, COP and WHO etc. With the creation of a joint platform of South Asian Countries, any country attending the meetings can watch the common interest of other country, based on joint decisions. European countries are using this strategy. Just for the preparation of standards, there is a pool of nearly 2,000 experts and they vote together to protect their interests during formation stage.

Instead of reactive actions, developing countries should become pro-active in formulating countervailing measures to oppose the restrictive practices of the developed countries. Developing countries should coordinate their efforts at the WTO and counteract the efforts of the developed countries for putting their own TBT.

South Asian countries and other developing countries should diversify their exports to regions other than those contemplating border carbon taxes, by creating conducive trading blocks. They should also work in the direction of reducing the carbon intensity of their manufacturing processes by improving energy efficiency, reducing wastages, greater use of recycled materials and improving productivity. This will further decrease the cost of their products. National Governments should also play a proactive role by policy measures to improve carbon efficiency of inputs and infrastructure. Defence preparedness should not be neglected, as this is the best bulwark against any possible threat. This will also help in keeping the supply routes safe. We should learn from history and not fall in the trap of developed countries again and lose our independence as happened during earlier times.

GEO-STRATEGIC PERSPECTIVE OF SINO-INDIAN TRANSBOUNDARY RIVER WATER ISSUES: THE IMPORTANCE OF COOPERATION

Maj Gen SVP Singh, Defence Analyst

Introduction

Water security is vital for the survival of nations. Humanity's supply of freshwater is finite, when one considers it represents less than one half of one percent of all the water on Earth. Throughout history humankind has endeavoured to control the water wealth be it politically, economically or militarily. Nations who controlled the world's sea lanes or the watersheds of major rivers commanded imperial power.[1] Starting from the ancient times, to the Agricultural and Industrial Revolutions, major civilisations controlled the waters of large rivers to promote economic prosperity—Egypt along the Nile and Mesopotamia along the Euphrates and the Tigris. In the Asian context, the Indus Valley civilization prospered astride the Indus River and ancient China built the Grand Canal to optimise the resources of the Southern Yangtse region with the Yellow River in the North.

World demand of water has increased six-fold from the 20th century. Correspondingly, disputes over trans-boundary rivers have also increased. Experts have predicted that wars in the 21st century will be fought over waters—the 'blue gold'.

What endangers triggering of hostilities? The United States Intelligence Community Assessment in its report on Global Water Security in February 2012, predicts that in the next 10 years due to lack of governance, surging population coupled with climate change would lead to draught, floods and water shortage.[2] This has inherent dangers of state failure. It states that use of water as a weapon will increase in the next decade with more powerful upstream nations impeding or cutting off downstream flow. Water will also be used within states to pressurise populations and suppress separatist elements.

Water problems will adversely affect production of food and energy generation, leading to downward economic development. According to UNESCO, there are 263 water basins transcending national boundaries in the world, 145 countries have territory within a trans-boundary basin and 21 lie within one. 12 countries have more than 95 percent of their territory within one or more trans-boundary basins.[3] There is perhaps hardly any accessible freshwater resource in the present day that is not being

---

1 Soloman, Steve; *Water: The Epic Struggle for Wealth, Power and Civilisation*, (New York: Harper Collins, 2010) p.16

2 https://s3.amazonaws.com/s3.documentcloud.org/documents/327371/report-warns-that-water-shortages-could-threaten.pdf

3 http://www.un.org/events/tenstories/06/story.asp?storyID=2900 (Accessed 25 June 2012)

engineered by nations, to their advantage hence 'water hegemonic'. The tussle to gain supremacy over the greater use of these shared waters is what threatens conflict. Nations therefore need to resolve water issues for the mutual benefit of their people.

The fiftieth anniversary of the 1962 Sino–Indian War has generated a spate of commentaries and seminars from experts. Though most of these introspections assure that 1962 will not be repeated, the moot point is, how India's capabilities compare with China now or a decade ahead. China's comprehensive national power (CNP), its economic strength, military power including the space and cyber advancements is far higher. Future conflict would likely be tri-service, over a larger theatre, with simultaneity of land, air and sea battles. Nuclear brinkmanship, outer space and cyberspace would also be active issues.

Of equal or greater concern is the dimension of a 'water war'. China's hydro power projects and river diversion plans on trans-boundary rivers and the paucity of fresh water in both countries is a major bone of contention. These projects threaten the ecological viability of river systems and would choke the flow of waters to the lower riparian India. This has the potential to escalate into a more serious dispute than the boundary disagreement. Water management between nations sharing trans-boundary water resources is a huge challenge. This paper argues that India needs to incorporate an overall agreement covering cross-border rivers and build cooperative river basin institutions. The manner in which it is confronted will determine the future macroeconomic growth and development of India and the region.

The paper analyses Sino-Indian Trans-boundary River Water Issues highlighting, the importance of Tibetan Waters; the prevalent South Asian scenario covering the potential for Inter-state water wars; the crisis rivers surfacing with China undertaking multifarious projects on the Rivers Brahmaputra and the Indus; the implications of these projects on India; and the way forward to a pragmatic approach. The paper precludes intra- state issues.

Importance of Tibet and its Waters

Tibet is the world's highest and largest plateau, covering an area of 2.5 million square kilometres, with an average elevation of more than 4,000 metres above sea level. The plateau stretches across 2,400 kilometres from east to west and 1,448 kilometres from north to south.

Due to its geostrategic centricity in Asia, Tibet is the principal watershed, a 'pivotal hydraulic theatre' to the Asian countries stretching in an arc from Afghanistan to Viet Nam. Referred to as the Third Pole because it contains the largest area of frozen water outside the Polar Regions, it is an oxygen-scarce landscape of enormous glaciers, huge alpine lakes, and waterfalls – a storehouse of freshwater. The Himalayas-Hindu Kush, Kunlun Shan, Tien Shan and Alps of Sichuan mountain ranges function as 'Water Towers of Asia'.[4] Its entire southern rim is flanked by the Himalayas, the world's highest mountain chain.

Ten important rivers originate in Tibet comprising the Brahmaputra, Indus, Sutlej, Karnali, Yangtze, Mekong, Huang Ho, Salween, Manas and Arun. About 90 percent of their runoff flows downstream to 11 countries: China, India (significantly three rivers), Bangladesh, Nepal, Bhutan, Pakistan, Thailand, Myanmar, Laos, Cambodia and Vietnam. The river systems impact the lives of about four-fifths of Asia's population, or 47 percent of the Worlds' population together providing drinking water, irrigation and power. These rivers bring fresh water to millions of Asians; hence the protection of these headwaters is vital.

The British Indian Empire threw up two competing empires for spheres of influence in Tibet. The Great Game was a strategic rivalry between the British and Russian empires for the mastery of Central Asia.[5] Tibet's geopolitical importance is based on its mass, its rich source of minerals, water and energy. Chinese geologists have also identified more than 130 minerals in Tibet 'with significant reserves of the world's deposits of uranium, chromites, boron, lithium, borax, and iron."[6]

Recent studies including by the Chinese Academy of Sciences have highlighted serious environmental challenges to the quantity and quality of Tibet's freshwater reserves, most of them caused by industrial activities. Deforestation has led to large-scale erosion and siltation. Mining, manufacturing, and other human activities are producing record levels of air and water pollution in Tibet. Together, these factors portend future water scarcity and

[4] http://www.lhassa.org/en/geography-of-tibet/mountain-chain.php (Accessed on 05 July 2012)

[5] http://tibet.net/2012/09/13/geopolitical-importance-of-tibet/ (accessed 05 July 2012)

[6] Tibet 2000: Environment and Development Issues by the Environment and Development Desk of the Department of Information and International Relations of the Central Tibetan Administration, Dharamsala, p. 86

adverse climate changes that could add to the region's volatility.[7]

Chinese rivers are polluted and silted and unable to provide China's 1.3 billion people with adequate supplies of freshwater. The Chinese have since long eyed Tibet's strategic water resources. They have planned building dams for hydropower and are spending billions of dollars to build a system of canals to tap water from the Himalayan snowmelt and glaciers and divert it to their water scarce northern and western regions.

Ironically in attempting to solve its own water crisis, China could potentially create widespread water shortages among its neighbours. The Intergovernmental Panel on Climate Change (IPCC) in its May 2007 report warned that "glaciers in the Himalayas are receding faster than in any other part of the world. If the present rate continues, the likelihood of them disappearing by the year 2035 or perhaps sooner is very high if the earth keeps getting warmer at the current rate". [8]

The Tibetan Government in Exile, in India, has identified the plateau's water as a strategic resource and criticised China's management of it. In a report earlier this decade, the exile government said China's water development plans, as well as global climate change, should cause concern across Asia, because it would "seriously decrease the water supplies of India, Bangladesh, the Indo-China nations and the Yangtze River Basin, especially in drought years."

The hydro-politics of this strategic region is under considerable stress and could be involved in future crises encompassing disputes over dams and river diversions, floods, water shortages and contamination. It is a challenge to both China and India, to manage shared water resources in a politically sustainable manner, without tensions or conflict. It is important to understand that "the likelihood of conflict rises as the rate of change within the basin exceeds the institutional capacity to absorb that change."[9]

South Asian Scenario

Trans-boundary Rivers—The Potential for Interstate Water Wars

The potential for interstate water wars in Asia is underlined by the existence of 57 trans-national river basins. China is the source of cross-border river flows to the largest number of countries in the world – from Russia to India, and Kazakhstan to the Indochina peninsula. China as an upper riparian controls major transnational basin resources and counts itself as an exporter of water to its neighbours in all cardinal directions. In South Asia, India, Pakistan, and Bangladesh are dependent on the trans-boundary inflow of river and aquifer waters from Tibet.[10] Due to population growth, rapid urbanisation, industrialisation and agriculture needs water resources are overstretched in South Asia and China.

Mao Zedong observed in 1952, that "the south has a lot of water, the north little. . . . If possible, it is alright to lend a little water." Mao's vision, to occupy Tibet served the dual purpose of dominating the Himalayas and in turn the major watersheds. This instilled the spirit of China's new water age, leading to implementation of grandiose hydraulic plans. Today, China is exploiting the water resources of Tibet for its arid regions and their hardened position on Arunachal Pradesh underlies its claims to almost 200 million cubic feet per second of water resources in the state.[11]

On the other hand, Nehru referring to the great strategic value of the water resources of the Himalayas, stated in the Indian parliament, "When I see a map of India and look at the Himalayan range, I think of the vast power concentrated there, which is not being used, and which could be used, and which really could transform the whole of India with exceeding rapidity..."[12] Despite this, water as a potential threat did not figure in his perception. Nehru had recorded in July 1949 that, "whatever may be the ultimate fate of Tibet in relation to China,

[7] http://www.csrwire.com/press_releases/15162-China-Tibet-and-the-Strategic-Power-of-Water-Pollution-and-Global-Warming-Threaten-Asia-s-Most-Important-Freshwater-Source# (accessed 07 July2012)

[8] Ibid

[9] Wolf, Aaron T, Chapter 1. Hydropolitical Vulnerability and Resilience: *Series Introduction*, p. 4, http://www.unep.org/dewa/Portals/67/pdf/asia.pdf (Accessed on 07 July 2012)

[10] Chellaney, Brahma; *Water: Asia's New Battleground* (New Delhi: HarperCollins, 2011) p. 246

[11] Sinha, Uttam Kumar, 14 June 2010, *Tibet's Water Challenge*, http://www.washingtonpost.com/wp- dyn/content/article/2010/06/13/AR2010061303331.html (accessed 03 August2012)

[12] Jawaharlal Nehru: *Independence and After: A Collection of Speeches, 1946-1949* (Delhi: Ayer Company Publishers, 1950) p. 152

I think there is practically no chance of any military danger to India from any change in Tibet.... I do not think there is any necessity for our Defence Ministry ..., to consider possible military repercussions on the India-Tibet frontier.[13] History however records differently and 60 years later, India appears to have come a full circle, with China fructifying its water diversion plans while India remains in a reactive mode. This is hurting India today.

At a regional level, institutional mechanisms are limited and multilateral agreements for water-sharing on the basis of a common regional framework do not exist. China refuses to join and engage in any dialogue on integrated watershed management in the region. It is significantly involved in water disputes with most of its riparian neighbours to include India, Myanmar, Russia, Kazakhstan and its client state North Korea. It does not have any treaty or agreement with its co-riparian states despite being a water exporter. China is a dialogue partner but not a member of Mekong River Commission (MRC) and is not bound to any legal obligations or rules. This clearly makes China water hegemonic. This has serious implications for India. Should China be the lone stakeholder to the waters in Tibet? What should the lower riparian nations do?

At the bilateral level in South Asia, a number of treaties exist but the hydrological contours of countries remain governed by resource nationalism. The Indus Waters Treaty (IWT) negotiated between India and Pakistan in 1960 despite having been taken to international courts by Pakistan, is an example of successful resolution of an international waters dispute. This has withstood the 1965, 1971 and Kargil Wars, notwithstanding Pakistani demands of larger share. The agreement works on the basis of separation of waters rather than a shared arrangement. A bilateral agreement between India and Bangladesh also exists for sharing dry-season flow in the Ganges though Bangladesh insists on allocation of additional waters. However, both nations have established a dialogue on flood management and hydropower generation. The Mahakali Treaty between India and Nepal paved the way for the construction of the Pancheshwar multipurpose hydropower project.[14] It includes cost sharing and a power purchase arrangement. The Indo–Bhutan agreement on the Chukha hydropower project includes payments made by India for power exports and is a significant source of revenue to Bhutan.

Water Dependency Ratio

The water dependency ratio is an index that measures the amount of water resources countries use from waters originating externally. The ratio highlights the potential vulnerability of shared waters to competing interests. The water dependency ratios of countries dependent on Tibetan waters reveal a sharp imbalance. Bangladesh and Pakistan, at 91 and 77 per cent respectively, are the two states most dependent on external waters. India has a dependency ratio of 34 per cent, which is a cause of water stress. However China has a dependency ratio of only one per cent, making it one of the most hydro-logically self-reliant countries, not only in Asia but also the world. See Table 1 for Water Resources and Dependency Ratio of Asian countries. Further, India is the lowest in per capita water storage, 200 cubic meters. In comparison China has 1,100 cubic meters per capita against a world average of 900 cubic meters per capita. See Table 2 for Total Water Availability per Capita.[15] Thus, for India adding storage is a critical infrastructure need, and it has plans to execute the river inter-linking project to store and convey water across the country. Despite the Supreme Court directive to proceed with the gigantic project, it faces major internal opposition.

Table 1: Countries in Asia—Water Resources and Dependency Ratio[16]

Country	*Total Internal Renewable Water Resources (km^3)*	*Total External Renewable Water Resources (km^3)*	*Dependency Ratio (%)*
Afghanistan	55	10	15
Bangladesh	105	1.106	91
Cambodia	121	356	75
China	2,812	17	1
India	1,261	636	34
Indonesia	2,838	0	0
Kazakhstan	75	34	31
Kyrgyzstan	46	-26	0
Laos	190	143	43
Malaysia	580	0	0
Mongolia	45	0	0
Myanmar	881	165	16
Nepal	198	12	6
Pakistan	55	170	77
Sri Lanka	50	0	0
Thailand	210	200	49
Uzbekistan	16	34	77
Vietnam	366	525	59

Source: Food and Agricultural Organization, *Aquastat Database*, 2008

[13] Chellaney, et al, p. 183

[14] Report, The *Waters of Third Pole, Sources of Threat Sources of Survival*, p. 23, http://184.172.177.95/~chinad/wp-content/uploads/2012/05/third_pole_full_report.pdf (Accessed on 08 July 2012)

[15] Asia Society, April 2009, *Asia's Next Challenge: Securing the Region's Water Future, A Report by the Leadership Group on Water Security in Asia*, pp15 & 21, http://asiasociety.org/files/pdf/WaterSecurityReport.pdf (Accessed on 01 October 2012)

[16] Asia Society, Transboundary Water Concerns in Asia, p 44, http://asiasociety.org/files/pdf/WaterSecurityReport.pdf (Accessed on 01 October 2012)

Table 2: Countries in Asia - Total Water Availability per Capita[17]

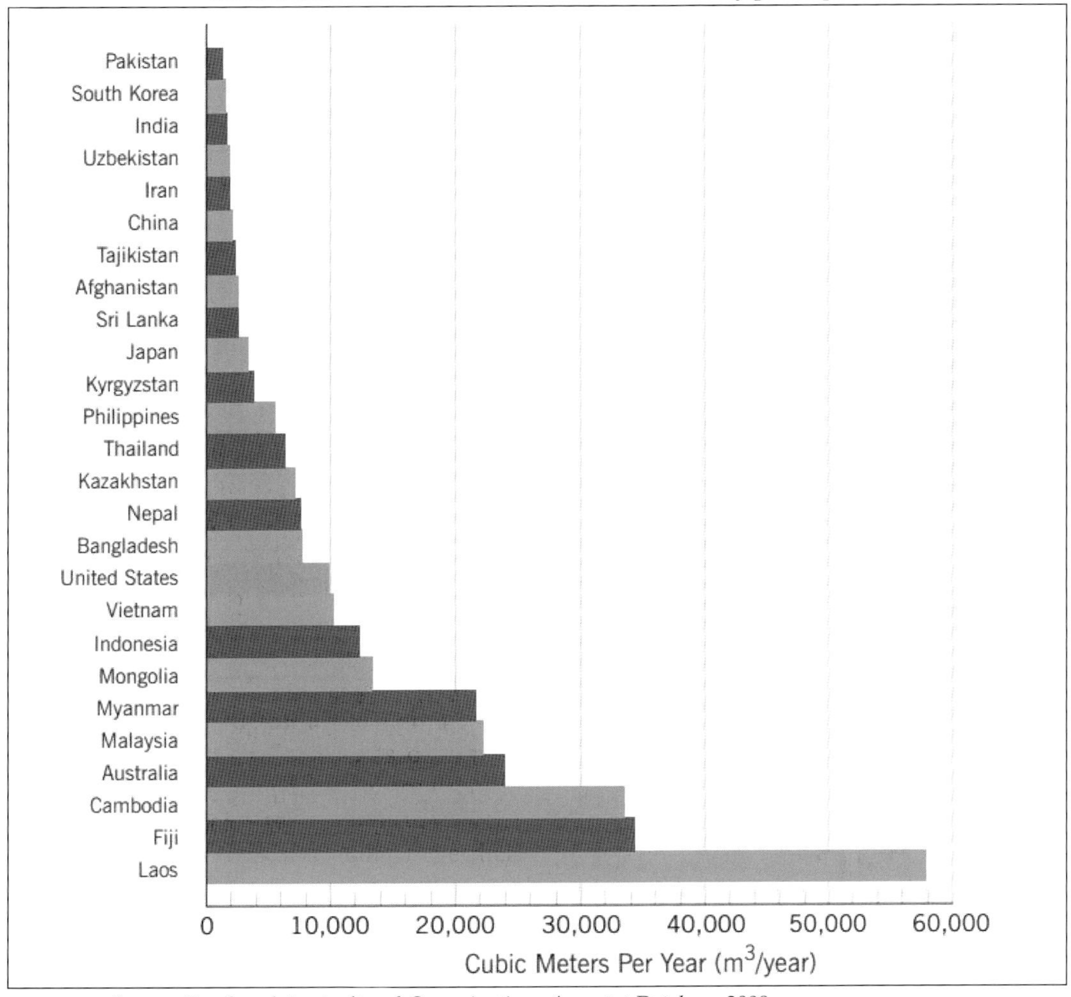

Source: Food and Agricultural Organization, *Aquastat Database*, 2008.

The Crisis Drivers

China's Hydro and River Diversion Projects

China faces severe problems on twin fronts of food and water. Both must be resolved for the country's political and social stability. Water is therefore crucial, firstly, to feed the 1.3 billion population and secondly, for hydropower plants to generate energy. In 2010, China overtook the United States as the world's largest energy consumer. China's power sector leans heavily on fossil fuels, 79 percent from coal, making it the largest coal consumer and carbon dioxide emitter. Hence the shift to hydropower and non- fossil fuels is a focal point for China. The 12th Five Year Plan targets an increase in the proportion of non-fossil fuels to 11.4 per cent by 2015, from 9.4 per cent in 2011.[18] By 2020, it plans to increase the energy sector by 15 percent. In a decade, China aims to have a 340 gigawatts hydropower capacity from the installed capacity of 198.3 GW in 2010.[19] To achieve this China has planned on extensive development of dams and river diversion projects.

In China, the south receives 80 per cent of rainfall whereas the industrial and population growth is in the north and east. Between 2000 and 2009, the freshwater reserves declined by 13 per cent. In order to curb these imbalances, drawing inspiration from Mao Zedong, China has taken up what may be the biggest water-diversion plan in history. This $65 billion plan called The South-North Water Diversion Project (SNWDP) will divert 45 billion cubic metres of water per year, roughly the average annual flow

[17] Ibid, p 44

[18] Shirodkar,Girish; *Playing Chinese Checkers with India's Hydro Sector,* Power Watch India, July 2012 http://www.sdg.com/publications/playing-chinese-checkers

[19] Zeng Ming,ed, 01January 2012, *China's 12th Five-Year Plan Pushes Power Industry in New Directions,* http://www.powermag.com/gas/Chinas-12th-Five-Year-Plan-Pushes-Power-Industry-in-New-Directions_4257.html

of the Yellow River along three channels in eastern, central and western China.[20] When finished; the work will link China's four main rivers—the Yangtze, Yellow, Huaihe and Haihe. Like the medieval Grand Canal, the SNWDP is an expression of China's traditional outlook to harness and conquer nature.

In the last 25 years, China has become the world's leading dam builder almost half of the world's estimated 45,000 large dams. Coupled with water diversion projects, China is responsible for huge human displacement and river alteration. It has used its rivers indiscriminately making them ecologically unsafe thus adversely affecting downstream countries. Further they have shifted focus from internal to international rivers, and graduated from large dams to building mega-dams. Among its newest dams on the Mekong is the 4,200 megawatt Xiaowan. It has lucrative contracts with Myanmar, Nepal, Cambodia, Laos, Mongolia and Kazakhstan to construct dams and hydropower stations on their rivers. The creation of upstream dams on international rivers such as the Brahmaputra and Mekong shows China is inflexible to the concerns of downstream nations.

China has the world's biggest dam, the Three Gorges Dam (TGD), started in 1994 having a capacity of 22,500 MW. The construction has caused serious environmental damage including water pollution, sedimentation and landslides and a forced resettlement of over one million people.

The Brahmaputra River

According to Tibet researcher Tashi Tsering, China has already constructed 10 dams on tributaries of the upper Brahmaputra, with three more under construction, seven more under consideration, and eight more proposed. The map showing the location of the existing or proposed sites is at Figure 1.[21] China apparently plans to build five major dams directly on the Brahmaputra mainstream. The first hydropower project, 510 MW Zangmu dam is expected to be completed by 2014.[22]

Figure 1: Hydropower Projects on the Yarlung Tsangpo (Upper Reaches of the Brahmaputra) in Tibet

India's attention was drawn by China's new project, at the Great Bend, the eastern-most point near Mount Namcha Barwa where the Brahmaputra River enters India. At this point, the Tsangpo falls 2,500 metres within a three kilometre length and also doubles its flow. This unique topography and major shift in water flow allows China to make two dams, at Motuo, with 38,000 MW and the Daduqia with 43,800 MW generating capacities. These mega projects would dwarf the size of Three Gorges dam.

[20] Report, The *Waters of Third Pole, Sources of Threat Sources of Survival*, p 29, http://184.172.177.95/~chinad/wp-content/uploads/2012/05/third_pole_full_report.pdf

[21] Shering,Tashi, 24 May 2010, *Damming Tibet's Yarlung Tsangpo-Brahmaputra and Other South Asian Rivers,* Tibetan Plateau Blog Spot, http://tibetanplateau.blogspot.in/2010/05/damming-tibets-yarlung-tsangpo.html (Accessed on 30 June 2012)

[22] Wirsing, Robert G; *The Brahmaputra:Water hotspot in Himalayan Asia, Global Water Forum*, June 2012, http://www.globalwaterforum.org/2012/06/02/the-brahmaputra-water-hotspot-in-himalayan-asia/(Accessed on 30 June 2012)

This venture comprises two projects. The building of a dam and the water diversion along the Great Western Route or the Shoutian Canal, This route is centred on the waters of the Brahmaputra, the Mekong and three tributaries on the Yangtze. The Shoutian Canal connects from Shoumatian on the Brahmaputra to Tianjin, the end point of the Yellow River. The diversion of waters smacks of Mao's plans. The re-routing of Tibetan waters through the Shoutian Canal was promoted by Guo Kai, a hydro-geologist. Chinese officialdom has also been guided by the book; 'Tibet's Water will Save China' published in November 2005 and authored by Li Ling, an ex-Army officer. This has been endorsed by the People' Liberation Army.[23] Some experts view the plans of re-routing the waters of the Brahmaputra as a declaration of war on India and Bangladesh. China true to its policy has officially denied the approval of this scheme.

The improved infrastructure in the Tibetan region comprising railroads, highways and airports coupled with the endorsement by feasibility studies of the Great Bend project has led China to renew its claims on Arunachal Pradesh, calling it 'Southern Tibet'. The strategic importance of this area cannot be overemphasised. Apart from being water rich, it is one of the most bio-diverse regions in the world having 3,700 plant species and is a heavily militarised zone.

The Indus River

China has built a medium scale dam on the River Indus at Ali (Gar) bordering Aksai-Chin and Demchok with an initial capacity to generate 11 megawatts of electricity. However, given its storage capacity and gradient factor, power generation can be doubled.

Gar is strategically located on the Tibet-Xinjiang Highway. It oversees trade and transit between Tibet, Ladakh and East Turkestan. It is also an alternative supply route from Lhasa and Golmud to Ladakh border. It is an important military base, bordering Ladakh, Aksai-Chin, Himachal Pradesh, Uttaranchal and Nepal. China, in pursuance of its policy of ethnic cleansing, has enhanced the troop's strength of Hans. The dam will facilitate expansion of the military base thus considerably reducing logistical costs to China. The international airport would also serve as an operational base to the Chinese air force.

The dam affects India adversely as the Indus provides energy and irrigation water for its large agrarian population. Apart from Ladakh, Gilgit-Baltistan will also face water shortfall and reduced power generation. There are fears that after realising the potential of Ali dam, China could next exploit building dams on River Sutlej, a major source of power generation and irrigation for Himachal Pradesh, Punjab, Haryana and Rajasthan. In Pakistan, the reduction of water will increase salinity, land erosion and sea-flooding which will severely damage the Indus Delta. The rise in water table has an inherent danger to flood Karachi and Thattha.[24]

Implications and Impact on India

> *"At least 500 million people in Asia and 250 million people in China are at risk from declining glacial flows on the Tibetan Plateau."*
>
> ***—Rajendra K. Pachauri, Chairman of the IPCC***

Impact of India's Policy Approach. Historically, a position upstream is always of supreme strategic importance both in peace and war, while downstream people are inescapably at the mercy of whoever controls the water supply. Indian polity on independence did not fully comprehend the inter-state river relations which would best serve the interests of the nation's water security. The annexation of Tibet by China in 1950 fundamentally changed the water map of Asia. China became a unique upper riparian nation for all the major river systems, originating from the Tibetan Plateau and flowing to Asian countries. Nehru was unable to visualise the threat to India's territorial and water interests with the loss of Tibet as a buffer. In 1954 under the Panch Sheel Treaty, India implicitly accepted China's annexation of Tibet without seeking or securing China's recognition of the then existing Indo–Tibetan border and with that forfeited all the British inherited extraterritorial rights and privileges in Tibet. Nehru perhaps did not perceive that this would seriously impact India's water interests in the future. Later in 2003, not only water but the territorial implications also escaped Vajpayee by signing the declaration in which India recognised the Tibetan Autonomous Region as part of the People's Republic of China thus surrendering the remaining Indian leverage on Tibet.[25] China subsequently in 2006 renewed its claim on Arunachal Pradesh with an eye on its water rich upper reaches. Tibet is also China's

---

[23] op cit, p 156

[24] *Sering, Senge H,* April 2010, *China Builds Dam on Indus near Ladakh,* Journal of Defence Studies, Vol 4. No 2, p.136-138, http://www.unpo.org/downloads/228.pdf (accessed 12 August 2012)

[25] Chellaney, Brahma, pp 182-184

nuclear base. Exercising the modern use of water as a tool of diplomacy and weapon, China will bargain hard, on the boundary dispute, specifically over its claims in Arunachal Pradesh.

Affect on India's Domestic Power Situation. India's power generation capacity is estimated to grow from 190 GW in 2012 to more than 300 GW by 2020. India has mainly depended on thermal power. Presently India has 39 GW of installed hydro capacity, and plans to tap the remaining 110 GW hydro potential. Hydropower generation is essential for emission control plans. The north east region accounts for an estimated 63,000 MW or 43 per cent of the total identified hydro potential of the country which is attributable to the large water flows through the Brahmaputra basin. However in real terms only two percent, 1158 MW of total identified potential has been developed as against 46 percent or 37,690 MW in rest of the country.[26]

Domestic bottlenecks notwithstanding, China remains the main cause for this sluggish development. Firstly because of their territorial claims, secondly due to the mushrooming of hydropower dams specifically the proposed Great Bend dam and the threat in being of diverting the Brahmaputra along the Great Western Route. An NGO in Assam claims that the construction of the Zangmu Dam on the Brahmaputra has already reduced the water flow by 30 percent. Thirdly, China has directly impeded development of major infrastructure in the northeast by opposing the $2.9 billion Asian Development Bank loan to India in March 2009 as it included funding of $ 60 million flood management in Arunachal Pradesh. India could face more such road blocks from China.

Dams and Reservoirs

Generally, run-of-the-river (ROR) type hydro projects are not a big concern, but the 'diversion' scheme is a serious issue. The adverse consequences on environment and ecology, of the planned 'Great Bend' dam and water diversion from the Brahmaputra River would be extensive Apart from the Tibet region, India and Bangladesh would be at the mercy of China for release of water during dry season and for protection from floods during the monsoons. In fact, the reverse may happen if it suits the Chinese interests.

The reservoir will sequester silt and deprive the downstream flood plains of high volume of water to the Sundarbans Delta and fertile nutrients which would be devastating for the 185 million people of India's North East and Bangladesh. World history is replete with societal declines and collapses caused by soil salination. Increased salinity in the delta will threaten the Forests of Sundari Trees, which is a UNESCO World Heritage site. Its adverse impact will also be felt in agriculture and fishing.

To illustrate, the TGD has drastically altered the local ecosystem and attenuated flow of the Yangtze River. There are recurrent landslides around the huge reservoir. The TGD has lowered productivity in the East China Sea. With 24 new dams coming up on Yangtze, it is already among the most dammed rivers of the world and the most polluted river of China. The Brahmaputra would be exposed to a similar threat, if the mega projects take off, it will provide great leverage to China.

Seismic

China's south-west lies in the world's most active tectonic zone of the Himalayan region. Large dams built in such high-risk areas are a threat from naturally occurring earthquakes. A report, published in Canadian NGO Probe International reveals that 48.2 percent of the dams lie in zones of high to very high seismic hazard, while 50.4 percent are in moderate seismic hazard. The rapid rate of dam construction in areas of high seismic hazard in western China could have disastrous consequences for both the economy and the people. Among the rivers affected are the Yarlung Tsangpo which directly affects India.

The Great Bend area lies in the high seismic geological fault line area. The 2008 Sichuan earthquake left over 70,000 dead and more than five million people homeless. Experts believe that the quake was triggered by China's new 156 meter high Zipingpu hydropower dam located five kilometres from the earthquake's epicentre. The critics also worry about reservoir induced seismicity wherein the pressure created by the weight of the reservoir water and the infiltration of water into fissures can cause landslides and tremors.[27]

[26] Op cit, Shirdodkar, Girish, p26

[27] Hongqiao, 29 October 2012, *Mega-dams in China's earthquake zones could have "disastrous consequences"*, http://www.chinadialogue.net/article/show/single/en/5261-Mega-dams-in-China-s-earthquake-zones-could-have-disastrous-consequences- (accessed 02 October 2012)

Floods

Events of recent past also highlight how vulnerable downstream areas are to upstreams in Tibet. In June 2000 the breach of a dam in Tibet led to floods that left over 100 people dead or missing in Arunachal Pradesh. Later in August, swollen lakes in Tibet caused severe flooding of the River Sutlej in Himachal Pradesh; it swept away about 100 bridges besides killing scores of people.

Migration and Food Shortages

Floods and water shortage, add other dimensions to the problem—migration of people and food shortages. Water shortage in the Ganges has affected the lives of millions in Bangladesh, forcing them to migrate to India. This has led to demographic and ethnic tensions in India's northeast specifically in Assam. Tempering with waters of the Brahmaputra would further aggravate these problems.

The crisis in the Himalayan River basins is not alone for India. Nepal, Bangladesh and Pakistan face a parallel threat of water and food shortages. The farmlands would diminish leading to likely migrations from these countries as well. India will have to contend with this issue on a regional level as a serious security threat. Any instability in the neighbouring countries will lead to further instability in the region having serious consequences.

Way Forward

Argument against Water War

Wars were fought in the twentieth century over land, for instance the Nazi Germany's *lebensraum* and over oil and energy of the Middle East. In the 21st century, South Asia is engulfed with problems of dwindling water resources due to climate change, population explosion and accompanying food shortages. Fresh water today is a national security asset. Though river waters transcend defined geographical boundaries of nation states, strategists argue that this century would be an era of 'hydrological warfare' in which rivers, dams and aquifers will be the resources to be fought over or controlled by the armies of the nations. The significance of water is such that it could switch gravity of military strategy from nuclear and missile warfare to one of 'hydraulic strategies'.

Historically, the only documented 'water war', traces back to 4,500 years between the Sumerian city states Lagash and Umma, over irrigation rights, in present day Iraq.[28] As per Aaron Wolf's research findings of five decades ending 1999, there have been no wars, 37 military acts between states, 30 of them involving Israel and its Arab neighbours and only seven minor skirmishes. Among military acts, in 1967 Israel destroyed Syrian structure on the headwaters of River Jordan with the aim to thwart an 'all Arab' water plan. In comparison, 145 water cooperation treaties were signed.[29]

Geo-strategy makes China, a natural hydro-hegemon of Asia, apart from sharing land borders with 14 countries, as an upper riparian it controls the flow of all rivers flowing out and which are the lifeline of the downstream nations. China is hydrologically one of the most highly self-reliant countries with a dependency ratio of only one percent but has an insatiable water appetite but its plans for harnessing and diversion of its river resources remain secretive.

The international law governing water management is not adequately defined and is contradictory. Those arguing in favour of water wars have also to answer for its strategic rationality, economic viability and pay offs that would accrue in terms of water resources. There is no doubt that water resources are at a premium which could lead to hostilities but in economic terms, going to war will be disastrous for human lives, development and the environment. Militarily, the downstream riparian will be at a disadvantage to go to war as it will involve occupation and control of population. Any damage to dams or head-works or installations carries inherent risks of flooding and environmental degradation, in the lower reaches. Downstream nations are, though, not always at a political disadvantage, for instance Egypt's greater influence and geopolitical strength in the world has facilitated to their larger share of Nile waters. However, it would be pragmatic to invest in water saving innovative technologies and building say desalination plants. China is economically more vibrant and militarily more powerful. The existing power asymmetry in CNPs of China and India is a critical factor in a competitive environment. India as an emerging regional power has therefore to define a wise and pragmatic path in 'hydro-politics' with China. However India must prepare for any future eventuality of a military conflict and speed up its modernisation and force expansion programs particularly in the mountains. It must build a military capability that would deter Beijing from trying to 'teach another lesson' to India. India's policy makers must take a serious note of this.

[28] Doyle Alister, 18 September 2006, "Water Wars" loom? But none in past 4,500 years, *The Environment in the News*, www.unep.org/cpi/briefs/2006Sept18.doc, (Accessed on 01 December 2012)

[29] Aaron T Wolf, 1998, Conflict and Cooperation along International Waterways, http:/www.transboundarywaters.orst.edu/publications/conflict_coop/# paper (accessed 30 November 2012)

Hydro-political Cooperation

India and China should not get involved in a twenty first century Asian cold war. Both need to develop deeper institutional linkages and structures, to address their bilateral differences in a comprehensive manner and jointly identify a roadmap for cooperation. India has however to be aware that China, as an upper riparian, with greater power, equitable agreements will be hard to bargain. China will seek higher benefits. Such has been the case with Turkey, in sharing the waters with Syria and Iraq. On the other hand China must realise that unilateral development of water resources projects would lead to increased tension and regional instability. Therefore sensitivity to mutual hydrologic concerns is vital to eliminate trust deficit.

By initiating cooperation on climate change, India and China have displayed an atypical characteristic to their tense relationship. Both have common fundamental positions on adherence to the Kyoto Protocol. The India-China-Nepal transboundary project to conserve the "highly diverse" and "environmentally fragile area is another positive. To chart out a stable and prosperous future the need is to set up institutional mechanisms and agreements to govern water management. The political leaders must endeavour for a 'water détente' cooperative model on the lines of the 'mutually assured doctrine' of the post nuclear cold war age. China is the fulcrum of any hydro-political cooperation in Asia. Salient issues to take forward the collaborative approach are discussed below:

- **Bilateral and Multilateral Treaties.** The riparian neighbours in South and Southeast Asia have mutual water pacts but China as seen earlier has no such water treaty with any co-riparian country. It is important for the lower riparian states affected by Chinese dam and river diversion projects to engage China in a dialogue at the bilateral and multilateral levels. The Lohit, Dibang, Dihang, Subansiri and Jia Bharali Rivers are lifelines to India's northeast, around 12 percent of the water flows in the Brahmaputra basin are from melting glacier flows. Utilization of Yarlung Tsangpo/Brahmaputra waters and to construct large dams on the to construct large dams on the same river system is a domestic compulsion for India and China. This need, which involves rivers and glaciers should be converted to one of bilateral cooperation and not competition. India should evolve a water resource sharing treaty of the Brahmaputra. This could be on the lines of the 1997 United Nations (UN) Convention on the Law of the Non-Navigational Uses of International Water Courses (UN Watercourses Convention) or the 1960 IWT between India and Pakistan. The IWT too could be factored in as it has withstood tumultuous times.
- **Tibet's Water as a 'Commons'.** China has build dams on shared rivers of Tibet as it is not constrained by any legally binding water sharing or water management treaties. There is no clear accepted international law on shared waters. While India abstained, China along with Turkey and Burundi voted against the UN Watercourses Convention in the UN General Assembly in 1997. However, to benefit downstream people, India must spread global awareness on the requirements of two billion downstream people. There is a necessity to redefine Tibetan water sources as a 'commons' which would be a momentous step towards preserving and sharing these waters. Though this proposal clashes with national jurisdictions, it merits consideration for future requirements of South and Southeast Asia. There is a need to push for the two principles of 'equitable use' and 'no significant harm'. India should take the lead to introduce the 'commons' principle in the UN reports and mechanisms on transboundary waters.[30]
- **Regional Convention for the Himalayan River Basins.** A plausible way to move forward is to formalize regional cooperation on shared water courses in the Himalayan River Basin. This should address the unique concerns of glacier dependent rivers. Basin agreements should be structurally dynamic. Presently four transnational river basins in Asia are having treaties comprising Indo- China nations of the Mekong, the Ganges between India and Bangladesh, the Indus between India and Pakistan, the Jordan between Israel and Jordan; all have seen a measure of success. Bangladesh has proposed a joint basin-wise management of the Brahmaputra with India and China. China and Bangladesh have agreed to discuss and share regular exchange of information on the use of the water resources of Brahmaputra. International awareness through the UN and India, an enlarged coalition on the Ganges-Brahmaputra-Meghna (GBM) river system involving Nepal,

[30] IDSA Task Force Report, September 2010, *Water Security for India: The External Dynamics*, p. 46, Institute of Defence Studies and Analysis, New Delhi,

Bangladesh and Bhutan can bring on China to create a river-basin approach. The MRC is a good example of river-basin cooperation.[31] China too will be required to start participating in bilateral and multilateral agreements on water issues.

- **Himalayan River Commission.** The Strategic Foresight Group has put forth setting up of The Himalayan River Commission (HRC), a forum to address problems and conflicts and to implement ideas. It includes India, China, Bangladesh and Nepal. It is perceived to be the next step of cooperation in the river basins. The suggested organisation is at Figure 4.[32] The HRC is proposed to function on the principles governing the Integrated River Basin Management.

- **Environmental and Hydrological Data Sharing.** As a lower riparian, India has to be simultaneously cautious and countervailing in its riparian relations with China. At a more practical level it has to continuously engage and open channels of communication with China on flood management. In 2002 India and China entered into agreements to share hydrological data for flood control and early warning systems on the Brahmaputra and subsequently on the Sutlej. Both countries are also cooperating on monitoring the melting of glaciers. What is crucial in these agreements is transparency, in which the Chinese have been inconsistent in sharing of information. The International Centre for Integrated Mountain Development is playing a significant role to step up cooperation in the region. In December 2009, the GBM and Indus River basins project was set up to cooperate on regional flood information system. This can be carried forward to create a regional framework for information sharing in areas such as disaster management.

- **Technological Partnerships.** Technology is the key to meet the water challenges. It is important is to set up mutual scientific and technological partnerships to optimise water efficiency, environmental protection and conservation strategies. Cooperation can be extended to setting up desalination plants, waste water treatment and recycling.

Figure 2: Himalayan Rivers Commission[33]

Himalayan Rivers Commission
(Rotating Presidency held at the political level Forum to address problems and conflicts, as well as a forum to implement ideas)

Ganges River Basin Organisation (Members – Bangladesh, India and Nepal)	**Brahmaputra River Basin Organisation** (Members – Bangladesh, China and India)	**Glaciers Commission** (Members – Bangladesh, China, India and Nepal)	**Agriculture Commission** (Members – Bangladesh, China, India and Nepal)	**Economic Activities Commission** (Will encompass all other aspects of the economy except for Agriculture e.g. trade and tourism)	**Joint Emergency Response Commission** (Members – Bangladesh, China, India and Nepal)	**Desertification Task Force** (Members – Bangladesh, China, India and Nepal)

Conclusion

India and China have had a turbulent relationship ever since China occupied Tibet in 1950. This changed the political map of South Asia and the Himalayas ceased to be the buffer. The most crucial geostrategic implication was that South Asian basins became hydrologically dependent on China. This strategic region will remain under water stress cum shortage. Future crises would be endangered by disputes over dam and river diversion plans on the Brahmaputra. Floods, drought, food shortages, climate change, population explosion and migration and pollution will continue to pose challenges to governance.

---

[31] Ibid, p.50

[32] Strategic Foresight Group. February 2011, *Himalayan Solution: Cooperation and Security in River Basins,* p. 30, http://www.strategicforesight.com/HimalayanSolutions.pdf

[33] Ibid.

Hydro-politics will remain the dominant issue of concern in the twenty first century. China will remain obsessed with water due to, firstly severe droughts it has faced and secondly it's declining fresh waters reserves. Both compounded in the last decade. Based on Mao's belief that 'man must conquer nature', Beijing perceives itself as a natural hydro-hegemon.

India's water position is more precarious than that of China. The second phase of China's water diversion program, of re-routing the Brahmaputra, if executed, will hurt India and Bangladesh grievously as it will environmentally devastate India's north-eastern plains. Some experts compare this project to be akin to a declaration of war. Transparency in sharing of hydrological data is critical to ensure that flash floods of the kind which occurred in the states of Arunachal Pradesh and Himachal Pradesh do not recur.

With a superior CNP, China wields tremendous power. Since international laws are weak in governance of waters, legally China's actions cannot be contested. For India the best way to manage the hydro-politics with China and other disputes is through cooperative approach and institutional mechanisms. Simultaneously India should rapidly build a deterrent military capability to thwart any aggressive designs from China.

BANGLADESH-INDIA RELATIONS: CHALLENGES TO SECURITY CONSTRUCT IN THE REGION

Dr. Sreeradha Datta, Director, Maulana Abul Kalam Azad Institute of Asian Studies, Kolkata, India

The prolonged discussions on a bilateral extradition treaty between India and Bangladesh are finally going to be given shape. The two sides are likely to sign a Revised Travel Agreement as well as an extradition treaty during the Indian Home Minister's forthcoming visit to Dhaka, in January 2013. Clearly, both sides are working on a mechanism towards repatriation of sentenced prisoners to either country apart from the festering issue of insurgents and criminals crossing over into each other's territory. Moreover, while expressing regret the two neighbours have also agreed not to resort to firing unless their side is fired upon or attacked by terrorists or armed criminals.

The above convergence has been possible with the mutual cooperation trajectory that began with the change of guard in Dhaka in 2008. The present Awami League government, headed by Sheikh Hasina Wajed, was voted to power through a thumping victory unprecedented in the recent history of Bangladesh. The country had come back from the altar of military rule to regaining its functional elected democracy once again. The 9th Jatiya Sangsad elections were held after nearly two years of postponement with Bangladesh finally going to the polls on 29 December 2008. The interim government, run by the army from behind, held the reins of governance. Thus India was keenly looking forward to a change. At the same time India, during the caretaker government (2007-2008), was able to recover to some extent the lost ground that it had experienced during the BNP coalition government in Dhaka (2001-2006). The triumph of democracy, along with the coming of a secular government in Bangladesh, gave India immense hope towards establishing stable bilateral ties.

Both India and Bangladesh seemed eager to grab the opportunity that the altered political conditions post-2008 threw up. Thus, the visit of the Bangladeshi Prime Minister to India, in January 2010, which opened up the panorama of cooperation, was much awaited. The joint communiqué that was signed during the visit was clearly a leap of faith that the two neighbours had taken. The cornerstone of the bilateral relations was the promise of shared prosperity. In the ensuing milieu heightened expectations were evident, both within India and Bangladesh.

The nearly 80percent voter turnout, many of who were first-time voters, which included a substantial strength of women, was a clear refection of the choice the Bangladeshis had made. The Awami League coalition's win with over three-fourths majority reposed the faith and belief of Bangladesh in its democracy and polity. Indeed, this victory was hailed as a game changer. It was nothing short of an extraordinary moment for Bangladesh when its secular fabric was brought back with zealous gusto.

The results were unprecedented. Winning 230 of Jatiya Sangsad's (national parliament) 299 seats and limiting Bangladesh Nationalist Party to a mere 27 seats was a historic win for the Awami League. Its victory was a cause of celebration for Bangladesh undoubtedly. India too basked in that joyous moment.

This paper argues that while India shares a warm relationship with the Awami League at present, it appears unclear whether India and Bangladesh have been able to establish the contours that can provide the basis of stable equitable ties. India and Bangladesh began on a firm and friendly footing, with commendable progress on security and trade issues. But the lack of progress on some outstanding issues between them hinders the two neighbours from realising the full bilateral potential of the relationship.

This paper also discusses the first few months of the Awami League assuming office when atmospherics on both sides were upbeat and it seemed that the bilateral ties were poised to take off as never before. The delay in implementations of several agreements have left the people of both the states disappointed and dissatisfied with the state of bilateral relations which has impacted upon the bilateral ties.

The paper further argues that, given the close proximity of India and the ruling coalition in Dhaka, domestic developments in Bangladesh will tend to influence the underlying perceptions about India. Given the ruling coalition's gradual waning of popularity Indo-Bangladesh relations are also affected. The bilateral relations are closely associated with the performance of the ruling coalition.

The final argument centres on the possibility of a security framework between the two neighbours which will be a precursor to a regional security paradigm. Over the course of the next few sections this paper examines whether India and Bangladesh can evolve a mechanism to address their mutual concerns as well as offer a security paradigm in the region.

I

Anti-terror Measures

Sheikh Hasina, soon after assuming powers, reiterated her promise to ensure that Bangladesh was wrested clean of terror elements. Simultaneously, Bangladesh conveyed its intention to address any anti-India activities that were carried out from Bangladeshi soil. A fresh probe into the Chittagong arms haul case of 2 April 2004 led to the arrest of former National Security Intelligence chiefs, Maj Gen (retd) Rezaqul Haider Chowdhury and Brig Gen (retd) Abdur Rahim. The confessional statements of Md. Hafizur Rahman and Din Mohammad, the two accused in the Chittagong arms haul case, had established beyond doubt the linkages between the Bangladesh security agencies and Indian militants. The complicity of the earlier BNP coalition government, officials as well as Indian north eastern terror groups, for whom the largest arms cache was intended, was clearly established in this case. India for long had maintained that not only have insurgents from the north east found safe havens in Bangladesh but that they have enjoyed the support of the Bangladeshi state as well.

For India, its most serious concern revolved around Bangladeshi insensitivity to the presence of Indian insurgents operating from Bangladeshi soil. Various terrorist attacks that had occurred in India pointed to Bangladeshi connections. More specifically, for long India had harboured grievances over Bangladeshi indifference towards its security concerns especially over illegal migration and the support that Indian north eastern insurgents enjoyed in Bangladesh. Bangladesh did not move against the insurgents as they were not perceived to be a source of domestic threats. On the contrary, successful commercial enterprises run by some of the insurgent leaders in and around the capital city gave many invested interests an opportunity to benefit from their presence inside Bangladesh. While in office, during 1996-2001, the Awami government was more sympathetic towards India's security concerns and had acted upon some of the militant training camps in hill tracts. Despite this India was unable to impress upon the Hasina government to extradite any of the leaders who were residing there. Earlier, in April 2000, Mohammad Nasim, Home Minister in Sheikh Hasina's government, had tacitly admitted that for long the Pakistani intelligence agency - the ISI - was training Indian militants on Bangladeshi soil. Arguably, the Awami League has certainly has been more receptive to India's security concerns but given the level of Directorate General of Forces Intelligence (Bangladesh) and Inter-Services Intelligence (Pakistan) nexus that functioned in Bangladesh, almost independent of the Prime Minister's Office, the actual efficacy of the political leadership can be questioned.

Undoubtedly, during 2001-6 the Khaleda Zia government, Bangladesh faced a worrying and violent phase. The growth of Islamic extremists led to large-scale violence and terrorism. The failure of the state in dealing with these and other violent attacks against various opposition leaders was obvious. The attack on opposition leader Sheikh Hasina that also proved fatal for former finance minister SMAS Kibria raised doubts about the ability and intentions of the Bangladeshi government to address some of its basic problems.

However, soon after taking over, the Awami League cabinet not only approved the passage of the Anti-Terrorism Ordinance, promulgated by the Caretaker Government on 9 June 2008 into law, but also initiated several measures to address the menace of terror faced by Bangladesh in the last few years. The Awami League government's initiative in addressing domestic terror also led to arrests of some Indian terrorists operating from within Bangladesh. The investigation into the Mumbai attack had thrown up links with not only Pakistan but also HuJI in Bangladesh. Earlier, on 27 May 2009, Abdul Rouf Daud Merchant, an operative of the mafia organisation headed by Dawood Ibrahim was arrested. Having fled to Bangladesh following his conviction for the killing of Indian film producer Gulshan Kumar, Merchant along with a few other operatives of the mafia network had been living in the country with false identities. This also led to arrest of Arif Hossain alias Chacha, another Indian fugitive from Dhaka in June 2009. The subsequent arrest of Moulana Mohammad Mansur Ali, an Indian national linked to the Pakistan-based militant group Lashkar-e-Taiba (LeT) from a *madrassa* in the Dakkhin Khan area of Dhaka on 20 July 2009 have reinforced the linkages. He was also involved in the attack on the American Centre in Kolkata on 22 January 2002. The arrest of Mufti Obaidullah, an Indian LeT member in Dhaka led to flow of further information of other Dawood-led LeT members.

Within months of taking over of the new government in Dhaka, ULFA 'Captain' Antu Chaudang, 'Second Lieutenant' Pradeep Chetia and Saurav were pushed back from the Meghalaya, Dawki border into India. In November 2009, Dhaka had facilitated 'the arrest and handed over' five top leaders of the banned outfit, including its 'Chairman' Arabinda Rajkhowa. In February 2010, Home Minster Chidambaram submitted a list of 50 wanted Indians who are said to be either hiding in Bangladesh or have been kept in detention. Dhaka had given Delhi a list of 100 criminals hiding in India. It included two convicted killers of Bangabandhu Mujibur Rahman and few accused of involvement in a grenade attack on the ruling Awami League in 2004.

Evidently, the newly elected Awami League attempted to tackle the problem decisively, both at the domestic and the bilateral level. Thus, of the five agreements signed during Sheikh Hasina's visit to India, in January 2010, three related to security issues:

- Agreement on Mutual Legal Assistance on Criminal Matters.
- Agreement on the Transfer of Sentenced Persons (those on death row were outside the purview of this agreement; also if a similar agreement existed with a third country, Bangladesh and India would provide transit facility for extradition of sentenced persons)
- Agreement on Combating International Terrorism, Organised Crime and Illicit Drug Trafficking (In the event of terrorist activities perpetrated in and against India and Bangladesh, the two countries can exchange intelligence and general information).

II

India Commits Support

Bangladesh's positive response to India's security concerns inevitably led to India's rising to the occasion. Thus India's credit line offer of US$ 1 billion was viewed as an reciprocal measure to address Bangladesh's economic concerns. The two leaders promised a common journey on the path of progress and economic development. A comprehensive bilateral road map was delineated during the Bangladeshi Prime Minister's visit to India within a year of her taking over in January 2010. The brief summary of the commitments for both states included;

For India:

- Indian security concerns were acknowledged with a firm commitment to address them.
- Transit through Bangladesh as well as access to Chittagong, Mongla and Ashuganj for one time transfer of Over Dimensional Cargo movement of its goods and other materials. India will construct a bridge over Feni River in Tripura to get access to the Chittagong port.

For Bangladesh:

- A billion-dollar line of credit from India for infrastructure development, the first state to ever have been given such financial support.
- An assured supply of 250 MW of power from India.
- Transit to Nepal and Bhutan.

The agreements to upgrade border land custom stations, introduce more trading points and opening up of border *haats* would be beneficial to both.

But over the next few months it became evidently clear that the trajectory fell far short of expectations. The delay in implementations of the projects led to dismay in Bangladesh. Once the agreements were inked, the critical challenge was to ensure the quick implementation of the projects. The fact that India and Bangladesh took eight months to work out the actual credit transfer did not find much favour from either side. The lethargy is mutual. India and Bangladesh finally inked the agreement US$ 1 billion loan in August 2010 with the visit of Indian Finance Minister Pranab Mukherjee to Dhaka. It has a 20-year repayment period on a rate of interest at 1.75 percent lower when compared to multilateral banks. Given the nature of projects agreed upon, a long gestation period is expected. But in the popular perception there is an inordinate delay in implementing the infrastructural projects, especially on the Bangladeshi side. Given the past history, Bangladeshi is keen to ensure that the bottlenecks, which are human or institutional deficiencies, need to be removed. The problem lies in the multi-layered decision-making processes and the entirety of the implementation machinery that begs reform. Subsequently, India was able to address several of the Bangladeshi grievances ranging from the large trade imbalance in India's favour, lack of progress on water sharing issues, non-ratification of the Indira-Mujib Land Boundary Agreement etc.

III

The Bangladesh Domestic Factor

With the passage of time, it has become clear that apart from few nuanced changes the overall bilateral policy towards Bangladesh remains the same irrespective of the government in New Delhi. The same cannot be argued for domestic political parties in Bangladesh. The ruling party and the opposition in Bangladesh are virulently on opposite sides over several issues especially with regards to India.

As mentioned earlier, although several agreements have been inked in early 2010, the delay in actual initiation and implementation obviously found little favour within Bangladesh. Indian Prime Minster Manmohan Singh's visit to Dhaka, in September 2011, was expected to smoothen out several outstanding issues. The large delegation of north eastern chief ministers and officials were supposed to be a force multiplier to the much awaited visit. But as events unfolded bilateral relations nosedived further. Dhaka was expecting India to reciprocate in large measures but felt let down given the sequence of events. Water will always remain a priority and a very emotive subject for Bangladeshis. The inability to sign any agreement on Teesta water sharing was disappointing for Bangladesh. The lack of any understanding on water turned Bangladeshi public opinion against India. The much awaited visit clearly floundered over this issue. The two sides were unable to complete the formalities for a transit agreement. The modalities first will have to be worked out then the infrastructural issues will have to be dealt with.

At the same time, some of the measures undertaken by the Bangladesh government have led to waning of its popularity. The Awami League coalition was unable to capitalise on the social capital that it had begun its tenure with. Several of the earlier issues that had negatively impacted upon Bangladesh were back on the surface again. The issue of corruption has been the bane of Bangladesh for decades and seems as entrenched as it always was. Despite the electoral campaign on anti-corruption measures the government did not pull all the stops as it had promised. As succinctly summed up ... 'the common people of Bangladesh are dismayed to see our motherland getting immersed in a sea of corruption! Our politicians have made politics a 'synonym' for corruption. Buying positions in the party hierarchy is considered to be the 'safest' and most 'lucrative' investment![1]

Evidently, Bangladeshi politics seem poised to be on a confrontational course all over again.[2] As in the past, the Opposition did not use the parliament to voice its opinion and street agitations and *hartals* were back with a vengeance. Whether it was over the cancellation of the 15th constitutional amendment and reinstatement of the caretaker government system, against price hike of fuel, the share market scam and repression of opposition leaders and activists or tracing its leader M Ilias Ali and his driver, who went missing, the situation was as hitherto once again. Within six months of the Awami League assuming power street agitations and protests were once again the tools of Opposition protests. While the Opposition has once again shown it ugly side the Awami League has not mended any of its ways too as expressed in an editorial... "We want to say in clear terms that the AL's policy towards the opposition, as exhibited in the last two days, is fundamentally undemocratic, legally

---

[1] Editorial, Mired in Corruption , 14 September 2012, *The Daily Star*, at http://www.thedailystar.net/newDesign/news-details.php?nid=249613

[2] Ali Riaz, *Inconvenient Truths about Bangladeshi Politics* (Dhaka: Prathama Prakashan, 2012). p. 158

untenable and practically unsustainable."[3]

Some of the political decisions taken in the last few months have not been very popular. The government turned down the recommendations of the special parliamentary committee on constitutional reforms to continue with the caretaker system for two more terms. Although the Supreme Court had declared 13th Amendment illegal, given the ground reality in Bangladesh, it necessitated the presence of a Caretaker Government. Also its proposal to the Election Commission to disqualify rebel candidates from contesting elections for two terms has not gone down well with the public.

The Bangladesh economy cannot keep up the pace it has achieved in the recent past. The lack of infra-structure—transport and communication—as well as shortage in gas and electricity supplies has all contributed to the downturn of the economy. Significantly, the lack of new investments does not bode well for an already sluggish economy. Indeed according to some studies Bangladesh will not be able to maintain its high GDP growth over the next few years.

Given the above and the Awami League losses in the 2011 municipality polls, the Narayanganj, Chittagong and Comilla city corporation polls, and the Tangail by-election has not been unnoticed. Evidently, the Awami League misjudged its huge support in 2008 election as 'license to rule instead of mandate to govern.[4]

Thus clearly, the Awami League government has not been able to maintain its popularity curve. Indeed annual media polls have reported on the plummeting of popular support. This has an inevitable fall out on India.

IV

The Non-Delivery

The breakthrough over the resolution of border issues during Indian Prime Minister Manmohan Singh's visit to Dhaka, including the demarcation of the contentious 6.1 km boundary and swapping enclaves and territories including 24-hour access to Dahagram, Angorpota enclaves through Tin Bigha corridor were largely glossed over due to the lack of any resolution over water sharing.[5] This also encouraged the opposition to take swipes at the ruling coalition. "If the government doesn't have the efficiency to bargain, nobody will give the country anything,"[6] Undoubtedly, anti-Indian sentiments run high within certain quarters of the country and political parties take advantage of the situation.[7]

Clearly, Sheikh Hasina was inhibited because she needed to show her people what India had given her before she could concede what India wanted. The domestic perception is in fact crucial to the outcome of what Bangladesh-India relations promised following Sheikh Hasina's historic visit. On the Indian side, there has been a clearly move in its perception about Bangladesh; it must consider Bangladesh's genuine interest in improving bilateral relations and that it is committed to addressing Indian security concerns. On connectivity, Bangladesh has shown the willingness to let its territory be used for India's interests.[8]

The difference in perceptionsm a vital ingredient in foreign policy-making, was wide and contrasting. Bangladesh was questioning motives, while India saw its several concessions to Bangladesh on trade and boundary issues, as its willingness to be large-hearted in dealing with smaller neighbours. Bangladesh was extremely disappointed over lack of consensus over the Teesta River while India continued to focus on other issues. From the Indian perspective, 'the Dhaka visit is our message to our smaller South Asian neighbours that India will not be niggardly or tight-fisted in its dealings with them but play a role that behoves its large size and strong economy.[9]

Indeed Bangladesh has already allowed India the use of Ashuganj port to bring large containers from

---

[3] Mahfuz Anam , 'Awami League's moral defeat, Government holds Dhaka city hostage,' March 13, 2012, *The Daily Star*, at http://www.thedailystar.net/newDesign/news-details.php?nid=226110

[4] Ali Riaz, *Inconvenient Truths about Bangladeshi Politics* (Dhaka: Prathama Prakashan, 2012). p. 162

[5] Some of the other resolutions that were reached during Singh's Dhaka visit included, Protection of Sundarbans tigers, Cooperation of railways on transit traffic for Nepal, Exchange of programmes by BTV and Doordarshan, Cooperation between Dhaka University and Jawaharlal Nehru University, Preservation of Sundarbans bio-diversity, Cooperation on renewable energy, Cooperation on fisheries, Cooperation on fashion technology

[6] Editorial, 'Poor bargain cost Teesta; She asks govt to be firm on Tipai issue, takes a swipe at Ershad', *The Daily Star* , 8 October 2011

[7] Ali Riaz, *Inconvenient Truths about Bangladeshi Politics* (Dhaka: Prathama Prakashan, 2012) p. 219

[8] M. Serajul Islam, 'Indo-Bangladesh relations: the importance of perception', *The Daily Star*, 9 October, 2010

[9] Larchis Mohan, 'Large-hearted' message from visit- Delhi sees Dhaka template for ties with other neighbours, *The Telegraph*, 6 December 2011 at http://www.telegraphindia.com/search/?cx=partner-pub-9104455251217860%3A2k8fyg-64or&cof=FORID%3A10&ie=ISO-8859-1&q=bangladesh&sa=Search&siteurl=www.telegraphindia.com%2F1111206%2Fjsp%2Ffrontpage%2Fstory_14845026.jsp

Calcutta port for despatch to Palatan in Tripura where a power plant is being built. India used the one-time concession for over-dimensional cargoes which are vital for the power station that would export energy to Bangladesh. The energy shortage of 1000-1500 megawatt gap in Bangladesh is rather acute and affecting the economy at several layers. Thus the plan to export power from Tripura to Bangladesh holds huge potential for bilateral cooperation. With both sides working out the detailed modalities involved, this would be one of the few bilateral deliverables shortly. Bangladesh is in dire need of meeting its demand and supply gap and the Indian positive presence in this sector will a beneficial factor for India.

Regional Way Ahead

The way ahead for India would be to engage its neighbours not only through the bilateral prism but also through a regional framework. When it comes to Bangladesh, history plays a critical role. It would be simplistic to assume that the genesis of the break-up of the subcontinent in 1947 and the division of Pakistan a quarter of a century later could be erased from memory. Anti-India sentiments have gained currency in Bangladesh. A host of differences with India have merely added a political flavour. The popular perception that India has been more comfortable with an Awami government in Dhaka fuelled this further. Thus a regional policy will add a greater degree of comfort when dealing with their giant neighbour, India.

However, the opposition will not spare any opportunity to embarrass the government and will look for areas of vulnerability. It is, therefore, important to manage the relationship and move away from a 'zero-sum game' mentality, to recognise that peace and cooperation create a positive-sum, win-win situation for all.[10]

The regional framework has greater acceptance and Bangladesh is also moving towards this end. They have been discussing this issue with Bhutan, Sri Lanka and the Maldives. 'One of the most significant developments in this regard has been the decision of the government to grant both Nepal and Bhutan use of the Chittagong and Mongla ports for transit trade to third countries.[11] Indeed, Bangladesh is keen to link up with Bhutan, Nepal and India and to extend it through Myanmar to the countries of Southeast Asia and beyond. Thus it has also offered use of two airports situated in the north of the country to Bhutan for its own use.[12] Nepal and Bangladesh trade through India has been successfully implemented.

Similarly, connectivity would also need to include telecom, IT, trade and financial sectors as well as specific measures for trade facilitation. The two sides have plans to further the energy trade. India has a two-pronged strategy in Bangladesh. One is to help them in running their existing projects and the second is to partner with them for setting up generation capacities.[13] Indian National Thermal Power Corporation plans to set up two imported coal-based power projects totalling 3,960MW in the country, at Khulna and Chittagong. India has also proposed setting up a liquefied natural gas (LNG) terminal as a joint venture in Bangladesh to create a power generation capacity of around 1,000MW.

According to Sheikh Hasina, with Bangladesh seeing the benefit of cooperating with India, the anti-India voices in Bangladesh will be subsumed in the din of mutual gain and benefits.[14] As two states with interlinked security concerns and future growth partners, India and Bangladesh need to become strategic dialogue partners. Correspondingly, India and Bangladesh have the potential to show how South Asian neighbours can change the rules of business. It will be a triumph of economics over political rhetoric not only between India and Bangladesh but in the entire region.

---

[10] 'India-Bangladesh ties a model for South Asia' The Hindu, 6 September , 2011 at http://www.thehindu.com/opinion/interview/article2427217.ece

[11] Govt slams Economist report, *The Daily Star*, August 5, 2011 http://www.thedailystar.net/newDesign/print_news.php?nid=197317

[12] Ibid

[13] Utpal Bhaskar & Elizabeth Roche, 'NTPC to set up two coal-based power plants in Bangladesh', *Financial Express*, 10 February 2010

[14] Bhaskar Roy, 'The lessons from Hasina's visit', *Sify* January 20, 2010

COUNTRY STUDIES

AFGHANISTAN

The Islamic Republic of Afghanistan (Dowlat-e Eslami-ye-Afghanestan) recognizes its independence day as 19 August, the date in 1919 when the country became fully independent of British rule. The background of the Afghan flag is three equal vertical sections of black, red, and green from left to right. In the centre of the flag in yellow is the national coat of arms, which portrays a mosque with a banner and a sheaf of wheat on either side. In the upper-middle part of the insignia are the lines "There is no God but Allah and Muhammad is his prophet" and "Allah is Great," together with a rising sun. The word "Afghanistan" and the year 1298 (the Muslim calendar equivalent of the year of independence, 1919) are located in the lower part of the insignia.

Recent History

In December 2001, Afghan leaders in exile signed the Bonn Agreement, forming an interim government, the Afghan Interim Administration, under the leadership of Hamid Karzai. In 2002 Karzai was selected president of the Transitional Islamic State of Afghanistan, whose ruling council included disparate leaders of the anti-Taliban Northern Alliance. A new constitution, written by a specially convened Loya Jirga, or constituent assembly of regional leaders, was ratified in early 2004. In October 2004, an overwhelming popular vote elected Karzai president of the Islamic Republic of Afghanistan. However, regional warlords and large areas of Afghanistan remained beyond the control of the Karzai government. Despite substantial international aid, the Afghan government, which included representatives from many factions, was unable to address numerous social and economic problems. The parliamentary elections of September 2005 gave regional warlords substantial power in both houses of the National Assembly, further jeopardising Karzai's ability to unite the country. The Bonn Agreement lapsed after the 2005 elections. The agreement's successor, the Afghanistan Compact, went into effect in January 2006 to set goals for international assistance in economic development, security, protection of human rights, and the fight against corruption and drug trafficking through 2010.

In the meantime, the resurgent Taliban intensified terrorist activities in areas beyond government control, particularly the south-eastern provinces. In mid-2006, North Atlantic Treaty Organisation (NATO) forces turned back a Taliban offensive aimed at Kandahar. However, beginning in 2007 the Taliban utilised safe havens in adjacent Pakistan to gradually restore and expand its control in Afghanistan. In early 2008, it controlled an estimated 10% of the country while the government controlled only an estimated 30%. Local tribes controlled the remaining territory. Despite U.S.-aided efforts to reduce cultivation of poppies for narcotics production, in 2007 and 2008 that crop accounted for an increasing percentage of Afghanistan's economy and was a major support of the Taliban. In mid-2008, a new International Conference in Support of Afghanistan reaffirmed international commitments to the country's economic and political stability but demanded improved coordination of aid and reduced corruption.

Capital	-	Kabul
Government	-	President Hamid Karzai
	-	Vice President Mohammad Fahim
	-	Vice President Karim Khalili
	-	Chief Justice Abdul Salam Azimi
Formation	-	Independence 19 August 1919
AREA	-	647,500 square kilometres
Population	-	30,419,928 (2012 estimate)
GDP (PPP)	-	$29.731 billion (2011 estimate) Per capita - $ 956
GDP (nominal)	-	$18.181 billion (2011 estimate) Per capita - $585
Defence Minister	-	Bismillah Khan Mohammadi
Chief of Staff	-	Lieutenant General Sher Mohammad Karimi
Commander ISAF	-	General John R. Allen (since 18 July 2011)

Meanwhile, widespread economic hardship increasingly weakened the Karzai government's support among the population.

The Taliban-led insurgency in Afghanistan has continued unabated and spread into new areas during 2008. Counterinsurgency efforts were forced to adapt to changes in Taliban tactics and seemed to make little overall headway. Without more positive developments and a more unified approach to the conflict, it seemed likely that some countries with troops deployed as part of the International Security Assistance Force (ISAF) mission under NATO command might begin to reappraise their commitments. Tensions within NATO over mission objectives have undermined the mission's effectiveness, and a broader debate is underway over how the international community should define 'success' in Afghanistan.

Despite a much publicised lack of troop numbers, ISAF forces were tasked for interdicting drug traffickers and destruction of opium factories within Afghanistan in a bid to hinder insurgents' sources of funds, while troops remained heavily engaged in combat and stabilisation operations across the country. Insurgents have moved into previously quiet provinces, increased their use of suicide bombing and of improvised explosive devices, and launched attacks on a number of high-value targets, including President Hamid Karzai and local government and security officials. The suicide attacks on the Serena Hotel in January 2008 and on the Indian Embassy have showed the relative ease with which insurgents move within Kabul. Explosively formed projectiles (EFP), similar to those employed in Iraq, have also been found in Afghanistan.

After suffering a series of defeats in open combat with international forces in the heartland areas of Helmand, Kandahar and Urzgan, insurgents established bases in areas where government and ISAF forces were fewer in number, such as the south-western provinces of Nimruz and Farah, while becoming more active in the north, especially in Badghis, Faryab, Faizabad and Badakhshan. There were also reports of significant Taliban presence in provinces near Kabul, such as Wardak. Insurgent operations focus on perceived areas of weakness such as the Afghan National Police (ANP), the members of which are poorly trained and equipped to protect themselves.

Meanwhile, the capacity of the Afghan National Army (ANA) remains limited in spite of improvements, and the force's manpower level remains below the desired total of 80,000, due to be reached in 2010. (The ANA, at full capacity and capability as currently envisaged, is planned to become a 'light infantry force of 15 brigades, including artillery, armour, commando, combat support, combat service support, an air corps, and the requisite intermediate commands and sustaining institutions).

Over five million Afghan refugees were repatriated in the last decade, including many who were forcefully deported from NATO countries. This large return of Afghans may have helped the nation's economy but the country still remains one of the poorest in the world due to the decades of war, lack of foreign investment, ongoing government corruption and the Taliban insurgency. According to a report by the United Nations, the Taliban and other militants were responsible for 76% of civilian casualties in 2009, 75% in 2010, 80% in 2011, 80% in 2012. In 2011 a record 3,021 civilians were killed in the ongoing insurgency, the fifth successive annual rise.

After the May 2011 death of Osama bin Laden in Pakistan, many prominent Afghan figures were assassinated, including Mohammed Daud Daud, Ahmed Wali Karzai, Jan Mohammad Khan, Ghulam Haider Hamidi, Burhanuddin Rabbani and others. Also in the same year, the Pak-Afghan border skirmishes intensified and many large scale attacks by the Pakistani-based Haqqani Network took place across Afghanistan. This led to the United States warning Pakistan of a possible military action against the Haqqanis in the Federally Administered Tribal Areas. The U.S. blamed Pakistan's government, mainly Pakistan Army and its ISI spy network as the masterminds behind all of this.

Attempts to turn Taliban fighters away from insurgency have met with limited success, though in the long run this would seem essential to any solution to Afghanistan's problems. The National Peace Commission was given the task of fostering reconciliation, but its mandate is unclear and the process is slow, allowing for the reconciliation only of individuals rather than groups. In anticipation of the 2014 NATO withdrawal and a subsequent expected push to regain power by the Taliban, the anti-Taliban United Front (Northern Alliance) groups have started to regroup under the umbrella of the National Coalition of Afghanistan (political arm) and the National Front of Afghanistan (military arm).

Geography

Location: Afghanistan is located in Central Asia, north and west of Pakistan, east of Iran, and south of Turkmenistan, Uzbekistan, and Tajikistan. The narrow Wakhan Corridor extends from north-eastern-most Afghanistan to meet with China. The land boundaries are with China (76 kilometres); Iran (936 kilometres); Pakistan (2,430 kilometres); Tajikistan (1,206 kilometres); Turkmenistan (744 kilometres); and Uzbekistan (137 kilometres).

Topography: The terrain of Afghanistan is dominated by rugged mountain ranges, which generally run from the northeast to the southwest. Mountains occupy all but the north-central and south-western regions of the country, which are dominated by plains. Nearly half the country has an elevation of 2,000 metres or more, and the highest peaks in the northeastern Hindu Kush range exceed 7,000 metres. Historically, mountain passes along the northeastern border with present-day Pakistan have been of great strategic importance. Significant parts of the southwestern plains region are desert.

Principal Rivers: The main rivers are the Amu Darya, 800 kilometres; the Harirud, 850 kilometres; the Helmand, 1,000 kilometres; and the Kabul, 460 kilometres. Afghanistan's chief tributaries to the Amu Darya, which forms much of the country's northern border, are the Koshk and the Qonduz.

Climate: Afghanistan's climate generally is of the arid or semi-arid steppe type, featuring cold winters and dry, hot summers. The mountains of the northeast have subarctic winter conditions. Farther south, monsoon effects moderate the climate near the Pakistan border and increase rainfall as far inland as central Afghanistan. The highest precipitation occurs in the Kabul region of the northeast. The highest temperatures and lowest precipitation are in the south-western plains region, where summer temperatures reach 49° C. Low temperatures in the north-eastern mountains range from –15°C in winter to 0° C in summer. The climate of the north-central Turkistan Plain is increasingly arid closest to the northern borders with Turkmenistan, Uzbekistan, and Tajikistan.

Natural Resources: Agricultural resources are primarily grazing land; fertile crop-growing land is concentrated in Kondoz Province in the north and Helmand Province in the south. Afghanistan is known to have major deposits of chrome, coal, copper, iron, and salt, as well as lesser amounts of a wide variety of minerals including gold, silver, and uranium. Natural gas is the most abundant hydrocarbon resource. Substantial oil deposits are recognised but not yet quantified. Water for all purposes is in critically short supply.

Land Use: Some 12.1% of Afghanistan's land is classified as arable; however, in the early 2000s a four-year drought cut that figure in half. In 2007 only 0.2% of the total was planted to permanent crops.

Environmental Factors: The environment of Afghanistan is assumed to have been spared large-scale disturbances until the Soviet invasion of 1979. Since that time, however, numerous events have caused severe damage. Afghanistan, which has no appreciable bodies of water, suffers from a limited freshwater supply that makes potable water unavailable to more than half the population. In recent years, groundwater quality has deteriorated because of agricultural and industrial runoff, and water quantity has been diminished by large-scale land clearing and desertification. Because of insufficient water treatment, the incidence of water-borne diseases is very high. Widespread overgrazing, soil erosion, salinisation, and water logging have reduced agricultural productivity. Although Afghanistan has little industry, particulate pollutants from the Aral Sea and industrial complexes in Iran, Turkmenistan, and Uzbekistan contaminate the atmosphere in northern Afghanistan. Chemical use and physical destruction in recent military conflicts have damaged the environment, and landmines and unexploded shells are residual hazards endangering an estimated 4 million Afghanis in 32 provinces. North-eastern Afghanistan is considered an earthquake hazard zone; in 1998 an earthquake along the Tajikistan border resulted in an estimated 4,000 fatalities.

Society

Population: Population assessment is difficult because many people do not have fixed residences. In 2008 the estimated population was 32.7 million. The population growth rate was 2.6% per year. The population is approximately 75% rural; in 2008 the six most populous cities accounted for less than 10% of the population. In 2006 net out-migration was 0.4 per 1,000 population. After heavy out-migration and internal displacement in the 1980s and 1990s, an estimated 2.5 million Afghans returned to Afghanistan in 2003-04 before the numbers began to decrease. The United Nations reported that in 2007 some 365,400 Afghanis returned to their country, bringing the total of repatriations since 2002 to 4.1 million. In 2007 more than 2 million Afghans were living in Pakistan and 1.5 million in Iran. In 2007 both countries, the main recipients of Afghan refugees, began preparations for large-scale deportation. Tajikistan closed its border with Afghanistan in 2007. Meanwhile, in that year insecure conditions in Afghanistan noticeably decreased the rate of return. In the early 2000s, hundreds of thousands were internally displaced within Afghanistan, mainly from rural to urban areas, because of drought and instability. In the first quarter of 2008, an estimated 13,000 people fled their homes as conflicts occurred in previously safe regions.

Ethnic Groups: The main ethnic groups are Pashtun, 42%; Tajik, 27%; Hazara, 9%; Uzbek, 9%; Aimak (a Persian-speaking nomadic group), 4%; Turkmen, 3%; and Baloch, 2%. The largest remaining nomadic group is the Kuchis, a Pashtun group whose population has dwindled to about 1.5 million since 1979. The Pashtuns are the major ethnic group in the south and the east, the Tajiks in the northeast. The predominant groups in north-central Afghanistan are the Hazaras, Tajiks, and Uzbeks.

Languages: More than 30 languages are spoken in Afghanistan. The official languages are Dari (Afghan Persian) and Pashtu. Dari is spoken by 50% of the population, and Pashtu is spoken as a first language by 35%. Turkic languages (primarily Turkmen and Uzbek) are spoken by 11% of the population. Of the languages spoken by smaller segments of the population, the most important are Balochi and Pashai. Many Afghans speak more than one language; Dari is the most common second language.

Economy

The economy of Afghanistan has improved significantly since 2002 due to the infusion of billions of US dollars in international assistance and investments, as well as remittances from expats. It is also due to dramatic improvements in agricultural production and the end of a four-year drought in most of the country. However, Afghanistan still remains one of the poorest and least developed countries in the world that is highly dependent on foreign aid. As of 2009, the nation's GDP is $14 billion and the GDP per capita is $1,000.

About half the population suffer from shortages of housing, clean drinking water, electricity and employment. The Government of Afghanistan and international donors have remained committed to improving access to these basic necessities by prioritising infrastructure development, education, housing development, jobs programs, medical care, and economic reform over the recent years. Historically, there has been a dearth of information and reliable statistics about Afghanistan's economy.

Agriculture. The Afghan economy continues to be overwhelmingly agricultural, despite the fact that only 12% of its total land area is arable and less than 6% currently is cultivated. Agricultural production is constrained by an almost total dependence on erratic winter snows and spring rains for water; irrigation is primitive. Relatively little use is made of machines, chemical fertilizer, or pesticides. The country's fruit and nut exports are at $113 million per year and could grow to more than $800 million per year in 10 years given the proper investment. Badghis and Samangan Province in the north of the country are famous for pistachio cultivation but the area lacks proper marketing and processing plants.

Wheat and cereal production is Afghanistan's traditional agricultural mainstay. The overall agricultural production dramatically declined following four years of drought as well as the sustained fighting and instability in rural areas. Some studies indicate that agricultural production and livestock numbers may only be sufficient to feed about half of the country's population. Shortages are exacerbated by the country's limited transportation network, which is currently being rebuilt. A report by the Food and Agriculture Organisation (FAO) states that Afghanistan was nearing self-sufficiency in grain production.

Livestock. The availability of land suitable for grazing has traditionally made animal husbandry an important part of the economy. There are two main types of animal husbandry: sedentary, practiced by farmers who raise both animals and crops; and nomadic, practiced by animal herders known as Kuchis. Natural pastures cover some 30,400 square kilometres but are being overgrased. The northern regions around Mazar-e Sharif and Maymanah were the home range for about six million karakul sheep in the late 1990s. Most flocks move to the highlands in the summer to pastures in the north. Oxen are the primary draft power and farmers often share animals for ploughing. Poultry are traditionally kept in most households.

Much of Afghanistan's livestock was removed from the country by early waves of refugees who fled to Pakistan and Iran. In 2001, the livestock population in Afghanistan had declined by about 40% since 1998. In 2002, this figure was estimated to have declined further to 60%. An FAO survey done in the northern regions in spring 2002 showed that in four provinces (Balkh, Juzjan, Sar-e Pol, and Faryab), there was a loss of about 84% of cattle from 1997 to 2002 and around 80% of sheep and goats. In recent years, USAID has been helping to improve animal husbandry in Afghanistan.

Fishing. The nation has plenty of water reserves and suitable climate for fish farming. Fishing takes place in the lakes and rivers, such as in Sarobi and Mahipar area. Fish constitute a smaller part of the Afghan diet today because fish farmers are unable to produce enough fish to keep up with the demands of customers. The annual catch was about 900 tons in 2003. Most fish and seafood is imported from neighbouring Pakistan, Iran, the United Arab Emirates and other countries. There are about 300 fish farms throughout the country and the largest one is at the Qargha.

Forestry. Afghanistan's timber has been greatly depleted, and since the mid-1980s, only about 3% of the land area has been forested, mainly in the east. Exploitation has been hampered by lack of power and access roads. Moreover, the distribution of the forest is uneven, and most of the remaining woodland is presently found only in mountainous regions in the southeast and south. The natural forests in Afghanistan are mainly of two types: dense forests of oak, walnut, and other species of nuts that grow in the southeast, and on the northern and northeastern slopes of the Sulaiman ranges; and sparsely distributed short trees and shrubs on all other slopes of the Hindu Kush. The dense forests of the southeast cover only 2.7% of the country. Roundwood production in 2003 was 3,148,000 cubic metres, with 44% used for fuel. The destruction of the forests to create agricultural land, logging, forest fires, plant diseases, and insect pests are all causes of the reduction in forest coverage. Illegal logging and clear-cutting by timber smugglers have exacerbated this destructive process.

Trade and industry. The current trade between Afghanistan and other countries is at US$5 billion a year. In 1996, legal exports (excluding opium) were estimated at $80 million and imports estimated at $150 million per year. Since the collapse of the Taliban government in 2001, new trade relations are emerging with the United States, Pakistan, Iran, Turkmenistan, the EU, Japan, Uzbekistan, India and other countries. The Afghan hand-woven rugs are one of the most popular products exported from the country. Other products include hand crafted antique replicas, precious and semi-precious stones as well as leather and furs.

Afghanistan is endowed with a wealth of natural resources, including extensive deposits of natural gas, petroleum, coal, marble, gold, copper, chromite, talc, barites, sulfur, lead, zinc, iron ore, salt, precious and semi-precious stones, and many other materials. In 2006, a U.S. Geological Survey estimated that Afghanistan has as much as 36 trillion cubic feet of natural gas, 3.6 billion barrels of oil and condensate reserves. According to a 2007 assessment, Afghanistan has significant amounts of undiscovered non-fuel mineral resources. Scientists also found indications of abundant deposits of coloured stones and gemstones, including emerald, ruby, sapphire, garnet, lapis, kunzite, spinel, tourmaline and peridot. In 2010, U.S. Pentagon officials along with American geologists have revealed the discovery of nearly $1 trillion in untapped mineral deposits in Afghanistan. Plans are being made by the Afghan government to begin extracting these but with the Taliban insurgency and the corruption there is no telling what will happen.

A memo from the Pentagon stated that Afghanistan could become the "Saudi Arabia of lithium" and its untapped minerals are worth at least $3 trillion. Afghanistan signed a copper deal with China in 2008, which to is a project that involves the investment of $2.8 billion dollars by China and an annual income of $400 million dollars to the Afghan government. The country's Ainak copper mine, in Logar province, is one of the biggest in the world and is expected to provide jobs to 20,000 Afghans. It is estimated to hold at least 11 million tonnes of copper. Experts believe that the production of copper could begin within two to three years and the iron ore in five to seven years as of 2010.

Economic development and recovery. Afghanistan embarked on a modest economic development program in the 1930s. The government founded banks; introduced paper money; established a university; expanded primary, secondary, and technical schools; and sent students abroad for education. In 1956, the government of Afghanistan promulgated the first in a long series of ambitious development plans. By the late 1970s, these had achieved only mixed results due to flaws in the planning process as well as inadequate funding and a shortage of the skilled managers and technicians needed for implementation.

The nation's banking system has improved recently with over 14 different banks operating as of 2003. They include Da Afghanistan Bank, Afghanistan International Bank, Kabul Bank, Azizi Bank, Pashtany Bank, Standard Chartered Bank, First Micro Finance Bank, and others. Money can be transferred electronically in and out of the country. A new law on private investment provides three to seven-year tax holidays to eligible companies and a four-year exemption from exports tariffs and duties.

The Afghan economy has been growing at about 10% per year in the last decade, which is due to the infusion of over $50 billion dollars in international aid and remittances from Afghan expats. It is also due to improvements made to the transportation system and agricultural production, which is the backbone of the nation's economy.

While the nations' current account deficit is largely financed with the donor money, only a small portion is provided directly to the government budget. The rest is provided to non-budgetary expenditure and donor-designated projects through the United Nations system and non-governmental organisations. The Afghan Ministry of Finance is focusing on improved revenue collection and public sector expenditure discipline. For example, government revenues increased 31% to $1.7 billion from March 2010 to March 2011.

One of the main drivers for the current economic recovery is the return of over 5 million expatriates, who brought with them fresh energy, entrepreneurship and wealth-creating skills as well as much needed funds to start up businesses. For the first time since the 1970s, Afghans have involved themselves in construction, one of the largest industries in the country. Some of the major national construction projects include the $35 billion New Kabul City next to the capital, the Ghazi Amanullah Khan City near Jalalabad, and the Aino Mena in Kandahar. Similar development projects have also begun in Herat in the west, Mazar-e-Sharif in the north and in other cities.

In addition, a number of companies and small factories began operating in different parts of the country, which not only provide revenues to the government but also create new jobs. Improvements to the business-enabling environment have resulted in more than $1.5 billion in telecom investment and created more than 100,000 jobs since 2003. The Afghan rugs are becoming popular again and this gives many carpet dealers around the country to expand their business by hiring more workers.

Afghanistan is a member of SAARC, ECO and OIC. It is hoping to join SCO soon to develop closer economic ties with neighbouring and regional countries in the so-called New Silk Road trade project. The nation's goal is to achieve an Afghan economy whose growth is based on trade, private enterprise and investment. Experts believe that this will revolutionize the economy of the region. Opium production in Afghanistan has soared to a record in 2007 with about 3 million people reported to be involved in the business but then declined significantly in the years following. The government started programmes to help reduce cultivation of poppy, and by 2010 it was reported that 24 out of the 34 provinces were free from poppy grow. In June 2012, India strongly advocated for private investments in the resource rich country and creation of suitable environment.

Government and Politics

Overview: Politics in Afghanistan has historically consisted of power struggles, bloody coups and unstable transfers of power. With the exception of a military junta, the country has been governed by nearly every system of government over the past century, including a monarchy, republic, theocracy and communist state. The constitution ratified by the 2003 Loya jirga restructured the government as an Islamic republic consisting of three branches, executive, legislative and judicial.

Afghanistan is currently led by President Hamid Karzai, who was elected in October 2004. The current parliament was elected in 2005. Among the elected officials were former mujahadeen, Taliban members, communists, reformists, and Islamic fundamentalists. 28% of the delegates elected were women, three more than the 25% minimum guaranteed under the constitution. This made Afghanistan, long known under the Taliban for its oppression of women, one of the leading countries in terms of female representation. Construction for a new parliament building began on 29 August 2005.

The Supreme Court of Afghanistan is currently led by Chief Justice Abdul Salam Azimi, a former university professor who had been legal advisor to the president. The previous court, appointed during the time of the interim government, had been dominated by fundamentalist religious figures, including Chief Justice Faisal Ahmad Shinwari. The court issued several rulings, such as banning cable television, seeking to ban a candidate in the 2004 presidential election and limiting the rights of women, as well as overstepping its constitutional authority by issuing rulings on subjects not yet brought before the court. The current court is seen as more moderate and led by more technocrats than the previous court, although it has yet to issue any rulings.

Judicial Branch: To replace the ad hoc system in place under the transitional government, the constitution of 2004 stipulated that the Supreme Court include nine justices appointed by the president, with approval of the Wolesa Jirga, for 10-year terms. Those justices have particular importance because they are responsible for managing the personnel, budgets, and policy decisions of the entire national, regional, and local court system. At the level below the Supreme Court are high and appeals courts. A National Security Court handles cases of terrorism and other threats to national security.

Administrative Divisions: The major sub-national administrative division is the province (*wilayat*), numbering 34 in 2008. The two newest provinces were added in 2004. Each province has between five and 15 districts. In 2006 some 361 districts were in existence, but the number changes frequently as districts split or combine. Each province has one designated provincial municipality; some but not all provinces also have a single rural municipality. The municipalities fall under the direct jurisdiction of the Ministry of Interior.

Politics and Political Parties: In the 2005 parliamentary election, among the elected officials were former mujahideen, Islamic fundamentalists, warlords, communists, reformists, and several Taliban associates. In the same period, Afghanistan reached to the 30th nation in terms of female representation in parliament. The last parliamentary election was held in September 2010, but due to disputes and investigation of fraud, the sworn in ceremony took place in late January 2011. After the issuance of computerised ID cards for the first time, which is a $101 million project that the Afghan government has launched, it is expected to help prevent major fraud in future elections and improve the security situation. President Karzai has declined to form a party to advance his programmes.

Mass Media

The media was tightly controlled under the Taliban and other periods in its history, and was relatively free in others. Under the Taliban, television was shut down in 1996, and print media were forbidden to publish commentary, photos or readers letters. The only radio station broadcast religious programmes and propaganda, and aired no music.

After the overthrow of the Taliban in 2001, press restrictions were gradually relaxed and private media diversified. Freedom of expression and the press is promoted in the 2004 constitution and censorship is banned, though defaming individuals or producing material contrary to the principles of Islam is prohibited. 400 publications are now registered and 60 radio stations, a major source of information, currently exist. Foreign radio stations, such as the BBC World Service, also broadcast into the country.

National Security

Overview: Beginning with the accession of the Karzai government in 2004, national security policy has aimed to establish a credible armed force, the Afghan National Army (ANA), and a national police force that will provide all conventional aspects of domestic security. The Afghan National Army currently has 134,000 (July 2010) soldiers with plans to reach 260,000 by 2014. The Afghan military is headquartered at the National Military Command Centre in Kabul. In October 2009, the United States announced it plans to spend $1.3 billion dollars by 2010 in upgrading and constructing several military bases for the Afghan army. This includes upgrades of more than $100 million to Bagram Air Base, the largest military base in the country, as well as a new $70 million dollar base in Farah near the border with Iran.

External Threat: The major external threat is the movement of hostile forces, military matériel, and terrorists from staging areas across Afghanistan's porous borders. After occurring regularly since 2002, such movement from Pakistan accelerated in 2006 and 2007. Beginning in 2007, clandestine arms shipments across the Iran border also were identified.

Defence Budget: $ 7.2 billion, which is 2.9% of the GDP.

Major Military Units: The military of Afghanistan is under the Ministry of Defence, which includes the Afghan National Army and the Afghan Air Force. It currently has about 180,000 active soldiers and is expected to reach 260,000 in the coming years. They are trained and equipped by NATO countries, mainly by the United States. The ANA is divided into 7 major Corps, with the 201st Selab ("Flood") in Kabul being the main one. The ANA also has a commando brigade which was established in 2007. The National Military

Academy of Afghanistan serves as the main educational institute for the military. A new $200 million Afghan Defence University (ADU) is under construction near the capital.

Major Military Equipment: Amounts and distribution of equipment, mostly Soviet-manufactured, are not known. In 2007 the army had main battle tanks, reconnaissance vehicles, armoured infantry fighting vehicles, armored personnel carriers, towed artillery, multiple rocket launchers, mortars, surface-to-surface missiles, recoilless rifles, antiaircraft guns, and surface-to-air missiles. The air force had six combat aircraft and seven support aircraft, to which it added in 2007 six Mi-17 transport helicopters, six Mi-35 helicopter gunships, and four An-32 transport aircraft.

Foreign Military Forces: Until September 2008, the coalition of foreign troops fighting Taliban and al Qaeda forces in Afghanistan was divided into two major commands: the U.S.-led Operation Enduring Freedom (OEF) and the North Atlantic Treaty Organisation (NATO)-led International Security Assistance Force (ISAF). For the first time in 2008, the OEF command was united with that of the ISAF, to improve force coordination. Some missions of the two forces continued to diverge, however. In 2008 about 19,000 U.S. troops had remained in the OEF, while 15,100 were assigned to the ISAF. Between 2005 and 2008, the ISAF increased from 9,000 troops to about 43,000, a number to which 40 countries contributed. Besides the United States, in 2008 the major contributing countries, in order of contingent size, were Britain, Germany, Canada, Italy, the Netherlands, and France. Previously concentrated in northern and western Afghanistan, in 2006 ISAF forces began moving into the southern province of Helmand and the central province of Uruzgan. The 2006 Afghanistan Compact called for NATO troops to remain through 2010 or until the Afghan armed forces reach their planned troop levels.

Status of the Insurgency. The Afghan Taliban-dominated insurgency has become increasingly dangerous and destabilising. Despite the loss of some key leaders, insurgents have adjusted their tactics to maintain momentum following the arrival of additional US forces in 2009. The Taliban was successful in its goal of suppressing voter turnout in key parts of the country. Since January 2007, the Taliban has increased its influence and expanded the insurgency outside the Pashtun belt, while maintaining most of its strongholds. The Taliban's expansion of influence into northern Afghanistan has made the insurgency a countrywide threat. As it has done elsewhere, the Taliban conducts military operations, shadow governance activities, and propaganda campaigns to solidify support among the populace and eliminate resistance to its presence. The insurgency also has increased the geographic scope and frequency of attacks. The lack of security in many areas coupled with a generally low government capacity and competency has hampered efforts to improve governance and extend development. Afghan leaders also continue to face the eroding effects of official corruption and the drug trade, which erode diminish public confidence in its already fragile institutions.

The Ministry of Interior has also remained largely ineffective. The country faces a chronic shortage of resources and of qualified and motivated government officials at the national and local level. In addition, continued insecurity undercuts the population's perceptions of the national government's long term prospects to either win the war, or to persuade tribal and other influential non-state actors to remain neutral or back insurgents. Kabul's inability to build effective, honest, and loyal provincial and district level institutions capable of providing basic government services and enabling sustainable, legal livelihoods erodes its popular legitimacy and has contributed to the influence of local warlords and the Taliban. Many Afghans perceive the police to be corrupt and more dangerous than the Taliban. The inflow of international funding connected to the international military presence and international reconstruction assistance has brought benefits but also has increased the opportunities for corrupt officials to profit from the counterinsurgency and stabilisation efforts in the country. The drug trade has a debilitating effect on the government's legitimacy, as criminal networks cooperate with insurgents and corrupt officials in ways that decrease security and the average Afghan's confidence that he will be treated fairly by the authorities.

The Drug Trade. The insidious effects of drug-related criminality continue to undercut the government's ability to assert its authority outside of Kabul, to develop a strong, rule-of-law based system, and to rebuild the economy. High wheat prices, low opium prices, and provincial-government-led efforts reduced poppy cultivation in Afghanistan to 131,000 hectares in 2009, down 17% from the 157,300 hectares cultivated in 2008. Potential opium production fell only 4%, however, to 5,300 metric tons, because good weather following a drought in 2008 increased yields. Potential heroin production is estimated at 630 metric tons, if the entire opium crop were processed. High wheat prices and low opium prices during the planting season in fall 2008 encouraged farmers to grow more wheat at the expense of poppy. Wheat prices were nearly three times higher than normal, driven by countrywide food production shortfalls, globally high prices for wheat, and a partial ban on wheat imports by Pakistan, Afghanistan's main wheat trading partner. Opium prices have been on a downward trend since 2004, most likely because of continued overproduction. Wheat prices have dropped by half since the fall 2008 planting season in response to an abundant Afghan wheat harvest last year and global price declines, reducing the profitability of wheat and probably making the crop less desirable than poppy to farmers. However, aggressive anti-poppy campaigns in some provinces and continued low opium prices caused by persistent overproduction may nevertheless convince some farmers to grow wheat and other licit crops instead of poppy. The Afghan Taliban in 2008 received up to $100 million in opium, cash, and goods and services from the opiate trade in Afghanistan, making the opiate trade the most important source of funding from inside Afghanistan for the Taliban-dominated insurgency.

Police: Increasingly after 2002, the police were the only defence for civilians against insurgent forces in many parts of the country. Thus police duties often include paramilitary activities that are vital to national defence. Plans call for Afghanistan to increase its police force, the Afghan National Police (ANP), to 82,000, including conventional, border, highway, and counternarcotics police. The ANP has received less training and resources than the Army and is beset by high rates of corruption and casualties and absenteeism. Limitations to the ANP's training, mentoring, and equipping, as well as to the abilities of a force trained to "hold" territory in those large parts of the country that have not been effectively "cleared" hinder its progress and effectiveness.

BANGLADESH

History

Bangladesh, formerly the East Wing of Pakistan, emerged as an independent nation in December 1971. One of the most divisive issues confronting Pakistan in its infancy was the question of what the official language of the new state was to be. Jinnah yielded to the demands that Urdu be Pakistan's official language. In East Pakistan, the dissatisfaction quickly turned to violence. (The Bengalis of East Pakistan constituted an estimated 54% of Pakistan's entire population). Jinnah visited East Pakistan on only one occasion after independence, shortly before his death in 1948. In the Constituent Assembly frequent arguments voiced the fear that the West Pakistani province of Punjab would dominate the nation. An ineffective body, the Constituent Assembly took almost nine years to draft a constitution, which was never put into effect.

At a 1966 Lahore conference of both the eastern and the western chapters of the Awami League, Mujib announced a controversial six-point political and economic programme for East Pakistani provincial autonomy. He demanded that the government be federal and parliamentary in nature, its members to be elected by universal adult suffrage with legislative representation on the basis of population; that the federal government have principal responsibility for foreign affairs and defence only; that each wing have its own currency and separate fiscal accounts; that taxation would occur at the provincial level, with a federal government funded by constitutionally guaranteed grants; that each federal unit could control its own earning of foreign exchange; and that each unit could raise its own militia or paramilitary forces.

Mujib's six points ran directly counter to greater national integration. It would divide Pakistan by encouraging ethnic and linguistic cleavages in West Pakistan, and would leave East Pakistan, with its Bengali ethnic and linguistic unity, by far the most populous and powerful of the federating units. It was tantamount to a call for independence.

On 25 March 1969 General Yahya Khan placed under martial law and assumed the titles of chief martial law administrator and president. He announced elections to take place on 7 December 1970 and East Pakistan was awarded 162 seats out of the 300-member National Assembly. On 12 November 1970, a cyclone devastated an area of almost 8,000 square kilometres of East Pakistan's mid-coastal lowlands and its outlying islands in the Bay of Bengal. It was perhaps the worst natural disaster of the area in centuries. As many as 250,000 lives were lost. Two days after the cyclone hit, Yahya arrived in Dhaka after a trip to Beijing, but he left a day later. His seeming indifference to the plight of Bengali victims caused a great deal of animosity.

The elections on 7 December 1970 were the first in the history of Pakistan in which voters were able to elect members of the National Assembly directly. In a convincing demonstration of Bengali dissatisfaction with the West Pakistani regime, the Awami League won all but 2 of the 162 seats allotted to East Pakistan in the National Assembly. Bhutto's Pakistan People's Party came in a poor second nationally, winning 81

Capital	-	Dhaka
Official language	-	Bengali
Government	-	Parliamentary Democracy
-		President Zillur Rahman
	-	Prime Minister Sheikh Hasina Wajed
	-	Speaker Abdul Hamid
Formation	-	Independence from Pakistan
	-	Declared 26 March 1971
	-	Victory Day 16 December 1971
Area	-	Total 147,570 square kilometres
Coastline	-	580 kilometres
Population	-	161,083,804 (2012 estimate)
	-	Density 1,033/square kilometre
GDP (PPP)	-	$282.229 billion (2011 estimate)
	-	Per capita $1,790
GDP (nominal)	-	$113.032 billion (2011 estimate)
	-	Per capita $700
Defence Minister	-	Sheikh Hasina Wajed
Chief of Army Staff	-	General Iqbal Karim Bhuiyan
Chief of Navy Staff	-	Vice Admiral Zahir Uddin Ahmed
Chief of Air Staff	-	Air Marshal Muhammad Enamul Bari

out of the 138 West Pakistani seats in the National Assembly. The Awami League's electoral victory promised it control of the government, with Mujib as the country's prime minister, but the inaugural assembly never met.

Yahya and Bhutto vehemently opposed Mujib's idea of a confederated Pakistan. Mujib was adamant that the constitution be based on his six-point programme. Bhutto, meanwhile, pleaded for unity in Pakistan under his leadership. As tensions mounted, Mujib suggested he become prime minister of East Pakistan while Bhutto be prime minister of West Pakistan. It was this action that triggered mass civil disobedience in East Pakistan. Yahya decided to ignore Mujib's demands and on 1 March 1 postponed indefinitely the convening of the National Assembly.

West Pakistani troops were sent to East Pakistan as tensions rose. Talks between Yahya and Muhib collapsed, and on March 23 Bengalis following Mujib's lead defiantly celebrated "Resistance Day" in East Pakistan instead of the traditional all-Pakistan "Republic Day." Yahya decided to "solve" the problem of East Pakistan by repression. On 25 March the Pakistan Army launched a terror campaign to intimidate the Bengalis into submission. Within hours a wholesale slaughter had commenced in Dhaka, with the heaviest attacks concentrated on the University of Dhaka and the Hindu area of the old town. Bangladeshis remember the date as a day of infamy and liberation. The Pakistan Army killed several hundred Bengalis. Mujib was captured and flown to West Pakistan for incarceration.

The West Pakistani press waged a vigorous but ultimately futile campaign to counteract newspaper and radio accounts of wholesale atrocities. The civil war was played down by the government-controlled press as a minor insurrection quickly being brought under control. After the tragic events of March, India became vocal in its condemnation of Pakistan. An immense flood of East Pakistani refugees, between 8 and 10 million according to various estimates, fled across the border into the Indian state of West Bengal. In April an Indian parliamentary resolution demanded that Prime Minister Indira Gandhi supply aid to the rebels in East Pakistan. She complied but declined to recognize the provisional government of independent Bangladesh.

On 4 December 1971 the Indian Army executed a 3-pronged pincer movement on Dhaka launched from West Bengal, Assam, and Tripura, taking only 12 days to defeat the 90,000 Pakistani defenders. On 6 December, India became the first nation to recognize the new Bangladeshi government.

At independence, Bangladesh was scarred by civil war. The new nation faced many other seemingly insurmountable problems inhibiting its reconstruction. The most glaring was the breakdown of law and order. In the wake of the war of independence, numerous bands of guerrillas roamed the countryside, fully armed and outside control of the government.

Despite substantial foreign aid, mostly from India and the Soviet Union, food supplies were scarce, and there was rampant corruption and black marketering. Mujib's economic policies also directly contributed to his country's economic chaos. His large-scale nationalisation of Bangladeshi manufacturing and trading enterprises and international trading in commodities strangled Bangladesh entrepreneurship in its infancy. However, at the time of the first national elections held in 1973 the Awami League won 282 out of 289 directly contested seats. After the election, the economic and security situations began to deteriorate rapidly, and Mujib's popularity suffered further as a result of what many Bangladeshis came to regard as his close alliance with India.

On the morning of 15 August 1975, Mujib and several members of his family were murdered in a coup engineered by a group of young army officers, most of whom were majors. The diplomatic status of Bangladesh changed overnight. One day after Mujib's assassination President Bhutto of Pakistan announced that his country would immediately recognize the new regime and offered a gift of 50,000 tons of rice in addition to a generous gift of clothing. India, however, suffered a setback in its relations with Bangladesh.

After several coups Ziaur Rahman, the Chief of Army Staff became the Chief martial Law Administrator of Bangladesh in November 1976. Zia made repatriate Major General Hussain Muhammad Ershad the deputy army chief of staff. Having consolidated his position in the army, Zia became president on 21 April 1977 and seemed to be supported by a majority of Bangladeshis.

In May 1977, with his power base increasingly secure, Zia drew on his popularity to promote a nineteen-point political and economic program. Zia focused on the need to boost Bangladeshi production, especially in food and grains, and to integrate rural development through a variety of programs, of which population planning was the most important. He heeded the advice of international lending agencies and launched an ambitious rural development program in 1977, which included a highly visible and popular food-for-work program.

One of the most important tasks Zia faced was to change the direction of the country. Zia altered the Constitution's ideological statement on the fundamental principles, in particular changing the Mujibist emphasis on secularism to "complete trust and faith in almighty Allah." While distancing Bangladesh from India, Zia sought to improve ties with other Islamic nations. Throughout his regime, Zia pursued an active foreign policy, and the legacy of his efforts continued to bear fruit in the late 1980s. In 1980 Zia proposed a conference for the seven nations of the subcontinent (Bangladesh, Bhutan, India, Maldives, Nepal, Pakistan, and Sri Lanka) to discuss the prospects for regional cooperation in a number of fields. This initiative was successful in August 1983 when the South Asian Association for Regional Cooperation (SAARC) was established.

In April 1978, Zia announced that elections would be held to "pave the way to democracy," adding that the Constitution would be amended to provide for an independent judiciary as well as a "sovereign parliament." Zia also lifted the ban on political parties. He was supported by a "national front," whose main party was the Jatiyo Ganatantrik Dal (National Democratic Party). As the candidate of the Jatiyo Ganatantrik Dal-led Nationalist Front, Zia won overwhelmingly, taking 76.7% of the vote. After campaigning by Zia, the Bangladesh Nationalist Party won 207 of the 300 seats in Parliament with about 44% of the vote.

Zia was assassinated in Chittagong on 30 May 1981, in a plot allegedly masterminded by Major General Manzur, the army commander in Chittagong. The army, under its chief of staff, Major General Ershad, remained loyal to the Dhaka government and quickly put down the rebellion, killing Manzur. In the trials that followed, a sizable number of officers and enlisted men received the death penalty for complicity.

After Zia's assassination, Vice President Sattar became acting president and, as the Constitution stipulates, called for new elections for president within 180 days. Although there was some speculation that Zia's widow, Begum Khalida Ziaur Rahman, and Mujib's daughter, Sheikh Hasina Wajed, would be candidates, Sattar ran against a number of political unknowns in the November election and won the presidential election with two-thirds of the vote. Immediately following the 1981 election, Ershad pushed Sattar for a constitutional role for the military in the governance of the country. On 24 March 1982, Ershad dismissed Sattar, dissolved the cabinet and the Parliament, and assumed full powers under martial law.

In January 1985, it was announced that parliamentary elections would be held in April, to be preceded by a partial relaxation of martial law: the Constitution was to be fully restored after the elections. In order to be eligible to contest the elections as a candidate in the presidential election in October 1986, Ershad Joined the Jatiya Dal, being elected as Chairman of the party and nominated as its presidential candidate. In the presidential election, which was boycotted by both the Bangladesh Nationalist Party (BNP) and the Awami League (AL), Ershad won an overwhelming victory.

In the Parliamentary elections, which were held in February 1991 the BNP alliance won an overall majority and, following discussions with the Jamaat-e-Islami, as a result of which the BNP was ensured a small working majority in the Jatiya Sangsad, Begum Khaleda Zia assumed office as Prime Minster. In September the BNP had gained an absolute majority in the Jatiya Sangsad, following the party's victory in a number of by-elections.

The main political parties are the Awami League and the Bangladesh Nationalist Party (BNP). The AL, which spearheaded the war of independence under Sheikh Mujib, is now led by his daughter, Sheikh Hasina. The differences between the AL and the BNP in terms of official economic policy have largely disappeared. While AL plays on its leading role during the war of liberation in 1971 and attacks those who opposed it, the BNP appeals more broadly to nationalist forces, drawing support from forces that had been on both sides of the liberation war.

On 11 January 2007, following widespread violence, a caretaker government was appointed to administer the next general election. The country had suffered from extensive corruption, disorder and political violence. The new caretaker government made it a priority to root out corruption from all levels of government. To this end, many notable politicians and officials, along with large numbers of lesser officials and party members, were arrested on corruption charges. The caretaker government held a fair and free election on 29 December 2008. Awami League's Sheikh Hasina won the elections with a landslide victory and took oath of Prime Minister on 6 January 2009. The ruling alliance got 230 seats among 300 seats in the parliament.

Geography

Bangla Desh is a country of 144,000 square kilometres with a land area 133,910 square kilometres. Its topography is of a broad deltaic plain besides the Chittagong Hills in the southeast, low hills in the northeast and modest-elevation highlands in the north and northwest.

Bangladesh is located in the low-lying Ganges-Brahmaputra River Delta or Ganges Delta. This delta is formed by the confluence of the Ganges (Padma), Brahmaputra (Jamuna), and Meghna rivers and their respective tributaries. The Ganges unites with the Jamuna (main channel of the Brahmaputra) and later joins the Meghna to eventually empty into the Bay of Bengal. The alluvial soil deposited by these rivers has created some of the most fertile plains in the world. Bangladesh has 58 trans-boundary rivers, making water issues politically complicated to resolve - in most cases as the lower riparian state to India. Most parts of Bangladesh are less than 12 metres (39 ft) above sea level, and it is believed that about 50% of the land would be flooded if the sea level were to rise by 1 metre.

The highest point in Bangladesh is in Mowdok range at 1,052 metres in the Chittagong Hill Tracts to the southeast of the country. A major part of the coastline comprises a marshy jungle, the Sundarbans, the largest mangrove forest in the world and home to diverse flora and fauna, including the Royal Bengal Tiger. In 1997, this region was declared endangered.

Straddling the Tropic of Cancer, Bangladeshi climate is tropical with a mild winter from October to March, a hot, humid summer from March to June. A warm and humid monsoon season lasts from June to

October and supplies most of the country's rainfall. Natural calamities, such as floods, tropical cyclones, tornadoes, and tidal bores occur almost every year, combined with the effects of deforestation, soil degradation and erosion. Cox's Bazar, south of the city of Chittagong, has a beach that stretches uninterrupted over 120 kilometres.

In September 1998 Bangladesh saw the most severe flooding the modern world has seen. Although only 1,000 people were killed, 30 million were made homeless and 130,000 cattle were killed, 50 square kilometres of land were destroyed and 11,000 km of roads were damaged or destroyed. 66% of the country was underwater. There were several reasons for the severity of the flooding. Firstly, there were unusually high monsoon rains. Secondly, the Himalayas shed off an equally unusually high amount of melt water that year. Lastly, trees that usually intercept rain water were cut down for fire wood or to make space for animals.

Population

Bangladesh is the 7th most populous nation in the world. With a land area of 144,000 square kilometres, the population density is remarkable. Bangladesh's population growth was among the highest in the world in the 1960s and 1970s, when the country grew from 50 to 90 million, but with the promotion of birth control in the 1980s, the growth rate slowed.

The majority ethnic group of Bangladesh is the Bengali people, comprising 98% of the population. The remainder are mostly Bihari migrants and indigenous tribal groups. There are thirteen tribal groups located in the Chittagong Hill Tracts, the most populous of the tribes are the Chakmas. The region has been a source of ethnic tension since the inception of Bangladesh. The largest tribal groups outside the Hill Tracts are the Santhals and the Garos (Achiks). There are also Kaibartta, Meitei,Mundas, Oraons, and Zomi ethnic groups. Human trafficking has been a lingering problem in Bangladesh and illegal immigration has remained a cause of friction with Burma and India.

The official and most widely used language in Bangladesh, as in West Bengal, is Bengali or Bangla. English is used as second language among the middle and upper classes and in higher education.

Health and education levels have recently improved. Most Bangladeshis are rural, living on subsistence farming. Health problems abound, ranging from surface water contamination, to arsenic contamination of groundwater, and diseases including malaria, leptospirosis and dengue. The literacy rate in Bangladesh is approximately 41%. There is gender disparity, though, as literacy rates are 50% among men and 31% among women.

Religion

The major religion practiced in Bangladesh is Islam (89.7%) and a sizable minority adheres to Hinduism (9.2%). About 96% of the Muslims are Sunni while over 3% are Shi'a. Ethnic Biharis are predominantly Shia Muslims. Other religious groups include Buddhists (0.7%, mostly Theravada), Christians (0.3%, mostly of the Roman Catholic denomination), and Animists (0.1%). Bangladesh ranks fourth after Indonesia, Pakistan, and India by the number of Muslims, with over 130 million. Islam is the state religion of Bangladesh.

Economy

Bangladesh has seen a dramatic increase in foreign direct investment. In order to enhance economic growth, the government set up several export processing zones to attract foreign investment. These are managed by the Bangladesh Export Processing Zone Authority. The insufficient power supply constitutes an obstacle to growth. According to the World Bank, "among Bangladesh's most significant obstacles to growth are poor governance and weak public institutions." In April 2010, Standard & Poor's awarded Bangladesh a BB- for a long term in credit rating which is below India and well over Pakistan and Sri Lanka in South Asia.

One significant contributor to the development of the economy has been the widespread propagation of microcredit by Muhammad Yunus (awarded the Nobel Peace Prize in 2006) through the Grameen Bank. By the late 1990s, Grameen Bank had 2.3 million members, along with 2.5 million members of other similar organisations.

Bangladesh government is planning for construction of the largest deep sea port in South Asia at Sonadia Island. The 500 billion taka project will be completed in multiple phases and enable Bangladesh to service the whole region as a maritime transport and logistics hub. India, China, Bhutan, Nepal and other neighbouring countries will be able to take full advantage of the strategic location and Bangladesh's LDC status for exporting their goods, which are manufactured in Bangladesh. Furthermore, with $7.5 billion a new international airport will be constructed. The airport is being modelled on Thailand's Suvarnabhumi Airport in size and capacity.

To ease the chaotic traffic congestion in the capital Dhaka the government plans to construct more expressways, freeways, and flyovers. There is a plan to build an overhead Rapid transit called Dhaka Metro, but the progress is slow and controversial because of contracts and agreements.

Recently the government of Bangladesh signed a deal with a Chinese company to provide high-speed modern DEMU trains and is also going to construct metro rail system and high-speed electric powered inter-city rail network. More airports, bridge (such as the multi-billion Padma Bridge project) national highways are also being constructed to facilitate trade and regional development.

Infrastructure

Rivers. Bangladesh has as extensive and complex network of some 700 rivers. The major systems are the Jamuna-Brahmaputra, Padma-Ganges, Surma-Meghna, and Padma-Meghna, all of which flow south into the Bay of Bengal. It is the primary transportation system employing nearly 300,000 small and medium-sized country boats, with about 8,430 kilometres of navigable waterways.

Roads. About 16,890 kilometres of motorable roads. Despite severe flooding, it is an important means of moving people and goods, with an extensive network of bridges and ferries cross numerous inland waterways all over the country.

Railroads. About 2,818 kilometres of track, operated by Bangladesh Railways.

Ports. Chittagong and Chalna are major freight-handling ports.

Airports. Largest near Dhaka (Zia International Airport) and at Chittagong and Sylhet.

Government and Politics

Bangladesh has a parliamentary form of government with a popularly elected prime minister. The 1972 Constitution amended numerous times to reflect new political realities as the country has also had a presidential form of government. There is a unicameral Parliament (known as Jatiyo Sansad, or House of the People) with 300 members.

Authoritarian or military regimes have run Bangladesh almost since its inception. The regime in power traditionally controls government and Parliament through a single national political party: under Sheikh Mujibur Rahman (1972-75), the Awami League (People's League); under Ziaur Rahman (1977-81), the Bangladesh Nationalist Party; and under Hussain Muhammad Ershad, and the Jatiyo Party (National Party). Numerous opposition parties joined periodically in fractious alliances against the party in power e.g. Awami League, centrist Bangladesh Nationalist Party, leftist Jatiyo Samajtantrik Dal (National Socialist Party), and conservative, pro-Islamic Jamaat e Islami (Congregation of Islam). Student and workers' wings of these parties are important players in national politics.

Two radical Islamist parties, Jagrata Muslim Janata Bangladesh (JMJB) and Jama'atul Mujahideen Bangladesh (JMB), were banned in February 2005. Bomb attacks taking place since 1999 have been blamed on those groups, and hundreds of suspected members have been detained in numerous security operations, including the head of those two parties in 2006. The first recorded case of a suicide bomb attack in Bangladesh took place in November 2005.

Foreign Policy

Bangladesh pursues a moderate foreign policy that places heavy reliance on multinational diplomacy, especially at the United Nations. In 1974 Bangladesh joined both the Commonwealth of Nations and the United Nations and has since been elected to serve two terms on the Security Council in 1978-79 and 2000-01. In the 1980s, Bangladesh played a lead role in founding the South Asian Association for Regional Cooperation (SAARC) in order to expand relations with other South Asian states.

India. Bangladesh's most important and complex foreign relationship is with India. This relationship is formed by historical and cultural ties and is strengthened because of India's involvement in liberating the people of Bangladesh from Pakistan. This forms an important part of the domestic political discourse. Bangladesh's relationship with India began on a positive note because of India's assistance in the independence war and subsequent reconstruction. Throughout the years, the relationship between the two countries has fluctuated for a number of reasons. A major source of tension between Bangladesh and India is the Farakka Dam. However, both countries recognize the importance of good relations, regional security and South Asian economic integration. In 2009, Bangladeshi security forces launched a crackdown on Indian insurgents hiding in the country's border regions, captured and deported the leaders of several insurgent groups. Bangladesh and India have also agreed to develop regional connectivity and economic integration, along with Nepal and Bhutan. India's eastern states, as well as Nepal and Bhutan, are keen to gain access to Bangladesh's Chittagong and Mongla ports.

China. Bangladesh enjoys very warm ties with the People's Republic of China, and particularly in the past decade, there has been increased economic cooperation between them. Between 2006 and 2007, trade between the two nations rose by 28.5% and there have been agreements to grant various Bangladeshi commodities tariff-free access to the Chinese market. Cooperation between the Military of Bangladesh and the People's Liberation Army is also increasing, with joint military agreements signed and Bangladesh procuring Chinese arms which range from small arms to large naval surface combat ships such as the Chinese Type 053H1 Missile Frigate.

Pakistan. Pakistan was hostile to Bangladesh in the early 1970s, but by 1974 it was apparent that the new nation would stand on its own, and Pakistan recognised Bangladesh. Diplomatic relations were established in January 1976, followed by the reestablishment of communications and transportation links. Two major areas of disagreement between Bangladesh and Pakistan stem from the dislocations resulting from the independence struggle. The first concerned the finances of united Pakistan. After the war, Bangladesh claimed that it deserved a share of the US$4 billion worth of pre-independence exchange, bank credit, and movable assets protected in West Pakistan. In a 1975 agreement, Bangladesh accepted half of Pakistan's pre-1971 external debt, but asset sharing issues remain unresolved. The second issue concerns the emigration of nearly 540,000 Biharis (non-Bengali Muslims) to Pakistan after the war.

Myanmar. It is the only nation besides India that shares a border with Bangladesh. Relations between the two countries have generally been cordial, but relations deteriorated in 1978 and 1979 when 150,000 Bengali-descent Muslims flooded into Bangladesh from Myanmar. It brought to light anti-Bengali

feelings in western Myanmar. Intervention by the UN led to a negotiated repatriation of the refugees and the reestablishment of good relations. Later talks led to the demarcation of the land boundary between the two countries. Bangladesh and Myanmar have also settled their maritime boundary.

The United States. The US is a major development partner of Bangladesh, and has given over five billion dollars in aid since 1972. The two countries also cooperate in counter-terrorism and promote regional cooperation in South Asia. Bangladesh participated in the US-led coalition during the 1991 Gulf War to liberate Kuwait, and supports the US-led reconstruction of Afghanistan. The US Military has also engaged in disaster management and relief operations in Bangladesh, in the aftermath of several devastating floods and cyclones, including the 1991 Bangladesh cyclone and Cyclone Sidr. On the economic front, the US is Bangladesh's largest export destination. American companies are also the largest foreign investors in Bangladesh, with major investments in the country's natural gas reserves by Chevron and Conoco Philips.

Armed Forces

Since its establishment in 1972, immediately after independence in 1971, the military of Bangladesh was not required to fight any war against an external force. It has, however, faced a troubled situation in maintaining law and order in the Chittagong Hill Tracts of the country for a protracted period of time since 1980s. The role of the Navy in containing smuggling through the seaways is insignificant. However, in November 2008, Bangladesh Navy effectively staved off economic aggression by Myanmar in the seas of Bangladesh. Occasionally the military forces have been called to participate in social activities like rehabilitation of people following a flood or cyclone. Since 2002, it has been involved in maintaining law and order situation within the country. This was institutionalised through formation of a military based police force called Rapid Action Battalion, RAB in short, of Bangladesh Police.

Since the 1990s, it has earned international reputation by working as part of UN Peace Keeping Missions in different countries of the world. In popular perception, the Bangladesh military is a privileged class of the society and recognised as a disciplined and well-trained national institution that can tackle critical national phases. However assassination of two presidents of the country in 1975 and 1981 and overthrow of an elected government in 1982 by the military has rendered it a potential opponent to the political and democratic system of the country. In 1996 too, the military made a mobilisation without presidential authority. Yet, all political government in effect patronize the military, reflected in higher budgetary provision and enhancement of seniority vis-a-vis civil bureaucrats. Critics often call into question the necessity of a full-fledged military in a small country like Bangladesh, engulfed by India on three sides.

The budget allocated for the military is considered inordinately high that leaves lesser resources for country's growth and development. In all, the role of the military is opaque. However, its power-base remains unquestionable. The Bangladesh military killed President Sheikh Mujibur Rahman in 1975 and President Ziaur Rahman in 1981. It toppled the democratically elected government of the country and captured state power in 1982. Besides the illegitimate and bloody incidents of 1975, 1981 and 1982, the military determined the course of the country politics after the end of the Bangladesh Nationalist Party (BNP) regime in October 2006. The change-over of January 2007, popularly known is considered as a silent coup, when Professor Iajuddin Ahmed was made to declare state of emergency and resign as Chief Adviser of the Caretaker government.

On the morning of 25 February 2008 more than one thousand personnel of the Bangladesh paramilitary force, Bangladesh Rifles (BDR) staged a mutiny at its headquarters in Dhaka at Pilkhana. For the next 33 hours, the mutineers held the BDR HQ, keeping several officers and civilians as hostage. Initially confined to Pilkhana, the mutiny spread to other outposts of BDR. There were reports of disobedience or violence from at least twelve other BDR outposts. The killings, however, were confined only to the HQ. By the end of the mutiny, 74 people including 56 officers had lost their lives. The mutiny shocked the entire nation leaving a question mark on the state of security in Bangladesh.

In addition to traditional defence roles, the military has been called on to provide support to civil authorities for disaster relief and internal security during periods of political unrest. Bangladesh contributed 2,300 troops during Operation Desert Storm in 1991, and is the world's largest contributor (10,736) to UN peacekeeping forces.

Environmental Challenges

Threats to the environmental security of Bangladesh are a cause of concern. They are floods, salinity, siltation, and cyclones. The dry season leads to recession of water in the Ganges, which affects Khulna and other neighbouring districts causing increased salinity in the rivers and streams, posing a serious threat to agriculture and industrial activities. Salinity also affects the flora and fauna in the Sunderbans forests. According to experts, the soil character of Bangladesh is undergoing changes because of siltation and salinity. Bangladesh holds the view that construction of barrage, in India, upstream of the river has aggravated the situation.

Periodic floods also cause destruction to agriculture, roads and human lives affecting the economic and social life of Bangladesh. Also, the level of arsenic in the ground water has reached a dangerous level. According the experts Bangladesh is in the midst of the biggest mass poisoning in history, having more than five times the amount considered acceptable in 46 districts.

BHUTAN

Bhutan is a landlocked nation in the Himalaya Mountains. Its flag is rectangular and divided diagonally from the lower left side corner. The upper part is yellow, symbolising the secular power of the king, while the lower part is orange, representing the Buddhist religion. Across the middle a white dragon (druk) is depicted, which symbolizes purity. The jewels held tightly in the dragon's claws symbolize wealth. The roaring mouth represents the strength of deities protecting the country.

Bhutan has a land boundary of 1,075 kilometres (China 470 kilometres, India 605 kilometres). Bhutan is one of the most isolated and least developed nations in the world. Nonetheless, it has been described as the happiest least developed country on earth. Foreign influences and tourism are heavily regulated by the government to preserve the country's traditional culture and national identity. The landscape ranges from subtropical plains in the south to the Himalayan heights in the north, with some peaks exceeding seven thousand metres. Mahayana Buddhism is the state religion and the population is predominantly Buddhist, with Hinduism being the second most dominant. Thimphu is the capital and largest city.

History

Until the early 17th century, Bhutan existed as a patchwork of minor warring fiefdoms when the area was unified by the lama and military leader Shabdrung Ngawang Namgyal. To defend the country against intermittent Tibetan forays, Namgyal built a network of impregnable dzong (fortresses), and promulgated a code of law that helped to bring local lords under centralised control.

During the 1870s, power struggles between the rival valleys of Paro and Trongsa led to civil war in Bhutan, eventually leading to the ascendancy of Ugyen Wangchuck, the ponlop (governor) of Tongsa. From his power base in central Bhutan, Ugyen Wangchuck defeated his political enemies and united the country following several civil wars and rebellions in the period 1882-85.

In 1907, an epochal year for the country, Ugyen Wangchuck was unanimously chosen as the hereditary king of the country by an assembly of leading Buddhist monks, government officials, and heads of important families. The British government promptly recognised the new monarchy, and in 1910 Bhutan signed a treaty which "let" Great Britain "guide" Bhutan's foreign affairs. In reality this did not mean much. It also did not seem to apply to Bhutan's traditional relations with Tibet. The greatest impact of this treaty seems to be the perception that it meant Bhutan was not totally sovereign. After India gained independence from the United Kingdom on 15 August 1947, Bhutan became one of the first countries to recognize India's independence. A treaty similar to the one of 1910 was signed on 8 August 1949 with India.

In 1953, King Jigme Dorji Wangchuck established the country's legislature—a 130-member National Assembly—to promote a more democratic form of governance. In 1965, he set up a Royal Advisory Council, and in 1968 he formed a Cabinet. In 1971,

Capital	-	Thimphu
Official language	-	Dzongkha
Government	-	Constitutional democratic monarchy
	-	King Jigme Khesar Namgyel Wangchuck
	-	Prime Minister Jigme Y. Thinley
Area	-	38,394 square kilometres
Population	-	742,737 (2012 estimate) Density 18/ square kilometre
GDP (PPP)	-	$4.287 billion (2011 estimate) Per capita $6,112
GDP (nominal)	-	$1.488 billion (2011 estimate) Per capita $2,121
Chief Operations Officer	-	Maj Gen Batoo Tshering

Bhutan was admitted to the United Nations, having held observer status for three years. In July 1972, Jigme Singye Wangchuck ascended to the throne at the age of 16 after the death of his father, Dorji Wangchuck.

In the 1980s, in order strengthen Bhutan's identity as a nation, the "one nation, one people" campaign was started to foster greater integration of the peripheral ethnic and cultural groups into main stream Bhutanese society. The age old code of conduct, known as Driglam namzha and usage of the official national language Dzongkha was promoted. Around the same time, a nation-wide census revealed a huge influx of illegal immigrants of Nepali origin, into Southern Bhutan. When the government attempted to remove the illegal settlers, there was a violent backlash; numerous acts of terrorism were carried out against government schools, hospitals, offices and neutral Southern Bhutanese. In order to re-establish order in the south, the government was forced to draft many young men and able bodied civil servants into a militia force. Eventually order was restored; along with the illegal settlers, a number of political dissidents and Southern Bhutanese who had rebelled against the country, fled to Nepal, where they were admitted into United Nations run camps and given refugee status. Despite the best efforts of the governments of Bhutan, Nepal and India, as well as outside parties such as the United Nations, European Union and the United States, a viable solution to this problem proves to be still elusive.

In 1998, King Jigme Singye Wangchuck introduced significant political reforms, transferring some of his powers to the Prime Minister and allowing for impeachment of the King by a two-thirds majority of the National Assembly. In late 2003, the Bhutanese army successfully launched a large-scale operation to flush out anti-India insurgents who were operating training camps in southern Bhutan.

In 1999, the government lifted a ban on television and the Internet, making Bhutan one of the last countries to introduce television. In his speech, the King said that television was a critical step to the modernisation of Bhutan as well as a major contributor to the country's Gross National Happiness (Bhutan is the only country to measure happiness) but warned against the misuse of television which may erode traditional Bhutanese values. Some believe it has indeed affected Bhutan in a negative way.

Bhutan is a predominantly Buddhist country, with the religion forming an integral part of everyday life. A new constitution was presented in early 2005 which will be put up for ratification by a referendum before coming into force. King Jigme Singye Wangchuck introduced significant political reforms, transferring most of his administrative powers to the Council of Cabinet Ministers. On 14 December 2006, Jigme Singye Wangchuck announced that he was abdicating his throne. Bhutan entered a new era of democracy, starting with its first elections in 2008. On 6 November 2008, 28-year old Jigme Khesar Namgyel Wangchuck, eldest son of King Jigme

Singye Wangchuck, was crowned King of the Himalayan Kingdom, becoming the world's youngest reigning monarch and head of the newest democracy.

On 8 February 2007, the Indo-Bhutan Friendship Treaty was substantially revised. Whereas in the Treaty of 1949 Article 2 read as "The Government of India undertakes to exercise no interference in the internal administration of Bhutan. On its part the Government of Bhutan agrees to be guided by the advice of the Government of India in regard to its external relations." In the revised treaty it now reads as "In keeping with the abiding ties of close friendship and cooperation between Bhutan and India, the Government of the Kingdom of Bhutan and the Government of the Republic of India shall cooperate closely with each other on issues relating to their national interests. Neither Government shall allow the use of its territory for activities harmful to the national security and interest of the other." The revised treaty also includes in it the preamble "Reaffirming their respect for each other's independence, sovereignty and territorial integrity;" an element that was absent in the earlier version. The Indo-Bhutan Friendship Treaty of 2007 strengthens Bhutan's status as an independent and sovereign nation.

The new democratic system comprises an upper and lower house, the latter based on political party affiliations. Elections for the upper house (National Council) were held on 31 December 2007, while elections for the lower house, the 47-seat National Assembly, were held on 24 March 2008. Two political parties, the People's Democratic Party (PDP) headed by Sangay Ngedup, and the Druk Phuensum Tshogpa (DPT) headed by Jigmi Thinley, competed in the National Assembly election. The Druk Phuensum Tshogpa won the elections taking 45 out of 47 seats in the parliament. Judicial power is vested in the courts of Bhutan. The Chief Justice is the administrative head of the Judiciary.

Economy

The Ngultrum is the currency of Bhutan and its value is pegged to the Indian rupee. The rupee is also accepted as legal tender in the country. Incomes of over Nu 100,000 per annum are taxed, but very few wage and salary earners qualify. Bhutan's inflation rate was estimated at about 3% in 2003. Bhutan has a Gross Domestic Product of around USD 2.913 billion (adjusted to Purchasing Power Parity).

Though Bhutan's economy is one of the world's smallest, it has grown very rapidly with about 8% in

2005 and 14% in 2006. This was mainly due to the commissioning of the gigantic Tala Hydroelectricity project. As of March 2006, Bhutan's per capita income was US$ 1,321 making it one of the fastest growing in South Asia. Bhutan's standard of living is growing faster than that of its neighbouring countries and is one of the highest in South Asia. Bhutan's small economy is based on agriculture, forestry, and the sale of hydroelectric power to India. Agriculture provides the main livelihood for more than 80% of the population. Agrarian practices consist largely of subsistence farming and animal husbandry. Handicrafts, particularly weaving and the manufacture of religious art for home altars are a small cottage industry and a source of income for some.

A landscape that varies from hilly to ruggedly mountainous has made the building of roads, and other infrastructure, difficult and expensive. This, and a lack of access to the sea, has meant that Bhutan has never been able to benefit from significant trading of its produce. Bhutan does not have a railway system, though Indian Railways plans to link up southern Bhutan with its vast network under an agreement signed in January 2005. The historic trade routes over the high Himalayas, which connected India to Tibet, have been closed since the 1959 military takeover of Tibet (although smuggling activity still brings Chinese goods into Bhutan).

The industrial sector is minimal, production being of the cottage-industry type. Most development projects, such as road construction, rely on Indian contract labour. Agricultural produce includes rice, chillies, dairy (yak) products, buckwheat, barley, root crops, apples, and citrus and maize at lower elevations. Industries include cement, wood products, processed fruits, alcoholic beverages and calcium carbide.

Government revenues total 122 million ($146 million), though expenditures amount $152 million. 60% of the budget expenditure, however, is financed by India's Ministry of External Affairs. Bhutan's exports - principally electricity, cardamom, gypsum, timber, handicrafts, cement, fruit, precious stones and spices - total $154 million. Imports, however, amount to $196 million, leading to a trade deficit. Main items imported include fuel and lubricants, grain, machinery, vehicles, fabrics and rice. Bhutan's main export partner is India, accounting for 87.9% of its export goods. Bangladesh (4.6%) and the Philippines (2%) are the other two top export partners. As its border with Tibet is closed, trade between Bhutan and China is now almost non-existent. Bhutan's import partners include India (71.3%), Japan (7.8%) and Austria (3%).

Demographics

Among the Bhutanese people, several principal ethnic groups may be distinguished. The second dominant group is the Ngalops, a Buddhist group based in the western part of the country. Their culture is closely related to that of Tibet. Much the same could be said of the Sharchops ("Easterners")the dominant group, who are associated with the eastern part of Bhutan (but who traditionally follow the Nyingmapa rather than the official Drukpa Kagyu form of Tibetan Buddhism). They are called the Eastern Bhutanese and Western Bhutanese respectively. In modern times, with improving transportation infrastructure, there has been much intermarrying between Easterners and Westerners, due to the closeness of their cultures and traditions. In the early 1970s, intermarriage between the Lhotsampas and main stream Bhutanese society was encouraged by the government.

The national language is Dzongkha, one of 53 languages in the Tibetan language family. The script, here called Chhokey ("Dharma Language"), is identical with the Tibetan script. A number of Nepali dialects are spoken in parts of southern Bhutan. Khengkha is spoken in central Bhutan. In the schools English is the medium of instruction and Dzongkha is taught as the national language. 24 languages are currently spoken in Bhutan, all of them in the Tibeto-Burman family, except Nepali, an Indo-Aryan language. Till the 1980's the government sponsored the teaching of Nepali in schools in Southern Bhutan. However, after the violent insurgency in the south, Nepali was removed from the curriculum. The languages of Bhutan are still not well-characterised, and several have yet to be recorded in an in-depth academic grammar. English now has official status as well.

The literacy rate is only 42.2% (56.2% of males and 28.1% of females), 14-year olds and younger comprise 39.1%, while people between 15 and 59 comprise 56.9%, and those over 60 are only 4%. The country has a median age of 20.4 years. Bhutan has a life expectancy of 62.2 years (61 for males and 64.5 for females) according to the latest data from the World Bank. There are 1,070 males to every 1,000 females in the country

Military and Foreign Affairs

The Royal Bhutan Army is Bhutan's military service. It includes the Royal Bodyguard and the Royal Bhutan Police. Membership is voluntary, and the minimum age for recruitment is 18. The standing army numbers about 6,000 and is trained by the Indian Army. It has an annual budget of about US$13.7 million—1.8% of the GDP.

Though the 1949 Treaty with India is still sometimes misinterpreted to mean that India controls Bhutan's foreign affairs, Bhutan today handles all of its foreign affairs itself including the sensitive (to India) border demarcation issue with China. Bhutan has diplomatic relations with 22 countries, including the European Union, with missions in India, Bangladesh, Thailand and Kuwait. It has two UN missions, one in New York and one in Geneva. Only India and Bangladesh have residential embassies in Bhutan, while Thailand has a consulate office in Bhutan.

By a long standing treaty, Indian and Bhutanese citizens may travel to each other's countries without a passport or visa using their national identity cards instead. Bhutanese citizens may also work in India without legal restriction. Bhutan does not have formal diplomatic ties with its northern neighbour, China, although exchanges of visits at various levels between the two have significantly increased in the recent past. The first bilateral agreement between China and Bhutan was signed in 1998, and Bhutan has also set up consulates in Macau and Hong Kong. Bhutan's border with China is largely not demarcated and thus disputed in some places.

On 13 November 2005, Chinese soldiers crossed into Bhutan under the pretext that environmental conditions had forced their retreat south from the Himalayas. The Bhutanese government allowed this incursion (after the fact) on humanitarian grounds. Soon after, the Chinese began building roads and bridges within Bhutanese territory. Bhutanese Foreign Minister Khandu Wangchuk took up the matter with Chinese authorities after the issue was raised in Bhutanese parliament. In response, Foreign Ministry spokesman Qin Gang of the People's Republic of China has said that the border remains in dispute (completely ignoring the original official pretext for the incursion) and that the two sides continue to work for a peaceful and cordial resolution of the dispute.

Security issues

Bhutan is bounded on three sides by India. From east to west, the Indian states of Sikkim, West Bengal, Assam, and Arunachal Pradesh border Bhutan. In view of the long-standing political disputes and border confrontations between India and China, Bhutan has long been part of India's strategic defence plan. In the view of some Indian strategists, Bhutan is a weak link in India's defence against China.

The key document guiding relations with India is the Treaty of Friendship between the Government of India and the Government of Bhutan of 1949. The ten-article treaty, in force in perpetuity, calls for peace between the two countries and assures Indian non-interference in Bhutan's internal affairs in return for Bhutan's agreeing "to be guided by the advice of the Government of India in regard to its external relations". It also guarantees free trade between the countries and duty-free transit across India of Bhutan's imports. Furthermore, the treaty assures the rights of citizens of each country and the extradition of criminals seeking refuge in either country.

Events in Tibet have had causal effects on Bhutan-Indian relations. The Indo-Bhutanese border was delineated in the Treaty of Peace of 1865 between Bhutan and Britain, but it was not until the period between 1973 and 1984 that a detailed delineation and demarcation was made. Border demarcation talks with India generally resolved disagreements except for several small sectors, including the middle zone between Sarbhang and Geylegphug and the eastern frontier with Arunachal Pradesh.

In the 1960s Bhutan joined international organisations. It first became a member of the Colombo Plan in 1962, which put the kingdom into contact with member states throughout South Asia and Southeast Asia for fostering cooperative economic development. UN membership was achieved in 1971. A founding member of SAARC in 1983, Bhutan has also established relations with the Coordination Bureau of the Nonaligned Countries (the headquarters of the Nonaligned Movement), the Group of 77, the Asian Development Bank, and the European Community. In 1975 Bhutan and four other landlocked Asian countries (Afghanistan, Laos, Mongolia, and Nepal) were granted a special status as "least developed landlocked countries" by the UN Economic and Social Commission for Asia and the Pacific (ESCAP) in coordination with the United Nations Conference on Trade and Development (UNCTAD) and UNDP. Despite these organisations' intentions to assist Bhutan and the other countries in dealing with international transit problems, Bhutan declined to participate in their work.

Perhaps the most significant international participation Bhutan embarked on in the 1980s was membership in SAARC. Bhutan became involved in useful working group discussions on agriculture and livestock, rural development, meteorology, telecommunications, science and technology, health and population, transportation, postal cooperation, and trade and industrial cooperation.

CHINA

The outbreak of revolution on 10 October 1911 signalled the collapse of the Qing Dynasty (1644-1911), which was formally replaced by the government of the Republic of China on 12 February 1912. The People's Republic of China was officially established on 1 October 1949, replacing the Republic of China government on mainland China.

The flag of China is red with a large yellow five-pointed star and four smaller yellow five-pointed stars (arranged in a vertical arc toward the middle of the flag) in the upper hoist-side corner. The colour red symbolizes the spirit of the revolution, and the five stars signify the unity of the people of China under the leadership of the Chinese Communist Party.

Since the introduction of economic reforms in 1978, China has become the world's fastest-growing major economy. As of 2012, it is the world's second-largest economy, after the United States, by both nominal GDP and purchasing power parity (PPP), and is also the world's largest exporter and second-largest importer of goods. On a per capita income basis, China ranked 90th by nominal GDP and 91st by GDP (PPP) in 2011, according to the IMF. China is a recognised nuclear weapons state and has the world's largest standing army, with the second-largest defence budget. In 2003, China became the third nation in the world, after the former Soviet Union and the United States, to independently launch a successful manned space mission. China has been characterised as a potential superpower by a number of academics, military analysts, and public policy and economics analysts.

History

The communist takeover of the mainland in 1949 set the scene for building a new society built on a Marxist-Leninist model replete with class struggle and proletarian politics fashioned and directed by the CCP. The People's Republic of China was barely established when it perceived a threat from the United States, which was at war in North Korea, and elected to support its neighbour, the new communist state, the Democratic People's Republic of Korea. The Chinese People's Volunteer Army invaded the Korean Peninsula in October 1950 and, along with its North Korean ally, enjoyed initial military success and then a two-year stalemate, which culminated in an armistice signed on 27 July 1953. Meanwhile, China seized control of Tibet. It also had embarked on a political rectification movement against "enemies of the state" and promoting "class struggle" under the aegis of agrarian reform as part of the "transition to socialism."

Periods of consolidation and economic development facilitated by President Liu Shaoqi (1898-1969) and Premier Zhou were severely altered by disastrous anti-intellectual (such as the Hundred Flowers Campaign, 1957), economic (the Great Leap Forward, 1958-59), and political (the Great Proletarian Cultural Revolution, 1966-76) experiments directed by Mao and his supporters. During this time, China had broken with the Soviet Union by 1959, fought a border war with India in 1962, and skirmished with Soviet troops in 1969. The 1976 death of Mao ended the extremist influence in the party, and, under the leadership of Deng Xiaoping and his supporters,

Capital	-	Beijing
Largest city	-	Shanghai
National language	-	Standard Mandarin (spoken)
	-	Simplified Chinese (written)
Ethnic groups	-	91% Han; 11+ minor ethnic groups; 55 recognised minorities
Government	-	Single-party communist state
	-	President Xi Jinping
	-	Premier Li Keqiang
Legislature	-	National People's Congress
Establishment	-	People's Republic of China proclaimed 1 October 1949
Area	-	9,596,960 square kilometres
Coastline	-	14,500 kilometres
Population	-	1,347,351,000 (2011 estimate)
	-	Density 139.6/square kilometre
GDP (PPP)	-	$11,299 trillion (2011 estimate)
	-	Per capita $8,382
GDP (nominal)	-	$7,298 trillion (2011 estimate)
	-	Per capita $5,413
Defence Minister	-	General Lian Guanglie
Chief of General Staff	-	General Chen Bingde
Chief of Navy	-	Admiral Wu Shengli
Chief of Air Force	-	General Ma Xiaotian
Chief of Missile Forces	-	Gen Jing Zhiyuan

China began a period of pragmatic economic reforms and opening itself to the outside world.

Reform-era activities began in earnest in 1978 and eventually made China one of the largest world economies and trading partners as well as a regional military power. The Four Modernisations (agriculture, industry, science and technology, and national defence) became the preeminent agenda within the party, state, and society. The well-being of China's people increased substantially, especially along coastal areas and in urban areas involved in manufacturing for the world market. Yet, politics, the so-called "fifth modernisation," occurred at too slow a pace for the emerging generation. The democracy movement, however, was violently suppressed by the military in the 1989 Tiananmen incident.

In the years after Tiananmen, conservative reformers led by Deng protégé Jiang Zemin endured and eventually overcame world criticism. When Deng went into retirement, the rising generation of technocrats ruled China and oversaw its modernisation. Political progress gradually occurred. Term limits were placed on political and governmental positions at all levels, succession became orderly and contested elections began to take place at the local level. Tens of thousands of Chinese students went overseas to study; many returned to participate in the building of modern China, some to become millionaires in the new "socialist economy with Chinese characteristics."

As the 21st century began, a new generation of leaders emerged and gradually replaced the old. Hu Jintao emerged—by 2004—as the preeminent leader (president of China, chairman of both the state Central Military Commission and party Central Military Commission, and general secretary of the CCP). A concern is that the benefits of economic development has not been distributed evenly, resulting in a wide development gap between urban and rural areas. As a result, under President Hu Jintao and Premier Wen Jiabao, the Chinese government initiated policies to address these issues of equitable distribution of resources, though the outcome remains to be seen. More than 40 million farmers have been displaced from their land, usually for economic development, contributing to the 87,000 demonstrations and riots across China in 2005. Living standards have improved significantly but political controls remain tight. In addition, preparations for a major Communist Party leadership change in late 2012 were marked by factional disputes and political scandals, such as the fall from power of Chongqing official Bo Xilai.

Geography

China has a total of 22,117 kilometres of land boundaries with 14 other nations. These borders include. Afghanistan (76 kilometres), Bhutan (470 kilometres), Burma (2,185 kilometres), India (3,380 kilometres), Kazakhstan (1,533 kilometres), North Korea (1,416 kilometres), Kyrgyzstan (858 kilometres), Laos (423 kilometres), Mongolia (4,677 kilometres), Nepal (1,236 kilometres), Pakistan (523 kilometres), Russia (4,300 kilometres), Tajikistan (414 kilometres), and Vietnam (1,281 kilometres). China's coastline extends 14,500 kilometres from the border with North Korea in the north to Vietnam in the south. China is involved in a complex dispute with Malaysia, Philippines, Taiwan, Vietnam, and possibly Brunei over the Spratly (Nansha) Islands in the South China Sea. China also occupies the Paracel (Xisha) Islands, which are also claimed by Vietnam and Taiwan, and asserts a claim to the Japanese-administered Senkaku Islands (Diaoyu Tai) in the Pacific Ocean.

Most of the mountainous and militarised boundary with India is in dispute. China's de facto administration of the Aksai Chin section of Kashmir is the subject of a dispute between China and India. India does not recognize Pakistan's ceding lands to China in a 1964 boundary agreement. In October 2004, China signed an agreement with Russia on the delimitation of their entire 4,300-kilometre-long border, which had long been in dispute.

Principal Rivers. Mountains cover 33% of China's landmass, plateaus 26%, basins 19%, plains 12%, and hills 10%. Thus, 69% of China's land is mountains, hills, and highlands.

China has 50,000 rivers totaling some 420,000 kilometres in length and each having a catchment area of more than 100 square kilometres. Some 1,500 of these rivers each have catchment areas exceeding 1,000 square kilometres. Most rivers flow from west to east and empty into the Pacific Ocean. The Yangzi (Changjiang or Yangzte River), which rises in Tibet, flows through Central China, and, having traveled 6,300 kilometres, enters the Yellow Sea near Shanghai. The Yangzi has a catchment area of 1.8 million square kilometres and is the third longest river in the world after the Amazon and the Nile. The second longest river in China is the Huanghe (Yellow River), which also rises in Tibet and travels circuitously for 5,464 kilometres through North China before reaching the Bo Hai Gulf on the north coast of Shangdong Province. The Heilongjiang (Heilong or Black Dragon River) flows for 3,101 kilometres in Northeast China and an additional 1,249 in Russia, where it is known as the Amur. The longest river in South China is the Zhujiang (Pearl River), which is 2,214 kilometres long.

Natural Resources. China has substantial mineral reserves and is the world's largest producer of antimony, natural graphite, tungsten, and zinc. Other major minerals are bauxite, coal, crude petroleum, diamonds, gold, iron ore, lead, magnetite, manganese, mercury, molybdenum, natural gas, phosphate rock, tin, uranium, and vanadium. With its vast mountain ranges, China's hydropower potential is the largest in the world.

Land Use. 14.86% (about 1.4 million square kilometres) of China's land is arable. About 1.3% (some 116,580 square kilometres) is planted to permanent crops. With comparatively little land planted to permanent crops, intensive agricultural techniques are used to reap harvests that are sufficient to feed the world's largest population and still have surplus for export. An estimated 544,784 square kilometres of land is irrigated.

Environmental Factors. The major current environmental issues in China are air pollution (greenhouse gases and sulfur dioxide particulates) from over reliance on coal, which produces acid rain; water shortages, particularly in the north; water pollution from untreated wastes; deforestation; an estimated loss of 20% of agricultural land since 1949 to soil erosion and economic development and desertification. Deforestation has been a major contributor to China's most significant natural disaster - flooding. China's national carbon dioxide (CO2) emissions are among the highest in the world and increasing annually. The CO2 emissions are estimated at 2.8 billion tons. These amounts cited by the UN are more than double those of India and Japan but still less than half those of the United States. China's ozone depleting potential also is high. The CO2 emissions are mostly produced by coal-burning energy plants and other coal-burning operations. Better pollution control and billion-dollar cleanup programmes have helped reduced the growth rate of industrial pollution.

Time Zone. Although China crosses all or part of five international time zones, it operates on a single uniform time, China Standard Time (CST; Greenwich Mean Time plus eight hours), using Beijing as the base.

Society

Population. The most densely populated provinces are in the east. Jiangsu (712 persons per square kilometre), Shangdong (587 persons per square kilometre), and Henan (546 persons per square kilometre). Shanghai is the most densely populated municipality at 2,646 persons per square kilometre. The least densely populated areas are in the west, with Tibet having the lowest density at only 2 persons per square kilometre. Sixty-two percent of the population lived in rural areas in 2004, while 38% lived in urban settings. About 94% of population lives on approximately 46% of land. In the long term, China faces increasing urbanisation; according to predictions, nearly 70% of the population will live in urban areas by 2035.

Demography. China has been the world's most populous nation for many centuries. China now has an increasingly aging population; it is projected that 11.8% of the population in 2020 will be 65 years of age and older. Based on 2006 estimates, China's age structure is 0-14 years of age—20.8%; 15-64 years—71.4%, and 65 years and older—7.7%. Estimates made in 2006 indicate a birthrate of nearly 13.3 births per 1,000 and a death rate of 6.9 per 1,000.

Ethnic Groups. Besides the majority Han Chinese, China recognizes 55 other nationality or ethnic groups, numbering about 105 million persons, mostly concentrated in the northwest, north, northeast, south, and southwest but with some in central interior areas. Based on the 2000 census, some 91.5% of the population was classified as Han Chinese (1.1 billion). The other major minority ethnic groups were Zhuang (16.1 million), Manchu (10.6 million), Hui (9.8 million), Miao (8.9 million), Uighur (8.3 million), Tujia (8 million), Yi (7.7 million), Mongol (5.8 million), Tibetan (5.4 million), Bouyei (2.9 million), Dong (2.9 million), Yao (2.6 million), Korean (1.9 million), Bai (1.8 million), Hani (1.4 million), Kazakh (1.2 million), Li (1.2 million), and Dai (1.1 million). All nationalities in China are equal according to the law.

Languages. The official language of China is standard

Chinese or Mandarin (Putonghua, which means standard speech, based on the Beijing dialect). Because of the many ethnic groups in China, numerous minority languages also are spoken. All of the Chinese dialects share a common written form that has evolved and been standardised during two millennia and serves as a unifying bond amongst the Han Chinese. The government has aggressively developed both shorthand Chinese and Pinyin (phonetic spelling) as ways to increase literacy and transliterate Chinese names. The Pinyin system was introduced in 1958 and was approved by the State Council in 1978 as the standard system for the romanisation of Chinese personal and geographic names.

Religion. The traditional religions of China are Confucianism, Daoism, and Buddhism. Confucianism is not a religion, although some have tried to imbue it with rituals and religious qualities, but rather a philosophy and system of ethical conduct that since the 5th century B.C. has guided China's society. Kong Fuzi (Confucius in Latinized form) is honored in China as a great sage of antiquity whose writings promoted peace and harmony and good morals in family life and society in general. Ritualized reverence for one's ancestors, sometimes referred to as ancestor worship, has been a tradition in China since at least the Shang Dynasty (1750-1040 B.C.). In 2005 the Chinese government acknowledged that there were an estimated 100 million adherents to various sects of Buddhism and some 9,500 and 16,000 temples and monasteries, many maintained as cultural landmarks and tourist attractions. Approximately 8% of the population is Buddhist, approximately 1.5% is Muslim, an estimated 0.4% belongs to the government-sponsored "patriotic" Catholic Church, an estimated 0.4 to 0.6% belongs to the unofficial Vatican-affiliated Roman Catholic Church, and an estimated 1.2 to 1.5% is registered as Protestant. Most adherents of Islam are members of the Uighur and Hui nationality people.

Education and Literacy. The population has had on average only 6.2 years of schooling, but in 1986 the goal of nine years of compulsory education by 2000 was established. The education system provides free primary education for five years, starting at age seven, followed by five years of secondary education for ages 12 to 17. Since free higher education was abolished in 1985, applicants to colleges and universities compete for scholarships based on academic ability. Private schools have been allowed since the early 1980s. In 2003 China supported 1,552 institutions of higher learning (colleges and universities) and their 725,000 professors and 11 million students. While there is intense competition for admission to China's colleges and universities among college entrants, Beijing and Qinghua universities and more than 100 other key universities are the most sought after. The literacy rate in China is 90.9%, based on 2002 estimates.

Economy

As of 2012, China has the world's second-largest economy in terms of nominal GDP, totalling approximately US$7.298 trillion according to the International Monetary Fund (IMF). However, China's 2011 nominal GDP per capita of US$5,184 puts it behind around ninety countries (out of 183 countries on the IMF list) in global GDP per capita rankings. If PPP is taken into account in total GDP figures, China is again second only to the United States—in 2011, its PPP GDP reached $11.299 trillion, corresponding to $8,382 per capita.

From its founding in 1949 until late 1978, the People's Republic of China was a Soviet-style centrally planned economy, without private businesses or capitalism. To propel the country towards a modern, industrialised communist society, Mao Zedong instituted the Great Leap Forward in the early 1960s, although this had decidedly mixed economic results. Following Mao's death in 1976 and the consequent end of the Cultural Revolution, Deng Xiaoping and the new Chinese leadership began to reform the economy and move towards a more market-oriented mixed economy under one-party rule. Agricultural collectivisation was dismantled and farmlands were privatised to increase productivity. Modern-day China is mainly characterised as having a market economy based on private property ownership, and is one of the leading examples of state capitalism.

Under the post-Mao market reforms, a wide variety of small-scale private enterprises were encouraged, while the government relaxed price controls and promoted foreign investment. Foreign trade was focused upon as a major vehicle of growth, leading to the creation of Special Economic Zones (SEZs), first in Shenzhen and then in other Chinese cities. Inefficient state-owned enterprises (SOEs) were restructured by introducing western-style management systems, with unprofitable ones being closed outright, resulting in massive job losses. By the latter part of 2010, China was reversing some of its economic liberalisation initiatives, with state-owned companies buying up independent businesses in the steel, auto and energy industries.

Since economic liberalisation began in 1978, China's investment- and export-led economy has grown almost a hundredfold and is the fastest-growing major economy in the world. Between 2007 and 2011, China's economic growth rate was equivalent to all of the G7 countries' growth combined.

China is the third-most-visited country in the world, with 55.7 million inbound international visitors in 2010. It also experiences an enormous volume of domestic tourism; an estimated 740 million Chinese holidaymakers travelled within the country in October 2012 alone. China is a member of the WTO and is the world's second-largest trading power behind the US, with a total international trade value of US$3.64 trillion in 2011. Its foreign exchange reserves reached US$2.85 trillion by the end of 2010, an increase of 18.7% over the previous year, making its reserves by far the world's largest. China owns an estimated $1.6 trillion of US securities. China, holding US$1.16 trillion in US Treasury bonds, is the largest foreign holder of US public debt. China is the world's third-largest recipient of inward foreign direct investment (FDI), attracting $115 billion in 2011 alone, marking a 9% increase over 2010. China also increasingly invests abroad, with a total outward FDI of $68 billion in 2010.

China's success has been primarily due to manufacturing as a low-cost producer. This is attributed to a combination of cheap labour, good infrastructure, relatively high productivity, favourable government policy, and a possibly undervalued exchange rate. The latter has been sometimes blamed for China's huge trade surplus (US$262.7 billion in 2007) and has become a major source of dispute between China and its major trading partners—the US, EU, and Japan—despite the yuan having been de-pegged and having risen in value by 20% against the US dollar since 2005. China is moreover widely criticised for manufacturing large quantities of counterfeit goods—in 2005, the Asia Business Council alleged that the counterfeiting industry accounted for 8% of

China's GDP at the time.

The state still dominates in strategic "pillar" industries (such as energy and heavy industries), but private enterprise (composed of around 30 million private businesses) has expanded enormously; in 2005, it accounted for anywhere between 33% to 70% of national GDP, while the OECD estimate for that year was over 50% of China's national output, up from 1% in 1978. The Shanghai Stock Exchange has raised record amounts of IPOs, and its benchmark Shanghai Composite index has doubled since 2005. SSE's market capitalisation reached US$3 trillion in 2007, making it the world's fifth-largest stock exchange.

China now ranks 29th in the Global Competitiveness Index, although it is only ranked 135th among the 179 countries measured in the Index of Economic Freedom. In 2011, 61 Chinese companies were listed in the Fortune Global 500. Measured by total revenues, three of the world's top ten most valuable companies are Chinese, including fifth-ranked Sinopec Group, sixth-ranked China National Petroleum and seventh-ranked State Grid (the world's largest electric utilities company).

China's middle-class population (defined as those with annual income of at least US$17,000) has reached more than 100 million as of 2011, while the number of super-rich individuals worth more than 10 million yuan (US$1.5 million) is estimated to be 825,000. The number of US dollar billionaires in China doubled from 130 in 2009 to 271 in 2010, giving China the world's second-highest number of billionaires. China's retail market was worth RMB 8.9 trillion (US$1.302 trillion) in 2007, and is growing at 16.8% annually. China is also now the world's second-largest consumer of luxury goods behind Japan, with 27.5% of the global share.

In recent years, China's rapid economic growth has contributed to severe consumer inflation, causing the prices of basic goods to rise steeply. Food prices in China increased by over 21% in the first four months of 2008 alone. To curb inflation and moderate rising property prices, the Chinese government has instituted a number of fiscal regulations and amendments, raising interest rates and imposing limits on bank loans. In September 2011, consumer prices rose by 6.1% compared to a year earlier, marking a reduction in inflation from the peak of 6.5% in July 2011. A side-effect of increased economic regulation was a slowdown in overall growth—China's quarterly GDP growth fell to 9.1% in October 2011, down from 9.5% in the previous quarter, and sank to 8.1% in April 2012. By October 2012, amid a

manufacturing slowdown and increasing turmoil in global markets, China's quarterly GDP growth rate had fallen to 7.4%.

The Chinese economy is highly energy-intensive and inefficient—on average, industrial processes in China between 20% and 100% more energy than similar ones in OECD countries. China became the world's largest energy consumer in 2010, but still relies on coal to supply about 70% of its energy needs. Coupled with lax environmental regulations, this has led to massive water and air pollution, leaving China with 20 of the world's 30 most polluted cities. Consequently, the government has promised to use more renewable energy, planning to make renewables constitute 30% of China's total energy production by 2050. In 2010, China became the largest wind energy provider in the world, with a total installed wind power capacity of 41.8 GW. In January 2011, Russia began scheduled oil shipments to China, pumping 300,000 barrels of oil per day via the Eastern Siberia—Pacific Ocean oil pipeline.

Communications

China currently has the largest number of active cellphones of any country in the world, with over 1 billion users as of May 2012. It also has the world's largest number of internet and broadband users. By December 2010, China had around 457 million internet users, an increase of 19% over the previous year, and by the end of 2011 the number of internet users had exceeded 500 million. According to the China Internet Network Information Center (CNNIC), China's average internet connection speed in 2011 was 100.9 kbit/s, less than half of the global average of 212.5 kbit/s.

China Telecom and China Unicom, the country's two largest broadband providers, accounted for 20% of global broadband subscribers, whereas the world's ten largest broadband service providers combined accounted for 39% of the world's broadband customers. China Telecom alone serves 55 million broadband subscribers, while China Unicom serves more than 40 million. The massive rise in internet use in China continues to fuel rapid broadband growth, whereas the world's other major broadband ISPs operate in the mature markets of the developed world, with high levels of broadband penetration and rapidly slowing subscriber growth. Several Chinese telecommunications companies, most notably Huawei and ZTE, have become highly profitable in overseas markets, but have also been accused of spying for the Chinese military.

Infrastructure

Transportation in mainland China has undergone intense state-led development since the late 1990s. The national road network has been significantly expanded through the creation of a network of expressways, known as the National Trunk Highway System (NTHS). By the end of 2011, China's expressways had reached a total length of 85,000 ki;ometres, second only to the network of the United States. Private car ownership is growing rapidly in China, which surpassed the United States as the world's largest automobile market in 2009, with total car sales of over 13.6 million. Analysts predict that annual car sales in China may rise as high as 40 million by 2020. A side-effect of the rapid growth of China's road network has been a significant rise in traffic accidents, mostly caused by poorly enforced traffic laws—in 2011 alone, around 62,000 Chinese died in road accidents.

China also possesses the world's longest high-speed rail network, with over 9,676 kilometres of service routes. Of these, 3,515 kilometres serve trains with top speeds of 300 kilometres/hour. In 2011, China produced its first high-speed trains built entirely without foreign assistance. China intends to operate approximately 16,000 kikometres of high-speed rail lines by 2020.

As of 2012, China is the world's largest constructor of new airports, and the Chinese government has begun a US$250 billion five-year project to expand and modernize domestic air travel. However, long-distance transportation remains dominated by railways and charter bus systems. Railways are the vital carrier in China; they are monopolised by the state, and divided into various railway bureaux in different regions. Due to huge demand, the system is regularly subject to overcrowding, particularly during holiday seasons, such as Chunyun during the Chinese New Year. The Chinese rail network carried an estimated 1.68 billion total passengers in 2010 alone. In urban areas, bicycles remain an extremely common mode of transport, despite the increasing prevalence of automobiles—as of 2012, there are approximately 470 million bicycles in China.

Rapid transit systems are also rapidly developing in China's major cities, in the form of networks of underground or light rail systems. Hong Kong has one of the most developed public transport systems in the world, while Shanghai has a high-speed maglev rail line connecting the city to its main international airport, Pudong International Airport. China is additionally developing its own satellite navigation system, dubbed Beidou, which began offering commercial navigation services in mainland China in 2011, and is planned to offer global coverage by 2020.

Government and Politics

Executive Branch. The government is led by the State Council, the equivalent of a cabinet. There also are four vice premiers and five state councillors. In 2006 there were 22 ministries and four commissions subordinate to the State Council. In addition, the People's Bank of China (China's central bank) and the National Audit Office are part of the State Council system. The five-year terms of office run concurrently with those of the National People's Congress (NPC) and are limited to no more than two consecutive terms.

Legislative Branch. The National People's Congress (NPC) is the highest organ of state power and exercises the legislative power of the state. Deputies to the NPC are elected from the provinces, autonomous regions, centrally administered municipalities, special administrative regions, and the armed forces. Elections are conducted by the permanent body of the NPC, the Standing Committee, and normally are held at least two months before the end of the current NPC. Deputies serve five-year terms and meet annually for two or three weeks, typically in March or April; 2,979 deputies were elected to the current 10th NPC. The NPC is empowered to amend the constitution; supervise the enforcement of the constitution; and elect the president and vice president of the People's Republic, chairman of the state Central Military Commission, president of the Supreme People's Court, and procurator general of the Supreme People's Procuratorate. The NPC Standing Committee consists of a chairman, 15 vice chairmen, a secretary general, and 153 members, including the officers. Standing Committee members are not allowed to hold administrative, judicial, or procuratorial posts and, in practice, are often senior CCP and former state leaders and officials. As with the NPC membership, the chairman and vice chairmen may serve no more than two consecutive terms.

Judicial Branch. China has a four-level court system. At the top is the Supreme People's Court in Beijing. Lower courts are the higher people's courts in provinces, autonomous regions, and special municipalities; intermediate people's courts at the prefecture level and also in parts of provinces, autonomous regions, and special municipalities; and basic people's courts in counties, towns, and municipal districts. Special courts handle matters affecting the military, railroad transportation, water transportation, and forestry. Constitutionally, the court system exercises judicial power independently and technically is free of interference from administrative organs, public organisations, and individuals. The Supreme People's Court supervises the administration of justice by local courts and special courts, while courts at higher levels oversee the administration of courts at lower levels. At each level, the courts are "responsible to the organs of state power which created them." Judges are limited to two consecutive terms running concurrently with the National People's Congress or local people's congresses.

Administrative Divisions. China has 22 provinces, five autonomous regions, and four municipalities. The provinces are, in the northeast. Heilongjiang, Jilin, and Liaoning; in the north. Shandong, Hebei, Shanxi, and Shaanxi; in central China. Jiangsu, Anhui, Henan, Hubei, and Zhejiang; in the south. Hunan, Jiangxi, Fujian, Guangdong, and Hainan (an island in the South China Sea); in the southwest. Guizhou, Yunnan, and Sichuan; and in the northwest. Gansu and Qinghai. The autonomous regions—Guangxi Zhuang, Tibet (Xizang), Xinjiang Uighur, Inner Mongolia, and Ningxia Hui—are in border areas with large non-Han ethnic minority populations. The four municipalities—Beijing, Tianjin, Shanghai, and Chongqing—are directly controlled by the central government. China also has two special administrative regions (SARs), Hong Kong and Macau. Beijing also claims Taiwan as a province.

Electoral System. Under the Organic Law of the Village Committees, all of China's approximately 1 million villages hold competitive, direct elections for sub-governmental village committees. The revised law also explicitly transferred the power to nominate candidates to villagers themselves, as opposed to village groups or Chinese Communist Party (CCP) branches. Deputies to local people's congresses of provinces, centrally administered municipalities, and cities divided into districts are elected by the people's congress at the next lower level. Deputies to people's congresses of counties, cities not divided into districts, municipal districts, townships, ethnic townships, and towns are elected directly by their constituencies to five-year terms. The local congresses each have corresponding standing committees that exercise legislative authority when the full congresses are not in session. Elected leaders, however, remain subordinate to the corresponding CCP secretary, and most are appointed by higher-level party organisations. Although China's constitution guarantees suffrage for citizens age 18 and older, the CCP maintains a close watch on electoral democracy at the grassroots levels and controls the outcome of elections at other levels.

Mass Media. China's electronic mass media are regulated by the State Administration of Radio, Film, and Television, a subordinate agency of the Ministry of Information Industry. The Chinese Communist Party's Propaganda Department traditionally has played a large role as arbiter of standards for appropriate broadcasts. The People's Broadcasting Station transmits radio broadcasts in standard Chinese (Putonghua) and the various dialects and

minority languages throughout China. In 2004, 282 domestic radio stations and 774 short- and medium-wave radio relaying and transmitting stations operated, and many stations provided Internet access to some of their broadcasts. China National Radio, headquartered in Beijing, transmits programmes in standard Chinese, Kazakh, Korean, Mongolian, Tibetan, and Uighur. The government has been active in regulating newspapers. The Ministry of Information Industry regulates access to the Internet while the Ministry of Public Security and the Ministry of State Security monitor its use. A broad range of topics that authorities interpret as potentially subversive or as slanderous to the state, including the dissemination of anti-unification information or "state secrets" that may endanger national security, are prohibited by various laws and regulations. Internet service providers (ISPs) are restricted to domestic media news postings and are required to record information useful for tracking users and their viewing habits, install software capable of copying e-mails, and immediately abort transmission of material considered subversive. As a result, many ISPs practice self-censorship to avoid violations of the broadly worded regulations.

Foreign Relations

Sweden was the first western country to establish diplomatic relations with the People's Republic on 9 May 1950. In 1971, the PRC replaced the Republic of China as the sole representative of China in the United Nations and as one of the five permanent members of the United Nations Security Council. The PRC was also a former member and leader of the Non-Aligned Movement, and still considers itself an advocate for developing countries.

Under its interpretation of the One-China policy, the PRC has made it a precondition to establishing diplomatic relations that the other country acknowledges its claim to Taiwan and severs official ties with the Republic of China government; it has acted furiously when any country shows signs of diplomatic overture, or sells armaments to Taiwan. It also opposes publicised foreign travels by pro-Taiwan-independence ROC officials, and other separatist figures, such as the 14th Dalai Lama.

The PRC has been playing an increasing role in calling for free trade areas and security pacts amongst its Asia-Pacific neighbours. In 2004, the PRC proposed an entirely new East Asia Summit (EAS) framework as a forum for regional security issues that pointedly excluded the United States. The EAS, which includes ASEAN + 3, India, Australia and New Zealand, held its inaugural summit in 2005. The PRC is also a founding member of the Shanghai Cooperation Organisation (SCO), with Russia and the Central Asian republics.

In 2000 the U.S. Congress approved "permanent normal trade relations" (PNTR) with China, allowing Chinese exports in at the same low tariffs as goods from most other countries.[52] Both Bill Clinton and George W. Bush asserted that free trade would gradually open China to democratic reform. Bush was an advocate of China's entry into the World Trade Organisation (WTO). China has a significant trade surplus with the United States, its most important export market. U.S. politicians have recently argued that the Chinese yuan is undervalued, giving China an unfair trade advantage.

Sinophobic attitudes often target Chinese minorities and nationals living outside of China. Sometimes the anti-Chinese attitudes turn violent, such as the 13 May Incident in Malaysia in 1969 and the Jakarta riots of May 1998 in Indonesia, in which more than 2,000 people died. In recent years, a number of anti-Chinese riots and incidents have also occurred in Africa and Oceania. Anti-Chinese sentiment is often rooted in socio-economics.

Much of the current foreign policy is based on the concept of Five Principles of Peaceful Coexistence of Zhou Enlai - non-interference in other states' affairs, non-aggression, peaceful coexistence, and equality and mutual benefits. China's foreign policy is also driven by the concept of "harmony without uniformity" which encourages diplomatic relations between states despite ideological differences. This has led China to support states that are regarded as dangerous by Western nations, such as Zimbabwe, North Korea, or Iran. Conflicts with foreign countries have occurred at times in its recent history, particularly with the United States; for example, the US bombing of the Chinese embassy in Belgrade during the Kosovo conflict in May 1999 and the US-China spy plane incident in April 2001. Its foreign relations with many Western nations suffered for a time following the Tiananmen Square protests of 1989, though they have since recovered.

The relationship between China and Japan has been strained at times by Japan's refusal to acknowledge its wartime past to the satisfaction of the PRC. Another point of conflict between the two countries is the frequent visits by Japanese government officials to the Yasukuni Shrine. A joint historical study conducted by the PRC and Japan released a report in 2010 which pointed toward a new consensus on the issue of WWII atrocities.

Equally bordering the most countries in the world alongside Russia, the PRC was in a number of international territorial disputes. China's territorial disputes have led to localised wars in the last 50 years, including the Sino-Indian War in 1962, the Sino-Soviet border conflict in 1969, and the Sino-Vietnamese War in 1979. In 2001, the PRC and Russia signed the Sino-Russian Treaty of Friendship, which paved the way in 2004 for Russia to transfer Yinlong Island as well as one-half of Heixiazi to China, ending a long-standing Sino-Russian border dispute. Other territorial disputes include islands in the East and South China Seas, and undefined or disputed land borders with India and Bhutan.

While accompanying a rapid economic rise, the PRC since the 1990s seeks to maintain a policy of quiet diplomacy with its neighbours. It does so by keeping economic growth steady and participating in regional organisations and cultivating bi-lateral relations in order to ease suspicion over China's burgeoning military capabilities. The PRC has started a policy of wooing African nations for trade and bilateral co-operation. (There are no less than 750,000 Chinese nationals working or living in Africa). There are some discussions about whether China will become a new superpower in the 21st century, with certain commentators pointing out its economic progress, military might, very large population, and increasing international influence but others claiming it is headed for economic collapse.

National Security

Overview. The armed forces of China are officially and collectively known as the People's Liberation Army (PLA). With 2.3 million active troops, the People's Liberation Army (PLA) is the largest military in the world. The PLA consists of an army, navy, air force, and strategic nuclear force. The Chinese Communist Party (CCP) Central Military Commission sets policy for the PLA. The commission, which is chaired by China's president, has three vice chairmen, each a general in the PLA ground forces, and seven members representing various components of the PLA. Operational control is administered dually by the CCP Central Military Commission and the State Central Military Commission and the Ministry of National Defence. PLA headquarters is organised into the General Staff Department, General Political Department, General Logistics Department, and General Armaments Department.

China, with possession of nuclear weapons and delivery systems, is considered a major military regional power and an emerging military superpower. China is the only member of the UN Security Council to have limited power projection capabilities. As a consequence, it has been establishing foreign military relationships that have been compared to a 'String of Pearls'.

Much progress has been made in the last decade and the PRC continues to make efforts to modernize its military. It has purchased state-of-the-art fighter jets from Russia, such as the Sukhoi Su-30s, and has also produced its own modern fighters, specifically the Chinese J-10s and the J-11s. It has also acquired and improved upon the Russian S-300 surface-to-air missile systems, which are considered to be among the best aircraft-intercepting systems in the world, albeit Russia has since produced the new generation S-400 Triumf, with China reportedly already having spent $500 million on a downgraded export version of it. The PRC's armoured and rapid-reaction forces have been updated with enhanced electronics and targeting capabilities. In recent years, much attention has been focused on building a navy with blue-water capability.

Defence Budget. The official announced budget of the PLA for 2009 was $70 billion. However, the United States claims China does not report its real military spending. The Defense Intelligence Agency estimates that the real Chinese military budget for 2008 could be anywhere from US$105 to US$150 billion.

Internal Threat and Terrorism. Although the government defines the outlawed Falun Gong movement as the major internal threat and the People's Armed Police Force actively pursues its members, Falun Gong is, nevertheless, not classified as a terrorist group, and it has not committed or sponsored acts of violence. Muslim separatists in Xinjiang Uighur Autonomous Region present China with its most significant terrorist threat, which emerged in the late 1980s. In 2003 Beijing published an "East Turkistan Terrorist List," which labelled organisations such as the World Uighur Youth Congress and the East Turkistan Information Centre as terrorist entities. These groups openly advocate independence for "East Turkestan," and, although they have not been publicly linked to violent activity, the separatists have resorted to violence, bomb attacks, assassinations, and street fighting, which Beijing responds to with police and military action. The Tibet Autonomous Region has also seen unrest.

INDIA

The Republic of India (official Sanskrit name is *Bharat*) occupies much of the Indian subcontinent. On the north, India borders China, Nepal, and Bhutan, Pakistan in the west, and Bangladesh and Myanmar in the east. The Indian Ocean to the south, the Arabian Sea to the west, and the Bay of Bengal to the east form the country's coastline. Non-contiguous to the mainland are the Lakshadweep Islands in the Arabian Sea and the Andaman and Nicobar Islands located 1,300 kilometres from the mainland in the Bay of Bengal. India has 35 cities and urban agglomerations with more than 1 million persons. The most populous cities are Mumbai (16.4 million people), Kolkata (13.2 million), New Delhi (12.8 million), Chennai (6.4 million), Bangalore (5.7 million), Hyderabad (5.5 million), and Ahmadabad (4.5 million).

India's national flag has three horizontal bands. The upper band is saffron in colour, the lower is green, and the middle is white with a 24-spoke dark blue wheel in its centre. The saffron symbolizes courage, sacrifice, and renunciation; the white represents purity and truth; and the green signifies faith and fertility. The wheel is the Dharma Chakra, an ancient Buddhist symbol used by the Indian king Ashoka to represent the "wheel of law."

Historical Background

On 15 August 1947, the country was partitioned into India and Pakistan, which led to massive migration of Hindus and Muslims and substantial communal conflict. Furthermore, the British had left India with a rudimentary industrial and scientific base; tremendous poverty; a large and growing population; social cleavages along caste and economic lines; and contentious territorial boundaries that have led to armed conflicts with Pakistan (1947 to 1949, 1965, 1971, 1999), China (1962), and numerous insurgent groups.

In spite of such difficulties, India can count a number of successes. India has maintained a democratic political system. India has developed an educational infrastructure that has trained one of the world's largest scientific and technical populations. Using Green Revolution agricultural technologies, the country has become self-sufficient in food production. A combination of socialist planning and free enterprise from the 1950s to the 1970s led to substantial industrialisation with the goal of making India economically self-sufficient. In the 1980s and 1990s, socialist economic planning and import substitution industries were slowly replaced by liberalisation measures, a large middle class emerged, information technology developed into an important economic sector, and economic growth has been impressive. India has also become influential in international political and economic matters and appears set to continue those trends.

Numerous problems remain, however, such as substantial poverty, large income gaps between wealthy and poor, a large mass of people who lack the skills to participate in the new economy, and numerous insurgencies that threaten the nation's territorial integrity. Some social issues remain unresolved, and the rise of Hindu nationalism has become a particularly contentious topic in both Indian

Capital	-	New Delhi
Official languages	-	Hindi, English (Constitutional languages – Assamese, Bengali, Bodo, Dogri, Gujarati, Hindi, Kannada, Kashmiri, Konkani, Maithili, Malayalam, Manipuri, Marathi, Nepali, Oriya, Punjabi, Sanskrit, Santhali, Sindhi, Tamil, Telugu, Urdu)
Government	-	Federal republic, parliamentary democracy
	-	President Pranab Mukherjee
	-	Prime Minister Manmohan Singh
	-	Chief Justice Altamas Kabir
Formation	-	Independence 15 August 1947 Republic 26 January 1950
Area	-	3,287,263 square kilometres
Coastline	-	7,516 kilometres
Population	-	1,210,193,422 (2011 census) Density 371/square kilometre
GDP (PPP)	-	$4.457 trillion (2011 estimate) Per capita $3,693
GDP (nominal)	-	$1.848 trillion (2011 estimate) Per capita $1,388
Defence Minister	-	AK Antony
Defence Secretary	-	Shashi Kant Sharma
Chief of Army Staff	-	General Bikram Singh
Chief of Navy Staff	-	Admiral Devendra Kumar Joshi
Chief of Air Staff	-	Air Chief Marshal Norman Anil Kumar Browne

society and politics. Some observers believe India is facing difficulties in the political capacity to address these problems. Intense multi-party political competition over numerous economic and social issues has resulted in often-fragile coalitions of political parties, and no single political party has held a parliamentary majority since 1989. The government changed nine times from December 1989 to the elections in May 2009 in which the Indian National Congress returned to power under Prime Minister Manmohan Singh. Increasing pluralism of political parties, growing diversity in interest-group representation, and substantial ideological divisions among parties are significant obstacles in policy implementation.

Geography

India's exact size is subject to debate because some borders are disputed. The Indian government lists the total area as 3,287,260 square kilometres and the total land area as 3,060,500 square kilometres; the United Nations lists the total area as 3,287,263 square kilometres and total land area as 2,973,190 square kilometres. In either case, India is the seventh largest country in the world.

Land Boundaries. Land boundaries total 15,200 kilometres. India shares common borders with Pakistan (3,325 kilometres; the Jammu and Kashmir border is 1,085 kilometres), China (line of actual control is 3,439 kilometres), Bhutan (605 kilometres), Nepal (1,690 kilometres), Burma (1,452 kilometres), and Bangladesh (4,339 kilometres). Although India and Sri Lanka do not share a land boundary, the narrowest distance between the two countries is only 64 kilometres across the Palk Strait. Most of Jammu and Kashmir is contested with Pakistan, and the Aksai Chin area of Jammu and Kashmir is disputed with China, as is the border of Arunachal Pradesh in northeast India. Nepal claims a 75-square-kilometre area called Kalapani. Possession of recently emerged New Moore Island (South Talpatty) in the Bay of

Bengal has been disputed by Bangladesh, and much of the border with Bangladesh is not demarcated.

Coastline. India's total coastline is 7,516 kilometres in length, which comprises 5,422 kilometres for the mainland, 132 kilometres for the Lakshadweep Islands, and 1,962 kilometres for the Andaman and Nicobar Islands. The Indian peninsula juts 1,980 kilometres into the Indian Ocean. 50% of the Indian Ocean basin lies within a 1,500 kilometre radius of India, a reality that has strategic implications.

Maritime Claims. Under the 1982 United Nations Convention on the Law of the Sea, India has a 200 nautical mile exclusive economic zone, a 12 nautical mile territorial sea, a 24 nautical mile contiguous zone, and a legal continental shelf extending to a depth of 2,500 metres or to the end of the continental margin. India has 1,197 islands in the Indian Ocean. (572 in the Andaman and Nicobar—38 of which are inhabited and 23 in the Lakshadweep—10 of which are inhabited. In addition, there are 447 islands off the Western coast and 151 islands off the Eastern Coast).

Topography. There are three main geological regions, the Indo-Gangetic Plain and the Himalayas—collectively known as North India—and the Peninsula, or South India. India has diverse physiological regions that include highlands, plains, deserts, and river valleys. The country's highest elevation is 8,598 metres at Kanchenjunga, which is the third highest mountain in the world and located in the Himalayas.

Principal Rivers. India's longest rivers are the Brahmaputra and Indus, which are both 2,896 kilometres long, although neither is entirely within India. Other major rivers are the Ganga (2,525 kilometres), Godavari (1,465 kilometres), Kaveri (Cauvery, 800 kilometres), Krishna (1,401 kilometres), Mahanandi (851 kilometres), Narmada (1,312 kilometres), and Yamuna (1,370 kilometres).

Climate. Climate in India varies significantly from the permanently snow-capped Himalayas in the north to the tropics in the south. The country has four seasons. December to February is relatively dry and cool, March to May is dry and hot, from June to September predominating southwest maritime winds bring monsoon rains to most of the country, and in October and November there are retreating dry monsoons originating from the northeast. Average temperatures range from 12.5° C to 30° C in the northwest, 17.5° C to 30° C in the north and northeast, and 22.5° C to 30° C in the south. Average annual rainfall is around 1,000 to 1,500 millimetres for much of the country, but can be quite low in some parts of the northwest (150 to 300 millimetres annually) and very high in the northeast and along the west coast (1,500 to 2,500 millimetres annually).

Natural Resources. Commercially important natural resources include arable land, bauxite, chromite, coal (fourth-largest reserves in the world), diamonds, iron ore, limestone, manganese, mica, natural gas, petroleum, and titanium ore.

Land Use. The total arable land and land planted under permanent crops combined is about 1,697,000 square kilometres, and total irrigated land is about 548,000 square kilometres. The total of non-arable land and land not under permanent crops is about 1,276,190 square kilometres.

Environmental Factors. India is vulnerable to various natural hazards, particularly cyclones and annual monsoon floods, and various combinations of poverty, population growth, increasing individual consumption, industrialisation, infrastructural development, poor agricultural practices, and poor resource distribution have led to substantial human transformation of India's natural environment. An estimated 60% of cultivated land suffers from soil erosion, water logging, and salinity. It is also estimated that between 4.7 and 12 billion tons of topsoil are lost annually from soil erosion. From 1947 to 2002, average annual per capita water availability declined by almost 70% to 1,822 cubic meters, and overexploitation of groundwater is problematic in the states of Haryana, Punjab, and Uttar Pradesh. Forest area covers 19.4% of India's geographic area (63.7 million hectares). Nearly half of the country's forest cover is found in the state of Madhya Pradesh (20.7%) and the seven states of the northeast (25.7%); the latter is experiencing net forest loss. Forest cover is declining because of harvesting for fuel wood and the expansion of agricultural land. These trends, combined with increasing industrial and motor vehicle pollution output, have led to atmospheric temperature increases, shifting precipitation patterns, and declining intervals of drought recurrence in many areas. The Indian Agricultural Research Institute has estimated that a 3° C rise in temperature will result in a 15 to 20% loss in annual wheat yields. These are substantial problems for a nation with such a large population depending on the productivity of primary resources and whose economic growth relies heavily on industrial growth.

Society

Ethnic Groups. The exact number of ethnic groups depends on source and method of counting, and scholars estimate that only the continent of Africa exceeds the linguistic, cultural, and genetic diversity of India. 72% of the population is Indo-Aryan, 25% Dravidian, and 3% Mongoloid and other. Each of these groups can be further subdivided into various combinations of language, religion, and caste. About 16% of the total population is "untouchable" (Scheduled Castes is the more formal, legal term; *Dalit* is the term preferred by "untouchables" and roughly translates to downtrodden); around 8% of the population belongs to one of 461 indigenous groups (often called Scheduled Tribes for legal purposes, although the term *adivasi* is commonly used).

Languages. The total number of languages and dialects varies by source and counting method, and many Indians speak more than one language. The Indian census lists 114 languages (22 of which are spoken by one million or more persons) that are further categorised into 216 dialects or "mother tongues" spoken by 10,000 or more speakers. An estimated 850 languages are in daily use, and there are more than 1,600 dialects. Hindi is the official language and the most commonly spoken, but not all dialects are mutually comprehensible. English also has official status and is widely used in business and politics, although knowledge of English varies widely. The teaching of Hindi and English is compulsory in most states and union territories. 22 languages are legally recognised by the constitution for various political, educational, and other purposes - Assamese, Bengali, Bodo, Dogri, Gujarati, Hindi, Kannada, Kashmiri, Konkani, Maithili, Malayalam, Manipuri, Marathi, Nepali, Oriya, Punjabi, Sanskrit, Santhali, Sindhi, Tamil, Telugu, and Urdu. The most commonly spoken languages are Hindi (40.2% of the population), Bengali (8.3%), Telugu (7.9%), Marathi (7.5%), and Tamil (6.3%).

Religion. Approximately 80.5% of the population is Hindu, 13.4% Muslim, 2.3% Christian, 1.9% Sikh, 0.8% Buddhist, and 0.4% Jain; another 0.6% belongs to other faiths, such as Zoroastrianism and numerous religions associated with Scheduled Tribes. The Indian constitution confers religious freedom for individuals and prohibits religious discrimination, but in spite of this, there have been enduring tensions among religious communities, most notably between Hindus and Muslims.

Education and Literacy. In 2000 the adult literacy rate (% aged 15 or older) was 58.5% (72.3% for males, 44.4% for females). These figures have all nearly doubled since 1961 and are higher than in most other South Asian nations. In 2001 the combined primary, secondary, and tertiary enrolment ratio was 55% of

Geosynchronous Satellite Launch Vehicle (GSLV)

the population of official school age for the three levels. Total government expenditures on education in 2001 were 13.2% of all government expenditures and 4% of GDP. Government expenditures on education have increased steadily, as have the number of educational institutions from the primary to the university level. The majority of states and union territories have free education up to the seventh-grade level, and the majority of primary schools are government funded and managed. 34% of secondary institutions are government funded but privately managed, and 25% are privately managed without government funding.

Health. National health indicators are generally lower than in many developing countries but have shown dramatic improvement nationwide, although there are variations among states in India. An estimated 21% of the total population is malnourished. In 2001 public health expenditures were 3.1% of total general government expenditures but only 17.9% of total health expenditures. By contrast, private expenditures were 82.1% of total health expenditures. Furthermore, total health expenditures per capita represented 5.1% of GDP The population's health is also a function of the relatively low number of health personnel and low level of infrastructure, which are on a par with many countries in Sub-Saharan Africa.

Welfare. Generally, central government welfare expenditures are a substantial portion of the official budget, and state and local governments play important roles in developing and implementing welfare policies. In 2000 union government expenditures on social services (includes education, health, family welfare, women and child development, and social justice and empowerment), rural development, and basic minimum services were approximately US$7.7 billion, which was 11.1% of total government expenditures and 1.7% of GDP. Furthermore, the union and state governments maintain a plethora of reserved seats in various political and education institutions for lower castes, indigenous persons, and others based on their percentage of the population.

Economy

From the 1950s to the 1980s, India followed socialist-inspired policies. The economy was shackled by extensive regulation, protectionism, and public ownership, leading to pervasive corruption and slow growth. Since 1991, the nation has moved towards a market-based system. The policy change in 1991 came after an acute balance of payments crisis, and the emphasis since then has been to use foreign trade and foreign investment as integral parts of India's economy.

With an average annual GDP growth rate of 5.8% for the past two decades, the economy is among the fastest growing in the world. It has the world's second largest labour force, with 516.3 million people. In terms of output, the agricultural sector accounts for 28% of GDP; the service and industrial sectors make up 54% and 18% respectively. Major agricultural products include rice, wheat, oilseed, cotton, jute, tea, sugarcane, potatoes; cattle, water buffalo, sheep, goats, poultry; fish. Major industries include textiles, chemicals, food processing, steel, transport equipment, cement, mining, petroleum, machinery, software. India's trade has reached a relatively moderate share 24% of GDP in 2006, up from 6% in 1985. India's share of world trade has reached 1%. Major exports include petroleum products, textile goods, gems and jewellery, software, engineering goods, chemicals, leather manufactures. Major imports include crude oil, machinery, gems, fertilizer, and chemicals.

India's annual small-car exports have surged fivefold in the past five years. India's GDP is US$1.237 trillion, which makes it the twelfth-largest economy in the world or fourth largest by purchasing power adjusted exchange rates. India's nominal per capita income US$1,068 is ranked 128th in the world. In the late 2000s, India's economic growth has averaged 7½% a year, which will double the average income in a decade.

Despite India's impressive economic growth over recent decades, it still contains the largest concentration of poor people in the world, and has a higher rate of malnutrition among children under the age of three (46% in year 2007) than any other country in the world. The percentage of people living below the World Bank's international poverty line of $1.25 a day (PPP, in nominal terms Rs. 21.6 a day in urban areas and Rs 14.3 in rural areas in 2005) decreased from 60% in 1981 to 42% in 2005. Even though India has avoided famines in recent decades, half of children are underweight, one of the highest rates in the world and nearly double the rate of Sub-Saharan Africa.

According to the World Bank, as of 2011, the Indian economy is nominally worth US$1.848 trillion; it is the tenth-largest economy by market exchange rates, and is, at US$4.457 trillion, the third-largest by purchasing power parity, or PPP. With its average annual GDP growth rate of 5.8% over the past two decades, and reaching 6.1% during 2011-12, India is one of the world's fastest-growing economies. However, the country ranks 140th in the world in nominal GDP per capita and 129th in GDP per capita at PPP. India's recent economic model is largely capitalist. India has been a member of WTO since 1 January 1995.

The 487.6-million worker Indian labour force is the world's second-largest, as of 2011. The service sector makes up 55.6% of GDP, the industrial sector 26.3% and the agricultural sector 18.1%. Major agricultural products include rice, wheat, oilseed, cotton, jute, tea, sugarcane, and potatoes. Major industries include textiles, telecommunications, chemicals, pharmaceuticals, biotechnology, food processing, steel, transport equipment, cement, mining, petroleum, machinery, and software. In 2006, the share of external trade in India's GDP stood at 24%, up from 6% in 1985. In 2008, India's share of world trade was 1.68%; In 2011, India was the world's tenth-largest importer and the nineteenth-largest exporter. Major exports include petroleum products, textile goods, jewellery, software, engineering goods, chemicals, and leather manufactures. Major imports include crude oil, machinery, gems, fertiliser, and chemicals. Between 2001 and 2011, the contribution of petrochemical and engineering goods to total exports grew from 14% to 42%.

Averaging an economic growth rate of 7.5% for several years prior to 2007, India has more than doubled its hourly wage rates during the first decade of the 21st century. Some 431 million Indians have left poverty since 1985; India's middle classes are projected to number around 580 million by 2030. Though ranking 51st in global competitiveness, India ranks 17th in financial market sophistication, 24th in the banking sector, 44th in business sophistication, and 39th in innovation, ahead of several advanced economies, as of 2010. With 7 of the world's top 15 information technology outsourcing companies based in India, the country is viewed as the second-most favourable outsourcing destination after the

United States, as of 2009. India's consumer market, currently the world's eleventh-largest, is expected to become fifth-largest by 2030.

India's telecommunication industry, the world's fastest-growing, added 227 million subscribers during the period 2010-11. Its automotive industry, the world's second fastest growing, increased domestic sales by 26% during 2009-10, and exports by 36% during 2008-09. Power capacity is 250 gigawatts, of which 8% is renewable. The Pharmaceutical industry in India is among the significant emerging markets for global pharma industry. The Indian pharmaceutical market is expected to reach $ 48.5 billion by 2020. India's R & D spending constitutes 60% of Biopharmaceutical industry. India is among the top 12 Biotech destinations of the world. At the end of 2011, Indian IT Industry employed 2.8 million professionals, generated revenues close to US$100 billion equalling 7.5% of Indian GDP and contributed 26% of India's merchandize exports.

Despite impressive economic growth during recent decades, India continues to face socio-economic challenges. India contains the largest concentration of people living below the World Bank's international poverty line of US$1.25 per day, the proportion having decreased from 60% in 1981 to 42% in 2005. Half of the children in India are underweight, and 46% of children under the age of three suffer from malnutrition. The Mid-Day Meal Scheme attempts to lower these rates. Since 1991, economic inequality between India's states has consistently grown: the per-capita net state domestic product of the richest states in 2007 was 3.2 times that of the poorest. Corruption in India is perceived to have increased significantly, with one report estimating the illegal capital flows since independence to be US$462 billion. Driven by growth, India's nominal GDP per capita has steadily increased from US$329 in 1991, when economic liberalisation began, to US$1,265 in 2010, and is estimated to increase to US$2,110 by 2016; however, it has always remained lower than those of other Asian developing countries such as Indonesia, Iran, Malaysia, Philippines, Sri Lanka, and Thailand, and is expected to remain so in the near future.

Infrastructure

India's transportation infrastructure has undergone tremendous change since independence. While traditional, non-mechanised transport means are still quite common, roads, railroads, ports, and aviation continue to expand. India now has the world's second largest road network, and its rail network is among the most used in the world for passengers and freight.

Furthermore, increasing incomes and government liberalisation measures have contributed to tremendous growth in the numbers of automobiles, two- and three-wheeled vehicles, private and public buses, and urban rail networks. However, there are significant, accompanying problems with pollution, increasing traffic density, unauthorised transportation providers, and high numbers of traffic fatalities.

Roads. There were about 3.3 million kilometres of roads by 2002, of which 1.4 million kilometres were surfaced and more than 1 million kilometres were covered with gravel, crushed stone, or earth. More than 150 highways are rated as national highways and carry about 40% of road traffic on a total length of 65,569 kilometres. Around 85% of all passenger traffic and 70% of all freight traffic travel by road. By 2007, highways have expanded by 13,146 kilometres, with road projects aimed at linking the country's major cities and spanning the entire country north-south and east-west. Modes of road transport are a mix of traditional and modern means. Urban transit is dominated by motor vehicles, with increasing use of automobiles, minibuses, buses, trucks, and particularly two- and three-wheeled vehicles.

Railroads. All railroads are government-owned and operated by Indian Railways. In 2002 total route length was 63,028 kilometres and double and multiple tracks resulted in a total track length of 108,706 kilometres. Of the total track length, 86,526 kilometres were 1.676-millimeter gauge, 18,529 kilometres were 1.000-millimeter gauge, and 3,651 kilometres were 0.762- and 0.610-millimeter gauge. About 16,000 kilometres were electrified, mostly 1.676 millimetre gauge. The rail system includes 7,566 locomotives, 37,840 coaches, 222,147 freight wagons, 6,853 stations, and nearly 116,000 bridges. Both passenger and freight carriage continue to expand annually, and the rail system is the fourth most heavily used in the world, both for passengers and freight. For the financial year 2004, Indian Railways carried 557 million freight tons and more than 5 billion passengers. There are some high-speed routes and increasing use of them. Most rolling stock and other components are still domestically produced, but they are increasingly manufactured through commercial agreements with foreign companies. There have been major government investments in modernisation since the early 1990s, but Indian Railways has also experienced dwindling government budgetary support and has suffered from the dual role of being both a public utility and a commercial enterprise.

Ports. India has 12 major ports and 185 minor and intermediate ports along the country's coastline. There are also 7 shipyards under the control of the central government, 2 shipyards controlled by state governments, and 19 privately owned shipyards. The major ports handled 344.6 million tons of cargo for the financial year 2004, with Chennai, Vishakhapatnam and Kandla carrying the greatest tonnage. Major ports can collectively handle 390 million tons of cargo annually, and port operations have improved since the mid-1990s. All major ports, except one (Ennore), are government administered, but private-sector participation in ports has increased. In 2000 there were 102 shipping companies operating in India, of which five were privately owned and based in India and one was owned by the government (Shipping Corporation of India). In 2000 there were 639 government-owned ships, including 91 oil tankers, 79 dry cargo bulk carriers, and 10 cellular container vessels. Indian-flagged vessels carried about 15% of overseas cargo at Indian ports.

Inland and Coastal Waterways. India has approximately 14,500 kilometres of inland waterways, but their transportation potential is vastly underused. More than 3,600 kilometres are navigable by large vessels, although only about 2,000 kilometres are used. For purposes of navigational development and conservation, three inland waterways have been declared national waterways. The Allahabad-Haldia portion of the Ganga-Bhagirathi-Hooghly rivers (1,620 kilometres), the Sadiya-Dhubri section of the Brahmaputra River (891 kilometres), and a combination of western canals (205 kilometres).

Civil Aviation and Airports. The government owns two airlines (Air India and Indian Airlines) and one helicopter service (Pawan Hans), and there are twelve privately owned airlines. Private airlines account for about 45% of domestic air traffic, and the government has divested more than 50% of the equity in both government-owned airlines. Of 288 airports, 208 have permanent-surface runways, and there are two runways of more than 3,659 meters. The Airports Authority of India administers 126 airports - 11 international, 89 domestic, and 26 for defence purposes.

Pipelines. In 2003 India had an estimated 5,798 kilometres of gas pipelines, 1,195 kilometres for liquid petroleum gas, 5,613 kilometres for oil, and 5,567 kilometres for refined products. India and Iran have discussed constructing a gas pipeline, but the Indian government and oil industry analysts have expressed concerns about the pipeline's security because of its proposed route through conflict-prone areas of Pakistan.

Telecommunications. India is witnessing its greatest period of change in communications, with shifts from government to private providers and greater public use of various technologies. From 1995 to 2003, the number of Internet users increased from 250,000 to 18.4 million. Since the late 1990s, the number of telephones, mobile phones, and personal computers has increased substantially. In 2004 there were 40.9 million telephones and 26.2 million mobile phones, and in 2003 there were an estimated 7.5 million personal computers. Some basic telephone services were opened to private-sector competition in 1994, and portions of state-owned telecommunications services have been purchased by private entities. Government-owned radio (All India Radio) and television (Doordarshan) networks have extensive national and local coverage, but domestic and international private television networks are increasingly prolific through cable and satellite.

Government and Politics

India is a democratic republic with a system of government legally based on the often-amended 1950 constitution. The central government is also known as the union government, and its structure is much like the British parliamentary system, with distinct, but interrelated executive, legislative, and judicial branches. State governments are structured much like the central government, and district governments exist in a variety of forms. The Indian parliament is a bicameral legislature composed of a lower house (the Lok Sabha or House of the People), with 543 popularly elected members and 2 members appointed by the President and an upper house (the Rajya Sabha or Council of States), with 12 appointed members and 233 members elected by state and union territory assemblies. Lok Sabha members serve five-year terms, and Rajya Sabha members serve six-year terms, with one-third of members up for election every two years. The legislature passes laws on constitutionally specified matters, such as central government finances and constitutional amendments. The two houses have the same powers, but the Rajya Sabha's power in the legislative process is subordinate to the Lok Sabha. India has both a prime minister and a president. Members of parliament and state legislative assemblies elect the president. Prime ministers are leaders of the majority party in parliament but are formally appointed by the president. In 2004 Manmohan Singh became prime minister. Over time, political power has become increasingly concentrated in the prime minister and Council of Ministers (cabinet), although they are responsible to the parliament. The president's duties are mostly ceremonial, although the president formally approves the prime minister and also approves the Council of Ministers based on the prime minister's advice. Furthermore, all bills require presidential approval before becoming law. The vice president is ex officio chairperson of the Rajya Sabha and acts in place of the president when the president is unable to perform his or her duties.

Judicial and Legal System. The Supreme Court is the top legal entity, and it is composed of a chief justice appointed by the president and 25 associate judges also appointed by the president in consultation with the chief justice. The Supreme Court has numerous legal powers, such as appellate jurisdiction over all civil and criminal proceedings, with the potential of influencing interpretation of the constitution. The parliament and Supreme Court have maintained a contentious relationship on issues related to judicial review and parliamentary sovereignty. Below the Supreme Court are high courts, followed by a hierarchy of subordinate courts, and some states also have *panchayat* (village level) courts that decide civil and criminal matters. Some high courts serve more than one state, and all are independent of state legislatures and executives. The judiciary is regarded as slow and cumbersome but is also widely respected and often takes an activist role in protecting citizens' rights.

Administrative Divisions. There are 28 states and 7 union territories including the national capital territory of New Delhi. State boundaries are often based on language or other social characteristics, and union territories tend to be geographically smaller and less populous than states. States and union territories contain 601 districts that are further subdivided into townships containing from 200 to 600 villages. The union government exercises greater control over union territories than over states. Relationships between some state governments and the union government have been contentious, particularly when state governments are run by political parties that oppose the governing party or coalition in parliament. The tremendous variations in economic and social development among states suggest that state governments can have a greater influence on their populations than the union government. However, the union government exercises considerable influence on states through numerous financial resources and its authority to assume control of states during times of emergency (called President's Rule).

Electoral System. The Election Commission is the independent government body that supervises parliamentary and state elections, which are massive and sometimes marred by violence. Elections for state assemblies and the Lok Sabha are held every five years unless called earlier, such as through a no-confidence vote of the government by the Lok Sabha. Indeed, elections are often held before the five-year limits because governments have often had difficulty staying in power for the full five-year term. In the 2004 general elections, there were more than 687,000 polling stations and 671.5 million voters. Since 1952, there have been 14 general elections, with voter turnout ranging from 55 to 64% of eligible voters. The legal voting age is 18. National and state legislative elections are similar to the British House of Commons and United States House of Representatives, in which members gain office by winning a plurality of votes in their local constituency. There are 543 parliamentary constituencies. The number of constituencies for state legislatures ranges from 32 to 403, with a total of 4,120 state constituencies nationwide.

Politics and Political Parties. From 1947 until 1989, the left-of-centre Indian National Congress and its factions dominated national politics. In the 1990s, the centre-right Bharatiya Janata Party (BJP) and the centrist Janata Dal emerged as influential political parties, although Congress returned to power in May 2004. There are numerous national and state parties. Among the best known and most prominent are Akali Dal, All-India Anna DMK (AIADMK), Asom Gana

Parishad, Bahujan Samaj Party (BSP), Bharatiya Janata Party (BJP), Communist Party of India (CPI), Communist Party of India-Marxist (CPI-M), Dravida Munnetra Kazhagam (DMK), Indian National Congress, Rashtriya Janata Dal (RJD), Samajwadi Party, Samata Party, Shiv Sena, and Telugu Desam. Since the late 1960s, minority parties in Parliament have often been majority parties in state legislatures. Since 1989, single political parties have generally failed to win a parliamentary majority. As a result, parliament is often run by coalitions of political parties.

Mass Media. India has more newspapers than any other nation, and newspaper readership annually grows by millions. There are a few state-run newspapers, but most print media are privately owned. There are more than 5,600 daily newspapers and more than 46,000 non-daily newspapers and print periodicals. In 2002 the government allowed print media to be up to 26% foreign owned, but the most powerful publishers are joint stock companies that frequently have other commercial and industrial holdings. Government authorities control most television channels, yet the growth of private FM and television stations has marked a shift away from mostly state-run electronic media such as Doordarshan (television) and All India Radio. Foreign television channels are available through cable television or Indian broadcasters. An estimated 42.3% of Indian households have a television, and 52.2% of those have cable or satellite transmission. Similarly, the number of Internet users has rapidly to an estimated 18.4 million users in 2003. India has a high degree of press and speech freedom.

Foreign Relations. India's Ministry of External Affairs is the governmental body that is officially responsible for making and implementing foreign policy, although India's prime ministers have often exercised substantial influence in foreign policy decision making. India's parliament and armed forces historically have had very limited roles in the formulation of foreign policy. India is the second most populous country and the world's most-populous democracy and recently has one of the fastest economic growth rates in the world. With the world's tenth largest military expenditures, and eleventh largest economy by nominal rates or fourth largest by purchasing power parity, India is considered to be a regional power, and a potential global power. It is India's growing international influence that increasingly gives it a more prominent voice in global affairs.

India has a long history of collaboration with several countries and is considered a leader of the developing world. India was one of the founding members of several international organisations, most notably the United Nations, the Non-Aligned Movement, the Asian Development Bank and the G20 industrial nations. India has also played an important and influential role in other international organisations like East Asia Summit, World Trade Organisation, International Monetary Fund (IMF), G8+5 and IBSA Dialogue Forum. Regional organisations India is a part of include SAARC and BIMSTEC. India has taken part in several UN peacekeeping missions and is the second-largest troop contributor to the United Nations. India is currently seeking a permanent seat in the UN Security Council, along with the G4 nations.

Post-Cold War shifts in military power and concerns with terrorism have led India to create stronger bilateral relations with China, Israel, the United States, and other nations. The Ministry of External Affairs has generally been most concerned with relations with neighbouring Nepal, Sri Lanka, and particularly Pakistan on issues concerning unresolved borders, natural resource distribution, immigration, and insurgent activity. India's security concerns have been most pronounced with Pakistan. In spite of these difficulties, tensions between India and Pakistan have periodically thawed, and the two countries have demonstrated interest in resolving their enduring dispute over Jammu and Kashmir.

As promotion of democracy around the world is one of the most important foreign policy objectives of the USA, India—as the largest democracy of the world - can hardly be ignored by the USA. Cooperation in promotion of democracy in the world has become one of the most important facets of Indo-USA relations in recent times.

Major International Treaties. India is a signatory to numerous international treaties. India is not a party to the Treaty on the Non-Proliferation of Nuclear Weapons (NPT) or the Missile Technology Control Regime. Indian governments have argued that the NPT does not reduce nuclear weapons proliferation by states already possessing nuclear weapons and that the NPT denies non-nuclear states the right to have nuclear weapons.

National Security

The prime minister and Council of Ministers formulate national security policy. Below this level is the civilian bureaucracy, which exercises important influence, primarily through the Defence Minister's Committee of the cabinet. The third tier of defence policy making is the Chiefs of Staffs Committee. These three levels are supported by intelligence organisations, scientific and technical advisory committees, defence production, and research and development groups. There are three military services—army, navy, and air force—and a number of paramilitary and reserve forces. The army has been the dominant service in terms of both percentage of budget allotted to the armed forces and percentage of persons serving in the armed forces.

India maintains the third-largest military force in the world. The President of India is the supreme commander of the Indian Armed Forces. India maintains close defence cooperation with Russia, Israel and France, who are the chief suppliers of arms. The Defence Research and Development Organisation (DRDO) oversees indigenous development of sophisticated arms and military equipment, including ballistic missiles, fighter aircraft and main battle tanks, to reduce India's dependence on foreign imports. India became a nuclear power in 1974 after conducting an initial nuclear test, and further underground testing in 1998. India maintains a "no first use" nuclear policy. On 10 October, 2008 Indo-US civilian nuclear agreement was signed, prior to which India received IAEA and NSG waivers, ending restrictions on nuclear technology commerce with which India became de facto sixth nuclear power in world.

Service chiefs and military officers continually suggest that the military should have greater input into defence policymaking and national security, and generally such a role is not viewed as a threat to civilian control of the military. Since 2001, the government has established the Defence Intelligence Agency (DIA), the Defence Acquisitions Council (DAC, which now controls the DRDO), and the National Security Council (NSC), which suggests that India has rethought its defence policymaking structure. The government has also proposed creating a Chief of Defence Staff. However, these changes have yet to make a major impact.

Foreign Military Relations. Indian peacekeeping forces have been sent to Sri Lanka from 1987 to 1990 and to the Maldives in 1988. Indian military and police contingents have participated in United Nations (UN) peacekeeping forces in Angola, Bosnia and Herzegovina, Cambodia, Democratic Republic of the Congo, Costa Rica, Cyprus, Dominican Republic, El Salvador, Ethiopia and Eritrea, Gaza, Guatemala, Honduras, Iraq, Korea (during the Korean War), Kuwait, Laos, Lebanon, Liberia, Mozambique, Namibia, Nicaragua, Rwanda, Sierra Leone, Somalia, Vietnam, West New Guinea (West Irian), Yemen, and Yugoslavia. India has also provided police personnel and monitors for UN peacekeeping operations in Angola, Bosnia and Herzegovina, Cambodia, Haiti, Kosovo, Mozambique, Sierra Leone, and Western Sahara.

Foreign Military Forces. The only foreign military forces in India are with the United Nations Military Observer Group in India and Pakistan (UNMOGIP), which has 45 military observers from 9 countries stationed in Jammu and Kashmir.

External Threat. External security threats come from neighbouring countries and insurgents using foreign border areas as havens for activities in India. Countries such as Bangladesh, Bhutan, and Sri Lanka present no conventional military threat to India, but their inability to police and control areas bordering India has provided Indian insurgents with havens. Indian government and military officials have publicly expressed concern about the political instability in its neighbourhood. As far as external threats posed by other countries, popular opinion tends to regard Pakistan as the principal enemy, largely because of the Kashmir conflict and Pakistan's suspected links to numerous South Asian militant groups. However, the defence establishment generally regards China as the chief external threat, because of perceived Chinese attempts to isolate India militarily and diplomatically from the rest of Asia and perceived Chinese efforts to prevent India from becoming a permanent member of the UN Security Council. While China-India border issues remain unresolved from the Indian point of view, Sino-Indian relations have improved.

Internal Threats and Terrorism. India's top security concerns are mostly internal. Much of the national security apparatus is directed to maintaining territorial integrity as dozens of groups push for varying degrees of political or social autonomy, sometimes violently. India treats separatism with extreme concern given the possibility that successful separatism may establish a precedent that other groups might seek to follow. Internal threats can be categorised as religiously oriented conflict or ethnic violence, usually with separatist objectives. Separatist violence periodically escalates in Jammu and Kashmir. Numerous separatist insurgent groups are active in the northeast. Left-wing Extremism (Naxalite) remains the largest internal security threat to India.

Human Rights. Although human rights problems exist in India, the country is generally not regarded as among the world's serious human rights violators. Human rights problems appear to be acute in areas and periods of communal violence, and security forces, insurgents, and various ethnic-based groups have all been accused of human rights violations in Jammu and Kashmir, Gujarat, Maharashtra, Uttar Pradesh, and various north-eastern states. Both international human rights organisations and India's National Human Rights Commission have questioned the impartiality of police and judicial authorities in various locales. On the other hand, human rights groups have praised India's repeal of the Prevention of Terrorism Act, which both the newly elected government and international organisations criticised as enabling human rights abuses by security forces. Indian media routinely address controversial issues, such as political corruption and discrimination against women, sexual minorities, indigenous peoples, and "untouchables." In response to cyber-crime and cyber-terrorism perpetrated by parties in both India and Pakistan, India passed the Information Technology Act of 2000, which allows cyber cafés and Internet users homes to be searched without warrants at any time as part of criminal investigations.

INDONESIA

The Republic of Indonesia (the word Indonesia was coined from the Greek *indos*—for India—and *nesos*—for island) proclaimed independence on 17 August 1945, from the Netherlands. The Hague recognised Indonesian sovereignty on 27 December 1949. Estimates of the size of Indonesia's total area vary. Officially, the Indonesian government says the total land area is 1.9 million square kilometres and total sea area, 7.9 million square kilometres, including an exclusive economic zone. The Indonesian flag has two equal horizontal bands of red (top) and white.

History

The struggle between the Dutch colonial government and the Indonesian nationalist movement was well under way when the Japanese occupied the Indies in 1942. They remained until the end of World War II in August 1945.

On 17 August 1945, Sukarno and Mohammad Hatta proclaimed the independent Republic of Indonesia with Sukarno as president and Hatta as vice president. Allied forces (mostly British and British Indian troops) did not arrive until six weeks later, by which time the republic had begun to establish itself and nationalist pride had burgeoned. The period October-December 1945 was filled with violent conflict in which Indonesians made it clear they would defend their independence with their lives. The republic survived two Dutch "police actions" and an internal communist rebellion, and on 27 December 1949, The Hague formally recognised the sovereignty of a federated republic, which a year later was formed into a unitary Republic of Indonesia.

The years following the struggle for independence were characterised by political and economic difficulty, regional dissidence, attempted assassinations and coups d'état, military-civilian conflict, and economic stagnation. A period of Guided Democracy was announced in 1959 by Sukarno, who in September 1963 proclaimed himself president-for-life and presided over a political system in which the civilian nationalist leadership, much of the Islamic leadership, the large Indonesian Communist Party (PKI), and the army were all at odds. This tense and hostile atmosphere was broken on 30 September 1965, with what appears to have been an attempted PKI coup against the Sukarno government. The precise circumstances remain unclear, but the immediate result was that a "New Order" coalition of students, intellectuals, Muslims, and the army brought about a military-dominated government that removed Sukarno and permitted a broad and deadly assault on communists, especially on Java, Bali, and Sumatra. On 11 March 1966, power was transferred from a seriously ill Sukarno to Suharto, an army officer. The PKI was formally banned the following day and Suharto became the acting president, and the New Order era began.

The New Order era, which lasted for more than 30 years, has a mixed record. Like Guided Democracy, it was authoritarian, but it was more successful in bringing stability to the nation. Unlike Guided Democracy, its economic achievements were enormous and the well-being of the majority of Indonesians undeniably improved, e.g. average life expectancy increased from 46 to 65.5 years. On the

Capital	-	Jakarta
Official language	-	Bhasha Indonesian
Government	-	Presidential republic
	-	President Susilo Bambang Yudhoyono
	-	Vice President Boediono
Formation	-	Independence from the Netherlands Declared 17 August 1945 Acknowledged 27 December 1949
Area	-	1,909,569 square kilometres
Population	-	237,424,363 (2011 estimate) Density 123.76/square kilometre
Coastline	-	54,716 kilometres
GDP (PPP)	-	$1,124 trillion (2011 estimate) Per capita $4,666
GDP (nominal)	-	$845.680 billion (2011 estimate) Per capita 3,508
Defence Minister	-	Purnomo Yusgiantoro
C-in-C Armed Forces	-	Admiral Agus Suhartono
Chief of Army Staff	-	General Pramono Edhie Wibowo
Chief of Navy Staff	-	Admiral Soeparno
Chief of Air Staff	-	Air Chief Mshl Imam Sufaat

other hand, the state's heavy involvement in banking and industry, especially the petroleum and natural gas sectors, worked against competition and encouraged corruption on a large scale. Suharto provided strong leadership, but he did not provide for a wise transition and, in his last years, clung to power and favoured family and friends. East Timor, which had been forcibly annexed by Indonesia in 1976, saw bitter conflict between the Indonesian military and local independence movements. When the Asian financial crisis hit in 1997-98, the New Order lost the economic justification that had guaranteed much of its public support, and there was a widespread call for Suharto to step down. He resigned on 21 May 1998, little more than two months after being elected for his seventh term as president.

Suharto was succeeded by Bucharuddin Jusuf Habibie, who sought first to resolve the East Timor situation and begin a new and more open electoral process. In 1999, following Indonesia's first freely contested parliamentary elections since 1955, Abdurrahman Wahid, well-known as both a progressive intellectual and as leader of Indonesia's largest Muslim became president. His quirky leadership style and questions about both his competency and his health, brought increasing opposition and eventually serious threats of impeachment. He was dismissed from office in July 2001 in favour of Megawati Sukarnoputri, the vice president and head of the Indonesian Democratic Party of Struggle (PDI-P). Megawati, Sukarno's eldest daughter, was decisively defeated in the September 2004 presidential runoff election by the Democratic Party candidate, retired army general Susilo Bambang Yudhoyono. Yudhoyono was sworn in as president in October 2004. In the last five years the economy has performed strongly. Although relations among different religious and ethnic groups are largely harmonious, sectarian discontent and violence has occurred. A political settlement to an armed separatist conflict in Aceh was achieved in 2005.

Geography

Topography. Indonesia's land boundaries total 1,758 kilometres, including 1,107 kilometres with Malaysia,

820 kilometres with Papua New Guinea, and 288 kilometres with East Timor. Indonesia's coastline totals 54,716 kilometres on the Indian Ocean, Strait of Malacca, South China Sea, Java Sea, Sulawesi Sea, Maluku Sea, Pacific Ocean, Arafura Sea, Timor Sea, and other smaller seas. Indonesia is the largest archipelagic nation in the world. It encompasses 17,508 islands. About 6,000 of these islands are named, and about 1,000 are permanently settled. The five main islands are Java, Kalimantan, Papua (formerly called Irian Jaya), Sumatra, and Sulawesi. There are two major archipelagos, Nusa Tenggara and Maluku, and about sixty smaller archipelagos. The larger islands of Indonesia are mountainous, with some peaks reaching 3,800 metres above sea level on the western islands and as high as 5,000 metres on Papua. The highest point is Puncak Jaya (5,030 metres) on Papua. The region is tectonically unstable with some 400 volcanoes, of which 100 are active.

Principal Rivers. Indonesia's waterways total 21,579 kilometres. The principal rivers are the Musi, Batanghari, Indragiri, and Kampar rivers on Sumatra; the Kapuas, Barito, and Mahakam rivers on Kalimantan; the Memberamo and Digul rivers on Papua; and the Bengawan Solo, Citarum, and Brantas rivers on Java, which are used primarily for irrigation.

Climate. Indonesia's maritime equatorial climate typically produces high, even temperatures and heavy rainfall; temperature variations are generally due to elevation and time of day, while rainfall may vary across the archipelago as a result of many different factors, among them monsoon patterns, which themselves vary according to location. Average temperatures at or near sea level range from about 23° C to 31°C. In most of the country, rainfall is comparatively heavy throughout the year, with a pronounced rainy season roughly between December and March. East of Surabaya, however, a dry season is increasingly noticeable, especially between June and October.

Natural Resources. Petroleum and natural gas are among Indonesia's most important natural resources. Indonesia is the world's largest exporter of liquefied natural gas. Most petroleum production is on central Sumatra, but Java also has significant production, and there are substantial proven offshore reserves. There are also large coal reserves. Other significant minerals are bauxite, copper, gold, iron, manganese, nickel, sulfur, silver, and tin. An important non-mineral resource is timber.

Land Use. 11.3% (206,753 square kilometres) of Indonesia's total land area is arable, and land planted in permanent crops, including an irrigated area of

48,150 square kilometres, represents 7.2% of the total (132,051 square kilometres). There are 1,619,687 square kilometres of non-arable land and land not under permanent crops.

Environmental Factors. Indonesia's geography leaves the nation vulnerable to severe flooding, unpredictable drought and plant pest attacks, volcanic activity, and earthquakes, which are sometimes associated with tidal waves (tsunami). The most important environmental issues associated with human activities are forest degradation (unregulated cutting, fires, smoke and haze, and erosion); water pollution from industrial wastes and sewage; air pollution from motor vehicles and industry in urban areas, and generally from smoke and haze caused by forest fires; and threats to biodiversity and rare plant and animal species.

Time Zones. Indonesia has three time zones.

Society

Population. Indonesia has the world's fourth largest population after China, India, and the United States, totaling an estimated 238,452,952 in July 2004, with a 1.5% annual growth rate. 69% of the population lives in rural areas. Java is one of the most densely populated areas in the world, with more than 120 million people, or some 945 persons per square kilometre. By contrast, the most densely populated Outer Islands have 90 persons or fewer per square kilometre. Jakarta, on the western end of Java, is the largest city, with an estimated population of 12 million.

Ethnic Groups. Indonesia is a culturally diverse nation. Ethnic identities are not always clear, stable or agreed upon; ethnic groups may appear or profess to be more distinct socially or culturally than they actually are. There are about 350 recognised ethno-linguistic groups in Indonesia, 180 of them located in Papua; 13 languages have more than a million speakers. Javanese are 45% of the population, Sundanese 14%, Madurese 7.5%, coastal Malays 7.5%, and others 26%.

Languages. The official national language is Bahasa Indonesia, a modified form of Malay, with an estimated 17 million to 30 million mother-tongue speakers and more than 140 million second-language speakers or readers. Additionally, as many as 725 other languages and dialects are spoken. Since independence, and particularly since 1965, English has replaced Dutch as the main Western language spoken and is widely used in government and business circles.

Religion. Indonesia has the largest Islamic population of any nation. Most Indonesians (88%) count themselves as Muslims and observe Islamic practices to varying degrees; another 5% of Indonesians are Protestant, 3% are Roman Catholic, 2% are Hindu, 1% are Buddhist, and 1% observe other religions. In some remote areas, animism is practiced. The constitution guarantees religious freedom for the five religions (the first five mentioned) recognised by the state. In 2002 the People's Consultative Assembly rejected a proposal to introduce Islamic law as a constitutional requirement.

Health. Indonesia had a three-tiered system of community health centers in the late 1990s, with 0.66 hospital beds per 1,000 population, the lowest rate among members of the Association of Southeast Asian Nations (ASEAN). In the mid-1990s, there were 16 physicians per 100,000 population in Indonesia, 50 nurses per 100,000, and 26 midwives per 100,000. Both traditional and modern health practices are employed. Government health expenditures are about 3.7% of the GDP. There is about a 75.25% ratio of public to private health-care expenditures. Human immuno-deficiency virus/acquired immune deficiency syndrome (HIV/AIDS) has posed a major public health threat since the early 1990s. Other health hazards are dengue fever and avian influenza.

Economy

Indonesia has a mixed economy in which both the private sector and government play significant roles. The country is the largest economy in Southeast Asia and a member of the G-20 major economies. The industry sector is the economy's largest and accounts for 46.4% of GDP (2010), this is followed by services (37.1%) and agriculture (16.5%). However, since 2010, the service sector has employed more people than other sectors, accounting for 48.9% of the total labour force, this has been followed by agriculture (38.3%) and industry (12.8%). Agriculture, however, had been the country's largest employer for centuries.

According to World Trade Organisation data, Indonesia was the 27th biggest exporting country in the world in 2010, moving up three places from a year before. Indonesia's main export markets (2009) are Japan (17.28%), Singapore (11.29%), the United States (10.81%), and China (7.62%). The major suppliers of imports to Indonesia are Singapore (24.96%), China (12.52%), and Japan (8.92%). In 2005, Indonesia ran a trade surplus with export revenues of US$83.64 billion and import expenditure of US$62.02 billion. The country has extensive natural resources, including crude oil, natural gas, tin, copper, and gold. Indonesia's major imports include machinery and equipment, chemicals, fuels, and foodstuffs. And the country's major export commodities include oil and gas, electrical appliances, plywood, rubber, and textiles.

In the 1960s, the economy deteriorated drastically as a result of political instability, an inexperienced government and economic nationalism. By the time of Sukarno's downfall in the mid-1960s, the economy was in chaos with 1,000% annual inflation, shrinking export revenues, crumbling infrastructure, factories operating at minimal capacity, and negligible investment. Following President Sukarno's downfall in the mid-1960s, the New Order administration brought a degree of discipline to economic policy that quickly brought inflation down, stabilised the currency, rescheduled foreign debt, and attracted foreign aid and investment. Indonesia was until recently Southeast Asia's only member of OPEC, and the 1970s oil price raises provided an export revenue windfall that contributed to sustained high economic growth rates, averaging over 7% from 1968 to 1981.

Following further reforms in the late 1980s, foreign investment flowed into Indonesia, particularly into the rapidly developing export-oriented manufacturing sector, and from 1989 to 1997, the Indonesian economy grew by an average of over 7%. Indonesia was the country hardest hit by the Asian financial crisis of 1997-98. Against the US dollar, the rupiah dropped from about Rp. 2,600 to a low point of 14,000, and the economy shrank by 13.7%. The Rupiah stabilised in the Rp. 8,000 to 10,000 range, and a slow but significant economic recovery has ensued. However, political instability, slow economic reform, and corruption slowed the recovery. Since 2007, however, with the improvement in banking sector and domestic consumption, the national economic growth has been 6% annually and this helped the country weather the 2008-09 global recession. The Indonesian economy performed strongly during the

Global Financial Crisis and in 2011, its GDP grew by 6.5 percent. The country regained its investment grade rating in late 2011 after losing it in the 1997. However, as of 2010, an estimated 13.3% of the population lived below the poverty line, and the unemployment rate was 7.1%.

Infrastructure

Roads. Indonesia has a total of 342,700 kilometres of roads, mostly (about 60%) located on Java, Madura, Bali, and Sumatra; 158,670 kilometres (46%) were paved, of which 27,358 kilometres were classified as main roads and 40,490 kilometres as secondary roads. Another 184,030 kilometres (54% of the total) were unpaved. About 32% of the roads were classified as highways. There are smaller networks of roads on Sulawesi and Kalimantan, while smaller islands often have limited roads within or connecting major settlements. Urban transit is dominated by motor vehicles; the use of automobiles (there were 3.4 million in use in 2002), buses, minibuses, and motorcycles is widespread, even in seemingly remote areas.

Railroads. Track length totalled 6,458 kilometres in 2002, of which 125 kilometres were electrified. All rail facilities were government-owned and -operated until 1991, when government liberalisation created a public corporation, now called PT Kereta Api, which operates Indonesian Railways. The corporation possesses almost total commercial freedom, with the exception of some passenger fares that remain fixed by the government, but it continues to face financial problems as the rising demand for its services is coupled with shortfalls in investment and revenues. However, some of this demand has been met by private passenger and freight service operators that have entered the market since 1995. All railroads are narrow gauge, with 5,931 kilometres 1.067 meter gauge, and 497 kilometres 0.750 meter gauge in 2002. Some 211 kilometres of roadbed are double-track, and 125 kilometres of 1.067 gauge electrified, all on Java.

Ports. Indonesia has 379 ports and harbours controlled by the Ministry of Communications for international and inter-island trade. The four main ports are at Tanjung Priok (near Jakarta), Tanjung Perak (near Surabaya), Belawan (Medan), and Makassar (South Sulawesi). Other major ports are at Cilacap, Cirebon, and Semarang (all on Java), Kupang (Timor), and Palembang (Sumatra). Some 127 ports are classified as capable of handling international shipping.

Inland and Coastal Waterways. Inter-island transportation is critical to domestic commerce. Traditional sailing craft are widely used, but they increasingly are motorised. The merchant fleet is composed of 718 ships of 1,000 gross registered tons or more. These ships include, by type, the following. cargo (398),

refrigerated cargo (2), container (57), bulk carrier (47), roll on/roll off (15), petroleum tanker (128), chemical tanker (13), specialised tanker (12), liquefied natural gas (6), passenger (10), passenger/cargo (13), short-sea passenger (9), vehicle carrier (7), and livestock carrier (1). There also are 35 oceangoing vessels, 259 inter-island vessels, more than 1,000 modernised local-use vessels, almost 4,000 traditional vessels, and 1,900 special bulk carriers. River transport plays a major role in eastern Sumatra, Kalimantan, and Papua. Most of Indonesia's major rivers are at least partly navigable, but those on Java are used primarily for irrigation.

Civil Aviation and Airports. The government owns one airline, Garuda Indonesia, and one smaller subsidiary, Merpati Nusantara Airlines. Civil aviation as a private-sector venture has greatly increased from one private airline in 1993 to 27 private domestic airlines by 2004. In 2003 there were an estimated 661 airports in Indonesia, of which 154 had paved runways (four with more than 3,000-metre runways) and 507 had unpaved runways. Six of the larger airports can accommodate wide-bodied aircraft. Additionally, there were 22 heliports in 2003. Indonesia had a fledgling domestic turbo-prop airliner industry under development under the government-owned Indonesia Aerospace in the late 1990s, but it reached only a prototype-level of production.

Pipelines. In 2003 Indonesia had 672 kilometres of condensate, 125 kilometres of condensate/gas, 8,183 kilometres of gas, 7,429 kilometres of oil, 66 kilometres of oil/gas/water, 1,329 kilometres of refined products, and 72 kilometres of water pipelines.

Telecommunications. Indonesia has been a pioneer

in national satellite communications since 1975. A third generation of satellites, known as Palapa C1 and C2, was launched in 1996; these satellites provide a number of inter-island and international telecommunications services. In 2002 there were some 7.8 million telephones and 11.7 million mobile cellular telephones in use, producing a ratio of some 91 units per 1,000 people. International telephone service was widely available. Radio and television were long dominated by government networks, but private stations have been on the rise since the early 1990s. As of 1998, there were 678 AM, 43 FM, and 82 shortwave radio stations and more than 31 million radios. In 2000 more than 31.7 million television receivers were in use. Estimates vary as to the number of Internet users in Indonesia—between nearly 4 million and 8 million. By 2002 there were more than 2.3 million personal computers, producing a ratio of 11.9 units per 1,000 people.

Government and Politics

Indonesia is a republic based on limited separation of powers among the executive, legislative, and judicial branches. The constitution of 1945 is in force, but, based on a constitutional amendment of August 2002, beginning with the 2004 presidential elections, the once powerful, party-centred presidency is subject to popular election and limited to two five-year terms. Prior to the 2004 elections, the People's Consultative Assembly (Majelis Permusyawaratan Rakyat—MPR) chose the president and vice president, who were not necessarily from the same political party. Under the new law, the president and vice president are elected on a single ticket and the winning ticket must win more than 50% of the popular vote and at least 20% of the vote in half of the provinces. If these percentages are not met, a second-round runoff election is held. The president is both chief of state and head of government.

The MPR, the highest authority of the state, has both elected and appointed members. Under the amendment that surrendered its presidential election powers, the MPR also replaced its 200 non-elected members (representatives of provinces and various social groups) with elected members of a new legislative body, the 200-seat House of Regional Representatives (Dewan Perwakilan Daerah—DPD), which was established by constitutional amendment in 2001. The DPD joins the existing 500-seat House of People's Representatives (Dewan Perwakilan Rakyat— DPR) in a bicameral, all-elected legislature. The members of both houses make up the MPR. The highest court of the land is the Supreme Court (Mahkamah Agung), composed of justices appointed by the president from a list of candidates approved by the legislature. In 2004 the Supreme Court was preparing to assume administrative responsibility for the lower-court system, currently run by the Ministry of Justice and Human Rights. Under the Supreme Court is a quadripartite judiciary of general, religious, military, and administrative courts. Appeals can be made, sequentially, from a district court to a high court to the Supreme Court. A separate Constitutional Court was established in 2003. The Supreme Audit Board (Badan Permeriksa Keuangan) oversees accountability of public finance and is independent of the chief executive, but its members are chosen by the president.

The judicial branch is theoretically equal to the executive and legislative branches and has the right of judicial review over laws passed by the DPR, as well as government regulations and presidential, ministerial, and gubernatorial decrees. In practice, however, the judiciary is less influential than the executive and legislative branches, and it has often been heavily influenced by the executive branch. Indonesia has not accepted compulsory International Court of Justice jurisdiction.

Administrative Divisions. Indonesia has 30 provincial-level units. 27 provinces (*propinsi*), two special regions (*daerah istimewa*; Aceh and Yogyakarta), and one special capital city region (*daerah khusus*; Jakarta). Since January 1, 2001, when central control over local affairs was lessened, the 357 districts (*kabupaten*) and municipalities (*kotamadya*)—the first-level provincial subdivisions—became the administrative units responsible for providing most government services. Following a 1999 referendum agreed to by the legislature, and a period of United Nations stewardship, the province of Timor Timur became the independent nation of the Democratic Republic of Timor-L'este (East Timor) on 20 May 2002.

Provincial and Local Government. Provinces (*propinsi*) are divided into districts or regencies (*kabupaten*), which are further divided into subdistricts (*kecamatan*). There also are some municipalities or city governments (*kotamadya*) that are on the same administrative level as the districts and others that are on the subdistrict level. The lowest level of the administrative hierarchy is the village (*desa*). The chief executives are provincial governors, district or regency heads, mayors of cities, and village heads. Legislation is handled by provincial and district parliaments. Under the revised election laws, governors, mayors, and district heads (regents) were to be directly elected for the first time in 2004.

Judicial and Legal System. The legal system is based on Roman-Dutch law, modified by indigenous concepts and by new criminal procedures and election codes. There are 2,418 district courts, each of which has a panel of judges that conducts trials by posing questions, hearing evidence, deciding on guilt or innocence, and assessing punishment. Both the defence and prosecution can appeal verdicts. Arbitrary arrest and detention are prohibited, but the government lacks adequate enforcement mechanisms, and authorities have routinely violated the Criminal Procedures Code. The code provides prisoners with the right to notify their families promptly, and specifies that warrants must be produced during an arrest. Exceptions are allowed if, for example, a suspect is caught in the act of committing a crime. The law allows investigators to issue warrants; at times, however, authorities make arrests without warrants.

Politics and Political Parties. Whereas the official government party, Golkar, once held an absolute majority, there are now numerous parties vying for power, and none enjoys national majority support. These parties include the Crescent Moon and Star Party (PBB), Democratic Party (PD), Indonesia Democratic Party-Struggle (PDI-P), National Awakening Party (PKB), National Mandate Party (PAN), Prosperous Justice Party (PKS), and United Development Party (PPP).

Mass Media. The constitution provides for freedom of speech and freedom of the press; however, the government has a history of restricting these rights in practice. Private press in current operation includes nearly 50 daily newspapers, dozens of magazines, 10 foreign press bureaus, and five private commercial television stations. There are also 10 foreign press bureaus, two government radio stations (Radio Republik Indonesia and Voice of Indonesia), one government news agency (Antara), and one independent national news agency (Kantorberita Nasional Indonesia). The government does not restrict Internet usage or content.

Foreign Relations. Indonesia is a charter member of the Nonaligned Movement, which was established in September 1961. The April 1955 Asian-African Conference—held in Bandung, Indonesia—was an important milestone in the development of the Nonaligned Movement's goal of independence from the Cold War superpowers (the United States and the Soviet Union) and the former colonialist powers and put Indonesia on the international stage for a time. As the Sukarno era progressed, however, Indonesia's government was at odds with the Dutch over West New Guinea (now called Papua) and increasingly hostile toward neighbouring Malaysia to the point that Sukarno withdrew Indonesia from the United Nations when Malaysia was appointed a non-permanent member of the Security Council in 1964. In 1967 Indonesia participated in establishing a new officially nonaligned grouping of neighbours, the Association of Southeast Asian Nations (ASEAN), which was friendly toward the Western powers. Its secretariat was placed in Jakarta, and its first secretary general was an Indonesian.

The commemoration of the 30th anniversary of the Bandung Conference in 1985 saw Indonesia's full reemergence on the world stage, allowing Jakarta to project itself as a leading voice in the Nonaligned Movement and providing it with an extra-regional platform for claiming proper international standing. Indonesia's diplomatic relations with China had been reinstituted in 1990. Indonesia continues to play an important role in ASEAN affairs. Indonesia's most contentious regional relations are those with Australia, mostly over the situation in East Timor.

Separatist movements in the provinces of Aceh and Papua have led to armed conflict, and subsequent allegations of human rights abuses and brutality from all sides. Following a sporadic thirty-year guerrilla war between the Free Aceh Movement (GAM) and the Indonesian military, a ceasefire agreement was reached in 2005. In Papua, there has been a significant, albeit imperfect, implementation of regional autonomy laws, and a reported decline in the levels of violence and human rights abuses, since the presidency of Yudhoyono.

National Security

Armed Forces. The Indonesia Armed Forces (Tentara Nasional Indonesia—TNI) component services are the Army (TNI—Angkatan Darat), 265,000; Navy (TNI—Angkatan Laut); and Air Force (TNI—Angkatan Udara). There is a reserve force of 400,000. With the transition to democratic rule beginning in 1998, the government endeavoured to undertake steps to reform the TNI in order to improve public opinion about the military and to bring the military under civilian control. Among such steps were the devolution of the national police from the armed forces to the Office of the President and official transfer of responsibility for internal security from the TNI to the police in April 1999, focusing the military's attention on national defense rather than domestic policing. Another important reform was a provision that military personnel had to retire or resign before occupying an elected or appointed civilian government position. However, the TNI successfully resisted transformation of its territorial command structure because of threats of terrorism and separatism, and because it needs this structure to support its huge business empire, from which it obtains an estimated two-thirds of its funding (the government budget provides only one-third of the funds needed to operate and equip the military and national police). After several years in disrepute because of revelations of extensive human rights abuses, the TNI has regained much of its lost prestige. Many Indonesians appear to favour military firmness as the country is facing terrorist, separatist, and ethnic conflict as well as a moribund economy.

Foreign Military Relations. Indonesia enjoys cordial military-to-military relations with a wide range of nations. Its closest ties are with fellow members of Association of Southeast Asian Nations (ASEAN). Formerly close ties to the United States, Australia, and some European countries became strained in the 1990s over human rights issues; many countries cut back their military relations with the TNI after the rampage of army and army-supported militia forces in East Timor in 1999. Because of arms sales embargoes imposed by its primary sources in the United States, Indonesia has turned to Russia and other nations of the former Soviet Union, South Korea, and Poland, among others, for major arms purchases.

Human rights and political issues have also affected sales of foreign military equipment to Indonesia, but such tensions eased after East Timor gained independence in 2002. In 1992 the U.S. Congress terminated grant military training assistance (International Military Education and Training—IMET) after learning of Indonesian military human rights abuses in East Timor. This restriction was partially relaxed in 1995, but assistance was suspended again in 1999 as a result of violence following the referendum on East Timor's separation from Indonesia.

External Threat. Indonesia has no conventional external threat to its security. The primary outside threat is that of international terrorism. Terrorists belonging to the regional terrorist group Jemaah Islamiyah (Community of Islam) have conducted a number of recent bomb attacks, including the bombing of two night clubs on Bali in October 2002 that killed 202 people and injured more than 300, while a bombing at the Marriott Hotel in Jakarta in August 2003 killed 12 people and injured 150. Other threats to Indonesian security include piracy, particularly in the Strait of Malacca, smuggling, and maritime poaching.

Internal Threats and Terrorism. There are two general threats to Indonesian domestic security: terrorism and ethnic and religious conflict. The terrorists causing the greatest problems in Indonesia are members of the regional group, Jemaah Islamiyah (Community of Islam). Although Jemaah Islamiyah operates primarily in Indonesia, it has operational units in peninsular Malaysia, Singapore, Australia, and Papua New Guinea. Jemaah Islamiyah has perpetrated significant terrorist acts and is believed to have strong links with al-Qaeda. The government announced at the time of the October 2002 Bali bombings that terrorism was "a real and potential threat to national security" and has called upon the public to confront domestically based terrorists.

Centre-region relations have been perennially problematic, with the government continuing to experience difficulties in maintaining order and the rule of law in outlying regions. The most pressing threats are separatists in Aceh and Papua (formerly Irian Jaya). The major insurgent groups are Gerakan Aceh Merdeka (GAM—Free Aceh Movement), which wants an independent Islamic state in Aceh and has an estimated strength of 2,000 armed activists; and Organisasi Papua Merdeka (OPM—Free West Papua Movement), which seeks independence for Papua and has an estimated 150 activists.

Other regions also experienced outbreaks of violence, some of them very serious, after 1996. These include religious violence in Maluku and Central Sulawesi, ethnic violence over land use and local power in Kalimantan and other locales, and violence involving both political-religious hostility as well as hysteria about the misuse of supernatural powers in East Java. There have been many incidents of anti-Chinese riots in urban areas, some of them very destructive. On several occasions, most notably in 2001, radical Muslim groups have "swept" parts of Jakarta, cities in central Java, and other tourist areas, threatening Westerners.

MALAYSIA

Malaysia is a federation of 13 states and three federal territories in Southeast Asia. The country consists of two geographical regions divided by the South China Sea. Peninsular Malaysia (or West Malaysia) on the Malay Peninsula shares a land border on the north with Thailand and is connected by the Johore-Singapore Causeway and the Malaysia-Singapore Second Link to the south with Singapore. It consists of nine sultanates (Johor, Kedah, Kelantan, Negeri Sembilan, Pahang, Perak, Perlis, Selangor and Terengganu), two states headed by governors (Malacca and Penang), and two federal territories (Putrajaya and Kuala Lumpur). Malaysian Borneo (or East Malaysia) occupies the northern part of the island of Borneo, bordering Indonesia and surrounding the Sultanate of Brunei. It consists of the states of Sabah and Sarawak and the federal territory of Labuan.

Its land boundaries total 2,669 kilometres with Brunei (381 kilometres), Indonesia (1,782 kilometres) and Thailand (506 kilometres). Its coastline extends 4,675 kilometres. Putrajaya is the newly created administrative capital for the federal government of Malaysia, aimed in part to ease growing congestion within Malaysia's capital city, Kuala Lumpur. Kuala Lumpur remains the seat of parliament, as well as the commercial and financial capital of the country.

The Malaysian flag has 14 equal horizontal stripes of red (top) alternating with white (bottom); there is a blue rectangle in the upper hoist-side corner bearing a yellow crescent and a yellow 14-pointed star (the crescent and the star are traditional symbols of Islam).

Malaysia adopted its Constitution on 31 August 1957 (amended on 16 September 1963)

History

Britain established its first colony in the Malay peninsula in 1786, with the lease of the island of Penang to the British East India Company by the Sultan of Kedah. In 1824, the British took control of Malacca following the Anglo-Dutch Treaty of 1824 which divided the Malay archipelago between Britain and the Netherlands, with Malaya in the British zone. In 1826, Britain established the crown colony of the Straits Settlements, uniting its three possessions in Malaya: Penang, Malacca and Singapore. The Straits Settlements were administered under the East India Company in Calcutta until 1867, when they were transferred to the Colonial Office in London.

During the late 19th century, many Malay states decided to obtain British help in settling their internal conflicts. The commercial importance of tin mining in the Malay states to merchants in the Straits Settlements led to British government intervention in the tin-producing states in the Malay Peninsula. British gunboat diplomacy was employed to bring about a peaceful resolution to civil disturbances caused by Chinese gangsters, and the Pangkor Treaty of 1874 paved the way for the expansion of British influence in Malaya. By the turn of the 20th century, the states of Pahang, Selangor, Perak, and Negeri Sembilan, known together as the Federated Malay States were under the de facto control of British Residents appointed to advise the Malay rulers. The British were "advisers" in name, but in reality they

Capital	-	Kuala Lumpur Putrajaya (administrative centre)
Official languages	-	Bahasa Malaysia, English
Ethnic groups	-	54% Malay, 25% Chinese, 7.5% Indian, 11.8% other
Government	-	Federal constitutional elective monarchy and Federal parliamentary democracy
	-	Head of State Tunku Abdul Halim
	-	Prime Minister Najib Tun Razak
Formation	-	Independence from Britain - 31 August 1957 Federation (with Sabah, Sarawak and Singapore) 16 September 1963
Area	-	329,847 square kilometres
Coastline	-	4,675 kilometres
Population	-	28,334,135 (2010 census) Density 86/ square kilometre
GDP (PPP)	-	$472.942 billion (2012 estimate) Per capita $16,186
GDP (nominal)	-	$278.680 billion (2012 estimate) Per capita $10,446
Defence Minister	-	Datuk Seri Ahmad Zahid Hamidi
Chief of Defence Forces	-	General Dato' Sir Azizan Ariffin
Chief of Army	-	General Tan Sri Dato' Sri Hj
Chief of Navy	-	Admiral Tan Sri Abdul Aziz Bin Hj Zafar
Chief of Air Force	-	General Tan Sri Dato' Sri Rodzali bin Daud

exercised substantial influence over the Malay rulers.

The remaining five states in the peninsula, known as the Unfederated Malay States, while not directly under rule from London, also accepted British advisors around the turn of the 20th century. Of these, the four northern states of Perlis, Kedah, Kelantan and Terengganu had previously been under Siamese control. On the island of Borneo, Sabah was governed as the crown colony of British North Borneo, while Sarawak was acquired from Brunei as the personal kingdom of the Brooke family, who ruled as White Rajahs.

Following the Japanese occupation of Malaya during World War II, popular support for independence grew. Post-war British plans to unite the administration of Malaya under a single crown colony called the Malayan Union foundered on strong opposition from the Malays, who opposed the emasculation of the Malay rulers and the granting of citizenship to the ethnic Chinese. The Malayan Union, established in 1946 and consisting of all the British possessions in Malaya with the exception of Singapore, was dissolved in 1948 and replaced by the Federation of Malaya, which restored the autonomy of the rulers of the Malay states under British protection.

During this time, rebels under the leadership of the Communist Party of Malaya launched guerrilla operations designed to force the British out of Malaya. The Malayan Emergency, as it was known, lasted from 1948 to 1960, and involved a long anti-insurgency campaign by Commonwealth troops in Malaya. Against this backdrop, independence for the Federation within the Commonwealth was granted on 31 August 1957.

In 1963 Malaya along with the then-British crown

colonies of Singapore, Sabah (British North Borneo) and Sarawak formed Malaysia. The Sultanate of Brunei, though initially expressing interest in joining the Federation, withdrew from the planned merger due to opposition from certain segments of the population as well as arguments over the payment of oil royalties and the status of the Sultan in the planned merger.

Independence was marred by conflict with Indonesia (Konfrontasi) over the formation of Malaysia, Singapore's eventual exit in 1965, and racial riots in 1969. The Philippines also made an active claim on Sabah in that period based upon the Sultanate of Brunei's cession of its north-east territories to the Sultanate of Sulu in 1704. The claim is still ongoing. After the racial riots of 1969, the controversial New Economic Policy—intended to increase the share of the economic pie owned by the bhumiputras ("indigenous people", which includes the majority Malays, but not always the indigenous population) as opposed to other ethnic groups—was launched by Prime Minister Tun Abdul Razak. Malaysia has since maintained a delicate ethno-political balance, with a system of government that has attempted to combine overall economic development with political and economic policies that favour Bhumiputras.

Geography

The two distinct parts of Malaysia, separated from each other by the South China Sea, share a largely similar landscape in that both West and East Malaysia feature coastal plains rising to often densely forested hills and mountains, the highest of which is Mount Kinabalu at 4,095.2 metres on the island of Borneo. The local climate is equatorial and characterised by the annual southwest (April to October) and northeast (October to February) monsoons.

The Strait of Malacca, lying between Sumatra and Peninsular Malaysia, is arguably the most important shipping lane in the world. Malaysia's natural resources include tin, petroleum, timber, copper, iron ore, natural gas, and bauxite. Malaysia is the world's primary exporter of natural rubber and palm oil, which together with sawn logs and sawn timber, cocoa, pepper, pineapple and tobacco dominate the growth of the sector. Palm oil is also a major generator of foreign exchange.

The country has 5.46% of arable land of which 17.54% is under permanent crops. Irrigated land covers an area of 3,650 square kilometres. Natural hazards include flooding, landslides, forest fires. Environmental issues include air pollution from industrial and vehicular emissions; water pollution from raw sewage; deforestation and smoke/haze from Indonesian forest fires.

Tin and petroleum are the two main mineral resources that are of major significance in the Malaysian economy. Malaysia was once the world's largest producer of tin until the collapse of the tin market in the early 1980s. In the 19th and 20th century, tin played a predominant role in the Malaysian economy. It was only in 1972 that petroleum and natural gas took over from tin as the mainstay of the mining sector. Meanwhile, the contribution by tin has declined. Petroleum and natural gas which were discovered in oilfields offshore Sabah, Sarawak and Terengganu have contributed much to the Malaysian economy particularly in those three states. Other minerals of some importance or significance include copper, gold, bauxite, iron-ore and coal together with industrial minerals like clay, kaolin, silica, limestone, barite, phosphates and dimension stones such as granite as well as marble blocks and slabs. Small quantities of gold are produced.

In 2004, Minister in the Prime Minister's Department, Datuk Mustapa Mohamed, revealed that Malaysia's oil reserves stood at 4.84 billion barrels while natural gas reserves increased to 89 trillion cubic feet. The government estimates that at current production rates Malaysia will be able to produce oil up to 18 years and gas for 35 years.

Malaysia has a bio-diverse range of flora and fauna, and is also considered one of the 17 mega-diverse countries.

Society

Malaysia is a multi-ethnic, multi-cultural and multilingual society. The population as of February 2007 is 26.6 million consisting of 62% Malays, 24% Chinese, 8% Indians, with other minorities and indigenous peoples. Malay is the national language of the country. In the past, Malays wrote in Sanskrit or using Sanskrit-based alphabets. After the 15th century, Jawi (a script based on Arabic) became popular. Over time, Romanised script overtook Sanskrit and Jawi as the dominant script. This was largely due to the influence of the colonial education system, which taught children in Romanised writing rather than in Arabic script.

By constitutional definition, all Malays are Muslim. About 30% of the population are Malaysians of Chinese descent. Malaysians of Indian descent comprise about 8% of the population. About 90% of the Indian community is Tamils but various other groups are also present, including Malayalis, Punjabis and Gujaratis. There are also various non-Malay peoples who are designated as indigenous, mostly in East Malaysia. These make up about 7% of the population.

Non-Malay indigenous groups make up more than half of the state of Sarawak's population—constitute about 66% of Sabah's population—and also exist in much smaller numbers on the Peninsula, where they are collectively known as Orang Asli. The non-Malay indigenous population is divided into dozens of ethnic groups, but they share some general cultural similarities. Population distribution is uneven, with some 20 million residents concentrated on the Malay Peninsula, while East Malaysia is relatively less populated.

Due to the rise in labour intensive industries, Malaysia has 10 to 20% foreign workers with the uncertainty due in part to the large number of illegal workers, mostly Indonesian. There are a million legal foreign workers and perhaps another million unauthorised foreigners. The state of Sabah alone has nearly 25% of its 2.7 million population listed as illegal foreign workers.

Although the Malaysian constitution theoretically guarantees religious freedom, in practice the situation is not so simple. All ethnic Malays are Muslim as defined in the Malaysian constitution. Additionally, all non-Muslims who marry a Muslim must renounce their religion and convert to Islam. Meanwhile, Non-Muslims experience restrictions in activities such as construction of religious buildings and the celebration of certain religious events in some states. Malaysians tend to personally respect one another's religious beliefs, with inter-religious problems arising mainly from the political sphere. However, there is a growing divide because many Chinese and Indians feel oppressed by recent religiously-related political sentiments that threaten freedom of religion.

Healthcare

Malaysian society places importance on the expansion and development of healthcare, putting 5% of the government social sector development budget into public healthcare—an increase of more than 47% over the previous figure. This has meant an overall increase of more than RM 2 billion. With a rising and aging population, the Government wishes to improve in many areas including the refurbishment of existing hospitals, building and equipping new hospitals, expansion of the number of polyclinics, and improvements in training and expansion of telehealth. Over the last couple of years they have increased their efforts to overhaul the systems and attract more foreign investment.

The Malaysian healthcare system requires doctors to perform a compulsory three years service with public hospitals to ensure the manpower of these hospitals is maintained. Recently foreign doctors have also been encouraged to take up employment here. There is still, however, a compound shortage of medical workforce, especially that of highly trained specialists resulting in certain medical care and treatment only available in large cities. Recent efforts to bring many facilities to other towns have been hampered by lack of expertise to run the available equipment made ready by investments.

The majority of private hospitals are in urban areas and, unlike many of the public hospitals, are equipped with the latest diagnostic and imaging facilities. Private hospitals have not generally been seen as an ideal investment—it has often taken up to ten years before companies have seen any profits. However, the situation has now changed and companies are now looking into this area again, particularly in view of the increasing interest by foreigners in coming to Malaysia for medical care and the recent government focus to develop the health tourism industry.

Government and Politics

Malaysia is a federal constitutional elective monarchy. The federal head of state of Malaysia is the Yang di-Pertuan Agong, commonly referred to as the King of Malaysia. The Yang di-Pertuan Agong is elected to a five-year term among the nine hereditary Sultans of the Malay states; the other four states, which have titular Governors, do not participate in the selection.

The system of government in Malaysia is closely modelled on that of the Westminster parliamentary system, a legacy of British colonial rule. In practice however, more power is vested in the executive branch of government than in the legislative, and the judiciary has been weakened by sustained attacks by the government during the Mahathir era. Since independence in 1957, Malaysia has been governed by a multi-party coalition known as the Barisan Nasional (formerly known as the Alliance).

Legislative power is divided between federal and state legislatures. The bicameral parliament consists of the lower house, the House of Representatives or Dewan Rakyat (literally the "Chamber of the People") and the upper house, the Senate or Dewan Negara (literally the "Chamber of the Nation"). The 219-member House of Representatives are elected from single-member constituencies that are drawn based on population for a maximum term of 5 years. All 70 Senators sit for 3-year terms; 26 are elected by the 13 state assemblies, 2 representing the federal territory of Kuala Lumpur, 1 each from federal territories of Labuan and Putrajaya, and 40 are appointed by the king. Besides the Parliament at the federal level, each state has a unicameral state legislative chamber whose members are elected from single-member constituencies. Parliamentary elections are held at least once every five years, with the last general election being in March 2004. The cabinet is chosen from among members of both houses of Parliament and is responsible to that body.

State governments are led by chief ministers (Menteri Besar in Malay states or Ketua Menteri in states without hereditary rulers), who is a state assembly member from a majority party in the state assemblies.

Administrative divisions. Putrajaya is the administrative capital of Malaysia. The country has 13 states (Johor, Kedah, Kelantan, Melaka, Negeri Sembilan, Pahang, Perak, Perlis, Pulau Pinang, Sabah, Sarawak, Selangor, and Terengganu) and one federal territory with three components (city of Kuala Lumpur, Labuan, and Putrajaya)

Judiciary. The legal system is based on English common law. Judicial review of legislative acts in the Supreme Court is at the request of the supreme head of the federation. Malaysia has not accepted jurisdiction of the International Court of Justice. Islamic law is applied to Muslims in matters of family law. Judges to the Federal Court are appointed by the paramount ruler on the advice of the prime minister)

Economy

Southeast Asia has been a centre of trade for centuries. Various items such as porcelain and spices were actively traded even before Malacca and Singapore rose to prominence. Later, as the British started to take over as administrators of Malaya, rubber and palm oil trees were introduced for commercial purposes. Over time, Malaysia became the world's largest major producer of tin, rubber, and palm oil. These three commodities, along with other raw materials, firmly set Malaysia's economic tempo well into the mid-20th century.

Instead of relying on the local Malays as a source of labour, the British brought in Chinese and Indians to work in on the mines, plantations and fill up the void in professional expertise. Although many of them returned to their respective home countries after their agreed tenure ended, some remained in Malaysia and settled permanently.

As Malaya moved towards independence, the government began implementing economic five-year plans, beginning with the First Malayan Five Year Plan in 1955. Upon the establishment of Malaysia, the plans were re-titled and renumbered, beginning with the First Malaysia Plan in 1965.

In the 1970s, Malaysia began to imitate the four Asian Tiger economies (Republic of Korea (South Korea), Republic of China (Taiwan), then British Crown Colony of Hong Kong and the Republic of Singapore) and committed itself to a transition from being reliant on mining and agriculture to an economy that depends more on manufacturing. With Japanese investment, heavy industries flourished and in a matter of years, Malaysian exports became the country's primary growth engine. Malaysia consistently achieved more than 7% GDP growth along with low inflation in the 1980s and the 1990s. Today, Malaysia is one of the world's largest computer hard disk manufacturing sites.

Malaysia is a relatively open state-oriented and newly industrialised market economy. The state plays a significant but declining role in guiding economic activity through macroeconomic plans. In 2007, the economy of Malaysia was the 3rd largest in Southeast Asia and 29th largest economy in the world by purchasing power parity with a growth rate of 5% to 7% since 2007.

Since the 1980s the industrial sector has led Malaysia's growth. The Malaysian economy recovered from the 1997 Asian Financial Crisis sooner than neighbouring countries, and has since recovered to the levels of the pre-crisis era. Inequalities exist between different ethnic groups, with a major issue being that the Chinese minority accounts for 70% of the country's market capitalisation, even though it only makes up about one third of it.

International trade, facilitated by the adjacent Strait of Malacca shipping route and manufacturing are both key sectors of the country's economy. Malaysia is an exporter of natural and agricultural resources, the most valuable exported resource being petroleum. At one time, it was the largest producer of tin, rubber and palm oil in the world. Manufacturing has a large influence in the country's economy, although Malaysia's economic structure has been moving away from it. In an effort to diversify the economy and make Malaysia's economy less dependent on exported goods, the government has pushed to increase tourism in Malaysia. As a result tourism has become Malaysia's third largest source of income from foreign exchange, although it is threatened by the negative effects of the growing industrial economy, with large amounts of air and water pollution along with deforestation affecting tourism. Malaysia has developed itself into a centre of Islamic banking. Knowledge-based services are also expanding. Malaysia's rapid economic growth and prosperity is reflected by the Petronas Towers, the headquarters of the national oil giant in Kuala Lumpur and, at one time, the tallest building in the world. While the pace of development today is not as rapid, it is seen to be more sustainable.

Infrastructure

The infrastructure of Malaysia is one of the most developed in Asia. Its telecommunications network is second only to Singapore's in Southeast Asia, with 4.7 million fixed-line subscribers and more than 30 million cellular subscribers. The country has seven international ports, the major one being the Port Klang. There are 200 industrial parks along with specialised parks such as Technology Park Malaysia and Kulim Hi-Tech Park. Fresh water is available to over 95 per cent of the population. During the colonial period, development was mainly concentrated in economically powerful cities and in areas forming security concerns. Although rural areas have been the focus of great development, they still lag behind areas such as the West Coast of Peninsular Malaysia. The telecommunication network, although strong in urban areas, is less available to the rural population.

Malaysia's road network covers 98,721 kilometres and includes 1,821 kilometres of expressways. The longest highway of the country, the North-South Expressway, extends over 800 kilometres between the Thai border and Singapore. The road systems in East Malaysia are less developed and of lower quality in comparison to that of Peninsular Malaysia. Malaysia has 118 airports, of which 38 are paved. The country's official airline is Malaysia Airlines, providing international and domestic air service alongside two other carriers. The railway system is state-run, and covers a total of 1,849 kilometres. Relatively inexpensive elevated Light Rail Transit systems are used in some cities, such as Kuala Lumpur. The Asean Rail Express is a railway service that connects Kuala Lumpur to Bangkok, and is intended to eventually stretch from Singapore to China.

Traditionally, energy production in Malaysia has been based on oil and natural gas. The country has 13 GW of electrical generation capacity. However, the country only has 33 years of natural gas reserves, and 19 years of oil reserves, while the demand for energy is increasing. In response, the government is expanding into renewable energy sources. Sixteen per cent of electricity generation is hydroelectric, the remaining 84 per cent being thermal. The oil and gas industry is dominated by state owned Petronas, and the energy sector as a whole is regulated by the Energy Commission of Malaysia, a statutory commission that governs the energy in the peninsula and Sabah.

National Security

Malaysia's strategic interests are viewed from three-tiers encompassing the areas of immediate vicinity, regional and global. The areas of its immediate vicinity comprise the land territories, territorial waters, airspace, the Exclusive Economic Zone (EEZ), the Straits of Malacca and its approaches, and the Straits of Singapore as well as the sea and air lines of communication connecting Peninsular Malaysia and Sabah and Sarawak.

The regional areas of interest to Malaysia cover Southeast Asia, including Andaman Islands as well as the South China Sea. Malaysia views any development affecting the region as invariably impinging her security and development. This is particularly significant as Malaysia shares either common land or sea boundaries or both with most of the ASEAN states. Any infringement to the region's security, whether in the form of intra-regional or extra-regional conflicts, will have consequential effects on Malaysia's security.

Malaysia's growing trade links, new markets for its products, increasing foreign investment and the acquisition of private enterprises with worldwide interests have broadened its interests beyond the immediate vicinity and the region. In view of this, it is in Malaysia's interest to ensure that global peace is maintained. Taking cognizance of its strategic and competing interests, Malaysia's defence revolves around the fundamental principles of Self-Reliance, Regional Cooperation and External Assistance.

Malaysia has asserted sovereignty over the Spratly Islands together with China, Philippines, Taiwan, Vietnam, and Brunei. Malaysia was not party to the March 2005 joint accord among the national oil companies of China, the Philippines, and Vietnam on conducting marine seismic activities in the Spratly Islands. Disputes continue over deliveries of fresh water to Singapore, bridge construction Singapore's land reclamation, maritime boundaries, and Pedra Branca Island/Pulau Batu Putih. Both parties agreed to arbitration on the island dispute within three years. The ICJ awarded Ligitan and Sipadan islands, also claimed by Indonesia and Philippines, to Malaysia but left the maritime boundary in the hydrocarbon-rich Celebes Sea in dispute, resulting in confrontations in March 2005 over concessions to the Ambalat oil block.

Separatist violence in Thailand's predominantly Muslim southern provinces prompted measures to close and monitor its border with Malaysia to stem terrorist activities. Philippines retains a claim to Malaysia's Sabah State in northern Borneo. In 2003, Brunei and Malaysia ceased gas and oil exploration in their disputed offshore and deepwater sea beds and negotiations have stalemated prompting consideration of international adjudication. Malaysia's land boundary with Brunei around Limbang is in dispute.

Piracy remains a problem in the Malacca Strait besides the issue of refugees from Indonesia and Burma. Malaysia is a regional transit point for some illicit drugs, though drug trafficking is prosecuted vigorously and carries severe penalties.

Even though it recognises the importance of regional cooperation and external assistance, Malaysia believes that self-reliance should continue to be the cornerstone of its defence. In this regard Malaysia will strive towards enhancing and developing its Armed Forces capabilities as well as promoting defence consciousness and patriotism among its citizens.

Armed Forces

In the early 1990s, Malaysia undertook a major programme to expand and modernize its armed forces. The role of the MAF is to defend the sovereignty and strategic interests of Malaysia from all forms of threat. It is responsible to assist the civilian authorities to overcome all international threats, preserve public order, assist in natural disasters and participate in national development programmes.

REPUBLIC OF MALDIVES

The Republic of Maldives, is an island nation consisting of a group of atolls in the Indian Ocean. The Maldives is located south of India's Lakshadweep islands, and about seven hundred kilometres south-west of Sri Lanka. The Maldives' twenty-six atolls encompass a territory featuring 1,192 islets, roughly two hundred of which are inhabited by local communities. The Maldives is the smallest Asian country in terms of population. It is also the smallest predominantly Muslim nation in the world.

The name "Maldives" derives from the Sanskrit maladvipa, meaning "garland of islands". Originally the inhabitants were Buddhist, but Islam was introduced in 1153. It later became a Portuguese (1558), Dutch (1654), and British (1887) colonial possession. In 1965, the Maldives obtained independence from Britain, and in 1968 the Sultanate was replaced by a Republic. However, in thirty-eight years, the Maldives have seen only three Presidents. Historically, Maldives had a strategic importance because of its location on the major maritime routes of the Indian Ocean. Sri Lanka and India have had cultural and economic ties with it for centuries.

History

Maldivian tradition suggests that the first settlers were Dravidian people, probably fishermen from the southwest coast of the Indian Subcontinent and the western shores of Sri Lanka. Buddhism came to the Maldives at the time of Emperor Ashoka's expansion and became the dominant religion until the 12th century AD. According to a legend, a prince named Koimala from India entered the Maldives from the North (Ihavandhu) and became the first king from the House of Theemuge. The ancient Maldivian Kings promoted Buddhism and the first Maldive writings and artistic achievements in the form of highly developed sculpture and architecture are from that period. The conversion to Islam began from the end of the 12th century AD. Over the centuries, the islands have been visited and their development influenced by sailors and traders from countries on the Arabian Sea and the Bay of Bengal.

From 1887 to 1965, Maldives was ruled by a succession of sultans. They were hereditary until 1932. Maldives remained a British crown protectorate until 1953 when the sultanate was suspended and the First Republic was declared under the short-lived presidency of Muhammad Amin Didi. Muslim conservatives in Male ousted his government, and during a riot over food shortages, Didi was beaten by a mob and died on a nearby island. In 1956 Britain obtained permission to reestablish its wartime airfield on Gan in the southernmost Addu Atoll on a 100-year lease and a payment of £2,000 a year, as well as some 44 hectares on Hitaddu for radio installations. In 1960 Maldives allowed Britain to continue at Gan and the Hitaddu for a thirty-year period, with the payment of £750,000 over the period of 1960 to 1965 for the purpose of Maldives' economic development.

In 1959 the inhabitants of the three southernmost atolls protested against the government. They formed the United Suvadive Republic and elected, Abdullah Afeef as president and Hithadhoo as capital of this

Capital	-	Malé
Official language	-	Dhivehi
Government	-	Presidential republic
	-	President Mohammed Waheed Hassan Manik
	-	Speaker of the Majlis Abdulla Shahid
	-	Chief Justice Ahmed Faiz
Formation	-	Independence from United Kingdom - 26 July 1965
Area	-	298 square kilometres
Population	-	328,536 (2012 estimate) Density 1,102/ square kilometre
GDP (PPP)	-	$2.841 billion (2011 estimate) Per capita $8,731
GDP (nominal)	-	$1.944 billion (2011 estimate) Per capita $5,973
Minister of Defence and National Security	-	Colonel (Retired) Mohamed Nazim
Chief of Defence Force	-	Major General Ahmed Shiyam

republic. On 26 July 1965, Maldives gained independence from Britain, who retained the use of the Gan and Hitaddu facilities. After independence from Britain in 1965, the sultanate continued to operate for another three years under King Muhammad Fareed. On 11 November 1968, the monarchy was abolished and replaced by a republic, although this was a cosmetic change without any significant alteration in the structures of government. The official name of the country was changed from Maldive Islands to the Maldives in a progressive manner. Tourism began to be developed on the archipelago about five years later.

Elected to replace Nasir for a five-year presidential term in 1978 was Maumoon Abdul Gayoom, a former university lecturer and Maldivian ambassador to the United Nations. The peaceful election ushered in a period of political stability and economic development. The local populace benefited from increased tourism and the corresponding increase in foreign contacts involving various development projects. Gayoom's popularity remained strong, allowing him to win three more presidential terms, receiving more than 95 percent of the vote as the government did not allow any legal opposition.

During the 1970s, the economic situation in Maldives suffered a setback when the Sri Lankan market for Maldives' main export of dried fish collapsed. Adding to the problems was the British decision in 1975 to close its airfield on Gan in line with its policy of abandoning defence commitments east of the Suez Canal. A steep commercial decline followed. As a result, the popularity of Nasir's government suffered and the twenty-year period of authoritarian rule under Nasir abruptly ended in 1978 when he fled to Singapore. A subsequent investigation revealed that he had absconded with millions of dollars from the state treasury.

In November 1988, a group of Maldivians headed by Mr. Lutfee a small time businessman used Tamil mercenaries from Sri Lanka to stage a coup against President Gayyoom. After an appeal by the Maldivian government for help, the Indian military intervened against the mercenaries in order to reinstate Gayyoom in power. On the night of 3 November 1988, the Indian Air Force airlifted a parachute battalion group from Agra and flew them non-stop over 2,000 kilometres to the Maldives. The Indian paratroopers landed at Hulule and secured the airfield and restored the Government rule at Malé within hours. The brief, bloodless operation, labelled Operation Cactus, also involved the Indian Navy.

On 26 December 2004, the Maldives were devastated by a tsunami following the 2004 Indian Ocean earthquake. Only nine islands were reported to have escaped any flooding, while fifty-seven islands faced serious damage to critical infrastructure, fourteen islands had to be totally evacuated, and six islands were decimated. A further twenty-one resort islands were forced to shut down due to serious damage. The total damage was estimated at over 400 million dollars or some 62% of the GDP. A total of 108 people, including six foreigners, reportedly died in the tsunami. The destructive impact of the waves on the low-lying islands was mitigated by the fact there was no continental shelf or land mass upon which the waves could gain height. The tallest waves were reported 14 feet high.

Geography

The Maldives holds the record for being the flattest country in the world, with a maximum natural ground level of only 2.3 metres, though in areas where construction exists this has been increased to several metres. Over the last century, sea levels have risen about 20 centimetres. The ocean is likely to continue rising and this threatens the existence of Maldives. The Indian Ocean is particularly important for its diverse sea life and coral reefs, and the Maldives are among the richest locations in this regard.

Demographics

The Maldivian ethnic identity is a blend of the cultures reflecting the peoples who settled on the islands, reinforced by religion and language. Some social stratification exists on the islands. It is not rigid, since rank is based on varied factors, including occupation, wealth, Islamic virtue, and family ties. Traditionally, instead of a complex caste system, like the Vedic one, there was merely a distinction between noble (bçfulhu) and common people in the Maldives. Members of the social elite are concentrated in Malé. Outside of the service industry, this is the only location where the foreign and domestic populations are likely to interact. The tourist resorts are not on islands where the natives live, and casual contacts between the two groups are discouraged.

A census has been recorded since 1905, which shows that the population of the country remained around 100,000 for the first seventy years of the last century. Following independence in 1965, the health status of the population improved so much that the population doubled by 1978, and the population growth rate peaked at 3.4% in 1985. By 2005, the population had reached 300,000, although the census in 2000 showed that the population growth rate had declined to 1.9%. Life expectancy at birth stood at 46 years in 1978, while it has now risen to 72 years. Infant mortality has declined from 127 per thousand in 1977 to 12 today, and adult literacy stands at 99%. Combined school enrolment stands in the high 90s.

The Maldives has one of the highest birth rates in the world. The result is that many islands have become overpopulated and are completely covered by homesteads. About 70,000 foreign nationals live in the country, mainly from the neighbouring South Asian countries of India, Sri Lanka, Bangladesh and Nepal.

Language and Culture

Maldivian culture is derived from a number of sources, the most important of which are its proximity to the shores of Sri Lanka and southern India. Thus the population is mainly a mix of Indo-Aryan, Dravidian and Semitic from the anthropological point of view. The official and common language is Dhivehi. The present-day written script is called Thaana and is written from right to left. English is used widely in commerce and increasingly as the medium of instruction in government schools. The language is from Indo-Iranian Sanskritic origin, which points at a later influence from the north of the sub-continent.

After the long Buddhist period of their history, Maldivians converted to Sunni Islam in the mid-12th century. Islam is the official religion of the entire population, as adherence to it is required for citizenship. In the island culture there are a few elements of African origin as well from slaves brought to the court by the royal family and nobles from their hajj journeys to Arabia in the past. There are islands like Feridhu and Maalhos in Northern Ari Atoll, and Goidhu in Southern Maalhosmadulhu Atoll where many of the inhabitants trace their ancestry to released African slaves.

Economy

In ancient times the Maldives were renowned for the cowries, coir rope, dried tuna fish (Maldive Fish), ambergris (Maavaharu) and coco de mer (Tavakkaashi). Local and foreign trading ships used to load these products in the Maldives and transport them to other harbours in the Indian Ocean.

Today tourism and fisheries form the two key

components of the Maldivian economy. The country's shipping, banking and manufacturing sectors are growing at a considerable pace. Among the South Asian nations, the Maldives has the second highest per-capita GDP at 3,900 USD (2002 figure). Major trading partners include India, Sri Lanka, Thailand, Malaysia and Singapore. The development of tourism has fostered the overall growth of the country's economy. It has created direct and indirect employment and income generation opportunities in other related industries. Today, tourism is the country's biggest foreign exchange earner, contributing to 20% of the GDP. With eighty-seven tourist resorts in operation. The year 2006 recorded 467,154 tourist arrivals.

The mechanisation of the traditional fishing boat called "Dhoni" in 1974 was a major milestone in the development of the fisheries industry and the country's economy in general. A fish canning plant was installed in the island of Felivaru in 1977, as a joint venture with a Japanese firm. Moreover, the opening up of the Exclusive Economic Zone (EEZ) of the Maldives for fisheries has further enhanced the growth of the fisheries sector. Today, fisheries contribute over fifteen percent of the GDP and engage about thirty percent of the country's work force. It is also the second-largest foreign exchange earner after tourism.

Airports with two permanent-surface runways exist at Male and Gan. Air Maldives is national airline. Maldives has minimal domestic and international facilities with one television station; and one Indian Ocean International Telecommunications Satellite Corporation (Intelsat) earth station.

The major daily newspaper is Haveeru (North Side) in Male. Aafathis, is another daily in Dhivehi and English. Maldives also has a number of weekly and monthly publications as well as several news agencies and publishers. Hindi-language films, newspapers, and magazines from India are popular. The government radio station Voice of Maldives, established in 1962, broadcasts to the entire country in Dhivehi and English.

Administrative Divisions

The Maldives have been divided into 21 administrative divisions (20 administrative atolls and Malé city). In addition to a name, every administrative division is identified by the Maldivian code letters, such as "Haa Alif" for Thiladhunmati Uthuruburi (Thiladhunmathi North); and by a Latin code letter. The first corresponds to the geographical Maldivian name of the atoll. The second is a code

adopted for convenience. It began in order to facilitate radio communication between the atolls and the central administration. As there are certain islands in different atolls that have the same name, for administrative purposes this code is quoted before the name of the island, for example: Baa Funadhoo, Kaafu Funadhoo, Gaafu-Alifu Funadhoo. Since most Atolls have very long geographical names it is also used whenever the name of the atoll has to be quoted short, for example in the atoll website names.

Each atoll is administered by an Atoll Chief (Atholhu Veriyaa) appointed by the President. The Ministry of Atoll Administration and its Northern and Southern Regional Offices, Atoll Offices and Island Offices are collectively responsible to the President for Atolls Administration. The administrative head of each island is the Island Chief (Katheeb), appointed by the President. The Island Chief's immediate superior is the Atoll Chief.

Politics

Politics in the Maldives takes place in the framework of a presidential republic, whereby the President is the head of government. The President heads the executive branch and appoints the cabinet. The President is nominated to a five-year term by a secret ballot of the Majlis (parliament), a nomination which is confirmed by national referendum.

The unicameral Majlis of the Maldives is composed of fifty members serving five-year terms. Two members from each atoll are elected directly by universal suffrage. Eight are appointed by the president, which is the main route through which women enter parliament. The country introduced political parties for the first time in its history in July 2005, six months after the last elections for the parliament. Nearly thirty-six members of the existing parliament joined the Dhivehi Raiyyathunge Party (the Maldivian People's Party) and elected President

Gayoom as its leader. Twelve members of parliament became the Opposition and joined the Maldivian Democratic Party. Two members remained independent.

In the first multi-party elections in the country the Presidential elections were held in the Maldives on 8 and 28 October 2008. On 8 October, no candidate gained more than 50% of the vote; a runoff was held on 28 October between Maumoon Abdul Gayoom and Mohamed Nasheed and his running mate, Dr. Mohammed Waheed Hassan. Nasheed and Dr. Waheed won the election, unseating long time incumbent Gayoom. The election was the first one held democratically in the history of the Maldives.

Tourism

The Maldives archipelago possesses a truly unique geograph. Nature has fragmented the archipelago into 1,190 tiny islands that occupy a mere one per cent of its 90,000 square kilometres of territory. Only 185 islands are home to its 300,000 population, while the other islands are used entirely for economic purposes of which tourism and agriculture are the most dominant. Tourism accounts for 28% of GDP and more than 60% of the Maldives' foreign exchange receipts. Over 90% of government tax revenue comes from import duties and tourism-related taxes. The development of tourism has fostered the overall growth of the country's economy. It has created direct and indirect employment and income generation opportunities in other related industries. The first tourist resorts were opened in 1972 with Bandos island resort and Kurumba Village.

The emergence of tourism in 1972 transformed the economy of the Maldives, moving rapidly from dependence on fisheries to tourism. In just three and a half decades, the industry has become the main source of income and livelihood of the people of the Maldives. Tourism is also the country's biggest foreign currency earner and the single largest contributor to the GDP. Today, there are 92 resorts in the Maldives hosting 600,000 tourists annually.

National Security

The Maldives National Defence Force is the combined security organisation responsible for defending the security and sovereignty of the Maldives, having the primary task of being responsible for attending to all internal and external security needs of the Maldives, including the protection of the Exclusive Economic Zone and the maintenance of peace and security. The National Security Service of about 2,000 members performs army, police, and maritime duties. The Republic of Maldives has no armed forces, faces no internal or external threat and is not involved in any international dispute. Threat perceptions include global factors like the threat to the environment, ozone depletion and global warming. Maldives has a Coast Guard Force with 400 Personnel.

As a result of the coup attempt in November 1988, the Maldives undertook a review of its defence requirements by overhauling and modernising its NSS. It added six British vessels to its existing force, doubled the infantry to 2,000 men under arms, acquired four armoured cars and tried to improve its airborne surveillance. It also decided to create the Defence Intelligence Services to monitor external and internal developments.

Maldives has traditionally sought to maintain an independent status, while preserving cordial relations with all members of the world community. The purpose is to keep the Indian Ocean area at peace. It joined the UN in 1965 and the World Bank and the IMF in 1978. In connection with its concern over the security of the Indian Ocean area, Maldives became a founder of the South Asian Association for Regional Co-operation in 1985.

Maldives' first-ever terror strike occurred on 29 September 2007, when an Islamist cell triggered an explosive device in Male's Sultan Park. Investigators discovered that the cell had connections with Lashkar-e-Taiba operatives at the Jamia Salafiyya in Faisalabad—a seminary that has produced key Lashkar commanders.

MYANMAR

Burma, officially the Union of Myanmar, is the largest country by geographical area in mainland Southeast Asia. Myanmar achieved independence from Britain on 4 January 1948, as the "Union of Burma." It became the "Socialist Republic of the Union of Burma" on 4 January 1974, before reverting to the "Union of Burma" on 23 September 1988. On 18 June 1989, the State Law and Order Restoration Council adopted the name "Union of Myanmar." This was recognised by the United Nations, but not by the US Government as this decision was not approved by any sitting legislature.

The flag of Myanmar is red with a blue rectangle in the upper hoist-side corner bearing, 14 white five-pointed stars encircling a cogwheel containing a stalk of rice; the 14 stars represent the seven administrative divisions and seven states. It is bordered by China on the north, Laos on the east, Thailand on the southeast, Bangladesh on the west, and India on the northwest, with the Bay of Bengal to the southwest. One-third of Myanmar's total perimeter, 1,930 kilometres, forms an uninterrupted coastline.

Myanmar's diverse population has played a major role in defining its politics, history and demographics in modern times. Its political system remains under the tight control of the State Peace and Development Council, the military government led, since 1992, by Senior General Than Shwe. The Burmese military has dominated government since General Ne Win led a coup in 1962 that toppled the civilian government of U Nu. The country's culture, heavily influenced by neighbours, is based on Theravada Buddhism intertwined with local elements.

History

The Mon people are thought to be the earliest group to migrate into the lower Ayeyarwady valley and, by the mid-900s BC, were dominant in southern Burma. The Mons became one of the first in South East Asia to embrace Theravada Buddhism. The Tibeto-Burman speaking Pyu arrived later in the 1st century BC, and established several city states and established a small kingdom in Bagan in 849. Prosperous from trade, Bagan kings built many magnificent temples and pagodas throughout the country—many of which can still be seen today. Bagan's power slowly waned in 13th century and the Bagan empire was irreparably broken up into several small kingdoms:

- The Burman kingdom of Ava or Innwa (1364-1555), the successor state to three smaller kingdoms founded by Burmanized Shan kings, controlling Upper Burma.
- The Mon kingdom of Hanthawady Pegu or Bago (1287–1540), founded by a Mon-ized Shan King Wareru (1287–1306), controlling Lower Burma.
- The Rakhine kingdom of Mrauk U (1434–1784), in the west.
- Several Shan states in the Shan hills in the east and the Kachin hills in the north.

The Burmese under King Anaukpetlun (1605-1628) established a smaller kingdom based in Ava covering Upper Burma, Lower Burma and Shan states, but it experienced a slow and steady decline for the next 100 years.

Capital	-	Naypyidaw
Largest city	-	Yangon (Rangoon)
Official language	-	Burmese Recognised languages: Jingpho, Kayah, Karen, Chin, Mon, Rakhine, Shan
Government	- - -	Unitary presidential constitutional republic President General Thein Sein Vice President Sai Mauk Kham Nyan Tun
Formation	-	Independence 4 January 1948 (from UK) New Constitution 30 March 2011
Area	-	676,578 square kilometres
Coastline	-	1,930 kilometres
Population	-	60,280,000 (2010 estimate) Density 73.9/square kilometre
GDP (PPP)	-	\$82.679 billion (2011 estimate) Per capita \$1,324
GDP (nominal)	-	\$51.925 billion (2011 estimate) Per capita \$832
Minister of Defence	-	Lt General Wai Lwin
C-in-C Armed Forces	-	Vice Senior General Min Aung Hlaing
C-in-C Army	-	General Soe Win
C-in-C Navy	-	Admiral Nyan Tun
C-in-C Air Force	-	General Myat Hein
C-in-C Air Defence	-	Brig Gen Myint Hiaing

King Bodawpaya (1782–1819) attempted to extend his kingdom towards India and captured then independent kingdom of Assam in 1819. The new conquests brought the Burmese adjacent to the British India. The British defeated the Burmese in the First Anglo-Burmese War (1824–26). Burma had to cede Assam, Manipur, Rakhine (Arakan) and Tanintharyi (Tenessarim).

In 1852, the British attacked a much weakened Burma during a Burmese palace power struggle. After the Second Anglo-Burmese War, the British captured the remaining coastal provinces: Ayeyarwady, Yangon and Bago, naming the territories as Lower Burma.

The Third Anglo-Burmese War (1885) resulted in Upper Burma and Lower Burma being reunited, and Burma was administered as a single province within British India despite Burma's independent history and traditions. To stimulate trade and facilitate changes, the British brought in Indians and Chinese who quickly displaced the Burmese in urban areas. To this day Yangon and Mandalay have large ethnic Indian populations. Railroads and schools were built, as well as a large number of prisons including the infamous Insein Jail, then as now used for political prisoners. Burmese resentment was strong and was vented in violent riots that paralysed Yangon on occasion all the way until the 1930s. Much of the discontent was caused by a perceived disrespect for Burman culture and traditions, for example, what the British termed the Shoe Question: the colonisers' refusal to remove their shoes upon entering Buddhist temples or other holy places.

On 1 April 1937, Burma became a separately administered territory, independent of the Indian administration. The vote for keeping Burma in India, or as a separate colony divided the populace, and laid the ground work for the insurgencies to come after independence. In the 1940s, the Thirty Comrades, commanded by Aung San, founded the Burma Independence Army. The Thirty Comrades received training in Japan.

During World War II, Burma became a major frontline in the Southeast Asian Theatre. The British administration collapsed ahead of the advancing Japanese troops but, by July 1945, the British had retaken the country. Although many Burmese fought initially for the Japanese, some Burmese also served in the British Burma Army. The Burma Independence Army under the command of Aung San and the Arakan National Army fought with the Japanese from 1942-44, but switched allegiance to the Allied side in 1945.

In 1947, Aung San became Deputy Chairman of the Executive Council of Burma, a transitional government. But in July 1947, political rivals assassinated Aung San and several cabinet members. On 4 January 1948, the nation became an independent republic, named the Union of Burma, with Sao Shwe Thaik as its first President and U Nu as its first Prime Minister. Unlike most other former British colonies and overseas territories, it did not become a member of the Commonwealth. A bicameral parliament was formed, consisting of a Chamber of Deputies and a Chamber of Nationalities.

Democratic rule ended in 1962 when General Ne Win led a military coup d'état. He ruled for nearly 26 years and pursued policies under the rubric of the Burmese Way to Socialism. In 1988, General Saw Maung staged a coup d'état and formed the State Law and Order Restoration Council (SLORC). In 1989, SLORC declared martial law after widespread protests. The military government finalised plans for People's Assembly elections on 31 May 1989.

In May 1990, the government held free elections for the first time in almost 30 years. The National League for Democracy (NLD), the party of Aung San Suu Kyi, won 392 out of a total 489 seats, but the election results were annulled by SLORC, which refused to step down. Led by Than Shwe since 1992, the military regime has made cease-fire agreements with most ethnic guerrilla groups. In 1997, the State Law and Order Restoration Council was renamed the State Peace and Development Council (SPDC).

On 23 June 1997, Myanmar was admitted into the Association of Southeast Asian Nations (ASEAN). On

27 March 2006, the military junta, which had moved the national capital from Yangon to a site near Pyinmana, officially named it Naypyidaw, meaning "city of the kings".

Mass public demonstrations started on 18 August 2007, when the government raised the price of gas and diesel oil by 500% in order to cover a budget deficit that resulted from a salary hike for civil servants. The junta's move of the Burmese capital to Pyinmana may also have contributed to the budget deficit.

On 19 September 2007, several hundred monks staged a protest march in the city of Sittwe. Larger protests in Rangoon and elsewhere ensued over the following days. Security became increasingly heavy handed, resulting in a number of deaths and injuries. By 28 September, internet access had been cut and journalists reputedly warned not to report on protests. Internet access was restored on 5 October.

The constitution of Burma, its third since independence, was drafted by its military rulers and published in September 2008. The country is governed as a presidential republic with a bicameral legislature, with a portion of legislatures appointed by the military and others elected in general elections. The current head of state, inaugurated as President on 30 March 2011, is Thein Sein.

The legislature, called the Pyidaungsu Hluttaw, is bicameral and made up of two houses: The 224-seat upper house Amyotha Hluttaw (House of Nationalities) and the 440-seat lower house Pyithu Hluttaw (House of Representatives). The upper house consists of 224 members of which 168 are directly elected and 56 are appointed by the Burmese Armed Forces while the lower house consists of 440 members of which 330 are directly elected and 110 are appointed by the armed forces. The major political parties are the National League for Democracy, National Democratic Force and the two backed by the military: the National Unity Party, and the Union Solidarity and Development Party.

Burma's army-drafted constitution was approved in a referendum in May 2008. The results, 92.4% of the 22 million voters with an official turnout of 99%, are considered suspect by many international observers and by the National league of democracy with reports of widespread fraud, ballot stuffing, and voter intimidation.

The elections of 2010 resulted in a victory for the military-backed Union Solidarity and Development Party and various foreign observers questioned the fairness of the elections. One criticism of the election was that only government sanctioned political parties were allowed to contest in it and the popular National League for Democracy was declared illegal and is still barred from political activities.

However, immediately following the elections, the government ended the house arrest of the democracy advocate and leader of the National League for Democracy, Aung San Suu Kyi, and her ability to move freely around the country is considered an important test of the military's movement toward more openness. After unexpected reforms in 2011, NLD senior leaders have decided to register as a political party and to field candidates in future by-elections.

In October, 2010, a new flag was adopted and the official name of the country changed to "Republic of the Union of Myanmar", replacing the old "Union of Myanmar" from 1989.

On 9 November 2010, Myanmar's ruling junta stated that the Union Solidarity and Development Party won 80% of the votes. This claim is widely disputed by pro-democracy opposition groups, asserting that the military regime engaged in rampant fraud to achieve its result. On 13 November 2010 the military authorities in Burma released the pro-democracy leader, Aung San Suu Kyi.

Geography

Myanmar has an area of 678,500 square kilometres (land: 657,740 square kilometres and water: 20,760 square kilometres). Its land boundaries total 5,876 kilometres with Bangladesh (193 kilometres), China (2,185 kilometres), India (1,463 kilometres), Laos (235 kilometres) and Thailand (1,800 kilometres). It has a coastline of 1,930 kilometres. It has a strategic location near major Indian Ocean shipping lanes.

The climate of Myanmar is characterised as tropical monsoon with cloudy, rainy, hot, humid summers (southwest monsoon, June to September) and less cloudy, scant rainfall, mild temperatures, lower humidity during winter (northeast monsoon, December to April).

The terrain comprises central lowlands ringed by steep, rugged highlands. The highest point is Hkakabo Razi (5,881 metres). Myanmar's natural resources include petroleum, timber, tin, antimony, zinc, copper, tungsten, lead, coal, some marble, limestone, precious stones, natural gas and hydropower. 14.92% of the land is arable with only 1.31% under permanent crops. Irrigated land comprises 18,700 square kilometres. Myanmar is prone to natural hazards like destructive earthquakes and cyclones. Flooding and landslides are common during rainy season (June to September). The country also experiences periodic droughts. Current environmental issues include deforestation and industrial pollution of air, soil, and water. Inadequate sanitation and water treatment also contribute to disease

The Ayeyarwady delta, which is approximately 50,400 square kilometres in area, is largely used for rice cultivation. In the north, the Hengduan Shan mountains form the border with China. Three mountain ranges, namely the Rakhine Yoma, the Bago Yoma, and the Shan Plateau exist within Myanmar, all of which run north to-south from the Himalayas. The mountain chains divide Myanmar's three river systems, which are the Ayeyarwady, Thanlwin, and the Sittang rivers. The Ayeyarwady River, Myanmar's longest river, nearly 2,170 kilometres long, flows into the Gulf of Martaban. Fertile plains exist in the valleys between the mountain chains. The majority of Myanmar's population lives in the Ayeyarwady valley, which is situated between the Rakhine Yoma and the Shan Plateau.

Myanmar's slow economic growth has contributed to the preservation of much of its environment and ecosystems. Forests, including dense tropical growth and valuable teak in lower Myanmar, cover over 49% of the country. Other trees indigenous to the region include rubber, acacia, bamboo, ironwood, mangrove, coconut and betel palm. In the highlands of the north, oak, pine and various rhododendrons cover much of the land. The lands along the coast support all varieties of tropical fruits. In the Dry Zone, vegetation is sparse and stunted.

People

The major Burmese ethnic groups are Burman 68%, Shan 9%, Karen 7%, Rakhine 4%, Chinese 3%, Indian 2%, Mon 2%, other 5%. The religions are Buddhist 89%, Christian 4% (Baptist 3%, Roman Catholic 1%), Muslim 4%, animist 1%, other 2%. Burmese is the major languages, though minority ethnic groups have their own languages. Myanmar has an estimated population of 47,382,633. The median age is 27 years with a population growth rate of 0.81%.

Myanmar has a population of about 55 million. Current population figures are rough estimates because the last partial census was taken in 1983. No trustworthy nationwide census has been taken in Myanmar since 1931. There are over 600,000 registered migrant workers from Myanmar in Thailand, and millions more work illegally. Burmese migrant workers account for 80% of Thailand's migrant workers. Myanmar has a population density of 75 persons per square kilometre, one of the lowest in Southeast Asia. Refugee camps exist along Indian-Burmese, Bangladeshi-Burmese and Burmese-Thai borders while several thousand are in Malaysia. Conservative estimates state that there are over 295,800 refugees from Myanmar, with the majority being Rohingya, Kayin, and Karenni.

Myanmar is ethnically diverse. The government recognizes 135 distinct ethnic groups. While it is extremely difficult to verify this statement, there are at least 108 different ethno-linguistic groups in Myanmar, consisting mainly of distinct Tibeto-Burman peoples, but with sizable populations of Daic, Hmong-Mien, and Austroasiatic (Mon-Khmer) peoples. The Bamar form an estimated 68% of the population. 10% of the population are Shan. The Kayin make up 7% of the population. The Rakhine people constitute 4% of the population. Overseas Chinese form approximately 3% of the population. Mon, who form 2% of the population, are ethno-linguistically related to the Khmer. Overseas Indians comprise 2%. The remainder are Kachin, Chin, Anglo-Indians and other ethnic minorities. Included in this group are the Anglo-Burmese. Once forming a large and influential community, the Anglo-Burmese left the country in steady streams from 1958 onwards, principally to Australia and the U.K. Today, it is estimated that only 52,000 Anglo-Burmese remain in Myanmar.

Government and Politics

Executive branch. Myanmar is governed by a strict military regime. The Chief of State and Chairman of the State Peace and Development Council (SPDC) is Senior General Than Shwe (since 23 April 1992). The head of government is Prime Minister, General Soe Win (since 19 October 2004). The cabinet is overseen by the SPDC (military junta), so named on 15 November 1997. It assumed power on 18 September 1988 under the name State Law and Order Restoration Council (SLORC).

Legislative branch. Myanmar has a unicameral People's Assembly or Pyithu Hluttaw (485 seats; members elected by popular vote to serve four-year terms). Elections were last held on 27 May 1990, but the Assembly was never allowed by the military junta to convene. In the elections the number of seats won (party-wise) were - NLD 392 (opposition), SNLD 23 (opposition), NUP 10 (pro-government), others 60.

Judicial branch. Remnants of the British-era legal system are in place, but there is no guarantee of a fair public trial; the judiciary is not independent of the executive.

Major political parties in Myanmar are the National League for Democracy and the Shan Nationalities League for Democracy, although their activities are heavily regulated and suppressed by the military government. Many other parties, often representing ethnic minorities, exist.

Human Rights. Several human rights organisations have reported on human rights abuses by the military government. They have claimed that there is no independent judiciary in Myanmar. The military government restricts Internet access through software-based censorship that limits the material citizens can access on-line. Forced labour, human trafficking, and child labour are common. The military is also notorious for rampant use of sexual violence as an instrument of control, including systematic rapes and taking of sex slaves as porters for the military. A strong women's pro-democracy movement has formed in exile, largely along the Thai border and in Chang Mai.

Administrative Divisions

Myanmar is divided into seven states and seven divisions.

The Divisions are:

- Ayeyarwady Division
- Bago Division
- Magway Division
- Mandalay Division
- Sagaing Division

- Tanintharyi Division
- Yangon Division

The States are:

- Chin State
- Kachin State
- Kayin (Karen) State
- Kayah (Karenni) State
- Mon State
- Rakhine (Arakan) State
- Shan State

Economy

Under British administration, Myanmar was one of the wealthiest countries in Southeast Asia. It was once the world's largest exporter of rice. Myanmar also had a wealth of natural and labour resources. It produced 75% of the world's teak and had a highly literate population.

Myanmar is a resource-rich country, which suffers from pervasive government controls, inefficient economic policies and rural poverty. Steps in the early 1990s to liberalize the economy after decades of failure under the "Burmese Way to Socialism" stalled, and liberalisation measures were rescinded. Myanmar does not have monetary or fiscal stability. The economy suffers from serious macro-economic imbalances, inflation, multiple official exchange rates overvaluing the Burmese kyat, and a distorted interest rate regime.

After a parliamentary government was formed in 1948, Prime Minister U Nu disastrously attempted to make Burma a welfare state and adopted central planning. Rice exports fell by two thirds and mineral exports by over 96%. Plans were partly financed by printing money, which led to inflation. The 1962 coup d'état was followed by an economic scheme called the Burmese Way to Socialism, a plan to nationalise all industries, with the exception of agriculture. The catastrophic programme turned Burma into one of the world's most impoverished countries. Burma's admittance to Least Developed Country status by the UN in 1987 highlighted its economic bankruptcy.

After 1988, the regime retreated from totalitarian rule. It permitted modest expansion of the private sector, allowed some foreign investment, and received needed foreign exchange. All fundamental market institutions are suppressed. Private enterprises are often co-owned or indirectly owned by state.

Inflation is a serious problem for the economy. In recent years, both China and India have attempted to strengthen ties with the government for economic benefit. Many nations, including the United States and Canada, and the European Union, have imposed investment and trade sanctions on Burma. The United States has banned all imports from Burma. Foreign investment comes primarily from People's Republic of China, Singapore, South Korea, India, and Thailand.

The major agricultural product is rice which covers about 60% of the country's total cultivated land area. Rice accounts for 97% of total food grain production by weight. Through collaboration with the International Rice Research Institute 52 modern rice varieties were released in the country between 1966 and 1997, helping increase national rice production to 14 million tons in 1987 and to 19 million tons in 1996. By 1988, modern varieties were planted on half of the country's rice lands, including 98 percent of the irrigated areas.

Today, the country lacks adequate infrastructure. Goods travel primarily across the Thai border, where most illegal drugs are exported and along the Ayeyarwady River. Railways are old and rudimentary, with few repairs since their construction in the late 19th century. Highways are normally unpaved, except in the major cities. Energy shortages are common throughout the country including in Yangon. Burma is also the world's second largest producer of opium, accounting for 8% of entire world production and is a major source of illegal drugs, including amphetamines. Other industries include agricultural goods, textiles, wood products, construction materials, gems, metals, oil and natural gas. The Norwegian company Seadrill owned by John Fredriksen is involved in offshore oil drilling, expected to give oil and oil export revenues.

The Union of Myanmar's rulers depend on sales of precious stones such as sapphires, pearls and jade to fund their regime. Rubies are the biggest earner; 90% of the world's rubies come from the country, whose red stones are prized for their purity and hue. Thailand buys the majority of the country's gems. Burma's "Valley of Rubies", the mountainous Mogok area, 200 kilometres north of Mandalay, is noted for its rare pigeon's blood rubies and blue sapphires. Many U.S. and European jewellery companies, including Bulgari, Tiffany, and Cartier, refuse to import these stones based on reports of deplorable working conditions in the mines. Human Rights Watch has encouraged a complete ban on the purchase of Burmese gems based on these reports and because nearly all profits go to the ruling junta, as the majority of mining activity in the country is government-run.

Since 1992, the government has encouraged tourism in the country. However, fewer than 750,000 tourists enter the country annually. Aung San Suu Kyi has requested that international tourists not visit Burma.

The junta's forced labour programmes were focused around tourist destinations which have been heavily criticised for their human rights records. Burma's Minister of Hotels and Tourism Maj-Gen Saw Lwin has stated that the government receives a significant percentage of the income of private sector tourism services. Much of the country is completely off-limits to tourists, and the military very tightly controls interactions between foreigners and the people of Burma, particularly the border regions. They are not to discuss politics with foreigners, under penalty of imprisonment, and in 2001, the Myanmar Tourism Promotion Board issued an order for local officials to protect tourists and limit "unnecessary contact" between foreigners and ordinary Burmese people.

Transportation

Myanmar has 85 airports, with 21 having paved runways. The country has 2,056 kilometres of gas pipelines and 558 kilometres of oil pipelines. The railways extend over 3,955 kilometres (most of it narrow gauge). The roadways extend 27,000 kilometres (paved - 3,200 kilometres; unpaved - 23,800 kilometres. Its waterways extend 12,800 kilometres.

The merchant marine of Myanmar has 34 ships (1000 GRT or over) 402,724 GRT/620,642 DWT, that include bulk carriers—8, cargo—18, passenger—2, passenger/cargo—3, roll on/roll off—2 and specialised tanker—1. (9 are foreign-owned: Germany 5, Japan 4). The major ports and terminals are Moulmein, Rangoon and Sittwe.

Armed Forces

Myanmar's armed forces are known as the Tatmadaw, which numbers 488,000. The Tatmadaw comprises the Army, the Navy, and the Air Force. The military is very influential in the country, with top cabinet and ministry posts held by military officers. Although official figures for Burmese military spending are not available, the Stockholm International Peace Research Institute, in its annual rankings, ranked Myanmar in the top 15 military spenders in the world. The country imports most of its weapons from Russia, Ukraine, China and India.

National Security

Over half of Myanmar's population consists of diverse ethnic groups with substantial numbers of kin beyond its borders. Despite continuing border committee talks, significant differences remain with Thailand over boundary alignment and the handling of ethnic rebels, refugees, and illegal cross-border activities. Civil wars have been a constant feature of Myanmar's socio-political landscape since independence in 1948. They are predominatly struggles for ethnic and sub-national autonomy and fighting has predominately taken place in areas around the ethnically Burman core region of the country where the majority of country's population resides. Ongoing conflicts include fighting between Kachin Independence Army and the government in Kachin State, the Rohingya armed groups in Arakan State as well as Shan, Lahu and Karen minority groups in the eastern half of the country. In 2005 Thailand sheltered about 121,000 Burmese refugees. Karens also protest Thai support for a Burmese hydroelectric dam on the Salween River near the border. Environmentalists in Myanmar and Thailand continue to voice concern over China's construction of hydroelectric dams upstream on the Nujiang/ Salween River in Yunnan Province.

Myanmar has about 550,000-1,000,000 refugees and internally displaced persons due to government offensives against ethnic insurgent groups near its borders. Most of them are ethnic Karen, Karenni, Shan, Tavoyan, and Mons. Myanmar is the world's second largest producer of illicit opium (estimated production 292 metric tons). The cultivation is estimated to be over 30,900 hectares. Lack of government will to take on major narco-trafficking groups and lack of serious commitment against money laundering continues to hinder the overall anti-drug effort. Myanmar is the major source of methamphetamine and heroin for regional consumption. The country is currently under Financial Action Task Force countermeasures due to continued failure to address its inadequate money-laundering controls.

Myanmar is building a research nuclear reactor near May Myo (Pyin Oo Lwin) with help from Russia. Myanmar is one of the signatories of the nuclear non-proliferation pact since 1992 and a member of the IAEA since 1957. The military junta had informed the IAEA in September 2000 of its intention to construct the reactor. The research reactor outbuilding frame was built by ELE steel industries limited of Yangon and water from Anisakhan/BE water fall will be used for the reactor cavity cooling system.

NEPAL

Nepal is a landlocked nation in South Asia, bordering the People's Republic of China to the north and India to the south, east and west. Nepal previously had the distinction of being the world's only Hindu state, with over 80% of the people following this faith. However, on 18 May 2006 Nepal was declared a secular state.

The national flag consists of two vertically stacked crimson red triangles with blue borders. The upper portion has an eight-pointed disc rising out of a white crescent moon, and the bottom portion has a white sun. The moon and sun symbolize the eternal eyes of god, the red colour represents energy in action, and the blue border signifies Nepal's peaceful nature.

History

Founded in 1559, Gorkha was one among the hill states until the rule of Prithvi Narayan Shah (1743–75), when the Nepalese state was established. An astute military strategist, Shah obtained financial assistance and armaments from India and then created alliances with neighbouring states or purchased their neutrality. In fact, his forces even managed to repel British troops. On 29 September 1768, Gorkha troops entered Kathmandu during religious celebrations and took it without a fight. Intrigue and infighting among the royalty continued until 1846, when Jang Bahadur Kunwar, a military commander, established a dynasty of prime ministers that ruled until 1951. The Rana dynasty was a parallel monarchy in which the pre-eminent authority was the prime minister, a hereditary position. The monarchy was reduced to a ceremonial position that legitimised Rana rule and monarchs were either exiled or kept under house arrest. Rampant nepotism and inefficient administration handicapped political development. The Ranas provided some positive development, such as eliminating slavery, establishing schools and factories. On 8 January 1951, the last Rana oligarch, Mohan Shamsher, agreed to restore the king to power and hold elections. In February 1951, King Tribhuvan (r. 1911–55) returned to power.

From February 1951 numerous short-lived governments ruled either under an interim constitution or under King Tribhuvan and his successor, Mahendra (r. 1955–72). The kings regularly dismissed uncooperative or poorly functioning ministries and continually postponed elections. After popular protests, the king allowed the first national elections in February 1959. The Nepali Congress won. But the king dismissed this government in 1960, and instituted a *panchayat* (village council) government, a four-tiered system of representative government with traditional village-level councils at the local level and the National Panchayat at the national level. King Mahendra died in January 1972, and his successor, Birendra (r. 1972–2001), adopted a more liberal approach to government.

In May 1980, King Birendra held a national referendum on the *panchayat* system. He interpreted the narrow margin of support (54.7 percent voted in favour) as a need for political change. He allowed direct elections to the National Panchayat and Nepal once again underwent tumultuous change. Nepal's improving relations with China placed stress on its

Capital	-	Kathmandu
Official language	-	Nepali Recognised languages: Maithili, Nepal Bhasa, Bhojpuri, Tharu, Gurung, Tamang, Magar, Awadhi, Sherpa, Kiranti and other 100 different indigenous languages.
Government	-	Federal Republic
	-	President Ram Baran Yadav
	-	Prime Minister Baburam Bhattarai
	-	Chief Justice Khil Raj Regmi
Formation	-	Kingdom declared 21 December 1768
	-	State declared 15 January 2007
	-	Republic declared 28 May 2008
Area	-	147,181 square kilometres
Population	-	29,331,000 (2010 estimate) Density 199.3/square kilometre
GDP (PPP)	-	$39,899 billion (2012 estimate) Per capita $1,383
GDP (nominal)	-	$17,921 billion (2012 estimate) Per capita $627
Defence Minister	-	Bijaya Kumar Gachchhadar
Chief of Army Staff	-	General Gaurav Shumsher JB Rana

relations with India, and for this and other reasons India terminated trade and transit treaties in March 1989. After a long and rich history, during which the country splintered and coalesced under a variety of absolute rulers, Nepal became a constitutional monarchy in 1990. A new constitution was promulgated on 9 November 1990, with provisions for basic human rights, adult franchise, and a multiparty democracy with the king as a constitutional monarch. Elections were held in May 1991, and the Nepali Congress came to power.

This arrangement caused increasing instability, both in the parliament and, since 1996, throughout large swathes of the country that have been fought over by Maoist insurgents. The civil conflict has continued for nearly a decade, in which the Communist Party of Nepal (Maoist) killed, expelled, and threatened government officials, landlords, and others it charged with economic and political oppression. Initially, the government largely ignored the conflict, but by 2000 the conflict expanded to nearly two-thirds of the country. Unstable political institutions and worsening civil conflict weakened the government's capacity to address economic, social, and other problems. Factional fighting within and among political parties led to rapid changes in government and prompted parties to spend time and resources on maintaining or acquiring power. In 1994 the Nepali Congress was defeated in midterm elections, and the Communist Party of Nepal (Unified Marxist-Leninist) formed a minority government that lasted nine months. A coalition government led by the Nepali Congress came into power in September 1995 with Sher Bahadur Deuba as prime minister. This coalition remained in power until 2002, but contentious relations with opposition parties and within the coalition undermined the coalition's stability.

In one of the most remarkable events in Nepal's history, Crown Prince Dipendra killed the king, queen, and other royal family members on 1 June 2001, reportedly over his choice of a bride. The crown passed to Gyanendra, Dipendra's uncle, who adopted a firm approach to political issues. When cease-fire talks with the Maoists ended in November 2001, King Gyanendra declared a state of emergency and sent the army into the conflict. This action intensified the conflict. The king dissolved parliament in May 2002 and later unconstitutionally released Deuba's government and assumed executive powers. In the face of unstable governments and a Maoist siege on the Kathmandu Valley in August 2004, popular support for the monarchy began to wane. A seven-party alliance government was installed, whose primary task is to change the constitution.

Following the 2006 democracy movement, the king agreed to relinquish the sovereign power back to the people and reinstated the dissolved House of Representatives on 24 April 2006. Using its newly acquired sovereign authority, on 18 May 2006, the newly resumed House of Representatives unanimously passed a motion to curtail the power of the king and declared Nepal a secular state.

The Maoist leader, Pushpa Kamal Dahal, known as "Prachanda", became the first prime minister of the Federal Democratic Republic of Nepal, having won an overwhelming vote in the Constituent Assembly elected in April. The first meeting of the Constituent Assembly on 28 May 2008 overwhelmingly voted for the abolition of the monarchy in the country and declared Nepal a Federal Democratic Republic. It thus abolished the 239-year-old monarchy. In June 2008 former King Gyanendra Shah departed from the palace, remaining in the country as an ordinary citizen.

The turning point in the change in Nepal was the April 2006 people's movement, when hundreds of thousands took to the streets for 19 successive days. The king was compelled to hand power back to the political parties, while a peace agreement emerged that ended the conflict, bringing the Maoists into an interim parliament and government and promising elections to a Constituent Assembly.

The people's movement also took the lid off social pressures often disregarded by Nepal's elites. Although established as a unitary Hindu kingdom, with politics directed from the Himalayan foothills, today around half the population live in the fertile southern plains and more than one-third are from over 50 indigenous, largely non-Hindu communities.

The Nepali Congress (NC) candidate Dr. Ram Baran Yadav was elected as the first President of republican Nepal, securing a comfortable majority in the presidential election held on 21 July 2008. The Communist Party of Nepal (Maoist) won the largest number of seats in the Constituent Assembly election held on 10 April 2008 and formed a coalition government which included most of the parties. Although acts of violence occurred during the pre-electoral period, election observers noted that the elections themselves were markedly peaceful.

The newly elected Assembly met in Kathmandu on 28 May 2008, and, after a polling of 564 Constituent Assembly members, 560 voted to form a new Government, with the monarchist Rastriya Prajatantra Party, which had four members in the assembly, registering a dissent note. At that point, it was declared that Nepal had become a secular and inclusive democratic republic. The King was thereafter given 15 days to vacate the Narayanhiti Royal Palace, in order to re-open it as a public museum.

However, political tensions and consequent power-sharing battles have continued in Nepal. In May 2009, the Maoist-led government was toppled and another coalition government with all major political parties barring the Maoists was formed. Madhav Kumar Nepal of the Communist Party of Nepal (Unified Marxist-Leninist) was made the Prime Minister of the coalition government.

On 27 May 2012, the country's Constituent Assembly failed to meet the deadline for writing a new constitution for the country. Prime Minister Baburam Bhattarai announced that new elections will be held on 22 November. One of the main obstacles has been disagreement over whether the states which will be created will be based on ethnicity.

Geography

Nepal is a landlocked country with India to the east, south, and west and China to the north. Its total land area is 147,181 square kilometres. Its boundary with China is 1,236 kilometres and with India is 1,690 kilometres. Nepal and China have no territorial disputes, but Nepal and India have several: possession of a 75-square-kilometre area called Kalapani, further complicated by its proximity to the Chinese border; the boundary of the Maha Kali River (Sarda River in India), with ramifications for development and distribution of hydropower and water resources; possession of 209 hectares of land after changes in the course of the Mechi River; and sovereignty over several areas comprising nearly 600 square kilometres along the border.

Mountains and rugged hills cover nearly 75 percent of Nepal. It has three main physiographic regions that run laterally across the country. In the south, the plains of the Terai Region cover about 23 percent of Nepal's total area and are the main agricultural and most densely populated region. The Hill Region covers about 42 percent of the total area and consists of hills, flat lands, and valleys. Farther north, the Himalayan Region covers nearly 35 percent of the total area with 200 peaks more than 6,000 metres in elevation and 13 peaks more than 8,000 metres high, including Sagarmatha (Mount Everest), the world's highest mountain (8,850 metres). Eight out of ten world's highest mountains are in Nepal. Nepal's major river systems are—from east to west—the Kosi (513 kilometres), Narayani (332 kilometres), and Karnali (507 kilometres) are major tributaries of the Ganges in India. Nepal lies within a subtropical monsoon climate zone. Climatic conditions and precipitation vary with elevation, ranging from tropical in the Terai plains to alpine and tundra in the northern mountain areas. Nepal's natural resource base is insufficient for its economic needs, and "scenic beauty" is seen as one of the most commercially important resources. Fuel resources are especially scarce. Permanent crop cultivation has reduced the proportion of land used for forest harvesting. Nepal has numerous environmental problems.

Society

No anthropological or linguistic survey of the population has ever been conducted. The names of ethnic groups are derived from the language they speak, and ethnic identity is based on various combinations of national origin, region, language, religion, and caste. The demographic composition is Hindus (59 percent), indigenous Janajatis (31 percent), Newars (5.5 percent), Muslims (4.3 percent), and others - Sikhs, Bengalis, Marwaris, and Jains (0.2 percent). Nepal has 92 languages spoken as mother tongues. Many languages are rarely spoken outside of specific areas, but knowledge of more than one language is common. Nepali is the national language and the most common mother tongue (spoken by 48.6 percent of the population), as well as the most common second language. Maithili is the second most common mother tongue (12.3 percent), and English is increasingly prominent as well as compulsory in public schools and universities.

Groups are the Brahman-Hill 12.5%, Magar 7%, Tharu 6.6%, Tamang 5.5%, Newar 5.4%, Kami 3.9%, Yadav 3.9%, other 32.7%, unspecified 2.8%. Nepali is the national language with 47.8% of the population speaking it as their first language. Other languages include Maithili 12.1%, Bhojpuri 7.4%, Tharu (Dagaura/Rana) 5.8%, Tamang 5.1%, Nepal Bhasa 3.6%, Magar 3.3%, Awadhi 2.4%, other 10%, White 2.6% unspecified 2.5%. Differences between Hindus and Buddhists have been in general very subtle and academic in nature due to the intermingling of Hindu and Buddhist beliefs. Both share common temples and worship common deities and many of Nepal's Hindus could also be regarded as Buddhists and vice versa. Gurkhas are from Nepal. Buddhism was relatively more common among the Newar. Among the other natives of Nepal, those most influenced by Hinduism were the Magar, Sunwar, Limbu and Rai. Hindu influence is less prominent among the Gurung, Bhutia, and Thakali groups, who employ Buddhist monks for their religious ceremonies.

Health indicators are poor by international standards, especially in rural areas. Disease prevalence is higher than in other South Asian countries. Nepal's Human Development Index (HDI) was 0.504 in 2002, ranking Nepal 140 out of 177 countries. Health-care facilities, hygiene, nutrition, and sanitation generally are poor and beyond the means of most, particularly in rural areas. Provision of health services is constrained by low government spending, rugged terrain, and lack of health education (which lowers the demand for health services).

Economy

Prior to 1990 economic relations were in the form of cross-border trade with India and China. Since 1990, the government has adopted market-oriented policies with greater liberalisation of the domestic economy and trade focusing on privatising state industries and creating joint-venture projects, particularly in financial institutions. The economy is characterised by dependence on agriculture, a poor export base, unbalanced regional development, dependence on foreign aid, excessive government control and regulation, and inefficient public enterprises and administration.

Hilly and mountainous terrain in the northern two-thirds of the country has made the building of roads and other infrastructure difficult and expensive. There were just over 8,500 km of paved roads, and one 59 km railway line in the south. Aviation is in a better state, with 48 airports, ten of them with paved runways. There is less than one telephone per 19 people; landline services are not adequate nationwide but concentrated in cities and district headquarters; mobile telephony is in a reasonable state in most parts of the country with increased accessibility and affordability.

Tourism is an important component of the economy, but the security situation has hurt the industry. Since the early 1990s, the government has abolished travel restrictions in some remote areas, constructed numerous tourist centres, and allowed access to 263 mountains. Most goods come either from or through India. Trade disputes with India have exacerbated a perpetual trade deficit and reduced Nepalese exports to India. Major imports include petroleum products, textiles, vehicles, fertilizer, crude palm oil, and machinery. More than 50 percent of imports come from India. Other important sources of imports are Singapore, China, Malaysia, and Indonesia.

Agriculture accounts for about 40% of Nepal's GDP, services comprise 41% and industry 22%. Agriculture employs 76% of the workforce, services 18% and manufacturing/craft-based industry 6%. Agricultural produce—mostly grown in the Terai region bordering India—includes tea, rice, corn, wheat, sugarcane, root crops, milk, and water buffalo meat. Industry mainly involves the processing of agricultural produce, including jute, sugarcane, tobacco, and grain. Its workforce of about 10 million suffers from a severe shortage of skilled labour. The spectacular landscape and diverse, exotic cultures of Nepal represent considerable potential for tourism, but growth in this hospitality industry has been stifled by recent political events. The rate of unemployment and underemployment approaches half of the working-age population. Thus many Nepali citizens move to India in search of work; the Gulf countries and Malaysia being new sources of work. Nepal receives US$50 million a year through the Gurkha soldiers who serve in the Indian and British armies and are highly esteemed for their skill and bravery. The total remittance value is worth around US$1 billion, including money sent from the Persian Gulf and Malaysia, who combined employ around 700,000 Nepali citizens. A long-standing economic agreement underpins a close relationship with India. The country receives foreign aid from India, Japan, the United Kingdom, the United States, the European Union, China, Switzerland, and Scandinavian countries. Poverty is acute; per-capita income is less than US$470. The distribution of wealth among the Nepalis is consistent with that in many developed and developing countries: the highest 10% of households control 39.1% of the national wealth and the lowest 10% control only 2.6%.

Infrastructure

Nepal's transportation system is poor. The mountainous terrain physically constrains development of the transportation network, and the government has lacked funds to maintain, improve and expand the transportation infrastructure, which has thus relied heavily on foreign funding. The transportation infrastructure is concentrated in the central and eastern parts of the Terai. Roads are Nepal's principal transportation mode. The total road length is 17,217 kilometres, including 4,781 kilometres paved, 4,703 kilometre gravel-covered, and 7,643 kilometres classified as fair weather roads.

Nepal's railroad system is small, outdated, and declining in use and quality. Two rail lines link to railheads in India. The passenger traffic is about 1.7 million per year and freight traffic, 21 tons. The railroad has lost money for years because of low fares, overstaffing, and political intervention. Civil aviation has been slow to develop. In 2005 Nepal had 44 airports of varying standards and only one international airport, Tribhuvan, near Kathmandu. The number of international tourists arriving by air was 288,356 in 2004.

Telecommunication penetration is now about 61.42% with mobile being 54.46%. Twelve months earlier the mobile penetration was 38.31%,so this represents a growth rate of 42.15% for the mobile sector. However, the growth of fixed line telephony has been very low. Similarly, the numbers of subscribers to data/internet services represents 17.53% penetration rate. Most of the data service is accounted by GPRS users. Twelve months earlier the data/internet penetration was 10.05%, thus this represents a growth rate of 74.77%. In the broadcast media, the state operates 2 television stations as well as national and regional radio stations. There are roughly 30 independent TV channels registered, with only about half in regular operation. Nearly 400 FM radio stations are licensed with roughly 300 operational.

Government and Politics

Executive Branch: Executive power is held by the Council of Ministers, which is headed by the prime minister. The Council of Ministers is responsible for the general administration of the country. The Council of Ministers has a central secretariat consisting of 22 ministries and the secretariat of the National Planning Commission.

Legislative Branch: Nepal's legislature consists of a bicameral parliament. The lower house of parliament, the House of Representatives (Pratinidhi Sabha), has authority over the Council of Ministers and is regarded as the more powerful of the two houses. It has 205 members directly elected for five-year terms. The prime minister is the leader of the majority party and the country's chief executive. The upper house, the National Council (Rashtriya Sabha), has 60 members, appointed or indirectly elected to six-year terms.

Judicial Branch: The 1990 constitution established a three-tier court system consisting of 75 district courts, 16 appellate courts, and the Supreme Court. Village and municipal bodies may exercise quasi-judicial functions for minor offenses. The judiciary is widely regarded as becoming more autonomous, but it suffers from large case backlogs, insufficient finances and personnel, political intervention, poor demarcation of jurisdiction between courts, and biases based on caste and economic status.

Administrative Divisions: Nepal is divided into 14 zones and 75 districts, grouped into 5 development regions. Each district is headed by a fixed chief district officer responsible for maintaining law and order and coordinating the work of field agencies of the various government ministries. The 14 zones are:

Bagmati	Bheri	Dhawalagiri
Gandaki	Janakpur	Karnali
Koshi	Lumbini	Mahakali
Mechi	Narayani	Rapti
Sagarmatha	Seti	

Foreign Relations: Nepal's foreign policy has been directed toward preserving autonomy and addressing domestic economic and security issues. Nepal's most substantive international relations are with international economic institutions, such as the Asian Development Bank, the International Monetary Fund, the World Bank, and the South Asian Association for Regional Cooperation. The country also maintains strong political relations with India and China, usually attempting to balance one against

the other. Relations with India are fraught with trade and border disputes and Indian suspicions that Nepalese and Pakistani rebels use Nepal as a haven to attack India. Relations with Bhutan have been strained since 1992 over the nationality and possible repatriation of refugees from Bhutan.

Armed Forces

Nepal's military consists of the Nepalese Army which includes the Nepalese Army Air Service, (the air force unit under it), and the Nepalese Police Force. Most of the equipment and arms are supplied by the India. Nepal has close ties with both of its neighbours, India and China. In accordance with a long standing treaty, Indian and Nepalese citizens may travel to each others' countries without a passport or visa. Nepalese citizens may work in India without legal restriction. Although Nepal and India typically have close ties, from time to time Nepal becomes caught up in the problematic Sino-Indian relationship. India considers Nepal as part of its realm of influence, and views Chinese aid with concern.

Nepal Army's participation in the UN peacekeeping operations spans a period of 50 years covering 31UN Missions are, in which over (61,094 Nepalese soldiers have served in support of UN peacekeeping endeavours. The Nepal Army has contributed Force Commanders, military contingent, military observers and staff officers. Its most significant contribution has been of peace and stability in Africa. It has demonstrated its capacity of sustaining large troop commitments over prolonged periods. Presently, Nepal is ranked as the fourth largest troop contributing country to the UN.

PAKISTAN

The Republic of Pakistan borders Iran to the southwest, Afghanistan to the west and north, China to the northeast, and India to the east. The Arabian Sea marks Pakistan's southern boundary. Pakistan's exact size is debated because of its disputed border with India. According to the United Nations, the country has a total area of 796,095 square kilometres. This figure, however, does not include the Pakistan-administered portions of Jammu and Kashmir and the Northern Areas, with areas of 11,639 square kilometres and 72,520 square kilometres, respectively.

Pakistan proclaimed independence on 14 August 1947, from Britain. Pakistan's flag is green with a narrow vertical white band on its left side. A white crescent and star are in the centre of the green band. Green signifies the Muslim majority, white denotes minorities, the crescent represents progress, and the star symbolizes light and knowledge.

Pakistan shares borders with Afghanistan (2,430 kilometres), China (523 kilometres), India (2,912 kilometres), and Iran (909 kilometres). Afghanistan disputes the legitimacy of its border with Pakistan, and at times Afghanistan's governments have argued that all Pashtun (Pakhtun) territory in Afghanistan and Pakistan should be under Afghan control. Pakistan and India have disputed possession of Jammu and Kashmir since 1947, and the issue remains unresolved despite numerous cease-fire agreements. Jammu and Kashmir is split between the two countries by a border called the Line of Control. Pakistan's coastline totals 1,064 kilometres along the Arabian Sea.

Pakistan's history has been characterised by periods of military rule and political instability. It is still an undeveloped nation that faces problems with high levels of poverty and illiteracy. It is the sixth most populous country in the world and has the second largest Muslim population in the world after Indonesia. It also has the second largest Shia Muslim population in the world. The country is listed among the Next Eleven economies and is the world's only Muslim-majority nuclear-powered country.

History

Muhammad Iqbal conceived the concept of a Muslim homeland called Pakistan ("Land of the Pure") in the 1920s, but the establishment of Pakistan was most advanced by Mohammad Ali Jinnah, a Bombay lawyer who proved to be a shrewd leader of the Muslim League political party. Jinnah claimed that India contained two nations, one Hindu and one Muslim, and that Muslims could not safely exist in a Hindu-dominated India. The degree to which Jinnah's objectives were motivated by religion is still debated, but his ideas resonated with Muslims who felt politically, economically, and socially discriminated against and with Muslims having theological interests in an Islamic state.

Pakistan was born as a bifurcated state in August 1947, divided by 1,600 kilometres of Indian soil and by economic and social divisions between a largely Bengali East Wing and a heavily Punjabi and Sindhi West Wing. The country also faced problems with absorbing millions of Muslim refugees from India, addressing substantial poverty, and establishing both

Capital	-	Islamabad
Official languages	-	Urdu (National); English (Government)
Regional languages	-	Punjabi, Pashto, Sindhi, Seraiki, Brahui and Balochi
Government	-	Parliamentary Federal Republic
	-	President Asif Ali Zardari
	-	Prime Minister Raja Pervaiz Ashraf
	-	Chief Justice Iftikhar Muhammad Chaudhry
Formation	-	Independence from Britain - 14 August 1947
	-	Islamic Republic - 23 March 1956
Area	-	796,095 square kilometres (disputed)
Coastline	-	1,046 kilometres
Population	-	180,440,000 (2012 estimate) Density 227/square kilometre
GDP (PPP)	-	$488.580 billion (2011 estimate) Per capita $2,787
GDP (nominal)	-	$210.566 billion (2011 estimate) Per capita $1,201
Defence Minister	-	Naveed Qamar
Chairman Joint Chiefs of Staff	-	General Khalid Shameem Wynne
Chief of Army Staff	-	Gen Ashfaq Parvez Kayani
Chief of Navy Staff	-	Admiral Muhammad Asif Sandila
Chief of Air Staff	-	Air Chief Marshal Tahir Rafik Butt
Commander Strategic Forces	-	Lt Gen Syed Absar Hussain

a functioning government and a sense of national unity over a geographically and ethnically divided state.

The founding fathers, Mohammad Ali Jinnah and Liaquat Ali Khan, passed away by 1951, and their deaths were precursors to the subsequent series of short-lived governments that changed just as often by military coup as by election. Pakistan was initially governed by a Constituent Assembly responsible for drafting a constitution and issuing legislation until the constitution went into force. However, the constitution's drafting was delayed by disagreements over how different regions would be represented and how the state would embody Islamic principles. Legislative paralysis prompted Governor General Ghulam Mohammad to dismiss the Constituent Assembly in 1954. This action is now seen as the beginning of "viceregal" politics in Pakistan, in which the military and civil bureaucracy, not elected officials, govern the country and maintain substantial influence over society and the provinces. A new Constituent Assembly wrote the first constitution in 1956 and reconstituted itself as the Legislative Assembly. However, regional rivalries between East and West Pakistan and ethnic and religious tensions threatened political stability, and on 7 October 1958, President Iskander Mirza disbanded the Legislative Assembly. Later that month, Mirza himself was overthrown by General Mohammad Ayub Khan.

Ayub Khan saw himself as a reformer who would bring much-needed stability to the country, and he started by establishing a system of local governments called Basic Democracies for communities to have meaningful input into politics. But Ayub quickly lost interest and turned toward the civil bureaucracy for policy advice and formation. A new constitution was promulgated in 1962, and it established a weak legislature (the National Assembly) and a president with substantial legislative, executive, and financial powers. Possibly the most notable event of Ayub's tenure was a 17-day war with India in 1965 over the Kashmir dispute. The 1965 war had the unintended consequences of interrupting impressive economic growth and deflating the military's confidence in its own abilities. Amid worsening societal and political problems, substantial popular opposition, and his own declining health, Ayub Khan resigned in 1969.

Subsequently, General Agha Mohammad Yahya Khan became president and chief martial law administrator, and he attempted to reinstitute parliamentary democracy. However, festering tensions over representation in the National Assembly led to civil war between East and West Pakistan in 1971. With Indian assistance, East Pakistan seceded and became the independent nation of Bangladesh. At the same time, India and West Pakistan fought a 14-day war which ended in a cease-fire agreement. Largely as a result of Pakistan's military losses, Yahya resigned in 1971, and Zulfiqar Ali Bhutto was appointed president, becoming the first civilian head of government in nearly two decades.

Bhutto lifted martial law, and a new constitution came into effect in August 1973. The constitution was heavily concerned with the role of Islam, the distribution of power between the federal and provincial governments, and the division of responsibilities between the president and prime minister, the latter assuming greater authority than before. Bhutto nationalised numerous industries, and the government's heavy involvement in the economy would have enduring economic repercussions. The country appeared to be democratising, but political opposition grew against Bhutto's repression of political opponents and alleged voting irregularities. In July 1977, Bhutto was overthrown, and General Mohammad Zia ul-Haq became chief martial law administrator. Bhutto eventually was sentenced to death on charges of conspiring to murder a political opponent and was executed in 1979.

Zia adapted the structure of Ayub Khan's Basic Democracies to a new system of local governments and also adopted various measures to create an Islamic state. When the Soviet Union invaded Afghanistan in 1979, Pakistan became the recipient of numerous Afghan refugees and large-scale foreign aid from the United States, China, Saudi Arabia, and others. The refugees and financial assistance continued until the war's end in 1989. Zia officially terminated martial law in 1985 by assuming the presidency and reinstating the 1973 constitution. However, he also added the Eighth Amendment, which empowered the president to appoint and dismiss the prime minister and provincial governors and to dissolve the national and provincial legislatures. When Zia died in an airplane crash in August 1988, Benazir Bhutto - head of the Pakistan People's Party (PPP) and daughter of Zulfiqar Ali Bhutto - became prime minister. Pakistan thus became the first Muslim country with a female head of government.

Bhutto's government was plagued by ethnic conflict, severe economic problems, and a lack of legislative support. In October 1990, Mian Nawaz Sharif, leader of the Islamic Democratic Alliance (IDA), became prime minister and faced the same problems that troubled Bhutto. In 1993 Bhutto's PPP won the National Assembly, and she once again became prime minister. However, in 1996 President Farooq Leghari dismissed Bhutto on charges of corruption, and in 1997 Nawaz Sharif replaced her. In 1998 India conducted nuclear tests, and two weeks later Pakistan reacted by detonating five nuclear devices. Many countries responded with condemnation and sanctions, but Pakistan felt that it finally possessed sufficient deterrent force against its perennial rival, India. Deterrence failed to hold, however, and in October 1999 India and Pakistan engaged in a limited conflict (the Kargil War), which Pakistan was widely seen as precipitating because of its suspected support of militants who entered Indian-held Kashmir from Pakistani-held Kashmir. The conflict proved to be embarrassing for the government, and, with the economy suffering tremendously, General Pervez Musharraf overthrew Nawaz Sharif on 12 October 1999.

Musharraf became both president and chief of army staff, and he further consolidated his power through various legal measures. After the 11 September 2001 terrorist attacks in the United States, Musharraf's government benefited from an infusion of economic and military aid, because Pakistan is seen as an important ally in the war on terrorism. However, Pakistan was widely suspected of complicity in a terrorist attack on India's parliament in December 2001. In an April 2002 national referendum, Musharraf's tenure as president was extended to 2007. In late 2004, Musharraf reneged on a previous commitment to relinquish his position as chief of army staff, much to the chagrin of many secular and religious political parties, who demanded that elections be held in early 2005.

In the 2007 general elections, the Pakistan Peoples Party (PPP) won 123 seats in the 342-seat National Assembly and Sharif's party came second with 91, while Pervez Musharraf's party came a poor third with 54 seats. Sharif's Pakistan Muslim League (Nawaz) won 8 provincial assembly seats, while the

PPP won 7 provincial seats.

On 28 November 2007, nearly nine months before his resignation as president, Musharraf stepped down as army chief due to growing domestic and international pressure. Musharraf's appointee as army chief was General Ashfaq Kayani, a former chief of the powerful Inter-services Intelligence (ISI) and subsequently vice chief of the army. Soon after taking over, Kayani began slowly to reduce the army's role in civilian affairs, which had increased enormously under Musharraf. Within ten months of taking over as army chief, Kayani had selected six of the nine powerful corps commanders of Pakistan.

On 18 February 2008, Pakistan held general elections after Benazir Bhutto's assassination postponed the original date of 8 January 2008. The Pakistan Peoples Party won the majority of the votes and formed an alliance with the Pakistan Muslim League (N). On 7 August 2008, the PPP and the Pakistan Muslim League (N) agreed to force Musharraf to step down and begin his impeachment. Asif Ali Zardari and Nawaz Sharif, announced sending a formal request or joint charge sheet that he steps down, and impeach him through parliamentary process upon refusal. On 18 August 2008, in a speech defending his record, Musharraf announced his resignation.

By 9 September 2008 a new democratically elected political establishment came to power in Pakistan, ending nine years of military rule originating in the coup led by Army Chief General Pervez Musharraf, on 12 October 1999. Following a six-week emergency declared by Musharraf on 3 November 2007 (the President's grip on power had been weakened by public unrest led by lawyers), elections to the National Assembly and the four provincial assemblies took place on 18 February 2009. These elections had been delayed by six weeks due to the assassination, on 27 December 2007, of Benazir Bhutto, a former prime minister and the leader of the largest opposition party, the Pakistan People's Party (PPP). The new coalition government, formed largely by the PPP and the Pakistan Muslim League (Nawaz) led by former Prime Minister Nawaz Sharif, elected Yousaf Raza Gilani, a senior PPP politician, as prime minister on 24 March 2009. On 9 September Asif Ali Zaradari was sworn in as the president, completing the country's turbulent transition to democracy.

President Zardari's top priority is to fight terrorism and Islamist militancy in the Federally Administered Tribal Areas (FATA) of Pakistan bordering Afghanistan. With his government focusing on a three pronged policy towards the tribal areas comprising political dialogue, development and the

use of force, military operations have had mixed results. The United States has expressed reservations about negotiating with Pakistan Taliban (Tehrik-e-Taliban Pakistan—TTP) militants, fearing it would reinforce the status of the tribal areas as a sanctuary for al-Qaeda and the Afghan Taliban in planning cross-border attacks into Afghanistan.

Notwithstanding US pressure on Pakistan to use its army and frontier corps more actively and effectively in the tribal areas and Swat in the Khyber-Pakhtunkhwa Province, Pakistani security forces in general remain unable or unwilling to effectively counter the resurgent Afghan and TTP militants, though there are over 112,000 troops deployed in the area. This has led to allegations of official Pakistani complicity—particularly by serving or retired members of the ISI—in providing assistance to the Afghan Taliban, which Pakistan has denied. Speculation has also arisen that the ISI provided Afghan Taliban militants details of the US military campaign, which in some cases enabled the fighters to escape US missile strikes in the tribal areas, and that the ISI was involved in the deadly suicide car bomb attack carried out by Jalaluddin Haqqani's Afghan Taliban, on the Indian Embassy in Kabul on 7 July 2008; this was denied by the Pakistan government.

Pakistan's military operations targeting the Taliban and al-Qaeda in the Bajaur Agency of the tribal areas have been relatively more effective. Since the start of the offensive in August 2008, the military's objective has expanded from defending its administrative headquarters at Khar to securing Bajaur Agency against the TTP. As a result of these operations an estimated 220,000 people were displaced from the area. At the same time, government backed tribal lashkars (militias) have begun mounting offensives against the Taliban, though their success appears limited so far. By the end of 2009, more than 3 million Pakistani civilians have been displaced by the ongoing conflict in North-West Pakistan between the government and Taliban militants.

Pakistan's major challenge is to build a consensus against terrorism and Islamist extremism among the political establishment. To effectively pursue the campaign on terror, the Pakistani military will need to balance growing US pressure for military strikes in the tribal areas with the Pakistani army's decreasing tolerance for such attacks. It also needs to ensure that the ensuing domestic political turbulence, heightened by the growing economic crisis, does not place the government at risk from the army. Since 2004, Pakistani armed forces are engaged in fighting against Pakistani Taliban groups. Militant groups have engaged in suicide bombings in Pakistani cities, killing more than 3,000 civilians and armed personnel in 2009 alone.

Geography

Topography. Pakistan has a diverse array of landscapes spread among nine major ecological zones. Its territory encompasses portions of the Himalayas, Hindu Kush and Karakoram mountain ranges, making it home to some of the world's highest mountains, including K2, which at 8,611 metres above sea level is the world's second highest peak. Inter-mountain valleys make up much of the North-West Frontier Province, and rugged plateaus cover much of Balochistan Province in the west. In the east, expansive, irrigated plains along the Indus River cover much of Punjab and Sindh provinces, which have deserts as well (Cholistan in Punjab, Thar in Sindh).

Principal Rivers. The main rivers are the Indus (2,749 kilometres within Pakistan) and its tributaries. the Chenab (730 kilometres), Ravi (680 kilometres), Jhelum (611 kilometres), and Sutlej (531 kilometres). The navigable portions of these rivers are generally small and unconnected as a result of seasonal variations in water flows and the presence of substantial irrigation structures.

Natural Resources. Economically important natural resources include arable land, chromite, coal, copper, fireclay, gypsum, iron, limestone, oil, natural gas, rock salt, and silica sand.

Land Use. More than 40% of the working population is employed in agriculture, yet the per capita amount of agricultural land is declining, and there are significant natural limitations to increasing the quantity of arable land. The country's total land area is 79.6 million hectares, but only 59.3 million hectares have been surveyed. Out of the surveyed land area, 24.6 million hectares are classified as not available for cultivation, 3.6 million hectares are forest area, and 9.2 million hectares are unused but believed to be cultivable. Approximately 22 million hectares are used for cultivation, of which nearly 16 million hectares are actually sown, with the remainder left fallow. About 13.5 million hectares of the sown area are irrigated, and 6.5 million hectares are sown more than once per year. Most cultivable and irrigated land is located in the eastern provinces of Punjab and Sindh around the Indus River and its tributaries. Pakistan has an extensive but inefficient canal system for irrigation, and much of the crop area is rain fed, but precipitation tends to be unevenly distributed throughout the year.

Environmental Factors. Numerous environmental problems threaten the economy and the population's health, and there is little indication of their abatement. The availability of natural resources is limited by the dry climate and mountainous terrain, substantial population growth is increasing pressure on the resource base, and resource management has suffered from the emphasis on rapid economic growth and often-unregulated forms of economic productivity. As a result, human transformation of the environment is manifest in several problems. Population growth and poor water infrastructure have reduced per capita water availability from 53,000 cubic metres to 1,200 cubic metres, and heavy reliance on firewood has contributed to the world's second highest rate of deforestation. Poor agricultural practices have led to soil erosion, groundwater degradation, and other problems that have hindered crop output and contributed to health problems for rural communities. Solid waste burning, low-quality fuels, and the growing use of fuel-inefficient motor vehicles have contributed to air pollution that in some cities—such as Islamabad, Lahore, and Rawalpindi—has exceeded levels deemed safe by the World Health Organisation. The government has expressed concern about environmental threats to economic growth and social development and, since the early 1990s, has addressed environmental concerns with new legislation and institutions such as the Pakistan Environment Protection Council. Only 0.04% of the government's development budget goes to environmental protection.

The 2010 Pakistan floods began in July 2010 following heavy monsoon rains in the Khyber Pakhtunkhwa, Sindh, Punjab and Balochistan regions of Pakistan and affected the Indus River basin. At one point, approximately one-fifth of Pakistan's total land area was underwater. According to Pakistani government data the floods directly affected about 20 million people, mostly by destruction of property, livelihood and infrastructure, with a death toll of close to 2,000. The number of individuals affected by the flooding exceeds the combined total of individuals affected by the 2004 Indian Ocean tsunami, the 2005 Kashmir earthquake and the 2010 Haiti earthquake.

Society

Population. Pakistan has a large, mostly rural population with a high rate of growth. The population growth rate expects it to double approximately every 26 years. The population is clustered in the eastern provinces of Punjab and Sindh, which contain 78.6% of the total population.

Ethnic Groups. Ethnic groups in Pakistan generally are categorised according to various combinations of religion, language, and sometimes tribe. Punjabis are the largest linguistic group (44.2% of the population) and often are divided into three occupational castes. Rajputs, Jats and Arains. Pakhtuns (15.4%) are the dominant ethnic group in the North-West Frontier Province, but Pakhtuns belong to different tribes or kinship groups and have no central governing authority. Sindhis (14.1%) are dominant in Sindh and are divided into occupational and caste groupings. Balochis (3.6%) are dominant in Balochistan and are divided into various eastern and western tribes. Other ethno-linguistic groups include the Seraikis, who live mostly in Punjab; Urdu-speaking Muhajirs, refugees from India and their descendants who migrated to Pakistan during the 1947 partition and are concentrated in Sindh; and Brahuis, a Dravidian language group in Sindh and Balochistan.

Languages. Urdu is the national language and the language of most print media. English has official status and often is regarded as the language of the elite and upwardly mobile. Urdu and English often are used in government and business. Punjabi is the most common language, spoken by 44.2% of the population, followed by Pakhtu (15.2%), Sindhi (14.1%), Siraiki (10.5%), Urdu (7.8%), and Balochi (3.8%). Smaller linguistic groups include the Hindko in the North-West Frontier Province, the Farsi-speaking Hazaras of Balochistan, and the Brahuis in Sindh and Balochistan. Language often articulates ethnic identity, and provincial boundaries are linguistically based. Urdu has been promoted as a means of unifying ethnic groups, but it is the mother tongue of only the Muhajirs. Furthermore, many groups perceive the establishment of Urdu as the national language as threatening to their employment potential, political participation, and ethnic identity.

Religion. The overwhelming majority of the population (96.3%) is Muslim, of whom approximately 95% are Sunni and 5% Shia. Sunnis and Shias are subdivided into numerous sects. Approximately 1.6% of the population is Hindu, 1.6% is Christian, and 0.3% belongs to other religions, such as Bahaism and Sikhism. Some 0.2% of the population is Ahmadiyya (also known as Qadiani), a small but influential sect that maintains some Islamic beliefs but is considered heretical by orthodox Muslims and is not recognised as Muslim by Pakistani law. The country was founded to promote religious freedom, and the constitution guarantees freedom of religion. However, Islam is the state religion, and the constitution states that religious practice is "subject to law, public order, and morality." The government also has Islamic institutions such as the Federal Shariat Court and the Council of Islamic Ideology, which advise politicians on the congruence of legislation with Islamic injunctions. It is debatable whether the government has established such institutions for religious or political reasons, but the government has promoted Islam as a means of unifying numerous ethnic groups. Nevertheless, political, economic, and religious differences have been manifested in occasionally violent conflicts between religious communities, particularly between Sunni and Shia militias.

Education and Literacy. Pakistan has low indicators of educational attainment, and education has been under-funded for decades. In 2001 the government announced plans to institute universal primary education by 2010 and 78% literacy by 2011. Free primary education is a constitutional right and is compulsory in every province except Balochistan. In addition to public and private schools, an indeterminate number of mosque-administered madrassas provide free room, board, and theological education, which makes them an attractive option for poor families. Some madrassas are suspected of having links to religious militants, prompting the government to announce its intention of establishing greater regulation over these institutions.

Economy

Despite being a very poor country in 1947, Pakistan's economic growth rate was better than the global average during the subsequent four decades, but imprudent policies led to a slowdown in the late 1990s. Throughout the 1990s, Pakistan's economy suffered for a number of reasons, but from 2002 to 2004 the economy has recovered as a result of changes in government policies and the resumption of international lending. Economic statistics do not reflect the reality of the economy, because official economic data omit the informal economy, which is estimated to equal about 30% of the formal economy. Since independence, economic growth rates have been impressive but also have fluctuated widely. These fluctuations have occurred largely because successive governments have emphasised different sectors through changes in subsidies, regulations, and state ownership of industry. The government has shifted from state ownership of many industries and heavy regulation of the private economy to privatisation of some state industries, deregulation, facilitation of capital flows, and reforms of the financial system and monetary policy. Still, lax fiscal and monetary policies, infrastructural deficiencies, a poorly developed human resource base, and persistent market distortions that benefit a small elite of landowners, industrialists, and others undercut economic potential.

The structure of the Pakistani economy has changed from a mainly agricultural base to a strong service base. Agriculture now only accounts for roughly 20% of the GDP, while the service sector accounts for 53% of the GDP. Significant foreign investments have been made in several areas including telecommunications, real estate and energy. Other important industries include apparel and textiles (accounting for nearly 60% of exports), food processing, chemicals manufacture, and the iron and steel industries. The economic crisis of 2008 led Pakistan to seek more than $100 billion in aid in order to avoid possible bankruptcy. This was never given to Pakistan and therefore it had to depend on a more aggressive fiscal policy, backed by the IMF.

Mining and Minerals. Mining and minerals historically have been a weak economic sector. Since 2000 mining and quarrying have accounted annually for around 1.4% of GDP and employed an estimated 0.1% of the working population. Chromite is the only metallic ore that has been exploited on a commercial scale, but the country has substantial deposits of copper and iron ores as well. Pakistan also has significant deposits of non-metallic ores such as anhydrite, dolomite, gypsum, limestone, marble, and rock salt.

Industry and Manufacturing. Since the mid-1960s, the industrial sector has produced 19 to 25% of GDP, accounting for 24.5% of GDP in 2004. Manufacturing and construction dominate the industrial sector, accounting for around 19% of GDP. Various liberalisation reforms have been pursued since the early 1980s but have been hindered by substantial corruption, frequent raw material shortages, the government's tendency to provide generous concessions to particular sectors and a burdensome tax structure that has helped promote the development of the informal economy.

Energy. Economic growth, population growth, and rising urbanisation have increased energy demand, much of which is met by imported energy sources because of the country's limited domestic energy resources. Coal has provided around 5% of total domestic energy supply for decades, but most is of poor quality and generally is used in brick kilns. With regard to non-traditional sources, oil and natural gas have provided around 37 to 43% of total energy supplies each since the late 1970s, and the country is attempting to expand hydropower production. For decades, Pakistan has depended heavily on oil imports. Domestic oil provided 6.7% of total energy supplies, and domestic recoverable petroleum reserves have fallen to less than 50% of their estimated original amount. However, natural gas production has nearly doubled to 2.7 million cubic feet per day, providing 43.8% of the total energy supply. The government has considered pipelines that could import around 1.5 billion cubic feet of gas per day, but these plans are still under review. Hydropower has declined from 17.7% of total energy supply to 11.3%.

Services. The services sector accounts for about 50% of Pakistan's annual GDP. From 2000 to 2004, transportation, wholesale and retail trade, finance, public administration, defence, and services collectively provided about 52% of GDP. Services alone were about 9 to 10% of GDP. The services sector has suffered from many of the same problems as the industrial sector, such as political corruption and crippling tax rates, and sectoral growth has been limited by a dearth of educational resources and skilled labour.

Balance of Payments. Pakistan has had balance of payments difficulties for decades, largely as a result of current account deficits due to trade deficits.

External Debt. Estimates of the size of Pakistan's external debt vary by source. However, observers generally believe that the combination of poor tax administration, high government expenditures, and heavy dependence on external funds has resulted in massive fiscal deficits that, at times, have nearly crippled the economy and rendered Pakistan one of the world's most indebted countries.

Foreign Aid. The economy is heavily dependent on bilateral and multilateral aid, which substantially influences economic growth. After 11 September 2001, the United States and other countries dropped economic sanctions against Pakistan because of its potential role in the war on terrorism. Prior to 2000, Pakistan had never completed an International Monetary Fund (IMF) lending programme because of government unwillingness to comply with loan package conditions and political issues such as nuclear weapons tests or difficulties in Kashmir.

The growth of non-agricultural sectors has changed the structure of the economy, and agriculture now only accounts for roughly 20% of the GDP. The service sector accounts for 53% of the country's GDP, with wholesale and retail trade forming 30% of this sector. Large amounts of foreign investments have been made into several industries. The top industries in Pakistan are telecom, software, automotives, textiles, cement, fertilizer, steel, ship building, and more recently, aerospace.

Pakistan has accomplished many engineering feats such as construction of the world's largest earth filled dam Tarbela, the world's twelfth largest dam Mangla, as well as, with collaboration with China, the world's highest international road: the Karakoram Highway. There are also additional dams planned such as Kalabagh Dam, Diamer-Bhasha Dam, Munda, Akhori and Skardu Katzara.

Infrastructure

Roads. Roads, road traffic, and motor vehicles all have increased substantially since the early 1990s. According to government statistics, from 1994 to 2003 total road length increased from 196,877 to 251,845 kilometres, and highways increased, from 104,001 to 151,028 kilometres. The total number of registered motor vehicles also increased from 3.5 million to 5.2 million, including 2.5 million motorcycles, 1.3 million automobiles, and 178,000 trucks. In the early 1990s, the government announced plans to shift passenger and freight traffic from roads to rail, but the declining quality and quantity of rail service continues to prompt increases in private and commercial use of roads.

Railroads. The railroad system is publicly owned, but government funding has been insufficient to maintain the system. Government figures indicate that operating revenues exceeded operating expenses from 1994 to 2003, but the deterioration in the quantity and quality of service suggests that major problems persist. From 1994 to 2003, the quantity of track kilometres fell from 8,775 to 7,791 kilometres, and route kilometres dropped from 12,625 to 11,515 kilometres. Of the track kilometres, 7,346 kilometres were 1.676-millimeter gauge, and 445 kilometres were 1.000-millimeter gauge. Passenger journeys peaked at 85 million in 1989 and declined until 1999, after which they increased to 72.4 million in 2003. Freight tonnage fell from 8 million tons in 1994 to 6.2 million tons in 2003. In the same period, the number of locomotives decreased from 676 to 577, and the quantity of coaches fell from 2,831 to 1,843. A proposed rail line connecting Pakistan with Iran has been stalled because of a lack of funding.

Ports. According to government statistics, the tonnage handled by ports increased from 30 million tons in 1994 to 41.2 million tons in 2003. In the same period, the number of twenty-foot-equivalent-units (TEUs) increased from 409,670 to 615,826. In 2004 Pakistan had two ports, Karachi and Port Qasim, both of which were upgraded in the 1990s. Karachi handles approximately 60% of import and export cargo and is linked by a daily container train to an inland terminal at Lahore. Port Qasim handles about 40% of import and export cargo. The first phase of a multipurpose port located at Gwadar on the Balochistan coast is operational, with a second phase under construction. A deepwater port at Keti Bandar, 100 kilometres southeast of Karachi, is planned as part of a private power project.

Civil Aviation and Airports. Since the 1980s, the air network has expanded. Pakistan has 50 airports with permanently surfaced runways. Karachi, Lahore, Peshawar, Quetta, and Rawalpindi handle both international passenger and cargo flights, and Multan and Turbat handle international cargo. The major international airline is government-owned Pakistan International Airlines, and four other private airlines offer international passenger and cargo services.

Pipelines. The government currently is considering several proposed gas pipelines linking Pakistan with Afghanistan, India, Iran, Turkmenistan, and others. These proposals are still under consideration, partly because the proposed routes would go through areas of periodic civil unrest. Pakistan has a gas pipeline network with coverage of 56,400 kilometres in 1050 towns. It has nearly 1600 CNG stations and the gas throughput in Pakistan is 38 MMSCMD per day. The number of gas customers in Pakistan is estimated at 19 lakh, and Pakistan runs vehicles on CNG whose number is estimated at 15.60 lakh.

Telecommunications. From 1991 to 2002, the estimated number of radios increased only slightly from 10 to 10.2 million, and the estimated number of televisions was unchanged at 2.1 million. The government runs both Azad Kashmir Radio, with three stations, and Pakistan Broadcasting Corporation, with 35 stations. Three private radio stations also are in operation. Government-run Pakistan Television Corporation maintains four domestic television channels, and there are three private television broadcasters. Foreign channels are available by satellite and cable. Domestic phone service is poor. In the early 2000s, Pakistan had approximately 3.7 million telephones, 8 million cellular telephones, 600,000 personal computers, and 500,000 Internet users.

Government and Politics

Overview. The government is based on the much-amended constitution of 1973, which was suspended twice (in 1977 and 1999) and reinstated twice (in 1985 and 2002). According to the constitution, Pakistan is a federal parliamentary system with a president as head of state and a prime minister as head of government. The legislature, or parliament, is the Majlisi- Shoora (Council of Advisers), consisting of the Lower House, which is often called the National Assembly, and the Upper House, or Senate. National Assembly members are directly elected for five-year terms. Senate members are elected by provincial assemblies, with equal representation from each of the four provinces as well as representatives from the Federally Administered Tribal Areas and Islamabad Capital Territory. Both the Senate and National Assembly may initiate and pass legislation, but only the National Assembly can approve federal budgets and finance bills. However, parliament often has had little real political power. For example, in 2003 the only bill passed by the National Assembly was the national budget. Executive power lies with the prime minister and president. The prime minister is an elected member of the National Assembly and is the leader of the National Assembly's dominant party or coalition. However, the prime minister also is appointed formally by the president. The prime minister is assisted by a cabinet of ministers who are appointed by the president on the prime minister's advice. An electoral college composed of members of the national and provincial legislatures elects the president for a five-year term, and no individual may hold the office for more than two consecutive terms. By law the president must be a Muslim. The president acts on the advice of the prime minister but has the power to prevent passage of non-finance bills and may dissolve the National Assembly if he concludes that the government cannot operate according to the constitution. The Senate, however, cannot be suspended.

Politics in Pakistan often have not operated according to the constitution. The military and Civil Service of Pakistan frequently have been the pre-eminent actors in the country's power structure. Moreover, there has been some concern that Pakistan could become a "failed state" because of the apparent inability of any single entity to control the country, the weakened productivity of a population beset by years of economic difficulties, and continuing problems of communal conflict and terrorism. Ethnic and provincial tensions often are manifested in rivalries between political parties, and several governments have been ended by assassination or military coup rather than by formal, electoral change.

Religion has played an important role in politics, and religious differences have been very salient in Pakistani government and civil society. The government has consistently been faced with tensions of whether and how to synthesize Islamic principles into an essentially secular and Western form of government.

Administrative Divisions. Pakistan has four provinces—Balochistan, North-West Frontier Province, Punjab, and Sindh—and numerous federally administered areas. Provincial boundaries correspond with areas of numerically dominant linguistic groups, and provinces are divided into a total of 26 divisions that are further subdivided into 101 districts. Federally administered areas include the capital (Islamabad) and 13 Federally Administered Tribal Areas (FATAs).

Judicial and Legal System. The legal system is derived from English common law and is based on the much-amended 1973 constitution and Islamic law (sharia). The Supreme Court, provincial high courts, and other courts have jurisdiction over criminal and civil issues. The president appoints the Supreme Court's chief justice and formally approves other Supreme Court justices as well as provincial high court judges on the advice of the chief justice. The Supreme Court has original, appellate, and advisory jurisdiction, and high courts have original and appellate jurisdiction. The Federal Shariat Court determines whether laws are consistent with Islamic injunctions. Special courts and tribunals hear particular types of cases, such as drugs, commerce, and terrorism. Pakistan's penal code has limited jurisdiction in tribal areas, where law is largely derived from tribal customs.

Mass Media. Print media are published in 11 languages, but most are published in Urdu and Sindhi, and English language publications are numerous. The press generally publishes free from censorship and has played an active role in national elections, but journalists often exercise self-censorship as a result of arrests and intimidation by government and societal actors. Most print media are privately owned, but the government controls the National Press Trust, a major newspaper publisher, and the Associated Press of Pakistan, one of the two major news agencies.

Foreign Relations. Pakistan's primary foreign policy objectives are protection from external threats and the preservation of territorial integrity. Foreign alliances often have been based on mutual—and sometimes ephemeral—strategic interests. Contentious relations with India dominate foreign relations and are largely due to perennial tensions over Kashmir, which was the basis of wars in 1948, 1965, 1971, and 1999. Various talks have eased tensions but not mutual suspicions. China has perhaps been Pakistan's most consistent ally because of shared antipathies of other countries, such as India and Russia, but in the 1990s China assumed a more distant relationship as a result of India's growing military prowess, Russia's military decline, and other factors. China is alleged to have supplied Pakistan with nuclear weapons material, ostensibly to counter India's nuclear weapons. Relations with Afghanistan have been harmonious and tense, often simultaneously. The two countries have a disputed border, but Pakistan supported insurgents in Afghanistan against Soviet occupation in the 1980s and was a key ally of the Taliban in the 1990s. Since their 1971 war, Pakistan and Bangladesh typically

have had close ties based largely on shared opposition to India. Relations with Islamic Middle Eastern countries generally have been close, but ties with largely Shia Iran have been strained. For countries outside South Asia and the Middle East, relations generally are based on Pakistan's perceived strategic value in the international system. After 11September 2001, the United States and other countries saw Pakistan as an important ally in fighting international terrorists operating in Afghanistan, and international aid increased substantially. Pakistan's relations with the United States have resumed the closeness of the 1980s. However, Pakistan's relations with the United States have had important ramifications for the government's domestic support, particularly among some religious parties who perceive the government as acting against Islamic injunctions.

Armed Forces

The Pakistan Armed Forces consists of approximately 619,000 active personnel in the army (550,000), air force (45,000), and navy (24,000), as well as 513,000 reserves. Under the 1973 constitution, the federal government controls the armed forces, and the president is the commander in chief. The Ministry of Defence has a permanent staff of civil servants headed by the defence secretary general, and the minister of defence is a civilian member of the prime minister's cabinet. The Joint Chiefs of Staff Committee deals with problems concerning military aspects of state security and is charged with integrating and coordinating the army, navy, and air force. The committee's secretariat acts as the principal link between the service headquarters and the Ministry of Defence.

The Directorate for Inter-Services Intelligence (ISI) is of particular importance at the joint services level because it manages covert operations outside of Pakistan and because it has been involved in domestic politics, usually to keep track of the incumbent regime's opponents. The chief of the army staff (COAS) is the key power holder in the armed forces and is also one of the triumvirate that runs the country, along with the prime minister and president. The COAS usually operates from army headquarters in Rawalpindi. The military is forbidden constitutionally from acting independently of the elected political leadership in domestic matters. However, from 1947 to 2004 military generals have acted as head of state for nearly 30 years, and in times of civilian government the armed forces have routinely intervened on domestic and foreign policy issues. The military justifies its consistent involvement in politics as protection from malign foreign interests and corrupt and incompetent politicians. Although public opinion surveys are rare, it appears that the public dislikes military rule, yet consistently has a more favourable view of the military than of elected officials.

Because the military conducts its affairs with carefully defended secrecy, the degree to which army officers and personnel are religiously motivated is debated. However, Western analysts tend to conclude that whereas the military increasingly sees itself as serving Islam, the institution's decision making is still largely secular. Military intervention in politics is designed to limit civilian involvement in sensitive matters, such as Kashmir, nuclear disarmament, internal military personnel decisions, and defence spending. The military also is extensively involved in the economy, and military enterprises produce approximately 3% of the gross national product. Military enterprises include the Army Welfare Trust (AWT), whose assets include the Askari Bank, one of the country's largest financial institutions, and the Fauji Foundation, which is the country's biggest conglomerate. These and other military financial institutions often are exempt from taxes and regulations covering the manufacturing sector and asset disclosure.

With regard to military strategy, the military's budget and personnel have reduced strategy to largely defensive objectives, such as limited offensive tactics in bordering areas (particularly Kashmir), use of irregular forces, and deterring and countering possible attacks from foreign powers (particularly India). The military's history of far lower military expenditures and capabilities than India has prompted the military to attempt to impose high costs on India to force its withdrawal from Kashmir. Furthermore, the military hopes that its nuclear capabilities can reduce the disadvantages of its conventional forces. However, the theoretical deterrence between nuclear powers has not limited military engagement between India and Pakistan—as exemplified by the 1999 Kargil War—and analysts believe that Pakistan's military strategy historically has suffered from overly optimistic assessments of potential success and underestimations of diplomatic and military losses, as well as a lack of contingency planning.

Foreign Military Relations. Pakistan has sought to become an important actor in international politics, but its foreign military alliances often are intended to address matters with bordering countries. Other countries have established alliances with Pakistan to address their own strategic interests in South and Central Asia, and these alliances have tended to be ephemeral. Pakistan's military relationship with China started in the 1970s as a way of countering India, but China has softened its relations since India's military strength has increased. Still, Pakistan and China maintain a military relationship, including periodic joint military exercises. United States aid in the 1980s was significantly reduced after the Soviet Union pulled out of Afghanistan in 1989 but resumed after the 11 September 2001, terrorist attacks. Moreover, in March 2004 the United States granted Pakistan status as a major non-North Atlantic Treaty Organisation ally, which provides access to U.S. military equipment and cooperation. In fact, the United States is one of the largest suppliers of military equipment to Pakistan along with China and Russia. Pakistan's military relations with India have been contentious, and the two countries fought a limited conflict in Kashmir in 1999. However, under the 1999 Lahore Agreement the two countries provide each other with advance notification of missile tests, and in 2003 and 2004 they engaged in several high-level discussions that have eased tensions.

External Threat. The military and public generally view India as the nation's primary security threat, and opposition to India is often a greater source of social cohesion than either Islam or Urdu. India's far greater military capabilities have been a source of both fear and frustration, and many suspect that this imbalance has prompted Pakistan to engage Indian forces indirectly through supporting insurgents morally, financially, or otherwise. India is not the country's only security concern, as Pakhtun and Balochi irredentist movements in Pakistan's western provinces have contributed to sometimes-tense relations with neighbouring Afghanistan.

Police. Provincial governments are charged with police administration in their respective jurisdictions, and provincial police forces operate independently. The federal government is largely uninvolved in provincial police administration but controls police in federally administered and tribal areas. The federal minister of interior supervises police nationwide, and the Police Service of Pakistan (PSP) selects, trains, and assigns senior officers to provincial or central government agencies. Although service in the PSP is competitive and well paid, lower ranking police personnel often have accused of routine extortion, violating civil liberties, and acting to preserve the tenure of government officials rather than the rule of law. The quantity of overall crime and various types of crime (such as murder and banditry) have increased steadily over the years, and the extensive availability and use of automatic weapons in Pakistani society is often referred to as the "Kalashnikov Culture." The population generally does not perceive the police to be effective against crime or publicly accountable.

Internal Security and Terrorism. Pakistan has numerous categories of terrorism and internal threats, with most insurgent groups identifying themselves as religious or ethnic separatists. Some political parties represent distinct religious and ethnic communities, and rivalries among these parties have been violent. Violence between religiously identified groups is rarely based solely on differing religious doctrines but rather the different social, political, and economic statuses that correlate with religion. There are also concerns that Pakistan's nuclear arsenal could be seized by insurgents in an event such as a coup or assassination of the nation's president. However, the government claims that it has enacted security measures to prevent such a threat and that the numerical and political superiority of religious moderates over religious extremists is a substantial obstacle to the latter's access to Pakistan's nuclear weapons.

Human Rights. The government's human rights record is generally regarded as poor by domestic and international observers, although there have been some improvements since 2000. Security forces use excessive and sometimes lethal force and are complicit in extrajudicial killings of civilians and suspected militants. The police and military have been accused of engaging in physical abuse, rape, and arbitrary arrest and detention, particularly in areas of acute conflict. Although the government has enacted measures to counter these problems, abuses continue. Furthermore, courts suffer from lack of funds, outside intervention, and deep case backlogs that lead to long trial delays and lengthy pretrial detentions. Many observers contend that Pakistan's legal code is largely concerned with crime, national security, and domestic tranquility and less with the protection of individual rights. Provincial and local governments have arrested journalists and closed newspapers that report on matters perceived as socially offensive or critical of the government. Journalists also have been victims of violence and intimidation by various groups and individuals. In spite of these difficulties, the press publishes freely, although journalists often exercise self-restraint in their writing.

SINGAPORE

The Republic of Singapore is a city-state located on the south-central coast of the island of Singapore. 137 kilometres north of the equator, it consists of 63 islands. The country is highly urbanised with very little primary rainforest remaining, although more land is being created for development through land reclamation. It is separated from Malaysia by the Straits of Johor to its north and from Indonesia's Riau Islands by the Singapore Strait to its south. Singapore is the world's fourth leading financial centre and a cosmopolitan world city, playing a key role in international trade and finance. The port of Singapore is one of the five busiest ports in the world.

The Singaporean flag has two equal horizontal bands of red (top) and white; a vertical white crescent (closed portion toward the hoist side), partially enclosing five white-point stars arranged in a circle, positioned near the hoist side of the red band. The red band symbolizes universal brotherhood and the equality of men; the white band, purity and virtue. The crescent moon represents a young nation on the rise, while the five stars stand for the ideals of democracy, peace, progress, justice, and equality.

Singapore has a long history of immigration. It has a diverse population made up of Chinese, Malays, Indians, Asians of various descents, and Caucasians. 42% of the population in Singapore are foreigners who work and study there. Foreign workers make up 50% of the service sector. The country is the second most densely populated in the world after Monaco and is the most globalised country in the world.

History

The island of Singapore was known to mariners for centuries as an entrepôt and supply point for Malay, Thai, Javanese, Chinese, Indian and Arab traders. In 1819 Sir Thomas Stamford Raffles arrived as the lieutenant governor of the British enclave of Bencoolen (Bengkulu on the west coast of Sumatra) and an agent of the British East India Company. He obtained permission from the local Malay official to establish a trading post. He called it Singapore, after its ancient name, and opened the port to free trade and free immigration on the south coast of the island at the mouth of the Singapore River. At the time, Singapore had about 1,000 inhabitants. By 1827 Chinese had become the most numerous of Singapore's various ethnic groups.

In the 20th century, Singapore became a major point of disembarkation for hundreds of thousands of labourers brought in from China, India, the Dutch East Indies, and the Malay Archipelago, bound for tin mines and rubber plantations to the north. Singapore prospered as financial institutions, transportation, communications and government infrastructure expanded rapidly to support the booming trade and industry of the British Empire.

Japan attacked Malaya in December 1941, and by February 1942 the Japanese had taken control of both Malaya and Singapore. They renamed Singapore *Sh Çnan* ("Light of the South") and set about dismantling the British establishment. During the 1942-45 occupation period, a favourable view of the colonial

Capital	-	City of Singapore
Official languages	-	English; Chinese; Malay; Tamil
Government	-	Parliamentary republic
	-	President Tony Tan Keng Yam
	-	Prime Minister Lee Hsien Loong
	-	Speaker of Parliament Michael Palmer
	-	Chief Justice Chan Sek Keong
Formation	-	Founding 6 February 1819
	-	Self-government 3 June 1959
	-	Independence from Britain 31 August 1963
	-	Merger with Malaysia 16 September 1963
	-	Separation from Malaysia 9 August 1965
Area	-	Total 710.2 square kilometres
Coastline	-	151 kilometres
Population	-	5,183,700 (2011 census) Density 7,315/square kilometre
GDP (PPP)	-	Total $314.911 billion (2011 estimate) Per capita $59,711
GDP (nominal)	-	Total $259.849 billion (2011 estimate) Per capita $49,270
Minister for Defence	-	Ng Eng Hen
Chief of Defence Forces	-	Lieutenant General Neo Kian Hon
Chief of Army	-	Major General Ravinder Singh
Chief of Navy	-	Rear Admiral Ng Chee Peng
Chief of Air Force	-	Major General Ng Chee Meng

relationship had lapsed among the local population and upon the return of the British, resulted in demands for self-rule. In 1946 Singapore became a separate crown colony with a civil administration.

In 1957 Malaya was granted independence, and the next year the British Parliament elevated the status of Singapore from colony to state and provided for new local elections. The PAP swept the elections held in May 1959, and Lee Kuan Yew was installed as the first prime minister. In 1962 Singaporean voters approved the PAP's merger plan with Malaya, and on 16 September 1963, Singapore joined Malaya and the former British territories on the island of Borneo—Sabah and Sarawak—to form the independent Federation of Malaysia.

Between 1963 and 1965, Singapore was an integral part of the Federation of Malaysia. Lee declared Singapore's independence from Britain on 31 August 1963; dissolved the Legislative Assembly; and called for an election to obtain a new mandate for the PAP pro-merger government. In the end, the merger failed. As a state, Singapore did not achieve the economic progress it had hoped for, and political tensions escalated between Chinese-dominated Singapore and Malay-dominated Kuala Lumpur, the capital of Malaysia.

After separation from Malaysia on 9 August 1965, Singapore was forced to accept the challenge of forging a viable nation—the Republic of Singapore—on a small island with few resources beyond the determination and talent of its people. Under the leadership of Lee Kuan Yew and the PAP, the new nation met the challenge.

In 1967, Singapore joined Brunei, Indonesia, Malaysia, the Philippines, and Thailand in forming the Association of Southeast Asian Nations (ASEAN) for the purpose of promoting regional stability, economic development, and cultural exchange. In 1968 Britain announced its decision to withdraw from its military bases in Singapore within three years. By the 1970s, Singapore had achieved status as a world leader in shipping, air transport, and oil refining. Singapore was no longer dependent on peninsular Malaysia for its economic prosperity.

In the 1970s through the 1990s, Singapore experienced sustained economic growth. Along with Hong Kong, South Korea, and Taiwan, it was called one of the "Four Tigers" of Asian economic prosperity. Labour-intensive industries were relocated to other ASEAN nations and were replaced by high-technology industries and services. The PAP developed a stable and corruption-free government, marked by strong central development planning and social policies. Despite authoritarian governmental practices and one-party dominance, the PAP maintained its large popular mandate. A Singaporean identity, distinct from that of the Malay and Chinese, emerged as the nation increasingly integrated itself into the global economy. In 1990 Lee Kuan Yew stepped down as prime minister, and Goh Chok Tong, the first deputy prime minister and first minister of defence, took over as part of the succession to a new generation of leaders. After 14 years in office, in 2004 Goh stepped down in favour of Lee Hsien Loong, the minister of finance and son of Lee Kuan Yew. The elder Lee agreed to stay on as minister mentor and Goh as senior minister in order to oversee the transition of the new generation of leaders. Lee Hsien Loong was confirmed in office in a democratic election held on 6 May 2006.

Geography

Singapore is located in Southeast Asia between Malaysia and Indonesia at the narrowest point of the Strait of Malacca, one of the world's strategic sea routes connecting the Indian Ocean with the South China Sea. Lying off the southern tip of the Malay Peninsula, Singapore is connected to Malaysia by a causeway. The land area is 699 square kilometres; and water area is 10 square kilometres, for a total national area of 709 square kilometres. The area has increased through land reclamation and landfill projects along the coast. Since 1988 the total land area has increased by some 63 square kilometres.

Singapore is an island nation with no land boundaries. Malaysia lies to the north across the Johore Strait and Indonesia to the south across the Strait of Malacca. Singapore comprises one main island and 58 islets. The total coastline is 193 kilometres. Since 1988, the coastline has increased by 55 kilometres as a result of extensive land reclamation and landfill projects. The forest cover is only about 4,000 hectares, or 6.6% of the land area. The gently undulating central plateau contains a water catchment area and a nature preserve.

Only two degrees north of the equator, Singapore has a tropical climate. There are two monsoon seasons, the north-eastern (dry) monsoon from December to March and the south-western (wet) monsoon from June to September. Even between the monsoon seasons, afternoon and early evening thunderstorms frequently occur.

Singapore has no irrigated land, and none of the land is planted to permanent crops. More than 60% of the land is devoted to residential, industrial, commercial, institutional, and infrastructure spaces. The major environmental issues are industrial pollution, limited freshwater resources, waste disposal, and seasonal smoke and haze resulting from forest fires in Indonesia.

Society

Population. Singapore's population was reported at 4,351,400 in July 2005. Of this total, 3,553,500 were citizens or permanent residents. In 2005 the annual population growth rate, based on total residents, was 1.9%, and population density was estimated at 6,222 persons per square kilometre. Ethnic Chinese make up 76.8% of the population. The remainder of Singapore's population is Malay (13.9%), Indian (mostly Tamil, 7.9%), or other (1.4%).

Languages. Singaporeans speak many different languages, and the majority speak at least two languages. Malay is the national language and one of the four official languages, along with Chinese, Tamil, and English. Chinese is the majority language, spoken by about 76% of the population. Since 1979 the government has promoted fluency in Mandarin Chinese. Other languages, in order of use, are Malay (about 15%), English (about 9%), and Tamil (about 4%).

Religion. Buddhists and Daoists make up 51.0% of the total, or 64.4% of the Chinese population and 13.9% of the "other" ethnic composition. Islam has the second largest following at 14.9%, or 99.6% of the Malay population. Christians represent 14.6% and Hindus 4.0%, or about 55.5% of the Indian population.

Education and Literacy. Literacy is estimated at 95% overall, and 57.8% of Singaporeans have secondary school diplomas or even higher qualifications. Singaporean students consistently rank in the top five in the world in the two major international assessments of mathematics and science knowledge. Singaporean students were ranked first in the 2011 Trends in International Mathematics and Science Study conducted by the International Association for the Evaluation of Educational Achievement and have been ranked top three every year since 1995. The country's two main public universities, the National University of Singapore and Nanyang Technological University, are among the top 100 in the world.

Health. The state of health in Singapore is good by international standards. Rising standards of living, high levels of education, good housing, safe water supply and sanitation, quality medical services, and the active promotion of preventive medicine all have helped to significantly boost the health of Singaporeans. Two health care delivery "cluster" systems are available to Singaporeans. The western cluster, the National Healthcare Group, provides comprehensive public health care through a network of four hospitals, one national centre, nine polyclinics, three specialty institutes, nine business divisions, and more than 11,000 staff members. The eastern cluster, Singapore Health Services, offers three hospitals, five national specialist centres, a network of primary health care clinics, and more than 12,000 staff members. Traditional Chinese medicine also is widely practiced.

Welfare. The Central Provident Fund is Singapore's compulsory national social security savings plan. It was established in 1955 to ensure the financial security of all workers either retired or no longer able to work. Citizens and permanent residents are eligible to participate. The government makes major expenditures for "social development."

Economy

In 2009, the Economist Intelligence Unit ranked Singapore the tenth most expensive city in the world in which to live—the third in Asia, after Tokyo and Osaka. Singapore is the 5th wealthiest country in the world in terms of GDP (PPP) per capita. In December 2008, the foreign exchange reserves of this small island nation stood at around US$174.2billion. The Singapore government, with approval from the President, announced in March 2009 that it would tap into its official reserves for the first time ever and withdraw some S$4.9 billion. The funds were then used as part of the US$20.5 billion. In January 2009, Singapore's official reserves stood at US$170.3 billion.

The economy depends heavily on exports refining imported goods, especially in manufacturing. Manufacturing constituted 26% of Singapore's GDP

in 2005.The manufacturing industry is well-diversified into electronics, petroleum refining, chemicals, mechanical engineering and biomedical sciences manufacturing. Singapore is the busiest port in the world in terms of tonnage shipped. Singapore is the world's fourth largest foreign exchange trading centre after London, New York City and Tokyo. Singapore has been rated as the most business-friendly economy in the world, with thousands of foreign expatriates working in multi-national corporations. The city-state also employs tens of thousands of foreign blue-collared workers from around the world.

Singapore is a popular travel destination, making tourism one of its largest industries. About 9.7 million tourists visited Singapore in 2006. The Orchard Road district is the centre of shopping hub in Singapore. To attract more tourists, the government decided in 2005 to legalise gambling and to allow two Integrated Resorts to be developed at Marina South and Sentosa. Cuisine has been heavily promoted as an attraction for tourists.

Singapore is also growing its medical tourism sector. 230,000 foreigners sought medical care in the country in 2003 and Singapore Medical services are aiming to serve one million foreign patients annually by 2012. In doing so it is hoped to generate $3 billion in revenue and create at least 13,000 new jobs within the health industries.

Singapore is considered to be having the best quality of life in Asia and eleventh overall in the world. It possesses the world's ninth largest foreign reserves. The country also maintains armed forces that are technologically advanced and well-equipped. After a contraction of -6.8% in the 4th quarter of 2009, Singapore is now the fastest-growing economy in the world, with GDP growth of 17.9% in the first half of 2010.

Industry and Manufacturing. Industry accounted for 33.6% of the gross domestic product (GDP) in 2005. Singapore's primary industries in order of value are electronics, chemicals, oil drilling equipment, petroleum refining, rubber processing and rubber products, processed food and beverages, ship repair, and offshore platform construction. Manufacturing output grew by 12.8% in 2005 and employed 20.5% of the workforce.

Energy. Although Singapore is 100% dependent on imports of oil and natural gas, it ranks as one of the world's top three crude oil refining and trading hubs. Singapore's crude oil refining capacity is estimated at 1.3 million barrels per day. However, India, Malaysia, and Thailand are challenging Singapore's regional petroleum refining dominance. In keeping with government policy, natural gas usage is rising rapidly.

Banking and Finance. The Monetary Authority of Singapore is responsible for regulating the country's banking and investment sector. In May 2006, Singapore had about 500 local and foreign financial services companies, including 108 commercial banks and 154 insurance companies. Singapore's stock exchange, the Singapore Exchange (SGX), has separate divisions for the trading of securities and derivatives.

Labour. Of 2.3 million Singaporeans employed at the end of 2005, 68.7% worked in services, 20.5% were employed in manufacturing, 10.1% were employed in construction, and 0.7% were employed in other sectors. According to the Ministry of Manpower, the annual average unemployment rate for 2005 was 3.1%.

Foreign Economic Relations. Located on the strategic Strait of Malacca, Singapore is a major trading hub and home to the world's busiest port. The nation's prosperity has been built on a free trade policy.

Imports. Singapore's imports totalled around US$210.7 billion in 2005. Machinery and equipment, mineral fuels, chemicals, and foodstuffs are Singapore's major import commodities. The major import partners in 2005 were Malaysia (13.7%), the European Union (11.6%), the United States (11.6%), China (10.3%), Japan (9.6%), Taiwan (5.9%), Indonesia (5.2%), Saudi Arabia (4.5%), South Korea (4.3%), and Thailand (3.8%).

Exports. Singapore's exports totalled US$241.9 billion in 2005. The major exports are machinery and equipment (especially electronic components and parts), consumer goods, chemicals, and mineral fuels and petroleum products (processed for re-export). The major export partners in 2005 were Malaysia (13.2%), the European Union (12.0%), the United States (10.2%), Hong Kong (9.4%), China (8.6%), Japan (5.5%), Thailand (4.1%), Taiwan (3.9%), and South Korea (3.5%). Singapore maintains a favourable balance of trade.

Foreign Investment. Foreign direct investment (FDI) in Singapore totalled US$15.36 billion in 2005. Most investment is concentrated in manufacturing, financial services, and commerce and comes primarily from the United Kingdom (16.1%), the US (15.4%), and Japan (13.5%).

Infrastructure

Roads. Since Singapore is a small island with a high population density, the number of private cars on the road is restricted so as to curb pollution and congestion. Car buyers must pay for duties one-and-a-half times the vehicle's market value and bid for a Singaporean Certificate of Entitlement (COE), which allows the car to run on the road for a decade. Car prices are generally significantly higher in Singapore than in other English-speaking countries and thus only one in 10 residents owns a car. Singapore has a road system covering 3,356 kilometres, which includes 161 kilometres of expressways. The Singapore Area Licensing Scheme, implemented in 1975, became the world's first congestion pricing scheme, and included other complementary measures such as stringent car ownership quotas and improvements in mass transit. Upgraded in 1998 and renamed Electronic Road Pricing, the system introduced electronic toll collection, electronic detection, and video surveillance technology.

Railroads. Singapore has only 23 kilometres of railroad track, all operated by Malaysian Railways and technically located on Malaysian territory per an agreement brokered in 1965. The line provides passenger service three times daily from Singapore's Keppel Station across a 1.2- kilometre causeway that spans the Johore Strait to the Malaysian mainland and Kuala Lumpur. Weekly luxury train service also is available from Keppel Station to Chang Mai and Bangkok, Thailand, with connections to Kuala Lumpur.

Rapid Transit. Singapore's principal public mass transit system is operated by Singapore Mass Rapid Transit (SMRT) Corporation, which also runs light rail, bus, and taxi services. The system has 16 underground stations, 34 elevated stations, and one station at grade and operates on two lines, the North-South and East- West lines. The Bukit Panjang Light Rail Transit system is a fully automated service that carried 37,800 passengers per day in FY 2005, using some 7.8 kilometres of elevated guide ways and serving 14 stations. More than 1 billion passengers ride on SMRT and SBS Transit buses. SBS Transit, which started as a bus company (Singapore Bus Services) in 1973, began light rail and its mass rapid transit operations in 2003. By 2005 SBS was operating two mini-metro light-rail feeder lines and one full metro line—the North East Line—with 14 operational underground stations and 20 kilometres of track. SBS and SMRT metro lines intersect at key interchange points. Most Singaporean residents travel by foot, bicycles, bus, taxis and train. Two companies run the public bus and train transport system—SBS Transit and SMRT Corporation. There are almost a dozen taxi companies, who together put out 25,000 taxis on the road. Taxis are a popular form of public transport as the fares are relatively cheap compared to many other developed countries.

Ports. Singapore is a major international transport hub in Asia, positioned on many sea and air trade routes. The Port of Singapore, managed by port operators PSA International and Jurong Port, was the world's second-busiest port in 2005 in terms of shipping tonnage handled, at 1.15 billion gross tons, and in terms of containerised traffic, at 23.2 million twenty-foot equivalent units (TEUs). It is also the world's second-busiest, behind Shanghai, in terms of cargo tonnage with 423 million tons handled. In addition, the port is the world's busiest for transhipment traffic and the world's biggest ship refuelling centre.

Civil Aviation and Airports. Singapore is an aviation hub for Southeast Asia and a stopover on the Kangaroo route between Sydney and London. There are eight airports in the country, and Singapore Changi Airport hosts a network of 80 airlines connecting Singapore to 200 cities in 68 countries. It has been rated one of the best international airports by international travel magazines, including being rated as the world's best airport for the first time in 2006 by Skytrax.

Pipelines. Singapore had 139 kilometres of natural gas pipelines in 2004.

Telecommunications: Telecommunications policy, regulation, and promotion are the responsibility of a government agency, Infocomm Development Authority of Singapore. Postal and telecommunications services are provided by Singapore Telecommunications (SingTel), which is 68% owned by Temasek Holdings, a government holding company that is 32% privately owned. Seventeen FM stations and two shortwave stations broadcast to some 2.6

million radios. Seven television broadcast stations are in operation, and more than 1.3 million televisions were in use. Singapore had 1.85 million landline telephones and 4.2 million cellular phones (equivalent to some 978 subscribers per 1,000 population) in use in 2005. The highly touted telephone system uses submarine cables to Malaysia (both Peninsular Malaysia and Sabah), Indonesia, and the Philippines, as well as two earth satellite stations relaying to Intelsat satellites (one each) positioned over the Indian and Pacific oceans.

Government and Politics

Singapore is a parliamentary republic. The constitution for the State of Singapore promulgated on 3 June 1959, was amended in 1965 at independence. The presidency is largely ceremonial, and the prime minister is the most powerful political figure. The current Prime Minister, Lee Hsien Loong, however, has been in office since 2004, and serves under the advice of his father, long-time prime minister and now minister mentor, Lee Kuan Yew. The People's Action Party (PAP), founded in 1954, has governed without serious opposition since 1959.

Executive Branch. The largely ceremonial president and head of state is assisted by the Council of Presidential Advisers (CPA), a body established by constitutional amendment in 1991. The president is required to consult the CPA before he vetoes the government budget or appoints government nominees to key posts. In other matters, such as withholding assent to certain bills passed by parliament, appointments to statutory boards, and withholding concurrence in regard to detention of persons in times of national emergency, the president may use his discretion on consulting the CPA. The CPA has six members: two appointed by the president at his discretion, two nominated by the prime minister, one put forward by the chief justice of the Supreme Court, and another suggested by the chairman of the Public Service Commission. CPA members are appointed to initial six-year terms and can be reappointed for additional four-year terms.

The head of government is the prime minister. There is no set tenure for the office of prime minister. On the advice of the prime minister, the president appoints the other members of the cabinet. The cabinet, responsible collectively to the Parliament, oversees government policies and day-to-day administration of the affairs of state.

Legislative Branch. The unicameral 84-seat Singapore Parliament is modeled after the Westminster system of parliamentary democracy where members are voted in at regular general elections and the leader of the majority party is invited by the president to assume the post of prime minister. The prime minister then selects ministers from elected members of Parliament to form the cabinet, which in turn runs the executive branch of government. Parliament sits for five years from the date of its first session after a general election. Members are elected by universal suffrage. The constitution provides for group representation in Parliament of the Malay, Indian, and minority communities.

Judicial Branch. The judicial branch is headed by a Supreme Court, whose chief justice is appointed by the president on the advice of the prime minister. Other Supreme Court judges then are appointed by the president on the advice of the chief justice. The Supreme Court consists of the Court of Appeals and the High Court. Supreme Court judges or former Supreme Court judges can sit as judges on the Court of Appeals and the High Court, as designated by the president after consultation with the prime minister. Subordinate courts include criminal courts, criminal mentions courts (at which charges are first placed), and traffic, night, coroners', civil, and family courts, plus various other tribunals and services that support the subordinate court system. Although Singapore's laws are inherited from English and British Indian laws, and includes many elements of English common law, the government has also chosen not to follow some elements of liberal democratic values. There are no jury trials and there are laws restricting the freedom of speech that may breed ill will or cause disharmony within Singapore's multiracial, multi-religious society. Criminal activity is often punished with heavy penalties including heavy fines or caning and there are laws which allow capital punishment in Singapore for first-degree murder and drug trafficking. The Singapore government argues that Singapore has the sovereign right to determine its own judicial system and impose what it sees as an appropriate punishment, including capital punishment for the most serious crimes.

Administrative Divisions. Singapore is a unitary state with no administrative divisions. It has no provincial or local government although there are some advisory bodies.

Politics and Political Parties. The majority party, which has been in power since 1959, is the People's Action Party (PAP). Of the opposition parties, only the Workers' Party of Singapore (WP) and the Singapore Democratic Alliance (SDA), an umbrella group, hold seats in Parliament. The SDA consists of the Singapore National Malay Organisation (Pertuhan Kebangsaan Melayu Singapura—PKMS), National Solidarity Party (NSP), Singapore's People's Party (SPP), and Singapore Justice Party (SJP).

Mass Media. The media industry is regulated by the government's Media Development Authority. All newspapers in Singapore are required by law to be public companies and are regulated by the government. Major daily newspapers are published in various languages. English-language publications include the venerable *Straits Times*, founded in 1845; *Business Times*; and three tabloids, *The New Paper*, *Streats*, and *Today*. Chinese-language newspapers include *Lianhe Wanbao*, *Lianhe Zaobao*, *Shin Min Daily News*, and *Toh Lam Hhat*. Two other dailies are the Malay *Berita Harian* and Tamil *Tamil Murasu*. Weekly newspapers are offered in English and Malay, and most newspapers can be accessed on the Internet. There also is a lively magazine circulation with 17 domestic English, one Malay, and nine Chinese titles. Most broadcasting is produced by radio and television companies owned by the Media Corporation of Singapore and Radio Corporation of Singapore.

Foreign Relations. Singapore seeks to maintain a credible defensive military to support its foreign policy. It promotes good relations with its neighbours and any nation wishing to establish friendly relations. As a founding member of the Association of Southeast Asian Nations (ASEAN), Singapore is committed to maintaining a secure peaceful environment in and around Southeast Asia and in the Asia-Pacific region. After breaking off a long-term diplomatic relationship with the Republic of China on Taiwan in 1990, Singapore established relations with the People's Republic of China.

National Security

The Singapore Armed Forces (SAF) utilises

technology as "force multipliers", especially in the area of C[4]I integration, which will enable its various units to fight in an integrated manner. The Army, Air Force and Navy are linked via advanced data-links and networks to enable coordinated attacks and support for various units and forces. Technology is an important element in the SAF's transformation into a 3rd Generation Fighting Force.

The SAF acknowledges that technology is crucial for overcoming the limitations of Singapore's small population. Having consistently had one of the largest defence budgets in the Asia-Pacific region, Singapore has focused on maintaining its spending on sophisticated and superior weaponry. Research and experimentation to develop a technological edge began as early as 1971, even though the SAF then had only rudimentary capabilities. The effort started off with a three-man team. The SAF devotes considerable resources to defence research and development (R&D) and experimentation - 5% and 1% of the defence budget, respectively. Singapore's education system has also produced national servicemen who can be trained to operate SAF's sophisticated platforms and systems.

The SAF has the Murai Urban Training Facility (MUTF) to hone the SAF's networked urban operations capability. The MUTF resembles a typical town and allows the soldiers to train realistically in an urban setting. Singapore has also an established military manufacturing industry which is responsible for the design and development of the following military hardware:

- PRIMUS—Self Propelled Howitzer
- Bionix II Infantry Fighting Vehicle (An upgrade of the Bionix AFV)
- MATADOR—Unguided Short Range Anti-Armour Weapon
- PEGASUS—Light Weight Howitzer
- SAR 21—Singapore Assault Rifle
- Formidable-Class Stealth Frigate—Warships designed with stealthy characteristics, equipped with advanced combat systems and with longer endurance

Because of the scarcity of open land on the main island, training involving activities such as live firing and amphibious landings is often carried out on smaller islands, barred to civilian access. This also avoids risk to the main island and the city. However, large-scale drills are considered too dangerous to be performed in the area, and since 1975 have been performed in Taiwan. Training is also held in about a dozen other countries.

Due to airspace and land constraints, the Republic of Singapore Air Force (RSAF) maintains a number of overseas bases in Australia, the United States, and France. The RSAF's 130 Squadron is based in RAAF Base Pearce, Western Australia, and its 126 Squadron is based in the Oakey Army Aviation Centre, Queensland. The RSAF has one squadron—the 150 Squadron—based in Cazaux Air Base in southern France. The RSAF also has a few overseas detachments in the United States, in San Diego, California, Marana, Arizona, Grand Prairie, Texas and Luke Air Force Base, among others

Foreign Military Relations. Singapore provides facilities for servicing foreign naval vessels, but its official policy disallows the establishment of a naval base on the island by another country. Singapore supports a strong US military presence in the Asia-Pacific region. Most of Singapore's major military imports have been purchased from the United States.

External Threat. Singapore faces a potential military threat from Malaysia if historical tensions were to re-emerge. In particular, Singapore fears that the Malaysian state of Johore could cut off its water supply, an act that would be regarded as a casus belli. Singapore also is concerned about the possibility of a terrorist strike.

Terrorism. Singapore perceives a threat from international terrorist organisations. It maintains a high level of readiness and cooperation in the area of counterterrorism. Particular emphasis has been placed on protective and preventive actions against attacks on critical infrastructure, cyber terrorism, and chemical and biological attacks. Maritime piracy, long a problem in the immediate area, is of special concern to Singapore.

Human Rights. The Ministry of Home Affair's Internal Security Department enforces the Internal Security Act as a counter to potential espionage, international terrorism, threats to racial and religious harmony, and subversion. The government maintains effective control over all security activities, but there are some reports of human rights abuses of detainees by security forces. The government generally respects the human rights of its citizens, but, nevertheless, retains broad powers to limit citizen rights and to handicap the political opposition. Caning, in addition to imprisonment, has been a routine punishment for numerous offenses. Preventive detention has been used to deal with espionage, terrorism, organised crime, and narcotics. Citizens' privacy rights occasionally have been infringed, and the government has restricted freedom of speech and freedom of the press and limited other civil and political rights. Government pressure to conform has resulted in the practice of self-censorship by journalists. The government has instigated court proceedings and defamation suits against political opponents and critics. Such suits have consistently been decided in favour of the government, a phenomenon that inhibits political speech and action and leads observers to believe that the ruling party uses the judicial system for political purposes.

SRI LANKA

Sri Lanka is an island nation located about 31 kilometres off the southern coast of India. It declared its Independence from the United Kingdom on 4 February 1948 and became a Republic on 22 May 1972. Its largest city is Colombo.

Due to its location in the path of major sea routes, Sri Lanka is a strategic naval link between West Asia and South East Asia, and has been a centre of Buddhist religion and culture from ancient times. Today, the country is a multi-religious and multi-ethnic nation, with nearly a third of the population following faiths other than Buddhism, notably Hinduism, Christianity and Islam. The Sinhalese community forms the majority of the population, with Tamils, who are concentrated in the north and east of the island, forming the largest ethnic minority. Other communities include the Muslim Moors and Malays and the Burghers.

Famous for the production and export of tea, coffee, rubber and coconuts, Sri Lanka boasts a progressive and modern industrial economy and the highest per capita income in South Asia. The natural beauty of Sri Lanka's tropical forests, beaches and landscape, as well as its rich cultural heritage, make it a world famous tourist destination. Sri Lanka has one of the fastest economic growth rates of the world.

History

One of the first written references to the island is found in the Indian epic Ramayana, which described the emperor Ravana as monarch of the powerful kingdom of Lanka, which was created by the divine sculptor Vishwakarma for Kubera, the treasurer of the Gods. The main written accounts of the country's history are the Buddhist chronicles of Mahavansa and Dipavamsa. The earliest-known inhabitants of the island were probably the ancestors of the Wanniyala-Aetto people, also known as Veddahs and numbering roughly 3,000. Linguistic analysis has found a correlation of the Sinhalese language with the languages of the Sindh and Gujarat, although most historians believe that the Sinhala community emerged well after the assimilation of various ethnic groups. From the ancient period date some remarkable archaeological sites including the ruins of Sigiriya, the so-called "Fortress in the Sky".

Since ancient times Sri Lanka was ruled by monarchs, most notably of the Sinha royal dynasty that lasted over 2000 years. The island was also infrequently invaded by South Indian kingdoms and parts of the island were ruled intermittently by the Chola dynasty, the Pandya dynasty, the Chera dynasty and the Pallava dynasty. The island was also invaded by the kingdoms of Kalinga (modern Orissa) and those from the Malay Peninsula. Buddhism arrived from India in the 3rd century BCE, brought by Bhikkhu Mahinda, who is believed to have been the son of Mauryan emperor Ashoka. Mahinda's mission won over the Sinhalese monarch Devanampiyatissa of Mihintale, who embraced the faith and propagated it throughout the Sinhalese population.

Sri Lanka had always been an important port and trading post in the ancient world, and was increasingly frequented by merchant ships from the

Capital	-	Sri Jayawardenapura-Kotte
Largest city	-	Colombo
Official languages	-	Sinhala, Tamil
Ethnic groups	-	73.9% Sinhalese; 12.6% Tamil; 7.4% Moors; 5.2% Indian Tamil; 0.5% Others
Government	-	Democratic Socialist Republic
	-	President Mahinda Rajapaksa
	-	Prime Minister D.M. Jayaratne
	-	Chief Justice Shirani Bandaranayake
Area	-	Total 65,610 square kilometres
Coastline	-	1,340 kilometres
Population	-	20,277,597 (2012 census) Density 323/square kilometre
GDP (PPP)	-	Total $116.5341 billion (2011 estimate) Per capita $5,673
GDP (nominal)	-	Total $59,095 billion (2011 estimate) Per capita $2,877
Defence Minister	-	Gotabhaya Rajapakse
Chief of Army	-	Lieutenant General Jagath Jayasuriya
Chief of Navy	-	Vice Admiral D.W.A.S. Dissanayake
Chief of Air Force	-	Air Marshal Harsha Abeywickrama

Middle East, Persia, Burma, Thailand, Malaysia, Indonesia and other parts of Southeast Asia. The islands were known to the first European explorers of South Asia and settled by many groups of Arab and Malay merchants. A Portuguese colonial mission arrived on the island in 1505 headed by the Lourenço de Almeida the son of Francisco de Almeida. At that point the island consisted of three kingdoms, namely Kandy in the central hills, Kotte at the Western coast, and Yarlpanam (Anglicised Jaffna) in the north. The Dutch arrived in the 17th century. Although much of the island came under the domain of European powers, the interior, hilly region of the island remained independent, with its capital in Kandy. The British East India Company established control of the island in 1796, declaring it a crown colony in 1802, although the island would not be officially connected with British India. The fall of the kingdom of Kandy in 1815 unified the island under British rule.

European colonists established a series of tea, cinnamon, rubber, sugar, coffee and indigo plantations. The British also brought a large number of indentured workers from Tamil Nadu to work in the plantation economy. The city of Colombo was established as the administrative centre, and the British established modern schools, colleges, roads and churches that brought Western-style education and culture to the native people. Increasing grievances over the denial of civil rights, mistreatment and abuse of natives by colonial authorities gave rise to a struggle for independence in the 1930s. During World War II, the island served as an important Allied military base.

Following the war, popular pressure for independence intensified. On 4 February 1948 the country won its independence as the Commonwealth of Ceylon. Don Stephen Senanayake became the first Prime Minister of Sri Lanka. In 1972, the country became a republic within the Commonwealth, and the name was changed to Sri Lanka. On 21 July 1960 Sirimavo Bandaranaike took office as prime minister, and became the first female head of government in post-colonial Asia and the first female prime minister in the world.

From 1983 to 2009, there was an on-and-off civil war

against the government by the Liberation Tigers of Tamil Eelam (LTTE), a separatist militant organisation who fought to create an independent state named Tamil Eelam in the North and East of the island. Both the Sri Lankan government and LTTE have been accused of various human rights violations.

The Sri Lankan government's military offensive against the LTTE intensified amidst cautious optimism that the group was on the verge of military defeat. On 16 January 2008 the government formally withdrew from the 2002 ceasefire on the basis that it was already dead in practice and that, rather than constraining the LTTE, it had given it time to rearm. This decision led to the withdrawal of the Norwegian-led Sri Lanka Monitoring Mission (SLMM).

Having successfully defeated the LTTE in the east by mid July 2007, the government's military strategy appeared to be to defeat them militarily by capturing their final stronghold in the north and then to negotiate a political settlement with the civilian Tamil community. In July 2008, Sri Lanka's army chief, Lt Gen. Sarath Fonseka, publicly announced that the LTTE had lost their conventional fighting capacity and would be defeat by mid-2009, indicating a delay in an earlier estimate of June 2008. Notwithstanding the offer of a unilateral ceasefire by the LTTE during the South Asian Association for Regional Cooperation (SAARC) Summit in Colombo (26 July-4 August 2008), the government refused to enter into any agreement with the militants.

The unrelenting government military offensive from August 2008 against the LTTE included the use of combat aircraft and helicopter gunships along with troops on the ground to regain territory. On 19 May 2009, the President of Sri Lanka officially claimed an end to the insurgency and the defeat of the LTTE, following the death of Velupillai Prabhakaran and much of the LTTE's other senior leadership. After the civil war ended the government of Sri Lanka called for re-development of the country. There are 300,000 Tamils that need to be resettled.

Geography

The island of Sri Lanka lies in the Indian Ocean, to the southwest of the Bay of Bengal and to the southeast of the Arabian Sea. It is separated from the Indian subcontinent by the Gulf of Mannar and the Palk Strait. According to Hindu mythology, a land bridge to the Indian mainland, known as Rama's Bridge, was constructed during the time of Rama by the *vanara* architect Nala. Often referred to as Adam's Bridge, it now amounts to only a chain of limestone shoals remaining above sea level. According to

geological surveys, this is a natural causeway which was formerly complete, but was breached by a violent storm in 1480. The teardrop-shaped island consists mostly of flat-to-rolling coastal plains, with mountains rising only in the south-central part. Amongst these are Sri Pada (Adams Peak) and the highest point Pidurutalagala, at 2,524 meters (8,281 ft). The Mahaweli Ganga (Mahaweli river) and other major rivers provide fresh water to the population.

Sri Lanka's climate can be described as tropical, and quite hot. Its position between 5 and 10 north latitude endows the country with a warm climate, moderated by ocean winds and considerable moisture. The mean temperature ranges from a low of 16°C in Nuwara Eliya in the Central Highlands to a high of 32°C in Trincomalee on the northeast coast, where temperatures may reach 38°C. The average yearly temperature for the country ranges from 28° to 30°C. The rainfall pattern is influenced by the monsoon winds of the Indian Ocean and Bay of Bengal. Some of the windward slopes receive up to 2,500 millimetres (98 in) of rain per month, but the leeward slopes in the east and northeast receive little rain. Periodic squalls occur and sometimes tropical cyclones bring overcast skies and rains to the southwest, northeast, and eastern parts of the island.

Government and Politics

The Constitution of Sri Lanka establishes a democratic, socialist republic in Sri Lanka, which is also a unitary state. The government is a mixture of the presidential system and the parliamentary system. The President of Sri Lanka is the head of state, the commander in chief of the armed forces, as well as head of government, and is popularly elected for a six-year term. In the exercise of duties, the President is responsible to the Parliament of Sri Lanka, which is a unicameral 225-member legislature. The President appoints and heads a cabinet of ministers composed of elected members of parliament. The

President's deputy is the Prime Minister, who leads the ruling party in parliament and shares many executive responsibilities, mainly in domestic affairs.

Members of parliament are elected by universal (adult) suffrage based on a modified proportional representation system by district to a six-year term. The primary modification is that, the party that receives the largest number of valid votes in each constituency gains a unique "bonus seat." The president may summon, suspend, or end a legislative session and dissolve Parliament any time after it has served for one year. The parliament reserves the power to make all laws. On 1 July 1960 the people of Sri Lanka elected the first-ever female head of government in Prime Minister Sirimavo Bandaranaike. Her daughter Chandrika Kumaratunga served multiple terms as prime minister and as president from 1999 to 2005.

President Mahinda Rajapaksa, the fifth President, began his second term on 19 November 2010. In the election held two years before the end of his first six year term, he won with 57.8 per cent of the votes. His success in Presidential and Parliamentary Elections in January and April, 2010 came after a series of sweeping victories in elections to eight Provincial Councils by the United People's Freedom Alliance (UPFA) led by him. The UPFA now has an over two-thirds majority in parliament.

Administrative divisions

Sri Lanka is divided into 9 provinces and 25 districts. Each province is administered by a directly-elected provincial council, as under:

Province	*Capital*	*Districts*
Central	Kandy	Kandy, Matale, Nuwara Eliya
North Central	Anuradhapura	Anuradhapura, Polonnaruwa
Northern	Jaffna	Jaffna, Kilinochchi, Mannar, Vavuniya,
Mullativu Eastern	Trincomalee	Ampara, Batticaloa, Trincomalee
North Western	Kurunegala	Kurunagala, Puttalam
Southern	Galle	Galle, Hambanthota, Mathara
Uva	Badulla	Badulla, Monaragala
Sabaragamuwa	Ratnapura	Kegalle, Rathnapura
Western	Colombo	Colombo, Gampaha, Kaluthara

The districts are further subdivided into Divisional Secretariats, and these in turn to Grama Sevaka divisions.

Economy

In the 19th and 20th centuries, Sri Lanka became a plantation economy, famous for its production and export of cinnamon, rubber and Ceylon tea, which remains a trademark national export. The development of modern ports under British rule raised the strategic importance of the island as a centre of trade. During World War II, the island hosted important military installations and Allied forces. However, the plantation economy aggravated poverty and economic inequality. From 1948 to 1977 socialism strongly influenced the government's economic policies. Colonial plantations were dismantled, industries were nationalised and a welfare state established. While the standard of living and literacy improved significantly, the nation's economy suffered from inefficiency, slow growth and lack of foreign investment.

From 1977 the UNP government began incorporating privatisation, deregulation and promotion of private enterprise. While the production and export of tea, rubber, coffee, sugar and other agricultural commodities remains important, the nation has moved steadily towards an industrialised economy with the development of food processing, textiles, telecommunications and finance. By 1996 plantation crops made up only 20% of export, and further declined to 16.8% in 2005 (compared with 93% in 1970), while textiles and garments have reached 63%. The GDP grew at an average annual rate of 5.5% during the early 1990s, until a drought and a deteriorating security situation lowered growth to 3.8% in 1996. The economy rebounded in 1997–2000, with average growth of 5.3%.

2001 saw the first recession in the country's history, as a result of power shortages, budgetary problems, the global slowdown, and continuing civil strife. Since the separatist war ended in May 2009 the Sri Lankan stock market has shown marked gains to be among the three best performing markets in the world. The Colombo Stock Exchange reported the highest growth in the world for 2003, and today Sri Lanka has the highest per capita income in South Asia.

In April 2004, there was a sharp reversal in economic policy after the government headed by Ranil Wickremesinghe of the United National Party was defeated by a coalition made up of Sri Lanka Freedom Party and the leftist-nationalist Janatha Vimukthi Peramuna called the United People's Freedom Alliance. The new government stopped the privatisation of state enterprises and reforms of state utilities such as power and petroleum, and embarked on a subsidy programme called the Rata Perata economic programme. Its main theme to support the rural and suburban SMEs and protect the domestic economy from external influences, such as oil prices, the World Bank and the International Monetary Fund.

Sri Lanka still lags behind some of its neighbours including Maldives and Mauritius but is ahead of its giant neighbour India. Its economy grew by an average of 5% during the 1990s during the 'War for Peace' era. According to the Sri Lankan central bank statistics, the economy was estimated to have grown by 7% last year, while inflation reached 20%. Parts of Sri Lanka, particularly the South and East coast, were devastated by the 2004 Asian Tsunami. The economy was briefly buoyed by an influx of foreign aid and tourists, but this was disrupted with the re-emergence of the civil war resulting in increased lawlessness in the country and a sharp decline in tourism. But following the end of the three-decade long separatist war in May 2009 tourism has seen a steep uptick. Also the end of war has ensured the rule of law in the whole of the island.

Demographics

Population density is the greatest in western Sri Lanka, especially in and around Colombo. There is a small population on the island of the Wanniyala-Aetto people, also known as Veddahs. These are believed to be the oldest and indigenous ethnic group to inhabit the island. The Sinhalese people form the largest ethnic group in the nation, composing approximately 81.9% of the total population. Tamils are concentrated in the North, East, Central and Western provinces of the country. Tamils who were brought as indentured labourers from India by British colonists to work on estate plantations, nearly 50% of whom were repatriated following independence in 1948, are called "Indian Origin" Tamils. They are distinguished from the native Tamil population that has resided in Sri Lanka since ancient times. Indian Tamils make up 5.1% of the Sri Lankan population and, Sri Lankan Tamils 4.3%. There is a significant population (8.0%) of Moors, who trace their lineage to Arab traders and immigrants from the Middle East. Their presence is concentrated in the cities and the central and eastern provinces. There are also small ethnic groups such as the Burghers (of mixed European descent) and Malays from Southeast Asia.

Languages and Religion

Sinhalese and Tamil are the two official languages of Sri Lanka. English is spoken by approximately 10% of the population, and is widely used for education, scientific and commercial purposes. Members of the Burgher community speak variant forms of Portuguese Creole and Dutch with varying proficiency, while members of the Malay community speak a form of creole Malay that is unique to the island.

Sri Lanka also enjoys significant religious diversity. Approximately 69% of Sri Lankans are adherents of Buddhism. Theravada Buddhism is the predominant school, with distinctive sects being widely followed. Buddhism in Sri Lanka has been deeply influenced by indigenous faiths and traditions, as well as the influences of prevailing Buddhist schools in South East Asia. The ancient and famous Sri Dalada Maligawa or "Temple of the Tooth" is the principal Buddhist Temple in Sri Lanka, and by tradition houses the Tooth of Buddha. Hinduism is practiced by 7.9% of the population, mainly from the Tamil community. Christianity is practiced by 7% of the population, especially by Burgher people though most Christians are Sinhalese or Tamils. While most Sri Lankan Christians are Catholics, there are also significant numbers who adhere to Dutch Reformed Church and the Anglican Communion. Islam in Sri Lanka is practiced by 8.5% of the population and its adherents are almost entirely Moors and Malays.

Transportation

The railroads are government owned; about 1,944 kilometres of track; network extends radically from Colombo to northern, eastern, and southern coastal cities. Deep water ports are at Colombo, Trincomalee and Galle. Sri Lanka has 14 airfields.

Education

With a literacy rate of 92%, and 83% of the total population having had Secondary Education, Sri Lanka has one of the most literate populations amongst developing nations. An education system which dictates 9 years of Compulsory Schooling for every child is in place, with 99% of the children entering the first grade. In 1942 a special education committee proposed extensive reforms to establish an efficient and quality education system for the people. In recent decades, a large number of private and international schools have been established across the nation. The International Baccalaureate and General Certificate of Secondary Education are popular education programmes.

Most secondary schools in Sri Lanka provide education from grades 1 to 13 in the same institution. Students sit for the GCE Ordinary Level Examination (O/Levels) in grade 11 and the GCE Advanced Level Examination (A/levels) in grade 13. These schools are modelled on British colleges and universities. A majority of them are public, but a number of elite private schools do exist. While most reputed schools centred around large cities are usually single-sex institutions, rural schools tend to be coeducational.

Sri Lanka has a number of large public universities. They include the University of Colombo, the University of Kelaniya, the University of Sri Jayewardenepura, the University of Moratuwa, the University of Peradeniya, the University of Jaffna, the University of Ruhuna, the Eastern University of Sri Lanka, the Rajarata University of Sri Lanka, the Sabaragamuwa University of Sri Lanka, the Wayamba University of Sri Lanka and the Uva Wellassa University of Sri Lanka.

Armed Forces

The Sri Lanka Army has approximately 200,000 regular personnel, approximately between 20,000–40,000 reserve personnel and 18,000 National Guardsmen and comprises 13 operational divisions, one air-mobile brigade, one commando brigade, one special forces brigade, one independent armoured brigade, three mechanised infantry brigades and over 40 infantry brigades. From the 1980s to 2009 the army was engaged in the Sri Lankan civil war.

In November 2007, 114 members of the 950 member Sri Lankan Army peacekeeping mission in Haiti were accused of sexual misconduct and abuse. 108 members, including 3 officers of the 950-member-strong Sri Lanka peacekeeping contingent were implicated in alleged misconduct and sexual abuse.

The Sri Lanka Navy has four regional headquarters; Colombo (NAV WEST), Boossa (NAV SOUTH), Trincomalee (NAV EAST), and Karanger (NAV NORTH). The SLN recently set up OM NOR CEN, a headquarters to command naval units performing defence measures on land; especially in areas recaptured from rebels. The Sri Lanka Navy's primary mission is guarding the coastline, particularly in the island's north and east.

The Sri Lanka Air Force played a major role throughout the Sri Lankan Civil War. The SLAF operates more than 160 aircraft and has a projected trained strength of 27,400 airmen and 1,300 officers, who are from both regular and reserve service. The Sri Lanka Air Force has expanded to specialize mainly in providing air-support to ground forces, troop landing, and carrying out air strikes on rebel-held areas in the Northern and Eastern theatres, but is also capable of high- and low-level air defence.

Security Issues

The strategic importance of Sri Lanka emanates from its geo-strategic location in the Indian Ocean. Trincomalee, on the eastern coast of Sri Lanka, is one of the best natural harbours in the world. Adequate support facilities in terms of port and other infrastructure also exist in Sri Lanka to meet medium scale repairs and refits. Incumbent on the creation of facilities at Trincomalee, Sri Lanka has the potential to emerge as the maritime hub in the region for shipping traffic. Sri Lanka is in fact better placed to provide bunkering and other facilities to ships than Singapore, which has emerged as a maritime hub.

India has been extremely sensitive about the role of extra-regional players in Sri Lanka, which is separated from it by the narrow 24-kilometre wide Palk Strait. Given its geographical proximity, Sri Lanka is within the Indian security orbit. The common Tamil ethnicity in the two countries exerts a gravitational pull. Happenings in Sri Lanka, therefore, have direct bearing on India. The insurgency in Sri Lanka has its ramifications on the internal politics and security in the state of Tamil Nadu in India. India cannot afford to have any sort of military rivalry in its backyard. Though Indian has a policy of non-interference in Sri Lankan affairs, the geographical and cultural linkages make it an indispensable factor in the peace process. The bottom line for Indian security planners is that Indian can acquiesce to a divided Sri Lanka only at its own peril.

THAILAND

The Kingdom of Thailand is located in the centre of peninsular Southeast Asia. Burma is to the west, Laos to the north and east, Cambodia to the southeast, and Malaysia to the south. The south coast of Thailand faces the Gulf of Thailand, while the Isthmus of Kra is bordered on the west by the Andaman Sea (part of the Indian Ocean) and on the east by the Gulf of Thailand. Thailand has islands in the Andaman Sea and Gulf of Thailand. The largest, with provincial status, is Phuket, off the west coast; on the gulf side, the largest islands are Samui and Pangan.

The total land boundary is 4,863 kilometres in length, including borders with Burma (1,800 kilometres), Laos (1,754 kilometres), Cambodia (803 kilometres), and Malaysia (506 kilometres). A dispute between Thailand and Laos over MeKong River islands continues to delay completion of an agreement on the demarcation of their boundary. Thailand has significant differences with Burma over the alignment of their boundary. There are disputed sections of the Thai - Cambodia border where border markers are missing. Land mines, the remnants of former conflicts, are still to be found—sometimes with lethal consequences—along Thailand's borders with Cambodia and Laos. Although Thailand has no actual border dispute with Malaysia, terrorist and insurgent activities in the frontier area lead to frequent border closures and tight security. The coastline is 3,219 kilometres long (750 kilometres on the Andaman Sea and 2,469 kilometres on the Gulf of Thailand).

History

The traditional founding date of Thailand is 1238. Unlike other nations in Southeast Asia, Thailand was never colonised. Its flag consists of five horizontal bands of red (on top), white, blue (double width), white, and red. The red stripes represent unity of the nation, the white strips represent purity of religion, and the blue stripe in the centre represents the king.

In the 9th century B.C., Mon and Khmer people established kingdoms that included large areas of what is now Thailand. Much of what these people absorbed from contacts with South Asian peoples—religious, social, political, and cultural ideas and institutions—later influenced the development of Thailand's culture and national identity. In the 2nd century B.C., the Hindu-led state of Funan in present-day Cambodia and central Thailand had close commercial contact with India and was a base for Hindu merchant-missionaries. In the southern Isthmus of Kra, Malay city-states controlled routes used by traders and travelers journeying between India and Indochina (present-day Cambodia, Laos, and Vietnam).

In 1238 a Tai chieftain, Sri Intraditya, declared his independence from Khmer overlords and established a kingdom at Sukhothai in the Chao Phraya Valley in central Thailand. The people of the central plain took the name *Thai*, which means "free," to distinguish themselves from other Tai people still under foreign rule. The Kingdom of Sukhothai was completely absorbed by the rising new Thai Kingdom of Ayutthaya by 1438.

The city-state of Ayutthaya was founded in 1350 and established its capital in 1351 on the Chao Phraya

Capital	-	Bangkok
Official language	-	Thai
Government	- - -	Parliamentary democracy and Constitutional monarchy King Bhumibol Adulyadej Rama IX Prime Minister Yingluck Shinawatra
Constitutional monarchy	-	24 June 1932
Constitution	-	24 August 2007
Area	-	513,120 square kilometres
Coastline	-	3,219 kilometres
Population	-	66,720,153 (2011 estimate) Density 132.1/square kilometre
GDP (PPP)	-	$616.783 billion (2011 estimate) Per capita $9,396
GDP (nominal)	-	$345.649 billion (2011 estimate) Per capita $5,394
Defence Minister	-	Air Chief Marshal Sukampol Suwannathat
Chief of Armed Forces	-	General Thanasak Patimaprakorn
Chief of Army	-	General Prayuth Chan-ocha
Chief of Navy	-	Admiral Surasak Runroengrom
Chief of Air Force	-	Air Chief Marshal Prajin Jantong

River in central Thailand, calling it Ayutthaya, after Ayodhaya, the Indian city of the hero Rama in the Hindu epic *Ramayana*. In 1360 Ramathibodi (r. 1351-69) declared Theravada Buddhism as the official religion and compiled a legal code based on Hindu legal texts and Thai custom that remained in effect until the late nineteenth century. Ayutthaya became the region's most powerful kingdom, eventually capturing Angkor and forcing the Khmer to submit to Thai suzerainty. Rather than a unified kingdom, Ayutthaya was a patchwork of self-governing principalities and tributary provinces ruled by members of the royal family who owed allegiance to the king. The king, however, was an absolute monarch who took on god-like aspects. This belief in a divine kingship continued until the 18th century. The kingdom became increasingly sophisticated as new social, political, and economic developments took place.

Real reform occurred during the reign of Chulalongkorn (Rama V, r. 1868-1910). He introduced currency based taxes and a conscription-based regular army. In 1893 a centralised state administration replaced the semi-feudal provincial administration. The regime established European style schools for children of the royal family and sen government officials, promising civil servants, anc military officers to Europe for further education. Th first railroad line was opened between Bangkok anc Ayutthaya in 1897 and extended farther north in 190 and 1909. To the south, rail connections were mad in 1903, linking with British rail lines in Malaya Although much diminished in territory by the 1910s Siam preserved its independence, and the kingdon served as a buffer state between the British anc French colonies.

Siam joined the Allies in declaring war agains Germany during World War I (1914-18) and sent small expeditionary force to the European wester front. These actions won Siam favourabl amendments to its treaties with France and Britai at the end of the war. Siam also gained, as spoils o war, impounded German ships for use in its merchan marine. Siam took part in the Versailles peac conference in 1919 and was a founding member o the League of Nations.

In May 1946, a new constitution was promulgated. I

called for a bicameral legislature with a popularly elected lower house and an upper house elected by the lower house. The name Siam was officially restored. The civilian government's failure eventually led to the restoration of the military faction in a coup in November 1947. In 1955 SEATO's headquarters was established in Bangkok, and Thailand offered the United States the use of Thai military bases.

Anti-communism influenced Thailand's foreign affairs, and in 1961 Thailand, the Philippines, and newly independent Malaya (since 1963, Malaysia) formed the Association of Southeast Asia (ASA). In 1967 Thailand became a founding member of the Association of Southeast Asian Nations (ASEAN), a broader regional cooperative organisation that replaced the ASA.

The period from 1976 till 1992 saw military rule and limited Parliamentary government. Strict censorship continued, and the regime tightly controlled labour unions and purged suspected communists from the civil service and educational institutions. As a result, many students joined the communist insurgency.

In March 1992, with a new constitution in force new elections were held. Coups and elections continued periodically till 2006. The first-ever elections to the Senate were held in 2000, and, in January 2001 one party—the Phak Thai Rak Thai (Thai Loves Thai Party)—won an absolute majority in the House of Representatives. Because of widespread allegations of illegal election practices, new polling took place in February in some constituencies. The Thai Rak Thai, having merged with another party, since the January election, still won absolute majority of seats, but a coalition government—with the New Aspiration Party and Chat Thai—was established. Police Lieutenant Colonel Thaksin Chinnawat became prime minister. The Thai Rak Thai was further strengthened in 2002 when it absorbed many members of the New Aspiration Party.

In February 2005, the Thai Rak Thai won a 75% majority in the House of Representatives elections, and, for the first time, a single-party government was formed. The following year, however, there were mass protests calling for Thaksin's resignation over corruption issues. He called for early parliamentary elections in April 2006 that were boycotted by the major opposition parties and declared unconstitutional in May. Amidst growing protests, and without meeting much resistance, a military junta overthrew the interim government of Thaksin Shinawatra on 19 September 2006. The junta abrogated the constitution, dissolved Parliament and

the Constitutional Court, detained and later removed several members of the government, declared martial law, and appointed one of the king's Privy Counsellors, General Surayud Chulanont, as the Prime Minister. The junta later wrote a highly abbreviated interim constitution and appointed a panel to draft a permanent constitution. The junta also appointed a 250-member legislature, called by some critics a "chamber of generals" while others claimed that it lacks representatives from the majority. In this interim constitution draft, the head of the junta was allowed to remove the prime minister at any time. The legislature was not allowed to hold a vote of confidence against the cabinet and the public was not allowed to file comments on bills. This interim constitution was later surpassed by the permanent constitution on 24 August 2007.

Martial law was partially revoked in January 2007. The ban on political activities was lifted in July 2007 following the 30 May dissolution of the Thai Rak Thai party. The new constitution was approved by a referendum on 19 August, which led to a return to democratic elections on 23 December 2007. The People's Power Party (Thailand), led by Samak Sundaravej formed a government with five smaller parties. Following several court rulings against him in a variety of scandals, and surviving a vote of no confidence, and protesters blockading government buildings and airports, in September 2008, Sundaravej was found guilty of conflict of interest by the Constitutional Court of Thailand (due to being a host in cooking TV programme), and ended his term in office. He was replaced by PPP member Somchai Wongsawat. On 2 December 2008, Thailand's Constitutional Court found the ruling Peoples Power Party guilty of electoral fraud, which led to the dissolution of the party according to the law. After defections from smaller parties the opposition Democrats Party was able to form a government, a first for the party since 2001. The leader of the

Democrat party, and former leader of the opposition, Abhisit Vejjajiva was appointed and sworn-in as the 27th Prime Minister, together with the new cabinet on 17 December 2008.

In April 2010, a set of new violent protests by the Red Shirt opposition movement, possibly backed financially by fugitive former Prime Minister Thaksin Shinawatra, resulted in 87 deaths (mostly civilian and some military) and 1,378 injured. When the army tried to disperse the protesters, it was met with automatic gunfire, grenades, and fire bombs from the opposition faction in the army, known as the "watermelon". This resulted in the army returning fire with rubber bullets and some live ammunition. During the time of the "red shirt" protests against the government, there were numerous grenade and bomb attacks against government offices and the homes of government officials.

On 3 July 2011, the oppositional Pheu Thai Party led by Yingluck Shinawatra (the youngest sister of Thaksin Shinawatra) won the general election by a landslide (265 seats in the House of Representatives). They could form a coalition government presided over by Yingluck.

Geography

Topography. In the north, the chief topographic features are high mountains along the borders with Burma and Laos and extending down the Isthmus of Kra to the southern border with Malaysia. The central plain, which extends to the Gulf of Thailand, is a lowland area drained by the Chao Phraya and its tributary rivers. The upland Khorat Plateau in the northeast drains into the River Mun. The narrow, tropical Isthmus of Kra runs from mainland Thailand to the border with peninsular Malaysia.

Principal Rivers. The principal river is the Chao Phraya, which, with its tributaries, drains about 33% of the national territory and flows south into a delta at Bangkok. The Mun and many other smaller upland rivers are tributaries of the Mekong, which forms the border between Thailand and Laos before flowing into Cambodia and Vietnam and into the South China Sea. Together, the Chao Phraya and Mekong systems sustain Thailand's agricultural economy and provide waterways for inland navigation.

Climate. A tropical country, Thailand has three distinct seasons. The first is a hot and dry season from February to May, with an average temperature of 34°C and 75% relative humidity. This season is followed by a rainy, cooler season brought by the southwest monsoon from June to September, with an average daily temperature of 29°C and 87% relative humidity. A cooler, dry season, caused by the northeast monsoon, lasts from November to January with temperatures ranging from 32°C to less than 20°C and lower relative humidity. The Isthmus of Kra is always hot and humid and has the heaviest rainfall. The lightest rainfall is in the northeast.

Natural Resources. Thailand's major natural resources are fluorite, gypsum, lead, lignite, natural gas, rubber, tantalum, tin, and tungsten. Renewable resources include fish and timber.

Land Use. Roughly 20% of Thailand is covered by mountains and hills, the steepness of which generally precludes agriculture. Arable land accounts for nearly 27.5% of the total area. About 6.9% is planted to permanent crops with 49,860 square kilometres irrigated.

Environmental Factors. The depletion of the water table around Bangkok has led to land subsidence. Despite the annual southwest monsoon, Thailand is subject to drought. Other environmental issues include air pollution from vehicle emissions, water pollution from organic and factory wastes, deforestation, soil erosion, and wildlife population depletion from illegal hunting.

Society

Population. The largest population is in the northeast, with 20.7 million inhabitants and a population density of 122.9 persons per square kilometre. The central region, excluding Bangkok, has the next largest population, with 14 million inhabitants and a density of 137.8 persons per square kilometre. Bangkok itself has a population of 6.3 million inhabitants and a population density of 4,038 persons per square kilometre.

Ethnic Groups. People of Thai ethnicity make up 75% of the population. Another 14% are ethnic Chinese, and 4% are Malay, leaving 7% as uncategorised. Additionally, Thailand has refugees from Burma, many of them ethnic, non-Thai-speaking Karen who fled their country in the face of fighting between Karen rebels and Burmese troops.

Languages. Nearly 94% of the people speak Tai-Kadai (Daic) languages, with Thai (in various dialects) being predominant and the national and official language. Another 2% speak Austro-Asiatic languages, 2% speak Austronesian languages, 1% speak Tibeto-Burman languages, and 0.2% speak Hmong-Mien languages. Standard Thai is based on the dialect spoken in the Chao Phraya Valley. The Thai alphabet, with 44 consonants and 32 vowels, originated during the reign of King Ramkhamhaeng

(Rama the Great, r. 1279-98) and is an adaptation of Mon and Khmer scripts derived from Indian Devanagari. Some 74 languages are spoken in Thailand, including numerous Thai dialects plus English, which is the secondary language among the well educated and is widely understood.

Religion. The predominant religion is Theravada Buddhism, representing about 94% of the practicing population and about 90% of all Thai people. Muslims represent 4.6%; Christians, 0.7%; Hindus, 0.1%; and Sikhs, Baha'i Faith, and others, 0.6%. Religious instruction is required at both the primary and secondary education levels.

Education and Literacy. The Ministry of Education supervises public and private education. The literacy rate in Thailand is 92.6%.

Health. Human immunodeficiency virus/acquired immune deficiency syndrome (HIV/AIDS) is a serious problem in Thailand. The Thai government has launched a well-funded, politically supported, and pragmatic response to the epidemic. Major infectious diseases in Thailand also include bacterial diarrhea, hepatitis, dengue fever, malaria, Japanese encephalitis, rabies, and leptospirosis.

Welfare. Thailand has social welfare and social insurance systems. Social welfare involves welfare services aimed at the poor, persons with disabilities, children, the elderly, women, minority hill tribes, and other disadvantaged individuals. The social insurance system provides sickness, maternity, disability, death, dependent child, old age, and unemployment benefits. There also is a social security system for private-sector employees and medical security and pension systems for public-service employees, employees of national enterprises, and military personnel.

Economy

Thailand is an emerging economy and considered as a newly industrialised country. After enjoying the world's highest growth rate from 1985 to 1996—averaging 12.4% annually—increased pressure on Thailand's currency, the baht, in 1997, the year in which the economy contracted by 1.9% led to a crisis that uncovered financial sector weaknesses and forced the Chavalit Yongchaiyudh administration to float the currency, however, Prime Minister Chavalit Yongchaiyudh was forced to resign after his cabinet came under fire for its slow response to the crisis. The baht was pegged at 25 to the US dollar from 1978 to 1997; however, the baht reached its lowest point of 56 to the US dollar in January 1998 and the economy contracted by 10.8% that year. This collapse prompted the Asian financial crisis.

Thailand's economy started to recover in 1999, expanding 4.2% and 4.4% in 2000, thanks largely to strong exports. Growth (2.2%) was dampened by the softening of the global economy in 2001, but picked up in the subsequent years owing to strong growth in Asia, a relatively weak baht encouraging exports and increasing domestic spending as a result of several mega projects and incentives of Prime Minister Thaksin Shinawatra, known as Thaksinomics. Growth in 2002, 2003 and 2004 was 5-7% annually. Growth in 2005, 2006 and 2007 hovered around 4-5%. Due both to the weakening of the US dollar and an increasingly strong Thai currency, by March 2008, the dollar was hovering around the 33 baht mark.

Thailand exports an increasing value of over $105 billion worth of goods and services annually. Major exports include Thai rice, textiles and footwear, fishery products, rubber, jewellery, cars, computers and electrical appliances. Thailand is the world's no.1 exporter of rice, exporting more than 6.5 million tons of milled rice annually. Rice is the most important

crop in the country. Thailand has the highest percentage of arable land, 27.25%, of any nation in the Greater Mekong Subregion. About 55% of the arable land area is used for rice production.

Substantial industries include electric appliances, components, computer parts and cars, while tourism in Thailand makes up about 6% of the economy. Prostitution in Thailand and sex tourism also form a de facto part of the economy. Cultural milieu combined with poverty and the lure of money have caused prostitution and sex tourism in particular to flourish in Thailand. One estimate published in 2003 placed the trade at US$4.3 billion per year or about 3% of the Thai economy. According to research by Chulalongkorn University on the Thai illegal economy, prostitution in Thailand in the period between 1993 and 1995 made up around 2.7% of the GDP. It is believed that at least 10% of tourist dollars are spent on the sex trade.

Thailand functions as an anchor economy for the neighbouring developing economies of Laos, Burma, and Cambodia. Thailand's recovery from the 1997-98 Asian financial crisis depended mainly on exports, among various other factors. Thailand ranks high among the world's automotive export industries along with manufacturing of electronic goods.

Forty-nine percent of Thailand's labour force is employed in agriculture, however this is less than the 70% employed in 1980. Agriculture has been experiencing a transition from labour intensive and transitional methods into a more industrialised and competitive sector.[64] Between 1962 and 1983, the agricultural sector grew by 4.1% on average a year and continued to grow at 2.2% between 1983 and 2007. However, the relative contribution of agriculture to GDP has declined while exports of goods and services have increased. As of December 2011, the unemployment rate in Thailand stands at 0.4%.

Agriculture, Forestry, and Fishing. In 2006 agriculture, forestry, and fishing contributed less than 10% of gross domestic product (GDP) but employed about 39% of the workforce. Thailand is the world's leading exporter of rice and a major exporter of shrimp. Other agricultural products include coconuts, corn, rubber, soybeans, sugarcane, and tapioca. In 1985 Thailand officially designated 25% of the nation's land area for protected forests and 15% for timber production. Protected forests have been set aside for conservation and recreation, while production forests are available for the forestry industry.

Mining and Minerals. Thailand's major minerals include fluorite, gypsum, lead, lignite, natural gas, rubber, tantalum, tin, and tungsten. The main mineral export is gypsum.

Industry and Manufacturing. Thailand is becoming a centre of automobile manufacturing for the Association of Southeast Asian Nations (ASEAN) market. The expansion of the automotive industry has been a boon for domestic steel production. Thailand's electronics industry faces competition from Malaysia and Singapore, while its textile industry faces competition from China and Vietnam.

Energy. As of January 2007, proven oil reserves totalled 290 million barrels, and proven natural gas reserves were 14.8 trillion cubic feet. In 2003 recoverable coal reserves totaled 1,492.5 million short tons.

Services. In 2006 the services sector, which ranges from tourism to banking and finance, contributed 45.2% of gross domestic product (GDP) and employed 38% of the workforce.

Tourism. Tourism makes a larger contribution to Thailand's economy (typically about 6% of GDP) than that of any other Asian nation. One of the negative side effects of Thailand's tourism industry is a burgeoning sex tourism industry and a related threat from human immunodeficiency virus/acquired immune deficiency syndrome (HIV/AIDS).

Infrastructure

Roads. Estimates vary on the length of roads in Thailand. According to one estimate, Thailand has 57,403 kilometres of roads, 56,542 kilometres of which were paved and 861 kilometres, unpaved. Streets in Bangkok are frequently gridlocked, with an overabundance of motor vehicles flowing into the central city via expressways.

Railroads. Railroads are operated under the State Railway of Thailand. In 2005 the system totaled an estimated 4,071 kilometres of narrow-gauge (1.000-metre gauge) track. Freight traffic is considered an important part of Thailand's domestic container transport to and from seaport and inland terminals.

Ports. Thailand's ports in order of size are Bangkok, Laem Chabang, Pattani, Phuket, Sattahip, Si Racha, and Songkhla. The Thai merchant fleet comprises 400 ships of 1,000 gross registered tons or more, including 145 cargo carriers, 91 petroleum tankers, 60 bulk carriers, 32 refrigerated cargo ships, 29 liquefied gas ships, 21 container ships, 14 chemical tankers, 6 passenger/cargo ships, 1 passenger ship, and 1 specialised tanker.

Inland and Coastal Waterways. Thailand has some 4,000 kilometres of navigable inland waterways, 92% of which, or 3,701 kilometres, are navigable by boats with drafts up to 0.9 metres. Thailand's long coastlines lend themselves to intercoastal trade.

Civil Aviation and Airports. Thailand has an estimated 108 airports and three heliports. Bangkok International Airport at Don Muang, 24 kilometres north of the capital, is an important regional hub for pass-through flights and as a destination. About 80 airlines provide service to the Bangkok International Airport and carry a reported 25 million passengers and 700,000 tons of cargo a year. Since 1977, Thai

Airways has been fully owned by the Thai government.

Pipelines. Thailand has 3,760 kilometres of gas pipelines and 379 kilometres of refined products pipelines.

Telecommunications. In 2002 the Thai government formed a new Ministry of Information and Communications to oversee all aspects of telecommunications. The ministry also is responsible for implementing the country's information technology policy, called IT 2010, which is designed to strengthen Thailand's telecommunications infrastructure as a means of promoting overall economic development. Thailand's telecommunications network suffers from delays and other shortfalls in the provision of telephone services as a result of inadequate investment. The quality and availability of telephone service are much better in Bangkok and other cities than in rural areas. Mobile telephones are much more prevalent than landline phones. State entities, including the police and military, and government allies own almost all television and radio stations and play an important role in determining programming content. The government's Public Relations Department requires that all Thai radio stations carry 30 minutes of official news prepared by Radio Thailand, the government's national radio network, twice daily. Radio Thailand has seven networks that specialize in such areas as news and information, public affairs, social issues, education, and foreign-language broadcasts. Thailand has five television channels, two of which are run by the central government, two by the army, and one by a private enterprise. Altogether, Thailand has 204 AM radio stations, 334 FM radio stations, 6 shortwave stations, and 111 television broadcast stations. Additionally, there are between 2,000 and 3,000 community radio stations, many of which operate outside the law by using frequencies restricted to government entities.

Government and Politics

Thailand is a constitutional monarchy with a democratically elected bicameral legislature.

Executive Branch. The constitutional monarch and head of state, since 9 June 1946, is King Bhumibol Adulyadej (Rama IX of the Chakri Dynasty). The Privy Council, which is still provided for in the interim constitution, is an 18-member constitutional body that advises the king on matters of legislation, government affairs, clemency, awards, and other matters requiring the king's signature. Under the interim constitution, executive governmental power

is exercised through a cabinet headed by a prime minister appointed by the king (with the concurrence of the Council for National Security (CNS) chairman) and the 19 members of the Council of Ministers who head major ministries.

Legislative Branch. Legislative power is exercised through a bicameral National Assembly composed of the House of Representatives (Saphaputhan Ratsadon) and Senate (Wuthisapha). All legislative matters of national policy received the approval of the National Assembly and the signature of the king before becoming law. Members of both houses served four-year terms. The number of representatives is determined by the size of the population.

Judicial Branch. Thailand has a three-level court system collectively known as the Courts of Justice. At the top is the Supreme Court of Justice. Below it are the Court of Appeal and, at the third level, the Courts of First Instance, over which the Supreme Administrative Court, which was established in 1999, presides. The Courts of First Instance include the Central Administrative Court and 16 regional administrative courts. A new Constitutional Tribunal, composed of justices from the Supreme Court of Justice and the Supreme Administrative Court, was established on 1 October 2006, to replace the functions of the Constitutional Court. Judges of the Supreme Court of Justice and the Supreme Administrative Court are subject to Senate approval. Other judges are members of the career civil service and are not subject to parliamentary review. Administrative appellate and supreme administrative courts operate at higher levels. A separate Military Court deals with military personnel and persons arrested during periods of martial law. Islamic sharia courts hear civil cases involving members of the Muslim minority.

Administrative Divisions. Thailand has 76 provinces (*changwat*), including Bangkok Municipality. The provinces are divided into 795 districts (*amphoe*), 81 sub-districts (*king amphoe*), 7,255 rural administrative sub-districts (*tambon*), and 69,866 villages (*muban*).

Electoral System. There are no elections for the heads of state and government. The monarchy is hereditary and based on the Palace Law of Succession enacted in 1924, which allows the king to appoint his heir. If he has failed to do so, the Privy Council nominates an heir for National Assembly consideration. Officially, the king appoints the prime minister, who is normally the leader of the party that had an outright majority or organised a majority coalition in the House of Representatives. The Senate is also elected by popular vote for non-party candidates.

Politics and Political Parties. Active political parties include the Phak Prachathipat Party (Democratic Party); Phak Mahachon Party (Great People's Party); Phak Chat Thai Party (Thai Nation Party); and Thai Rak Thai Party (Thai Loves Thai Party).

Foreign Relations. Thailand's foreign policy includes support for the Association of Southeast Asian Nations (ASEAN) in the interest of regional stability and emphasis on a close and longstanding security relationship with the United States. It has signed but not ratified the United Nations Law of the Sea Treaty.

National Security

Armed Forces Overview. Under normal operating circumstances, the minister of defence and the supreme commander of the armed forces are at the top of the chain of command and maintain control; however, real power is held by the three service chiefs.

Foreign Military Relations. A long-standing ally of the United States, Thailand signed numerous bilateral defence and mutual security agreements between 1950 and 2003. Most Thai military equipment is from the United States, the United Kingdom, and China.

External Threat. Thailand faces a number of external threats from cross-border activities. Those on the border with Burma involve the handling of ethnic rebels, refugees, and illegal crossings, often related to drugs and arms trafficking. There have been periodic armed border clashes between Thai and Burmese border guards. Some 98,000 Karen refugees live in camps on the Thai side of the Burma-Thailand border, and rebel members of this group have skirmished with Thai troops. Similarly, separatist insurgents in predominantly Muslim southern Thailand allegedly have operated from neighbouring Malaysia, leading to cooperation between the two governments and Malaysian arrests of separatist ringleaders. Thailand has periodically closed border areas where communist Cambodian insurgents at odds with the Phnom Penh government control neighbouring territory. The Cambodian government has accused Thailand of complicity with the insurgents.

Terrorism. Thailand has been confronted with terrorist violence, primarily in the predominantly Muslim southern provinces of Narathiwat, Pattani, and Yala, which border Malaysia. This separatist violence has led to border closures and security tightening with neighboring Malaysia to inhibit terrorist activities. During 2006 violence in the southern provinces, and particularly violence aimed at public school teachers, sporadically forced the temporary closure of public schools and disrupted the educational process in those areas. Fears of terrorism against Thailand's own tourist resorts are another cause of concern.

Human Rights. Trafficking in women and children and forced prostitution and labour are serious problems in Thailand. It is conservatively estimated that between 200,000 and 300,000 men, women, and children—but particularly women and young girls—are engaged in prostitution as part of Thailand's illegal sex tourism industry. Of these, between 30,000 and 40,000 prostitutes are under the age of 18 years; this figure does not include foreign migrants, many of whom come from Burma, Cambodia, China, and Laos. Thai and migrant women also are trafficked to Japan, Malaysia, Singapore, Bahrain, Australia, South Africa, Europe, and the United States for prostitution and sweatshop labour. Men, women, and children from China and Southeast Asian neighbours also are trafficked for sweatshop, fishery, construction, farm, and industrial labour.

MILITARY BALANCE

AFGHANISTAN

Active	170,700 Paramilitary 136,100

Afghan National Army ***165,700***

	Five Regional Commands
Forces by Role	
Army	201 Corps (Kabul); 2 brigades in Kabul and 1 in Kunar 203 Corps (Gardez); 1 brigade each at Gardez, Khost and Paktika 205 Corps (Kandahar); 1 brigade each at Kandahar, Helmand and Zabul 207 Corps (Herat); 1 brigade plus 1 battalion *(kandak)* each at Shindin and Farah 209 Corps ((Mazar-e-Sharif); 1 brigade with battalions *(kandaks)* at Kunduz, Mazar-e-Sharif and Faryab) 215 Corps (1 commando battalion, 3 infantry brigades) 111 Division (Kabul) (2 infantry brigades)
Reaction Force	1 mechanized brigade (part of 201 Corps) with 1 infantry, 1 mechanised infantry *(kandak)* 1 armoured *(kandak)* and 1 support battalion
Commando	1 brigade with 5 independent battalions *(kandaks)* (one per corps)
Special Forces	1 Special Operations division (1 Special Forces group); 1 commando brigade with 3 commando battalions
Equipment by Type	
Tanks	**MBT**: T-62; T-54/T-55
Reconnaissance	**APC** 173; APC (T) 173 M113A2
Artillery	**Towed** 109: 122mm 85 D-30; 155mm 24 M114A1; **Missiles** SSM SS-1 Scud
Anti-tank	**RCL: 73mm**: SPG-9; **82mm**: B-10; **Guns: 85mm**: D-48
Air Defence	**SAM**: SA-13 *Gopher* SP/SA-7 *Grail* MANPAD; **Guns 100mm; Towed**: KS-19; **14.5mm** 23mm**; Self-Propelled**: ZSU-23-4; **Towed**: ZU-23; **37mm Towed**: M-1939; **57mm Towed**: S-60; **85mm Towed**: M-1939 *KS-12:* **Missiles Tactical**: FROG-7; Scud

Afghan National Army Corps ***5,000***

3 bases	Kabul, Kandahar and Shindad
Equipment by Type	
Aircraft	**Transport**: 41: Medium 20 G-222 (C-27A) Light 9: 3 *Cessna* 182; 12 *Cessna* 208B **Training** 2 L-39 *Albatross*
Helicopters	**Anti-tank**: 11 Mi-35; **Support:** 6 MD-530F; 33 Mi-17

Afghan National Police 136,100 (under control of Ministry of Interior)

Includes Afghan Uniformed Police	80,000
Afghan National Civil Order Police	13, 000
Afghan Border Police	25,000
Afghan Anti-Crime Police	7,000

International Security Assistance Force (ISAF) led by NATO is deployed in all regions since October 2006, with contributing NATO nations filling identified posts.

BANGLADESH

Army: *126,150*

Forces by Role	
Armour	1 brigade (2 armoured regiments); 6 independent regiments
Infantry	7 division headquarters; 17 brigades (*total:* 68 infantry battalions)
Special Forces	1 commando battalion
Artillery	20 regiments
Engineers	1 brigade
Signals	1 brigade
Aviation	2 squadrons
Air Defence	1 brigade
Equipment by Type	
Tanks	232: **Main Battle tanks** 174 Type-59; 58 Type-69 **Light tanks** 8 Type-62
Armoured Personnel Carriers	248: APC (T) 134 MT-LB; APC (W) 92; 75 BTR-80; 17 *Otocar*; PPV 22 *Cobra*
Artillery	815: **Towed** 343: 170 105 mm; 114 Pack (Howitzer;) 111 122 mm; 62 130 mm; 472 Mortars 81 mm; 82 mm; 120 mm
Anti-Tank	**Recoilless** 238 106 mm M-40A1
Aircraft	6; 5 Cessna 152; 1 Piper *Cheyenne*
Air Defence	**Surface-to-Air Missiles** Man-portable QW-2: some HN-5A; **Guns Towed** 164 37 mm; 34 Type-59 (S-60); 132 Type 65/74

Navy: *16,900*

Forces by Role
Headquarters located at Dhaka

Equipment by Type	
Frigates	5; **FFGHM** 1: 1 *Bangabandhu* (ROK Modified *Ulsan*) with 2 twin launchers with Otomat Mk 2 AShM, 2 triple 324mm TT, 1 76mm gun (capacity: 1 AW109E helicopter) **FFG** 1: 1 *Osman* (PRC *Jianghu I*) with 2 quad launchers with HY-2 (CSS-N-2) *Silkworm* AShM, 2 RBU 1200, 2 twin 100mm gun **FF** 3: 2 *Abu Bakr* (UK Leopard) with 2 twin 115mm gun 1 *Umar Farooq* (UK *Salisbury* – training role) with 3 *Squid*,1 twin 115mm gun
Patrol & Coast Combatants	42 **PSOH** 2 *Bijoy* (UK *Castle*) **PCFG** 4 *Durdarsha* (PRC *Huangfeng*) with 4 single launchers with HY-2 (CSS-N-2) *Silkworm* AShM **PCO** 6: 1 *Madhumati* (*Sea Dragon*); 5 *Kapatakhaya* (UK *Island*) **PCC** 3: 2 *Meghna* (fishery protection); 1 *Nirbhoy* (PRC *Hainan*) with 4 RBU 1200 **PBFG** 5 *Durbar* (PRC *Hegu*) with 2 single launchers with SY-1 AShM **PBFT** 4 *Huchuan* (PRC) with 2 single 533mm TT each with YU 1 Type 53 HWT **PBF** 4 *Titas* (ROK *Sea Dolphin*) **PB** 14: 2 *Akshay*; 1 *Barkat* (PRC *Shanghai III*); 1 *Bishkali*; 2 *Karnaphuli*; 1 *Salam* (PRC *Huangfen*); 7 *Shaheed Daulat* (PRC *Shanghai II*)
Mine Countermeasures	5; **MSI** 3: 4*Shapla* (UK *River*); **MSO** 1: 1 *Sagar*
Amphibious Craft	11: 2 **LCU**; 3 **LCVP**; 5 **LCM** (*Yuchin*); 1 **LSL**

Logistics and Support	11; **AOR** 2 (coastal); **AR** 1; **AG** 1; **ATF** 1; **AGHS** 2 *Agradoot;* 1 *Anushandhan;* **YTM** 3
Training	1 *Shaheed Ruhul Amin*
Aviation	Light Helicopters 2AE109E *Power*
Facilities	Bases - Chittagong, Dhaka, Kaptai, Khulna and Mangla

***Air Force:* 14,000**

Three major bases: **Bashar** (consists of Dhaka–Tejgaon and Dhaka-Kurmitola); **Matiur Rahman** (Jessore) and **Zahurul Haque** (Chittagong). **Kurmitola** is the main fast Jet fighter / FGA base. Tejgaon houses two helicopter squadrons. **Jessore** houses the transport squadrons, the Air Force Academy and the Flying Training Wing. **Bogra** has the flying instructors' school; **Chittagong** has a combat training / light attack squadron plus a helicopter squadron. Flying hours 17,000 +/year.

Forces by Role

FGA	2 squadrons with F-7 MB, F-7B G (recce capable), FT-7 BG, FT-7B *Airguard;* A-5C (Q-5III) *Fantan;* 1 OCU with L-39 ZA *Albatross;* FT-6 MiG-19 UTI) *Farmer*
Fighter	1 squadron with MiG-29 *B* / MiG-29UB *Fulcrum*
Transport	1 squadron with An-32 *Club;* 1 squadron with C-130B *Hercules*
Helicopters	5 squadrons with Mi-17 / MI-171/MI-171Mi-IV Hip; Bell 206L Long Ranger-4; Bell 212 Huey
Training	1 training school with PT-6 (CJ-6) basic training; T-37B *Tweet* (jet conversion training); Bell 206L *Long Ranger-4* (helicopter training)

Equipment by Type

Aircraft	76 combat capable; **FGA** 59+ : 41 F-7MB /F-7BG (recce capable) / FT-7BG/ FT-7B *Airguard;* 18 A-5C (Q-5III) *Fantan;* 10 FT-6 (MiG-19 UTI) Farmer; **FTR** 8:6 MiG-29 *Fulcrum* ; 2 MiG-29 UB *Fulcrum;* **TPT** 7:3 *An-32 Club+* ; 4 C-130B *Hercules* ; **TRG** 30: 8 L-39ZA *Albatross;* 10 PT-6 (CJ-6); 12 T-37B *Tweet*
Helicopters	**Support** 17: MI-17 (Mi-8MT) *Hip H* **Utility** 13; Bell 206L *LongRanger;* 11 Bell 212
Tactical Missiles	**AAM**: some AA-2 *Atoll*

***Paramilitary* 63,900**

Ansars	20,000
Armed Police	5,000 rapid action force
Bangladesh Rifles	38,000; Border Guard; Paramilitary 41 battalions
Coast Guard	900
Patrol &Coastal Combatants	10; **PFC** 2 *Shaheed Bishkail;* **PCI** 1 *Bishkali;* **PCR** 5 *Pabna;* **PB** 2 *Meghna*

BHUTAN

Royal Bhutan Army ***10,000***

Forces by Role

Royal Bhutan Army	No.1 Wing	-	Tendu
	No.2 Wing	-	Damthang
	No.3 Wing	-	Goinichawa
	No.4 Wing	-	Yonphula
	No. 5 Wing	-	Samchi
	No. 6 Wing	-	Wangdi
	No. 7 Wing	-	Paro
	No. 8 Wing	-	Samchi
	No. 9 Wing	-	Geylephug
	No. 10 Wing	-	Deothang
	No. 11 Wing	-	Rimte
	No. 12 Wing	-	Wangdi
	No. 13 Wing	-	Deothang
	No. 14 Wing	-	Nanglam
	No. 15 Wing	-	Thimpu (Rbg)
	No. 16 Wing	-	Gelegphug
	Training Wing	-	Tenchholing
Independent Companies	9 (Ha, Damthang, Gumchawa, Punakha, Kalikhola, Thimphu (2), Khakthang and Deothang)		
Special Forces	(six companies)		
Wangchuk Lo Dzong Military Training School	Ha		
Royal Bodyguards	Three companies - Royal Palace (Thimpu)		
Forest Guards			
Army Aviation	1 Dornier DO-28; 7 Mil Mi-28 helicopters		
Royal Bhutan Police			
Police Training Centres	3 (Jigmiling, Geylephug and Zilnon Namgyeling)		
Airport Security Unit	Paro		

CHINA

Armed Forces **2,285,000**	**Army 1,600,000; Navy 255,000; Air Force 330,000 Strategic Missile Forces 100,000, Paramilitary 660,000**
Organisations by Service	
Strategic Missile Forces	Second Artillery Force (100,000+)
Offensive	28 launch brigades within 6 missile bases; organization varies by missile type; one testing and one training base 1 ICBM brigade with DF-4 3 ICBM brigade with DF-5A 1 ICBM brigade with DF-31 2 ICBM brigade with DF-31A 1 IRBM brigade with DF-3A 1 MRBM brigade with DF-21 6 MRBM brigade with DF-21A 2 MRBM brigade with DF-21C 1 MRBM brigade with DF-21D 4 SRBM brigade with DF-11A 4 SRBM brigade with DF-15 2 SSM brigade with DH-10
Missiles	**Strategic** 470 **ICBM** 66: 12 DF-31 (CSS-9) (1 brigade); 24 DF-31A (CSS-9 Modified) (2 brigades); 10 DF-4 (CSS-3) (2 brigades); 20 DF-5A (CSS-4 Modified) (3 brigades) **IRBM** 2 DF-3A (CSS-2 Mod) **MRBM** 122: 80 DF-21 (CSS-5) (5 brigades); 36 DF-21 (CSS-5 Modified) (2 brigades); 2 DF-3A (CSS-Modified) (1 brigade); 6 DF-21D (CSS-5 Mod 4 - ASBM) **SRBM** 216: 108 DF-11/M-11 **(**CSS-7 Modified**)** (4 brigades); 96 DF-15/M-9 (CSS-6) 225 (6 brigades) **LACM** 54: 54 CJ-10 (DH-10) (2 brigades)
Navy	**Submarines Strategic; SSBN 3** 1 *Xia* (with 12 JL-1 (CSS-N-3) strategic SLBM); 2 *Jin* (capacity 12 JL-2 (CSS-NX-4) strategic SLBM *(two more being built)*
Defensive Radar	**Strategic**: phased array radar; detection and tracking radars (covering Central Asia and Shanxi (northern border)) located at Xinjiang
Space	**Satellites** 40 **Communications** 4: 3 *Fenghuo* (*Zhongxing* – dual use telecom satellites for civil/military communications); 1 *Chinasat* 1A (*Zhongxing* 1A – reported dual use satellite for civil/military communications) **Navigation/Positioning/Timing** 10: 2 *Beidou*-1; 1 *Beidou*-2(M); 3 *Beidou*-2(G); 4 *Beidou*-2 (IGSO) ISR 15: 1 *Haiyang* 2A; 12 *Yaogan Weixing* (remote sensing); 2 *Zhangguo Ziyuan* (ZY-2 - remote sensing) **ELINT/SIGINT** 11: 8 *Shijian* 6 (4 pairs - reported ELINT/SIGINT role)
People's Liberation Army **800,000**	
Group Army	18 (strength from 30-65,000), organization varies, normally with 2-3 mechanized/motorized infantry division/brigade, 1 armoured division/ brigade, 1 artillery division / brigade, 1 SAM/AAA or AAA brigade; combat readiness category varies with 10 GA at Category A and 8 at Category B (reorganization to brigade structure still in progress). Five Regions have rapid reaction units (RRU). The PLA air has 3 RRU airborne divisions and

the Navy two marine brigades. 31st, 38th, 39th, 42nd and 54th GA have received air regiments that have in the past been MR or MD assets)

Military Regions

7: North East–Shenyang Military Region 250,000
Army; 3 groups ((Heilongjiang, Jilin, Liaoning Military District): 2 armoured, 1 mechanized, 4 motorized, 1 artillery division; 2 armoured, 5 motorized, 3 artillery, 1 SAM/ AAA, 3 AAA, 1 anti-tank brigade

North–Beijing Military Region 300,000; Army; 3 groups ((Beijing, Tianjin Garrison, Inner Mongolia, Hebei, Shanxi Military District): 2 armoured, 1 mechanized, 5 motorized, 1 artillery division; 3 armoured, 7 motorized infantry, 4 artillery, 2 SAM/AAA, 3 AAA brigade; 1 anti-tank regiment

West–Lanzhou Military Region 220,000: Army; 2 groups ((incl Ningxia, Shaanxi, Gansu, Qing-hai, Xinjiang, South Xinjiang Military District): 1 armoured, 2 motorized infantry, 1 artillery division; 1 armoured, 2 motorized infantry, 1 artillery, 1 AAA brigade; 1 anti-tank regiment

South-West–Chengdu–Military Region 180,000
Army 2 Group Army (13,14) (Chongqing Garrison), Sichuan, Guizhou, Yunnan, Tibet MD): 1 GA (13) 2 motorized (149th Div RRU), 1 artillery division, 1 armoured brigade, 1 AD brigade, 1 aviation regiment, 1 engineer regiment; 1 GA (14) (4 motorized, 1 artillery division, 2 armoured brigades, 1 artillery, 2 AD brigades); 2 mountain infantry brigades, 1 EW regiment, 1 aviation regiment, 1 special operations unit

South–Guangzhou Military Region 180,000: Army; 2 groups (Hubei, Hunan, Guangdong, Guangxi, Hainan Military District): 1 mechanized, 3 motorized infantry, 1 artillery division; 2 armoured, 1 artillery, 1 SAM/AAA, 1 AAA brigade. Hong Kong: 7, 000 with 1 infantry brigade (3 infantry, 1 mechanized infantry, 1 artillery regiment, 1 engineer battalion), 1 helicopter unit

Centre–Jinan Military Region 190,000 Army; 3 groups ((Shandong, Henan Military District): 2 armoured, 1 mechanized infantry, 3 motorized infantry, 1 artillery division; 1 armoured, 1 mechanized infantry, 4 motorized infantry, 2 artillery, 2 SAM/AAA, 1 AAA brigade, 1 anti-tank regiment

East–Nanjing Military Region 250,000: Army; 3 groups ((Shanghai Garrison, Jiangsu, Zhejiang, Fujian, Jiangxi, Anhui Military District): 2 armoured, 1 mechanized infantry, 3 motorized infantry, 1 artillery division; 1 armoured, 4 motorized infantry, 2 artillery, 2 SAM/AAA, 1 AAA brigade; 1 anti-tank regiment

Forces by Role

Military Region	7 commands; 18 Group Army HQs
Armoured	9 armoured divisions, 8 armoured brigades, 1 OPFOR brigade
Mechanised Infantry	7 mechanized infantry divisions, 7 mechanized infantry brigades, 2 (high altitude) mechanized infantry brigades, 2 independent regiments
Motorized Infantry	10 motorized infantry divisions, 3 (high altitude) motorized infantry divisions, 1 (jungle) motorized infantry division, 19 motorized infantry brigades, 2 (high altitude) motorized infantry brigades
Infantry	2 infantry regiments, 5 (border) independent regiments
Mountain Infantry	2 mountain infantry divisions, 2 (independent) brigades
Airborne	1 (manned by AF) corps (3 airborne divisions, 35,000 airborne)
Amphibious	2 amphibious assault divisions, 1 amphibious armoured brigade
Artillery	2 artillery divisions, 17 artillery brigades
SSM	1 independent brigade; 9 (coastal defence) regiments
Air Defence	21 air defence brigades; 1 independent regiment
Engineers	1 independent brigade, 13 engineer regiments, 1 pontoon bridge brigade, 2 pontoon bridge regiments
Signals	50 regiments
EW	5 EW regiments

Aviation	1 aviation brigade; 9 aviation regiments, 2 (independent) regiments (training)
Security	2 (Guards) divisions

Equipment by Type

Tanks	**MBT** 7,400+: 4,300 Type-59/Type-59D/Type-59-II; 300 Type-79; 500 Type-88A/B; 1,500 Type-96/Type-96A; 300 Type-96G; 500 Type-98A/Type-99; some Type-99A2 **LT TK** 800: 200 Type-05 AAAV ZTD-05; 400 Type-62; 200 Type-63A **AIFV** 2,350: 500 Type-04 (ZBD-04); 250 Type-05 AAAV (ZBD-05); 700 Type-86/Type-86A (WZ-501); 750 Type-92; 150 Type-92A **APC** 2,700 **APC (T)** 2,000: 1,650 Type-63/Type-63C; 350 Type-89 **APC (W)** 700: 100 Type-09 (ZBL-09); 500 Type-92B; 100 WZ-523
Artillery	12,462+ **SP** 1,785: 122mm 1,371: 1,296 Type-70-I/Type-89/Type-07 PLZ-07; 75 Type-09 (PLC-09) 152mm 324 Type-83; **155mm** 126 Type-05 (PLZ-05) **Towed** 6,176: 122mm 3,800 Type-54-1 (M-30) M-1938/Type-83/Type-60 (D-74)/Type-96 (D-30); 130mm 234 Type-59 (M-46)/Type-59-I; 152mm 2,106 Type-54 (D-1)/Type-66 (D-20); 155mm 150 Type 88 WAC-21 **Gun/Mor** 150+: 120mm 150+: 100 2S23 NONA-SVK; 50+ PLL-05 **MRL** 1,770+ **SP** 1,716+: 107mm some 122mm 1,620 Type-81/Type-89; 300mm 96 Type-03 PHL-03 **Towed** • 107mm 54 Type-63 **Mor** 2,586 **Towed** 81mm Type-W87; 82mm Type-53 (M-37)/Type-67/Type-82; 100mm Type-71 (reported); 120mm Type-55 (incl SP); 160mm Type-56 (M-160)
Anti-Tank	**Missiles SP** 276 HJ-9 *Red Arrow* 9 **Man-portable** HJ-73A/HJ-73B/HJ-73C/HJ-8A/HJ-8C/HJ-8E **RCL** 3,966: 75mm Type-56; 82mm Type-65 (B-10)/Type-78; 105mm Type-75; 120mm Type-98 **RL** 62mm Type-70-1 **Guns** 1,730: 100mm 1,658: 1,308 Type-73 (T-12)/Type-86; 350 Type-02 PTL02 120mm up to 72 Type-89 SP
Aircraft	**Transport** 8 Medium 3 Y-8 Light 5 Y-7
Helicopters	**Anti-Tank** 16 Z-10 **MRH** 401: 22 Mi-17 *Hip H*; 33 Mi-17-V5 *Hip H*; 24 Mi-17-V7 *Hip H*; 8 SA316 *Alouette III*; 8 SA342L *Gazelle*; 80 Z-9/9B; 200 Z-9 WA; 26 Z-9W **Transport** 234 Heavy 21: 4 Mi-26 *Halo*; 7 SA321 *Super Frelon*; 10 Z-8 Medium 145: 50 Mi-8T *Hip*; 69 Mi-171; 8 Mi-172; 18 S-70C2 (S-70C) *Black Hawk* Light 68: 53 AS350 *Ecureuil*; 15 EC120
UAV	ISR • Heavy BZK-005; WZ-5 Medium ASN-105; ASN-206 Light ASN-104; W-50 Unknown WZ-6 BZK-006
Air Defence	SAM 290+: **SP** 290: 200 HQ-7A; 60 9K331 Tor-M1 (SA-15 *Gauntlet*); 30 HQ-6D *Red Leader* **Man-portable** HN-5A/HN-5B *Hong Nu*; FN-6/QW-1/ QW-2 **Guns** 7,700+ **SP** 25mm Type-95/Type-04; 35mm Type-07 37mm Type-88; 57mm Type-80 **Towed** 23mm Type-80 (ZU-23-2); 25mm Type-85;

	35mm Type-90 (GDF-002); 37mm Type-55 (M-1939)/ Type-65/Type-74; 57mm Type-59 (S-60); 85mm Type-56 (M-1939) KS-12; 100mm Type-59 (KS-19)
Radar	**Land** *Cheetah*; RASIT; Type-378
	Missiles AShM HY-1 (CSS-N-2) *Silkworm*; HY-2 (CSS-C-3) *Seersucker*; HY-4 (CSS-C-7) *Sadsack*
	ASM KD-10
ARV	Type-73; Type-84; Type-85; Type-97; Type-654
	VLB KMM; MTU; TMM; Type-84A
	MW Type-74; Type-79; Type-81-II; Type-84
Reserves	
Infantry	18 infantry divisions (3 brigades; 3 regiments)
Artillery	3 divisions (6 brigades)
Engineers	10 regiments
Anti-tank	1 brigade
Air Defence	17 divisions (6 brigades; 6 regiments)
Logistic	8 brigades
Signals	10 regiments
Chemical	8 regiments

Navy 215,000; 40,000 conscript (total 255,000)

North Sea Fleet	HQ located at Qingdao; Responsible for coastal defence from DPRK border (Yalu River) to south of Lianyungang (approx 35°10´N); equates to Shenyang, Beijing and Jinan Military Region, and to seaward 9 coastal defence districts **Support bases:** Qingdao(HQ), Lushun
East Sea Fleet	HQ located at Dongqian Lake (Ninsbo); Responsible for coastal defence from south of Lianyungang to Dongshan (approx 35°10´N to 23°30´N); equates to Nanjing Military Region, and to seaward 7 coastal defence districts **Support Bases:** Fujian, Zhousnan, Dongqian Lake (Ninsbo)
South Sea Fleet	HQ located at Guangzhou; Responsible for coastal defence from Dongshan (approx 23°30´N) to Vietnam border; equates to Guangzhou Military Region, and to seaward (including Paracel and Spratly Islands) **Support Bases:** Yulin, Guangzhou, Zuanjiang

Equipment by Type

Submarines	71: **Strategic SSBN** 3: 1 *Xia* (capacity 12 JL-1 (CSS-N-3) strategic SLBM); 2 *Jin* (capacity 12 JL-2 (CSS-NX-4) strategic SLBM **Tactical** 68 **SSN** 5: 3 *Han* (Type 091) with YJ-82 AShM, 6 single 533mm TT 2 *Shang* (Type 093) with 6 single 533mm TT (3rd vessel in build) SSG 1 mod *Romeo* (Type SSG) with 6 YJ-1 (CSS-N-4) *Sardine* AShM, 8 single 533mm TT (test platform) **SSK** 52: 12 *Kilo* (2 Project 877, 2 Project 636, 8 Project 636N) with 3M54 *Klub* (SS-N-27B *Sizzler*) ASCM; 6 single 533mm TT with up to 18 Test-71/96 HWT 20 *Ming* (4 Type 035, 12 Type 035G, 4 Type 035B) with 8 single 533mm TT 16 *Song* (Type 039/039G) with YJ-82 (CSS-N-8) *Saccade* ASCM, 6 single 533mm TT 4 *Yuan* (Type 039A/B) with 6 533mm TT SS 1 *Golf* (SLBM trials)

Principal Surface Combatants 78

Destroyers **13**

DDGHM 11:

4 *Hangzhou* (RUS *Sovremenny*) with 2 quad launcher with 3M80/3M82 *Moskit* (SS-N-22 *Sunburn*) AShM, 2 3K90 *Uragan* (SA-N-7 Grizzly) SAM, 2 twin 533mm ASTT,
2 RBU 1000 *Smerch* 3, 2 twin 130mm gun,(capacity
either 1 Z-9C (AS-565SA *Panther*) helicopter or 1 Ka-28 *Helix* A helicopter)

2 *Luyang* (Type 052B) with 4 quad launcher YJ-83 AShM, 2 single launcher with 3K90 *Uragan* (SA-N-7 *Grizzly*) SAM, 2 triple 324mm TT with Yu-7 LWT, 1 100mm gun, (capacity 1 Ka-28 *Helix* A hel)

2 *Luyang II* (Type 052C) with 2 quad launcher with YJ- 62 AShM, 8 sextuple VLS with HHQ-9 SAM, 2 triple 324mm TT with Yu-7 LWT, 1 100mm gun, (capacity 2 Ka-28 Helix A helicopter)

1 *Luhai* (Type 051B) with 4 quad launcher with YJ-83 AShM, 1 octuple launcher with HQ-7 SAM, 2 triple 324mm ASTT with Yu-7 LWT, 1 twin 100mm gun, (capacity 2 Z-9C (AS-565SA Panther)/Ka-28 Helix A helicopter)

2 Luhu (Type 052) with 4 quad launcher with YJ-83 AShM, 1 octuple launcher with HQ-7 SAM, 2 triple 324mm ASTT with Yu-7 LWT, 2 FQF 2500, 1 twin 100mm gun, (capacity 2 Z-9C (AS-565SA Panther) helicopter)

DDGM 2:

2 *Luzhou* (Type 051C) with 2 quad launcher with YJ-83 (C-803) AShM; 6 sextuple VLS with SA-N-20 *Grumble* SAM, 1 100mm gun, 1 helicopter landing platform

Frigates **65**

FFGHM 25:

2 *Jiangkai* (Type 054) with 2 quad launcher with YJ-83 AShM, 1 octuple launcher with HQ-7 SAM, 2 triple 324mm TT with Yu-7 LWT, 2 RBU 1200, 1 100mm gun, (capacity 1 Ka-28 *Helix* A/Z-9C (AS-565SA *Panther)* helicopter)

9 *Jiangkai II* (Type 054A) with 2 quad launcher with YJ-83 AShM, 1 32-cell VLS with HQ-16 SAM (reported), 2 triple 324mm TT with Yu-7 LWT, 2 RBU 1200, 1 76mm gun, (capacity 1 Ka-28 *Helix* A/Z-9C (AS-565SA *Panther*) helicopter)

4 *Jiangwei I* (Type 053H2G) with 2 triple launcher withYJ-83 AShM, 1 sextuple launcher with HQ-61 (CSA-N-2)SAM, 2 RBU 1200, 1 twin 100mm gun, (capacity: 2 Z-9C (AS-565SA *Panther*) helicopter)

10 *Jiangwei II* (Type 053H3) with 2 quad launcher with YJ-83 AShM, 1 octuple launcher with HQ-7 SAM, 2 RBU 1200, 2 100mm gun, (capacity: 2 Z-9C (AS-565SA *Panther*) helicopter)

FFGH 1:

1 *Jianghu IV* (Type 053H1Q - trg role) with 1 triple launcher with SY-1 (CSS-N-1) *Scrubbrush* AShM, 4 RB 1200, 1 100mm gun, (capacity: 1 Z-9C (AS-565SA *Panther*) helicopter)

FFGM 2:

2 *Luda* mod (Type 051DT) with 2 quad launcher with YJ-1 (CSS-N-4) *Sardine* AShM, 1 octuple launcher with HQ-7 *Crotale* SAM, 2 FQF 2500, 2 twin 130mm guns, (mine laying capability)

FFG 37:

9 *Jianghu I* (Type 053H) with 2 triple launcher with SY-1 (CSS-N-1) *Scrubbrush* AShM, 4 RBU 1200, 2 100mm gun

8 *Jianghu II* (Type 053H1) with 1 triple launcher with SY-1 (CSS-N-1 *Scrubbrush* AShM, 2 RBU 1200, 1 twin 100mm gun, (capacity 1 Z-9C (AS-565SA) Panther hel)

3 *Jianghu III* (Type 053H2) with 8 YJ-1 (CSS-N-4)

Sardine AShM, 4 RBU 1200, 2 twin 100mm gun
6 *Jianghu V* (Type 053H1G) with 1 triple launcher with SY-1 (CSS-N-1) *Scrubbrush* AShM, 2 RBU 1200, 1 twin 100mm gun
9 *Luda* (Type 051/051D/051Z) with 2 triple 324mm ASTT, 2 FQF 2500, 2 twin 130mm gun
1 *Luda II* (Type 051G) with 2 triple launcher with HY-2 (CSS-N-2) *Silkworm* AShM, 2 triple 324mm ASTT, 1 twin 130mm gun, (mine-laying capability)
1 *Luda III* (Type 051G II) with 2 triple launcher with HY-2 (CSS-N-2) *Silkworm*/YJ-1 (CSS-N-4) *Sardine* AShM, 4 twin launcher with YJ-1 (CSS-N-4) *Sardine* AShM, 2 triple 324mm ASTT, 2 twin 130mm gun

Patrol and Coastal Combatants 211
PCFG 76+
65+ *Houbei* (Type 022) with 2 quad launcher with YJ-83 (C-803) AShM
11 *Huangfen* (Type 021) with 2 twin launcher with HY-2 (CSS-N-3 *Seersucker*) AShM
PCG 26
6 *Houjian* (Type 037/II) with 2 triple launcher with YJ-1 (CSS-N-4 *Sardine*) AShM
20 *Houxin* (Type 037/IG) with 2 twin launcher with YJ-1 (CSS-N-4 *Sardine*) AShM
PCC 75
3 *Haijui* (Type 037/I) with 4 RBU 1200 (20 eff.)
50 *Hainan* (Type 037) with å4 RBU 1200 (20 eff.)
22 *Haiqing* (Type 037/IS) with 2 Type-87 (12 eff.)
PB 34+ *Haizui/Shanghai III* (Type 062/I)

Mine Warfare 73

Mine Countermeasures 88
MCO 7: 6 *Wochi*; 1 *Wozang*
MSO 16 T-43
MSC 16 *Wosao*
MSD 49: 4 *Futi*-class (Type 312); 42 in reserve; 3 (other)
Minelayers • ML 1 *Wolei*

Amphibious

Principal Amphibious Vessels LPD 1 *Yuzhao* (Type 071) (capacity 2 LCAC or 4 UCAC
plus supporting vehicles; 500–800 troops; 2 helicopters - 2 further vessels launched)

Landing Ships 87
LSM 61:
10 *Yubei* (capacity 10 tanks or 150 troops)
1 *Yudeng* (Type 073) (capacity 6 tk; 180 troops)
10 *Yuhai* (capacity 2 tk; 250 troops)
30 *Yuliang* (Type 079) (capacity 5 tk; 250 troops)
10 *Yunshu* (Type 073A) (capacity 6 tk)
LST 26:
7 *Yukan* (capacity 10 tk; 200 troops)
9 *Yuting* (capacity 10 tk; 250 troops; 2 hel)
10 *Yuting II* (capacity 4 LCVP; 10 tk; 250 troops)
Landing Craft 151
LCU 120 *Yunnan*
LCM 20 *Yuchin*
LCAC 1
UCAC 10

Logistics and Support 205: **AORH** 5: 2 *Fuqing*; 2 *Fuchi*; 1 *Nanyun;*
AOT 50; 7 *Danlin*; 20 *Fulin*; 2 *Shengli*; 2 *Jinyou*; 18 *Fuzhou*
AO L5 *Guangzhou;*
AS 8: 1 *Dazhi*; 5 *Dalang*; 2 *Dazhou*

ASR 1 *Dajiang* with 2 SA-321 *Super Frelon;*
ARS 2: 1 *Dadong;* 1 *Dadao;*
AG 6: 4 *Qiongsha* (capacity 400 troops); 2 *Qiongsha* (hospital conversion);
AK 23: 2 Yantai; 2 Dayun; 6 Danlin; 7 Dandao; 6 Hongqi
AWT 18: 10 *Leizhou;* 8 *Fuzhou;*
AGOR 5: 1 *Dahua;* 2 *Kan;* 1 *Bin Hai;* 1 *Shuguang;*
AG1 1 *Dadie;*
AGM 5 (space and missile tracking);
AGS 6: 5 *Henlai;* 2 *Ganzhu;*
AGB 4: 1 *Yanbing;* 3 *Yanha;*
ABU 7 *Yannan*
ATF 51: 4 *Tuzhong;* 10 Huiju; 1 *Daozha;* 17 *Gromovoy;* 19 *Roslavl;*
AH 1 *Daishan*
TRG 2: 1 *Shichang;* 1 *Daxin*
YDG 5 *Yen Pai*

Naval Aviation **26,000**

<u>Forces by Role</u>

Bomber	2 regiments with H-6D/H6M
	1 regiment with H-6D/H-5
Fighter	1 regiment with SU-30KM2
	1 regiment with J-7E, 2 regiments J-81/J-8F
	1 regiment with 24 J-7II
FGA	1 regiments with J10-AS
	1 regiment with J-11B/BS
	1 regiments with Su-30Mk2
Attack	2 regiments with JH-7
	3 regiments with JH-7A
ELINT/ Reconnaissance	1 regiment with Y-8J/Y-8JB
Maritime Patrol	1 regiment with SH-5
Transport	2 regiments with Y-8/Y-7
Training	1 regiment with HY-7/K-8
	1 regiment with HY-7/HJ-5
	1 regiment with CJ-6
	1 regiment with JJ-6/JJ-7
Helicopters	1 regiment with Mi-8; Ka-28; Ka-31
	1 regiment with AS365; Ka-28; Z-8; Z-8A/JH/S

<u>Equipment by Type</u>

Aircraft

311 combat capable
Bombers 50: 20 H-5; 30 H-6G
Fighter 72: 24 J-7E *Fishbed*; 24 J-8F *Finback*; 24 J-8H *Finback*
FGA 172+: 120 JH-7/JH-7A; 24 J-10A/S; 4+ J-11B/BS; 24 Su-30MK2 *Flanker*
ASW 4 SH-5
ELINT 7: 4 Y-8JB *High New* 2; 3 Y-8X
AEW&C 6: 4 Y-8J; 2 Y-8W *High New* 5
ISR 7 HZ-5
TKR 3 H-6DU
TPT 66: Medium 4 Y-8 Light 62: 50 Y-5; 4 Y-7; 6 Y-7H; 2 Yak-42
TRG 106+: 38 CJ-6; 5 HJ-5*; 21 HY-7; 14 JJ-6*; 4 JJ-7; 12 JL-8; 12+ JL-9

Helicopters

ASW 28: 13 Ka-28 *Helix* A (6 more on order); 25 Z-9C
AEW 2 Ka-31
SAR 2 Z-8S

	Transport 46 Heavy 38: 15 SA321 *Super Frelon*; 20 Z-8/Z-8A; 3 Z-8JH Medium 8 Mi-8 *Hip*
Missiles	**AAM** • IR PL-5; PL-9; R-73 (AA-11 *Archer*) SARH PL-11 IR/SARH R-27 (AA-10 *Alamo*) ARH R-77 (AA-12 *Adder*) ASM Kh-31A (AS-17B *Krypton*); YJ-61 (CAS-1 (improved) *Kraken*); YJ-8K (CSS-N-4 *Sardine*); YJ-83K (CSSC-8 *Saccade*)
Bombs	Conventional: Type-200-4/Type-200A Laser-Guided: LS-500J; TV-Guided: KAB-500KR; KAB-1500KR

Marines 10,000

Forces by Role

Army	3 (amphibious role) divisions
Marine Infantry	2 brigades (*each:* 1 infantry battalion, 1 AD battalion, 1 (armoured) mechanized infantry battalion, 2 amphibious reconnaissance battalions, 2 artillery battalions, 2 tank battalions)

Equipment by Type

Tanks	**Light tanks** 150 Type-63A
APC	**APC (T)** 60 Type-63; **APC (W)** Type-92
Artillery	**Towed: 122mm** Type-83; **MRL 107mm** Type-63
Anti-tank	**Missiles** HJ-73, HJ-8
Air Defence	**SAM MANPAD** HN-5 *Hong Nu/Red Cherry*

Air Force 330,000

The PLA Air Force (PLAAF) branches - Aviation, SAM, AAA and Airborne.

Military region air force (MRAF)	7; Beijing, Shenyang, Lanzhou, Jinan, Nanjing, Guangzzhou, Chengdu 13 division level command posts (within a MRAF are aviation division, ground-to-air missile divisions (brigades and regiments), anti-aircraft artillery brigades (regiments), radar brigades (regiments) and other support troops.
Air Divisions	29 (including up to 4 regiments, each with 10-15 aircraft, 1 maintenance unit, transport and training aircraft) are distributed between the military regions.
Headquarters Air Force	1 air division (34th,VIP Transport) with Il-76 MD, Tu-154M, B-747, CRJ200, Y8, Y7, An-30; 100th, 101st, 102nd Regiments; Air Force Flight Test Regiment
North Beijing MRAF	1 air division (7th fighter) including 19th Regiment (Zhangjiakou) with J-11, 21st Regiment (Zhangjiakou) with J-7B air division (15th fighter / attack) including 43rd Regiment (Hairen) with J-7C, 44th Regiment (Lingqiu) with Q-5, 45th Regiment-J-7D; 1 air division (24th fighter) including 70th Regiment (Yangkun, Tianjin) with J-8A/E, 71st Regiment (Zunhua) with J-8, 72nd Regiment (Yangkun) with J-8; Flight Test & Training Centre (Hebei, Cangzhou) including 4 Regiment with Su-30, Su-27/J-11, J-8C, J-10, J-17E, JJ-7; 4th Air Academy (Hebei, Shijiazhuang / Baoding) including 4 regiments with K-88, JJ-5, CJ-6; 6th Air Academy Hebei, Zhuzhou) including 3 Regiment with JJ-5, Cj-6; Air Defence; 3 SAM division (5th, Beijing, with S300, HQ0, HQ2), (6th Beijing, with HQ7, HQ2), 7th Tianjin, with HQ2,

AAA); 1 SAM Regiment (7th Guangxi, Liaoning, with HQ2); Independent AAA regiment at Guangdong, Huangpu

Northeast-Shenyang MRAF

1 air division (1st fighter) including 1st regiment (Anshan) with J-11/J-11B, 2nd Regiment with J-8F, 3rd Regiment (Anshan) with J-8A; 1 air division (11th attack) (Jilin, Siping) including 31st Regiment with Q-5D, 33rd Regiment with Q-5D; 1 air division (21st fighter) including 61st Regiment (Heilongjiang, Mudanjiang) with J-8H; 1 air division (30th fighter) including civilian/ PLAAF base (Liaoning, Dalian), 88th Regiment with J08A/E, 890th Regiment with J-8F, 90th Regiment with J 7E; 4th Reconnaissance Regiment (Yuhong chang) with JZ-8; MRAF Training Bases; 1st Air Academy (Heilongjiang, Harbin) including 2 Regiments with H-5, HJ-5, An-30, An-26, CJ-6, 3rd Air Academy (Liaoning, Jinzhou) including 2 Regiments with JJ-5, CJ-6 7th Air Academy (Jilin) Including 3 Regiments with K-8, JJ-5, CJ-6

West-Lanzhou MRAF

1 air division. (6th fighter) including 16th Regiment (Ningxia, Yinchuan) with J-11, 18th Regiment (Yinchaun) with J-7E, 139th Regiment (Tianshui with J-7; 1 air division (36th bomber) Shangxi, Wugong/Lintong) including 106th Reconnaissance / bomber Regiment with Y8H-1 Aerial Survey Regiment; 107th Regiment with H-6E, 108th Regiment with H-6A; 1 air division (37th fighter) (Xinjiang, Urumqi) including 109th Regiment with J-8H, 110th Regiment with J-7E, 111th Regiment with J-7G; 5th Air Academy (Gangsu, Wuwei) including 3 Regiments with CJ-6, JJ-5; 8th Air Academy (Xinjiang, Shuquan) Including 3 Regiments with C6, JJ-5; PLAFF Missile Testing Regiment (Gansu, Dinxi) with JJ-6; J-7B; Air Defence; 6th SAM brigade (Gangu, Lanzhou) with HQ2, AAA, 6th SAM Regiment (Xinjiang)with HQ2E, 41st Radar Regiment (Xinjiang, Hetian)

Centre – Ninan MRAF

1 air division (5th attack) Shangdong, Weifang) including 13th Regiment with Q-5E; 14th Regiment with JH-7A; 1 air division (12th fighter) (Shangdong, Jinan) including 34th Regiment with J-8B, 35th Regiment with J-8B, 36th Regiment with J-76; 1 air division (19th fighter) Henan, Zhengshou) including 55th Regiment with J-11, 56th Regiment with J-11, 57th Regiment with J-7E; 1st Reconnaissance Regiment (Shangdong, Wendeng) with JZ-6.

East-Nanjing MRAF

1 air division (3rd fighter) including 7th Regiment with J-10, 8th Regiment with J-7E, 9th Regiment with Su-30MKK; 1 air division (10th bomber) including 28th Regiment (Anqing) with H-6E, 29th Regiment (Nanjing) with H-6E, 30th Regiment (Nanjing) with Y-8D; 1 air division (14th fighter) (Jiangxi, Nangchang, Xiangtang) including 40th Regiment (Nangchang, Xi-angtang) with J-11A, 41st Regiment (Jiojiang) with J-7H; 1 air division (26th Special Mission) Wuxi, Jiangsu, Suzhou, Guangfu) including 1 regiment with KJ-2000, 1 regiment (Reconnaissance) with JZ-8F; 1 air division (28th attack) (Zhejiang-Hangzhou) including 82 Regiment with J8-7A, 83rd Regiment with Q-5D, 84th Regiment with Q-5D; 1 air division (29th fighter) Zhejiang, Quzhou) including 85th Regiment with Su-30 MKK, 86th Regiment with J-7C, 87th Regiment with J-8B/D; MRAF Trg Base; 3rd Reconnaissance regiment with JZ-6; 13th Air Academy (Anhui, Bingbu) with K-8, JJ-5, CJ-6; Air Defence: 4 SAM Brigade (2nd, Fujian, Xianyou with S300, HQ9), (3rd, Shanghai with HQ7, HQ2), (4th Jiangsu, Nanjing with HQ9, HQ7), (8th, Shanghai with HQ9).

South-Guangzou MRAF

1 air division (2nd fighter) (Guangdong, Zhanjiang Suxi) including 4th Regiment (Liuzhou) with J-7B, 5th Regiment (Qifengling) with J-10, 6th Regiment (Zhangjiang Suxi) with J-11; 1 air division (8th bomber/ tkr) Hunan, Leiyang) including 22nd Regiment with H-6E, 23rd Regiment with H-6U; 1 air division (9th fighter) Guangdong, Shaoguan) including 25th

Regiment with J-8B, 26th Regiment with J-8D, 27th Regiment with J-7B Regiment (Henan, Kaifeng) with IL-76/MD, 38th Regiment (Wuhan, Wangjiadun) with An-26/Y-8, 39th Regiment (Hubei, Dunyang) with IL-76/MD; 1 air division (18th fighter) Hunan, Changhsa) including 52nd Regiment (Wuhan, Shangpo) with J-7B, 54th Regiment (Changsha, Datuopu) with Su-30MKK; 1 air division (42nd fighter) Guanxi, Nanning) including 124th Regiment (Baicetiangyang) with J-7B, 125th Regiment (Nanning) with J-7H, 2nd Independent Reconnaissance Regiment (Jiangxi, Taihe) with JZ-6; Air Defence; 4 SAM Brigade (9th, Hunan, Huaibei with HQ2, AAA), (10th Guangdong, Guangzhou with HQ2), (11th, Guangdong with HQ7, AAA), (7th Guangxi, Nanning with HQ2), Independent AAA Regiment (Guangdong, Huangpu) with AAA

Southwest-Chengdu MRAF 1 air division (4th airlift) (Chengdu, Qionglai) with An-26/Mi-17 helicopter; 1 air division (33rd fighter) (Chongqing, Baishiyi) including 97th Regiment with J-7E, 98th Regiment with J-7B, 99th Regiment with J-11; air division (44th fighter) Yunnan, Kunming) including 130th Regiment with J-7BV; 131st Regiment with J-7B, 132nd Regiment with J-10; 2nd Air academy (Sichuan, Jiajiang) with H-5, HJ-5, CJ-5.

<u>**Forces by Role**</u>

Bomber
2 regiments with H-6/K (with YJ-63 cruise missile)
2 regiments with H-6A/M
1 (nuclear ready) regiment with 20 H-6 (Tu-16) *Badger*

Fighter
10 regiment with J-7 Fishbed
8 regiments with J-7E *Fishbed*
5 regiments with J-7G *Fishbed*
1 regiments with J-8B *Finback*
2 regiments with J-8F *Finback*
4 regiments with J-8H *Finback*
1 regiment with Su-27SK/UBK *Flanker*
6 regiments with J-11/*Su-27UBK*
4 regiment with *J-11B/BS*

Fighter/Ground Attack
3 regiments with *Su-30MKK Flanker*
6 regiments with *J-10A/S*

Ground Attack
3 regiments with *JH-7A*
5 regiments with *Q-5C/D/E Fantan*

Electronic Warfare
1 regiment with Y-8CB/G/XZ
1 regiment with Y-8CB/G

ISR
2 regiments with JZ-6
1 regiments with JZ-8 *Finback*
1 regiment with JZ-8F *Finback*
1 regiment with Y-8H1

Airborne EW & Control 1 regiment with KJ-200/KJ-2000/Y-8T

Combat Search & Rescue 1 regiment with Mi-171; Z-8

Tanker 1 regiment with H-6U

Transport
1 (VIP) regiment with B-737; CRJ-200/700
1 (VIP) regiment with B-737; Tu-154M; Tu-154M/D
1 regiment with Il-76MD *Candid B*
3 regiments with Y-7
3 regiments with Y-8

Training
1 regiment with H-6H
Some regiments with CJ-6/-6A/-6B; H-5; HJ-5; Y-7; JL-8 (K-8); JJ-5; JJ-6; JJ-7

Transport Helicopters Some regiments with AS332 *Super Puma* (VIP); *Bell* 214; Mi-8; *Hip*; Z-9;

Air Defence
3 SAM division
2 mixed SAM/ADA division

9 SAM brigade
2 mixed SAM/ADA brigade
2 ADA brigade
9 independent SAM regiments
1 independent ADA regiments

Equipment By Type

Aircraft

1,693 combat capable
Bombers up to 82 H-6A/E/H/K/M
Fighter 890: 240 J-7 *Fishbed;* 192 J-7E *Fishbed;* 120 J-7G Fishbed; 24 J-8B *Finback;* 48 J-8F *Finback;* 96 J-8H *Finback;* 95 J-11; 43 Su-27SK *Flanker;* 32 Su-27UBK *Flanker*
FGA 415+: 200+ J-10A/S; 70+ J-11B/BS Flanker; 72 JH-7/JH-7A; 73 Su-30MKK *Flanker*
Anti-tank 120 Q-5C/D/E *Fantan*
EW 13: 4 Y-8CB *High New* 1; 7 Y-8G *High New* 3; 2 Y-8XZ *High New* 7
ELINT 4 Tu-154M/D *Careless*
ISR 99: 48 JZ-6; 24 JZ-8 *Finback;* 24 JZ-8F *Finback;* 3Y-8H1
AEW&C 8+: 4+ KJ-200; 4 KJ-2000 C2 5: 2 B-737; 3 Y-8T *High New* 4
Tanker 10 H-6U
Transport 320+
Heavy 10 Il-76MD *Candid* B Medium 40+ Y-8; Light 239: 170 Y-5; 41 Y-7/Y-7H; 20 Y-11; 8 Y-12 PAX 31: 9 B-737 (VIP); 5 CRJ-200; 5 CRJ-700; 12 Tu-154M *Careless*
Training 490: 400 CJ-6/-6A/-6B; 50 JJ-7; 40 JL-8

Helicopters

MRH 22: 20 Z-9; 2 Mi-17-V5 *Hip H*
Transport 82+: Heavy 18+ Z-8 (SA321) Medium 6+ AS-332 *Super Puma* (VIP); 4 *Bell* 214; 50 Mi-8 *Hip;* 4+ Mi-171 UAV • ISR • Heavy CH-1 *Chang Hong; Chang Kong* 1; *Firebee Light Harpy*

SAM

3 divisions located in North
2 brigade located in South
1 brigade located in North-East
2 brigades located in East
1 brigade located in South West;
Missiles 600+
SP 300+: 24 HD-6D; 60+ HQ-7; 32 HQ-9; 24 HQ-12 (KS-1A); some HQ-16; 32 S-300PMU (SA-10B *Grumble*); 64 S-300PMU1 (SA-20 *Gargoyle*); 64 S-300PMU2 (SA-20 *Gargoyle*)
Towed 300+ HQ-2 (SA-2) *Guideline* Towed/HQ-2A/HQ-2B (A)
Guns 16,000 100mm/85mm
Missiles AAM • IR PL-2B; PL-5B/C; PL-8; R-73 (AA-11 *Archer*);
SARH PL-11
IR/SARH R-27 (AA-10 *Alamo*); ARH PL-12; R-77 (AA-12 *Adder*)
ASM KD-88; Kh-29 (AS-14 *Kedge*); Kh-31A/P (AS-17 Krypton); Kh-59 (AS-18 Kazoo); YJ-91 (Domestically produced Kh-31P variant)
LACM YJ(KD)-63; CJ-10 (in development)

15th Airborne Corps

Special Forces — 1 SF unit
Reconnaissance — 1 reconnaissance regiment
Air Manoeuvre — 2 AB divisions (2 AB regiment; 1 artillery regiment)
1 AB division (1 AB regiment; 1 artillery regiment)

Combat Support	1 signals group
Combat Service Support	1 logistics group
Equipment	**AIFV** 130+ Type-03 (ZBD-03) **Artillery**108+ **Towed** • 122mm å54 Type-96 (D-30) **MRL** • **Towed** • 107mm å54 Type-63 **Mortars** some 82mm **Anti-tank** • **SP** some HJ-9 *Red Arrow* 9

Equipment By Type	
Aircraft	1,653 combat capable
Bombers	82 H-5,F-5,F-5B (Il-28) *Beagle*; H-6 (Tu-16) *Badger*; H-6E/H-6F/H-6H; 12 H-6H; 46 (with YJ-63 cruise missile)
Fighters	**1,540:** 124 J-7 *Fishbed*; 192 J-7B *Fishbed*; 48 J-7H *Fishbed*; 48 J-7C *Fishbed*; 144-7E *Fishbed*; 48 J-7G *Fishbed*; 32 J-8 Finback; 68 J-8A *Finback*; 132 J-8B finback; 60 J-8D *Finback*; 20 J-8E (*Finback*; 48 J-8F *Finback*; 72 J-8H *Finback*; 84+ J-10; 116J-11 (Su-27SK) *Flanker*;
FGA	**283:** 73 Su-30MKK Flanker; 18+ J-11B Flanker; 72 JH-7/JH-7A; 120Q-5/Q-5D/Q-5E *Fantan*
Reconnaissance	**120:** 72 JZ-6 (MiG-19R); 24 JZ-8 *Finback*; 24 JZ-8F *Finback*
AEW	**9:** Y-8
Tanker	**18**: 10 HY-6; 8 IL-78M
Transport	296+: 4 An-12 *Cub* 1; B-737 15: 15 B-737-200 (VIP) CL-601 *Challenger* 5 Il-18 *Coot* 2; Il-76 13: 13 Il-76MD *Candid B*; Tu-154 17+: 17+ Tu-154M *Careless*; Y-11 20 Y-12 8 Y-5 (An-2) *Colt* 170 Y-7 (An-24) *Coke*/Y-7H (An-26) *Curl* 41
Survey	**3:** Y-8H1
Training	**522:** 400 CJ-6/-6A/-6B; 50 JJ-7; 40 JL-8 (K-8); 32 Su-27UBK *Flanker*
Helicopters	**Support** 56: 6 AS-332 *Super Puma* (VIP); 50 Mi-8 *Hip* **Utility** 24; AS-365 20: 20 Z-9 (AS-365N) *Dauphin 2;* 4 Bell 214
UAV	CH-1 *Chang Hong; Chang Kong 1*; BQM-34 *Firebee*; *Harpy*
Air Defence	**SAM** 1,578+: SP 1,078+: 60+ HQ-7; 24 HQ-9 S-300PMU (SA-10) 994: 850 S-300PMU1 (SA-10B) *Grumble*/S-300PMU2 (SA-10C) *Grumble*; 144 S-300PMU2 (SA-10C) *Grumble*/SA-10D *Grumble;* HQ-2 (SA-2) *Guideline* Towed/HQ-2A/HQ-2B(A) 500+; **Guns 16,000:** 16,000 100mm/85mm; **Missile Tactical** 4,500+
ASM	AS-14 *Kedge*; sAS-17 *Krypton*; AS-18 *Kazoo*; YJ-63
AAM	**4,500+:** 100 AA-12 *Adder*; 1,200 P-27 (AA-10) *Alamo*; 3,200 P37 (AA-11) *Archer*; PL-12; PL-2B; PL-5B; PL-8
Cyber	*The PLA has devoted much attention to information warfare over the past decade, both in terms of battlefield EW and wider, cyber warfare capabilities. The main doctrine is the 'Integrated Network Electronic Warfare' document, which guides PLA computer network operations and calls for the combination of network warfare and EW tools at the start of a conflict in order to paralyse (or at least degrade) an opponent's C4ISR capabilities. China's cyber assets fall under the command of two main departments of the General Staff Department (GSD). Computer network attacks and EW would in theory come under the 4th Department (Electronic Countermeasures), and computer network defence and intelligence gathering comes under the 3rd Department (Signals Intelligence). The 3rd Department is supported by a variety of 'militia units' comprising both military cyber warfare personnel and civilian hackers. In 2011, the PLA said that a much-reported 'Cyber Blue Team' was a body designed to improve the PLA's 'ability to safeguard internet security.'*

Paramilitary — ***660,000 active***

People's Armed Police — ***660,000***

*Internal Security **400,000*** — 14 (mobile) divisions
22 (mobile) independent regiments
some firefighting and garrison units

Border Defence — ***260,000*** 30 divisions HQ
110 (border) regiments
20 (marine)

Equipment by Type
Patrol and Coastal Combatants 154+
PCO 16; **PB/PBF** 138+

China Marine Surveillance — Patrols China's EEZ

Equipment by Type
Patrol and Coastal Combatants 68+
PSO 6; **PCO** 14; **PB/PBF** 48+

Maritime Safety Administration (MSA)
Various tasks including aid to navigation
Equipment By Type
Patrol and Coastal Combatants 207+
PB 207+

Fisheries Law Enforcement Command (FLEC)
Enforces Chinese fishery regulations
Equipment by Type
Patrol and Coastal Combatants 133+
PSO 4; **PCO** 11; **PB/PBF** 118+

Ministry of Public Security

Police — *45 divisions (14 each with 4 regiments, remainder no standard organisation; 1–2 divisions per province)*

Commissars 69,000+

UN Peacekeeping

Observers: Ivory Coast, Cyprus, Democratic Republic of Congo, Gulf of Aden, Lebanon, Liberia, Middle East, South Sudan, Sudan, Western Sahara, Timor-Leste

Missions: Democratic Republic of Congo (1 engineer company; 1 field hospital); **Lebanon** (1 engineer company; 1 field hospital); **Liberia** (1 engineer company; 1 transport company; 1 field hospital); **Sudan** (2 engineer companies; 1 transport company; 1 field hospital)

CHINA – MILITARY REGIONS

Shenyang MR (North East)
Land Forces
(Heilongjiang, Jilin, Liaoning MD)
16th Group Army
(1 armoured div, 2 motorised infantry div, 2 motorised infantry brigade, 1 artillery brigade, 1 AD brigade, 1 engineer regiment)
39th Group Army
(1 armoured div, 1 mechanised infantry div, 1 mechanised infantry brigade, 1 motorised infantry div; 1 artillery brigade, 1 AD brigade, 1 aviation regiment)
40th Group Army
(1 armoured brigade, 2 motorised infantry brigade, 1 artillery brigade, 1 AD brigade, 1engineer regiment)
Other Forces
(1 SF unit; 1 motorised infantry brigade; 1 EW regiment)

Shenyang MRAF
1st Fighter Division
(1 fighter regiment with J-11B; 1 FGA regiment with J-10A; 1 fighter regiment with J-8F)
11th Attack Division
(1 attack regiment with JH-7A; 1 attack regiment with Q-5D)
21st Fighter Division
(1 fighter regiment with J-7E; 1 fighter regiment with J-8H; 1 fighter regiment with J-7H)
30th Fighter Division
(2 fighter regiment with J-7E; 1 fighter regiment (forming) with J-11B)
Other Forces
(1 EW regiment with Y-8CB/G; 1 ISR regiment with JZ-8; 3 training schools with An-30/CJ-6/H-5/HJ-5/JJ-5/K-8/Y-7; 1 (mixed) SAM/ADA brigade; 1 SAM brigade)

Beijing MR (North)
Land Forces
(Beijing, Tianjin Garrison, Inner Mongolia, Hebei, Shanxi MD)
27th Group Army
(1 (OPFOR) armoured brigade, 2 mechanised infantry brigade, 2 motorised infantry brigade, 1 artillery brigade, 1 AD brigade, 1 engineer regiment)
38th Group Army
(1 armoured div, 2 mechanised infantry div, 1 artillery brigade, 1 AD brigade, 1 engineer regiment, 1 aviation regiment)
65th Group Army
(1 armoured div, 1 mechanised infantry div, 1 motorised infantry brigade, 1 artillery brigade, 1 AD brigade, 1 engineer regiment, 1 aviation regiment)
Other Forces
(1 SF unit, 2 (Beijing) guard div; 1 motorised infantry brigade; 1 ADA brigade)

North Sea Fleet Naval Aviation
7th Naval Air Division
(1 training regiment with JL-9, 1 FGA regiment with JH-7A)
Other Forces
(1 bomber regiment with H-5; H-6DU/G; Y-8X; 1 transport regiment with Y-7/Y-8)

Beijing MRAF
7th Fighter Division
(1 fighter regiment with J-11; 1 fighter regiment with J-7G; 1 fighter regiment withJ-7)
15th Fighter/Attack Division
(1 fighter regiment with J-7; 1 attack regiment with Q-5C)
24th Fighter Division
(1 fighter regiment with J-8F; 1 FGA regiment with J-10A)

Other Forces

(1 Flight Test Centre with Su-30, Su-27/J-11, J-8C, J-10, J-7E, JJ-7 (on rotation); 1 training base with J-7B, JJ-7; 2 training schools with CJ-6/JJ-5/K-8; 3 SAM div; 1 (mixed) SAM/ADA div)

Other Forces

34th VIP Transport Division

(1 transport regiment with B-737; CRJ200/700; 1 transport regiment with B-737; Tu-154M; Tu-154M/D; 1 transport regiment with Y-7; 1 (flight test) regiment)

Lanzhou MR (West)

Land Forces

(Ningxia, Shaanxi, Gansu, Qing-hai, Xinjiang, South Xinjiang MD)

21st Group Army

(1 armoured div, 1 motorised infantry div (RRU), 1 artillery brigade, 1 AD brigade, 1 engineer regiment)

47th Group Army

(1 armoured brigade, 1 mechanised infantry brigade, 2 (high altitude) motorised infantry brigade, 1 artillery brigade, 1 AD brigade, 1 engineer regiment)

Xinjiang MD

(1 (high altitude) mechanised div, 2 independent mechanised infantry regiment, 3 (high altitude) motorised div, 1 artillery brigade, 1 AD brigade, 1 engineer regiment, 1 aviation brigade)

Other Forces

(1 SF unit; 1 EW regiment)

Lanzhou MRAF

6th Fighter Division

(1 fighter regiment with J-11; 1 fighter regiment with J-7E; 1 fighter regiment with J-7)

36th Bomber Division

(1 surveillance regiment with Y8H-1; 1 bomber regiment with H-6M; 1 bomber regiment with H-6E)

37th Fighter Division

(1 fighter regiment with J-8H; 1 fighter regiment with J-7G; 1 fighter regiment (forming) with J-11B)

Other Forces

(2 training school with CJ-6, JJ-5; PLAAF Missile Test regiment with JJ-6, J-7B; 1 (mixed) SAM/ADA div; 1 SAM brigade; 4 independent SAM regiment)

Jinan MR (Centre)

Land Forces

(Shandong, Henan MD)

20th Group Army

(1 armoured brigade, 1 mechanised infantry brigade, 1 motorised infantry brigade, 1 artillery brigade, 1 AD brigade, 1 engineer regiment)

26th Group Army

(1 armoured div, 3 motorised infantry brigade, 1 artillery brigade, 1 AD brigade, 1 aviation regiment)

54th Group Army

(1 armoured div, 2 mechanised infantry div (RRU), 1 artillery brigade, 1 AD brigade, 1 aviation regiment)

Other Forces

(1 SF unit; 1 EW regiment)

North Sea Fleet

Coastal defence from DPRK border (Yalu River) to south of Lianyungang (approx 35°10´N); equates to Shenyang, Beijing and Jinan MR, and to seaward; HQ at Qinguardao; support bases at Lushun, Qinguardao. 9 coastal-defence districts

2 SSBATTALION; 3 SSN; 23 SS; 2 DDGHM; 2 DDGM; 2 FFGHM; 2 FFGM; 1 FFGH; 10 FFG; 1 ML; 20 PCFG/PCG; 9 LS; 7 MCMV

North Sea Fleet Naval Aviation

5th Naval Air Division

(1 FGA regiment with JH-7A; 1 fighter regiment with J-8F)

Other Forces

(1 EW/ISR/AEW regiment with Y-8J/JB/W; 1 MP regiment with SH-5; 1 hel regiment with AS365; Ka-28; SA321; Z-9)

Jinan MRAF

5th Attack Division

(1 attack regiment with Q-5E; 1 attack regiment with JH-7A)

12th Fighter Division
(1 fighter regiment with J-8B; 2 fighter regiment with J-7G)
19th Fighter Division
(1 fighter regiment with Su-27SK; 1 fighter regiment with J-7; 1 fighter regiment with J-11B)
Other Forces
(1 ISR regiment with JZ-6; 4 SAM battalion)

Nanjing MR (East)
Land Forces
(Shanghai Garrison, Jiangsu, Zhejiang, Fujian, Jiangxi, Anhui MD)
1st Group Army
(1 armoured brigade, 1 amphibious mechanised div, 1 motorised infantry brigade, 1 artillery div, 1 AD brigade, 1 engineer regiment, 1 aviation regiment);
12th Group Army
(1 armoured div, 3 motorised infantry brigade (1 RRU), 1 artillery brigade, 1 AD brigade, 1 engineer regiment);
31st Group Army
(1 (amphibious) armoured brigade, 2 motorised infantry div (including 1 RRU), 1 motorised infantry brigade, 1 artillery brigade, 1 AD brigade, 1 aviation regiment)
Other Forces
(1 SF unit; 1 SSM brigade)

East Sea Fleet
Coastal defence from south of Lianyungang to Dongshan (approx 35°10´N to 23°30´N); equates to Nanjing Military Region, and to seaward; HQ at Ningbo; support bases at Fujian, Zhoushan, Ningbo. 7 coastal defence districts
16 SS; 4 DDGHM; 14 FFGHM; 12 FFG; 35 PCFG/ PCG; 27 LS; 22 MCMV

East Sea Fleet Naval Aviation
4th Naval Aviation Division
(1 FGA regiment with Su-30Mk2; 1 FGA regiment with J-10AH)
6th Naval Aviation Division
(2 FGA regiment with JH-7; 1 bomber regiment with H-6G)
Other Forces
(1 heliborne regiment with Mi-8; Ka-28; Ka-31)

Nanjing MRAF
3rd Fighter Division
(1 fighter regiment with J-7E; 1 FGA regiment with J-10A; 1 FGA regiment with Su-30MKK)
10th Bomber Division
(2 bomber regiment with H-6A; 1 EW regiment with Y-8CB/G/XZ)
14th Fighter Division
(1 fighter regiment with J-11; 2 fighter regiment with J-7E)
26th Special Mission Division
(1 AEW&C regiment with KJ-200/KJ-2000/Y-8T; 1 CSAR regiment with M-171/Z-8; 1 ISR regiment with JZ-8F)
28th Attack Division
(1 attack regiment with JH-7A; 2 attack regiment with Q-5D)
29th Fighter Division
(1 FGA regiment with Su-30MKK; 1 fighter regiment with J-11; 1 fighter regiment with J-8H)
Other Forces
(1 training school with K-8, JJ-5, CJ-6; 3 SAM brigade; 1 ADA brigade; 2 independent SAM regiment)

Guangzhou MR (South)
Land Forces
(Hubei, Hunan, Guanguardong, Guangxi, Hainan MD)
41st Group Army
(1 armoured brigade, 1 mechanised infantry div (RRU), 1 motorised infantry div, 1 artillery brigade, 1 AD brigade, 1 engineer regiment)
42nd Group Army
(1 armoured brigade, 1 amphibious mechanised div (RRU), 1 motorised infantry div, 1 artillery div, 1 AD brigade, 1 aviation regiment)

Other Forces

(1 SF unit; 1 motorised infantry brigade; 1 (composite) motorised infantry brigade (Composed of units drawn from across the PLA and deployed to Hong Kong on a rotational basis); 1 AD brigade; 1 SSM brigade; 1 EW regiment)

South Sea Fleet

Coastal defence from Dongshan (approx 23°30´N) to VNM border; equates to Guangzhou MR, and to seaward (including Paracel and Spratly Islands); HQ at Zuanjiang; support bases at Yulin, Guangzhou
1 SSBATTALION; 2 SSN; 18 SS; 5 DDGHM; 9 FFGHM; 15 FFG; 40 PCFG/PCG; 1 LPD; 51 LS; 10 MCMV

South Sea Fleet Naval Aviation

8th Naval Aviation Division

(1 FGA regiment with J-11B; 1 bomber regiment with H-6G; 1 fighter regiment with J-7E)

9th Naval Aviation Division

(1 fighter regiment with J-8H, 1 FGA regiment with JH-7A)

Other Forces

(1 transport regiment with Y-7; Y-8; Z-8; Z-8JH/S; Z-9)

Guangzhou MRAF

2nd Fighter Division

(1 fighter regiment with J-7G; 1 FGA regiment with J-10; 1 fighter regiment with J-11)

8th Bomber Division

(1 tanker regiment with H-6U; 1 bomber regiment with H-6H; 1 bomber regiment with H-6K)

9th Fighter Division

(1 FGA regiment with J-10; 1 fighter regiment with J-7; 1 fighter regiment with J-8H)

13th Transport Division

(1 transport regiment with Y-8; 1 transport regiment with Y-7; 1 transport regiment with Il-76MD)

18th Fighter Division

(1 fighter regiment with J-7; 1 FGA regiment with Su-30MKK)

42nd Fighter Division

(2 fighter regiment with J-7)

Other Forces

(1 ISR regiment with JZ-6; 4 SAM Brigade, 1 ADA brigade, 1 independent ADA regiment)

Other Forces

Marines

(2 marine brigade)

15th Airborne Corps

(3 AB div)

Chenguardu MR (South-West)

Land Forces

(Chongqing Garrison, Sichuan, Guizhou, Yunnan, Tibet MD)

13th Group Army

(1 armoured brigade, 1 (high altitude) mechanised infantry div (RRU), 1 motorised infantry div, 1 artillery brigade, 1 AD brigade, 1 engineer regiment, 1 aviation regiment)

14th Group Army

(1 armoured brigade, 1 (jungle) motorised infantry div, 1 motorised infantry div, 1 artillery brigade, 1 AD brigade)

Other Forces

(1 SF unit; 1 (high altitude) mechanised infantry brigade; 2 mountain infantry brigade; 1 EW regiment)

Chenguardu MRAF

4th Transport Division

(2 transport regiment with Y-8; 1 transport regiment with Y-7)

33rd Fighter Division

(1 fighter regiment with J-7E; 1 fighter regiment with J-11)

44th Fighter Division

(1 fighter regiment with J-7; 1 FGA regiment with J-10)

Other Forces

(1 training school with H-5, H)

INDIA

<u>Organisations by Service</u>	
Strategic Forces Command	In charge of all nuclear assets
<u>Forces by Role</u>	2 Missile Groups with SS-150/SS-250/SS-350 *Prithvi;* 1 Missile Group with *Agni I* 1 Missile Group with *Agni II*
<u>Equipment by Type</u>	
Strategic Missiles	**IRBM** 80-100 *Agni I;* 20-25 *Agni-II; Agni III* **SRBM** SS-150 *Prithvi* I/SS-250 *Prithvi* II missiles produced each year; SS-250 *Dhanush* (naval); PJ-10 *Brahmos*. Some Indian Air Force assets (such as *Mirage 2000* H/ *Su-30 MkI*) in strategic role

***Army* 1,130,000**

<u>Forces By Role</u>	
Regional Commands	Northern (Udhampur) Western (Chandimandir) Central (Lucknow) Southern (Pune) Eastern (Kolkata) South Western (Jaipur)
Training Command	ARTRAC (Shimla)
Corps HQ	13; (3 strike corps, 10 holding corps)
Armoured	Three divisions (*each:* 3 armoured brigades; one SP artillery brigade with 1 medium regiment, 2 SP artillery regiments) 8 independent armoured brigades 60 armoured regiments (10 regiments each with 45 T-90S; 35 regiments each with 45 T-72M1; 8 regiments each with 45 T-55; 7 regiments each with 45 *Arjun)*
Mechanised Infantry	25 battalions
Infantry	4 RAPID (Reorganised Army Plains Infantry Divisions) (*each:* one armoured brigade, two mechanised infantry brigades, two infantry brigades) 18 infantry divisions (*each:* one artillery brigade, 3-5 infantry brigades); 8 independent brigades; 14 mountain divisions (*each:* 1+ artillery brigade and 3-4 infantry brigades); 2 independent mountain brigades; 319 battalions
Special Forces / Airborne	1 independent para brigade; 8 Special Forces battalions; 5 airborne battalions
Artillery	3 divisions (*each:* 2 artillery brigade with 3 medium artillery and 1 composite SATA/MRL regiments); 15 independent artillery brigades **Medium artillery** 80 regiments **Self-Propelled medium artillery** 3 regiments **Field artillery** 82 regiments **Self-Propelled field artillery** 3 regiments **Mountain artillery** 51 regiments **Mortar** 10 regiments **MRL** 5 regiments **SSM** 2 regiments; 1 *Agni* regiment; 1 *BrahMos* regiment
Engineers	4 brigades; 56 regiments
Helicopters	14 squadrons

Anti-tank helicopters	5 squadrons
Air Defence Artillery	6 brigades 5 regiments with 320 ZU-23-2 (some Self-Propelled) 30 regiments with 1,920 L40/70 (*each:* 4 Air Defence batteries); 12 SAM regiments; 2 groups (*each:* 2-5 SAM batteries)
Territorial Army	6 Ecological battalions 37 Departmental units (from government ministries) 25 Infantry battalions 20 Air Defence regiments with 1,280 L40/60

Equipment by Type

Tanks	3,233+ 124 *Arjun*; 715 T-55 (being retired); 1,950 T-72M1; 444+ T-90S; (1,100 various models in store)
Reconnaissance	110 BRDM-2 each with AT-4 *Spigot*/AT-5 *Spandrel*; *Ferret* (used for internal security duties along with some indigenously built armoured cars)
AIFV	1,455+ 350+ BMP-1; 980 *Sarath* (BMP-2); 125 BMP-2K APC 649+ APC (W) 157+ OT-62/OT-64; PPV 179: 165 *Casspir*; 14 *Yukthirath* MPV
Artillery	9,682+ **SP** 20+: 130mm 20 M-46 *Catapult*; 152mm 2S19 *Farm* **Towed** 2,970+: 105mm 1,350+: 600+ IFG Mk1/Mk2/Mk3 (being replaced); up to 700 LFG; 50 M-56 122mm 520 D-30; 130mm 600 M-46; (500 in store) 155mm 500: 300 FH-77B; 200 M-46 (upgrade) **MRL** 192: 122mm 150 BM-21/LRAR 214mm 14 *Pinaka*; 300mm 28 9A52 *Smerch* **Mortars** 6,520+ **SP** 120mm E1 **Towed** 6,520+: 81mm 5,000+ E1 120mm 1,500 AM-50/E1 160mm 20 M-58 *Tampella*
Anti-tank	**Missiles** SP 9K111 (AT-4 *Spigot*); 9K113 (AT-5 *Spandrel*) **Man-portable** 9K11 (AT-3 *Sagger*) (being phased out); 9K111 (AT-4 *Spigot*); 9K113 (AT-5 *Spandrel*); *Milan 2*; RCL 84mm *Carl Gustav*; 106mm 3,000+ M40A1 (10 per inf bn)
Helicopters	**MRH** 232: 40 *Dhruv*; 12 *Lancer*; 120 SA315B *Lama* (*Cheetah*); 60 SA316B *Alouette III (Chetak)*
Air Defence	**SAM** 3,500+ **SP** 680+: 180 2K12 *Kub* (SA-6 *Gainful*); 50+ 9K33 *Osa* (SA-8B *Gecko*); 200 9K31 *Strela-1* (SA-9 *Gaskin*); 250; 9K35 *Strela-10* (SA-13 *Gophe*r) **Man-portable** 2,620+: 620 9K32 *Strela-2* (SA-7 *Grail* – being phased out)‡; 2,000+ 9K31 *Igla-1* (SA-16 *Gimlet*) **Guns** 2,395+ **SP** 155+: 23mm 75 ZSU-23-4; ZU-23-2 (truck-mounted); 30mm 20-80 2S6 *Tunguska* **Towed** 2,240+: 20mm *Oerlikon* (reported); 23mm 320 ZU-23-2; 40mm 1,920 L40/70
UAV	**ISR** Medium 26: 14 *Nishant*; 12 *Searcher* Mk I/Mk II
Radar	**Land** 38+: 14 AN/TPQ-37 *Firefinder*; BSR Mk.2; 24 *Cymbeline*; EL/M-2140; M113 A1GE *Green Archer* (mor); **MUFAR**; *Stentor*
Amphibious	2 LCVP
Missiles	**IRBM** 24+: 12 *Agni* I (80-100 msl);12 *Agni-II* (20-25 msl); some Agni-III **SRBM** 30: 30 SS-150 *Prithvi I*/SS-250 *Prithvi II* **LACM** 8–10 PJ-10 *BrahMos*
AEV	BMP-2; FV180
ARV	T-54/T-55; VT-72B; WZT-2; WZT-3

VLB	AM-50; BLG-60; BLG T-72; Kartik; MTU-20; MT-55;*Sarvatra*
MW	910 MCV-2

Navy ***58,350 (including 7,000 Naval Aviation and 1,200 Marine Commandos)***

Forces by Role	
Fleets	Fleet HQ New Delhi Western (Mumbai) Eastern (Vishakhapatnam) Southern (Kochi)
Equipment by Type	
Submarines	**Tactical** 15 **SSN** 1 *Chakra* (RUS *Nerpa*) with 4 single 533mm TT with 3M54 *Klub* (SS-N-27 *Sizzler*) SLCM, 4 single 650mm TT with T-65 HWT; (RUS lease agreement) **SSK** 14 4 *Shishumar* (GER T-209/1500) with 8 single 533mm TT 4 *Sindhughosh* (FSU *Kilo*) with 6 single 533mm TT (of which 2 undergoing phased refit of 3M54 Klub (SS-N-27 *Sizzler*) SLCM) 6 *Sindhughosh* (FSU *Kilo*) with 6 single 533mm TT with 3M54 *Klub* (SS-N-27 *Sizzler*) SLCM
Principal Surface Combatants	21
Aircraft Carrier	**CV** 1; 1 *Viraat* (UK *Hermes*) (capacity 30 *Sea Harrier* FRS Mk1 FGA aircraft each with *Sea Eagle* tactical ASM;7 Ka-27 ASW helicopter/*Sea King* MK42B ASW helicopter)
Destroyers	10 **DDGHM** 6 3 *Delhi* with 4 quad launcher with 3M-24 *Uran* (SS-N-25 *Switchblade*) AShM, 2 single launcher with 3K90 *Uragan* (SA-N-7 *Gadfly*) SAM, 5 single 533mm ASTT, 1 100mm gun, (capacity either 2 *Dhruv* helicopter /Sea King Mk42A ASW helicopter) 3 *Shivalik* with 1 octuple VLS with 3M54 *Klub* (SSN-27 *Sizzler)* ASCM, 1 octuple VLS with *Barak* SAM, 6 single launcher with 3K90 *Uragan* (SA-N-7 *Gadfly*) SAM, 1 76mm gun, (capacity 1 *Sea King* Mk42B ASW helicopter) **DDGM** 5 2 *Rajput* (FSU *Kashin*) with 2 twin launcher with R-15M *Termit* M (SS-N-2C Styx) AShM, 2 twin launcher with M-1 *Volna* (SA-N-1 *Goa*) SAM, 5 single 533mm ASTT, 2 RBU 6000 *Smerch* 2, 1 76mm gun, (capacity 1 Ka-25 *Hormone*/ Ka-28 *Helix* A helicopter) 1 *Rajput* (FSU *Kashin*) with 2 twin launcher with PJ-10 *BrahMos* ASCM, 2 single launcher with R-15M *Termit* M (SS-N-2C *Styx*) AShM, 2 twin launcher with M-1 *Volna* (SA-N-1 *Goa*) SAM, 5 single 533mm ASTT, 2 RBU 6000 *Smerch* 2, 1 76mm gun, (capacity 1 Ka-25 *Hormone*/Ka-28 *Helix* A helicopter) 2 *Rajput* (FSU *Kashin*) with 1 octuple VLS with PJ-10 *BrahMos* ASCM, 2 twin launcher with R-15M *Termit* M (SS-N-2C *Styx*) AShM, 2 octuple VLS with *Barak* SAM. 1 twin launcher with M-1 *Volna* (SA-N-1 Goa) SAM, 5 single 533mm ASTT, 2 RBU 6000 Smerch 2, 1 76mm gun, (capacity 1 Ka-25 *Hormone*/Ka-28 *Helix* A helicopter) **Frigates** 10 **FFGHM** 9 3 *Brahmaputra* with 4 quad launcher with SS-N-25 *Switchblade* AShM, 1 octuple VLS with *Barak* SAM, 2 triple 324mm ASTT, 1 76mm gun, (capacity 2 SA316B *Alouette III (Chetak)/Sea King* Mk42 ASW helicopter) 3 *Godavari* with 4 single launcher with R-15 *Termit* M (SS-N-2D *Styx*) AShM, 1 octuple VLS with *Barak* SAM, 2 triple 324mm ASTT, 1 76mm gun, (capacity 2 SA316B *Alouette III (Chetak)/Sea King* MK42 ASW helicopter) 3 *Talwar* I with 1 octuple VLS with 3M54 *Klub* (SS-N-27 *Sizzler*) AShM, 6

single launcher with 3K90 *Uragan* (SA-N-7 *Gadfly*) SAM, 2 twin 533mm ASTT, 2 RBU 6000 *Smerch* 2, 2 CADS-N-1 *Kashtan* CIWS, 1 100mm gun, (capacity 1 *Dhruv*/Ka-31 *Helix B* AEW helicopter /Ka-28 *Helix A* ASW helicopter)
FFH 1
1 *Nilgiri* with 2 triple 324mm ASTT, 2 twin 114mm gun (capacity 1 SA316B *Alouette III (Chetak)* helicopter / *Sea King* Mk42 ASW helicopter)

Patrol & Coastal Combatants 61

Corvettes 26
FSGM 22
4 *Khukri* with 2 twin launcher with R-15M *Termit* M (SSN- 2C Styx) AShM, 2 twin launcher with 9K32M *Strela*-2M (SA-N-5 *Grail*) SAM, 1 76mm gun, 1 helicopter landing platform (For *Dhruv*/SA316 *Alouette III (Chetak))* 4 *Kora* with 4 quad launcher with 3M24 Uran (SS-N-25 *Switchblade*) AShM, 1 quad launcher with 9K32M *Strela*-2M (SA-N-5 *Grail)* SAM, 1 76mm gun, 1 hel landing platform (For *Dhruv*/SA316 *Alouette III (Chetak))*
12 *Veer* (FSU *Tarantul*) with 4 single launcher with R-15 *Termit* M (SS-N-2D *Styx*) AShM, 2 quad launcher (manual aiming) with 9K32M *Strela*-2M (SA-N-5 *Grail*), 1 76mm gun
2 *Prabal* (mod *Veer*) each with 4 quad launcher (16 eff.) each with 3M24 *Uran* (SS-N-25 Switchblade) AShM, 1 quad launcher (manual aiming) with 9K32M Strela-2M (SA-N-5 *Grail*) SAM, 1 76mm gun
FSM 4
4 *Abhay* (FSU *Pauk II*) with 1 quad launcher (manual aiming) with 9K32M Strela-2M (SA-N-5 *Grail*) SAM, 2 twin 533mm ASTT, 2 RBU 1200, 1 76mm gun
PSOH 6 *Sukanaya* (capacity 2 HAL *Chetak*)
PCC 16: 6 *Trinkat* SDB MK 5; 5 SDB Mk 3; 10 *Car Nicobar*
PBF 8 *Super Dvora*
PB 5: 3 *Plascoa* 1300 (SPB); 2 SDB Mk 3

Mine Warfare 8

MSO 8 *Pondicherry* (FSU *Natya*)

Amphibious 17

LPD 1; *Jalashwa* (US *Austin* Class) (capacity up to 6 support helicopters); either 9 LCM or 4 LCM and 2 LCAC; 5 LCVP; 930 troops)
LS 10
LSM 5 *Kumbhir* (FSU *Polnocny* C) (capacity 5 MBT or 5 APC; 160 troops)
LST 5: 2 *Magar* (capacity 15 MBT or 8 APC or 10 trucks; 500 troops; 3 *Magar* Mod (capacity 11 MBT or 8 APC or 10 trucks; 500 troops)
Landing Craft: **LCU** 6 *Vasco da Gama* MK2 / 3 LC (capacity 2 APC; 120 troops)

Logistics and Support 49

AORH 3: 1 *Aditya* (mod *Deepak*); 2 Deepak; 1 *Jyoti;*
AOL 6
ASR 1
AWT 2
AGOR 1 *Sagardhwani*
AGHS 8 *Sandhayak;*
AGS 1 *Makar*
ATF 1
AP 3 *Nicobar*
AX 4 1 *Krishna* (UK *Leander*) 1 *Tir*; 2 AXS;
YPT 1
YDT 3
YTL/YTM 15

Facilities

Bases Mumbai, Vishakhapatnam, Kochi (Cochin), Karwar (under construction), Chennai (under construction), Kolkata (under construction), Port Blair (Andaman Islands)
Naval airbases at Arakonam and Goa

Naval aviation 7,000

Forces by Role	
Air	HQ (Arakonam)
FGA	1 squadron with *Sea Harrier* FRS MK51 1 squadron with MiG-29K *Fulcrum*
ASW	5 squadrons with Ka-31 *Helix B*; Ka-25 *Hormone*; Ka-28 (Ka-27PL) *Helix A*; *Sea King* MK42A/*Sea King* MK42B; HAL *Chetak* (SA-316B) *Alouette III*
Maritime Reconnaissance	2 squadrons with Il-38 *May*; Tu-142M *Bear F*; Do-228-201; B-2 *Defender*
Search and Rescue (several in SAR role)	1 squadron with *Sea King* MK42C; HAL *Chetak* (SA-316B) *Alouette III*
Transport	1 squadron with HAL-784M
Communications	1 squadron with Do-228 1 squadron with HS-748M (HAL-784M)
Training	2 squadrons with HJT-16 MKI *Kiran*; HJT-16 MKII *Kiran II*; HPT-32 *Deepak*
Transport Helicopter	1 squadron with UH-3H *Sea King*
UAV	1 squadron with *Searcher* Mk II, 4 *Heron*

Equipment by Type	
Aircraft	31 combat capable **Fighter** 11 Mig-29K *Fulcrum* **FGA** 11 *Sea Harrier* FRS MK51 **ASW** 9 5 Il-38 *May*; 4 Tu-142M *Bear* **MP** 14 Do-228-201 **Transport** 37: 17 BN-2 *Islander*, 10 Do-228, 10 HS-748 HAL-784M **Training** 12: 6 HJT-16 MKI, 6 HJT-16 MKII *Kiran II6*
Helicopters	**AEW** 9: 9 KA-31 *Helix B* **SAR** 6: 6 *Sea King* MK42C **MRH** 53: 4 Dhruv; 26 SA316B *Alouette III (Chetak)*; 23SA319 *Alouette III* **Utility** 49+; *Dhruv* ALH, 6 HAL *Chetak* (SA-316B), 25 *Alouette III*; (some in SAR role)
UAV	12: 8 *Searcher* Mk II, 4 *Heron*
Missiles	**ASM**: *Sea Eagle*; KH-35/*Sea Skua* **AAM**: R-550 *Magic 2*/R-550 *Magic* tactical AAM

Marines	1,200; Amphibious 1 brigade; Commando 1 (marine) force *Sagar Prahari Bal* (SPB) newly raised

Command Headquarters

Western	- Mumbai
Southern	- Kochi
Eastern	- Vishakhapatnam
Andaman and Nicobar	- Port Blair (Joint Command)

Air Force 127,000

Regional Air Commands	Western (New Delhi) Central (Allahabad) Southern (Trivandrum) Eastern (Shillong) South Western (Gandhinagar)

Forces by Role	
Fighter	3 squadrons with MiG-29B *Fulcrum*, MiG-29UB *Fulcrum*
FGA	4 squadrons with *Jaguar* IB/IS 8 squadrons with MiG-21bis/*Bison* 4 squadrons with MiG-21M/MF *Fishbed* 6 squadrons with MiG-27ML *Flogger* 7 squadrons with Su-30 MK1 *Flanker* 3 squadrons with M-2000H (M-2000E) *Mirage*

Maritime attack	1 squadron with *Jaguar* S (I) with *Sea Eagle* ASM
AEW/AWACS	1 squadron with IL-76 TD *Phalcon*
Reconnaissance	1 squadron with Gulfstream IV
Transport	7 squadrons with An-32 *Cline* 1 squadron with B-737; B-737BBJ; EMB-145BJ 4 squadrons with Do-228; HS-748 2 squadrons with Il-76 *Candid* 1 squadron with C-130J *Super Hercules*
Tankers	1 squadron with Il-78 *Midas*
Anti-tank helicopters	2 squadrons with Mi-25 *Hind D*/Mi-35 *Hind*
Helicopters	2 squadrons with ALH *Dhruv* 9 squadrons with Mi-8 *Hip* 6 squadrons with MI-17 *Hip H*/ Mi-17 IV 1 squadron with 10 Mi-26 *Halo* 1 squadron with Mi-26 (Halo) 3 squadrons with HAL *Cheetah* (SA-315B) Lama 5 squadrons with HAL *Chetak* (SA-315B)
Training	some squadrons with HJT-16 MKI *Kiran*; HPT-32 *Deepak*; MiG-21; Mig-21bis; Mig-21M/MF; Mig-21FL; Mig—27Ml; Mig-23BN; Jaguar IS/2-IM; *Hawk* Mk132 AJT 56
UAV	5 squadrons with *Searcher* MK II
SAM	25 squadrons with S-123M *Pechora* (SA-3B) *Goa* 6 squadrons with OSA-AK (SA-8B *Gecko*) 10 flt with SA-18 *Gimlet*

Equipment by Type

Aircraft	798 combat aircraft **Fighter** 64: 57 MiG-29 *Fulcrum*; 7 MiG-29UB *Fulcrum*; FGA 698: 14 *Jaguar* IB; 82 *Jaguar* IS; 10 *Jaguar* IM; 31 *MiG-21bis*; 119 MiG-21 *Bison*; 54 MiG-21M *Fishbed*; 16 MiG-21MF *Fishbed*; 40 MiG-21U/UM *Mongol*; 127 MiG-27ML *Flogger* J2; 40 *Mirage* 2000E (2000H) **AEW&C:** 3 IL-76 TD *Phalcon* **Reconnaissance:** 3 *Gulfstream* IV SRA-4 **Tanker:** 6 IL-78 *Midas* **Transport** 217: 24 II-76 Candid; 105 An-32 Cline; 6 B-707; 4 B-737; 20 BAe-748; 51 Do-228; 4 EBM-135BJ; **PAX** 33: 6 B-707; 4 B-737; 3 B-737bBJ; 20 HS-748 **Training** 212: 36 Hawk Mk 132AJT; 120 HJT-16 MKI; 56 HJT-16 MKII Kiran II
Helicopters	**Anti-Tank:** 20 Mi-25 *Hind D*/Mi-35 *Hind* **Support** 210; 0 *Dhruv*; 4 Mi-26 Halo (Hy Tpt); 102 Mi-8, 72 Mi-17 (Mi-8 MT) Hip H; 60 HAL *Cheetah* (SA-315B) *Lama* SA-315; 48 HAL *Chetak* (SA-316B) *Alouette* III
UAV	some *Searcher* MK II
Air Defence	**SAM** S-125 *Pechora* (SA-3B) *Goa* **SP** 9K33 Osa-AK (SA-8B) *Gecko* **Man-portable** 9K310 *Igla-1* (SA-16 *Gimlet*)
Missiles	**ASM** AM-39 *Exocet*; AS-11; AS-11B (ATGW); AS-12 *Kegler*; AS-17 *Krypton*; As-30; AS-7 *Kerry*; *Sea Eagle* **ARM** AS-11; AS-11B (ATGW); AS-12 *Kegler;* AS-17 *Krypton* **AAM** AA-10 *Alamo*; AA-11 *Archer*; AA-12 *Adder*; AA-7 *Apex*; AA-8 *Aphid*; R-550 *Magic*; Super 530D

Coast Guard ***9,550***

(under Director General – Ministry of Defence)

Regional Commands Mumbai, Chennai, Port Blair (11 districts)

Forces by Role

Air	9 squadrons

Equipment by Type

Patrol & Coastal Combatants	63 **PSOH** 9: 2 *Sankalp*; 4 *Samar*; 1 *Samudra*, 2 *Vishwast* **PCO** 7 *Vikram* **PCC** 16: 8 *Priyadarshini*; 1 *Rani Abbakka* (additional vessels in build); 7 *Sarojini-Naidu* **PBF** 8 *Interceptor* **PB** 23: 7 *Jija Bai* (mod) 1; 6 *Tara Bai*; 10 (various) **Amphibious** UCAC 6 *Griffon* 8000
Aircraft	**Transport** 24: 24 Do-228
Helicopters	**Utility SA-316** 17: 17 HAL *Chetak* (SA-316B) *Alouette*
Cyber	*National agencies include the Computer and Emergency Response Team (CERT-In), which has authorised designated individuals to carry out penetration tests against infrastructure. The Defence Information Assurance and Research Agency (DIARA) is mandated to deal with cyber-security related issues of the armed services and defence ministry. All services have their own cyber security policies, and headquarters maintain information security policies. In 2005, the Indian Army raised the Army Cyber Security Establishment and in April 2010 set up the Cyber Security Laboratory at the Military College of Telecommunications Engineering in Mhow (under the Corps of Signals). There is no Indian national cyber security strategy.*

Rashtriya Rifles (Ministry of Defence)	***65,000*** 60 battalions (in 20 Sector HQ)
Paramilitary	***1,300,600***
Assam Rifles	64,000; Ministry of Home Affairs 7 HQ; 42 battalions
Border Security Force	**208,000**; Ministry of Home Affairs. 157+ battalions Small arms, light artillery, some anti-tank weapons **Artillery: Mortars** 942 81 mm **Aircraft**: some transport (air support)
Central Industrial Security Force	94,000 (lightly armed security guards only) Ministry of Home Affairs; Guards public-sector locations
Central Reserve Police Force	230,000 Ministry of Home Affairs Internal security duties, only lightly armed, deployable throughout the country 2 Mahila (women) battalions 125 battalions 13 rapid action force battalions
Defence Security Corps	31,000 (provides security at Defence Ministry sites)
Indo Tibetan Border Police	36,324

Ministry of Home Affairs	Tibetan border security SF/guerrilla warfare and high altitude warfare specialists; 30 battalions
National Security Guards	7,357 Anti-terrorism contingency deployment force, comprising elements of the armed forces, CRPF and Border Security Force
Special Protection Group	3,000
Railway Protection Force	70,000
Shastra Seema Bal	31,554 Guards Indo-Nepal/Bhutan borders
Special Frontier Force	10,000 Mainly ethnic Tibetans
Special Protection Group	3,000 Protection of VVIPs
State Armed Police	450,000 For duty primarily in home state only Some battalions with infantry weapons and equipment 24 (India Reserve Police; Commando-trained) battalions
Reserve organisations	
Civil Defence	500,000 Fully trained in 225 towns in 32 states Some units for NBC defence
Home Guards	487,821 reservists (actual) (515,000 authorised) In all states except Arunachal Pradesh and Kerala; men on lists, no training. Not usually armed in peacetime -weapons held in state armouries. Used for civil defence, rescue and fire-fighting teams in wartime.
Paramilitary special battalions	6 battalions to protect tea plantations in Assam
Foreign Missions	Afghanistan (2 companies for protection for road construction project) Arabian Gulf and Indian Ocean (2 FFG on maritime security operations) Tajikistan (Forward Operating Base) Farkhar
UN Missions	**Observers** (Ivory Coast, Democratic Republic of Congo, Sudan, Timor-Leste, Lebanon, Syria/Israel, Tajikistan) **Peace Keeping** Democratic Republic of Congo (3 mechanised infantry battalions; 1 infantry battalion; 1 helicopter unit; 1 field hospital) Lebanon (1 infantry battalion; 1 field hospital) South Sudan (1 infantry battalion; 1 engineer company; 1 aviation unit; 1 transport company; 1 field hospital)

INDONESIA

***Armed Forces* 302,000**	Army 233,000; Navy 45,000 Air Force 24,000 Paramilitary 280,000 (Terms of service 2 years; Selective conscription authorized) Reserves 400,000

Organisations by Service

Army 233,000

Military Area Commands	**12** Provincial (*KOREM*) and District (*KODIM*) Commands **Kodam Iskandar Muda**, Aceh **Kodam I**/Bukit Barisan, North Sumatra, West Sumatra, Riau and Riau Islands. **Kodam II**/Sriwijaya, South Sumatra, Jambi, Bengkulu, Bangka Belitung and Lampung. **Kodam Jaya**, Jakarta, Bekasi and Tangerang. **Kodam III**/Siliwangi, West Java and Banten. **Kodam IV**/Diponegoro, Central Java and Yogyakarta. **Kodam V**/Brawijaya, East Java. **Kodam VI**/Tanjungpura, Kalimantan island (Borneo). **Kodam VII**/Wirabuana, Gorontalo, and Sulawesi. **Kodam IX**/Udayana, Bali, East Nusa Tenggara and West Nusa Tenggara. **Kodam XVI**/Pattimura, Maluku and North Maluku. **Kodam XVII**/Trikora, West Irian Jaya and Papua.

Forces by Role

Cavalry	8 battalions
Light	2 brigades (6 battalions)
Infantry	60 battalions
Airborne	5 battalions
Field Artillery	10 battalions
Engineers	8 battalions
Aviation / Composite	1 composite aviation squadron
Helicopters	1 squadron
Air Defence	7 battalions

Special Forces Command	**(*KOPASSUS*)** 5,000 **Special Forces**: 3 groups (*total:* 2 commando/parachute units, 1 counter-terrorist unit (Unit 81) 1 training unit, 1 (intelligence) SF unit

Strategic Reserve Command **(*KOSTRAD*)** 40,000

Armoured	2 battalions
Infantry	2 division HQ; 3 brigades (9 battalions); 1 independent brigade
Airborne	3 brigades
Field Artillery	2 regiments (6 battalions)
Air Defence	1 regiments (2 battalions)
Engineers	2 battalions

Equipment by Type

Tanks	Light tanks 350: 275 AMX-13 (being upgraded); 15 PT-76; 60 Scorpion 90
Reconnaissance	**142**: 55 Ferret (13 upgraded); 69 Saladin (16 upgraded); 18 VBL

Armoured Fighting Vehicles	11 BMP-2; **APC** 241: F80 BTR-40; 34 BTR-50PK**;** 22 *Commando Ranger*; 45 FV603 *Saracen*; 60 LAV-150 *Commando*
Artillery	1010: **Towed** 135; 120 M-101; 10 M-56; 155mm 5: 5 FH-2000; **Mortars** 875: 81mm 800; 120mm 75: 75 Brandt
Anti-Tank	**Recoilless** 135: 106mm M-40 45: 45 M-40A1; 90mm 90: M-67 **Rocket launcher** 89mm 700: 700 LRAC
Aircraft	**Transport** 11: 3 DHC-5 *Buffalo*; 6 NC-212 (CASA 212) *Aviocar*; 2 Rockwell *Turbo Commander* 680
Helicopters	**Anti-tank** 2: 6 Mi-35 Hind; **Support** 16 Mi-17 *Hip*; **Utility** 37: 8 Bell 205; 12 NB-412 (Bell 412) *Twin Huey*; 17 NBO-105 (BO-105); **Training** 12 Hughes 300C
Air Defence	**Missiles** 68: 51 Rapier; 17 RBS-70; **Guns Towed** 413: 20mm 121: 121 Rh 202; 40mm 36: 36 L/70; 57mm 256: 256 S-60
ARV	9: 2 AMX-13; 6 AMX-VCI; 3 BREM-2; Stormer; T-54/T-55
VLB	12: 10 AMX-13; Leguan; 2 Stormer

Navy 45,000

Eastern Fleet	HQ located at Surabaya; 13 bases
Western Fleet	HQ located at Teluk Ratai (Jakarta); 10 bases
Commands	Riau (West); Papua (East); Makassar (Central)
Forward Operating Bases	1 Kupang (West Timor); 1 Tahuna (North Sulawesi)

Equipment by Type

Submarines	**Tactical** SSK 2: 2 *Cakra* each with 8 single 533mm TT with 14 SUT HWT
Principal Surface Combatants	11
Frigates	**FFGHM** 7 6 *Ahmad Yani* each with 2 Mk-141 Harpoon quad (8 eff.) each with RGM-84A *Harpoon* tactical SSM, 2 SIMBAD twin manual each with *Mistral* SAM, 2 triple 324mm ASTT (6 eff.) each with Mk 46 LWT, 1 76mm gun, (capacity either 1 HAS-21 *Wasp* ASW helicopter or 1 NBo-105 (Bo-105) utility helicopter) 1 *Hajar Dewantara* (training) with 2 twin (4 eff.) each with MM-38 *Exocet* tactical SSM, 2 single 533mm ASTT each with SUT HWT, (capacity 1 NBo-105 (Bo-105) utility helicopter) **FFGM** 4 4 *Sigma* each with 2 *Tetral* quad (8 eff.) *Mistral* SAM, each with 4 MM-40 *Exocet* Block II tactical SSM, 2 triple 324mm ASTT (6 eff.) 176mm gun, 1 helicopter landing platform
Patrol & Coastal Combatants	67
Corvettes	19 **FSGH** 1 1 *Nala* with 2 twin launcher with MM-38 Exocet AShM, 1 twin 375mm A/S mor, 1 120mm gun (capacity 1 lt helicopter) **FSG** 2 2 *Fatahillah* each with 2 twin launcher with MM-38 *Exocet* tactical SSM, 2 B515 ILAS-3/Triple 324mm ASTT (2-6 eff.) with 12 A 244 /Mk 46, 1 2 tube *Bofors* 375mm (2 eff.) 1 120 mm gun **FSM** 16 16 *Kapitan Patimurat* each with 4x1 400mm ASTT, Twin each with SA-N-5 *Grail* SAM 2 RBU 6000 *Smerch* 2(24 eff.), 1 57mm gun **PCFG** 4 *Mandau* each with 4 MM-38 Exocet tactical SSM **PCT** 4 Singa each with 2 Single 533mm TT **PCC** 4 *Kakap*; 4 *Todak* **PBG** 1 *Clurit* with 2 twin launcher with C-705 AShM **PB** 33 *1 Cucut*; 13 *Kobra*; 1 *Krait*; 8 *Sibarau*; 10 *Viper*

Mine Warfare	11: **MCC 2:** 2 *Pulau Rengat*; **MSC 8:** 8 *Palau Rote*
Amphibious	**LPD 5:** 1 *Dr Soeharso* (Ex-*Tanjung Dalpele*; capacity 2 LCU/LCVP; 13 tanks; 500 troops); 4 *Makassar* (capacity 2 LCU / LCVP; 13 tank; 500 troops; 2 AS332L *Super Puma* **LST 26**: 1 *Teluk Amboina* (capacity 16 tanks; 200 troops); 12 *Teluk Gilimanuk*; 7 *Teluk Langsa* (capacity 16 tanks; 200 troops); 6 *Teluk Semangka* (capacity 17 tanks); 200 troops) **Craft**: 54 LCU
Logistics and Support	32 **AGF 1** *Multatuli* **AORLH** 1 Arun (UK Rover) **AOT 3**: 2 *Khobi*; 1 *Sorong* **AKSL** 4 **AGOR** 7: 5 *Baruna Jaya*; 1 *Jalanidhi*; 1 *Burujulsad* **AGHS** 1 **ATF** 2 **AXS** 2 (Training) **AP** 8: 1 *Tanjung Kampani* (troop transport); 1 *Tanjung Nusanive* (troop transport); 5 *Karang Pilang* (troop transport) **YTM** 3

***Marines* 20,000**

Forces by Role

Special Forces	1 battalion
Marine	1st marine corps group (total: 3 marine battalions) based Surabaya 1 independent marine corps group (total: 2 battalions) based at Jakarta 1 marine brigade (total; 3 battalions) based at Teluk, Rata and Sumatra
Combat Support	1 Air Defence artillery regiment

Equipment by Type

Tanks	**Light tanks 55**: 55 PT-76
Reconnaissance	21 BRDM; **AIFV 34:** 24 AMX-10P; 10 AMX-10 PAC 90 APC APC (W), BTR, BTR-50 100: 100 BTR-50P
Artillery	62 **Towed** 50 105mm LG1 22: 22 LG1 MK II 122mm 28+: 28+ M-38 M-1938 **MRL** 140mm 12: 12 BM-14 **Mortars:** some 81mm
Air Defence	150 L/60/L/70 40mm, S-60 57mm

Naval Aviation 1,000

Aircraft	**MP** 23: 3 CN-235 MPA; 14 N-22B *Searchmaster* B; 6 N-22SL *Searchmaster* L **Transport** 15; CN-235 1: 1 CN-235M; DHC-5 *Buffalo* 2, NC-212 (CASA 212) 4: 4 CASA 212-200 *Aviocar*; PA-34 *Seneca* 4; Rockwell *Commander* 100 4 **Training** 6: 6 PA-38 *Tomahawk*
Helicopters	**ASW 9**: 9 HAS-1 *Wasp* **Support** AS-332 6: 6 NAS-322L (AS-332L) *Super Puma* **Utility 28;** EC-120 9: 9 EC-120B *Colibri*; NB-412 (Bell 412) *Twin Huey* 2 NBO-105 (BO-105) 17
Facilities	**Bases** at Belawan,Vayapura and Ujung Pandang

***Air Force* 24,000**

Operational Commands	2: East and West; plus Training Command (only 45% of aircraft operational)

Forces By Role	
Fighter	1 squadron with F-5E *Tiger* II; F-5F *Tiger* II 1 squadron with F-16A/B *Fighting Falcon*
FGA	1 squadron with Su-30 MKI *Flanker* (multi-role); Su-27SK *Flanker* 1 squadron with A-4E *Skyhawk*; TA-4H *Skyhawk*; TA-4J *Skyhawk* 2 squadrons with *Hawk* MK109; *Hawk* MK209
Reconnaissance	1 flight with OV-10F *Bronco*
Maritime Reconnaissance	1 squadron with B-737-200
Transport	5 squadrons with B-707; C-130B *Hercules*; C-130H *Hercules*; C-130H-30 *Hercules*; NC-212 (CASA 212) *Aviocar*; CN-235-110; *Cessna* 401; *Cessna* 402; F-27-400M Troopship; F-28-1000; F-28-3000; L-100-30; SC.7 3M *Skyvan* (survey); 4 *Cessna* 207 *Stationair*
Tanker	1 squadron with KC-130B *Hercules*
Training	3 squadrons with *Cessna* 172; AS-202 *Bravo*; *Hawk* MK53*; 7 KT-1B; SF-260M/SF-260W *Warrior*; T-34C *Turbo Mentor*; T-41D *Mescalero*
Helicopter	2 squadrons with S-58T; NAS-322L (AS-332L) *Super Puma* (VIP/CSAR); NAS-330 (SA-330) *Puma* (1 NAS-330SM VIP); EC-120B *Colibri*

Equipment By Type	
Aircraft	69 combat capable
Fighter	22: F-5 12: 8 F-5E *Tiger* II; 4 F-5F *Tiger* II; Su-30 2: 2 Su-30 MKI *Flanker* (multirole) F-16 10: 7 F-16A *Fighting Falcon*; 3 F-16B *Fighting Falcon* Su-27 2: 3 Su-27SK *Flanker* (AD)
Fighter Ground Attack	10: A-4 11: 11 A-4E *Skyhawk*; *Hawk* MK109 7; *Hawk* MK209 (FGA/fighter) 28; FAC OV-10 12: 12 OV-10F *Bronco*
Maritime Patrol	5: 3 B-737-200; 2 CN-235M-220 MPA
Tanker	KC-130 2: 2 KC-130B *Hercules*
Transport	40: B-707 1; B-737 3: 3 B-737-200; C-130 18: 8 C-130B *Hercules*; 4 C-130H *Hercules*; 6 C-130H-30 *Hercules*; CN-235 10: 10 CN-235-110: *Cessna* 401 5; *Cessna* 402 2; F-27 6: 6 F-27-400M Troopship; F-28 3: 1 F-28-1000; 2 F-28-3000; L-100 3: 3 L-100-30; NC-212 (CASA 212) *Aviocar*: 10; SC.7 3M *Skyvan*: 1 (survey) **Utility** 6: 2 *Cessna* 172; 4 *Cessna* 207 *Stationair* **Training 101:** AS-202 *Bravo* 39; *Hawk* MK53 7 KT-1 7: 7 KT-1B SF-260 19: 19 SF-260M/SF-260W *Warrior* T-34 20: 20 T-34C *Turbo Mentor* T-41 6: 6 T-41D *Mescalero* TA-4 3: 1 TA-4H *Skyhawk*; 2 TA-4J *Skyhawk*
Helicopters	**SAR** 10: 10 S-58T **Support** 16; AS-332 5: 5 NAS-322L (AS-332L) *Super Puma* (VIP/CSAR) NAS-330 (SA-330) *Puma* 11 (1 NAS-330SM VIP) **Utility** EC-120 12: 12 EC-120B *Colibri*
Missiles	**Tactical ASM**; AGM-65: some AGM-65G *Maverick* AAM AIM-9: AIM-9P *Sidewinder*

Special Forces (Paskhasau)

Special Operations	3 (*PASKHASAU*) Wings (total: 6 Special Operations squadrons); 4 independent companies; Reserves some 6,000 (to age 45)

Organisations by Service	
Army	3,200 (including 300 recalled reserves)

Forces by Role	
Infantry	7 battalion
Special Operations	1 company
Artillery	1 battery
Engineers	1 battalion

<u>**Equipment by Type**</u>

Artillery — **16: Towed** 85mm: 4 25-pdr (ceremonial); **Mortar**12 81mm

Helicopters — **Support** 1 AS-355 *Ecureuil*; **Utility** 1 AS-365 *Dauphin* 2

Navy **300**

<u>**Equipment By Type**</u>

Patrol and Coastal Combatants **9:** PCC 3: 3 *Kula*; PCI 6: 2 *Levuka*; 4 *Vai*

Logistics and Support **2:** AGHS (SVY) 1: 1 *Tovutu*; **Training** 1: 1 *Cagi Donu* (Presidential Yacht)

Facilities Bases located at Walu Bay and Viti 1 (Training)

Paramilitary ***280,000 active***

Naval Auxiliary Service

Patrol & Coastal Combatants **71**: **PCC** *65 Kal Kangen*; **PCI** 6 *Carpentaria*

Customs

Patrol & Coastal Combatants **PCC** 55

Marine Police

Patrol and Coastal Combatants **85: PSOH** 2 *Bisma*; **PCC** 14 *Bango*; **PC** 37; **PBI** 32

Police 280,000 (including 14,000 Police mobile brigade (BRIMOB) organised in 56 companies, including Counter terrorism unit (Gegana)
APC (W) 34 *Tactica*
Aircraft Transport 5: 2 *Beech* 18; 2 NC-212 (CASA-212) *Aviocar*; 1 Rockwell *Turbo Commander* 680
Helicopters Utility 22: 3 Bell 206 JetRanger; 19 NBO-105 (BO-105)

KPLP (Coast and Seaward Defence Command)
Responsible to Military Sea Communications Agency

Patrol & Coastal Combatants **11**; **PSO** 2 *Arda Dedali* ; **PCC** 9: 4 *Golok* (SAR); *5 Kujang*

Logistics and Support **ABU** 1 *Jadayat*

Reserve Organizations **Kamra People's Security** 40,000 (report for 3 weeks; basic training each year; part time police auxiliary)

UN Missions **Observers:** Georgia, Lebanon, Liberia, Nepal, Sudan, Democratic Republic of Congo, Haiti
Units: Democratic Republic of Congo (1 engineer coy), Lebanon (1 infantry battalion, 1 MP company, 1 field hospital)

MALAYSIA

***Armed Forces* 109,000**	(Army 80,000; Navy 14,000; Air Force 15,000) Paramilitary 24,600 Reserves 51,600 (Army 50,000, 1,000 Air Force 600) Paramilitary 244,700
***Army* 80,000**	
<u>Forces by Role</u>	2 Military Regions 1 HQ Field Command 4 Area Commands (divisions)
Armour	5 regiments
Mechanised infantry	1 brigade; (3 battalions; 1 engineer squadron); 5 regiments
Infantry	9 brigades; 36 battalions
Special Forces	1 brigade (3 Special Forces battalions)
Airborne	1 brigade (Rapid Deployment Force) (1 light tank squadron, 1 light artillery regiment, 3 airborne battalions)
Artillery	2 medium regiments 7 field artillery regiments 1 MRL regiment 1 locating regiment
Air Defence	3 regiments
Engineers	5 regiments
Helicopters	1 squadron
Reserves	
Territorial Army	Police 5 (highway safety) battalions Infantry 16 regiments
<u>Equipment by Type</u>	
Tanks	48 *Twardy* PT-91M **Light Tanks** 21 *Scorpion* 90
Reconnaissance	296: **AML** 130: 130 AML-60/AML-90; 92 *Ferret* (60 mod) 162 SIBMAS **AIFV** 44: 31 ACV 300 *Adnan (Bushmaster)*; 13 ACV300 *Andan*
APC	784 **APC (T)** 262: 149 ACV300 *Adnan* (including variants); 13 ACV300 *Adnan* AGL **APC (W)** 522: 32 *Anoa*; 300 *Condor* (including variants); 150 LAV-150 *Commando*/V-100 *Commando*; 30 M3 *Panhard*; 10 VBL
Artillery	454 **Towed** 134 105mm 130: 130 Model 56 pack howitzer 155mm 34: 12 FH-70; 22 G-5 **MRL** 36: 36 *ASTROS II* (equipped with 127mm SS-30) **Mortar** 254: 254 81mm SP 14: 4 K281A1; 10 ACV300-S; 120mm **SP** 8 ACV-S 81mm: 232
Anti-tank	**Man-portable** 60+: 18 AT-7 9K115 *Saxhorn*; 24 *Eryx*; 18 *Baktar Shikan* (HJ-8); METIS-M; C90-CRRB **RCL** 260: 106mm 24: 24 M-40; **84mm** 236: 236 *Carl Gustav* **RL 73mm** 584: 584 RPG-7 *Knout*

Amphibious Craft	**LCA** 165: 165 *Damen* assault craft 540 (capacity 10 troops)
Helicopters	**Utility** 20: 9 SA-316B *Alouette III;* 11 A109
Air Defence	**SAM** 15 *Jernas (Rapier 2000)* **MANPAD** 48+: *Anza;* SA-18 *Grouse (Igla); Starburst;* **Guns** 60: **35mm**: 24 GDF-005 towed **40mm**: 36 L40/70 towed

Navy 14,000

Forces by Role	Naval HQ located at Lumut with 3 Regional Commands Regional Command 1 Kuantan – East Coast Regional Command 2 Kota Kinabalu – Borneo Regional Command 3 Langkawi - West Coast
Equipment by Type	
Submarines	**Tactical SSK** 2 *Tunku Abdul Rahman* (*Scorpene*) each with 6 single 533mm torpedo tubes
Principal Surface Combatants	10
Frigates	10 **FFGHM** 2 2 *Lekiu* (capacity 1 *Super Lynx* utility helicopter) each with 2 B515 *ILAS-3* triple 324mm each with 1 *Sting Ray* LWT, 2 quad (8 eff.) each with 1 MM-40 *Exocet* tactical SSM, 1 *Sea Wolf* VLS with 16 *Sea Wolf* SAM **FFG** 2 2 *Kasturi* each with 2 twin (4 eff.) each with MM-38 Exocet tactical SSM, 1 Mle 54 *Creusot-Loire* 375mm Bofors (6 eff.), 1 100 mm gun, 1 helicopter landing platform **FF** 6 6 *Kedah* (MEKO) each fitted for MM-40 *Exocet* tactical SSM; each fitted for RAM CIWS and 1 76mm gun (Further 4 of class in build)
Patrol & Coastal Combatants	37
Corvettes	**FSGM** 4 4 *Laksamana* each with 2 B515 *ILAS-3* triple 324mm each with A244 LWT, 1 quad (4 effective) with 12 *Aspide* SAM, 3 twin (6 effective) each with 1 Mk 2 *Otomat* SSM, 1 76mm gun **PCFG** 4 4 *Perdana* (*Combattante* II) each with 2 single with 1 MM-38 *Exocet* tactical SSM, 1 57mm gun **PBG** 4 4 *Handalan* (Spica-M) each with 2 twin (4 eff.) each with MM-38 *Exocet* tactical SSM, 157mm gun **PBF** 17 *Tempur* **PB** 8: 6 *Jerong* (Lurssen 45); 2 *Sri Perlis*
Mine Warfare	**MCO** 4: 4 *Mahamiru*
Amphibious	**LS LST** 1: 1 *Sri Inderapura* (capacity 10 tanks; 400 troops) **AGHS (Survey) /AGOS** 2 **Amphibious Craft** 115: 115 LCM/LCU
Logistics and Support	**13: AOR** 2; **AG** 1; **ARS** 2; **ATG** 2; **Training AX** 1; **AXS** 1; **AP** 2

Naval Aviation 160

Helicopters	**ASW** 6 Super *Lynx;* **Utility** AS-555 *Fennec*
Special Forces	
Naval commandos	1 unit

Air Force 15,000

Air Operational HQ	2 Air Divisions Training and Logistics Command Integrated Area Defence Systems HQ

Forces by Role

Fighter	2 squadrons with MiG-29N (MiG-29) *Fulcrum*
FGA	1 squadron with F/A-18D *Hornet*
	1 squadron with *Hawk* MK108; *Hawk* MK208
FGA / Reconnaissance	1 squadron with F-5E *Tiger II*/F-5F *Tiger II*; RF-5E *Tigereye*
Maritime	1 squadron with Beech 200T *Maritime Patrol*
Special Forces	1 (Air Force Commando) unit (air field defence)
Transport	2 squadrons with KC-130H *Hercules* (tanker); C-130H *Hercules*; C-130H-30 *Hercules*; Cessna 402B (2 modified for aerial survey)
	1 (VIP) squadron with B-737-700 BBJ; BD700 *Global Express*; F-28 *Fellowship*; *Falcon* 900; 2 S-61N; S-70A *Black Hawk*; A-109
	1 squadron with 6 CN-235
Training	1 training school with MB-339A; MD3-160; PC-7 MK II *Turbo Trainer*; SA-316 *Alouette III*
Helicopters	4 (Transport/SAR) squadrons with S-61A-4 *Nuri*; S-61N; S-70A *Black Hawk*
SAM	1 squadron with *Starburst*

Equipment by Type

Aircraft	67 combat capable
Fighter	21: 8 F-5F *Tiger II; 11* MiG-29N *Fulcrum*
FGA	26: 8 F/A-18D *Hornet; 8 Hawk* MK108; 12 Su-30 MKM
Reconnaissance	2: 2 RF-5E *Tigereye*
Maritime	4: 4 Beech 200T *Maritime Patrol*
Tanker	2 KC-130H *Hercules*
Transport	32; 1 *Airbus* A319CT; 1 B-737-700 BBJ BD700 *Global Express* 1 C-130 12: 4 C-130H *Hercules*; 8 C-130H-30 *Hercules* CN-235 6 *Cessna* 402 9: 9 *Cessna* 402B (2 modified for aerial survey) F-28 *Fellowship; 1 Falcon* 900
Training	101: 15 *Hawk* MK208; 8 MB-339AB; 8 MB-339C; 20 MD3-160 2 MiG-29U *Fulcrum;* 30 PC-7/18; 30 PC-7 MK II *Turbo Trainer*
Helicopters	**ASW** 20 S-61A-4 *Nuri*
	Support 8: 4 S-61N; 4 S-70A *Black Hawk*
	Utility 9: 1 A-109; 8 SA-316 *Alouette III*
UAV	**Tactical** 3 *Eagle;* 150; *Aludra*
Air Defence	**SAM MANPAD**: *Starburst*
	Missile Tactical: ASM: AGM-65 *Maverick;* AGM-84D *Harpoon* **AAM**: AA-10 *Alamo*; AA-11 *Archer*; AIM-7 *Sparrow*; AIM-9 *Sidewinder*

***Paramilitary* 24,600**

Police-General Operations Force 18,000

Forces

Police	5 brigade HQ; 2 (Aboriginal) battalions; 19 battalions; 4 independent companies
Special Operations	1 battalion

Equipment by Type

Reconnaissance	100 S52 *Shorland* **APC (W)** 170: 140 AT105 *Saxon*; 30 SB-301

Malaysian Maritime Enforcement Agency (MMEA) 4,500

1 MMEA HQ Putrajaya with designated control for the Malaysian Maritime Zone, which is divided into 5 Maritime Regions (Northern Peninsula; Southern Peninsular; Eastern Peninsular; Sarawak; Sabah) and sub-divided into a further 19 Maritime Districts

<u>Equipment by Type</u>

Patrol & Coastal Combatants	**66**
	PSO 2 *Langkawi* with 1 hel landing platform
	PB 64: 15 *Gagah*; 4 *Malawali*; 2 *Nusa*; 1 *Peninjau*; 5 *Ramunia*; 2 *Rhu*; 4 *Semilang*; 15 *Sipadan* (*ex-Kris/Sabah*); 16 (various)
Logistics and Support	**AX** 1 *Marlin*
Aircraft	**MP 2** *Bombardier* 415MP
Helicopters	**MRH** 3 *Dauphin* AS-365

Marine Police *2,100*

<u>Equipment by Type</u>

Patrol & Coastal Combatants	**132**
	PBF 12 6 *Sangitan*; 6 *Stan Patrol*
	PB/PBR120
Logistics and Support	8: 2 AT; 6 Transport
Facilities	Bases at Kuala Kemaman, Penang, Tampoi and Sandakan

Police Air Unit

Aircraft	**Transport** 7: 7 PC-6 *Turbo-Porter* **Utility** 10: 4 Cessna 206; 6 Cessna 208 *Caravan I*
Helicopters	**Support AS-355** 2: 2 AS-355F *Ecureuil II* **Utility BELL 206** 1: 1 Bell 206L *Long Ranger*

Area Security Units (R) *3,500*

Auxiliary General Operations Force

Paramilitary	89 units
Border Scouts (R)	1,200 in Sabah and Sarawak
People's Volunteer Corps	240,000 reservists (some 17,500 armed)

Customs Service

Patrol & Coastal Combatants	**23**
	PBF 10
	PB 13

UN Missions	**Observers:** Democratic Republic of Congo, Lebanon, Liberia, Nepal, South Sudan, Sudan, Timor-Leste, Western Sahara
	Units: Lebanon (1 infantry battalion)

MYANMAR

Armed Forces *406,000 (Tatmadaw)*

Army *375,000*

Organization	
Regional Commands	12 (Myitkina, Lashio, Mandalay, Taunggyi, Monywa, Sittwe, Kengtung, Toungoo, Hainggyi, Yangon, Mawlamyine, Myeik); 4 regional operational commands, 14 military operational commands, 34 tactical op commands (TDC) Military Operations Command 1 (Kyaukme, Shan State) Military Operations Command 2 (Loilem, Shan State) Military Operations Command 3 (Mogaung, Kachin State) Military Operations Command 4 (Phugyi, Yangon) Military Operations Command 5 (Ann, Rakhine State) Military Operations Command 6 (Pyinmana, Mandalay) Military Operations Command 7 (Phekon, Shan State) Military Operations Command 8 (Dawei, Tanintharyi) Military Operations Command 9 (Kyauktaw, Rakhine) Military Operations Command 10 (Kyeekone, Mandalay) Military Operations Command 12 (Kawkareik, Kayin) Military Operations Command 13 (Bokpyin, Tanintharyi) Military Operations Command 14 (Mongsat, Shan State) Military Operations Command 15 (Buthidaung, Rakhine) Military Operations Command 16 (Theinni, Shan State) Military Operations Command 17 (Mongpan, Shan State) Military Operations Command 18 (Hehalsai, Shan State) Military Operations Command 19 (Ye, Mon State) Military Operations Command 20 (Kawthaung) Military Operations Command 21 (Bhamo, Kachin State)
Forces by Role	
Light Infantry	10 division headquarters; 100 infantry battalions
Armour	10 battalions
Airborne	1 brigade
Infantry	337 battalions (regional commands)
Artillery	22 artillery regiments; 37 independent companies
Engineers	6 combat engineers battalions; 54 field engineers battalions
Air Defence	7 battalions
Intelligence	40 companies
Signals	45 battalions
Equipment by Type	
Tanks	280 **MBT** 150: 50 T-72; 100 Type-63/Type-69 **Light Tanks** 105 Type-63 **Reconnaissance** 115: 45 *Ferret*; 40 Humber *Pig*; 30 *Mazda*
Armoured Personnel Carriers	361 **APC (T)** 331 Type-85; 55 Type-90 **APC (W)** 20 *Hino* **PPV** 10 MPV
Artillery	404 **SP** 155mm 30 B-52 NORA

	Towed 264: 105mm 132: 36 M-56; 96 M101; 122mm 100 D-30; 130mm 16 M-46; 140mm; 155mm 16 *Soltam* MRL 30+: 107mm 30 Type-63; 122mm BM-21 (reported); 240mm M-1991 (reported)
	MRL 80+: 107mm 30 Type-63; 122mm BM-21
	Mortars 80+: 82mm Type-53 (M-37); 120mm 80+: 80 Soltam; Type-53 (M-1943)
	Anti-Tank 1,000**:** RCL 1,000+; 106mm M-40A1; 84mm 1,000 Carl Gustav 73mm; RPG-7 *Knout*
	Guns 60; 57mm 6-Pdr; 76.2mm 17 pdr
Air Defence	**Missiles** HN-5 *Hong Nu/Red Cherry*; SA-16 *Gimlet*
	Guns 46: **SP** 57mm 12 Type-80; **Towed** 34: 37mm 25 Type-74; 40mm 10 M-1

Navy 16,000

Forces by Role

Headquarters located at Yangon

Organization

Regional Operations Commands 5 (Sittwe, Hainggyi Island, Yangon, Mawlamyine, Katan Island)

Irrawaddy Regional Command (Yangon)
Thanhklyet Soon Naval Base
Bassein Naval Base
Coco Island Base (Naval Radar Unit)
Danyawaddy Regional Command (Sittwe)
Kyaukpyu Naval Base
Thandwe (Sandoway) Naval Base
Panmawaddy Regional Command (Hainggyi Island)
Mawyawaddy Regional Command (Moulmein)
Tanintharyi Regional Command (Mergui)
Zadetkyi Island Naval Base
Mali (Tavoy) Naval Base
Palai Island Naval Base
Kadan Naval Base
Sakanthit Naval Base
Lambi Naval Base
Pearl Island Naval Base
Zadetkale Naval Base (Radar Unit)

Equipment by Type

Principal Surface Combatants 1	
Frigates	**FFG** 1 *Aung Zeya* (reported) with 2 twin launcher with C-802 AShM, 1 76mm gun
Patrol & Coastal Combatants	99
Corvettes	**FS** 3 *Anawrahta* each with 1 76mm gun
	PCG 6 H*ouxin* each with 2 twin (4 eff.) each with 4 C-801 (CSS-N-4) *Sardine* tactical SSM
	PBG 4 *Myanmar* each with 2 twin (4 eff.) each with 4 C-801 (CSS-N-4) *Sardine* tactical SSM
	PCO 2 *Indaw*
	PCC 9 *Hainan*
	PB 18: 3 PB-90; 6 PGM 401; 3 Swift; 2 *Nawara*t; 9 Y 302; 1 *Imp* Y-301
Amphibious Craft	18: 8 **LCU**; 10 **LCM**
Logistics and Support 18	**AOT** 1; **AK** 1; **AKSL** 5: **AGS** 2; **ABU** 1; **TPT** 9
Facilities	Bases located at Bassein, Mergui, Moulmein, Seikyi, Rangoon (Monkey Point), Sittwe
Naval Infantry	1 battalion

Air Force 15,000

Organization

Operational Commands	4 (Nampong, Mandalay, Hanthawady, Myike)
Training Command	1
Airbases	Pathein, Mingaladon, Myitkyinar, Myike, Namsang, Taungoo, Meikhtila, Shante (training and operations), Homemalin

Forces by Role

Fighter	3 squadrons with MiG-29B *Fulcrum*; F-7 (Mig-21F *Fishbed* C; FT-7 (JJ-7) Mongol A*: MiG-29 *UB Fulcrum**
FGA	2 squadrons with A-5M (Q-5II) *Fantan*
CCT	2 squadrons with G-4 *Super Galeb*; PC-7 *Turbo Trainer*; PC-9
Transport	1 squadron with An-12 *Cub*; F-27 *Friendship*; FH-227; PC-6A *Turbo Porter*/ PC-6B *Turbo Porter*
Training/Liaison	1 Squadron with Ce-550 *Citation II*; Cessna 180 *Skywagon*; K-8
Helicopters	4 squadrons with PZL W-3 *Sokol* Mi-17 (Mi-8MT) *Hip H*; PZL Mi-2 *Hoplite*; Bell 205; Bell 206 *Jet Ranger*; SA-316 *Alouette III*

Equipment by Type	136 combat capable aircraft
Fighter	69: *8 MiG-29B Fulcrum; 50 F-7 Airguard*
FGA	22 A-5M (Q-5II) Fantan
Transport	15: 2 An-12 *Cub*; 1 Ce-550 *Citation II*; 3 F-27 *Friendship*; 4 FH-227; 5 PC-6A *Turbo Porter* / PC-6B *Turbo Porter*
Utility	4 Cessna 180 *Skywagon*
Training	57: 10 FT-7 (JJ-7) Mongol A: 12 G-4 Super Galeb; 12 K-8; 2 MiG-29UB *Fulcrum*; 12 PC-7 *Tourbo Trainer*; 9 PC-9
Helicopters	**Support** 39: 10 PZL W-3 *Sokol*; 11 Mi-17 (Mi-8 MT) *Hip H**; 18 PZL Mi-2 *Hoplite* **Utility** 27: 12 Bell 205; 6 Bell *Jet Ranger*; 9 SA-316 *Alouette III*

Paramilitary 107,250

People's Police Force 72,000

People's Militia 35,000

People's Pearl and Fishery Ministry 250

Patrol & Coastal Combatants	11 **PCC** 3 *Indaw* **PCI** 8: *Carpentaria*; 3 *Swift*

PENTAGON'S SOUTH ASIA DEFENCE AND STRATEGIC YEAR BOOK

NEPAL

Army *95,750*

Forces by Role

Army	6 Division HQ; 1 (valley) command
Infantry	16 brigades (*total:* 63 infantry battalions; 32 independent companies
Special Forces	1 brigade (1 AB battalion, 1 mechanised battalion, 1 independent Special Forces battalion)
Rangers	1 battalion
Artillery	1 brigade (4 artillery regiments)
Air Defence	2 AD regiments; 4 independent AD companies
Engineers	5 engineer battalions
Royal Guards	1 MP battalion

Equipment By Type

Reconnaissance	40: 40 *Ferret*
Armoured Personnel Carriers	**APC (W)** 40: 40 *Casspir*
Artillery	109 **Towed** 39 75 mm 6 pack; 94 mm; 5 3.7 inch (mountain training), 105 mm 28; 8 L-118 Light Gun; 14 pack how **Mortars** 70+: 81 mm, 120 mm
Air Defence	**Guns** 32+; 14.5 mm Towed, ZPU 30: Type-56 (ZPU-4) 37 mm (PRC) 40 mm 2 L/60

Air Wing *320*

Aircraft	**Transport** 5: 1 BAe-748; 2 M-28 *SkyTruck*; 2BN2T *Islander*
Helicopters	**MRH** 9: 1 *Dhruv*; 2 *Lancer*; 3 Mi-17-1V *Hip H*; 1 SA315B *Lama* (*Cheetah*); 2 SA316B *Alouette III* **Transport** 3 Medium 1 SA330J Super *Puma Light* 2 AS350B2/B3 *Ecureuil*

Paramilitary *62,000*

Armed Police Force *Ministry of Home Affairs*	**15,000**
Police Force	**47,000**
UN Missions	**Observers:** Chad, Ivory Coast, Democratic Republic of Congo, Haiti, Liberia, Lebanon, Sierra Leone, South Sudan, Sudan, Timor-Leste **Units: Congo** (1 mechanised infantry battalion, 1 engineer company); **Haiti** (2 infantry battalions); **Lebanon** (1 infantry battalion); **Liberia** 1 MP platoon

PAKISTAN

Army 550,000

Strategic Assets	**National Command Authority** for control of nuclear weapons. It has two committees—Employment Control; and Development Control. The Strategic Plans Division (SPD) acts as the secretariat and formulates nuclear policy, strategy and doctrine, and strategic plans for deployment and employment.

Army Strategic Forces Command 12,000-15,000

Equipment by Type	
Strategic Missiles	60 **MRBM** 30 *Ghauri-I Hatf-V; Ghauri-II Hatf-VA; Shaheen-II Hatf-VI* 2; *Babur* **SRBM** 30 *Ghaznavi;* 50 *Hatf-III; Shaheen-I Hatf-IV; Hatf-VII;* **LACM** some *Babur Hatf-VIII*
Forces by Role	
Army	9 corps headquarters (Mangla, Multan, Lahore, Karachi, Rawalpindi, Peshawar, Quetta, Gujranwala, Bahawalpur) Northern Areas Command (Gilgit)
Armoured	2 divisions; 7 (independent) brigades
Mechanised	2 mechanised infantry divisions; 1 (independent) mechanised brigade
Infantry	18 divisions; 1 (area) command; 5 (independent) brigades
Special Forces	1 group (3 Special Forces battalions)
Artillery	9 (corps) brigades; 5 independent brigades
Engineers	7 brigades
Aviation	1 (VIP) squadron; 5 (composite) squadrons
Helicopters	10 squadrons
Air Defence	1 command; 3 Air Defence groups (8 Air Defence battalions)
Equipment by Type	
Tanks	2,411+: 265 MBT 2000 *Al-Khalid*; 320 T-80UD; 51 T-54/T-55; 1,100 Type-59; 400 Type-69; 275+ Type-85; (270 M48A5 in store)
Armoured Personnel Carriers	1,320 **APC (T)** 1,200: 1,100 M113; 100 Type 63 **APC (W)** 120 BTR-70/BTR-80
Artillery	4,607+ **SP** 510: 155mm 450: 150 M109/M109A2; 300 M109A5 203mm 60 M110/M110A2 **Towed** 1,659: 105mm 329: 216 M101; 113 M-56; 122mm 570: 80 D-30 (PRC); 490 Type-54 M-1938; 130mm 410Type-59-I; 155mm 322: 144 M114; 148 M198; 30 *Panter* 203mm 28 M115 **MRL** 88+ 107mm Type 81; 122mm 52+: 52 Azar (Type-83); some KRL-122 300mm 36 A100 **Mortars** 2,350+: 81mm; 120mm AM-50; M-61
Anti Tank	**SP** M901 TOW **Man-portable** 11,100: 10,500 HJ-8/TOW; 600 9K119 *Refleks* (AT-11 *Sniper*) **RCL** 75mm Type-52; 106mm M40A1 **RL** 89mm M20 **Guns** 85mm 200 Type-56 (D-44)
Aircraft	**ISR** 30 Cessna O-1E *Bird Dog*

	Transport Light 14: 1 Beech 200 *King Air*; 1 Beech 350 *King Air*; 3 Cessna 208B; 1 Cessna 421; 1 Cessna 550 *Citation*; 1 Cessna 560 *Citation*; 2 *Turbo Commander* 690; 4 Y-12(II)
	Training 90 Saab 91 *Safir* (50 obs; 40 liaison)
Helicopters	**Anti-tank** 42: 25 AH-1F *Cobra* with TOW; 16 AH-1S *Cobra*; 1 Mi-24 *Hind*
	MRH 114+: 10 AS550 *Fennec*; 6 AW139; 26 *Bell* 412EP *Twin Huey*; 40+ Mi-17 *Hip H*; 12 *SA315B Lama*; 20 SA319 *Alouette III*
	Transport 59 Medium 36: 31 SA330 *Puma* ; 4 Mi-171; 1 Mi-172
	Light 23: 5 Bell 205 (*UH-1H Iroquois*); 5 Bell 205A-1 (AB-205A-1); 13 Bell 206B *Jet Ranger II*
	Training 22: 12 Bell 47G; 10 Hughes 300C
UAV	**ISR** Light *Bravo; Jasoos; Vector*
Air Defence	**SAM**
	SP some M113 with RBS-70
	Man-portable 2,990+: 2,500 Mk1/Mk2; 60 FIM-92A Stinger; HN-5A; 230 Mistral; 200 RBS-70
	Guns Towed 1,934: 14.5mm 981; 35mm 248 GDF-002/GDF-005 (with 134 *Skyguard* radar units); 37mm 310 Type-55 (M 1939)/ Type-65; 40mm 50 L/60; 57mm 144 Type-59 (S-60); 85mm 200 Type-72 (M-1939) KS-12
Radar	**Land** AN/TPQ-36 *Firefinder* (arty, mor); RASIT (veh, arty); SLC-2
Missiles	**Strategic**
	MRBM up to 25 *Ghauri/Ghauri II (Hatf-5)*; some *Shaheen-2 (Haft-6* - in test)
	SRBM 50 *Ghaznavi (Hatf-3* - PRC M-11); up to 10 *Shaheen-1 (Hatf-4)*;
	LACM some *Babur (Hatf-7* - in development)
	Tactical • SRBM 105+: *105 Hatf-1*; some *Abdali (Hatf-2)*;
ARV	117+: 65 Type 653; *Al Hadeed*; 52 M88A1; T-54/T-55
VLB	M47M; M48/60
MW	*Aardvark* Mk II

***Navy* 22,000 (including 1,400 Marines and 2,000 Maritime Security Agency)**

Equipment by Type	
Submarines	8
	SSK 5: 2 *Hashmat* (French *Agosta* 70) each with 4 x1 533 mm ASTT each with 20+ F17P HWT/UGM- 84 *Harpoon* tactical USGW; 3 *Khalid* (French *Agosta* 90B) each with 1x533 mm ASTT each with SM-39 *Exocet* tactical USGW
	SSI 3: 3 MG110 SSI each with 2 single 533mm TT
Principal Surface Combatants	
Frigates	10
	FFGHM 3
	3 *Sword (PRC Type 054)* with 2 quad launcher with YJ-83 AShM, 1 octuple launcher with HQ-7 SAM, 2 triple 324mm ASTT with Mk 46 LWT, 1 76mm gun, (capacity 1 Z-9C *Haitun* helicopter)
	FFGH 4
	4 *Tariq* (UK *Amazon*) (capacity 1 *Lynx* Utility Helicopter) each with 2 single each with TP 45 LWT,2 Mk-141 *Harpoon* twin each with 1 RGM-84D *Harpoon* tactical SSM, 1 114 mm gun
	FFHM 2
	2 *Tariq* (capacity 1 *Lynx* Utility Helicopter) (D184, D186) each with 2 triple 324 mm ASTT (6 effective) each with Mk 46 LWT, 1 sextuple (6 effective) with LY-60 (*Aspide*) SAM, 1 114 mm gun;
	FFH 1
	1 *Alamgir* (US *Oliver Hazard Perry*) with 2 triple 24mm ASTT with Mk46 LWT, 1 76mm gun
Patrol & Coastal Combatants	12
	PBFG 2 *Zarrar* each with 4 single each with RGM-84 *Harpoon* AShM

	PBG 4: 2 *Jalalat* II with 2 twin launcher with C-802 (CSS-N-8 *Saccade*) AShM 2 *Jurrat* with 2 twin launcher with C-802 (CSS-N-8 *Saccade*) AShM **PBF 4**: 2 *Kaan* 15 **PB** 2: 1 *Larkana*; 1 *Rajshahi*
Mine Warfare	3: 3 *Munsif* (French *Eridan*)
Amphibious	**Landing Craft** • UCAC 4 *Griffon* 2000
Logistics and Support	11 **AORH** 2 1 *Fuqing* with 1 SA-319 Alouette III utility helicopter 1 *Moawin* with 1 Sea King MK45 ASW helicopter **AOT** 3: 1 *Attock*; 2 *Gwadar* **AGS** 1 *Behr Paima* **YTM** 4

<u>Facilities</u>

Bases	Karachi; Ormara; Gwadar
Marines	**1,400**
Commando	1 group
Naval aviation	Aircraft 7 combat capable **ASW** 9: 3 *Atlantic*, 4 P-3C *Orion* **MP** 6: F-27 MK 200MPA **Transport** 1 Hawker 850XP
Helicopters	**ASW** 12: 5 *Sea King Mk45* ASW; 7 Z-9C *Haitun* **Utility** 4; 4 SA-319B *Alouette III*
Missiles Anti-ship	AM-39 *Exocet*

Air Force ***70,000***

Regional Commands	Northern (Peshawar) Central (Sargodha) Southern (Faisalabad)

<u>Forces By Role</u>

Fighter	1 squadron with *Mirage* IIIEP/OD (*Mirage* IIID) 1 squadron with F-16A *Fighting Falcon*/F-16B 3 squadrons with F-7PG/ FT-7PG *Airguard* 2 squadrons with F-7PG/F-7P *Skybolt*
Fighter Ground Attack	2 squadrons with JF-17 *Thunder* (FC-1) 1 squadron with F-16C/D Block 52 *Fighting Falcon* 3 squadrons with *Mirage* 5 (5PA)
ASW	1 squadron with Mirage 5PA2/5PA3 with AM-39 *Exocet* AShM
AEW&C	1 squadron with Saab 2000/Saab 2000 *Erieye*
ELINT / ECM	1 squadron with *Falcon* 20F
SAR	6 squadrons with SA-316 *Alouette III* 1 squadron with Mi-171 (SAR/Liaison)
Tanker	1 squadron with Il-78 *Midas*
Transport	1 squadron with C-130/C-130B *Hercules* 1 VIP squadron with B-707; Cessna 560XL *Citation Excel*; CN-235M-220; F-27-200 Friendship; Falcon 20E; Gulfstream IVSP 1 (communications) squadron with EMB-500 *Phenom* 100; Y-12 (II)
Training	2 OCU squadrons with F-7P/FT-7P *Skybolt* 1 OCU squadron with *Mirage III/Mirage 5* 1 OCU squadron with F-16A/B *Fighting Falcon* 1 squadron with FT-5 1 squadron with K-8 *Karakoram* 2 squadrons with MFI-17 2 squadrons with T-37C *Tweet*

Surface to Air Missiles — 1 battery with CSA-1 (SA-2) *Guideline*; 9K310 *Igla-1* (SA-16 *Gimlet*)
6 batteries each with 24 *Crotale*

Equipment by Type

Aircraft — 453 combat capable

Fighter — 223: 29 FC-1/JF-17 *Thunder*; 50 *Mirage* III EP; 54 F-7PG (F-7 MG) *Airguard*; 75 F-7P *Skybolt*; 46 F-16A/F-16B *Fighting Falcon*; 12 F-16 C/D; (18 F-16CD; 12F-16 C6F-16D .

Fighter Ground Attack — 170: 12 F-16C Block 52 *Fighting Falcon*; 6 F-16D Block 52 *Fighting Falcon*; 29+ JF-17 *Thunder* (FC-1 - 150+ on order); 7 *Mirage IIID (Mirage IIIOD)*; 63 *Mirage IIIE* (IIIEP); 40 *Mirage 5* (5PA)/5PA2; 3 *Mirage 5D* (5DPA)/5DPA2; 10 *Mirage 5PA3* (ASuW)

ISR — 10 *Mirage* IIIRP (Mirage IIIR)

ELINT / ECM — 2 Da-20 *Falcon*; 4 ZDK-03 AWACS

AEW&C — 3: 2 Saab 2000 *Erieye* (2 more on order); 1 ZDK-03

Tanker — 4 Il-78 Midas

Transport — 34
Medium 16: 5 C-130B *Hercules*; 10 C-130/E *Hercules;* 1 L-100-20 **Light** 13: 1 Cessna 560XL *Citation Excel;* 4 CN-235M-220; 4 EMB-500 *Phenom* 100; 1 F-27- 200 *Friendship*; 2 Y-12 (II)
PAX 5: 1 B-707; 1 *Falcon 20E*; 2 *Gulfstream* IVSP; 1 Saab 2000

Training — 139: 39 K-8 Karakorum; 80 MFI-17B Mushshak; 20 T-37C Tweet

Helicopters — 19; 4 Mi-171, 15 SA-316 *Alouette III*

Missiles — 150
Towed: 144 *Crotale*; 6 CSA-1 (SA-2) *Guideline*
MANPAD: SA-16 *Gimlet*

Radar - Land — 51+: 6 **AR-1** (AD radar low level); *Condor* (AD radar high level); FPS-89/100 (AD radar high level);
MPDR 45: 45 MPDR 45/MPDR 60/MPDR 90 (AD radar low level);
TPS-43G (AD radar high level)**Type 514** (AD radar high level)

Anti-Ship Missiles — AGM-65 *Maverick*; AM-39 *Exocet*

Air-to-Air Missiles — AIM-9L *Sidewinder*/AIM-9P *Sidewinder*; R-Darter Super 530

Unmanned Aerial Vehicle — **MQ-1** Predator; ***Baaz***; ***Ababeel***

Facilities — 4 Radar air control sectors
7 Radar control and reporting station

Paramilitary *304,000 active*

Coast Guard

Patrol & Coastal Combatants — 5; **PB** 1; **PBF** 4

Miscellaneous Boats/Craft — 23

Frontier Corps — 65,000 under Ministry of Interior (Balochistan and Khyber Pakhtunkhwa)

Forces By Role

Armoured reconnaissance — 1 independent squadrons

Paramilitary — 11 regiments (*total:* 40 paramilitary battalions)

Equipment By Type

APC — **APC (W)** 45: 45 UR-416

Maritime Security Agency — 2,000

Principal Surface Combatants

Destroyers — **DD** 1: 1 *Nazim* (US *Gearing*) with 2 triple 324mm TT, 1 twin 127mm gun

Patrol & Coast Combatants	10 **PCO** 4 *Barkat* **PB** 6: 2 *Subquat* (PRC Shanghai); 1 *Sadaqat* (ex-PRC Huangfen) ; 3 (various)

***National Guard* 185,000**

Janbaz Force
Mujahid Force
National Cadet Corps
Women Guards

Northern Light Infantry Paramilitary	12,000 3 battalions
Pakistan Rangers	40,000 (Ministry of Interior)
UN Missions	**Observers:** Ivory Coast, Democratic Republic of Congo, Liberia, Sudan, Timor Leste, Western Sahara **Units**: **Ivory Coast** (1 Infantry Battalion; 1 Engineer Company; 1 Transport Company); **Democratic Republic of Congo** (3 Mechanised Infantry Battalions; 1 Infantry Battalion); **Liberia** (3 Infantry Battalions; 3 Engineer Companies; 1 Field Hospital); **Sudan** (1 Engineer Company)

SINGAPORE

Armed Forces *72,500*	(**Army** 50,000; **Navy** 9,000; **Air Force** 13,500) **Paramilitary** 93,800
	Reserves 312,500 (Army 300,000 5,000 Air 7,500) Paramilitary 44,000

Army 15,000; *35,000 conscripts (total 50,000)*

Forces by Role	
	1 Rapid Deployment division (1 infantry brigade, 1 amphibious brigade (3 amphibious battalions), 1 air mobile brigade) 1 division (mixed active/reserve formations) 3 Combined Arms division (each: 2 infantry brigades (each: 3 infantry battalions), 1 armoured brigade, 1 reconnaissance battalion, 2 artillery battalions, 1 AD battalion, 1 engineer battalion)
Reconnaissance	4 battalions
Infantry	8 battalions
Commando	1 battalion
Artillery	4 battalions
Engineer	4 battalions
Intelligence	1 battalion
Reserves	9 infantry brigades included in mixed active/inactive reserve formations listed above; 1 operational reserve division with an additional infantry brigade; People's Defence Force Commands with 12 infantry battalions
	Mechanised — 6 battalions Reconnaissance/light armoured — 6 battalions Infantry — 56 battalions Commando — 1 battalion Artillery — 12 battalions Engineer — 8 battalions
Equipment by Type	
Tanks	96: **MBT** 100 *Tempest (Centurion)*; 96 *Leopard*; 80-100 **Light tanks** 350 AMX-13 SM1
Reconnaissance	22 AMX-10 PAC 90
AIFV	**372:** 22 AMX-10 P 90; 100 AV-81 *Terrex*; 250 IFV-25; M-113A1/M-113A2 (some with 40mm AGL, some with 25mm gun)
APC	1,695: **APC (T)** 1,400+: 250 IFV-40/50; 700+ M113A1/M113A2; 400+ ATTC Bronco **APC (W)** 280: 250 LAV-150 Commando/V-200 Commando; 30 V-100 Commando PPV 15 *Maxx Pro Dash*
Artillery	798 **SP** 155mm 54 SSPH-1 *Primus* **Towed** 88: 105mm (37 LG1 in store); 155mm 88: 18 FH-2000; 18 Pegasus; 52 FH-88 **MRL** 227mm 18 HIMARS **Mortars** 638+ **SP** 90+ 81mm; 120mm 90: 40 on *Bronco*; 50 on M113 **Towed** 548 81mm 500 120mm 36 M-65 160mm 12 M-58 *Tampella*
Anti-tank	**Missile Man-portable** 60: 30 *Milan*; 30 *Spike* MR **RCL** 290: 84mm 200 Carl Gustav; 106mm 90 M40A1 **RL** 67mm *Armbrust*

Air Defence	**SAM** 75+
	SP *Mistral*; RBS-70; 9K38 *Igla* (SA-18 *Grouse*) (on V-200/M-113)
	Man-portable *Mistral*; RBS-70; 9K38 *Igla* (SA-18 *Grouse*)
	Guns 34
	SP 20mm GAI-C01
	Towed 34 20mm GAI-C01; 35mm 34 GDF (with 25 Super-Fledermaus fire control radar)
UAV	**ISR** Light Skylark
RADAR	**Land** AN/TPQ-36 *Firefinder*; AN/TPQ-37 *Firefinder* (arty, mor); 3 *ARTHUR* (arty)
AEV	80: 18 CET; 54 FV180; 8 M728
ARV	*Bionix; Bueffel*; LAV-150; LAV-300
VLB	*Bionix*; LAB 30; *Leguan*; M2; M3; 12 M60
MW	910-MCV-2; *Trailblazer*

Facilities

Training camps	3 (including infantry, artillery and armoured) located in Taiwan (Republic of China), 1 (artillery, combat engineers) located in Thailand; 1 located in Brunei

***Navy* 3,000**; *1,000 conscript; 5,000 active reservists (total 9,000)*

Equipment by Type

Submarines	**Tactical SSK** 6:
	3 *Challenger* each with 4 single 533mm TT
	1 *Challenger* (trg role) with 4 single 533mm TT
	2 Archer (SWE *Västergötland* class) (AIP fitted) with 6 single 533mm TT for *WASS Black Shark* LWT
Principal Surface Combatants	6
Frigates	**FFGHM** 6 *Formidable* each with 8 RGM-84 *Harpoon* SSM, 2 octuple (32 eff.) VLS with *Aster* 15 SAM, 1 76mm gun, (capacity for 1 S-70B *Sea Hawk*)
Patrol & Coastal Combatants	35
	Corvettes FSGM 6: 6 *Victory* each with 2 triple ASTT (6 effective), 2 octuple (16 effective) each with 1 *Barak* SAM, 2+ Mk 140 *Harpoon* quad (8 effective) each with 1 RGM-84C *Harpoon* tactical SSM, 1 76mm gun
	PCO 11: 6 *Fearless* each with 2 *Sadral* sextuple each with *Mistral* SAM 5 *Fearless* each with 2 *Sadral* sextuple each with *Mistral* SAM, 1 76mm gun
	PBF 6
	PBI 12
Mine Warfare	**MHC** 4: 4 *Bedok*
Amphibious	**LPD**: 4 *Endurance* (capacity 350 troops; 18 MBTs; 4 LCVP; 2 hel) (with hel deck) each with 2 Twin (4 effective) each with *Mistral* SAM, 1 76mm gun
	Landing Craft 34 LCU; LCU 100 LCVP
Logistics and Support	2
	AR 1 *Swift Review*
	Training 1

Facilities	**Bases** located at Changi and Tuas (Jurong)

Air Force *13,500; 3,000 conscript; 7,500 reservists (total 21,000)*

Forces by Role

Commands	5
	Air Defence and Operations Command (includes Air Operations Control Group, Air Defence Group, and Air Surveillance and Control Group) **Unmanned Aerial Vehicle (UAV) Command; Participation Command** (includes Helicopter Group and Tactical Air Support Group; Coordinators

airlift, close air support and maritime air surveillance, and also raises, trains and sustains RSAF helicopters, divisional ground based air-defence systems and tactical support elements)
Air Combat Command (includes Fighter Group and Transport Group)
Air Power Generation Command (controls air base support units including Field Defence squadrons).

Fighter Ground Attack 2 squadrons with F-5S *Tiger II*; 9 F-5T *Tiger II* (secondary GA role); 3 squadrons with F-16C *Fighting Falcon*/F-16D *Fighting Falcon*
1 squadron with F-155 G *Eagle*

Reconnaissance 1 squadron with 8 RF-5S *Tiger*

Reconnaissance /transport 1 squadron with 4 KC-130B *Hercules* (tanker/transport); 1 KC-130H *Hercules*; 5 C-130H *Hercules* (2 Elint); 1 squadron with 9 F-50 *Maritime Enforcer* (4 transport, 5 MR)

Airborne Early Warning 1 squadron with 4 E-2C *Hawkeye*

Tanker 1 squadron with 4 KC-135R *Stratotanker*

Training 1 squadron with F-16C/D at Luke AFB, AZ; AH-64D *Apache* located at Marana, (AZ), US-47D *Chinook* located at Grand Prairie, (TX)US; F-15 at Mountain Home (ID), US on F-15E, and then F-15SG 1 squadron with A-4 SU Super *Skyhawk*; TA-4SU *Super Skyhawk*; 1 squadron with PC-21

Helicopters 1 squadron with AB-205A (Bell 205A); UH-1H *Iroquois*;
1 squadron with CH-47SD *Super D Chinook*;
2 squadrons with AS-332M *Super Puma* (including SAR); AS-532UL *Cougar*;
2 squadrons with AH-64D *Apache*; AS-550A2 *Fennec*/AS-550C2 *Fennec*

Unarmed Aerial Vehicles 2 squadrons with *Searcher MkII*
1 squadron with *Hermes 450* (Staffed by personnel from all three services)

<u>**Equipment by Type**</u>

Aircraft 148 combat capable

Fighter 37: F-5 37: 28 F-5S *Tiger II*; 9 F-5T *Tiger II* (GA role)

Fighter Ground Attack 84: 24 F-15SG Eagle; 20 F-16C Fighting Falcon; 40 F-16D Fighting Falcon

Anti-tank 14: 4 A-4SU *Super Skyhawk*; 4 A-4SU; 10 TA-4SU *Super Skyhawk*; 4 A-4SU

Reconnaissance 8 RF-5S *Tiger*

Maritime Reconnaissance 9 F-50 *Maritime Enforcer* (4 transport, 5 MR)

Airborne Early Warning 4 G550-AEW

Tanker 5; 1 KC-130B *Hercules* (tanker/transport); 4 KC-135R *Stratotanker*

Transport 9; 5 C-130H *Hercules* (2 Elint); 4 F-50

Training 19 PC-21

Helicopters **Anti-tank** 19 AH-64D *Apache*
ASW 6 S-70B *Sea Hawk*
Support: 40: 18 AS-332M *Super Puma* (including 5 SAR)**;** 10 CH-47SD *Super D Chinook;*
Utility 54: 12 AS-532UL *Cougar;* 6 AB-205A (Bell 205A); 24 UH-1H *Iroquois*

UAV some *Hermes* 450; 40 *Searcher* MK II

Missiles **Tactical: ASM**; AGM-45 *Shrike; Hellfire*; AGM-65B/G *Maverick*; AGM-84 *Harpoon*; AM-39 *Exocet*
AAM: AIM-120C *AMRAAM* in store (US); AIM-7P *Sparrow*; AIM-9N *Sidewinder*AIM-9P *Sidewinde*r

Air Defence Group

<u>**Forces by Role**</u>

Air Defence 1 ADA squadron with *Oerlikon*
1 AD squadron with MIM-23 HAWK
1 AD squadron with *Rapier-Blindfire*

<u>**Equipment by Type**</u>

Missiles **Tactical ASM**: AGM-45 *Shrike* AGM-65; AGM-65B *Maverick*; AGM-65G *Maverick*; AGM-84 *Harpoon*; AAM AIM-120; AIM-120C *AMRAAM* in store (US)
AIM: AIM-7P *Sparrow;* AIM-9N *Sidewinder*/AIM-9P *Sidewinder*

Air Force Systems Bde

Forces by Role

AIR DEFENCE
1 AD squadron with radar (mobile)
1 AD squadron with LORADS

Divisional Air Def Arty Bde
Attached to army divs

Forces by Role

Air Defence
1 AD battalion with *Mistral*
1 AD battalion with 9K38 *Igla* (SA-18 *Grouse*)
3 AD battalion with RBS-70

Equipment by Type
SAM 36+
Towed *Mistral*; RBS-70
Man-portable 9K38 *Igla (SA-18 Grouse)*

Paramilitary *75,100 active*

Civil Defence Force *1,600 regulars, 3,200 conscripts, 23,000 reservists; 54,000+ volunteers; 1 construction brigade (2,500 conscripts)*

Singapore Police Force *8,500; 3,500 conscript; 21,000 reservists (total 33,000)*

Singapore Gurkha contingent *1,500* (6 companies)

Cyber
The Singapore Ministry of Defence has long identified the potential damage that could be caused by cyber attacks, with this concern perhaps more acute following its adoption of the Integrated Knowledge-based Command and Control (IKC2) doctrine, designed to aid the transition of Singapore's Armed Forces to a 'third generation' force. Meanwhile, Singapore established the Singapore Infocomm Technology Security Authority (SITSA) on 1 October 2009, as a division within the Internal Security Department of the Ministry of Home Affairs (MHA). Its main responsibilities will be dealing with cyber terrorism and cyber espionage, as well as operational IT security development.

Deployment Overseas

Australia
Air Force: 230 personnel
Aircraft: Training 27: 27 S-211
Helicopters: 12 AS-332 *Super Puma* Spt/AS-532 *Cougar* Utility
Facilities: School - 1 with 12 AS-332 *Super Puma* Spt/AS-532 *Cougar* utility (flying training) located at Oakey, 1 with 27 S-211 training aircraft (flying training) located at Pearce

Brunei
Air Force: 500 personnel; 1 helicopter detachment with 5 UH-1H *Iroquois*
Facilities: School - 1 (training)

France
Air Force: 200 personnel; some training squadron with 6 A-4SU *Super Skyhawk*; 10 TA-4SU *Super Skyhawk*

Taiwan (Republic of China)
Army: Training camp - 3 (including infantry, artillery and armoured)

Thailand
Army: Training camp - 1 (Artillery, combat engineers)

United States
Air Force: Aircraft • FGA 24: 12 F-16C *Fighting Falcon*/F-16D *Fighting Falcon* on lease located at Cannon AFB, (NM), US; 12 on lease located at Luke AFB, (AZ), US
Helicopters: Anti-tank AH-64: some AH-64D *Apache* located at Marana, (AZ); **Support: CH-47** 6+: 6+ CH-47D *Chinook* located at Grand Prairie, (TX)

United States Navy
Support facility located at Singapore USPACOM: 1 logistic support squadron located at Singapore

SRI LANKA

***Army* 117,900**

Forces by Role	
Divisional HQ	9
Armoured	3 regiments
Armoured Reconnaissance	3 regiments (battalions)
Air Mobile	1 brigade
Infantry	33 brigades
Special Forces	1 independent brigade
Commando	1 brigade
Field Artillery	3 (1 light, 1 MRL battery and 1 medium regiment)
Field Engineers	4 regiments
Signals	5 regiments

Equipment By Type	
Tanks	**MBT** 62: 62 T-55AM2/T-55A
Reconnaissance	15: 15 *Saladin*
AIFV	**BMP** 62: 13 BMP-1; 49 BMP-2;-
	APC (T) Type-85; 182 BTR-80
	APC (W) 31 *Buffel*; 21 FV603 *Saracen*; 105 *Unicorn*; 25 BTR-80/ BTR-80A
Artillery	908
	Towed 96: 122 mm; 130 mm 30 Type-59-I; 152 mm 46 Type-66 (D- 20)
	MRL 28; 122mm RM-70 *Dana*; 6 KRL-122
	Mortars 784: 520 81 mm; 209 82 mm; 55 120 mm M-43
Anti-tank	**RCL** 40; 10 105 mm M-65; 30 106 mm M-40;
	Guns 8 85 mm Type-56 (D-44)
UAV	1: 1 *Seeker*
Air Defence	**Guns Towed** 27; 24 **40 mm** L/40; 3 **94 mm**; 3 3.7 in
Radar	**Land** 2: 2 AN/TPQ-36 *Firefinder* (artillery)
ARV	16 VT-55
VLB	2 MT-55

***Navy* 15,000**

Forces by Role	
Headquarters	Colombo

Equipment by Type	
Patrol & Coastal Combatants	139
	PSOH 1 *Sayura* (IND *Vigraha*)
	PCG 2 *Nandimithra* (ISR *Sa'ar* 4) with 3 single launcher with 1 GII Gabriel II AShM, 1 76mm gun
	PCO 3: 1 *Reliance*; 2 *Sagara* (IND *Vikram*)
	PCC 1 *Jayesagara*
	PBF 87: 26 *Colombo*; 3 *Dvora*; 3 *Killer* (ROK); 6 *Shaldag*; 14 *Super Dvora* (Mk1/ II/III); 3 *Simonneau*; 5 *Trinity Marine*; 27 *Wave Rider*
	PB 18: 4 *Cheverton*; 2 *Prathapa* (PRC mod *Haizhui*); 3 *Ranajaya* (PRC *Haizhui*); 1 *Ranarisi* (PRC mod *Shanghai* II); 5 *Weeraya* (PRC *Shanghai* II); 3 (various)
	PBR 27
Amphibious	**Landing Ships • LSM** 1 *Yuhai* (capacity 2 tanks; 250 troops)
	Landing Craft 8
	LCU 2 *Yunnan*

	LCM 2
	LCP 3 *Hansaya*
	UCAC 1 M 10 (capacity 56 troops)
Logistics and Support	**2: 1 Transport;** 1 **Training**
Facilities	
Bases	Northern Command located at Kankesanthurai
	Southern Command located at Galle
	North Central Command located at Medawachiya
	HQ and Western Command located at Colombo
	Main base and Eastern Command located at Trincomalee

Air Force *28,000*

Forces by Role	
Fighter	1 squadron with *Chengdu* F-7BS/GS, FT-7
Fighter Ground Attack	1 squadron with MiG-27M *Flogger J2*; FT-7 (JJ-7) *Mongol A*, F-7M; FT-5 (MiG-17U) *Fresco*; MiG-23UB *Flogger C* (conversion trg);
	1 squadron with *Kfir* C-2; 2 *Kfir* C-7/*Kfir* TC-2
	1squadron with K-8 *Karakorum*
Transport	1 squadron with An-32B *Cline*; BAe-748;
	1 squadron with Beech 200 *Super King Air*; C-130K *Hercules*; Cessna 421C *Golden Eagle*; Y-12; Cessna 150; Bell 412 *Twin Huey* (VIP)
Anti-tank Helicopters	1 squadron with Mi-24V *Hind E*;
Training	1 squadron with PT-6 (CJ-6); K-8; SF-260TP
Utility Helicopters	1 squadron with MI-17 (Mi-8) *Hip H*;
	1 squadron with Bell 206 *Jet Ranger*
	1 (VIP) squadron with Mi-35P *Hind*; Bell 212
ISR UAV	1 squadron with *Blue Horizon*-2
	1 squadron with *Searcher II*
Equipment by Type	
Aircraft	31 combat capable
	Fighter 8: 3 F-7BS; 4 F-7GS; 1 FT-7
	FGA 16: 4 *Kfir* C-2; 2 *Kfir* C-7; MiG-27 4: 4 MiG-27M *Flogger J2*, 3 F-7M;
	Transport 23; 5 An-32B *Cline*; BAe-748 2 Beech 200 *Super King Air* 1; 2 C-130K *Hercules;* 6 Cessna 421C *Golden Eagle*;Y-12
	Training 14: 7 K-8 *Karakorum*; 7 PT-6
Helicopters	**Anti-tank** 11; MI-24 1: 1 Mi-24V *Hind E*; MI-35 12 Support MI-8 7: 3 MI-17 (Mi-8MT) *Hip H*
	Utility 12: 2 Bell 206 *JetRanger*; 2 Bell 212; 6 Bell 412 *Twin Huey* (VIP)
UAV	**Medium** some Blue Horizon-2; Searcher II
Air Defence	**Guns • Towed** 27: 40mm 24 L/40; 94mm 3 (3.7in)

Paramilitary *62,200*

Home Guard	13,000
National Guard	15,000
Police Force	30,200; 1,000 (women); 30,400 reservists (total 61,600)
Ministry of Defence Special Task Force	3,000 (anti-guerrilla unit)
UN Missions	**Observers**: Democratic Republic of Congo, South Sudan, Sudan, Western Sahara
	Units: Haiti (infantry battalion); Lebanon (1 infantry company)

THAILAND

Armed Forces 305,860	**(Army 190,000; Navy 69,860; Air Force 46,000)** **Paramilitary 113,700** **Reserves 200,000; Paramilitary 45,000**
Organisations by Service	
Army	*120,000; 70,000 conscript (total 190,000)* 4 Regional Army HQ 2 Corps HQ
Forces by Role	
Armoured Air Cavalry	1 regiment (3 air mob companies)
Rapid Reaction	1 force (1 battalion per region)
Cavalry	2 divisions; 1 independent regiment
Reconnaissance	4 companies
Mechanised Infantry	2 divisions
Armoured Infantry	3 divisions
Infantry	8 independent battalions
Special Forces	2 divisions
Light Infantry	1 division
Artillery	1 division
Air Defence Artillery	1 division (6 Air Defence Artillery battalions)
Engineers	1 division; 12 independent engineer battalions
Helicopters	some flights
Economic development	4 divisions
Psy Ops	1 battalion
Reserves	
Infantry	4 division HQ
Equipment by Type	
Tanks	283 **MBT** 53 M-60A3; 105 M-60 A1; 50 Type-69 (training in store); 105 M-48A5 **Light Tanks** 465: 24 M-41; 104 *Scorpion* (50 in store); 66 *Stingray*
Reconnaissance	32+: M1114 *HMMWV;* S52 32: 32 S52 Mk 3
Armoured Personnel Carriers	1,140 **APC (T)** 880; M-113 340: 340 M-113A1/M-113A3 Type-85 **APC (W)** 160: 18 *Condor;* LAV 142: 142 LAV-150 *Commando*
Artillery	2,555 **Towed** 577; 105mm 340; 24 LG1 MK II; 200 M-101 285: 285 M-101 -Mod/ M-101 105mm Towed; M-102 12; M-618A2 32; 130mm 15: 15 Type-59-I; 155mm 185; GHN-45 42: 42 GHN-45 A1; M-114 50; M-198 61; M-71 32; SP 155mm M-109 20: 20 M-109A2; MRL 130mm: some Type-85 **Mortars** 1,900 **SP** 33; 81mm 21 M125A3; 107mm M106A3; 120mm 12 M1064A3 **Towed** 1,867: 81mm; 107mm M106A1; 120mm 12 M1064
Anti-tank	**Missiles** 318+ **SP** 18 M-901A5 **Man-portable** 300 M47 *Dragon* **Recoilless** 180; 106mm 150: 150 M-40; 75mm 30: 30 M-20; **Rocket Launcher** M-72 *LAW*
Aircraft	**Reconnaissance: Observation** 40: 40 Cessna O-1A *Bird Dog* **Transport** 19; 2 Beech 1900C, Beech 200 *Super King Air* 2; CASA 212 *Aviocar* 2 *Jetstream* 41; 2 Short 330UTT 2

	Utility: U-17 10: 10 U-17B TRG 33 MX-7 18: 18 MX-7-235 *Star Rocket* T-41 15: 15 T-41B *Mescalero*
Helicopters	**Anti-tank** 3 AH-1F *Cobra*
	MRH 3 Mi-17V-5 *Hip H*
	Transport 175 Heavy 6 CH-47D *Chinook* Medium 7 UH-60L *Black Hawk Light* 162: 92 Bell 205 (UH-1H *Iroquois*); 28 Bell 206 *Jet Ranger*; 37 Bell 212 (AB-212); 3 *Enstrom* 480B
	Training: 42 Hughes 300C
Unarmed Aerial Vehicles	**Reconnaissance: Tactical**: *Searcher*
Air Defence	**SAM Static**: *Aspide*
	Man-portable: some FIM-43 *Redeye* HN-5: some HN-5A
	Guns 202 20mm 48
	SP 24: 24 M-163 *Vulcan*
	Towed 148: 24 M-167 *Vulcan* 37mm 52: 52 Type-74 40mm 78: 30 M-1 /M-42 SP; 48 L/70 57mm 24+: 6 Type-59 (S-60); 18+ non-operational
Radar	**Land**: 36; AN/TPQ *Firefinder* (Artillery, mortar); RASIT (vehicle, artillery)
ARV	43: 22 M88A1; 6 M88A2; 10 M113; 5 Type-653; WZT-4
VLB	Type-84
MW	*Bozena; Giant Viper*

***Navy* 44,010** *(including Naval Aviation, Marines, Coastal Defence); 25,850 conscript (total 70,600)*

Forces by Role

Air wing	1 division
Navy	Fleet HQ located at Sattahip
	Mekong River Operating Unit HQ at Nakhon Phanom

Equipment by Type

Principal Surface Combatants	10
Aircraft Carrier	**CVS** 1: 1 *Chakri Naruebet* (capacity 9 AV-8A *Harrier* FGA aircraft; 6 S-70B *Seahawk* ASW helicopters)
Frigates	10
	FFGHM 2:
	2 *Naresuan* (capacity either 1 S-70B-2 *Seahawk* ASW helicopters or 1 *Super Lynx* utility helicopters) each with 2 Mk 141 *Harpoon* quad (8 eff.) each with 1 RGM-84A *Harpoon* tactical SSM, 2 triple 324mm TT (6 eff.), 1 8 cell Mk 41 VLS with 1 RIM-7M *Sea Sparrow* SAM, 1 127mm gun
	FFGM 4
	2 *Chao Phraya* each with 4 twin (8 eff.) each with 1 CSS-N-4 *Sardine* tactical SSM, 2 (4 eff.) non-operational each with 1 HQ-61 (CSA-N-2) SAM non-operational, 2 RBU 1200 (10 eff.), 2 twin 100mm gun (4 eff.), 2 twin 37mm gun (4 eff.), 1 helicopters landing platform
	2 *Kraburi* (capacity 1 AB-212 (Bell 212) utility helicopters) each with 2 twin (4 eff.) each with 1 HQ-61 (CSA-N-2) SAM, 4 (8 eff.) each with 1 CSS-N-4 *Sardine* tactical SSM, 2 RBU 1200 (10 eff.), 1 twin 100mm gun (2 eff.), 2 twin 37mm gun (4 eff.)
	FFGH 2
	2 *Phuttha Yotfa Chulalok* (capacity 1 AB-212 (Bell 212) utility helicopters) (leased from US) each with 2 Twin ASTT (4 eff.) with 22 Mk 46 LWT, 1 Mk16 Mk 112 octuple with 1 RGM-84C *Harpoon* tactical SSM, tactical ASROC, 1 127mm gun
	FF 2:
	1 *Makut Rajakumarn* with 2 triple ASTT (6 eff.), 2 114mm gun
	1 *Pin Klao* with 6 x1 324mm ASTT, 3 76mm gun 2 *Tapi* each with 6 x1 324mm ASTT each with Mk 46 LWT, 1 76mm gun
Patrol & Coastal Combatants	83

PENTAGON'S SOUTH ASIA DEFENCE AND STRATEGIC YEAR BOOK

Corvettes	7 **FSG** 2 2 *Rattanakosin* each with 2 triple ASTT (6 eff.), 1 *Albatros* octuple with 1 Aspide SAM, 2 Mk 140 *Harpoon* quad (8 eff.) each with 1 RGM-84A *Harpoon* tactical SSM, 1 76mm gun **FS** 5 3 *Khamronsin* each with 2 triple ASTT (6 eff.), 1 76mm gun; 2 *Tapi* each with 6 single 324mm ASTT each with Mk 46 LWT, 176mm gun; 2 *Pattani* each with 176mm gun **PCFG** 6 3 *Prabparapak* each with 2 single each with 1 GI *Gabriel* 1 tactical SSM, 1 triple (3 eff.) with GI *Gabriel* 1 tactical SSM, 140mm gun, 157mm gun 3 *Ratchari* each with 2 twin (4 eff.) each with MM-38 *Exocet* tactical SSM, 176mm gun **PCO** 5: 3 *Hua Hin* each with 220mm gun, 176mm gun; 2 *Pattani* with 1 76mm gun **PCC** 9: 3 *Chon Buri* each with 276mm gun each with 140mm gun, 176mm gun; 6 *Sattahip* each with 140mm gun, 176mm gun **PCI** 47: 9 *Swift*; 10 T-11; 13 T-213; 3 T-81; 9 T-91 **PBF** 4 **PB** 52: 10 T-11; 9 *Swift*; 3 T-81; 9 T-91; 3 T-210; 13 T-213; 1 T-227; 3 T-991; 1 T-994
Mine Warfare	19 **MCC** 2: 2 *Bang Rachan* **MCM Support** 1 *Thalang* **MCO** 2 *Lat Ya* **MSC** 2 *Bangkeo* **MSR** 12
Amphibious	**LS** 8: **LS** 2 Prab 1 **LST** 6: 4 *Chang* (capacity 16 tanks; 200 troops) each with 6 40mm gun 2 *Sichang* (capacity 14 tanks; 300 troops) training each with 2 40mm gun, 1 helicopter landing platform **Landing Craft** 56 LCU 13: 3 *Man Nok*; 6 *Mataphun* (capacity either 3-4 MBT or 250 troops); 4 *Thong Kaeo* **LCVP** 12 **LCM** 24 **LCA** 4 **UCAC** 3 *Griffon* 100TD
Logistics and Support	14 **AORH** 1 *Similan* (1 helicopter), **AOR** 1 *Chula* **AOL** 5: 4 *Prong*; 1 *Samui* **AWT** 1 **ABU** 1 **TRG** 1 **YPT** 2 **YTM** 2
Facilities	Bases at Bangkok, Sattahip, Songkhla, Phang Nga, Nakhon and Phanom

***Naval Aviation* 1,2000**

Aircraft	39 combat capable
Fighter Ground Attack	7: 5 AV-8A *Harrier*; 2 TAV-8A *Harrier*

Reconnaissance	**Observation** 9: 9 *Sentry* 02-337 **MP** 10: 5 DO-228-212; 2 F-27 MK 200MPA*; 2 P-3T (P-3A) *Orion* **Transport** F-27 2: 2 F-27-400M *Troopship* **Utility** 8: 2 CL-215-III; 4 GAF N-24A *Search Master;* 1 UP-3T (UP-3A) *Orion*
Training	16: 14 **TA-7**; 4 TA-7C *Corsair II* TAV-8 2: 2 TAV-8A *Harrier*
Helicopters	**ASW** 8: 6 S-70B *Seahawk;* 2 S-76B Super Lynx 2 **Utility** 15: AB-212 (Bell 212) 5 Bell 214 5: 5 AB-214ST S-76 5: 5
Missiles	**Tactical ASM**: AGM-84 *Harpoon*

Marines *23,000*

Forces by Role

Reconnaissance	1 battalion
Amphibious assault	1 battalion
Infantry	2 regiments
Artillery	1 regiment (1 Air Defence Artillery battalion, 3 Field artillery battalions)
Marine	1 division HQ

Equipment by Type

APC	**APC (W) LAV** 24: 24 LAV-150 *Commando* **AAV** 33: 33 LVTP-7
Artillery	**Towed** 48: 36 105mm (reported); 12 GC-45 155mm
Anti-tank	**Missiles** 24+: some M47 *Dragon* **TOW** 24+: some; 24 HMMWV
Air Defence	**Guns** 14: 14 12.7mm

Air Force *46,000* — 4 air divisions, 1 Flying Training school

Forces by Role

Fighter	2 squadron with 35 F-5E *Tiger II*/F-5F *Tiger II*, 2 F-5B 3 squadrons with F-16A *Fighting Falcon* 1 squadron with L-39ZA/MP *Albatros*
FGA	1 squadron with *Gripen* C/D
Ground Attack	1 squadron with *Alpha Jet* 1 squadron with AU-23A *Peacemaker* 1 squadron with L-39ZA/MP *Albatros*
Reconnaissance/ELINT	1 squadron with 3 IAI-201 *Arava*, 2 Learjet 35A
AEW&C	1 squadron with Saab 340 *Erieye*
Transport	1 squadron with 9 Basler *Turbo-67;* 15 GAF N-22B *Nomad;* 1 squadron with 4 BAe-748; 3 G-222; 1 squadron with 7 C-130H *Hercules;* 5 C-130H-30 *Hercules*
VIP	1 (Royal Flight) squadron with A-310-324; Airbus A319CJ; 1 B-737-200; BAe-748; 737-400; Beech 200 *Super King Air*; SA-226AT *Merlin IV/IVA;* AS-532A2 *Cougar MKII;* AS-332L *Super Puma*; Bell 412 *Twin Huey*
Utility	1 squadron with L-392A
Liaison	1 squadron with Beech 65 *Queen Air*; Beech E90 *King Air*; Rockwell *Commander* 500; Cessna 150; T-41D *Mescalero*
Survey	1 squadron with 3 SA-226AT *Merlin IV/IVA;* GAF N-22B *Nomad*
Training	school with CT-4B/E *Airtrainer;* PC-9; Bell 206B *JetRanger II*
Helicopters	2 squadron UH-1H *Iroquois* 1 squadron Bell 412 *Twin Huey*

Equipment by Type

Aircraft	163 combat capable
FTR/FGA	87: **F-5** 49: 35 F-5E *Tiger II*/F-5F *Tiger II* (32 being upgraded), 2 F-5B **F-16** 50: 41 F-16A *Fighting Falcon;* 9 F-16B *Fighting Falcon*

PENTAGON'S SOUTH ASIA DEFENCE AND STRATEGIC YEAR BOOK

Transport	47: A-310 1: 1 A-310-324 A-319CJ 1B-737 3: 1 B-737-200; 2 B737-400 BAe-748 6 *Basler* Turbo-67 9 Beech 200 *Super King Air* 2 Beech 65 *Queen Air* 2 Beech 90 1: 1 Beech E90 *King Air* C-130 12: 7 C-130H *Hercules*; 5 C-130H-30 *Hercules* G-222 3 IAI-201 *Arava* 3 LEARJET 35 2: 2 *Learjet* 35A Rockwell *Commander* 500 3 SA-226 6: 6 SA-226AT *Merlin IV/IVA*
Utility	37: 22 AU-23A *Peacemaker*; 15 GAF N-22B *Nomad*
Training	123: 10 Alpha Jet; 29 CT-4B/E *Airtrainer*; 3 Cessna 150 L-39 46: 46 L-39ZA/MP *Albatros* PC-9 23 T-41 12: 12 T-41D *Mescalero*
Helicopters	**Support** 19: 3 AS-332L *Super Puma*; 3 AS-532A2 *Cougar MKII*; 13 Bell 212 **Utility** 28 Bell 206 6: 6 Bell 206B *JetRanger II* Bell 412 *Twin Huey* 2 UH-1 20: 20 UH-1H *Iroquois*
Missiles	**Tactical AAM**: AIM-120 *AMRAAM* **AIM-9**: AIM-9B *Sidewinder*/AIM-9J *Sidewinder Python III; ASM: AGM-65 Maverick*

Paramilitary *113,700 active*

Border Patrol Police *41,000*

Marine Police *2,200*

Patrol and Coastal Combatants 95

PCO 3: 1 *Srinakrin*
PCC 2 *Hameln*
PB 46: 2 *Chasanyabadee*; 1 *Yokohama*, 1 *Sriyanont*; 6 *Ital* Thai Marine; 1 *Burespadoogkit*; 3 *Cutlass*; 3 *Technautic* 38 (various)
PBR 46

National Security Volunteer Corps *45,000*

Police Aviation *500*

Aircraft	6 combat capable **ATK** 6 AU-23A *Peacemaker* **Transport** 16 Light 15: 2 CN-235; 8 PC-6 Turbo-Porter; 3 SC-7 3M Skyvan; 2 Short 330UTT **PAX** 1 F-50
Helicopters	**MRH** 6 Bell 412 Twin Huey **Transport** Light 67: 27 Bell 205A; 14 Bell 206 *Jet Ranger*; 20 Bell 212 (AB-212)

Provincial Police *50,000 (including 500 Special Action Force)*

Thahan Phran (Hunter Soldiers) *20,000*

Paramilitary 13 regiments

Volunteer Irregular Force

UN Missions **Observers**: Sudan

TABLE - CONVENTIONAL MILITARY STRENGTH: SOUTH ASIA

Country	*Regular*	*Paramilitary*	*Tanks (1)*	*APCs (2)*	*Combat Ac (3)*	*Attack Heptrs*	*Principal Surface Combatants (4)*	*Patrol and Coastal Combatants*	*Subs (5)*	*Amph (6)*
China	2,285,000	660,000	7,400	4,350	1,693	38	78	211	71	239
Indonesia	302,000	400,000	350	519	67	-	11	67	2	31
Malaysia	109,000	51,600	48	784	74	-	10	37	2	1
Myanmar	406,000	107,250	160	361	136	-	1	99	0	18
Singapore	72,500	312,500	96	1,695	148	19	6	35	5	4
Thailand	305,860	200,000	283	1,140	163	3	11	83	0	8
Afghanistan	170,700	136,100	no data	173	no data	13	0	0	0	0
Bangladesh	157,050	63,900	232	248	74	14	5	42	0	11
Bhutan	10,000	0	0	0	0	0	0	0	0	0
India	1,325,000	1,155,000	3,215	1,455	798	22	21	61	15	18
Nepal	95,750	62,000	0	53	0	-	0	0	0	0
Pakistan	642,000	304,000	2,411	1,320	453	42	10	12	8	0
Sri Lanka	160,900	5,500	62	221	31	11	0	139	0	1
Russia	1,027,000	20,000,000	23,000+	27,190+	2,080	1,589+	62	74	67	45+
USA	1,498,157	1,082,718	8,023+	28,454	4,269	5,289	106	16	71	32
Australia	54,747	19,915	149	1,728	109	113	12	14	6	3

Notes: All figures are estimates and include some equipment held in store. Figures are not shown for coast guard and paramilitary forces.

1. Main battle tanks.
2. Includes light tanks, light armoured vehicles, armoured personnel carriers, infantry mobility vehicles and infantry fighting vehicles.
3. Includes fighters, bombers and armed maritime patrol aircraft.
4. Includes corvettes, frigates, destroyers, cruisers and aircraft carriers.
5. Includes nuclear and conventional submarines.

Amphibious ship categories, including: tank landing ship, medium landing ship, heavy landing ship, amphibious landing platform, landing ship logistic and helicopter, landing ship dock, assault landing ship and landing ship helicopter and dock.

TERRORISM

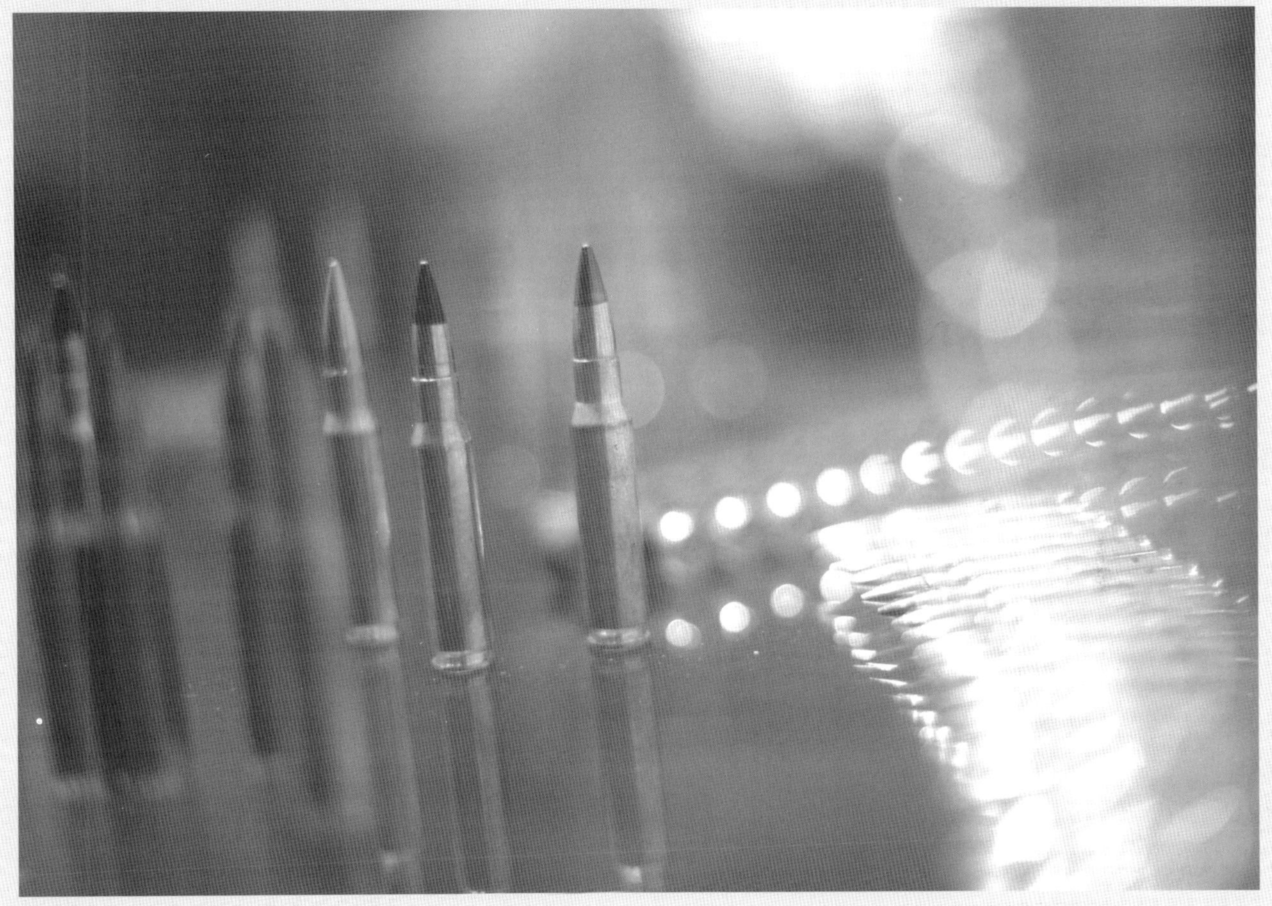

MILITANT GROUPS IN AFGHANISTAN

The major Afghan militant groups in the border areas are generally portrayed as falling into one of three categories: the original Taliban who are now resurgent; Hizb-e-Islami led by Gulbud-din Hekmatyar (HiG); and the HQN. However, these categories do not represent the totality of militant groups operating within Afghanistan because they ignore the presence of foreign militant groups of Central Asian and Arab origin that also operate in the region.

In fact, the situation is far more complex, because the interlocking agendas of anti-government insurgents and self-interested spoilers are fuelling the violence in Afghanistan. It is obvious that the Taliban are operating from within Pakistan. But less obvious is the role of the criminal networks, while a corrupt and weak government is providing an enabling environment to act with near impunity. Apart from the Taliban, there are others with vested interests who, for reasons of personal power, have no desire to see central authority spread in Afghanistan.

The presence of foreign fighters of Arab and Central Asian origin, Pakistani and Afghan tribes, and criminal networks, in Afghanistan is well documented. There is also evidence of coordination among these groups at the tactical and strategic levels but there is no unified leadership who operate in conformity with their local bases of support but their ideological distinctions are less clear:

(a) The northern front is dominated by HiG's presence based in the Afghan provinces of Nuristan, Kunar, Laghman and Nangarhar as well as across the border in Pakistan. Other groups such as the LeT, TNSM are also active on this front.

(b) The central front consists of a loose network of foreign fighters of Central Asian and Arab descent. They are located across the territory from Bajaur in Pakistani FATA to Khost, Paktia and Paktika in Afghanistan. The HQN has been active on this front as well.

(c) The Taliban dominates the southern front. This includes Balochistan and FATA in Pakistan and Helmand, Kandahar, Oruzgan and Zabol provinces in Afghanistan.

THE TALIBAN

Origins

After the withdrawal of the Soviet Union from Afghanistan, the *mujahideen* fought among themselves in rapidly fluctuating coalitions. It is at this point in time that the networks of *madaris* that had been established during the 1980s to provide *mujahideen* fighters and support to Afghan refugees achieved some autonomy and transmuted into a politico-religious movement under the charismatic leadership of Mullah Omar with the direct support from the Pakistani government. The men who joined this movement called themselves the Taliban (literally, students).

The capture of Herat in 1995, Kabul in 1996, and most of the North in 1998, consolidated the control of the Taliban over 90 percent of Afghanistan's population. Only Ahmed Shah Masoud, helped by the Russians and Iranians, resisted the Taliban in north-eastern Afghanistan. The death of Masoud, on 9 September 2001, marked the complete success of the Taliban. But the events of September 11 brought about the rapid downfall of the Taliban when the United States launched a military operation in Afghanistan after Mullah Omar refused to hand over bin Laden.

Since then the Taliban have regrouped in south and southeast Afghanistan along the Pakistan-Afghanistan border and re-emerged as a more sophisticated group often referred to as the "neo-Taliban". Factors explaining the resurgence of the Taliban include the reestablishment of their logistical base, external support, and the return of militants supporting their cause from abroad and funds from the narcotics trade. The insurgency in Afghanistan today is being driven by Taliban commanders from sanctuaries based in Pakistan.

Objectives

The Taliban movement had a twofold agenda. On the one hand, the Taliban were a puritan-religious movement, of a fundamentalist nature but with no political project beyond the implementation of the *sharia*. On the other hand, it was a movement sustained by Pashtun nationalism, which sought to re-establish the Afghan state, the traditional fief of the Pashtuns that was appropriated in 1992 by Masoud's Northern Alliance. The Taliban believe that the implementation of *sharia* law is the means by which such a state could be constructed because it would overcome tribal and ethnic differences.

However, after 9/11 a different set of objectives based on personal backgrounds, experiences, and circumstances motivated the objectives of the Taliban. The motivations that encourage insurgent behaviour are:

(a) retaliating against military action by foreign forces;
(b) resisting the invasion by these forces that threaten Afghan culture;
(c) resisting corruption in the government;
(d) attempting to gain leverage in the struggle of power as a consequence of being excluded; and
(e) exploiting the insurgency for criminal purposes such as extortion, narcotics, or self-aggrandizement.

Based on these motivations, the primary goal of the neo-Taliban is the withdrawal of foreign troops and the establishment of *sharia*, which has been equated with law and order, access to justice, and alternate form of government and an Islamic society.

Strategies and Tactics

Previously, the Taliban strategy was to forcefully implement *sharia* to re-establish the Afghan state. The resurgent Taliban have a different strategic aim, i.e. to overthrow the Afghan government and break the political will of the U.S. and NATO forces. In keeping with this aim, the neo-Taliban have adopted a different range of strategies. First, they have realised that they cannot face U.S. military with force on force so they have shifted their strategy toward a defensive posture by attacking soft targets, such as government officials, aid workers, and civilians. Second, they have been organizing vanguard teams of about 20-25 members, who prepare the ground for later escalation of militant activity. These teams are responsible for establishing a base among the local population, identifying those members of the population who would be sympathizers and supporters, and engaging in propaganda to disseminate the Taliban message. On occasion these teams have also carried out terrorist and guerrilla activities like attacking police-posts, ambushes, and bombings. The third strategy and arguably the most effective one is to demoralize the enemy through relentless attacks against the same targets. Suicide attacks have commonly been used as part of this strategy. Tactically, the neo-Taliban are characterised by improvements in telecommunications and by the use of more sophisticated weapons and fighting tactics.

In comparison to the "old Taliban," the neo-Taliban have distinguished themselves by developing a media strategy. Previously, the Taliban had banned music and television. They now use media technologies to disseminate their message and worldview. The neo-Taliban also have a media committee that is responsible for propaganda and corresponds with major radio stations and news channels. In fact, the Taliban also post their videos and publications online that encourage Muslims to join the Taliban and wage *jihad*. The main objectives of the media strategy are recruitment, indoctrination, funding, propaganda and psychological warfare.

Recruitment and Training

The defining characteristics of the Taliban movement in the 1990s were that its leadership was drawn from former *mujahideen*, many of whom were affiliated with *Harakat-e-Inqilaab-e-Islami* during the 1980s; many of the members were secular Pashtuns; and they accommodated armed Pashtuns who aligned themselves with the Taliban for reasons of expediency. The fact that the Taliban overlooked ideological inclinations when recruiting Pashtuns, shows that the Taliban represent a tribal movement.

Students from *madrassas* situated between Ghazni and Kandahar formed a major core of the Taliban movement. These madrassas had been linked since well before the war with Soviets to the Deobandi school of Sunni Islam. A typical *Talib* recruit is characterised as poor, with limited exposure to urban life, having conservative views and educated in a *madrassa*.

The leadership is still made up of the same men who formed the Taliban under Mullah Omar.

Their major sources for recruitment are:

(a) Pakistani-based *madrassas*.
(b) Villagers who have joined out of sheer expediency with financial incentives playing an important role.
(c) Members of the population who find the Taliban ideology appealing
(d) Members of disenfranchised and alienated communities who did not agree with the Taliban in principle but, disheartened by the current government's poor performance, consider the Taliban to be a viable alternative.

The Taliban have sometimes paid villagers (US$15 - $55 per day) to harass foreign and government troops with rocket attacks and shooting. Core members are paid (US$ 100 -$350 per day) as indemnity for their families.

The most important training camp used by the Taliban prior to the U.S. operation in Afghanistan was the Darunta Complex located near Jalalabad. Today, the neo- Taliban have established themselves on the Pakistani side of the border, and there are reports to suggest that the Taliban are sharing the training camps run by Pakistani militant groups such as the Hull,

Funding

Financially, the Taliban have had access to numerous sources of external funding including wealthy patrons in Saudi Arabia and Middle East and the Pakistani government. But other creative means to generate funds have also included tolls levied on the transport industry. The narcotics economy has hugely funded the Taliban, but this remains a bit of a controversy. It is not clear how much revenue is generated from the narcotics trade and whether it is a primary source of income for the Taliban. Field commanders are not involved in fund-raising, which implies that field commanders are not completely autonomous because they have to rely on the central leadership for resource allocation.

Organisation

The Taliban organisation was earlier made up of four components: the *Amir-ul-momineen* (Commander of the Faithful), the title given to Omar as the leader of the Taliban; the Supreme *Shura*, the highest decision making body, with ten members and based in Kandahar; the Military *Shura*, to plan strategy and implement tactical decisions though it had no authority to enforce its plans; and the Kabul *Shura*, which dealt with the daily governance in Kabul. The organisation became gradually centralised with Mullah Omar making unilateral decisions without consulting the various *shura*, and was destroyed by the U.S.-led military onslaught post-9/11.

Today the organisation of the Taliban involves two main tiers. The top tier includes the leadership dominated by Mullah Omar and his key associates, many of whom are based in Quetta and together compose the Quetta *Shura*. In this tier a second *shura*, based in Pakistan's FATA, revolves around the HQN. The second tier is made up of Taliban fighters.

The resurgent Taliban are a loose conglomeration of different networks that for reasons of convenience and to project a semblance of unity are known as the Taliban and consider Omar to be their leader. The organisation of the resurgent Taliban represents commander-solidarity networks that are based on comradeship, shared backgrounds and patronage links with the commander in the network. The networks are united in their opposition to the Karzai regime, willingness to wage *jihad* and a desire to establish an Islamic system. Their bonds of trust have been built over a number of years.

Networks and Affiliations

Al Qaeda is viewed as having played a major role in the development of the Taliban. It is during the Taliban regime in the 1990s that al Qaeda established itself as a transnational network with terrorist capabilities. In return for this safe haven in Afghanistan, al Qaeda has provided the Taliban with funding, training facilities, and militants to fight its battles. Most importantly, al Qaeda's global jihadist ideology has had the effect of rendering the ideological vision of the Taliban leadership more extreme. Post-9/11, however, an ideological divergence between al Qaeda and the Taliban has been noted, with the latter attempting to project itself as a responsible alternative to the Afghan government and being unwilling to attack the Pakistani state.

With the end of the Afghan war and the Pakistani

government realizing that their key player in Kabul, Gulbuddin Hekmatyar, was not of any use, the Pakistani ISI began to support the Taliban. (Pakistan's minister of interior, Naseerullah Babar, visited the Taliban in October 1994 and helped in the effort to take the city of Herat in 1995). As a consequence, there exists a pro-Taliban lobby in Pakistan consisting of army officers and Deobandi clerics. Pakistan is one of two countries that diplomatically recognised the Taliban government during the 1990s. However, after 9/11, while lending support to the Taliban, Pakistan has simultaneously aided the counter-insurgency efforts led by the U.S.

Recent Overtures

It is believed that the Taliban leadership and base deeply regret their past association with al Qaeida. Once a general ceasefire and/or political agreement are decided, the base would obey a call by Mullah Mohammad Omar – and only him – to completely renounce al Qaeda. This renunciation would need to be built into a larger agreement, allowing the Taliban to leverage their delinking themselves – step by step – from al Qaeda in exchange for some form of political recognition. Following renunciation, the Taliban would act to assure that al Qaeda is no longer able to operate on Afghan soil. The Taliban also appear to be open to setting-up a Joint Monitoring Commission staffed by Taliban representatives, ISAF and the Afghan Government to investigate reports of continued al Qaeda activity. However, the continuation of drone attacks both within Afghanistan and across the border in Pakistan severely complicates the task of maintaining the base's allegiance and the leadership's ability to control popular outrage.

The Taliban may be open to negotiating a ceasefire as part of a general settlement, and also as a bridge between confidence-building measures and the core issue of the distribution of political power in Afghanistan. This would require strong Islamic justification, obscuring any hint of surrender. In this context a ceasefire endorsed by Mullah Mohammad Omar has the greatest potential for success. A general ceasefire (closer to a larger plan for reconciliation) is preferred by the Taliban more than local- and district-level ceasefires (reintegrating local commanders and cadres). A general ceasefire with Mullah Mohammad Omar's backing would allow the Taliban to better deal with 'peace spoilers' and dissenters.

It is also amply clear that the Taliban will not negotiate with President Karzai or his administration, which is seen as corrupt and weak. Also, outright acceptance of the present Afghan constitution is widely considered as a non-starter. The Taliban would, perhaps, be willing to accept long-term US military presence and bases as long as they do not constrain Afghan independence and Islamic jurisprudence. In time, military presence could be transformed into mainly economic assistance. The Taliban leadership are keen to end all attacks on teachers and health-care workers, as evident in public statements and modern subjects such as mathematics and sciences are encouraged in both *madrassas* and schools more generally, as underlined in a Taliban policy document on education circulated in early 2012. The Taliban fully understand that their policies of the 1990s need to be re-configured in the face of rapidly changing social forces within current-day Afghanistan. Though co-education will not be tolerated, but models for both education and working environments could be adapted to accommodate strict segregation of men and women.

THE HAQQANI NETWORK (HQN)

Origins

Surprisingly little has been written about the HQN, an organisation contributing significantly to the insurgency in Afghanistan. Two reasons explain the lack of information available on the group: One, it is a secretive organisation that has revealed little about itself; and two, it is widely believed to be subsumed under the umbrella of the Afghan Taliban movement. The origins of the HQN are traced to Jalaluddin Haqqani whose achievements as a military commander during the Soviet Union's invasion of Afghanistan have given the HQN immense popularity in Loya Paktiya (Khost, Paktia, and Paktika provinces) and its base of operations in Miran Shah, North Waziristan. Jalaluddin Haqqani relinquished power to the Taliban in the mid-1990s and agreed to his appointment as the minister for borders and tribal areas in the Taliban government. But he has not fully accepted the authority of the Taliban and has remained an independent but allied force. Currently, Jalaluddin Haqqani's son Sirajuddin is the most senior commander of the HQN and manages the day-to-day affairs of the HQN.

After the U.S. attacks, Jalaluddin Haqqani and his forces retreated to their base in Miran Shah, North Waziristan in the FATA where a network of Haqqani-run *madaris* is located. Even though widely respected for their role in anti-Soviet jihad, the Haqqanis have faced a lack of acceptance from the tribal leaders in North Waziristan because Jalauddin Haqqani originally belongs to the Zadran tribe from Khost Province in Afghanistan.

Objectives

The HQN's primary objective is to carry out what commonly is termed a "*jihadi*-aligned resistance" to rid Afghanistan of international and government influence. It can also be argued that due to the success the HQN has had in benefiting from foreign assistance from ISI and CIA, a motivating factor to be part of insurgent activity may also be to maintain their position of privilege and influence in Loya Paktiya.

Strategies and Tactics

The HQN has demonstrated greater imagination, intent and capability for complex attacks than regular Taliban commanders. One of the factors explaining their effectiveness is their relationship with al Qaeda leaders, who facilitate the HQN's activities.

The HQN has also been implicated in an increasing the number of roadside and suicide bombings in both urban and rural Afghanistan. Its military tactics include the use of asymmetrical warfare, and guerrilla warfare using IEDs and mines.

Recruitment and Training

The HQN broadly consists of four types of members: "those who served under Jalauddin Haqqani during the Soviet era, those from Loya Paktia who joined the network since 2001, those from North Waziristan who have been associated with Haqqani *madaris*, and foreign (non-Pashtun) militants including Arabs, Chechens and Uzbeks ... the vast majority of HQN fighters belong to the Zadran tribe in particular from Haqqani's Mezi clan and its allies.

Whether the HQN ought to be considered a tribal network or not, is a debatable question. The HQN's recruitment from within their own tribal network does not imply that only those who are closely related can enter the upper ranks of the leadership. The HQN is an excellent example of a movement that has exploited its Pashtun identity to win support for itself. The tribal base of the HQN is a fault line in the Afghan insurgency led by the Taliban. While the HQN only recruits from Paktia Pashtun tribes, the Taliban leadership has recruited mainly from the Kandahari Pashtuns. This cleavage is important because the Paktiwal Pashtuns have openly resisted what is perceived as Kandahari dominance in the past.

Funding

The HQN's funds come from a variety of sources. First, contacts that were formed during the Afghan war are known to contribute to the HQN. Second, field commanders are expected to raise their own funds through donations, extortion, and taxation of cross-border trade. Third, the HQN has been implicated in a number of kidnappings for ransom schemes like that of the reporter David Rohde.

Organisation: The leadership of the HQN is based in Miran Shah, North Waziristan, and is often known as the "Miran Shah Shura," Sirajuddin Haqqani heads the *shura*, overseeing the group's political and military activities. He also established a liaison with Mullah Ornar's Quetta Shura, TTP, and al Qaeda. Sirajuddin is aided by his deputy commander (who coordinates militant activities) and political deputy (who is in charge of finances and weapons and ammunition acquisitions) in carrying out this leadership role. The organisation of the Miran Shah *Shura* can be described as tiered with a number of Haqqani family members that form the inner circle of leadership. The middle tier of the HQN's organisation is composed of field commanders who typically recruit the groups' lower tier-the rank and file-and ensure that HQN fighters are properly trained and indoctrinated in the HQN's religious ideology at Haqqani-run *madrassas*.

Networks and Affiliations

The HQN has the capacity to operate as an independent entity. It has links to Arab funding, al Qaeda, and the ISI such that if it chose, it could be autonomous of the Taliban. But the HQN has been prevented from taking such a step because it does not have a clearly defined area of control in Afghanistan. Its dominance in *Loya* Paktiya is questionable, which is why most HQN activities are launched from Miran Shah. Here too, the HQN's links with the ISI are resented by the local population, which has an anti-Pakistani government stance.

Jalaluddin Haqqani holds a position in the Quetta *Shura* of the Taliban, while his son Sirajuddin is the Taliban's senior military commander for Loya Paktia. Hence, one may conclude that the HQN is very much under the command of Omar. Yet its activities demonstrate that the network is often at odds with the policies of the Taliban. This is because the Taliban wants to avoid attacks that hurt its image of a respectable alternative to the present government. Hence, it seems that the relationship between the HQN and the Taliban may be strained in some instances, but is generally one of mutual benefit. While the HQN provides the Taliban with the foothold in *Loya* Paktia and North Waziristan, the Taliban provide the HQN with access to operate in areas beyond its local influence.

The relationship between the HQN and the TTP is

similarly complicated. Within North Waziristan, the HQN has been at odds with the local tribes, but has been closely allied with ex- TTP commander Hafiz Gul Bahadur. This alliance is useful because Bahadur has a tribal base which the HQN lacks, but more importantly, Bahadur, unlike the TTP has avoided a direct confrontation with Pakistani troops. Maintaining a neutral posture toward the Pakistani state is especially important because of HQN's links with the ISI. Jalaludin Haqqani was favoured by both the ISI and the CIA during the anti-Soviet jihad. The ISI's support to the HQN in terms of funding or training is not overt. But there is evidence to suggest that the HQN found a safe haven on Pakistani soil because of ISI help.

The HQN's interaction with foreign militants is also interesting. More recently, the HQN has received help from al Qaeda, which has facilitated the HQN's military operations by providing training, weapon expertise, arms, and funding. In return, the HQN has voluntarily provided shelter to al Qaeda militants and hid their weapons in Miran Shah. But apart from tactical cooperation, ideologically the HQN is at odds with al Qaeda. Its Pashtun profile lends the HQN a distinct nationalist rhetoric, which it exploits to retain influence in *Loya* Paktia and the FATA. It also does not agree with al Qaeda's global jihad or anti-Pakistan rhetoric. It is not clear whether these complicated relationships with al Qaeda and Quetta *Shura* Taliban are a source of tension among the HQN's leaders and field commanders.

HIZB-E-LSLAMI (ISLAMIC PARTY OF GULBUDDIN HEKMATYAR, OR HIG)

Origins

The *Hizb-e-Islami* of Afghanistan was formed by Gulbuddin Hekmetyar in the mid-1970s after it broke off from *Jamiyat-e-Islami* led by Rabbani. At the time, the HiG was one of the predominant Islamist parties in Afghanistan that was revolting against the Daud regime in Kabul. In the 1980s, the HiG became involved in resisting the Soviet occupation in Afghanistan. It was patronised by the Pakistani ISI and the United States to carry out its activities against the Soviet forces. After Soviet withdrawal from Afghanistan, the HiG attempted to forge a number of unsuccessful political alliances in a bid to capture power in Kabul. The HiG eventually reconciled and joined the Afghan government in 1996 instead of trying to take control itself. However, this was short-lived as HiG was soon driven from Kabul with the rise of the Taliban and Hekmatyar was forced into self-exile in Iran. After the 2001 US invasion of Afghanistan, Iran expelled Hekmatyar, who reportedly returned to Afghanistan in February 2002. Although Hekmatyar did not formally ally himself with either the Taliban or al Qaeda, he did pledge his support in the fight against U.S. and NATO forces. On February 19, 2003, the United States designated Hekmatyar a Specially Designated Global Terrorist but the HiG was not designated as a Foreign Terrorist Organisation. However, the activities of the group are closely monitored because it remains an active threat. The HiG's main area of operation is in the north-eastern provinces of Afghanistan and on the outskirts of Kabul. It also maintains a presence on a strategic highway connecting Afghanistan to Pakistan.

Organisation

During the Soviet occupation, the ISI and the CIA preferred to work with Hekmatyar because the HiG was perceived to be the most organised guerrilla force in terms of its communist-style, tightly-controlled hierarchical structure, superior recruitment pattern and religious zeal. Post-9/11, the HiG is still led by Hekmatyar but is considerably weaker, operating a loosely hierarchical organisation that is two-tiered. 1he first tier is concerned with logistic, financial, and political support, while the second tier is made up of fighters and field commanders. The U.S. military has estimated that HiG forces number between 400 and 600 fighters, although experts believe this number to be closer to 1,500.

The HiG split in the late 1970s, with Maulvi Mohammad Yunus Khalis's faction breaking away from the dominant group led by Hekmaytar. Similar factionalisation of the party has continued, with a group led by Khalid Farooqi splitting from the parent organisation and choosing to support the transitional regime of Hamid Karzai.

Networks and Affiliations

The Taliban and the HiG have operated in separate areas, but since Hekmatyar pledged his support to the Taliban, tactical cooperation between the two groups has been reported. However, the nature of the relationship between the Taliban and the HiG has been one of suspicion and competition. Tensions between the Taliban and the HiG have worsened in the past year. The Taliban has made aggressive inroads in the HiG's stronghold in north-eastern Afghanistan. Even though the HiG stood its ground, the Taliban have now surpassed the HiG as the dominant insurgent force in the region. Furthermore, there are reports that this tension between the HiG and the Taliban has been exploited by the Karzai government, which has repeatedly made overtures to HiG members to form pro-government militias to resist further Taliban expansion. The HiG has conditionally chosen to side with the government against the Taliban to prevent further loss of its influence in the region. But these negotiations have reached a stalemate because of Hekmatyar's insistence on U.S. troop withdrawal. The HiG's attempts to leverage its position have thus far been unsuccessful.

FOREIGN MILITANTS IN AFGHANISTAN

Foreign fighters assisting the Afghan insurgency are an amalgam of Muslim extremists, including the al Qaeda forces. The ranks of foreign fighters operating in this region are made up of two types of individuals: those from the Caucuses and Central Asia, such as the Chechens, Uzbeks, and Tajiks; and those who are Arab, such as the Egyptians, Saudis, and Libyans.

AL QAEDA (AQ)

Origins

Al Qaeda's roots in Afghanistan can be traced back to the days following the Soviet invasion. During the war, the Saudi government, in collaboration with the ISI and CIA, began transferring volunteers to Afghanistan to help the jihad effort. It was here that bin Laden encountered other militant fighters who would form the future leadership of the Taliban. In 1989, as the Soviet Union withdrew from Afghanistan, foreign militant fighters returned to their homes to launch Islamic campaigns there. One of them was bin Laden who went back to Saudi Arabia and returned to Afghanistan in 1996, which is when al Qaeda took shape as an organisation promoting a violent *jihad*.

Objectives

The *fatwa* that was issued by bin Laden on February 23, 1998, conveyed his worldview and objectives. His grievances were precise and political; namely the presence of U.S. forces in Saudi Arabia, the destruction of Iraq through sanctions, and the occupation of Palestine. In the name of jihad, bin Laden launched an attack on Americans. Bin Laden defined short-term, mid-term, and long-term goals for the group. Before 9/11, its immediate goal was the post-Gulf War withdrawal of U.S. troops from Saudi Arabia. The mid-term goal was the removal of apostate rulers of the Middle East and the creation of Islamic states that followed *sharia* law. The long-term goal was to unite these Islamic states to wage war on the United States and its allies. Bin Laden's agenda was original in advocating pan-Islamic unity, thereby functioning as a catchall group and attracting the widest possible support.

Strategies and Tactics

Al Qaeda's success lies in the way it has spread its network trans-nationally by cultivating agents who infiltrate Muslim communities to recruit, gather intelligence, and conduct operations. Every al Qaeda operation makes use of the extensive network that it has in place. It does so in three phases: First, intelligence teams carry out surveillance and the attack team rehearses the operation in a training camp. Second, safe houses, transportation, and ammunition are organised close to the target area through local agents. Finally, the strike team arrives and carries out the attack, after which it either withdraws or commits suicide.

Suicide is a preferred tactic of al Qaeda. Al Qaeda devotes much time and effort to programming its fighters for death exploiting the willingness of its fighters to die to drive fear into the enemy. It has the capacity to engage an enemy on several fronts simultaneously. This is because al Qaeda operates in a holistic way by politicizing and radicalizing Muslim societies. Al Qaeda therefore poses an ideological challenge that cannot be wiped away through military action.

Recruitment and Training

The military committee, which is a part of al Qaeda's high command, is responsible for both recruitment and training. While there is no formal procedure for recruitment, it is usually done by appointed agent-handlers outside Afghanistan. There are 14 mandatory qualifications required to be admitted as a member of al Qaeda and its associate groups: "knowledge of Islam, ideological commitment, maturity, self-sacrifice, discipline, secrecy, good health, patience, unflappability, intelligence, caution and prudence, truthfulness and wisdom, the ability to observe and analyze, and the ability to act.

Al Qaeda's training programme is contained in several training manuals that make up the multi-volume 7,000-page Encyclopaedia of Afghan Jihad. The curriculum taught (basic, advanced, or specialised) in a training program varies depending on the mission that has been assigned to a recruit.

Funding

Al Qaeda has developed a very complex financial network. Philanthropists, businesses, and other foundations in the United Arab Emirates (UAE) and Saudi Arabia are the primary sources of funding for al Qaeda. It operates legitimate institutions, including state and private charities, banks, and companies as front organisations to move funds through the *hawala* system of banking that evade government scrutiny. Al Qaeda also has a wide network of investments and small businesses so they can generate funds.

Organisation

Al Qaeda is characterised by a broad-based ideology, novel structure, robust capacity for regeneration, and a very diverse membership cutting across ethnicity, class, and national boundaries. A set of vertical and horizontal linkages make it possible for al Qaeda to maintain its extensive organisational network. A high command with a vertical leadership structure provides direction and tactical support to a horizontal network of compartmentalised cells and associate organisations. The utility of such an organisation for al Qaeda is twofold: (1) it provides mobility and capacity to regenerate; and (2) it allows for both direct and indirect control over a far-flung network.

Al Qaeda's high command is led by the *amir*, who presides over a *majlis-e-shura* (consultative council) and four operational committees-military, fatwa and Islamic study, finance and business, and media and publicity. Members of the *majlis-e-shura* are appointed by the amir and rotate from time to time. There is no set method of appointment and promotion within the organisation. Such decisions are made on merit, ability, and performance, although family friendships and nationality may also be taken into consideration.

Networks and Affiliations

While al Qaeda's network is extensive and transnational in nature, for the purposes of this review, we are interested in documenting al Qaeda's network in Afghanistan and Pakistan only. Al Qaeda's contribution to the Afghan insurgency since 2001 has been limited to the south-eastern and eastern provinces of the country. This is due to geography and to long-standing ties to local militants in these regions.

It is difficult to examine the nature of the relationship between the Taliban and al Qaeda because both are complex organisations made up of militants that are variably held accountable by the central leadership. Prior to 9/11, al Qaeda and Taliban had a cooperative relationship, but more recently a strategic divergence has been observed. There are two reasons for this development. First, al Qaeda's core organisational infrastructure has relocated from Afghanistan to the FATA where it has come to ideologically align itself more closely to Pakistani militant groups. Second, al Qaeda's objectives in the region are not just to resist U.S. and NATO forces, but also to attack the Pakistani government, which is viewed as apostate for allying itself with the U.S.-led War on Terrorism.

Al Qaeda functions as a "force multiplier" for local groups, supporting them with manpower, training, and propaganda skills. An example is al Qaeda's relationship with the TTP in the FATA. Ideologically, both groups employ the doctrine of *takfir* to justify their activities against the Pakistani state. Moreover, the global *jihadi* ideology resonates with both groups.

In the FATA, al Qaeda has also attempted to cooperate with other foreign militant groups - namely, the Libyan Islamic Fighting Group and a faction of the Islamic Movement of Uzbekistan, or IMU, called the Islamic Jihad Union (IJU) These groups do not necessarily share al Qaeda's vision and promote their own interests. In fact, due to their divergent goals and objectives, these groups compete over access to funding, weapons, and safe houses in the FATA and Balochistan.

The IMU includes Islamic militants from Uzbekistan and its Central Asian neighbours. The group was co-founded by a former Soviet soldier who served in the Soviet-Afghan war. IMU militants fought alongside the *mujahideen* during the Afghan war, which brought them closer to radical Islam. The Islamic Jihad Union, a splinter group of the IMU, is led by the Nadzimiddin Kamilidinovich. Their base is in North Waziristan in the Mir Ali area, from which they direct operations in Pakistan and Central Asia.

MILITANT GROUPS IN PAKISTAN

The makeup of the militant groups, and their networks, in Pakistan is complex. One typology, based on both the objectives and the local bases of these insurgent groups, can divide them into five categories of nonreligious and religious militant groups: sectarian, anti-Indian, Afghan Taliban, al Qaeda and affiliates, and Pakistani Taliban. Another typology would include non-religious militant groups with secessionist or anti-state goals. Militancy in Pakistan is not a homogeneous phenomenon and there are differences across militant groups in terms of structure, leadership, and objectives. Another typology can be based on the political and religious objectives of the militant groups and their sectarian affiliation: groups focused on Kashmir, such as the LeT, Hizb-ul-Mujahideen, and Al Badr; sectarian groups such as the SSP, the SMP, and the LeJ and anti-state groups such as Baloch nationalists. Still further, there are groups such as the Hull and the JeM that are involved in insurgent activities in Kashmir and also elsewhere. Even for the militant groups focused on Kashmir, the groups adhere to different sectarian orientations and their operations in Kashmir are shaped by different interests.

Another distinction that is drawn among militant networks in Pakistan is based on the local origins of the Punjabi Taliban and Pashtun Taliban networks. The Pashtun network includes those groups affiliated with the TTP. The Punjabi Taliban is a loose conglomeration of members belonging to banned militant groups of Punjabi origins-such as the JeM, the LeJ, and the SSP - that are sectarian and focused on jihad in Kashmir, but that also have developed strong connections with the TTP, Afghan Taliban, and other militant groups in the FATA. There are five ways in which the Punjabi Taliban can be distinguished from the Pashtun TTP:

- The Punjabi Taliban lack organisation and instead operate as a network of members from different groups.
- Many Punjabi militants benefited from patronage by the Pakistani government in the 1990s.
- The Punjabis are Sunnis belonging to the Deobandi or Ahl-e-Hadith sects.
- Punjabi militants differ in language and dress from the Pashtun Taliban and are educated, better equipped, and technologically savvier.
- The Punjabi Taliban are more prone to mercenary action than the Pashtun Taliban.

The distinction between anti-Indian groups and Afghan militant groups also overlap.

JAMAAT-E-ISLAMI (PARTY OF ISLAM, OR JI)

The JI is not a party of the *ulema* but an organisation represented by a diverse membership, including students, unions, and professional organisations. The JI is Pakistan's largest Islamic political party but its performance in politics has not been consistent. It experienced a peak in its political power under Zia's regime but following his death, its involvement in politics was impacted adversely. It lost its stronghold in Karachi during the 1990s winning only a few seats in the National Assembly. It is only as part of the MMA that the JI together with the JUI, formed the provincial government in the KPK and Balochistan from 2002 to 2007.

The JI has also been associated with militancy. JI volunteers entered the violent insurgency in the 1971 Bangladesh war of independence. Later, the JI was known to lend overt support to the Afghan *mujahideen* during the 1980s through its network of *madrassas*, charities, and businesses and so it came to influence the Islamist forces of Hekmatyar and Rabbani in Afghanistan. Although the JI has defined itself as a political ideological movement and does not want to be overtly linked to militancy, it has found a way around this by playing a role in the establishment of groups such as the Hizb-ul-Muiahideen (HM), a *jihadi* outfit active exclusively in Kashmir

The JI's student wing Islami Jamiat Tuleba (Islamic Society of Students, or IJT) has also been known to engage in militant activities on university campuses in Pakistan. The IJT was conceived as a missionary movement that would spread the JI's Islamist ideology among students. As one of its objectives, the IJT decided to purge university campuses in Pakistan of any overtly secular or left-leaning elements. This led to violent confrontations between the IJT and other student organisations. The IJT's activities emphasised ideological divisions among the supporters of Deobandi, Ahl-e-Hadith movements who formed their own student organisations. The IJT's most violent clashes occurred at Karachi University against the All Pakistani Mohajir Student Organisation during the 1980s. These clashes claimed the lives of some 80 student leaders between 1982 and 1988, after which General Zia banned all student union activities in Pakistan. The IJT also has a role in providing a source of recruits for JI -affiliated *jihadi* organisations in Kashmir.

Islamist Organisations of Militant and Non-militant Nature in Pakistan

	SUNNI ISLAM				SHI'A ISLAM
	Deobandi	*Ahl-e-Hadith*	*Barelvi*	*Modern Islamist*	
Political parties	Jamiat Ulema-e-Islam (Fazlur Rehman); Jamiat-Ulema-e-Islam (Sami-ul- Haq): Jamiat-Ulema-e-Islam (Ajmal Qadri)	Jamiat Ahl-e-Hadith	Jamiat Ulema-e-Pakistan (Noorani); Pakistan Awami Tehrik	Jamaat-e-Islami	Tehrik-e-Jafria Pakistan
Quietist movements	Tableeghi Jamaat	Markaz Da'wat-ul-lrshad	Da'waat-e-Islami		
Sectarian groups	Sipah-e-Sahaba Pakistan; Lashker-e-Jhangvi		Sunni Tehrik		Sipah-e-Muhammad Pakistan
Jihadi groups	Harkat-ul-Jihad-e-Islami; Harkat-ut-Ansar: Harkat-ul-Mujahideen; Jaish-e-Muhammad; Tehrik-e- Taliban Pakistan; Tehrik-e-Nifaaz-e-Shariati Muhammad; Lashkar-e-Islam: Ghazi Force	Lashkar-e-Taiba; Tehrik- ul-Mujahideen	Ansar-ul-Islarn (Khyber Agency)	Hizbul-Mujahideen; Al Badr	Hizb-ul-Momineen
Trusts and charity organisations	Al-Rashid Trust; Al-Akhtar Trust	Khair-un-Naas: Jamaat-ud-Da'waa; Rabita Trust	Barkati trust	Al-Khidmat Foundation	
Student Organisations	Jamiat Tuleba-e-Islam	Ahl-e-Hadith Youth Force: Ahl-e-Hadith Students Federation	Anjuman Tuleba-e-Islam	Islami Jamiat-e-Tuleba; Islami Jamiat Tulebaat	Imamia Student Organisation

HIZB-UL-MUJAHIDEEN (PARTY OF FREEDOM FIGHTERS, OR HM)

Origins

The HM is generally viewed as the militant wing of the JI that exclusively operates in Kashmir since its inception in 1989. It is also considered to be the largest Kashmiri militant group that advocates the liberation of Kashmir or that it should accede to Pakistan. However, the group's origins are mired in controversy. It is believed that the HM was formed by the ISI with the support of the JI to limit the growing influence of the Jammu and Kashmir Liberation Front (JKLF). Three people were instrumental in this process: JI leader in Jammu and Kashmir Maulana Saaduddin, the *amir* of JI Maulana Tufail, and General Zia-ul-Haq. Several smaller militant groups that sought financial and logistic support from the ISI -backed JI were merged in September 1989 to form the HM under the leadership of Ahsan Dar.

The HM, like any other *jihadi* group, has not been immune to differences in opinion over strategies and tactics within its leadership. This has given rise to a number of splinter groups. These include:

- Zia Tigers
- Maududi Squad
- Tehri k-e-Jihad-i-Islami
- Allah Tigers
- Al Hamza
- Ansarul Islam
- AI Badr

The Chief Patrons of the HM are Ahsan Dar and Syed Salahuddin. HM in Kashmir is led by Ghazi Nasiruddin. HM in Pakistan-administered Kashmir is led by Ghulam Nabi Nausheri. HM in Pakistan is led by Syed Salahuddin.

In the late 1990s the HM was superseded by the performance of groups such as the LeT and the JeM. However, it began to receive more attention since January 2002, when these groups were banned by the Pakistani government. The HM was designated a Foreign Terrorist Organisation by the United States in May 2003.

Objectives

The HM's main objective is to liberate Kashmir and to unite it with Pakistan although some of its cadres are known to support independence for Kashmir. The group aims to create awareness amongst Muslims about jihad; nurture the spirit of jihad by training young men to participate in Kashmiri jihad and to provide funds for those involved in jihad.

Strategies and Tactics

The HM's militant operations primarily target those of Indian origin or those having pro-Indian links. Its tactics include torture and assassinations. It also has the capacity to carry out raids, ambushes and jailbreaks.

Recruitment and Training

The recruitment process deems any individual wanting to liberate Jammu and Kashmir from Indian oppression as eligible to join the HM provided he understands the beliefs and goals of the organisation; conforms to the obligations of *sharia*; and takes an oath to this end. The HM has benefited from the JI's efficient organisational structure in Jammu and Kashmir to attract supporters, but its main sources of recruitment are the IJT and *madaris* run by the JI. HM cadres receive training at HiG training camps in Afghanistan.

Funding

The HM relies heavily on the JI for its funding. The JI collects donations from boxes placed all over Pakistan and Kashmir. It has also set up five different foundations to fund the HM's jihad and the families of martyrs who are killed in action. These foundations include the Kashmir Fund Kashmir Kafalat Fund; Al-Khidmat Foundation; Shuhada-e-Islam Foundation (Martyrs of Islam), and Islamic Mission Britain.

Organisation

There is no consensus on the number of HM cadres. The HM itself claims that it has 2,500 active *mujahideen* and a total of 13,000 members. It operates from its headquarters in Muzaffarabad in Pakistan-occupied Jammu and Kashmir. The HM's organisation is similar to an army. It is a highly organised and hierarchical structure, whose top tier is composed of a central council led by a commander in chief responsible for functions such as intelligence-gathering, planning logistics, finance, education, training and media. Below this tier there are either three or four battalions at the district level. Each battalion has three platoon companies led by a platoon commander. In turn, each platoon comprises three sections of 11 *mujahideen* each. In addition to this, the HM has a women's wing called Banaat-ul-Islam and has its own news agency called Kashmir Press International.

Networks and affiliations

The HM does not identify with the Taliban, al Qaeda, or any of the insurgent groups that operate in Afghanistan. However, there are some reports that claim that Hekmetyar's HiG has allowed HM cadres to receive training at its camps in eastern Afghanistan. The HM operates exclusively in Kashmir. It is known to have some networks with other *jihadi* groups in Kashmir through the *Shura-e-Jihad* and Muttahida Jihad Council.

DEOBANDI MILITANTS IN PAKISTAN

There are about 46 Deobandi organisations, but these are divided by functional differences. The political expression of Deobandi thinking is found in the JUI, which is further split into three factions led by Fazlur Rehman, Ajmal Qadri, and Sami-ul-Haq. These factions were created less due to ideological or strategic differences but more on personality differences among the faction leaders. Apart from the JUI, the SSP also participates in mainstream politics. Deobandi sectarian groups are active against the Shi'a, Barelvi, and Ahmadis.

HARKAT-UL-JIHAD-E-ISLAMI (ISLAMIC JIHAD MOVEMENT, OR HUJI)

Origins

The HuJI has been referred to as the original creator of Deobandi jihadi groups in Pakistan as it is the first *jihadi* organisation in Pakistan. There is another view that the precursor to Pakistani *jihad* was Massoud Alvi's *Jabha-Khalidia* that was founded in 1973 in Multan. (Massoud Alvi was a mentor to Fazlur Rehman Khalil, the founder of the HuM. Alvi's movement later became the *Jamiat-ul-Mujahideen* during the Afghan jihad. This is not to be confused with the HM offshoot of the same name in Kashmir.) In 1980, three students named Irshad Ahmed, Abdus Samad Sial and Muhammad Akhtar hailing from Karachi's *Jamia Uloom al-Islamia* left to participate in the Afghan jihad against Soviet occupation.

They called their group *Jamiat-ul-Ansar ul-Afghaneen* (Party of the Friends of the Afghan People) and allied themselves with Maulvi Nasrullah Mansur's *Harakat Inqilaab-e-Islami* and Yunus Khalis's faction of the *Hizb-e-Islami*. As a result they became the principal *jihadi* group to impart military training to Pakistani *madrassa* students wanting to participate in the Afghan *jihad*. These trainees were later organised as the HuJI Mir. The HuJI was established by the JUI and Tableeghi Jamaat in the initial stages of the Afghan *jihad* to run relief camps for the Afghan *mujahideen*. It is only as the war continued that the CIA, through the ISI, contacted the HuJI leadership to train its members to become militants against Soviet forces.

In the aftermath of Soviet withdrawal from Afghanistan, the HuJI turned its attentions toward Kashmir but due to internal disagreements among the leadership, the group split in 1991 resulting in the formation of *Harkat-ul-Mujahideen* (Movement of the Mujahideen, HuM) under the leadership of Maulana Fazlur Rehman Khalil. It is reported that this rift did not suit the Saudi patrons of the HuJI and so efforts were made in 1993 to unite the two groups in the form of *Harkat-ul-*Ansar (Movement of Friends, or HuA) under the leadership of Maulana Saadatullah Khan. (The HuA was most active in the jihad in Kashmir and is known to use the cover name of Al Faran for its terrorist activities). Another view suggests that this merger was facilitated by the ISU because it was at this stage that the ISI began to encourage collaboration between the HuA and the HM in Kashmir. However, this alliance lasted only four years. In 1997, the HuA was designated a terrorist organisation by the United States, which was a contributing factor for the group to once again split into the HuJI and the HuM. Since 9/11, the HuJI, under the leadership of Qari Saifullah Akhtar, has supported al Qaeda and the Taliban against the U.S.-led coalition forces.

The HuJI has carried out high-profile terrorist attacks but has claimed responsibility through previously unknown front groups. For example, the attack on Pakistan's ex-prime minister Shaukat Aziz was claimed by the Islambouli Brigade; the attack on Lt. Gen. Ahsan Saleem Hayat was claimed by Jundullah of Karachi.

Objectives

The HuJI is pan-Islamic in its objectives, i.e., to combat the worldwide oppression of Muslims by infidels ... and to give Muslims back their past glory, placing special emphasis on occupied Muslim territory such as Kashmir and Palestine. In the 1980s, the HuJI was focused on Afghan *mujahideen* fight against the Soviet invasion. Its goals are focused on Jammu and Kashmir and the broader Islamisation of Pakistani society.

Strategies and Tactics

The HuJI operations are similar to army manoeuvres, with a large number of militants directly confronting Indian forces rather than using guerrilla tactics. Its tactics include bombings, kidnappings, and armed attacks, mainly directed at Indian targets in Kashmir. Since 9/11, the HuJI expanded its sphere of activities and has been implicated in the January 2002 attack in Kolkata on the United States Information Service Office; the suicide attack that killed 11 French engineers in Karachi in 2005, and assassination attempts on Pakistani politicians and military.

Recruitment and Training

The HuJI recruits a majority of its personnel from religious schools run by Deobandi Ulema in Punjab and in the KPK. It also benefits from the proselytisation campaigns to solicit recruits. *Madrassa* students are attracted to the HuJI more than any other militant organisation because it adheres strictly to Deobandi principles; it has a large network so that recruiters are assigned almost immediately; and finally, because as an organisation it is close to the Taliban, which has meant greater access to jobs in the past.

The HuJI is held responsible for running six training camps (*ma'askar*) in Afghanistan and Pakistan. (These training camps include *Ma'askar* Mehmood Ghaznavi in Kotli, *Ma'askar* Abu Ubaida bin Jarrah in Gilgit, and *Ma'askar* Abu Haneefa in Mansehra in Pakistan. In Afghanistan, the HuJI runs *Ma'askar* Irshad in Jalalabad; *Ma'askar* Khalid Zubair Shaheed in Rashkor and another camp in Kirgha.) The HuA's training curriculum is followed by both the HuJI and the HuM as these organisations share members. The training curriculum is based on religious indoctrination and training in military practices. Apparently, the HuA places no conditions on its training, and a trainee is free to decide which militant organisation or which area of operation he wants to be a part of after his training is complete. The actual training program consists of a one-month course in techniques of weapons-handling and guerrilla warfare and a three-month course in advanced techniques of mountain warfare, map reading, and secure communications.

Funding

Funding is generated through the collection of donations from Pakistan and abroad. The HuJI also profits from the sale of small arms to smaller jihadi organisations.

Organisation

The HuJI is known to have an established network of offices in some 40 districts of Pakistan that are responsible for recruitment and funding. The organisational structure consists of five departments including *Da'wa-o-Irshad* (the Call to Islam), military operations, finance, broadcast, and organisation.

Networks and Affiliations

The HuJI has a wide transnational network. In fact, it prides itself for being the second line of defence of every Muslim country. A brochure of the HuJI claims that it has links with other militant groups in at least twenty-four countries. The HuJI has been directly linked to the Taliban and al Qaeda. The HuJI operatives fought alongside the Taliban during the jihad against the Soviets as a result of which close interpersonal relationships exist among the leaders of the two organisations. Within Pakistan the HuJI is linked to other militant groups that serve as fronts for HuJI activities such as Harkatul Jihad Brigade 111 in Kashmir. The 313 Brigade, led by Ilyas Kashmiri, has also been affiliated with the Hull. The Brigade claimed responsibility for the failed assassination attempt on President Musharraf in December 2003 after which Ilyas Kashmiri was arrested.

JAISH-E-MOHAMMAD (ARMY OF MOHAMMAD, OR JEM)

Origins

The JeM was founded in January 2000 by Masood Azhar who had formerly been an influential member of the HuM. Azhar had been implicated and arrested in the Indian airline hijacking in 1999 and upon his release split from the HuM to form his own group. The JeM received endorsements from influential Deobandi scholars and ideologues such as Mufti Nizamuddin Shamzai and Maulana Yusuf Ludhianvi claiming that the emergence of the JeM as a militant group that would refresh the *jihadi* cause ... and avoid the rifts that had emerged in the other groups. When the JeM first emerged, it established Jinks with the SSP and the LeJ and formally aligned itself with the JUI - F.

In December 2001, the JeM was designated a foreign terrorist organisation by the United States, after which it renamed itself *Tehrik-ul-Furqaan* (Movement of the True Standard) with Shamzai as the chief patron. This organisation was banned by the Musharraf government in 2002. Around the same time, a military commander of the JeM, Maulana Abdul Iabbar and other high profile members of the JeM demanding an increase in attacks on Western interests in Pakistan split from JeM to form the *Jamaat-ul-Furqan* (Party of the True Standard). This organisation claimed responsibility for the terrorist attacks on the Christian churches in Islamabad, Murree, and Taxila in 2002. In the aftermath of these attacks, Azhar confirmed the ouster of Abdul Jabbar from the JeM and that his organisation could not be held responsible for *Jamaat-ul-Furqaan's* activities. It was after this incident that Azhar once more renamed the JeM and called it Khudaam-ul-Islam (Movement of the Servants of Islam).

Aliases of the JeM include Army of Mohammed, Army of the Prophet, Mohammed, *Jaish-e-Mohammad* (Mohammed), *Jaish-e-Mohammad*, *Mujahideen-e-Tanzeem*, *Jaish-i-Mohammed* (Mohammad, Muhammad, and Muhammed), *Jeish-e-Mahammed*, Mohammed's Army, National Movement for the Restoration of Pakistani Sovereignty, and Army of the Prophet, *Tehrik-ul-Furqaan*.

Objectives

The JeM espouses a Sunni Deobandi ideology. In fact, Azhar has authored several important texts in Deobandi Islam. Through these texts, Azhar has attempted to motivate other Muslims to participate in jihad by regaling stories of Muslim conquests against unbelievers. However, the initial involvement of the JeM's leadership with the HuJI lends it a pan-Islamic ideology that is anti-Western, anti-Jewish and anti-Indian. The JeM's main objectives are centred on jihad in Kashmir.

Strategies and Tactics

The JeM was implicated in assassination attempts on President Musharraf in late 2003 and on the murder of journalist Daniel Pearl. However, most of the JeM's activity has been in Kashmir where it has carried out a number of *fidayeen* attacks on Indian security forces. The JeM is the first militant organisation to use suicide attacks in Kashmir. The JeM also publishes and widely disseminates its publications *Islah* (reform) and *Shamshir* (sword) as propaganda tools.

Recruitment and Training

The JeM primarily derives its strength from Punjab and is part of the Punjabi Taliban network. General estimates place the JeM's active ranks at around 5,000 with 1,500-2,000 fighters. The JeM regularly sends student teams for *tabligh* to *madrassas*, government schools, and colleges to recruit potential militants. The JeM is known to operate two major training camps in Balakot and Kabul.

Funding

It is widely understood that when the JeM split from the HuM, it took a lot of material resources from its parent organisation. But it also received support from other Sunni groups that gave the fledgling group seed money to start its operations. The JeM, like all other militant groups, depends on donations from supporters in Pakistan and Middle East and as an organisation is particularly adept at pamphleteering to solicit these donations. The Al-Rashid Trust founded by Maulana Abdul Jabbar of Jamia Binoria, Karachi, is strongly affiliated to the JeM. It is known to have provided nearly Rs 20 million, or US$(2008)250,000, as seed money for the creation of the JeM. The trust's network of mosques and *madrassas* in Afghanistan has facilitated the expansion of the JeM's activities. The Al-Akhtar Trust, a charitable organisation, supports the JeM among other militant organisations by collecting funds for the welfare of *mujahideen*. The JeM also makes a profit from the sale of sacrificial animal skins.

Organisation

The JeM's network in Pakistan is spread in more than 78 districts with its main offices in Karachi, Bahawalpur, and Multan. Its central decision-making body is the 12-member Majlis-e-Shura (Council of Advisers) headed by an *amir*. This body oversees the operations of seven other departments responsible for military operations, the release of captured *mujahideen*, recruitment, the families of the martyrs, enforcement of vice and virtue, revival of *Sunnah* and media.

Networks and Affiliations

The JeM is strongly linked to the Jamia Binoria, a *madrassa* in Karachi. *Ulema* from Jamia Binoria, Shamzai, and Ludhianvi helped in the formation of the JeM, headed by Azhar who is a former student and teacher at the *madrassa*. Due to its adherence to Deobandi principles, the JeM also established links with Pakistani sectarian organisations, the SSP and the LeJ. These groups share mentors and ideologues. The JeM is now included by analysts in the Punjabi Taliban network.

The JeM is believed to have close links with the Pakistani ISI, the Taliban, and al Qaeda who have all contributed finances and equipment to establish the JeM. The link with the Taliban is especially important to mention, since it was the Taliban who negotiated Azhar's release after the hijacking of the Indian airline in 1999. Several JeM members who defected from the HuJI and the HuM were closely connected to the Taliban leadership since the days of the Afghan war.

SIPAH-E-SAHABA (CORPS OF THE PROPHET'S COMPANIONS, OR SSP)

Origins

Maulana Hag Nawaz Ihangvi and his associates founded the SSP, initially known as the *Anjuman-e-Sipah-e-Sahaba* in September 1985 in Jhang, a district in western Punjab to counter the rising influence of Shi'ism in the wake of the Iranian Revolution. (Qari Zia-ur-Rehman Farooqi, Maulana lsrar-ul-Haq Qasimi, and Maulana Azam Tariq were founding members of the SSP and, after Jhangvi's death in 1993, served as leaders of the SSP). The SSP emerged from the JUI, which was in agreement with it over ideology but not method. There was no formal split and hence, the relationship between the JUI and the SSP has been very ambiguous. In fact, Jhangvi remained a member of the JUI eventually rising to the position of *naib-amir* (deputy leader). But Jhangvi had a more hard-line, militant, anti-Shi'a agenda than his contemporaries in the JUI and it is in 1989 that the SSP emerged as a separate organisation.

The SSP has operated as a political party in its own right by participating regularly in provincial and national elections; for instance, SSP leader Azim Tariq was a serving member of the National Assembly when he was assassinated in 2003. In 1996, the LeJ, led by Riaz Basra, emerged after dissension in SSP ranks led by Riaz Basra. It is widely believed that no formal split occurred but that the LeJ was the militant wing of the SSP. Besides the LeJ, the SSP also spawned a number of splinter groups, more militant in character than itself - the Jhangvi Tigers, AI-Haq Tigers, *Tanzeem-ul-Haq*, *Al-Farooq*, and the Al-Badr Foundation. In 2002, the SSP was one of the five militant organisations that were banned by the Musharraf regime. After the ban, the SSP continued to operate under the name Millat-e-Islamia Pakistan (Nation of an Islamic Pakistan). Currently Allama Ali Sher Ghazni is the patron-in-chief of the banned SSP with Maulana Zia-ul-Qasmi serving as the chair of the Supreme Council.

Objectives

Several factors explain the impetus behind the formation of the SSP. The most obvious reason was to counter Shi'a influence, and to curtail the organisational rise of the TNFJ, which was believed to be supported by the Iranian government. The roots of sectarian violence in Pakistan can be attributed to the Zia regime's drive toward Islamisation based on Sunni interpretations of Islam. A socio-economic explanation is that the SSP was formed in response to the domination of the Sunni Muslims by Shi'a landlords in Jhang. Ideologically, the SSP was created to demand the establishment of a Pakistani state that is based on Sunni, Hanafi Islam and emulated the rightly- guided caliphs of early Islam.

Strategies and Tactics

SSP extremists have mostly operated in two ways: targeted killings of prominent members of the Shi'a community and in particular TNFJ members and to attack worshippers in Shi'a mosques. The SSP has also not shied away from attacking symbols of the Iranian government. With time, SSP militants have started using more sophisticated weaponry to carry out their operations. A more subversive tactic to recruit and spread awareness of the SSP has been the dissemination of virulent anti-Shi'a literature in *madaris* and mosques. It publishes a monthly called Khilafat-e-Rashida (The Rightly Guided Caliphate). The SSP also organizes anti-shi'a rallies and campaigns.

SSP activists blamed Iran-backed Shi'a militants for the assassination of their leader Maulana Jhangvi in 1990. In December SSP militants killed Sadiq Ganji, Iran's consul general in Lahore. In January 1997, an Iranian cultural centre was set on fire. Other similar attacks led to the deaths of an Iranian diplomat and air force personnel. In retaliation, Shi'a militants carried out a bomb blast on Lahore High Court killing Jhangvi's successor, Zia-ur-Rehman.

Recruitment and Training

The core of the SSP's supporters is formed by Sunni peasantry in the rural areas of Jhang and by the merchant and trader classes in the urban centres. The *madrassas* are also a major recruiting ground for the SSP. Initially the SSP recruited from Deobandi and Ahl-e-Hadith *madrassas*, but over time the SSP has established its own *madrassa* network centered in Punjab and Karachi. SSP militants have been known to get *jihadi* training in Afghanistan while fighting alongside the Taliban against the Northern Alliance and the Hazarajat Shi'a population.

Funding

To fund its organisation and activities the SSP has relied on contributions from its supporters in the form of *zakat*. Although the SSP is rooted in rural Punjab, it relies heavily on Sunni businesspeople for its funding. The SSP also thrives on considerable financial and logistic backing from the Saudi government, which has wanted to curb Iran's influence over the Shi'a population in Pakistan.

Organisation

The SSP is a tightly organised group and has branches in 74 districts of Pakistan with approximately one million members. It also has an affiliated student wing and welfare trust. It maintains its headquarters in two of the largest Deobandi *madrassas*, Jarmiat-ul-Uloorn Eidgah in Bahawalnagar and Dar-ul-Uloom Faqirwali in Fort Abbas. From these two *madrassas* it coordinates the activities of 5,000-6,000 activists and a vast network of 500 local offices in Pakistan and abroad. The SSP has branches in several countries including Saudi Arabia, Bangladesh, Canada, and the United Kingdom.

Networks and Affiliations

The SSP has consisted of two loosely allied subgroups, namely the LeJ (a domestic anti-Shi'a group) and the JeM (an externalist face of the SSP). This is in keeping with the trend that newly emerging militant groups remain under the tutelage of established organisations until they develop required levels of proficiency and organisational salience.

The SSP also has links with the Taliban since many activists participated in the Afghan jihad and later helped Taliban forces fight the Northern Alliance and Shi'a population in Hazarjat, Afghanistan. After 9/11, the exploitation of sectarian differences in Kurram and Orakzai agencies in the FATA have also drawn SSP activists to support the TTP against the Shi'a population there. The SSP supports al Qaeda's agenda of global *jihad*. But there is no concrete evidence to suggest that a strategic or operational alliance exists between the SSP and al Qaeda.

The SSP is also linked to the ISI. It had the backing of the military regime when it first emerged in the 1980s. Furthermore, through its elected representatives the SSP has maintained close ties with the Pakistani state. It has also remained linked with other religious political parties, most notably the JUI and the JI through the *Milli Yekhjehati* Council (Council for National Unity).

LASHKAR-E-JHANGVI (ARMY OF JHANGVI, OR LEJ)

Origins

The LeJ is a radical offshoot of the SSP that was formed in 1996 by Riaz Basra, Akram Lahori, and Malik Ishaque. Perhaps, it was formed to function as the militant wing of the SSP to carry out attacks against the Shi'a community and became independent when it gained more proficiency. It is also believed that the LeJ was formed because a faction of extremist SSP members was dissatisfied with SSP leadership for moving away from Ihangvi's ideals resulting in a merger between Basra's organisation and the already existing SSP splinter groups Jhangvi Tigers, Al Haq Tigers, and Allah Akbar.

In October 2000, the LeJ split into two factions, one headed by Riaz Basra and the other led by Qari Abdul Hai (aka Qari Asadullah or Talha). The reason given for the split was a strategic difference over whether or not to resume sectarian strife that had receded considerably after Musharraf's coup in 1999. While Basra was in favour of resuming militant attacks on the Shi'a community, Hai opposed the plan. Musharraf attempted to curtail the violence that was unleashed by the LeJ by banning the group in August 2001. In 2002 during a shoot-out with the police, the leaders Riaz Basra and Asif Ramzi were killed in Multan and Karachi, respectively. This was a major setback for the LeT. Akram Lahori was appointed as Basra's successor, but he was taken into police custody two years later. The United States designated the LeJ as a foreign terrorist organisation in 2003.

Objectives

Many reasons have been given for the LeJ's split from the SSP ranging from accusations by the LeJ's membership that the SSP had deviated from Ihangvi's ideals; the rising violence of the Shi'a sectarian group, Sipah-e-Muhammad Pakistan; the assassinations of SSP leaders by Shi'a militant groups; and finally, to enable the LeJ to emerge as a militant organisation in its own right. However, the objectives of the LeJ remained the same as its parent organisation. Its primary objective was to attack Shi'a and Iranian targets in Pakistan. But after 9/11 the LeJ's activities have expanded to include wider Islamic *jihad* and the group has bought into the ideology of the al Qaeda.

Strategies and Tactics

LeJ is a unique militant organisation in that it shuns media exposure and operates as covertly as possible. It communicates through fax messages to accept responsibility for its activities and through its publication *Intiqaam-e-Haq*.

Initially, the LeJ's main strategy was to kill targets from moving motorbikes. As LeJ operatives have gained more training and have started using more advanced weapons, hit men use a combination of hand grenades to kill and create panic, automatic fire to strike those stampeding to safety and suicide detonations to finish themselves off and the rest. The LeJ times its attacks during daylight hours so that they make the evening news. It is known to favour suicide bombing. There are reports of the LeJ training female bombers to carry bombs concealing them under their *burkas* or in their handbags. The LeJ typically works alone, but is known to have collaborated with other militant groups like the JeM, for example, in the murder of Daniel Pearl. There is also evidence to suggest that HuM, LeJ and JeM militants have collaborated under the front name Al-Qanoon (The Law) as an ad hoc hit squad.

Basra used to make threatening phone calls to police officers who made attempts to investigate the LeJ's activities. These calls were effective in deterring police officers from investigating the LeJ, to the extent that police officers concealed their identities when interrogating SSP and LeJ operatives. The LeJ is also unique in its policy to assassinate those police officers who investigate their activities.

Recruitment and Training

The LeJ recruits primarily from mosques and *madrassas* that are linked to the Deobandi school of thought. The LeJ's leadership conducts a thorough whetting process before it recruits members. The criteria for selection are based on religious conviction, skill, and commitment to carry out *fidayeen* and suicide attacks. The LeJ recruits receive training at a camp located near Kabul and some have been trained at *Ma'askar* Khalid Bin Walid run by the HuJI.

Funding

Not much is known about the LeJ's financial resources. But like the SSP, the LeJ has also benefited from contributions made by other Deobandi groups and sympathizers in Saudi Arabia and Pakistan.

Organisation

When the LeJ was established, Riaz Basra was appointed as the *Salaar-e-Aala* (commander in chief) with 12 *Salaars* (sub-commanders) under his command. The LeJ's organisation is decentralised and similar to that of al Qaeda. The LeJ has adopted a cell-based structure because it has the advantage of providing increased security. Typically, a cell of three to seven members carries out a particular operation and is disbanded later. Due to this decentralised and compartmentalised configuration, it is difficult to determine the actual number of LeJ activists.

Networks and Affiliations

The Taliban have been a staunch ally of the SSP and the LeJ, allowing the latter to establish a training base in its territory. The LeJ has been implicated in attacks that were carried out in collaboration with other militant groups, namely the HuM and the JeM. There is a strong operational relationship between the LeJ and the Islamic Movement of Uzbekistan (IMU). These links were forged in Afghanistan when both groups were fighting the Northern Alliance on behalf of the Taliban. The Lej's endeavour to train female suicide bombers has provided evidence of links to the IMU, which the only organisation imparting such training.

TEHRIK-E-TALIBAN PAKISTAN (STUDENTS MOVEMENT OF PAKISTAN, OR TTP)

Origins

The TTP is the overarching organisation that presents a united front for Deobandi Sunni militants in the border area between Afghanistan and Pakistan. In December 2007, a number of militant groups formally came together under the leadership of Baitullah Mehsud from South Waziristan to attack U.S. and NATO forces in Afghanistan and targets within Pakistan.

TTP is also known as the Pakistan Taliban as opposed to the Afghan Taliban led by Mullah Omar. (The latter are also known as the Quetta *Shura*). The TTP is a catch-all name for ethnically Pashtun militants on the Pakistani side of the border. But this blurs the fractious and decentralised nature of the various militant groups. Not all militant groups operational in this area are members of the TTP. To refer to the TTP as the Pakistani Taliban is also misleading because it implies a distinction from the Afghan Taliban. This distinction is not useful for three reasons. First, the tribes inhabiting this region spill over onto both sides of the border. Second, some of the militant groups may have their headquarters in Pakistan but may only be operational in Afghanistan (e.g., the HQN and the HiG). Third, by referring to the Taliban as Pakistani implies that only the Pakistani government is responsible for countering the militant insurgency and that the so-called Afghan Taliban are someone else's responsibility.

The Afghan Taliban are understood to comprise the leaders of the former Taliban government of Afghanistan. These leaders are referred to as the "Quetta *Shura*" after the Pakistani city where they are based. The Quetta *Shura* is led by Mullah Omar. The HQN is also considered a part of the Afghan Taliban because of its tribal roots and operational capacity in Afghanistan, but it has deep roots in North Waziristan in the FATA.

Tribal militant groups operating in the FATA have become a militant force in their own right. Three events triggered small, militant groups to network with each other. First, Pakistani forces focused their attentions in the FATA on capturing foreign militants linked to al Qaeda, leaving these groups to operate freely. Second, the proscription of various Pakistani militant groups led many of their members to seek refuge in the FATA and to join Taliban ranks. Finally, most observers agree that the Pakistani government's military operation against Lal Masjid in 2007 triggered militancy in the region because it was perceived as an attack by the Pakistani government on its own people. These groups chose not to merge with the Quetta *Shura* led by Mullah Omar and instead developed their own identity. They differed from the Quetta *Shura* Taliban in their area of operation and volatile relationship with the Pakistani government. Not only did the TTP engage in military attacks within Pakistan, at other times it signed peace deals directly with the government.

Several systemic factors explain why these disparate groups came together despite their different backgrounds, tribal affiliations, and strategic inclinations. First, they are all linked by ideological and historical commonalities. A large number of these militants emerged out of Deobandi *madaris* located in Pakistan's KPK and Balochistan provinces and sought ideological guidance from the Taliban led by Omar. Many of them also fought alongside the Taliban as *mujahideen* to expel the Soviet forces from Afghanistan in the 1980s. Hence, militancy in the FATA has been described less as a cause than a symptom of radicalism in Pakistan's politics. Second, the Pakistani government's neglect of FATA's governance alienated the men who joined these groups looking for an alternative form of political structure. How these groups managed to expand their influence over the FATA and gain support locally is a separate question, one that is answered by political analysts in a number of ways. The most common explanation is that TTP exploited local grievances: socio-economic concerns among local Pakistanis; Pakistani government's failure to provide security and justice; and frustration with government corruption. It was less costly for local populations to acquiesce to the militant groups than actually confronting or opposing them.

Objectives

The main objectives of the TTP are to enforce *Sharia*, unite against NATO forces in Afghanistan and perform defensive *jihad* against the Pakistani army. However, within the TTP there are numerous disagreements regarding whether the Pakistani government ought to be viewed as a legitimate target of *jihadi* activity or not; whether foreign fighters ought to be included under the banner of the TTP; and what is the right balance between the number of operations that should be carried out in Afghanistan and Pakistan. These disagreements have led to a lack of cohesion within the TTP's organisation. Yet, what binds these groups together is a common purpose to establish an Islamic state in Pakistan that is based on *sharia* law, to resist any attempts that counter this goal and to support efforts to expel the coalition forces in Afghanistan. Their specific interpretation of *sharia* law, much like the Quetta *Shura* Taliban, is austere and manifested itself in the establishment of parallel *sharia* courts and in the reformation of society along rigid Deobandi lines (attacks on girl's schools, barbershops, and DVD and CD stores).

The TTP leadership does not participate in Kashmiri *jihad* because that does not help to advance their goals in Afghanistan or against the Pakistani government, which is mistrusted because of its collaboration with U.S. and NATO forces. The TTP justifies its attacks on fellow citizens and fellow Muslims by adopting the *takfiri* doctrine. Under this doctrine the Pakistani government, due to its allegiance to Western states, is regarded as apostate and corrupt.

Strategies and Tactics

To indicate their resentment toward the Pakistani government, the TTP has used a combination of intimidating local tribal leaders and targeting the limited administrative infrastructure in the tribal areas. Ironically, to spread their message, the TTP employs FM radio stations as the primary medium of communication.

The strategies adopted by the TTP to achieve their objectives include forging links with militant groups in Punjab and Karachi; exploiting the dissatisfaction of the local populace toward the Pakistani government to form a support base for itself; being willing to share power and to coexist with the Pakistani government so as not to give the latter any reason to take military action against the militants; exploiting sectarian differences to strengthen its Sunni constituency; presenting a united front under common names such as *Ittehad Shura-ul-Mujahideen* (United Council of Mujahideen) because it provides them with legitimacy and access to resources; and making deals with the Pakistani government.

Recruitment and Training

The TTP has two types of recruits: unemployed youth who are drawn to jihad as a way of gaining a livelihood or enhance their social importance; and local criminals who see jihad as a lucrative business. Those who are not ideologically motivated toward jihad have seen an opportunity to generate revenue by charging a price for providing shelter and support to militants. There are also a number of reports, which claim that a large number of TTP's members and senior leadership are recruited from Deobandi *madaris*. The average age of a member is 35, with little or no formal education and often not even from a *madrassa*. A majority of the members have a poor family background. The leaders of the TTP have been observed to have affiliations with the dominant religious parties in Pakistan-JUI and JI.

Funding

The TTP finances its organisation and its activities through extortion, smuggling, donations, and ransom money from kidnappings. The TTP, unlike the Quetta Shura Taliban, has not been averse to using advanced media technologies to solicit donations from local *madrassas*, businesspeople, and ordinary people who are afraid to confront the militants. Other methods of collecting funds are more unique to the TTP. For example, the TTP is connected to crime-networks such as Jundullah in Karachi. These criminals are provided with hit lists, money, and weapons to carry out bank robberies and kidnappings. The stolen money is then transferred via TTP money couriers to South Waziristan. The TTP has also carried out kidnappings for ransom targeting mostly businesspeople and aid-workers.» Similar to the Quetta *Shura* Taliban, the TTP has also relied on raising revenue from the narcotics trade, extortion rackets, and by levying taxes on the transport and timber industry. Merchants and truckers who require a secure transit corridor pay taxes, make contributions and lend support to the TTP. The TTP's leaders have also tapped valuable natural resources such as wood, gem stones, and marble, which can be quite profitable. The timber industry, for instance, lends support to extremists not just for its own protection but to prevent the government from closely monitoring its activity.

Organisation

The *majlis-e-shura* of the TTP has representation from all of the FATA's seven tribal agencies and from the KPK's settled districts of Swat, Bannu, Tank, Lakki Marwat, Dera Ismail Khan, Kohistan, Buner, and Malakand. Even though the TTP is a young organisation, it has strong operational capabilities. The total number of fighters is unknown. Various militant groups fighting under the umbrella of the TTP, based on their alleged goals are:

(a) *The Mehsud Group*: the core conglomerate of the Tehrik-e-Taliban, including Baitullah Mehsud's group and his affiliates across

FATA, as well as Maulana Fazlullah's Swat chapter, who have waged a jihad against the Pakistani state.

(b) *Muqami Taliban*: typically pro-government factions, including Maulvi Nazir (South Waziristan) and Gul Bahadur (North Waziristan), focused primarily on supporting the Afghan jihad.

(c) *Punjabi Taliban*: factions of groups previously focused on sectarianism inside Pakistan or the Kashmir/India jihad now networking with TTP.

(d) Niche groups with specific ambitions, e.g. Ghazi Force, now interlinked with TTP.

The breakdown of the insurgency in the FATA according to local power structures in each of the agencies and how they relate to the TTP is tabulated below:

North Waziristan	• HQN • Maulana Hafiz Gul Bahadur
South Waziristan	• TTP (Baitullah Mehsud- deceased) • Mullah Nazir • Turkistan Bhittani
Khyber	• Lei (Mangal Bagh) • Ansar-ul-Islam (Pir Saif-ur-Rehman) • TTP (Khyber)
Kurram	• TTP(Kurram)
Orakzai	• TTP(Orakzai) • LeJ • Ghazi Force
Bajaur	• TTP (Maulvi Faqir Muhd)
Mohmand	• TTP (Omar Khalid)

North Waziristan's Shawal region has served as a safe haven for numerous militants escaping from U.S.-led counterinsurgency operations. This agency is home to the HQN, Hafiz Gul Bahadur's group, al Qaeda, and Uzbek fighters. South Waziristan is the centre of TTP activity. "The leader of the TTP, Baituallh Mehsud, led the Mehsud tribe in South Waziristan. After Mehsud"s death, his close aide, Wali-ur Rehman, assumed the TTP command of the Mehsud tribe. The TTP's anti-Pakistan stance is a source of division among the agency's major tribes, the Mehsuds, Wazirs, and Bhittanis.

Khyber, Kurram, and Orakzai agencies came under the sway of the TTP when Hakimullah Mehsud assumed command of the region. Kurram agency with its large Shi'a population, is torn by Shi'a-Sunni violence that has been further fuelled by the TTP presence and the interference of the LeJ and the SSP. The conflict in Khyber agency is more a Deobandi-Barelvi clash between Mufti Shakir's *Lashar-e-Islam* (Army of Islam) and Pir Saif-ur-Rehrnans *Ansar-ul-Islam* (Friends of Islam) formed in 2006. Orakzai agency is controlled by a number of niche militant groups such as the Abdullah Azzam Brigade and the Ghazi Force that support the TTP cause.

Army of Islam (LeI) was inspired by a local tribesman, Haji Namdar, who founded the *Amr bil Maroof Nahi Anil Munkar* (Promotion of Virtue and Prevention of Vice, or AMNAM) in Khyber agency. The control of this group was taken over by Mufti Munir Shakir, who disseminated his militant rhetoric through FM radio broadcasts. Shakir was exiled in 2005, after which the LeJ was led by Mangal Bagh (a bus conductor and party activist). The LeJ was portrayed as a reformist organisation against criminal activity, drug trafficking, and gambling. Its major clash was with the Barelvi-oriented *Ansar-ul-Islam*, The LeJ under Bagh's leadership did not attempt to merge with the TTP. However, Pakistani military operations have indirectly had the effect of bringing Bagh and the TTP closer, with both organisations united in their effort against Pakistani security forces.

The Ghazi Force is named after the head cleric of Lal Masjid (Red Mosque) who was killed during the military siege on the mosque in Iuly 2007. Its founder, Fidaullah (arrested by Pakistani security forces in 2009), studied at a LaI Masjid seminary, and since 2007 has been encouraging his students to enter jihad and seek military training in Waziristan. The primary purpose of the Ghazi Force is to avenge the Pakistani military's raid on Lal Masjid. To achieve these ends it has collaborated with the TTP to carry out attacks on Islamabad and Rawalpindi. The group is based in Orakzai agency and has a training camp in Hangu, KPK. The Ghazi Force relies on a cell-based organisation and is believed to have 50 fighters mostly recruited from *madaris*. The Ghazi Force is anti-Shi'a, which means that there is a possibility of future collaboration with sectarian groups that operate on the same ideological lines. In a sense, the Ghazi Force is akin to a "franchise group" that has emerged out of the TTP.

Bajaur is home to a number of militant groups of which the TTP and the TNSM are most predominant. Bajaur's importance is augmented because of its ideal location to access trade routes between Pakistan and Afghanistan. Maulvi Faqir Muhammad is the TTP leader in this agency and is believed to have close links with Bin Laden's deputy, Zawahiri. Faqir Muhammad was originally a member of the JI and later joined the TNSM, which he left to join the TTP. Another key figure in Bajaur is Qari Zia-ur Rahman, an Afghan commander who leads a militia of trained fighters hailing from Uzbekistan, Chechnya, Turkmenistan, and Afghanistan. Other militant groups operating in Bajaur include the Jaish-e-Islami headed by Wali-ur Rehman, Karwan-e-Niamatullah, and Dr. Ismail's group are reportedly allied with Mehsud's TTP. In the aftermath of Mehsud's death in August 2009, Wali-ur Rehman took over as head of the Mehsud tribe of South Waziristan. The presence of international terrorist groups such as the Islami Jihad Union (IJU), IMU, and al Qaeda have also been traced to Bajaur agency.

Mohmand agency has been relatively peaceful because pro-Pakistani government tribal leaders still have some influence in the areas. The Taliban in Mohmand agency are led by Maulana Omar Khalid who rose to prominence during the Lal Masjid crisis when he captured a shrine in protest. The lack of organised opposition in Mohmand agency has allowed Omar Khalid to establish control. The Quetta Shura Taliban and the HiG also have a presence in Mohmand.

Militancy in Swat centres on the *Tehrik-e-Nifaz-e-Shariati-Mohammad* (Movement for the Enforcement of Islamic Law, TNSM). Unlike the FATA, Pakistani politics significantly influences militancy in Swat as this is a settled district in the KPK that participates in the national electoral system. Upon the formation of the TTP in December 2007, Fazlullah, the leader of the TNSM was appointed the leader of the rtr in Swat. The Lal Masjid crisis was used by Fazlullah as a pretext to launch an aggressive operation against Pakistani security forces in Swat. The confrontation reached such a point that the provincial government signed an agreement with Sufi Muhammad in February 2009 stipulating that *sharia* would be implemented in Swat. However, further escalation of violence prompted the Pakistani government to launch a military offensive against the TNSM in April 2009, which displaced nearly 2.5 million people.

The TNSM was originally founded in the early 1990s by Sufi Muhammad, Maulana Fazlullah's father-in-law. Muhammad rose to prominence as a local leader of the JI. After the U.S. invasion of Afghanistan in 2001, the TNSM mustered an army of 10,000 men to wage *jihad* against the U.S. and NATO forces. This operation was a complete disaster and many Pakistanis lost their lives. Muhammad was arrested by Pakistani security forces in 2002, clearing the way for Fazlullah to take over the leadership of the TNSM. Fazlullah cleverly combined dissatisfaction with the Pakistani government, anti-American sentiment, and religious rhetoric to build a constituency for himself.

Networks and Affiliations

As a direct consequence of Pakistan's collaboration with the U.S.-led Global War on Terrorism militant groups whose goals were driven more by Kashmir or by anti-Shi'a sectarianism are beginning to support the anti-Pakistani outlook of the TTP. These groups include the LeJ, the JeM, the SSP, and the HuM. However, these links are not new since many personal relationships were formed during the 1980s when the leaders of these groups interacted with each other in Deobandi *madaris* or had the opportunity to wage jihad against the Soviets. The so-called Punjabi Taliban network has provided logistic assistance to the TTP within Pakistan's heartland.

After the downfall of the Taliban regime in Kabul post 9/11, many Taliban were given shelter in the FATA by the tribes residing there. One of the factors explaining the hospitality afforded to the refugees is the Pashtunwali code. TTP's anti-Pakistan objectives are in direct conflict with the Quetta Shura and the HQN's efforts to accommodate the Pakistani government as they stage attacks inside Afghanistan. At the same time, the TTP and the Taliban led by Mullah Omar are deeply connected because of interpersonal relations and a shared history. But operational cooperation does not obscure their strategic differences. A third group that is often incorrectly lumped with the Taliban is the HiG. This organisation has an extensive base in the refugee camps in Peshawar, and therefore uses the routes through Khyber agency and training camps located in northern FATA.

Al Qaeda continues to operate in the FATA by building a close relationship with TTP militant groups. There is evidence to suggest that al Qaeda's organisational infrastructure is concentrated in North Waziristan and that it has been training its militants in the same training camps as the TTP. Finally, al Qaeda has provided tremendous ideological support to the TTP, support that the Quetta Shura has not been willing to provide. The al Qaeda has been vocal in its condemnation of the Pakistani state and therefore supports the anti-Pakistan activities of the TTP.

AHL-E-HADITH MILITANTS IN PAKISTAN

The number of Ahl-e-Hadith organisations is the smallest. There are 17 Ahl-e-Hadith organisations in Pakistan. The LeT is the most prominent militant organisation representing this sect.

L.ASHKAR-E-TAIBA (ARMY OF THE PURE, OR LET)

Origins

The *Markaz Da'watul-Irshad* (Centre for Preaching, or MDI) was set up in 1987 at Muridke in Punjab with the objective of assisting in jihad efforts in Kashmir and Afghanistan. This institution was founded by two professors, Hafiz Saeed and Zafar Iqbal. It is believed that Abdullah Azzam known for being bin Laden's ideological mentor also played a role as a founding member. The LeT was formed as the militant wing of the MDI in the late 1980s and began its militant activities in the eastern provinces of Afghanistan, but its attentions were soon refocused by the ISI toward Kashmir in the 1990s. There is evidence to suggest that the seed money of Rs 10 million, or US$(2005) 170,000, for the establishment of the MDI and the LeT came from bin Laden. The link between the LeT and bin Laden is Abdullah Azzam, widely acknowledged as bin Laden's mentor.

The LeT was declared a terrorist organisation by the United States in December 2001 and banned by Gen. Pervez Musharraf in the same year. In 2005 it was also proscribed by the United Nations. The ban triggered the separation of the MDI from the LeT and it was renamed *Jamaat-ud-Da'waa* (Party of the Calling, or TuD) under the leadership of Hafiz Saeed. Maulana Abdul Wahid Kashmiri was appointed the new chief of the LeT and was quick to announce that the LeT's base of operations had been shifted to Indian-Kashmir. While most informed observers are convinced that the TuD is a front organisation so that the LeT can continue its operations unabated, Saeed adamantly claims that there is no link between the LeT's operations and the JuD, the latter strictly being a charitable organisation. Since the ban, there have also been reports that the LeT has fractionalised on account of defections resulting from Saeed's pro-Pakistani government position.

Lashkar-e-Taiba is sometimes also known as "the Army of Medina." This is because Taiba is also the old name of Medina, the Saudi Arabian city. Other aliases for LeT include al-Mansoorain and Islami lnqilaabi Mahaaz (Islamic Revolutionary Front).

The most notable defection was of Maulana Zafar Iqbal, a founding member of the MDI, who has set up a charity organisation by the name of *Khair-un-Naas* (People's Welfare). The organisation has thus far not participated in any militant activity.

Objectives

According to an LeT pamphlet titled "Why Are We Waging Jihad?" the group has declared United States, India, and Israel to be existential threats to Islam, and as such has deemed *jihad* against all threats to Islam to be a religious obligation for all Muslims. The group's literature further justifies a perpetual state of jihad to avenge the loss of any territory that was once under Muslim rule.

An examination of the LeT's militant activities reveals three types of objectives - local, regional, and global. Locally, the LeT concentrates its activities in Kashmir, aiming to rid Kashmir of Indian domination; fomenting larger Hindu-Muslim discord in India and manipulating ethno-religious tensions in Kashmir to incite revolution across India. Regionally, the LeT aims to develop and strengthen a number Muslim-majority states surrounding Pakistan, forming links with other militant groups in Chechnya, Central Asia, India, Burma, and Bosnia. Finally, the LeT, since 2006-2007, is showing signs of expanding its interests beyond the subcontinent. It considers the United States and Israel to be the main enemies of Islam and to that end it has attempted to assist al Qaeda's global *jihad*.

Strategies and Tactics

In keeping with its primary objective to rid Kashmir of Indian presence, the LeT has spearheaded terrorist attacks in Jammu and Kashmir and in India. It has developed guerrilla style "hit and run" operations against Indian targets. Assaults are usually carried out with bombs, land mines, and improvised incendiary devices. This indicates that the LeT has had no compunction in targeting both civilian and security forces. LeT's hallmark modus operandi is a *fidayeen* attack. These have been misconstrued as suicide attacks, where the goal of the attacker is to die in the execution of the attack. However, a *fidayeen* is "one who must complete the mission in the worst circumstances" and who engages in combat during which dying is preferable to being captured. Hence, the goal is not to commit suicide but to kill as many of the enemy as possible until the mission is fulfilled, aborted, or been completed. However, the LeT always denies any role in a terrorist attack that kills civilians

A less violent strategy of the LeT to fuel its jihadist activities is the dissemination of propaganda and recruitment materials such as its monthly and weekly publications. These are distributed in mosques and *madrassas* in Pakistan and abroad. In the absence of efficient delivery of social services by the Pakistani state, the LeT has capitalised on the opportunity to spread its network by doing charitable work through the JuD. Within the headquarters of MDl, a network of social services is coordinated including schools, *madrassas*, and clinics.

The LeT routinely publishes on its website http://www.jamaatudda'wa.com. It also publishes an Urdu monthly, *Al Dawaa*; Urdu weeklies, *Al Jehad* and *Gazwa*; an English monthly, Voices of lslam; an Arabic monthly, *Al Rabat*; and an Urdu monthly for students, *Mujala-e-Tulaba*.

Recruitment and Training

The LeT has been known to recruit and train more militants than it actually needs so that it is never vulnerable to a massive strike. Over-recruitment also increases awareness of the organisation. Its recruitment offices are located throughout Pakistan. The LeT's recruits do not hail from the *madrassas* but tend to be better educated than the average militant from the other groups. A majority of LeT recruits have secondary education or even college degrees. Proselytisation campaigns at college campuses encourage potential recruits to attend congregations held at Muridke. A vast majority of the recruits are Punjabi, usually hailing from Lahore, Gujranwala, and Multan, districts that are all Ahl-e-Hadith strongholds.

Recruits traditionally go through a basic course for two to three weeks (*Daura-e-Am*) and three weeks of religious indoctrination in Ahl-e-Hadith faith (*Daura-e-Suffah*). This is followed by training in guerrilla warfare (*Daura-Khas*). It is only after *Daura-e-Khas* that a select few receive advanced training in specialised skills. It is not unusual for trainees to wait up to a year or more before they graduate to military training. In the meantime they undertake fundraising or proselytisation campaigns. There is a difference between the training given to the militant cadre and the *ulema* cadre. The latter are made to go through a 42-day course following a refresher course called *Bait-ur-Rizwan*. The military training phase is in three stages: a six-month induction period in which recruits learn basic field craft and weapons handling; four to five months of advanced training focusing on language proficiency, urban warfare, small unit tactics, sabotage and assassination; and finally, the tertiary stage, which is for a select few, is specialised training in suicide assaults, computer skills, field communication and explosive techniques.

The LeT has camps, recruitment centres, and offices spread across Pakistan and Pakistan-occupied Kashmir in Muzaffarabad. The LeT reportedly has 2,200 offices across Pakistan and trains its recruits in training camps run by the ISI. In some reports, the LeT is known to use training camps located in eastern Afghanistan in Kunar and northern Afghanistan in Nuristan that are shared with the HiG and al Qaeda. These camps are mainly used for weapons training.

Funding Sources

There are no accurate accounts of the LeT's assets. But it is known that funds are collected through three sources: donations; Islamic non-governmental organisations (NGOs), and sympathetic militant groups. The means used to secure these contributions include collection boxes and solicitation over the Internet. The LeT no longer deposits its funds into banks; instead it invests in legitimate front organisations in order to avoid the risk of bank accounts being frozen or seized . After the ban, the LeT has followed the practice of funnelling its funds through informal banking systems such as *hawala* through intermediaries outside Pakistan.

Since the 1990s the LeT has been recruiting and involved in fund-raising within the Pakistani expatriate community.

Organisation

The LeT's membership is believed to consist of approximately 500 core members, and 150,000 militant cadres, with 750 insurgents on the ground in Jammu and Kashmir. It has a hierarchical organisation resembling an army, with a chief commander, provisional commander, district commander, battalion commander, and so on. The group also has a policymaking body that is headed by an *amir*, and a *naib-amir* (vice chief). The current *amir* of the LeT is MauJana Abdul Wahid Kashrniri, and the operational commander is Zaki ur Rehman Lakhvi. Hafiz Saeed is still considered the ideological leader of the LeT, but he is more involved in running the JuD. The organisation is composed of cells of ten militants each. These militants typically serve on a contract basis receiving between Rs 10,000 to 20,000, or US$(2002) 150-300, per month in salary.

The LeT is also reported to have an extensive network of sleeper cells in Europe, Australia, and United States which are mainly responsible for fund-raising. However, these cells may potentially be used for staging attacks in the West.

Networks and Affiliations

The main reason for its enhanced potential is that the ISI has supported it in a number of ways. The ISI has been known to run some of the LeT's training camps as well as being the group's financier, weapons provider, and abetting the movement of LeT militants across the Line of Control (LoC) in Jammu and Kashmir. The ISI found that using the LeT as a proxy proved to be an effective strategy to combat India in Kashmir. The LeT's focus on Kashmir and its special relationship with the ISI has enabled it to remain relatively unaffected by counterterrorism measures implemented by the Pakistani government.

The LeT prefers to operate independently. But there is evidence to prove that it has operated alongside the Pakistani armed forces in Jammu and Kashmir during the Kargil war in 1999. The LeT has also collaborated with other Deobandi militant groups. There have been increasing reports of collaboration between the LeT and al Qaeda and pro-Taliban groups. While the LeT allows other *jihadi* actors to avail of its training facilities, it is averse to engaging in joint training programmes with Deobandi militant groups due to the ideological disagreement over the conduct of *jihad* within Pakistani territory. Yet the LeT has been known to engage with the Taliban, the TTP, and the JeM over tactics, information exchange and sharing of best practices.

The LeT's most dangerous affiliation is with the Indian Mujahideen and the Student Islamic Movement of India (SIMI), which has been suspected of involvement in the July 2006 Mumbai attacks. Not only is there evidence of the LeT recruiting from among SIMI cadres but also of collaboration on logistics in staging attacks within and beyond India.

The LeT has been known to collaborate with crime syndicates such as with Dawood Ibrahim's D-Company. This is a symbiotic relationship dependent on the provision of arms to carry out insurgencies for the LeT and a cover for the crime syndicate. This involvement with crime syndicates gives the LeT a degree of independence from the ISI as its primary provider of weapons. There is also documented circumstantial evidence that suggests that the LeT provided logistic and perhaps financial support through its network in Paris to Richard Reid, the al Qaeda 'shoe-bomber' to blow up American Airlines Flight 63 in 2001.

BARELVI MILITANTS IN PAKISTAN

Mainstream Sunni Barelvis are conspicuous in their absence from the militant *jihadi* terrain of Pakistan, even though ideologically Barelvis have defined themselves in opposition to Deobandi and Ahl-e-Hadith schools of thought. This seems odd given that the majority of the Sunni population in Pakistan identify themselves as being Barelvi Muslims and there are 43 Barelvi organisations that exist in Pakistan, of which 6 are political parties, 21 are sectarian groups, 12 are *jihadi* groups, 2 are Tablighi organisations, and 2 are educational.

Barelvi interests have been represented in mainstream politics by the JUP and Pakistan Awami Tehrik (PAT). The former was a member of the MMA, which formed the provincial government in the KPK and Balochistan from 2002 to 2007. The JUP like its Deobandi counterpart, the JUI, has also been prone to factionalisation. There are at least five different factions of the JUP that have been formed around individual personalities.

The Barelvi sect also has a quietist apolitical movement by the name of Da'wat-e-Islami that was created as a reaction to the Deobandi-oriented TJ by Maulana Ilyyas Qadri. Finally, to offset the dominance of the SSP as a Deobandi-oriented, anti-Shi'a, group, the Barelvis established the Sunni Tehrik.

SUNNI TEHRIK (MOVEMENT FOR THE SUNNIS)

Origins

Very little has been written about the Sunni Tehrik, perhaps because it is a smaller sectarian group that has limited its operations within Pakistan against other Sunni sects and does not have explicit anti-Western interests. The Sunni Tehrik was created by Mohammad Saleem Qadri in 1990 to counter the growing influence of Deobandi and Ahl-e-Hadith groups. Saleem Qadri was a member of the *Da'wat-e-Islami* and the JUP before he created the Sunni Tehrik. Unlike other sectarian groups that have been reviewed here, the Sunni Tehrik has not been banned, but its activities have been closely monitored by the Pakistani government since January 2002.

Objectives

The Sunni Tehrik claims to be a non-political organisation working to protect the interests of the Ahl-e-Sunnat, which is how the followers of the Barelvi sect refer to themselves. In its manifesto the Sunni, Tehrik also states that it will protect Ahl-e-Sunnat mosques and the believers from a distortion of their faith. Sunni Tehrik objectives stem from an opposition to the prevalence of Deobandi and Ahl-e-Hadith sects and the belief that Ahl-e-Sunnat can demand their rights only if they respond to the threat posed by Deobandi and Ahl-e-Hadith sectarian groups in a similar manner.

Strategies and Tactics

The Sunni Tehrik emerged as a sectarian organisation but its main targets were not the members of the Shi'a community but the Deobandi SSP and the Ahl-e-Hadith LeT. The main tactic used was to take control of mosques that were thought to have been wrongfully taken away from the Ahl-e-Sunnat sect. These episodes resulted in violence, rioting, and aggressive occupation of mosques.

Recruitment and Training

It is believed that the Sunni Tehrik recruits belong to a network of Barelvi *madrassas* called Zia-ul Quran who had refused to join the JUP.

Funding

The Barkati Foundation was set up to manage the finances of the Sunni Tehrik. Members of Sunni Tehrik contribute monthly donations. Money is also collected through the Milad fund, Jahez (dowry) fund, and *Tahafuz Ahl-e-Sunnat* (protection of Ahl-e-Sunnat) fund.

Organisation

After his murder in 2001, Saleem Qadri was replaced by Ghulam Abbas Qadri. The organisation does not have a provincial structure; instead, conveners of 14 divisional centres are directly accountable to the *amir*. These 14 divisional centres include Hyderabad, Sukkur, Nawabshah, Mullan, Bahawalpur, Bahawalnagar, Lahore, Sahiwal, Mian Chunnu, Sialkot, Gujrat, Turbat, Quetta, and Jaffrabad. The main hub of Sunni Tehrik activities is in Karachi.

SHI'A MILITANTS IN PAKISTAN

Efforts to organize representative groups for the Shi'a community began after the Zia government's Islamisation campaign during the 1980s. The *Tehrik-e-Nifaaz-e-Fiqah-e-Jaffriya* (Movement for the Implementation of Jaffriya Law, or TNFJ) was formed in April 1974 under the leadership of Allama Mufti Jaffer Hussain. He was succeeded by Allama Arif Al after he was murdered in 1988, leading to a split in the TNFJ. The disagreements within the TNFJ centred around two issues: one, the nomination of Sajjid Naqvi as Hussaini's successor; and two, whether the TNFJ should change its name to *Tehrik-e- Jaffriya Pakistan* (Movement of the Jaffriya Fiqh in Pakistan. or TJP). By changing the name it was hoped that the TJP could distance itself from the image of trying to impose Shi'a law on a Sunni population. However, within the TJP some members had a clear preference for militant activism leading to the creation of Sipah-e-Muhammad Pakistan (Soldiers of Muhammad. or SMP).The TJP was proscribed by the Musharraf regime in 2002 after which the organisation was renamed Islami Tehrik Pakistan (Islamic Movement of Pakistan, or ITP). It participated in the 2002 election as one of the six members of the MMA.

The TJP has several affiliated organisations, including Sipah-e-Abbas, Sipah-e-Ahl-Bait and youth bodies like the Imamia Students Organisation (ISO) and the lmamia Organisation. The ISO is a nationwide organisation of the Shi'a sect that endeavours to bring Shi'a students together on one platform. The ISO has a central office in Lahore but it manages a vast network all over Pakistan. Members of the ISO have reportedly played an active role in the Shi'a resistance against Sunni domination.

SIPAH-E-MUHAMMAD PAKISTAN (SOLDIERS OF MUHAMMAD, OR SMP)

Origins

Allama Ghulam Raza Naqvi announced the creation of the SMP in 1993. It was formed after the ISO became too violent and wanted to avenge the large number of activities that it had lost to the SSP. Between 1993 and 2001, the SMP was accused of involvement in some 250 incidents of terrorism and was proscribed by the Pakistani government in 2001.

Strategies and Tactics

The SMP is not very different in its strategies and tactics from the SSP. It maintains a network of mosques and *madrassas* to exert and extend its influence. It has also used its publications and party pamphlets as a way to spread its message and carry out anti-Sunni propaganda. Both have also used publications and pamphleteering as a way to disseminate their creed.

Recruitment and Training

The SMP has approximately 30,000 cadres, mostly based in Punjab and led by Allama Rai Jaffer Raza. The organisation has no training facilities outside of Pakistan and their cadres do not operate outside Pakistani territory. The sociological profile of an SMP recruit is rural or small-town, some education in the government-school system, religious studies at *madrassas* in Punjab or elsewhere in Pakistan and, not infrequently, in Iran and participation in the war in Afghanistan.

Organisation

The SMP's central organisation is based in Thokkar Niaz Baig in the suburbs of Lahore, but it has an elaborate network that allows it to operate in Karachi as well.

TERRORIST INCIDENTS: INDIA—2012

24 Jan — A total 676 militants belonging to seven militant formations surrendered along with 202 small and big arms at a function held at the indoor stadium inside the Sarusajai Sports Complex, in the presence of Union Home Minister P. Chidambaram and Chief Minister Tarun Gogoi. The militant outfits that surrendered were Adivasi People's Army (APA), All Adivasi National Liberation Army (AANLA), Santhal Tiger Force (STF), United Kukigam Defence Army (UKDA), Kuki Revolutionary Army (KRA), Kuki Liberation Army (KLA) and Hmar Peoples' Convention (HPC).

More than 18,000 militants have laid down arms since 2001 in Assam and more than INR 400 crores has been spent on paying incentives to these surrendered militants without achieving its goal. Further, majority of militants, who laid down arms since 2001, did not have any police cases against them and militant formation do not deposit all their weapons during the surrender.

12 Feb — Kamal Chauhan, a former Rashtriya Swayamsevak Sangh (RSS) worker arrested by the National Investigation Agency (NIA) confessed that he had planted bombs on board the Samjhauta Express in 2007. "Yes, I have done it on my will," Chauhan told journalists as he was being taken out after in-camera proceedings in the Panchkula court.

11 Mar — The former head of Britain's Special Intelligence Service, Nigel Inkster, categorically said that Inter-Services Intelligence (ISI) was behind the 2008 suicide bomb attack on the Indian embassy in Kabul, which killed 60 people. Inkster said the "evidence of ISI's involvement in the bombing was clear cut".

14 Mar — The Inter Services Intelligence (ISI) has admitted before a three-member bench of the Pakistan Supreme Court headed by Chief Justice Iftikhar Muhammad Choudhary to meddling in northeast India. Former ISI chief Asad Durrani made the admission before the bench during a hearing on the ISI's mandate. He also admitted ISI funding the Bangladesh National Party (BNP) during the 1991 general elections in Bangladesh.

18 Mar — Two Italians were abducted by the Communist party of India-Maoist (CPI-Maoist) cadres in the tribal-dominated Kandhamal-Ganjam region in Odisha. While the Maoists claimed responsibility for the abduction through some private news channels around midnight on 17 March, there are reports that the Italians may have been abducted on March 14 itself. Setting a deadline for 18 March evening the Maoists demanded an immediate halt to combing operations by Security Forces and withdrawal of cases against tribals who, they claim, were arrested as Maoists.

19 Mar — India handed over to Bangladesh a list of 51 camps and names of 22 Indian insurgent leaders to Bangladesh for action against them. These camps and leaders are operating from Bangladeshi territory.

3 Apr — Union Home Minister P. Chidambaram said that Pakistan has enough evidence to detain 26/11 mastermind and Jama'at ud Dawa (JuD) chief Hafiz Muhammad Saeed. Chidambaram said that India had handed over a complete dossier on Saeed, including compact discs containing his anti-India speeches and sought his voice samples.

21 Apr — The Communist Party of India-Maoist (CPI-Maoist) cadres abducted the District Magistrate of Sukma District after killing two of his bodyguards. The collector, Alex Paul Menon, was meeting a group of villagers for a Government outreach programme.

28 Apr — Increasing Talibanisation of Pakistan and shifting of terror focus from the Af-Pak region would pose a serious security threat to India in the next two years, Chief of Air Staff Air Chief Marshal N A K Browne said. "If the American troops and the International Security Assistance Force (ISAF) withdraw from Afghanistan as planned, 2013-14 are going to be crucial watershed years for India as far as the security of our western border is concerned," Browne hinted.

13 May — Seven persons, including six troopers of the Central Industrial Security Force (CISF) and the civilian driver, were killed in an ambush by the Communist Party of India-Maoist (CPI-Maoist) cadres in Dantewada District. The troopers, including a head constable and five constables, were on patrol duty guarding the National Mineral Development Corporation (NMDC) facility in Kirandul when armed Maoists ambushed them with heavy gunfire at around 9:30pm.

21 June — Six persons were killed in a gun battle between Naga militant groups that took place in the remote Haochong village, located about 68 kilometres North of Nungba Police Station, in Tamenglong District.

22 June — The Delhi Police arrested key plotter of the November 26, 2008 (26/11) Mumbai

(Maharashtra) attacks, Abu Jundal alias Abu Hamza alias Sayeed Zabi ud Deen alias Zabi Ansari alias Riyasat Ali at the Indira Gandhi International airport. According to reports, he is an Indian national who went to Pakistan for allegedly training people for the 26/11 attacks. He was arrested after being deported from Saudi Arabia.

Abu Jundal, who belonged to the Lashkar-e-Toiba (LeT), revealed that LeT founder and Jamaat-ud-Dawa (JuD) 'chief' Hafiz Mohammad Saeed was present in the Karachi (Pakistan) control room when the 26/11 masterminds were controlling the events.

29 June — The Chhattisgarh Police and the Central Reserve Police Force (CRPF) claim to have killed 20 cadres of the Communist Party of India-Maoist (CPI-Maoist) in two separate incidents in the State's Sukma and Bijapur Districts.

19 July — The handler of the 26 November 2008 (26/11) Mumbai terrorist attacks and Lashkar-e-Toiba (LeT) operative Syed Zabiuddin Ansari alias Abu Jundal has disclosed that LeT founder and Jamaat-ud-Dawa (JuD) chief Hafiz Mohammad Saeed used to often meet top Pakistan Army corps commanders in Pakistan to plan major terror strikes in India, including 26/11. In fact Jundal claims that at one such meeting, top Army officers categorically instructed Saeed that the Mumbai case (26/11) should be a fidayeen (suicide) attack, and that no one should be caught alive.

He also told his interrogators that the planning for 26/11 started long back but a final team to monitor the attack, with different tasks, was formed one year before the strike. Jundal, source said, was kept out of some meetings in which Saeed and Zakiur Rehman Lakhvi were present and he was given the task of teaching Hindi to the 10 terrorists and explaining the locations in Mumbai to them.

29 July — At least 61 persons killed in clashes between Bodos and Muslims in Assam. Kokrajhar, Chirang and Baksa Districts and parts of Dhubri and Bongaigaon District are affected. The number killed in various Districts is: Kokrajhar-28, Chirang-32 and Dhubri-1. About four-lakh violence-hit people are presently taking shelters in about 278 relief camps. The clashes started when founder president of All Bodoland Minority Students' Union (ABMSU) , Mohibul Islam and former leader of All Assam Minority Students' Union (AAMSU), Abdul Siddique Sheikh were seriously injured in the attack on 19 July.

1 August — The busy Junglee Maharaj Road in Pune (Maharashtra) witnessed four low-intensity blasts, injuring one person. The explosions took place between 7.37 and 8.15pm. Two other bombs were defused by the Anti-Terror Squad.

29 Sept — The Chief of the Central Reserve Police Force (CRPF) K Vijay Kumar said that 6,000 square kilometers of area, mostly in south Chhattisgarh, and adjoining areas of Odisha, Andhra Pradesh and Maharashtra, continue to remain almost completely out of bounds for the Security Forces. He, however, said with SFs have gained control over more than 5,000 square kilometers area in the last two years.

30 Sept — Attack on Lieutenant General K. S. Brar (Retd) in London (UK) by suspected radical Sikh elements supposedly working for welfare of incarcerated Sikh militants, as well as cyber sites openly promoting the Khalistan cause.

21 Nov — Mohammed Ajmal Amir Kasab, the lone surviving Lashkar-e-Toiba (LeT) terrorist from the 26 November 2008 (26/11) terror attack, was hanged to death at the Yerawada Prison in Pune (Maharashtra). Kasab was convicted and given capital punishment by the trial court on 6 May 2010, which was upheld by the Bombay High Court on 21 February 2011. The Supreme Court subsequently upheld the sentence on 29 August 2012. Kasab then filed the mercy petition which was rejected by the President Pranab Mukherjee on 5 November.

TERRORIST INCIDENTS: PAKISTAN—2012

5 Jan Tehreek-e-Taliban Pakistan (TTP) militants on January 5 killed 15 Frontier Constabulary personnel in Mir Ali area of North Waziristan Agency.

6 Jan At least six militants were killed and 12 got injured on January 6 after Lashkar-e-Islam and its rival Zakhakhel tribal force exchanged gunfire to gain control of a key base in Bazaar Zakhakhel area of Landikotal in Khyber Agency of Federally Administered Tribal Areas (FATA).

9 Jan 45 militants and 17 SF among 65 persons killed during the week in FATA

The dead bodies of 10 Frontier Constabulary paramilitary troops were recovered from Dabori town of Orakzai Agency.

10 Jan A powerful bomb planted in a pick-up van exploded at a petrol station in Jamrud bazaar in Khyber Agency, killing 35 persons, four of them Khasadar personnel, and injuring 78 others.

11 Jan At least 11 militants were killed and six others got injured when jet fighters pounded their hideouts in Jabba, Toor Semath, Akhunkot, and Mir Qalamkhel localities in Mamozai tehsil of Orakzai Agency.

12 Jan At least 15 militants were killed and several others got injured while there terrorist hideouts were destroyed in an air attack by Security Forces in different areas of Orakzai Agency in FATA.

16 Jan 40 civilians and 38 militants among 92 persons killed during the week in FATA.

Shahzain Bugti, a grandson of slain Akbar clan chieftain and former Chief Minister of Balochistan, Nawab Akbar Bugti, on January 16 announced head money for former Army dictator and President Pervez Musharraf. "We will give PKR 1 million in cash and a bungalow worth 100 million rupees to anybody who kills Musharraf. And we'll also provide him full security," Shahzain Bugti said. "The gallows are ready for Musharraf. There will be serious consequences, if the government does not arrest him upon his arrival," he warned.

23 Jan 34 militants and 15 SFs among 51 persons killed during the week in FATA

At least five militants were killed when a US drone fired two missiles on a house and a vehicle at Mohammad Khel and Degan village in Dattakhel area of North Waziristan Agency.

24 Jan Seven militants and two soldiers were killed during a clash in Jogi area of the Central tehsil in Kurram Agency.

25 Jan Twenty two militants and six soldiers were killed during a clash when Security Forces captured a Tehreek-e-Taliban Pakistan (TTP) stronghold in the Jogi area of Central tehsil of Kurram Agency in FATA.

28 Jan US Defence Secretary Leon Panetta acknowledged publicly for the first time that a Pakistani doctor provided key information to the US in advance of the Navy SEAL's assault on Osama bin Laden's compound in Abbottabad on 1 May 2011. Panetta acknowledged that Dr Shakeel Afridi had in fact been working for the US intelligence, collecting DNA to verify the 9/11 mastermind's presence.

31 Jan At least 35 militants and eight soldiers were killed in a gun-battle after a newly-established security check post was attacked in Jogi heights of Mamozai tehsil in Kurram Agency.

16 Frontier Corps personnel were killed and 3 others injured when BLA militants opened fire on three FC check posts in the Killi Pir Ismail area of Ziarat District.

1 Feb Army fighter jets pounded militant hideouts in the Mamozai area of Orakzai Agency before dawn, killing at least 20 TTP militants.

At least 15 personnel of the Frontier Corps (FC) were killed and 12 others were injured when militants belonging to the Baloch Liberation Army (BLA) attacked four FC check posts near Margat coalmines in Mach area of Bolan District.

2 Feb Three persons were killed when unidentified militants opened fire on a car in the Mashkil area of Quetta, the provincial capital of Balochistan.

3 Feb 18 militants and seven soldiers were killed and three others injured during a clash that broke out when a group of 40 Tehreek-e-Taliban Pakistan (TTP) militants attacked on Security Forces (SFs) check post in Shidano Dhand area of Kurram Agency in FATA.

6 Feb 85 militants and 18 SFs among 107 persons killed during the week in FATA.

33 SFs and seven civilians among 40 persons killed during the week in Balochistan.

SFs pounded militant hideouts with jet fighters, killing at least 15 and injuring eight militants in Khadezai, Mamozai and Torsamant areas of Upper Orakzai Agency.

8 Feb A US drone fired two missiles at a house suspected of being a militant hideout in the village of Tapi 15 kilometers east of in Miranshah in North Waziristan Agency, killing 10 suspected militants.

9 Feb A US drone fired two missiles that hit a compound located in Miranshah, the main town in North Waziristan Agency, killing four militants.

10 Feb Security Forces killed 11 militants and injured 19 others in a crackdown in the Mamozai area of Kurram Agency in FATA.

11 Feb An Anti-Terrorism Court was told that former Prime Minister Benazir Bhutto was killed on 27 December 2007 because she supported the Lal Masjid (Red Mosque) operation. Magistrate Taufiq Ahmed, who had recorded confessional statements of Rafaqat Hussain, Husnain Gul and Aitzaz Shah on 13 February 2008, said the accused told him that they wanted to kill only Bhutto and because of the deaths of 23 other people in the attack, which they regretted, they would accept any punishment awarded to them.

13 Feb 40 militants and three SFs among 43 persons killed during the week in FATA.

16 Feb Two US drone strikes killed at least 21 militants near the Afghan border in Miranshah, the main town of North Waziristan Agency.

17 Feb At least 43 Shias were reportedly killed while 36 others injured after a suicide bomber detonated his explosives just near the targeted mosque in the Kurmi bazaar of Parachinar, the main town of Kurram Agency

19 Feb At least nine members of Zakakhel lashkar (tribal militia) were killed and four others injured when a bomb planted by militants exploded at Stana checkpoint of Nari Baba area in Tirah Valley of Khyber Agency in FATA.

Eight militants and a security man were killed and four personnel, among them a captain, suffered injuries during a raid on a hotel at Rustam Bazaar in Wana, the headquarters of South Waziristan Agency.

A total of 231 bullet-riddled bodies were found by roadsides in Balochistan in 2011, said a report, titled Balochistan's Maze of Violence, compiled by the Centre for Research and Security Studies (CRSS), launched in Islamabad.

20 Feb 59 civilians and 49 militants among 112 persons killed during the week in FATA.

23 Feb At least 17 Tehreek-e-Taliban Pakistan (TTP) militants were killed in an air strike in Khadizai, Samarbazar and Bermela areas of Upper Orakzai Agency.

24 Feb Seven militants and three soldiers were killed when militants attacked troops deployed in Malikdeenkhel area of Khyber Agency.

26 Feb 10 militants and two security personnel were killed in a clash between Security Forces and militants in the Siplatoi area of South Waziristan Agency in FATA during a search operation.

Six Lashkar-e-Islam militants were killed when helicopter gunships targeted their hideouts in Nanagrosa and Nari Baba areas in Landikotal town of Khyber Agency.

27 Feb 44 militants and nine SFs among 61 persons killed during the week in FATA.

5 Mar 150 militants and 17 SFs among 172 persons killed during the week in FATA.

6 Mar At least 17 militants, including two al Qaeda 'commanders' and seven suicide bombers, were killed in separate SFs actions in Upper Orakzai and Malakhel area of Dabori in Orakzai Agency.

9 Mar At least 18 militants, among them six foreigners, were killed when US drones fired missiles on a compound and a vehicle in two different areas of South Waziristan Agency. Also, Tehreek-e-Taliban Pakistan (TTP) militants ambushed a military convoy, killing seven soldiers at Khar Qamar, 30 kilometres west of Miranshah, the main town of North Waziristan Agency.

The Government appointed Lieutenant General Zaheerul Islam as the new head of the Inter-Services Intelligence (ISI) to succeed Lieutenant General Ahmad Shuja Pasha.

Pakistan said it is not putting the "core issue" of Kashmir on the backburner as it works to normalise ties with India, and any final settlement between the two sides would be linked to realising the "aspirations of the Kashmiri people". "The Jammu and Kashmir dispute is about the people of Kashmir and their inalienable right to self-determination. Therefore, there is no question of freezing this issue or putting this core dispute on the backburner."

10 Mar Pakistani fighter jets bombed several terrorists' hideouts in the northwestern Orakzai Agency, near the Afghanistan border, killing 33 terrorists and injuring 23, military officials said. In another strike, four militant hideouts in the Khadezai and Mamozai areas of tribal region were destroyed by bombardment of jet fighters, killing at least 21 terrorists. Further, at least five militants were killed when they attacked a convoy of SFs after in Bara tehsil of Khyber Agency.

13 Mar US drones struck twice in the regions along the border with Afghanistan in South Waziristan Agency (SWA), killing 15 militants, including two senior 'commanders'. Further, three persons were killed by unidentified militants in Tirah Kukikhel near Spean Khwar in Khyber Agency.

14 Mar Eight civilians and six suspected militants, including an Afghan national, were killed during operation in Sipah area of Bara tehsil in Khyber Agency. In addition, at least six members of an anti-Taliban militia were killed and three others injured in an IED blast during a meeting of tribal elders at Kotkai village of Mamond tehsil in Bajaur Agency.

17 Mar 23 suspected militants were killed when Army planes targeted their positions in Dabori and Mamozai areas of Orakzai Agency. Also, eight terrorists were killed and several others were injured in aerial bombing in the areas of Samaa Bazaar, Toor Semath, Kagu Qamar, Mamuzai, Jabba, and Balaras of Orakzai Agency. Further, the volunteers of Tawheed-ul-Islam (TuI), a Zakhakhel-based group, killed three suspected

militants involved in bomb blasts at Zakhakhel and Tirah areas of Khyber Agency. Elsewhere, three women were killed in a roadside bomb explosion, while two others sustained injuries at Mundi Kas area in Bara tehsil.

Slain al Qaeda leader Osama bin Laden had ordered his followers in Afghanistan and Pakistan to attack the aircraft of USPresident Barack Obama. Bin Laden wanted to kill the US President because "Obama is the head of infidelity and killing him automatically will make (Vice President Joe) Biden take over the presidency," according to the documents.

18 Mar At least 26 terrorists were killed in air strikes by fighter jets in the bordering areas of Orakzai and Kurram Agencies in FATA.

Fourteen bullet-riddled bodies were found in Speen Qabar area of Bara tehsil in Khyber Agency, a day after Security Forces left the area after an operation. In addition, SFs resorted to indiscriminate firing and shelling in Mir Ali tehsil (revenue unit) of North Waziristan Agency, killing five civilians, one of them a child, after two military convoys were attacked.

19 Mar 94 militants and 51 civilians among 146 persons killed during the week in FATA.

20 Mar Provincial Agriculture Minister Asadullah Baloch of Balochistan National Party-Awami (BNP-Awami) claimed that over a 1,000 people have been abducted in the past four years in the province. "Abduction for ransom has become a lucrative business in Balochistan and people are joining this business en masse as Police and Law Enforcement Agencies (LEAs) have failed to book a single culprit," he said.

There has been a swift rise in the number of abduction for ransom in Lahore District. According to the figures available in a report, at least 400 cases of abductions have been registered till 20 March 2012. One reason for the rise in the crime is the failure of Law Enforcement Agencies to track down the abducted people, which, in a way, encouraged criminals to snatch people.

21 Mar French Police laid siege to an apartment block where a self-declared al Qaeda militant who boasted of having "brought France to its knees" with a wave of deadly attacks was holed up. Prosecutors said suspect Mohamed Merah, a 23-year-old Frenchman of Algerian descent, had fought off several police assaults on his flat and bragged to negotiators of having been trained by al Qaeda in Waziristan area of Pakistan on the Afghanistan-Pakistan border.

23 Mar At least 13 persons, including eight Lashkar-e-Islam (LI) militants, were killed and four others got injured when a TTP suicide bomber blew himself up at Dars Jumat mosque in Sandapal area of Bara tehsil in Khyber Agency.

Human rights violations increased manifold in 2011 according to a report released in Islamabad. The report State of Human Rights in 2011 launched by the Human Rights Commission of Pakistan, spoke of a gloomy scenario vis-à-vis administration of justice, law and order, jails and prisoners, freedom of movement, expression and thought, rights of women, children and workers, education and health as well as environment and status of refugees.

Major Haroon Ashiq, a former Pakistan Army commando, who became a key al Qaeda operative and an accused in several murder cases and abductions, walked free from his Rawalpindi prison cell after being acquitted by Anti-Terrorism Court in a murder case, with witnesses withdrawing their testimony in fear of reprisals. Major Haroon was accused of murdering Special Service Group (SSG) Major General Faisal Alvi on 19 November 2008 in Islamabad for opposing Taliban's peace agreement with the Pakistani Government.

24 Mar At least 12 militants and four soldiers were killed in a clash between Security Forces (SFs) and Tehreek-e-Taliban Pakistan (TTP) during a search operation in Shin Warsak area of South Waziristan Agency in Federally Administered Tribal Areas (FATA). In addition, 10 militants and three soldiers were killed after TTP militants stormed a check post in Khadizai area of Orakzai Agency. Also, at least eight militants were killed in Khyber Agency area in an explosion inside their hideout.

26 Mar 58 militants and 9 civilians among 76 persons killed during the week in FATA.

27 Mar Three American lawmakers espousing the cause of the people of Balochistan alleged that the Pakistani Government is a "radical Islamist" one and is providing weapons and resources to extremist groups. Seeking independence of Balochistan, the three Congressmen led by Dana Rohrabacher at a news conference held at the National Press Club in Washington claimed that Pakistan is not a friend of the US, but an American enemy. Rohrabacher said, "The Government of Pakistan is radical Islam. It has been providing weapons and resources to radical Muslim elements that again use them against Americans. All these years we thought that Pakistan is our friend. We now find out that are really our enemy."

28 Mar Pakistan has an "addiction" of "playing around" with militant groups against India, Michael Sheehan, Assistant Secretary of Defence for Special Operations/Low-Intensity Conflict, said. "They have an addiction to playing around with militia groups to achieve certain interests, particularly vis-a-vis India. That gets them in all kinds of trouble," Michael Sheehan told senators at a Congressional hearing.

29 Mar A US drone launched a missile attack on a militant compound in a market area of Miranshah, the main town in North Waziristan Agency, killing four Tehreek-e-Taliban Pakistan (TTP) militants and injuring two others.

2 Apr 41 civilians and one SF among 42 persons killed during the week in Sindh Nine persons, including an Awami National Party (ANP) activist and a women, were killed in the ongoing violence at different places of Karachi.

At least 10 persons, including one Senior Superintendent of Police (SSP) and an ANP worker, were killed in the ongoing spate of violence in Karachi.

10 people were killed and 17 others injured while 46 vehicles were set ablaze after the killing of two Muttahida Qaumi Movement (MQM) workers in PIB Police precincts in Karachi.

40 militants and two SFs among 42 persons killed during the week in FATA.

The Tehreek-e-Taliban Pakistan (TTP) introduced "moral policing" in parts of north-eastern Afghanistan, Afghan Police claimed. Key leaders of the TTP - including its 'commanders' in Swat, Bajaur Agency and Mohmand Agency - Maulana Fazalullah, Maulvi Faqir and Abdul Wali - and dozens of their loyalists had fled military operations and sought sanctuary in the Afghan Provinces of Nuristan and Kunar.

Slain al Qaeda chief Osama bin Laden spent nine years on the run in Pakistan after the 11 September 2001 attacks, and during that time he moved between five safe houses and fathered four children, at least two of whom were born in a Government hospital, his youngest wife, Amal Ahmad Abdul Fateh (30), told Pakistani investigators. She also told the investigators that after 9/11 she reunited with her husband in Peshawar (Khyber Pakhtunkhwa) in 2002. From Peshawar they went to Swat where they lived for about nine months. Later, they stayed for about two years in Haripur District before moving to Abbottabad.

Five Security Force personnel were killed when a group of Tehreek-e-Taliban Pakistan (TTP) militants from across the Afghanistan border attacked a security post at Olai checkpoint in Mohmand Agency. At least eight militants died when Security Forces retaliated.

3 Apr As many as 24 people lost their lives and another 55 were injured in a wave of sectarian violence across Gilgit-Baltistan, which erupted after clashes between Ahle Sunnat Wal Jamaat (ASWJ) and Police.

4 Apr Seven people were killed and three others injured when a passenger van was blown up in a roadside bomb blast at Shah Kas area in Jamrud tehsil of Khyber Agency.

5 Apr A suicide bomber targeted a senior Police Officer, Superintendent of Police Anwar Ahmed Khan, said to be a leading name in the crackdown on militants, killing four passers-by and injuring 17 others in the Malir area of Karachi. Earlier in a pre-dawn attack, three Policemen were shot dead in PIB Colony. Four more people were killed in different parts of Karachi.

9 Apr 37 civilians and four SFs among 43 persons killed during the week in Sindh. Five people, including an activist of Awami National Party (ANP), were killed in separate acts of target killing in Karachi on 4 April. Six persons were killed in Karachi on 6 April and at least 11 more persons were killed in Karachi on 7 April.

24 militants and nine civilians among 39 persons killed during the week in FATA.

Four militants and two soldiers were killed during a clash when a group of 20 militants attacked a military check post in the Khapyanga area of Kurram Agency.

Six Shias belonging to the Hazara community were killed and three others were injured when armed militants opened fire at a cobblers shop on Prince Road in Quetta.

11 Apr Lashkar-e-Islam militants shot dead five Zakkakhel tribe persons in Bara tehsil of Khyber Agency.

Four people, including two activists of the Jaye Sindh Qaumi Mahaz (JSQM), were shot dead by unidentified armed assailants in Karachi.

12 Apr Three people belonging to the Hazara community were shot dead and another wounded in separate incidents of target killings in the provincial capital Quetta.

13 Apr Over 181,000 have fled Khyber Agency of FATA, says UNHCR: More than 181,000 people have fled fighting between Government troops and Taliban or al Qaeda-linked militants in the Khyber Agency Areas of Federally Administered Tribal Areas (FATA), the United Nation High Commissioner for Refugees (UNHCR) said. "The number of people displaced by an ongoing government security operation in northwest Pakistan has now surpassed 181, 000," said a statement from the office of the UNHCR.

14 Apr Unidentified assailants riding motorcycles killed eight Shias, belonging to Hazara community, in two incidents of sectarian attacks in Quetta, the provincial capital of Balochistan.

16 Apr 19 militants and seven civilians among 30 persons killed during the week in FATA.

28 civilians and four militants among 33 persons killed during the week in Balochistan.

19 civilians and three militants among 24 persons killed during the week in Sindh.

17 Apr Nine persons, including a Shia man, the Vice Principal of Jinnah Polytechnic Institute, Imran Zaidi (55), were killed in separate incidents of violence in Karachi.

18 Apr The National Assembly Human Rights Committee (NAHRC) was told that more than 650 Shias in Quetta (Balochistan) and 450 in Dera Ismail Khan (Khyber Pakhtunkhwa) were targeted and killed recently. Mohammad Amin Shahidi, Deputy General Secretary of Wahdatul Muslimeen, a Shia organisation, informed the committee that more than 650 Shias in Quetta and 450 in Dera Ismail Khan were targeted and killed recently.

19 Apr Three people, including a Senior Assistant Editor of Dawn and an activist of Muttahida Qaumi Movement (MQM), were killed and several others were injured in different parts of Orangi Town in Karachi.

23 Apr 42 civilians and two militants among 44 persons killed during the week in Sindh.

29 Apr At least four persons, including a Policeman, were killed and 19 others injured during Police operation in Lyari area of Karachi, the provincial capital of Sindh.

30 Apr 21 civilians and nine militants among 37 persons killed during the week in Sindh.

4 May A suicide attack targeting Security Forces (SFs) on May 4 killed at least 29 persons, including seven Policemen, and injured over 72 others at Khar Bazaar in Khar town of Bajaur Agency.

A report released by UNESCO ranks Pakistan as the second-most dangerous country for journalists in 2010-2011. Mexico was the most dangerous, with 18 journalist fatalities in that time frame. Two Pakistani journalists were killed in 2006-2007, followed by six in 2008-2009 and 16 in 2010-2011, the report, "The Safety of Journalists and the Danger of Impunity," found. Forty-two journalists have been killed in Pakistan since 1992, according to the Committee to Protect Journalists.

5 May At least 10 persons were killed while one was injured when US drone attacked a house in Darr-e-Nishtar area of NWA early in the morning.

6 May Nine soldiers were killed and 12 more injured when unidentified militants ambushed a military convoy at Amin Checkpost, a security outpost on a hilltop outside Miranshah, in North Waziristan Agency (NWA) of FATA.

7 May 39 civilians and 19 SFs among 67 persons killed during the week in FATA.

27 civilians and nine SF among 44 persons killed during the week in Sindh.

13 May 39 persons were killed in two days of clashes between Security Forces and militants in Miranshah area of North Waziristan Agency (NWA).

14 May 41 militants and 26 SF among 83 persons killed during the week in FATA.

17 May Eight persons, including a MQM activist and two cadres belonging to Sunni Tehreek (ST), were killed in separate acts of target killings in Karachi.

21 May 29 militants and two civilians killed during the week in FATA.

26 civilians and three militants among 29 persons killed during the week in Sindh.

Five students were killed and 53 injured in a suicide attack that targeted a university bus near Federal Investigation Agency (FIA) office on Samungli Road in Quetta.

May 24 Six persons, including two political activists, were killed in separate acts of violence in Karachi.

25 May Seven passengers on a Swabi-bound bus were shot dead three others were wounded when armed militants opened fire on the bus on National Highway at Rinn Shakh, near Qazi Ahmed Taluka town in Shaheed Benazirabad District.

Three people, including an activist each from the Awami National Party (ANP) and the Muttahida Qaumi Movement (MQM) were killed in separate incidents of violence in Karachi.

28 May 55 militants and four civilians killed during the week in FATA.

41 civilians and one militant killed during the week in Sindh.

Six militants were killed and two others injured in a gunfight with Security Forces (SFs) in Gandi Tal area of Orakzai Agency.

28 May Eight persons, including a Superintendent of Police (SP) and his doctor friend, were killed and 14 others were injured in separate incidents of violence in various areas of Karachi

31 May 10 persons including Rangers Sub-Inspector (SI) were killed in separate incidents of violence and sectarian killing in Karachi.

1 Jun Militants attacked troops near the Nadir Mela area of Kurram Agency, leading to a shootout that killed six militants and injured two soldiers, including a captain.

2 Jun More than 30 militants were killed in clashes with Security Forces (SFs) in Tirah Valley of Khyber Agency.

4 Jun 103 militants and seven civilians killed during the week in FATA.

30 civilians and two SFs killed during the week in Sindh.

5 Jun 20 Tehreek-e-Taliban Pakistan (TTP) militants were killed in retaliatory fire by Security Forces (SFs) when a group of militants attacked the Salala checkpost along the Af-Pak international border in Mohammad Agency.

7 Jun 15 people, including five children, were killed and more than 48 got injured in a remote-controlled bomb blast outside a madrassa, Jamia Islamia Miftahul Uloom, near Bank Chowk on Sariab Link Road in Quetta.

8 Jun 21 persons were killed and over 40 others injured when a powerful bomb ripped through a bus carrying Government employees in

Gulbela area on the Charsadda Road in the jurisdiction of Daudzai Police Station in Peshawar. The Intelligence reports revealed that it was a suicide attack.

9 Jun 23 persons, including 18 members of a militant outfit, were killed in a fierce gun battle with Security Forces (SFs) in Chagai District.

Unidentified armed militants killed four a Policemen patrolling on Sariab Road in Quetta.

10 Jun 10 people, including one security official, were killed, and 10 others injured when terrorists fired rockets at a security check post in South Waziristan Agency of Federally Administered Tribal Areas (FATA).

11 Jun 71 militants among 75 persons killed during the week in FATA.

26 civilians and 20 militants killed during the week in Balochistan.

22 civilians among 25 persons killed during the week in Khyber Pakhtunkhwa.

14 Jun Nine persons, including a Police Officer, were killed and over a half dozen injured in different acts of target killings in Karachi.

15 Jun 11 people were shot dead and two others wounded in different parts of Karachi.

17 Jun Twelve people, including four Muttahida Qaumi Movement (MQM) activists and a woman, were killed in separate acts of violence and target killing in Karachi. Also, two people, including a Police constable and an activist of the MQM, were shot dead in the night.

18 Jun 48 civilians and six militants killed during the week in Sindh

29 civilians and 32 militants killed during the week in FATA.

25 people were killed when a car bomb hit a crowded bazaar in the town of Landi Kotal in Khyber Agency.

22 civilians among 25 persons killed during the week in Khyber Pakhtunkhwa.

21 Jun A bomb on a donkey cart killed three people at a Sufi shrine in Peshawar.

The Tehreek-e-Taliban Pakistan (TTP) claimed on June 22 that they had beheaded seven Security Force (SF) personnel, who were kidnapped after a clash with Security Forces (SFs) near Laddah in South Waziristan Agency (SWA) of Federally Administered Tribal Areas (FATA).

Three persons of the Bugti tribe, were killed when their motorcycle hit a landmine in Pat Feeder area of Dera Bugti District.

22 Jun 15 militants and one Security Force (SF) official were killed and two SFs were injured, when terrorists from Afghanistan attacked Karakar security check post (near Afghan border) in the Barawal area of Upper Dir District.

23 Jun Eight Sindhis, including a Policeman, were killed and another was injured in an attack by unidentified militants in Mill area of Sariab Road area of Quetta in Balochistan.

24 Jun Afghanistan-based Pakistan militants attacked a military convoy on June 24 in Upper Dir District of Khyber Pakhtunkhwa, resulting in the killing of at least 21 persons, including 11 militants and 10 soldiers.

4 Policemen were shot dead in an ambush at Bakra Mandi area of Eastern Bypass, on outskirts of Quetta, the capital of Balochistan.

25 Jun 26 militants and 11 SFs killed during the week in Khyber Pakhtunkhwa.

24 militants and 10 SFs killed during the week in FATA.

20 civilians and nine SFs killed during the week in Balochistan.

27 Jun The bullet-riddled body of chief of the anti-Taliban Bazidkhel Qaumi Lashkar (community militia), Fahim-ur-Rehman, who escaped at least seven attempts on his life since 2008, was found in his white Land Cruiser on the Ring Road of Peshawar on June 27. The bodies of his three close friends and associates, Altaf Bacha, Haji Niaz Muhammad and Rahim Lala, were also found in the vehicle.

Seven persons were killed and as many as 30 injured, when a remote-controlled bomb went off at the Sibi Railway Station of Sibi District.

28 Jun Eight troops, including a captain, were killed and three others injured in a remote-controlled bomb blast near Alhaj Market in Bara town of Khyber Agency.

14 persons, including two policemen and a woman, were killed and 30 others, including women and children, sustained injuries in a suicide attack on a bus of pilgrims coming from Iran, at Hazar Ganji area of Quetta.

2 Jul 48 militants and five civilians among 53 persons killed during the week in Khyber Pakhtunkhwa.

26 militants and 10 civilians among 44 persons killed during the week in FATA.

31 civilians and one militant among 32 persons killed during the week in Balochistan.

3 Jul Pakistan agreed to reopen its border to NATO supply convoys into Afghanistan after the United States (US) Secretary of State Hillary Clinton said that Washington was sorry for the loss of life in NATO aerial attack on Salala border check-post on 26 November 2011.

6 Jul 18 Punjabi-speaking persons, who were travelling to Iran, were shot dead and two others injured when Baloch Liberation Tigers (BLT) militants attacked their vehicles in the Basoli area of Turbat District.

8 Jul At least 14 persons were killed while seven others injured in a landmine blast in the Tooba Achakzai area near the Pak-Afghan border in the border town of Chaman in Balochistan.

Militants attacked a convoy of Security Forces (SFs) and killed four personnel, which was passing through Tiarza tehsil (revenue unit) of Serwakai sub-division of South Waziristan Agency in Federally Administered Tribal Areas (FATA).

9 Jul — 42 civilians and six militant among 51 persons killed during the week in Balochistan.

30 militants and eight civilians among 43 persons killed during the week in FATA.

29 civilians and four militant among 35 persons killed during the week in Sindh.

Unidentified militants killed eight security personnel at an Army camp near Wazirabad town in Gujranwala District hours after a protest march of the Difa-e-Pakistan Council (DPC) passed through the area.

Supreme Court Chief Justice Iftikhar Muhammad Choudhary said that every third missing person in Balochistan was picked up by the Frontier Corps (FC). He said the issue of missing persons needed to be addressed to solve the problem of Balochistan.

12 Jul — The Balochistan Levies found the bodies of seven coal miners who were abducted on 7 July, in the Degari area, some 28 kilometres from Quetta.

Militants shot dead nine Police and prison staff and wounded three others after storming a building in Ichra area of Lahore in Punjab where they were sleeping.

13 Jul — At least eight persons were killed and 22 others injured in a bomb blast during a political rally organised by the Awami National Party (ANP) in Kuchlak area of Quetta, the provincial capital of Balochistan.

Officials warned that the Tehreek-e-Taliban Pakistan (TTP) ban on polio would put 240,000 children at risk in Waziristan Agencies of Federally Administered Tribal Areas (FATA), if a vaccination campaign didn't start by the coming week. THE TTP and Hafiz Gul Bahadur group banned polio vaccinations in the Waziristan to protest against US drone attacks.

14 Jul — 13 persons, including Police and Navy personnel and a Muttahida Qaumi Movement (MQM) activist, were killed in incidents of target killing in Karachi.

18 Jul — 12 Shiite Muslims were killed when a roadside bomb hit their minibus at Spai village in the Orakzai Agency. Three bullet-riddled dead bodies were found in different areas of Bajaur Agency.

40 civilians and one SF among 41 persons killed during the week in Balochistan.

31 civilians and two SF among 33 persons killed during the week in Karachi.

17 SFs and three civilians among 20 persons killed during the week in Punjab

21 Jul — A suicide bomber detonated an explosive laden vehicle near the house of a pro-Government militant 'commander' Maulvi Nabi, killing at least nine persons, including four children, three of them being girls, and injuring 13 others, in a war of attrition between two militant outfits in Speen Tall area of Orakzai Agency.

Four people, including three members of the same family, died and eight others suffered injuries when an Improvised Explosive Device (IED) was detonated using a remote-controlled device near a pick-up truck in Doog Darra area of Upper Dir District.

23 Jul — 47 civilians and three SFs among 51 persons killed during the week in Karachi.

25 civilians and 16 militants among 42 persons killed during the week in FATA.

15 militants and nine civilians among 24 persons killed during the week in Khyber Pakhtunkhwa.

30 Jul — 68 militants and 17 civilians among 87 persons killed during the week in FATA.

13 Aug — 24 militants and six civilians among 35 persons killed during the week in FATA.

A remote-controlled bomb attack killed three soldiers in Mir Ali town of North Waziristan Agency.

14 Aug — Around 20 militants and five soldiers were killed in a clash in Ghaljo area of Orakzai Agency.

17 Aug — Eleven persons killed in separate incidents of target killing in Karachi.

20 Aug — 53 militants and six civilians among 65 persons killed during the week in FATA.

31 civilians and one SF among 32 persons killed during the week in Sindh.

32 civilians killed during the week in Khyber Pakhtunkhwa

27 Aug — 85 militants and 17 civilians among 102 persons killed during the week in FATA.

29 Aug — Nine SF personnel and six militants were killed while several others wounded in a clash between SFs and militants in Baba Ziarat locality of Ghat Badr, some 35 kilometers south of Ladha, in South Waziristan Agency.

3 Sep — 120 militants and 27 SF personnel among 153 persons killed during the week in FATA.

25 civilians and one SF among 26 persons killed during the week in Sindh.

7 Sep — 6 people were shot dead in separate acts of violence in Karachi.

10 Sep — 15 persons killed and 40 others injured in a suicide attack in a crowded Hamid Market in Kashmir Chowk area of Parachinar town, the headquarter of Kurram Agency.

13 Sep — 10 labourers were killed and another four sustained injuries in the Dasht area of Mastung District of Balochistan.

14 Sep — Eight persons were shot dead in separate incidents of target killing in different areas of Karachi.

17 Sep 24 civilians and nine militants among 33 persons killed during the week in FATA.

23 civilians and one SF among 25 persons killed during the week in Sindh.

23 civilians killed during the week in Balochistan.

18 Sep Nine persons, including a Jama'at-e-Islami (JeI) activist, were killed in Karachi.

19 Sept US sanctions against the Pakistan-based Haqqani Network of militants come into force following the Obama administration's decision to designate the group a "Foreign Terrorist Organisation".

24 Sep 51 militants and three civilians among 54 persons killed during the week in FATA.

39 civilians and three SFs among 44 persons killed during the week in Sindh.

28 Sep Six people were killed in separate incidents of violence in Karachi.

Offering a bounty of $ 100, 000 for the killing of the US film maker, who made "Innocence of Islam", an anti-Islam film, Railways Minister Ghulam Ahmad Bilour during a public meeting at the Mahabat Khan Mosque in Peshawar announced a bounty on the heads of the future blasphemers, too.

1 Oct 33 militants and three SFs among 36 persons killed during the week in FATA.

33 civilians and two SFs among 36 persons killed during the week in Sindh.

During a Difa-e-Pakistan (DPC) rally in Peshawar, a former Pakistani legislator and General Secretary of Jama'at Ulema-e-Islam-Sami (JUI-S), Ikramullah Shahid, announced a USD 200,000 bounty for the maker of the anti-Islam film released in the US.

3 Oct Three tortured bullet-riddled dead bodies of MQM activists were found from various parts of Karachi.

4 Oct Five persons, including a suspect, a Policeman and an Imambargah trustee, were killed in separate acts of violence in Karachi.

5 Oct Three persons, including an activist of Muttahida Qaumi Movement (MQM) and an active cadre of Sunni Tehreek (ST), were shot dead in separate incidents of violence in Karachi.

8 Oct 40 civilians and two militants among 43 persons killed during the week in Sindh.

18 militants and five civilians among 25 persons killed during the week in FATA

Six Pakistan People's Party (PPP) workers and a reporter of a TV channel were killed and 10 others, including three reporters and administrator of Khairpur Taluka Municipal Administration, injured when a group of unidentified assailants opened fire on a public meeting in Sadoro Janwari village in Khairpur District.

11 Oct 11 persons were killed and 21 others sustained critical injuries in a bomb blast on Nishtar Road in Sibi town (Sibi District).

13 Oct A suicide car-bomb attack killed 18 persons and injured 40 others in Darra Adam Khel town in Kohat District.

15 Oct 49 militants and 13 civilians SFs among 65 persons killed during the week in FATA.

23 civilians and nine SFs among 38 persons killed during the week in Khyber Pakhtunkhwa.

25 civilians and two militants among 29 persons killed during the week in Sindh.

16 civilians and three SFs among 19 persons killed during the week in Balochistan.

A guard of Balochistan Food Minister Asfandyar Khan Kakar and two militants were killed in an exchange of fire at the residence of the Minister in the Chaman Housing Scheme in Quetta.

16 Oct Four members of the Hazara community were shot dead in a sectarian attack in the Kabari Market scrap market of Quetta.

19 Oct Three personnel of Frontier Corps (FC) were killed and ten others, including five security men and a woman, were wounded in a remote-controlled blast at the Badini intersection area in Quetta.

22 Oct 18 civilians and 12 militants among 33 persons killed during the week in Sindh.

17 civilians and four SFs among 23 persons killed during the week in Balochistan.

20 militants and one civilian killed during the week in FATA.

25 Oct 5 members of Ahl-e-Sunnat-Wal-Jama'at (ASWJ) were shot dead in a sectarian attack at 'Gulzar-e-Habib' restaurant in FB area of Karachi.

29 Oct 25 militants and eight civilians among 33 persons killed during the week in FATA.

23 civilians and six militants among 32 persons killed during the week in Sindh.

31 Oct The Tehreek-e-Taliban Pakistan (TTP) went on a shooting rampage and killed four persons, including three ANP activists, including the party's Sherpao Colony ward President, outside the Al-Naseer PCO under Quaidabad Police Station in Karachi.

2 Nov 18 persons, including seven women and four children, were killed and five others injured as unidentified assailants fired indiscriminately at a local passenger van parked outside a petrol pump in the Jhalawan Complex area of the Khuzdar District.

5 Nov 38 civilians and three Security Force personnel among 43 persons killed during the week in Sindh.

28 militants and six civilians among 38 persons killed during the week in FATA.

27 civilians and one SF among 28 persons killed during the week in Balochistan.

10 Nov 19 persons, including six students of Deobandi School of thought, were killed in separate incidents of violence in Karachi.

12 Nov 58 civilians and 10 SFs among 73 persons killed during the week in Sindh.

15 Nov 32 civilians and four SFs among 40 persons killed during the week in Sindh

18 Nov 3 people were killed and over a dozen were injured in an Improvised Explosive Device (IED) blast near an imambargah at Abbas Town in Karachi.

19 Nov During a seminar, 'International Journalist Day', organised at the National Press Club (NPC) in Islamabad it was said that at least 91 journalists have been murdered across the country since 2000. It was told that Pakistan has become the third most dangerous country for journalists after Somalia and Syria.

21 Nov 20 mourners, including two minors, were killed and more than 30, including three Police personnel and five children, were wounded in a suicide blast at a Muharram procession. The procession was taken out from the Qasar-e-Shabbir Imambargah (Shia place of commemoration) in Dhok Syedan area on Misrial Road in Rawalpindi District.

5 Dec At least six militants were killed and eight others sustained bullet injuries when Lashkar-e-Islam (LI) militants attacked pro-government lashkar (militia), Tauheedul Islam (TI), post in Bukar area of Zakhakhel in Khyber Agency.

Three soldiers were killed and 20 others sustained injuries in a suicide blast near the Ziari Noor Camp on the Angoor Adda Road in South Waziristan Agency.

10 Dec 14 militants and seven SFs among 22 persons killed during the week in FATA

28 civilians and four SFs among 33 persons killed during the week in Sindh.

Nine persons—three Policemen, a soldier, two civilians and three suicide bombers - were killed while five others, including a Station House Officer (SHO), sustained injuries in a suicide attack targeting the Kakki Police Station in Bannu District.

15 Dec The Pakistan Air Force (PAF) base inside the Badshah Khan International Airport of Peshawar, provincial capital of Khyber Pakhtunkhwa, was attacked by militants, with a simultaneous rocket barrage, resulting in the killing of seven people, including five militants, and injuries to 40 others.

16 Dec Security Forces killed five militants - said to be Uzbeks - in a fierce encounter in Pawaki village, just one kilometre from the PAF base clearing the area off miscreants.

17 Dec 33 civilians and 11 Security Forces among 44 persons killed during the week in Sindh.

19 persons, among them women and children, were killed and 71 others injured when a powerful car bomb ripped through the Jamrud bazaar in Khyber Agency.

18 Dec 6 persons, including four women polio workers, were killed in separate incidents in Karachi.

20 Dec A local journalist and two other persons were shot dead when a group of armed assailants intercepted a bus coming from Quetta on its way to Punjab and opened fire on the passengers and abducted six passengers on Quetta-Sukkur highway in the Machh area of Bolan District.

21 Dec 3 persons, including an activist of Pakistan People's Party (PPP), a Shia community member and an Ahl-e-Sunnat-Wal-Jama'at (ASWJ) cadre were shot dead, while five people were injured in hand grenade attack in Karachi.

24 Dec 27 civilians and four militants killed during the week in Sindh.

23 civilians and nine militants killed during the week in FATA.

24 civilians and three SFs killed during the week in Balochistan.

11 persons, including six Pakistanis and five Afghan nationals were killed in Pothan area near Pakistan-Iran border in Gwadar District of Balochistan while trying to illegally cross into neighbouring Iran in three vehicles.

25 Dec At least 20 persons, including four Policemen, were killed in separate incidents in Karachi

29 Dec An explosion ripped through a passenger bus at the Cantonment Station of Karachi, killing six people and wounding 52 others, some of whom were in critical condition.

30 Dec A car bomb exploded near a convoy of buses taking Shia pilgrims to Iran, killing 20 persons and injuring 25, on the RCD Highway in the Dringer area in Mastung District of Balochistan.

Twenty-one tribal policemen believed to have been kidnapped by the Taliban were found shot dead in the Jabai area of Frontier Region Peshawar after being notified by one policeman who escaped. Another policeman was found seriously wounded. The 23 policemen went missing before dawn on 27 December, when militants armed with rocket-propelled grenades and automatic weapons attacked two posts in Frontier Region Peshawar. Two policemen were also killed in the attacks.

31 Dec 22 civilians and eight SFs among 30 persons killed during the week in Balochistan.

28 SFs and 12 militants among 47 persons killed during the week in FATA.

35 civilians and five SFs among 43 persons killed during the week in Sindh.

FEATURES

CHRONOLOGY OF ARMS CONTROL AND DISARMAMENT AGREEMENTS
In force, 1 January 2011

1925 Protocol for the Prohibition of the Use in War of Asphyxiating, Poisonous or Other Gases, and of Bacteriological Methods of Warfare (1925 Geneva Protocol)

1948 Convention on the Prevention and Punishment of the Crime of Genocide (Genocide Convention)

1949 Geneva Convention (IV) Relative to the Protection of Civilian Persons in Time of War

1959 Antarctic Treaty

1963 Treaty Banning Nuclear Weapon Tests in the Atmosphere, in Outer Space and Under Water (Partial Test-Ban Treaty, PTBT)

1967 Treaty on Principles Governing the Activities of States in the Exploration and Use of Outer Space, Including the Moon and Other Celestial Bodies (Outer Space Treaty)

1967 Treaty for the Prohibition of Nuclear Weapons in Latin America and the Caribbean (Treaty of Tlatelolco)

1968 Treaty on the Non-proliferation of Nuclear Weapons (Non- Proliferation Treaty, NPT)

1971 Treaty on the Prohibition of the Emplacement of Nuclear Weapons and other Weapons of Mass Destruction on the Seabed and the Ocean Floor and in the Subsoil thereof (Seabed Treaty)

1972 Convention on the Prohibition of the Development, Production and Stockpiling of Bacteriological (Biological) and Toxin Weapons and on their Destruction (Biological and Toxin Weapons Convention, BTWC)

1974 Treaty on the Limitation of Underground Nuclear Weapon Tests (Threshold Test-Ban Treaty, TTBT)

1976 Treaty on Underground Nuclear Explosions for Peaceful Purposes (Peaceful Nuclear Explosions Treaty, PNET)

1977 Convention on the Prohibition of Military or Any Other Hostile Use of Environmental Modification Techniques (Enmod Convention)

1977 Protocols I and II Additional to the 1949 Geneva Conventions and Relating to the Protection of Victims of International and Non- International Armed Conflicts

1980 Convention on the Physical Protection of Nuclear Material

1981 Convention on Prohibitions or Restrictions on the Use of Certain Conventional Weapons which may be Deemed to be Excessively Injurious or to have Indiscriminate Effects (CCW Convention, or 'Inhumane Weapons' Convention)

1985 South Pacific Nuclear Free Zone Treaty (Treaty of Rarotonga)

1987 Treaty on the Elimination of Intermediate-Range and Shorter- Range Missiles (INF Treaty)

1990 Treaty on Conventional Armed Forces in Europe (CFE Treaty)

1992 Treaty on Open Skies

1993 Convention on the Prohibition of the Development, Production, Stockpiling and Use of Chemical Weapons and on their Destruction (Chemical Weapons Convention, CWC)

1995 Treaty on the Southeast Asia Nuclear Weapon-Free Zone (Treaty of Bangkok)

1996 African Nuclear-Weapon-Free Zone Treaty (Treaty of Pelindaba)

1996 Agreement on Sub-Regional Arms Control (Florence Agreement)

1997 Inter-American Convention Against the Illicit Manufacturing of and Trafficking in Firearms, Ammunition, Explosives, and Other Related Materials

1997 Convention on the Prohibition of the Use, Stockpiling, Production and Transfer of Anti-Personnel Mines and on their Destruction (APM Convention)

1999 Inter-American Convention on Transparency in Conventional Weapons Acquisitions

1999 Vienna Document 1999 on Confidence- and Security- Building Measures

2006 ECOWAS Convention on Small Arms, Light Weapons, their Ammunition and Other Related Materials

2006 Treaty on a Nuclear-Weapon-Free Zone in Central Asia (Treaty of Semipalatinsk)

2008 Convention on Cluster Munitions

2010 Treaty on Measures for the Further Reduction and Limitation of Strategic Offensive Arms (New START, Prague Treaty)

AGREEMENTS NOT YET IN FORCE

1996 Comprehensive Nuclear-Test-Ban Treaty (CTBT)

1999 Agreement on Adaptation of the CFE Treaty

2010 Central African Convention for the Control of Small Arms and Light Weapons, Their Ammunition and All Parts and Components That Can Be Used for Their Manufacture, Repair and Assembly (Kinshasa Convention)

DRONE WARFARE (JOYSTICK WARS)

Introduction

Unmanned "drone" aircraft controlled from remote video consoles are being used in increasing numbers by the U.S. military in Afghanistan and by the CIA in Pakistan and other places outside of recognised war zones. Some analysts argue that the CIA strikes in Pakistan are illegal, while others say they comply with the laws of war. The spread of armed drones, along with resulting civilian deaths, is raising ethical concerns as well as questions about the effectiveness of drones. It is understood that the U.S. military now possesses over 7,000 drones, and more than 40 nations, including Iran and China, have drone technology. Unmanned aircraft are being used for everything from border control and environmental monitoring to drug interdiction and building inspections. Some policy experts worry that as drones expand worldwide, they not only could make the U.S. a more potent military force but also put it at greater risk of attack from enemies possessing the technology.

Technically, drones are pilotless planes that are pre-programmed to fly a set course and mission. Predators, Reapers and some other types of unmanned craft, on the other hand, are controlled remotely during flight by operators on the ground, typically at bases located in the U.S. However, the term "drones" is widely, if loosely, used to describe both types of unmanned craft.

Table 1: Drone Attacks in Pakistan

	2004-07	*2008*	*2009*	*2010*	*2011*	*2012*
Total Drone Strikes	9	34	53	90	59	28
Estimated Total Deaths	86-109	263-296	536	831	548	312

*Data till July 15, 2012

Source: "The Year of the Drone: An Analysis of U.S. Drone Strikes in Pakistan, 2004-2010", New America Foundation, 2010

The growing use of unmanned war-planes is part of a much broader embrace of drone technology for both military and civilian uses—everything from environmental monitoring and border patrol to drug interdiction and post-disaster searches. But it is the expanding robotic technology for war that is stirring the greatest debate. In recent years the U.S. military has spent billions of dollars to expand its fleet of unmanned planes. The U.S. Air Force is now training more pilots to fly unmanned planes than traditional fighter pilots.

Drone technology itself is astonishing in its capacity to reconnoitre and kill. In the case of the Predator and it's even more powerful brother, the Reaper, controllers sit at computer consoles at U.S. bases thousands of miles from harm's way and control the aircraft via satellite communication. With the ability to remain aloft for long hours undetected on the ground—Predators can fly at altitudes of about 50,000 feet—the planes can do everything from snap high-resolution reconnaissance photos of insurgents' vehicles to shoot Hellfire missiles at them.

Ethical Issues

A secret archive of classified military documents, controversially released in July 2010, by WikiLeaks revealed the lethal power of the Predator. As reported by The New York Times, in early winter 2008 a Predator spotted a group of insurgents suspected of planting roadside bombs near an American military outpost in Afghanistan. "Within minutes after identifying the militants, the Predator unleashed a Hellfire missile, all but evaporating one of the figures digging in the dark. When ground troops reached the crater caused by the missile, costing $60,000, all that was left was a shovel and a crowbar."[1]

The U.S. Air Force flies some 20 Predator and Reaper aircraft a day in Afghanistan, and allies such as Britain and Germany have their own fleets. The leaked incident reports show that missions include taking reconnaissance photos, gathering electronic transmissions, sending images of ongoing battles to field commanders and attacking militants with bombs and missiles, plus supporting U.S. Special Operations missions. "Killer drones are the future of warfare."[2]

But overshadowing that future is a fierce debate over how, where and by whom drones are being used. Of particular concern is the CIA's drone programme, which reportedly has targeted suspected militants in western Pakistan and other remote trouble spots where the United States is not engaged in open hostilities, including Yemen.

The CIA attacks have raised important legal questions about the role of targeted killing in the fight against the Taliban and Al Qaeda. U.S. officials contend that such killings are legal under established principles of self-defence, international laws of armed conflict and the Authorisation for Use of Military Force—the so-called "law of 9/11" passed by Congress following the 2001 terrorist attacks. But critics say CIA attacks inside Pakistan violate international laws of armed conflict because the U.S. is not at war with Pakistan, is not using its drones as part of Pakistan's own military operations and its drone strikes are carried out by civilians in secret far from active battlefields.

Targeted killings of terrorism suspects and the use of drones to carry them out, displace clear legal standards with a vaguely defined license to kill, the creation of a major accountability vacuum, and a 'Playstation' mentality to killing with drone technology.

The Predator programme represents a radically new and geographically unfounded use of state-sanctioned lethal force. Because of the CIA programme's secrecy, there is no visible system of accountability in place, despite the fact that the agency has killed many civilians inside a politically fragile, nuclear-armed country with which the U.S. is not at war."[3] The use of unmanned weapons to target individuals—and, for that matter, the targeting of individuals in general—raises many complex legal questions. It needs to be examined as to who can be a legitimate target, where that person can be legally targeted and when the risk of collateral damage is too high.

As the use of drones grows, some questions that policy makers, legal analysts and human-rights advocates need to weigh are:

- Is targeting suspected militants a matter of military necessity or do other reasonable alternatives, such as capture and arrest, exist?
- Is the intensity of the attacks along with any civilian casualties and collateral damage—proportional to the threat posed by the militants being targeted?
- Are drone operators working for the CIA—and not the U.S. military—in compliance with international law, including, under certain circumstances, the laws of war governing "lawful combatants"?
- Are suspected militants hiding in the Pakistani border region directly engaged in hostilities with the United States, making them legal targets for attack?
- Does it matter if the Pakistani government sanctions American drone strikes within its borders?

Answering such questions is made difficult because two separate legal principles may be used to address them. International Humanitarian Law—the so-called law of armed conflict—has been shaped by international agreement over many decades It gives "lawful combatants"—generally uniformed soldiers who are part of a country's armed forces—the right to strike other combatants or civilians who are taking direct part in hostilities The other is the principle of self-defence, under which nations may claim the right

[1] C. J. Chivers, et al . "View Is Bleaker than Official Portrayal of War in Afghanistan." The New York Times, 25 July 2010.

[2] Statement of Afsheen John Radsan before the House Subcommittee on National Security and Foreign Affairs, "Loftier Standards for the CIA's Remote-Control Killing," 28 April 2010, www.oversight.house.gov/images/stories/sub committees/NS_Subcommittee/4.28.10_Drones_ II/Hadsan_Statement_for_the_Record. pdf

[3] Jane Mayer, "The Predator War," *The New Yorker*, 26 Oct 2009, p.38

to use lethal force not only in an active combat zone but also outside it to protect vital national interests.

The organised terrorist enemy does not have conventional forces but plans and executes its attacks while hiding among civilian populations. That behaviour simultaneously makes the application of international law more difficult and more critical for the protection of innocent civilians. Many legal scholars view that U.S. drone attacks, even by the CIA inside Pakistan, are legitimate and legal under international law and/or the principle of self defence. The larger concern is that international law has fallen behind in the development of drone technology, particularly when that technology is deployed by non-military agents like the CIA. There need to be checks in place similar to those on conventional military operations.

However, other legal experts argue that drone strikes carried out by the civilian CIA and away from where the U.S military is engaged in active combat, are illegal. Members of the CIA, as civilians, are not "lawful combatants" under international law, meaning their drone killings are "unlawful." "The international community does not know when and where the CIA is authorised to kill, the criteria for individuals who may be killed, how it ensures killings are legal and what follow-up there is when civilians are illegally killed. In a situation in which there is no disclosure of who has been killed, for what reason and whether innocent civilians have died, the legal principle of international accountability is, by definition, comprehensively violated."[4]

How many civilians have died from drone strikes in Pakistan and elsewhere is something of a guessing game. With the CIA programme under a shroud of secrecy and the task of distinguishing friend from foe often difficult, especially along the Afghanistan-Pakistan border region, civilian casualties can't be determined with certainty—a factor that influences where various analysts come down on the effectiveness of drones as an anti-terror tool.

One analyst has concluded that "drone strikes produce more terrorists than they eliminate . . . would be a damning argument—if the data weren't simply bogus." She argued that the only public data on civilian casualties from drone attacks in Pakistan come from the Pakistani Taliban and that "high-level Pakistani officials have conceded to me that very few civilians have been killed by drones, and their innocence is often debatable."[5]

Yet critics of drone strikes argue that no matter how successful they may be at killing individual militants, they sow the seeds for new rounds of extremism and militancy. Of particular concern is the use of drones as part of a counterinsurgency strategy, an approach used in Afghanistan that has put a premium on protecting civilians as a way to promote the rule of law and choke off insurgent influence. "Targeted killings are one of America's few options left."[6]

Many military experts argue that drones are simply a new kind of weapon, not unlike machine guns and tanks once were. There is no prohibition under the laws of war on the use of technologically advanced weapons systems in armed conflict so long as they are employed in conformity with applicable laws of war. But some critics are concerned about the moral implications of using weapons that put civilians—but not the weapons' operators—at risk. According to the just-war principles, it is better to risk the lives of one's own combatants than the lives of enemy non-combatants. But this moral calculus is completely tossed aside in the case of drone warfare, since drone operators don't risk their lives at all. Footage of drone strikes and clips of combat scenes are available on You Tube, turning "war into a sort of entertainment, or 'war porn' as soldiers call it." [7]

The phrase—'to go to war'—for the last 5,000 years meant going to a place of such danger that you might never come home again, might never see your family. But for the individual now—not all, but for an increasing set—going to war is the act of waking up, getting in your car and driving to sit behind a computer screen and engaging in what is war, then driving home. It's different, and it presents new challenges for everything from leadership to stress management to crucial questions of personnel and promotion policies.

Development of Drones

Drone development proceeded in fits and starts after World War II. During the Vietnam War, which ended in 1975, an unmanned reconnaissance plane called

---

[4] 'U.N. expert criticizes 'illegal' targeted killing policies and calls on the U.S. to halt CIA drone killings," news release, United Nations Office at Geneva, 2 June 2010, www.unog.ch/ unog/websitc/news_media. nsf

[5] C. Christine Fair, "Drone Wars," *Foreign Policy*, 28 May 2010, www.foreignpolicy.com/ articles/2010/o5/ 28/drone_ wars.

[6] Daniel L. Hyman, "Do Targeted Killings Work?" *ForeignPolicy.com*, 14 July 2009, www.brookings.edu/opinions/2009/0714_targeted_ killings_hyman.aspx

[7] P.W. Singer, *Wired for War: The Robotics Revolution and Conflict in the 21st Century* (Penguin: 2009), pp. 320

the Fire Fly flew more than 3,400 missions, but 16 percent of the planes crashed.[8] In the late 1970s, the U.S. Army planned development of a small propeller-driven reconnaissance drone called the Aquila, but military planners kept adding expensive technological requirements. Finally, after spending more than $1 billion for a few prototypes, the military cancelled the project.[9]

The 1980s saw a resurgence in interest in unmanned aircraft. In the 1982 war in Lebanon, the Israeli Air Force used a drone called the Pioneer, powered by a 26-horsepower snowmobile engine. The U.S. Navy bought several, and the Reagan administration ramped up drone research.[10] During the 1991 Persian Gulf War, Pioneer planes sought out targets for shelling of Iraqi forces by ships. Consequently, the U.S. Defence Department spent more than $3 billion in the 1990s on unmanned aircraft.[11]

The Predator era began in the mid-1990s, driven by a constellation of developing forces. Among them the development of Global Positioning System (GPS) technology that uses satellites for pinpoint navigational accuracy: the growth and ubiquity of computer power and its increasing adoption by the military: pressure on the Pentagon to spend more efficiently on new battlefield technology; and political pressure to adopt unmanned systems, in part to reduce combat casualties and attract tech-savvy recruits into the armed forces.

However, early problems with the technology cast doubt on its reliability. An early version of the Predator was used for reconnaissance in 1995 during a NATO air campaign in the Balkans war against Bosnian Serbs. But it was unable to fly almost 60 percent of its missions because its wings iced up easily. In February 2001 a Hellfire laser-guided missile was successfully test fired from a Predator drone, and by the end of the year the September 11 terrorist attacks on the United States put the development and use of unmanned aircraft—particularly armed ones—into high gear.[12]

In the first year of war, armed Predators destroyed roughly 115 targets in Afghanistan.[13] Soon, their use outside of the Afghan battlefield opened a debate that continues today over targeted killings.

In November 2002, a Hellfire missile fired from a Predator based in Djibouti struck a vehicle speeding through a desert in Yemen, targeting Qaed Salim Sinan al-Harethi, a leader of Al Qaeda in Yemen and a suspect in the October 2000 bombing of the destroyer USS Cole. Also in the car were five other men, including a suspected Al Qaeda operative who held US citizenship.[14]

In whatever way legal analysts and administration officials have viewed drone strikes, one thing has been clear: The use of unmanned military aircraft has grown apace in the past half-dozen or so years, with a mix of strategic successes and failures and technological advantages and vulnerabilities.

Unmanned aircraft have been used to take out a number of so-called high-value terrorist targets, among them Baitullah Mehsud, Pakistan's Taliban chief, suspected in the assassination of former Pakistani prime minister Benazir Bhutto, who was killed by a CIA drone strike in summer 2009. Pakistan considered the Al Qaeda-Iinked Mehsud its No. 1 internal threat and his demise was a severe blow to extremists threatening the stability of Pakistan and a possible boost to U.S.-Pakistan cooperation in fighting insurgents who wreak havoc along the Afghan border."[15]

Pentagon accident reports reveal that the pilotless aircraft suffer from frequent system failures, computer glitches and human error. Air Force investigators continue to cite pilot mistakes, coordination snafus, software failures, outdated technology and inadequate flight manuals. Accident rates for drones are falling, but total mishaps are rising because the aircraft are being put to more and more use. At least 38 drones are in the air over Afghanistan at any one time, and flight hours more than tripled between 2006 and 2009. In 2010, drones flew 185,000 hours over Afghanistan and Iraq.

[8] Singer, *op. cit.*, pp. 54-55

[9] *Ibid*, p, 55.

[10] Andrew Callam, "Drone Wars: Armed Unmanned Aerial Vehicles," *International Affairs Review*, Winter 2010; www.iar-gwu.org/ node/144.

[11] Callam, op. cit

[12] Callam, op. cit

[13] Singer, op. cit., p. 55.

[14] Seymour M. Hersh, "Manhunt,' *The New Yorker*, 25 December 2002, www.newyorker.corm/ archive/2002/12/23/ 021223fa_fact.

[15] "Death of Taliban chief a blow to extremists," MSNBC, 7 Aug 2009, www.msnbc.rnsn.com/id/320879/

MQ-1B Predator		*MQ-9 Reaper*
Armed reconnaissance, surveillance and target acquisition	**Primary function**	Hunter-killer weapon system
14.8 m (48.7 ft)	**Wingspan**	20.1 m (66 ft)
8.2 m (27 ft)	**Length**	11 m (36 ft)
204 kg (450 lb)	**Payload**	1,701 kg (3,750 lb)
135-217 kph (84-135 mph)	**Cruise speed**	370 kph (230 mph)
1,240k, (770 miles)	**Range**	1,850 k (1,150 miles)
Two Hellfire missiles	**Weapons**	Combination of Hellfire, Paveway II and GBU-12 JDAM
Two: one pilot and one sensor operator; plus a mission co-ordinator when required	**Crew**	Two: one pilot and one sensor operator; plus a mission co-ordinator when required
$20m per system (includes four aircraft, ground control station and satellite link)	**Unit cost**	$53.5m per system (includes four aircraft, ground control station and satellite link)
130 -	**Active force – USAF** **RAF**	47 4

Two medium-sized drones currently in use in Afghanistan and Pakistan are the MQ-1B Predator and the MQ-9 Reaper. Each multi-million dollar Predator or Reaper system comprises four aircraft, a ground control station and a satellite link.They carry a wealth of sensors in their bulbous noses: colour and black-and-white TV cameras, image intensifiers, radar, infra-red imaging for low-light conditions and lasers for targeting. They can also be armed with laser-guided missiles.

The MQ-1B Predator (formerly called the RQ-1 Predator) was originally designed as an aircraft for intelligence-gathering, surveillance, identifying targets and reconnaissance. However, since 2002 it has been equipped with two Hellfire II missiles, meaning it can strike at a range of up to 8 kilometres. By contrast the newer MQ-9 Reaper was conceived as a "hunter-killer" system. It can carry four Hellfire missiles and laser-guided bombs such as Paveway II and GBU-12. Its cruise speed is 370 kph, much faster than the 217 kph of the Predator which is more vulnerable to being shot down at low altitudes—although the drones would usually be flown above the range of most of the weapons available to the Taliban.

Current Situation

Drones are used in situations where manned flight is considered too risky or difficult. They provide troops with a 24-hour "eye in the sky", seven days a week. Each aircraft can stay aloft for up to 17 hours at a time, loitering over an area and sending back real-time imagery of activities on the ground.

The Pentagon's 2011 budget included plans for a doubling of production of unmanned aircraft. In fact, the Air Force, for the first time, proposed buying more unmanned planes than conventional piloted combat craft. The Air Force planned to double production of the Reaper, and the Army planned to buy 26 extended-range Predators, according to the Los Angeles Times. Overall, the newspaper reported, Pentagon spending on Reapers and Predators will grow to $1.4 billion in 2011, up from $8775 million in 2010.[16] Drones not only are useful in dealing with international conflict but also for fighting drug trafficking and providing help in natural disasters.

In the longer term, military planners envision a massive expansion in the role of drones in combat operations. As the revolution in drone technology proceeds, manufacturers are working to figure out how to enhance the capability of unmanned aircraft.

A 2008 RAND Corporation study analysed terrorist groups that existed worldwide between 1968 and 2006 and concluded that military force was rarely the primary reason such groups ended. Rather, most ended because of operations carried out by local police or intelligence agencies or because they negotiated a settlement with their governments. These findings suggest that the U.S. approach to countering al Qaeda has focused far too much on the use of military force. Instead policing and intelligence

[16] Julian E. Barnes, "Pentagon budget calls for more unmanned aircraft," *Los Angeles Times*, 2 Feb 2010

should be the backbone of U.S. efforts.[17] Another question is whether the United States, with all of its pioneering technology in unmanned aviation, will itself fall prey to rogue actors who get their hands on the same technology.

The three main unmanned aerial vehicles (UAVs), or drones, used by the U.S. Air Force and the Central Intelligence Agency are the Predator, a medium-altitude craft that can shoot two laser-guided Hellfire missiles and take high-resolution reconnaissance photos; the Reaper, a larger version of the Predator that carries four Hellfire missiles; and the Global Hawk, a high-altitude, long-endurance craft that gathers and transmits reconnaissance and surveillance data.

Drone Pilots and Air Force Culture

There are fighter pilots and there are drone pilots. Between the two is a cultural gap that needs to be bridged. The clash between the two became especially apparent in 2006 after an air strike that killed Abu Musab al-Zarqawi—the Iraqi leader of an al Qaeda affiliate. After land-based crews of the unmanned Predator drone spent hundreds of hours searching for al-Zarqawi, an F-16 released a bomb that killed him.

The F-16 pilot received the Distinguished Flying Cross; the Predator pilots received thank you notes from a general based in the region. Military officials concluded that even though the drone crews engaged in missions of a combative nature, they weren't physically in combat and weren't in harm's way. Appreciation for drone pilots, however, is gradually changing, even within an Air Force culture that exalts fighter and bomber pilots.

Pilots of drones being flown in Afghanistan and Pakistan typically operate from bases in the United States, 7,500 miles away from the action. Operating a drone may be an enhanced version of the latest Xbox flight simulator, but there's no reset button. As an indication of the U.S. Air Force's commitment to drone warfare, it bought more unmanned aircraft than traditional fighter jets for the first time in 2010. However, the culture is still one dominated by aviators.

Military Utility of Drones

Armed drones lower the perceived costs of using lethal force in at least three ways.

a) Drones reduce the cost of using lethal force. Most drones are a bargain compared with the available alternatives. Manned aircraft expensive: Lockheed Martin's F-22 fighter jets cost about $150 million each; F-35s are $90 million; and F-16s are $55 million. But the 2011 price of a Reaper drone was $28.4 million, while Predator drones cost only about $5 million to make. Hellfire missiles cost less than $60,000 each.

b) Relying on drone attacks reduces the domestic political costs of using lethal force. Sending special operations forces after a suspected terrorist places the lives of military personnel at risk. In contrast, using armed drones eliminates all short-term risks to the lives of military personnel involved in the operations.

c) By reducing accidental civilian casualties, precision drone technologies reduce the perceived moral and reputational costs of using lethal force.

Limitations of Drones

Drones are only effective in attack roles when operating against targets with no air defence capabilities. Unlike a fighter jet pilot, drone operators cannot detect threats to the safety of their aircraft. Surface-to-air missiles therefore pose a much greater threat to drones than to other forms of military aviation.

The vulnerability of drones to ground fire could become a debilitating factor, if greater dependence is placed on drones in war-fighting. One of the biggest advantages of unmanned aircraft is their low acquisition cost, relative to manned aircraft. However, heavy losses to enemy fire would drive the overall cost of drone operations beyond sustainable levels. The United States had a similar experience when it attempted to use helicopters on a massive scale in Vietnam. Conversely, should efforts be made to enhance the operational sophistication of drones, per-unit costs will rise, making the loss of a drone a serious concern for military commanders. This would increase risk aversion.

In the final analysis, drones are popular because they present a low-cost option for locating and destroying low-tech adversaries. If they were to be upgraded to penetrate sophisticated air defence systems, their advantages vis-à-vis manned aircraft would fall away. Furthermore, drones have higher operating costs than manned aircraft, which in the long run, militates against greatly enhancing their use in

[17] Seth C Jones and Martin C. Libicki, "How Terrorist Groups End," Research Brief: Rand Corporation, 2008, www.rand.org/pubs/researchbriefs/RB9351/indexl.html.

warfare. They are also ten times more prone to crashing than fighter jets – a problem that can only be overcome through expensive technical upgrades.

Such considerations mean that drones have a niche role in contemporary military operations. They are by no means a transformative technology that has the potential to make manned flight obsolete. Expanded use of drones could even prove counterproductive, as it would threaten to lead to information overload. At present, Predator and Reaper drones in Afghanistan deliver around 400 hours of video footage daily to US forces. The transmission of this data to ground controllers based in the United States consumes vast amounts of communications bandwidth.

An illustration of the strain that drones pose to communications systems is provided by the fact that a single Global Hawk uses five times as much bandwidth as did all US forces involved in the 2001 invasion of Afghanistan. Although communications technology is presently being upgraded to cope with the demands posed by drone tasking and coordination, there are limits to which existing bandwidth can be expanded. This suggests that, even allowing for technological progress, there are limits to the potential use of drones in military operations. Furthermore, increased bandwidth also increases vulnerability to electronic counter-measures such as jamming.

Drones also have two undesirable side-effects. Firstly, they encourage senior commanders to micro-manage operations and insist that the latest imagery be provided to them before any action is taken. This stifles tactical initiative and lengthens the time between identification and elimination of a target. Secondly, commanders at both operational and tactical levels can grow so dependent on drone support that they refuse to deploy their troops without it. Convoy movements in Iraq and Afghanistan are now partially conditional on the availability of drone cover—a sign of poor morale.

Known Locations of U.S. Drone Bases

- Incirlik, Turkey
- Jalalabad Airfield, Afghanistan
- Khost Airfield, Afghanistan
- Kandahar Airfield, Afghanistan
- Shindand Airfield, Afghanistan
- Al-Udeid Air Base, Qatar
- Zamboanga, Philippines
- Al-Dhafra Air Base, United Arab Emirates
- Al-Anad Air Base, Yemen
- Arba Minch, Ethiopia
- Camp Lemonier, Djibouti
- Mahe, Seychelles

The Af-Pak Situation

The American military has launched the highest ever drone strikes this year in Afghanistan, according to U.S. Air Force statistics. It's essentially the same number of robotic attacks in Pakistan since the CIA-led campaign there began nearly eight years ago. And the increased strikes come as the rest of the war in Afghanistan is slowing down. The secret drone campaigns have drawn the most scrutiny because of the legal, geopolitical, and ethical questions they raise. But in Afghanistan the rise of the flying robots is largely occurring in the open, on an acknowledged battlefield where the targets are largely unquestioned and the attending issues aren't nearly as fraught.

The difference between the operations in Afghanistan and Pakistan come down to the fundamental differences between open military campaigns and covert campaigns run by the intelligence community. It shapes everything from the level of transparency to the command and control to the rules of engagements to the process and consequences if an air strike goes wrong. The military has 61 Predator and Reaper "combat air patrols," each with three or four robotic planes. The CIA's inventory is believed to be just a fraction of that: 30 to 35 drones total, although there is thought to be some overlap between the military and intelligence agency fleets.

Even the air war is shrinking. Overall surveillance sorties are down, from an average of 3,183 per month last year to 2,954 in 2012. (Drones flew 860 of those sorties in 2011, and now fly 761 per month today.) Missions in which U.S. aircraft fire their weapons have declined, too. It was 450 times per month on average in 2011. This year, the monthly total has dropped to 360.

In other words, drone strikes in Afghanistan now make up about 9 percent of the overall total of aerial attacks. Last year, it was a little more than 5 percent. The UAVs are growing in importance while the rest of the military campaign is receding.

Conclusion

Over-reliance on drones reflects a dangerous blurring of the boundaries between "war" and "non-war," with grave consequences for the rule of law. Whether one regards drone strikes as lawful acts of war or as extra-judicial killings depends wholly on how far one is willing to stretch the law of war in efforts to make it fit an increasingly unprecedented situation.

In the ultimate analysis, drones are a "short-term fix" approach to counterterrorism, one that relies excessively on eliminating specific individuals deemed to be a threat, without much discussion of whether this strategy is likely to produce long-term security gains.

In contexts other than counterinsurgency and counterterrorism, the effectiveness of drones is largely dependent on the operating environment. If air defence technology improves at a faster pace than drone technology, dependence on unmanned aircraft could prove ruinously expensive for most countries. Despite this, the US military is currently investing heavily in operational drones. At the moment, most of its drones are tactical ones, which are cheap and easily replaceable.

Drones are likely to be most useful when carrying out vital missions deemed too dangerous for manned aircraft, such as electronic warfare over hostile territory. Even their use on border policing has proven controversial, with one study finding that the results produced do not justify the costs involved. From a long-term perspective, improvements in drone technology are occurring too slowly and incrementally to justify labelling it a transformative phenomenon. Rather than replacing manned aircraft in the future, drones are likely to only complement them.

Drones have assumed a leading role in counterterrorism and counterinsurgency, and are projected to be of growing importance in future military operations. Their low cost makes them expendable and ideal for highly dangerous or politically sensitive missions. However, technical limitations as well as likely improvements in competing technologies, notably air defence systems, shall circumscribe the military role of drones. Although an integral part of future warfare, they are unlikely to fully replace manned aircraft and will instead, complement them.

MQ1 Predator drone armed with Hellfire missile Source: US Air Force

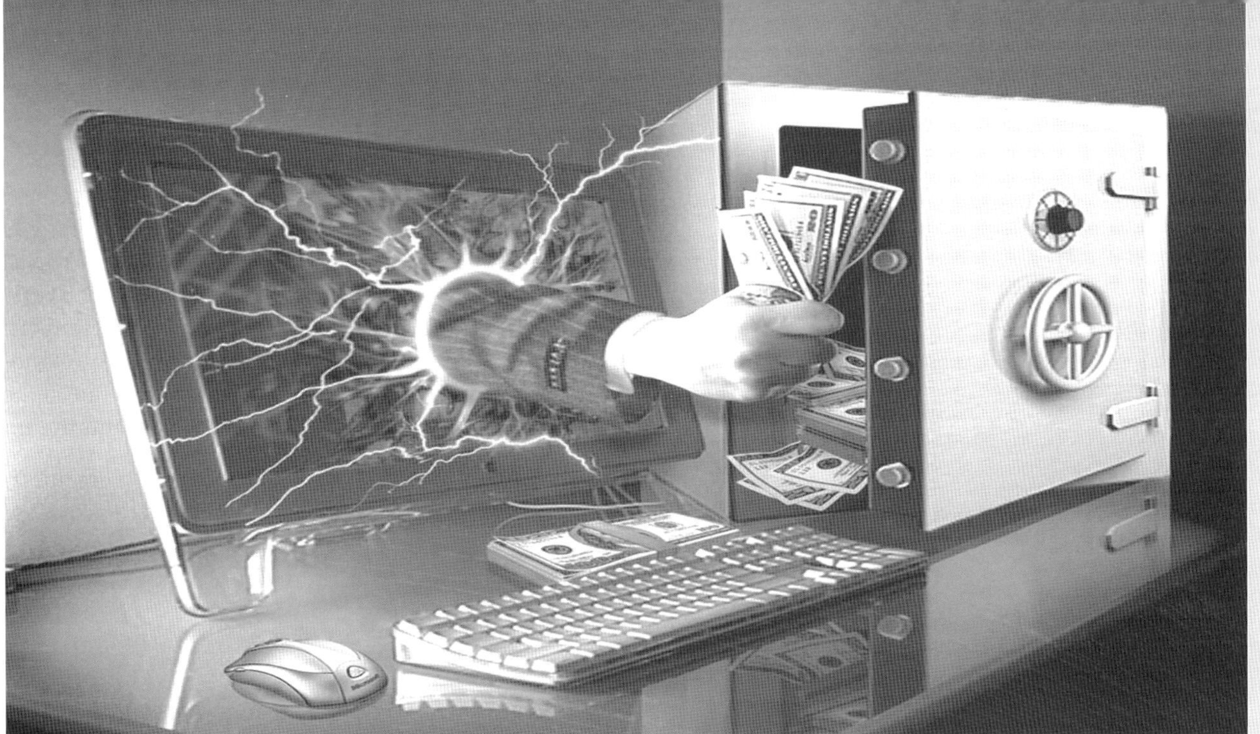

CYBER WARFARE

...there are terrorist threats in the cyber space, which is the fifth domain after land, sea, air and space. Much of our critical infrastructure lies in cyber space. Cyber crimes such as hacking, financial fraud, data theft, espionage etc. would, in certain circumstances, amount to terrorist acts. Our counter terrorism capacity must be able to meet the threats in cyber space. Since there are no boundaries in cyber space, how will the Central Government and the State Governments share the responsibility to face the threats in cyber space?[1]

Introduction

The world needs an open, resilient and secure Internet in partnership with private companies and governments around the world. The Internet has become a cornerstone of economic growth and innovation, a vital contributor to global communication and an integral part of the life of people in every corner of the globe. Yet, a range of cyber threats now endanger reliable access to information technology, as well as economic and national security interests of all countries. These threats include cyber warfare waged by both state and non-state actors, cyber espionage that steals valuable national secrets and the intellectual property of private companies, cyber crime involving vast amounts of money annually, and cyber agitation by those with political or ideological objectives. Policymakers across the political spectrum recognize the threat, but have not yet reached consensus about how to balance privacy and security, government regulation and private sector initiatives, and constraints on the Internet with the incredible freedom that has produced unprecedented economic and social gains. Debate on how and when to use offensive cyber weapons is in its infancy and the ways in which cyber conflicts may escalate are poorly understood.

The threat of cyber terrorism is real and growing, as global and national systems become increasingly interlinked and interdependent. Speculation about the potential threat of cyber attacks has been rife since the 1980s, and Government systems across the world have been targeted from time to time by politically motivated, mischievous and state-backed groupings. Definitional disputes abound, and it is not clear how many of these can be described as cyber terrorist 'attacks'. Nevertheless, cyber technology has become a crucial tool in the terrorist arsenal, and its use to directly engineer widespread, and potentially life threatening, disruptions cannot be overestimated.

Modern nations and advanced militaries around the world are intensifying their activities in cyberspace, which simultaneously constitutes a source of power and a soft underbelly. The infrastructures critical for the functioning of a state (electricity, communications, water, transportation, finance, and so on) all rely on this domain. Military command and control networks depend on cyberspace, as do all the most advanced technologies of the modern battlefield, such as

---

[1] Union Home Minister P. Chidambaram in his opening statement at the meeting of Chief Ministers on National Counter Terrorism Centre (NCTC) on 5 May 2012

intelligence gathering, processing and fusion systems, satellite use on the battlefield, use of autonomous fighting tools, real time integration of sensors to identify targets with fire systems, and more.

As an arena of warfare, cyberspace presents some unique features, including the ability to operate quickly, in thousandths of seconds, against enemies located far away, without risking the lives of combat personnel. The unique features of the domain also make it attractive for confrontation against a potential adversary. There can be confrontations in cyberspace (such as the 2007 attack on Estonia, attributed to Russia) and wars in which attacks in cyberspace are a component of a war effort (such as Russia's attack on Georgia in 2008). Attacks are occurring in cyberspace (on computerized systems) and cyberspace is being used as a means to damage the functionality of machines operating in the physical domain, e.g., the 2009 US Stuxnet attack against Iran's principal uranium enrichment facilities, which experts believe may stall Iran's nuclear programme by as much as five years. Stuxnet is indeed a cyber weapon and a tool threatening the whole existing system of international security.

Cyber war will likely play a part in every modern war. Indeed, both cyberspace attacks that have occurred and processes undertaken by states to prepare themselves in this domain indicate that the cyberspace arms race has already started. As part of this race, a number of states have, in recent years, established organisations dedicated to cyberspace as a domain of warfare, and security strategies for cyberspace have been formulated. At the same time, states are also faced with considerations regarding the constraints of cyber attacks and the risk of exposure to counterattacks, especially because defences are still not sufficiently strong.

There is also a growing international recognition that it is necessary to defend cyberspace and regulate its activities. This could be achieved through inter-state cooperation, adaptation of international law to cyberspace, and formulation of a compelling international treaty. Progress thus far has been slow, certainly not in pace with developments in cyberspace.

Cyberspace and Security

The term "cyberspace" defines a phenomenon that emerged with the linking of communications networks with computers and machines, which began in the 1970s; mass use of the internet and personal computers since the mid-1990s; and in the past decade, the comprehensive integration between computer systems and various communications systems and machines (such as in industry, transportation, and other fields), the mass use of handheld cellular devices, the flourishing of social networks on the internet, and more.

All of these have profoundly influenced society and the economy. Information technologies and cyberspace are rapidly changing the nature of the modern battlefield as well. The advanced technology on the battlefield includes intelligence systems, systems for information sharing and information fusion, the use of satellites on the battlefield, autonomous tools, real-time integration of target-seeking sensors with fire systems, and more. The development of cyberspace has also allowed extensive civilian coverage of a combat zone, partly by means of mobile cellular devices that provide anyone present in the area with the ability to document information, or alternatively, manipulate it. This information is transmitted instantly to internet networks, which in turn generates discussions in the social networks and affects public opinion. Thus arenas of war have become a space in which the public plays a central role and exerts—more so than in the past—its influence on the political stances of governments and international institutions, at times on the basis of nebulous information. This phenomenon has far reaching implications for everything having to do with the use of military force. It limits the ability to apply force but can also help enlist public opinion in favour of the use of force.

Definition

According to the International Telecommunications Union (ITU) of the United Nations, cyberspace is "the physical and non-physical terrain created by and/or composed of some or all of the following: computers, computer systems, networks and their computer programmes, computer data, content data, traffic data, and users." This definition implies that cyberspace entails three interdependent layers (See Table 1):

a) The human layer: the users of computerisation (communications and computers).
b) The logical layer: the software and bits. These move at the speed of light and represent information, instructions, cyberspace assets (such as valuable software, electronic funds), malware (such as Trojan horses), and more.
c) The physical layer: the network physical components, including hardware, mobile infrastructures, and stationary infrastructures, found on land, at sea, in the air, and in space.

Table 1: The Three Layers of Cyberspace

Layer	*Type of activity and its purpose*	*Contents (examples)*	*Developing trends (examples)*
The human layer			
The user	Human use of computerisation products	Reading, trading, investing, finding information, exchanging information, maintaining contact with friends, between citizens and government offices, crime, cyberwar	An increase in the phenomenon of user communities (WEB2) and the use of mobile and integrative devices (smart phones); the start of sophisticated internet use (WEB3)
The logical layer	Software activity		
Graphic user interface (GUI)	Translating information from user language to computer language (digital information) and back	Pages of text, pictures, videos, audio, buttons	Increase in types and levels of applications presented at the interface; rise in graphic presentation; transition to 3D
Applications software	Processing information from user interfaces, network management software	Instructions and flow charts in programming language (algorithms)	More applications; more and more layers of software between the hardware and user interface
Operating systems	Running software and translation from computer language to machine language	Information in programming language relevant to the layer	
The physical layer			
Hardware	Electromagnetic physical infrastructure doing machine operations	Chips, electronic cards, etc; electrical impulses	Growth in volume of information about electronic components, miniaturisation, mobility, flash memory
Communications and energy systems (electromagnetic infrastructure)	Providing conditions for existence and activity of computerisation in electromagnetic field	Infrastructure and maintenance; laying cables, computer tables, etc; RF signals, light and electricity waves	Growth in variety and spread of communications systems: cellular, Bluetooth, router, satellite, ocean cable. Improved energy utilisation and miniaturisation
Hardware and software carriers	Provide additional conditions to maintain cyberspace on land, at sea, in the air, and in space.		People carrying smart computers and phones; computer-embedded installations, systems, and tools; equipment with integrated processors and controllers; and devices with input options (scanners), sensors, and effectors. This is where the connection between cyberspace and the physical realms occurs.

Unlike definitions that view cyberspace as a fifth dimension, there is an approach that claims that cyberspace is one of seven domains, alongside air, space, sea, land, the electromagnetic domain, and the human domain. This approach distinguishes between cyberspace and the electromagnetic domain and counts the human layer as a dimension of its own. Cyberspace is an artificial domain realised by means of the electromagnetic domain that interfaces with physical domains by means of sensors and effectors. As such, cyberspace serves to empower the functionality of civilian and military systems operating in all domains while it also exposes them to cyberspace attacks.

Cyberspace as a Domain of Warfare

Some of the characteristics of the new domain of warfare include:

- ***The ability to act at nearly the speed of light, without traditional geographical limitations.*** This feature allows attackers the opportunity to execute long distance attacks in fractions of seconds without having to contend with the enemy in a physical arena. At the same time, cyberspace depends on the physical domain and the network infrastructures diffused in the physical space. On the defensive side, the possibility of a quick attack requires a foundation of dynamic defensive systems reacting automatically to attacks in real time and independent of human calculations.

- ***The ability to act in secret.*** Cyber attacks that have already occurred and information about strategies for action in cyberspace indicate that the attacker has the ability to operate in cyberspace anonymously—without leaving a signature—and hide behind others such as private hackers, criminal elements, or foreign agencies and nations. Thus, the use of cyberspace allows the attacker to minimize exposure, incrimination, and risk of counterattack, as it has been impossible to implicate the suspected nation in any of the cyber attacks carried out to date. In warfare in a kinetic battlefield it is usually clear who started, who attacked, and what space was conquered; none of this applies in cyberwar. This fact has contradictory implications: on the one hand, this may serve to limit counterattacks (there isn't anyone to respond to), yet there is also the potential for uncontrolled escalation. For example, should there be attacks causing fatalities and heavy damage to property, there will be political pressure to react against suspected elements even in the absence of solid evidence about the identity of the attacker.
- ***Cyber weapons can also be used as non-lethal weapons.*** The ability to cause heavy damage to the functioning of a state without destroying its physical infrastructures or killing people is considered an advantage of cyber weapons over strategic kinetic attacks (firepower). At the same time, cyber attacks can also cause a great deal of destruction and loss of human life by means of damaging systems located in physical domains but connected to cyberspace.

Cyberspace makes accessible targets not susceptible to attack by fire, such as:

a) Installations and systems (communications, command and control, etc.) located in areas difficult to access in a kinetic attack (because of distance, strong kinetic defences, concentrations of population, and so on).
b) Banking and finance. Today these are considered critical national infrastructures vulnerable to attack in cyberspace, both because of the nation's great dependence on financial systems and because of these systems' dependence on cyberspace. Damage to the financial system is liable to keep salaries from being deposited in banks, limit foreign trade, and even cause the economy to stop functioning.
c) Logistics and transportation systems, which today are computer-enabled.
d) National databases, i.e., in government ministries, the courts, universities, and so on.

Low risk to human life. Attacks in cyberspace entail little risk to the life of the attacker compared to military kinetic attacks in which risk to troops is one of the considerations likely to prevent an attack. This allows more audacity in the promotion of offensive ideas. For the party defending against attack, the limited risk to human life allows a fairly large scope of activity and even the ability to operate automatic defence mechanisms, without dependence on human calculations and, unlike kinetic defence systems, without risk to individuals on either side.

Selectivity. In certain attack scenarios, it is possible to attack specific targets within a certain domain without damaging additional entities. In other scenarios, however, it is difficult to control the scope of the attack and damage may spread beyond what was planned.

Virality. This feature touches on the tendency of viruses to replicate themselves unchecked and their ability to move through the web to different locations. This is a difficult challenge for an attacked party, which must prevent the virus from spreading. For the attacker this is an advantage in certain scenarios of widespread attack, as many additional effects may be created by means of a limited effort. However, this characteristic is liable to present a difficulty to the attacker who is interested in a focused and selective attack with tight control over attack results.

Standardisation of cyberspace. The cyber domain is based primarily on infrastructures made by global companies (e.g., Microsoft, Cisco, Check Point) that are located in every country and linked together. While the universal nature of the domain and the use of the same platforms (e.g., Unix and Windows operating systems) serve those constructing cyberspace, these features also entail a great deal of risk to an attacked party. For example, hacking of information security software or a technological database belonging to a global cyberspace company is liable to endanger every site where it is used. In March 2011, RSA, the information security company owned by the giant storage company EMC, announced it sustained damage by a sophisticated attack by hackers who managed to steal information on a secure ID apparatus serving to verify employee identity in organisations and governments around the world.[2] Such incidents endanger the effectiveness of security products shared by many corporations and governments.

Connectivity between cyberspace and devices operating in other domains. Using sensors it is possible to convert geographical, thermal, mechanical, and other data from physical domains into bits, and vice versa, and using effectors it is possible to convert directions transmitted over the bit web to actions in those domains. This connectivity allows a cyberspace attacker to generate effects in physical domains by attacking systems connected to cyberspace, such as computer embedded systems.

Reversibility—the ability to go back in time. It is possible to recover from a cyberspace attack by reversing computers backwards (resetting the time) with the help of backup systems. The more comprehensive and continuous the backup systems are, the more the return to the precise original configurations becomes possible. Restoration after a cyberspace attack is usually quick and cheap relative to physical destruction caused by massive fire attacks. However, certain cyberspace attacks are also liable to cause extensive physical damage that are less easily reversed. From the attacker's perspective, the advantage of this feature is that it allows the infliction of limited and temporary damage to an infrastructure under attack, e.g., a civilian infrastructure. The drawback to the attacker lies in the targeted party's ability to regroup and block tracks that were attacked and defend against tools used in prior attacks (making cyberspace weapons virtually disposable); this in turn will make it difficult for the attacker to generate cumulative damage and maintain attack continuity and strength. This is a major challenge to attackers who desire to reach strategic goals using extended and extensive cyberspace attacks.

High human ability to control cyberspace. Because cyberspace is an artificial, man-made domain, defenders should be able to control the sphere they have constructed. They should be able to anticipate the conditions in the domain, as opposed to the difficulty in anticipating conditions in other domains (e.g., weather). They can shut the domain down or limit its use: examples of attempts to limit the use of cyberspace may be found in China, Arab states, and Iran. The domain also allows both sides (attacker and attacked) to train with great ease and undertake simulations. In addition, it is easier for those attacked to rebuild an organised, ordered network quickly than a less organised network. Nonetheless, events unanticipated by the builders of the domain do occur in cyberspace, products of interactions between computers or the intensification of human errors. The features of the domain intensify the ability of insiders to act maliciously by means of cyberspace.

Integrated civilian-military domain. In many cases, military communications infrastructures are linked to civilian infrastructures. Hence, defending civilian infrastructures is also critical for military purposes. At the same time, militaries have cyberspace capabilities that may help defend civilian infrastructures. In democratic nations, this integration is a legal challenge for a threatened or attacked party in light of legislation in the field of individual rights, which makes it difficult to gather information and use military units in civilian cyberspace.

Connectivity and use of computerisation resources of other elements. Global communications networks allow an attacker to cross borders and move quickly to connected targets and even use the enemy's own computerisation resources to attack its systems. At the same time, connectivity allows the attacked party to make use of resources among friendly nations to identify attacks and foil them before they arrive at its own doorstep.

Mutual dependence between cyberspace and physical domains. Cyberspace has two-way interdependence with physical domains. Kinetic damage to physical infrastructures such as communications installations and power stations is liable to enhance cyberwar.

Ability to mass produce cyber weapons quickly and cheaply. From the moment a cyber weapon such as a worm or defence software is created, there is nothing stopping its mass replication, effortlessly and at low cost. This characteristic, which departs entirely from kinetic weapons, serves both the attacking and attacked parties.

Use of remote resources. Cyberspace allows users to reach human and computer resources in ways unfeasible in physical domains. Unlike the traditional battlefield in which soldiers are present in battle, soldiers and computer resources operating in cyberspace can be deployed in different locations and mobilised quickly by means of information technologies. This greatly improves the capabilities of using reserves in cyberspace.

Technological and operational depreciation. Technological developments and weaknesses in existing structures force frequent changes in defensive tools. Similarly, regular upgrade and

---

[2] "RSA Computerization Infrastructures Breached; Risk to Customer Information Security," *The Marker*, 19 March 2011.

development of defensive capabilities and the repair of breaches forces users to improve the tools for attack. This is a major drawback for the attacker because it must replace large amounts of means once they are obsolete.

Low entrance threshold. Cyberspace imposes few limitations on the construction of major cyber offensive capabilities, unlike the construction of armed forces based on kinetic forces. This is due to:

a) **Technology.** Technological means are free available in the market. Attackers can even buy defensive systems used by the enemy and invest in developing attack capabilities to the point of attaining technical superiority.
b) **Offensive knowledge.** A considerable amount of knowledge is also available on the free market, e.g., hackers and businesses provide attack services in cyberspace, mainly to test and drill defensive structures of companies and organisations.
c) **Low cost**. The capital needed to develop offensive capabilities is low compared to the capital needed to establish a modern conventional army.

In short, nations can establish cyberspace forces with advanced offensive capabilities at far lower costs than those required in constructing advanced kinetic forces. Organisations and groups can also acquire and operate cyber weapons, and all can hire civilians and private companies to work on their behalf.

The Strategic Environment

Security differences between cyberspace and physical domains demand the re-examination of traditional strategic concepts and their infusion with new meaning. The primary terms for the traditional battlefield also serve the cyberspace war domain: deterrence, defence, attack and so on. This may be a transitional lexicon that will be succeeded with new terms and concepts coined in the future.

The cyberspace strategic environment differs from the traditional strategic environment where it is customary to note geographical threats. The connection between cyberspace and geography has to do with the geographical spread of computer and network infrastructures. The concept of geography is therefore different in the cyberspace context. The attitude toward time in cyberspace also differs because of the speed with which bits move in the electromagnetic sphere.

Cyberspace is thus liable to enhance capabilities of previous enemies, while new and different enemies that had found it difficult to engage in conventional battles, whether because of distance or geographical separation (nations without common borders), might join them. Similarly, cyberspace creates different security opportunities and allows actors to tap allies in new ways on the basis of capabilities and presence. Consequently, and due to the priority different nations give to development of cyberspace capabilities, new balances of power between nations or non-state organisations (terrorist groups, nationalist or anarchist hacker groups) may emerge. As a result, cyberspace creates a unique and expand strategic environment.

In terms of security activities against enemies in cyberspace, it is customary to distinguish among three areas:

a) Penetrating enemy computerisation systems for the purposes of espionage. (This is not considered cyberwar).
b) Soft cyber warfare, i.e., activities in cyberspace designed to disrupt the enemy's functioning, such as psychological warfare, but not to cause destruction directly.
c) Cyberwar—activities in cyberspace, including attacks intended to cause direct damage or destruction to the enemy, such as damage to computerized systems or targets in physical domains, by means of attacking machines controlled through cyberspace or operating them in a manner that causes damage.

In all countries, the organisations charged with these activities are security services—militaries and intelligence gathering organisations. At the same time, defending cyberspace also involves many organisations within the civilian sector, including government ministries and offices as well as private companies (security, technology, and communications companies). Creating a joint, synchronized system among all them and allowing feedback between attackers and attacked is the central challenge for shaping cyberspace strategy at the national level.

Espionage

Espionage is designed primarily to gather intelligence in a clandestine manner. It is not intended to damage or disrupt enemy's systems, nor is it meant to affect the enemy directly (as long as the enemy remains unaware of the fact that its secrets have been uncovered). Using cyberspace for intelligence gathering has a long history which has three types of activity:

a) Intelligence gathering—military, state/political, technological, economic, and social—about the enemy's capabilities and intentions in peacetime and in war, in order to form situation assessments, formulate strategies, make decisions, and organize military and fighting forces.
b) Technological and economic intelligence gathering—including theft of technological and business secrets.
c) Gathering enemy cyberspace assets, such as stealing software and databases. This goes beyond knowledge theft and is closer to using looted weapons or stealing assets, and may therefore be viewed as soft cyberwar. Cyber asset theft can be effected through duplication and without removing any assets from the enemy's domain.

The first event in cyberspace espionage is understood to have occurred in the 1970s, when Russia managed to connect to ARPANET (the US Advanced Research Projects Agency Network, the precursor of the internet). It was revealed that within the framework of a military project financed by the United States at the Centre for Mathematical Studies in Geneva, the communications network modem had been connected to Moscow and was supplying the Russians with accessibility to the United States via the network.[3] Another example of a serious event of cyberspace espionage was described by US Deputy Secretary of Defence Lynn: "We learned the hard way in 2008 when a foreign intelligence agency used a thumb drive to penetrate our classified computer systems—something we thought was impossible. It was our worst fear: a rogue programme operating silently on our system, poised to deliver operational plans into the hands of an enemy."[4] This possibly refers to an intrusion attributed to China, when the plans for Lockheed Martin's future F-35 Lighting II fighter jet were stolen, including the plans for the electronic systems of the most advanced aircraft in the world, whose development had cost $300 billion.[5]

Soft Cyber Warfare: Informational Message Warfare

Informational message warfare is a type of soft warfare based on information manipulation. It is a central component in the fields of psychological warfare, fraud, propaganda, and disclosure of secret information. Its purpose is to affect the opinions and conduct of the enemy and its supporters in a way that is consistent with the goals of the initiator and without using kinetic force (firepower). The flip side of the same coin is public diplomacy, whose purpose is to supply information and present the rationale of an action to the domestic audience and friends, a move critical in gaining legitimacy for the use of force. Since the transition of the mass media to the internet in the 1990s, there has been a steady rise in the use made of cyberspace for informational message warfare and public diplomacy.

The great potency of informational message warfare is evidenced in testimony submitted before the United States Congress in March 2011 by General David Petraeus, Commander of the US Forces in Afghanistan (July 2010-July 2011). General Petraeus reported on the effort to increase espionage activities on social networks in order to fight radical ideologies and anti-US as well as anti-Western propaganda. As part of this effort, software is being developed that will allow stealth intervention in social networks. For example, an American company based in California won a tender issued by the US military to develop online management services that would allow one operator to manage ten fictitious identities on the internet simultaneously. All identities would be furnished with a detailed background history and use different servers around the world in order to create the impression those responders were located in different places. The software would allow intervention by impostor talk-backers and bloggers in discussions in Arabic and Farsi and other languages spoken in Pakistan and Afghanistan.[6]

The US Air Force is equipped with C-130 Hercules airplanes charged with carrying out psychological warfare missions, such as penetrating TV and radio broadcasts in enemy states and broadcasting messages against the regime and other messages meant for the local populations. The planes also serve as relay stations that allow the establishment of cell phone networks that can provide the population with cell phone and wireless internet services and allow for communication with the population should the regime attempt to cut off connectivity. In other words, this can take control of the electromagnetic field and cyberspace out of the hands of the regime and place it in the hands of an intervening party.[7]

---

[3] John Markoff, "A Code for Chaos," *New York Times*, 2 October 2010, based on Thomas C. Reed, a former secretary of the Air Force, in his book *At the Abyss: An Insider's History of the Cold War* (New York: Ballantine Books, 2004).

[4] Lynn, February 15, 2011.

[5] Siobhan Gorman, August Cole, and Yochi Dreazen, "Computer Spies Breach Fighter-Jet Project," *Wall Street Journal*, April 21, 2009.

[6] Yitzhak Ben-Horin, "War on the Web: Fictitious Bloggers Serving the US," *Ynet*, 18 March 2011.

[7] Anshel Pfeffer, "Weapon against Oppression. Plane for Internet Connection," *Haaretz*, 9 February 2011.

Soft Cyber Warfare: Sanctions

Cyberspace is an attractive domain for sanctions because technically it is relatively easy to enact operations that have a significant impact, such as preventing communications with foreign nations. At the same time, instituting effective cyberspace sanctions obligates the formation of a coalition of relevant nations. Cyberspace sanctions can be imposed as part of a package of sanctions in place against a rogue nation or as part of a general formulation of rules governing cyberspace.

Cyberwar

Cyberspace belligerency is an act of warfare against an enemy in the domain of cyberspace designed to cause harm to the enemy in order to damage its functioning and cause it to act according to a script dictated by the attacker. By itself, a cyberspace attack cannot wrest a decision or produce strategic achievements, such as occupying land by ground forces, but it is capable of striking critical enemy targets and capabilities. Cyber warfare or a cyber weapon, basically means that it is some kind of malware with code which is able to cause physical damage of critical infrastructure or at least a damage of computer systems, i.e. hardware.

A cyberspace attack is thus likely to be a component in every modern war in the future, alongside other force components. The unique features of cyberspace also make it attractive for the periods that separate conventional wars. Cyberspace attacks may serve the following functions:

a) A means of levelling pressure on the enemy to change its policies (e.g., the attack against Estonia attributed to Russia) between conventional wars.
b) Foiling security risks in the making, such as the development of non-conventional weapons.
c) Constructing attack capabilities as part of the balance of deterrence.
d) A counter-response—cyberspace attack against attackers or against nations that are the source of cyberspace attacks

Although the subject of attacks in cyberspace is not regulated by international law, offensive cyberspace activity could be considered an act of war, as opposed to cyberspace espionage, which does not involve immediate concrete damage and is not considered as such. Cyberspace attacks usually occur in the logical layer, but there is also offensive activity that makes use of the hardware component. One may distinguish between two types of attack: one is an attack in cyberspace designed to disrupt or damage the enemy's cyberspace (computers, networks, databases, etc.) in a way that prevents the enemy from taking advantage of the cyberspace domain for its own benefit. The other is using cyberspace to attack devices connected to it such as the Stuxnet attack in Iran.

Cyberspace attackers are in a better position than targeted parties. The attackers' advantage stems from the fact that the internet was fundamentally designed to be open and is built to ensure the flow of information and entry of new technologies, whereas network security was seen as being of secondary importance. These structural issues, which have contributed to the internet's development, have endowed attackers with an inherent advantage. This can be demonstrated by comparing anti-virus software to malware. A sophisticated anti-virus system (February 2011) has some 10 million lines of code compared to 1 million just a year ago. Nonetheless, malware with 125 million lines of code (its length as of one year ago) is capable of penetrating anti-virus software.

In the range of logical attacks, intrusions making use of malware differ from methods that are not penetrative by nature, such as DDoS (distributed denial-of-service) attacks. Malware of various types is typically inserted secretly into the enemy's computers, relying on the weaknesses of the defence system. The intrusion may be from without, through global, universal networks, or from within, through a secret agent in the organisation, or a combination—penetration of a local network via agents. In this family of malware there are software types such as worms and Trojan horses that allow the intruder to undertake a variety of information gathering or attack activities, such as: intelligence gathering stored in the enemy's computers (spyware), disruption of enemy computers, file erasure, control of files, and through them control of other networked computers and devices. Malware tends to spread to additional computers, sometimes in the service of the operator but sometimes randomly. Certain malware types can lie dormant in enemy computers until activated.

DDoS attacks are meant to disrupt enemy cyberspace. In attacks of this kind, websites under attack are flooded by a large number of simultaneous hits, to the point they can no longer bear the load, and crash. Such attacks use technical isolation (use of servers not identified with the attacking establishment) and humint (hackers) in order to avoid incrimination. Offensive use of hardware is yet another way to penetrate enemy cyberspace.

Defence in cyberspace is a new kind of challenge, in part because of the enemy's capability to attack with the speed of light. Moreover, a small breach of one weak link—whether human or technological—is enough to cause a defence already in place to fail. Indeed, cyberspace enhances a hostile element's ability to take advantage of breaches in the defensive systems, while security systems are often powerless against malicious acts by insiders who have permission to operate in the system. In addition lies the difficulty in identifying the attacker. When detecting a cyberspace intrusion, one cannot determine the purpose of the activity and therefore at the initial stage the distinction between espionage and an attempted attack in the domain may be difficult. The distinction between espionage and attack is important when considering a countermove, because nations go to war after being attacked but do not respond to espionage the same way, since espionage has traditionally not been considered an act of war.

Thus, it is clear that the concept of information security (whose purpose is to guard information from theft, destruction, and glitches) does not begin to cover cyberspace defence and the protection of systems linked to it, such as critical infrastructures and weapon systems. In reality, the most destructive actions—use of the domain in order to damage such systems—can be effected without damaging computer configurations in any way.

Prominent Cyber Attacks

The first cyber attack is said to have occurred when the CIA planted malware in an American-made computerized control system, which was then stolen by the Russians and transported to the USSR via Canada. The Soviets installed the control system on the trans-Siberian gas pipeline in July 1982; shortly afterwards, it exploded because the CIA had tampered with the software so that it would, according to the memoirs of Thomas Reed, "go haywire, after a decent interval, to reset pump speeds and valve settings to produce pressures far beyond those acceptable to pipeline joints and welds," producing "the most monumental non-nuclear explosion and fire ever seen from space." According to Reed, the purpose of the operation was to stop Soviet technology and intellectual property thefts. This event may be viewed as the opening salvo of cyberspace warfare.[8]

The first significant attacks on the modern network have been attributed to Russia. In 2007, many Estonian government websites were attacked and disabled for two days in an attack that made use of the DDoS method. For Estonia, one of the most advanced nations in the world in terms of computer and internet use, this was a serious blow to governability. The widespread use of computers was revealed as a weakness in light of the extensive attack that took place entirely in cyberspace. The Russian-attributed cyber attack was purportedly motivated by the Estonian government's decision to move a monument, erected in memory of World War II Red Army soldiers, from the capital, Tallinn, to the suburbs. The attack heightened awareness of cyberspace threats from enemy nations and made cyberwar a part of global consciousness.

In 2008, Georgia came under cyber attack in an event also attributed to Russia. This attack too made use of the DDoS method, damaging many public servers and shutting down government websites. Unlike the attack against Estonia, however, the attack on Georgia was not a stand-alone event: rather, it preceded the invasion of the country by Russian ground troops. The attack is an example of cyberwar serving as ancillary to an overall military effort.

The Stuxnet attack in Iran marked a new era in cyberwar. In September 2010 it was revealed that Iranian nuclear installations had been attacked and damaged by the Stuxnet worm that was inserted during the summer of 2009. Symantec, the global security company, which has published a comprehensive report on the attack, estimated that the worm had been adapted to damage specific frequency converters installed on Iran's uranium enriching centrifuges.[9]

Iranian President Ahmadinejad, admitting that the attack had occurred, tried to downplay its importance. Once the attack became public knowledge, Siemens put out a kit to discover and remove the worm, and the Iranians put a team together to remove it. In this case, too, there is no evidence linking anyone in particular to the attack. Some of the primary strategic analyses of the event are:

a) The Stuxnet attack differed from previous attacks because it was a far more sophisticated tool focused on a particular target, unlike prior attacks—attributed primarily to Russia—which made use of relatively primitive tools and a broad front.
b) The attack was the first event in the cyberwar era in which a cyber attack spilled over into the physical domain connected to cyberspace.

[8] Markoff, "A Code for Chaos"; "Cyberwar: War in the Fifth Domain," *The Economist*, July 1, 2010.

[9] Matan Mittelman, "Another Step in Exposing the Mystery Surrounding Stuxnet," *The Marker*, 16 November 2010.

That is, the attack embodies the notion of attacking systems outside the cyber domain by means of cyberspace.

c) The uniqueness attributed to this cyber attack is that Stuxnet was inserted into a common computer—Stuxnet is a Windows-based computer worm—in order to attack a specific professional system of controlling industrial equipment also found in systems such as the power grid, manufacturing equipment in industrial plants, gas pipelines, dams, and power stations. Prior to this event, cyber attacks focused only on internet websites, corporate networks, and military networks. In other words, the event demonstrated the potentially enormous damage a widespread cyber attack could have on these sophisticated tools.

d) The specific virus or a weapon of its type is liable to fall into the hands of elements that would make additional use of it, such as terrorist or criminal organisations.

In December 2011 Iran reported that its cyber warfare unit had successfully brought down an American unmanned aerial vehicle (UAV) - USAF RQ-170 Sentinel drone. This kind of plane has been designed to evade radar systems and from the view point of technology it is amongst the most recent types of advanced aircraft deployed by the US. Iranian authorities claim that the drone has been nearly fully decoded and its technology will be adapted into Iran's own arsenal.

A computer virus that wiped crucial business data from tens of thousands of computers at Middle Eastern energy companies over the summer of 2012 marked the most destructive cyber attack on the private sector to date. The so-called *Shamoon* virus which rendered permanently inoperable more than 30,000 computers at the Saudi Arabian state oil company Aramco and did similar damage to the systems of Ras Gas in Qatar, represented a significant escalation of the cyber threat. In the attack on Aramco, the virus replaced crucial system files with an image of a burning U.S. flag. It also overwrote the files with "garbage" data.

Cyber Terror

Experts agree that cyberspace can attract cyber terror, e.g., terrorist organisations causing critical installations to explode by means of viral control mechanisms. Terrorist organisations make extensive use of cyberspace for internal communications and propaganda, but not for cyber attacks.

Terrorist organisations may be avoiding attacks through cyberspace for several reasons. One, they have incomplete capabilities to attain the effects that would generate significant amounts of damage. Two, terrorist organisations currently prefer real, not virtual, blood-soaked suicide terrorism, which from their perspective yields much more than anonymous cyber terror. Three, there can be a conflict of interests. Terrorist organisations are not necessarily interested in changing the rules of cyberspace in light of their extensive use of the domain for their own benefit, such as managing their organisations, maintaining communications between activists, appealing to certain target audiences, and conducting informational message warfare. Four is a cost-benefit issue. While developing effective cyber weapons is less costly than building conventional armies, it is vastly more expensive than operating suicide bombers.

Cyber Terrorism in India

Cyber technology has played a role—albeit principally as a covert communication, propaganda or psychological warfare tool—in terrorist activities in India, for some time now. This includes prominent attacks in cities including Ahmedabad, Jaipur, Delhi, Mumbai and Varanasi, among others, over the past years.

Significantly, the perpetrators of the 26 November 2008, Mumbai terrorist attacks (26/11), which claimed 166 lives, made substantial use of cyber technology in preparing and mounting the operation. The entire (26/11) mission planning was done via Google Earth. The terrorists used cellular phone networks as command and control and social media to track and thwart the efforts of Indian commandos. An earlier report had noted that the Pakistan-backed Lashkar-e-Toiba (LeT) had used Voice-over Internet Protocol (VoIP) software to communicate with the 26/11 attackers on the ground and direct the large scale operation on a real-time basis. The attackers' handlers were apparently watching the attacks unfold live on television [and] were able to inform the attackers of the movement of security forces from news accounts and provide the gunmen with instructions and encouragement. The distinguishing feature of VoIP-based communications, which form the technical basis of popular communications software such as Skype and Vonage, is that audio signals are converted to data and travel through most of the Internet infrastructure in binary, rather than audio, format, making them near impossible to detect and proactively intercept.

After the terrorist attack on Delhi High Court on

7 September 2011, in which 15 persons were killed and another 87 were injured, investigative assistance was sought from the US and some south-east Asian countries, to trace back cyber linkages connected with the incident. Terrorists had hacked into unsecured wi-fi internet connections to send e-mails after the attack.

The Indian Mujahedeen (IM) has carried out over a dozen high profile attacks in the recent past. Before almost all of these attacks, IM activists sent out e-mails to various media organisations. Police traced e-mails sent by IM from Navin Computer in Sahibabad area of Ghaziabad District in Uttar Pradesh soon after the 13 May 2008, Jaipur blast, which claimed 80 lives. Three video clips attached to one of the e-mails showed two explosive-fitted bicycles moments before they were detonated. The e-mails were sent from two accounts—guru_al_hindi_jaipur@yahoo.co.uk and guru_al_hindi@yahoo.fr.

IM activists had hacked into the unsecured wi-fi internet connection of an American national, Kenneth Haywood, residing in the Sanpada area of Navi Mumbai, minutes before the 26 July 2008, Ahmedabad terror attack, which killed 53 people. An e-mail claiming the attack was sent prior to the blasts from his Internet Protocol (IP) address. After the 19 September 2010, Jama Masjid (Delhi) attack, Delhi Police confirmed, a day later, that the IM had sent a threat e-mail from the IP address of a computer in Mumbai. Investigations into the Varanasi (UP) blast of 7 December 2010, highlighted the need for 'wardriving' to detect threat mails posted by IM, allegedly from Mumbai. 'Wardriving' is used to search for wi-fi wireless networks with the help of a laptop from a moving vehicle, in order to detect unsecured wi-fi internet points that may be exploited.

The LeT has attained a significant degree of 'cyber efficiency', and has been making increasing use of VoIP for communications. LeT's 26/11 'master-mind', Zaki-ur Rehman Lakhvi, who is presently in a Rawalpindi (Pakistan) jail, is known to have been networking with LeT cadres from jail, using a private VoIP on his smart phone. "Lakhvi's compound serves as Lashkar's alternative headquarters," an unnamed top intelligence source disclosed. Pakistan-based LeT, which is headed by Hafiz Mohammad Saeed, started using VoIP as soon as the technology became common in the early 2000s. Highlighting the problems this creates, an unnamed intelligence source explained, "Earlier, we could intercept conversations on phone or locate Lashkar cadres based on their IP addresses through their emails. But now we're finding it tough to gather intelligence because Lashkar men hold audio or video conferences using private VoIP".

A number of Pakistani hacker groups, including 'Death to India', 'Kill India', and 'G-Force Pakistan', have openly circulated instructions for attacking Indian computers. Websites run by Nicholas Culshaw of Karachi, and another run by Arshad Qureshi of Long Beach, California, circulated malicious anti-Indian propaganda along with step-by-step instructions for hacking into thousands of Indian websites. Anti-Indian terrorist instructions were also hosted by http://62.236.92.165, http://209.204.7.131, and http://209.204.5.113. All these sites appear to be disabled now, but their architects quickly recreate new platforms.

On 3 December 2010, in a breach of security was detected on the Central Bureau of Investigation (CBI) website, which had been hacked by the 'Pakistan Cyber Army'. The CBI home page carried a message from the 'Pakistani Cyber Army' warning India not to attempt to attack their websites. It further claimed to have defaced another 270 Indian websites. India has been ranked fifth in the worldwide ranking of countries affected by Cyber Crime.

According to data maintained by the *National Crime Records Bureau* (NCRB), documenting the number of cyber crime cases and related arrests have been[10]:

Years	*Cyber Crime Cases*	*Arrests*
2007	217	154
2008	288	178
2009	420	288
2010	966	799

Further, the number of cases registered under Cyber Crime related sections of Indian Penal Code (IPC), along with the number of arrests, were given as:[11]

Years	*Cyber Crime Cases*	*Arrests*
2007	328	429
2008	176	195
2009	276	263
2010	356	294

A total of 90, 119, 252 and 219 Government websites, as reported and tracked by the *Indian Computer Emergency Response Team* (CERT-In), had been defaced by various hacker groups in the year 2008, 2009, 2010 and January–October 2011, respectively.[12]

[10] Information given to the the *Rajya Sabha* (Upper House of Parliament) by Minister of State for Communications and Information Technology, Sachin Pilot, on 26 March 2012.

[11] Ibid.

[12] Information given to the *Lok Sabha* (Lower House of Parliament), by Minister of State for Communications and Information Technology, Sachin Pilot, on 30 November 2011,

As far Government initiative is concerned, following the 26/11 attacks, the Information Technology Act, 2000, has been amended by Information Technology (Amendment) Act, 2008 with effect from 27 October 2009. The amended Act is a comprehensive Act and provides legal framework to fight all prevalent cyber crimes. Stringent punishment ranging from imprisonment of three years to life imprisonment and fine has been provided for various acts of cyber crime. On 16 May 2012, National Security Advisor Shiv Shankar Menon stated that the Government of India was in the 'final stages' of preparing the 'national cyber security architecture'.

Cyber crimes and the use of cyber space and technologies by terrorists are, currently, at worst, powerful facilitators for terrorist groups. In the main, they remain marginal irritants to the system. Nevertheless, the potential threat they constitute is grave, and this has been noticed by the Indian government. A decision has been taken to establish a National Cyber Coordination Centre, a full-fledged agency to counter this menace. A race is currently on, with terrorists, on the one hand, pushing the frontiers of cyber space to harness the most disruptive of tools possible, and state agencies, on the other, seeking to interdict them in this enterprise. It remains to be seen which side in the conflict has the greater coherence and more sustained motivation.

China and the Cyber Challenge

The Chinese approach affords a different strategic view of cyberspace. It sees cyberspace as a domain of opportunities whose potential requires, among other elements, the ability to carry out intrusions in order to engage in aggressive information gathering and attack.

As a superpower of 1.35 billion people, China sees digital technologies as a rare opportunity to promote its strategic, economic, and military capabilities and its standing. The local rapid spread of the internet and cellular communications is in part evidence of this perspective. Since the late 1990s, China's activity in cyberspace in terms of security has focused on espionage in the West and attacks on political opponents around the world. According to American research on China's cyberspace strategy, in recent years China has constructed military cyberspace capabilities designed to gain strategic advantages commensurate with its status as a superpower. China sees the development of military cyberspace capabilities as a necessary strategic element to redress its strategic inferiority vis-à-vis the United States in the conventional domains.

According to Western publications, China represents a danger to the West in several cyber-related areas:

- Intelligence gathering that can be turned to military advantage, theft of cyberspace assets (software and databases) for military and civilian use and more by means of intrusion from afar and close contact, including providing hardware components encrypted with malware. In 2009, there was a report of an intrusion into American computers attributed to China, during which the plans for the future F-35 Lightning II fighter jet were stolen.
- The development of offensive capabilities in cyberspace, liable to threaten advanced civilian and military infrastructures in Western nations. China's high technological and operational capabilities in terms of intelligence gathering in cyberspace may also be indicative of its offensive capabilities.
- The economic and cultural struggle in which China challenges Western values in global cyberspace, such as freedom of information and protection of intellectual property rights. China is said to be responsible for intrusions into the computers of commercial companies for the purpose of intelligence gathering as well as for attacks against opponents of the regimes. The United States has disclosed a number of reports in this context, including the comprehensive GhostNet report released by the Information Warfare Monitor in March 2009.[13] However, China has denied any connection to the invasive cyber activity attributed to it.

As part of its offensive approach, China is developing the capability to combine computer network attacks, electronic warfare, and kinetic blows (firepower) in order to destroy the enemy's communications systems (military and civilian) and create blind spots, which Chinese forces would then be able to exploit in real time. Command and control and logistical structures are also inviting targets for cyberspace attack because of their key to attaining military strategic objectives. Such attack operations would be used by the Chinese in the early stages of a confrontation, and perhaps even as part of a preventive move. Actions of this sort are considered a component of China's strategic deterrence, whereby

[13] Joel Harding, "China's Cyber Strategy – Too Much or Too Little?" *Infosec Island*, 10 January 2012.

this constitutes a nonviolent "small war" that does not necessarily require an enemy's response and is possibly capable of preventing the "big war." Personnel in the Chinese army contend that cyber weapons have the deterrent potential equal to that of nuclear weapons, only better: they cause no physical damage. The damage they do cause is controlled and pinpointed, and the weapons can be aimed at essentially unlimited ranges.

Experts in the field of cyberspace security feel that China is currently in the midst of a concerted effort to gather classified information from the West before the latter's cyberspace information security capabilities grow stronger. Partners in this effort are Chinese governmental cyberspace units, Chinese subcontractors, and elements active in cybercrime. There is evidence of connections between Chinese establishment sources and warlike or gathering activities carried out by hackers against American and other foreign targets. Moreover, the scope of the operations, the capabilities displayed and the types of objectives targeted indicate that these were state-sponsored events.[14]

China acts very differently to the idea of full freedom of action in cyberspace to its citizens, maintaining close control of its internal cyber domain, especially in order to prevent political subversion. China therefore views companies such as Google as enemies. In early 2011, China went so far as to increase its oversight of cyberspace as a result of lessons learned from the use made of cyberspace by protestors in the Arab nations for their revolutionary activities. In this sense, China's security services have an advantage in defending against external enemies because they enjoy complete freedom of action in cyberspace.

Furthermore, China has increased its protective measures against cyber attacks. In September 2011 the Supreme People's Court and Supreme People's Procuratorate issued legal interpretations on hacking and other internet crimes. They posited that a crime against information network poses a threat to both national security and public interests. They also stated than one million IP addresses in China were controlled from overseas in 2009, 42,000 websites were distorted by hackers, and in 2009, 18 million Chinese computers—about 30 per cent of computers infected worldwide—were infected by the Conficker virus every month.[15]

Cyber Security

The issue of cyber security is an important adjunct to the proliferation of new media. There is an increasing vulnerability to high value infrastructure like aviation, power and railways on cyber networks, which can be sabotaged through large scale computer attacks. Social media and mobile communications will increasingly become ubiquitous and integral to routine interactivity.

Cyber security will continue to emerge as a potential challenge in future. The endeavour to create a comprehensive organisational structure remains a critical requirement. However, it is equally important to run cyber education programmes through the virtual world as well as educational institutions and public awareness groups to enable greater understanding of the implications of the threat. This will enable better understanding of the threats involved and could result in participative counter-measures between the government and people using the networks. News reports in September 2012 revealed that Iranian hackers had successfully conducted massive distributed denial of service attacks against the websites of Bank of America and JPMorgan Chase & Co.

The pace of cyber espionage is accelerating. According to a 2011 report by the U.S. government, foreign hackers—including individuals and governments—are increasingly stealing military secrets, sensitive data, intellectual property and proprietary technologies that cost millions of dollars to develop and up to hundreds of millions of dollars in potential profits. Cyber crime is also growing. Though it is hard to establish concrete estimates of the cost of cyber crime, the security firm Symantec estimates that cyber crime costs companies $114 billion each year and as much as $274 billion if the costs of recovery time are included.

"Hacktivists" steal confidential information and use it to advance their own political or ideological agendas. In 2010 the group Wikileaks released thousands of sensitive U.S. diplomatic cables, the ripples of which are still being felt. Government cannot address these cyber threats without actively engaging the private sector, because private industry owns and operates the vast majority of cyber networks and critical infrastructure. The private sector is also the paramount source of technological innovations to prevent and respond to cyber threats.

14 "Chasing The Night Dragon," *Strategy Page* website, 8 March 2011.

15 See Cyber Crime Law, http://www.cybercrimelaw.net/Cybercrimelaw.html.

Conclusion

Efforts have been made to formulate an international treaty to regulate permitted cyberspace activity to defend global infrastructures, but it is unclear when such a treaty may be signed or the extent to which it may be effective.

Cyberspace is already an attractive battlefield because of its unique features and intrinsic importance to state functions. The relatively scanty history of cyber attacks is presumably due to restraints that discourage use of this domain for attack and the lack of sufficient preparedness for cyberwar. Such preparedness requires both defensive and offensive capabilities of a very high order. In order to generate wars in the new domain, appropriate security establishments are also required for development of capabilities in the field. Indeed, in recent years, nations have been working to accelerate their preparations to act in cyberspace and are building security establishments. This activity may be evidence that nations assume that the restraints currently keeping cyber attacks in check are temporary in nature; thus, nations cannot afford to risk being unprepared for war in the new domain. In any case, constructing capabilities may itself be accelerating the development of cyberspace as a domain of military warfare.

There is, therefore, a need for all nations to work with together along with the private sector to increase cyber security while simultaneously promoting Internet freedom; pass legislation that protects critical infrastructure and facilitates the sharing of threat information while assuaging the concerns of privacy advocates and the business community; work on plans on when and how to use cyber weapons, while considering the precedents these decisions will set ; and, develop a cyber security workforce and encourage the development of hardware, software and networks that will be less vulnerable to cyber attacks.

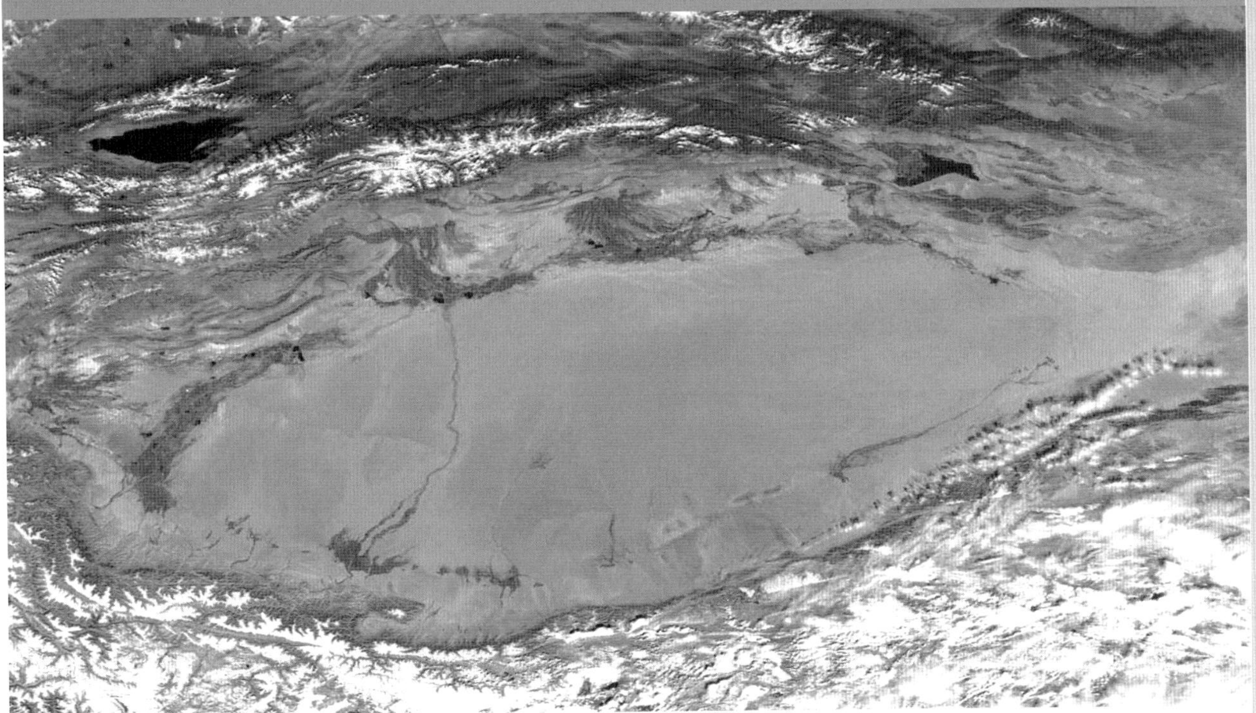

THE UIGHUR MOVEMENT: CHINA'S INSURGENCY IN XINJIANG

Background

The history of China and central Asia is rife with religious and territorial conflict. In the seventh century (CE 742), a predominantly Turko-Mongolian steppe nomadic tribe known today as the Uighurs migrated eastward from eastern Turkey towards the oases of modern-day Xinjiang province of China and have remained there for the last 1,270 years. Throughout this time, this population has endured the hardships of political, economic, cultural, ethnic, and religious persecution ranging from nomadic tribal disputes to unrelenting and brutal aggression from the Chinese government.

The culture and identity of the Uighur people of Xinjiang have been shaped by geographic, cultural, and historic interactions with China and surrounding civilisations and Uighur identity has evolved in such a way that the Uighurs can neither acculturate comfortably into China, as Beijing would like, nor effectively resist the Chinese state, as Uighur nationalists and militants would like.

Of significant importance are three separate periods of Uighur uprisings in response to Chinese policies and military action designed to crush expansion of Islam: the 1846 rebellion during the Qing Dynasty; the Uighur rebellions of 1931-34 and 1940-49 resulting in two separate instalments of the East Turkistan Republic; and between 1990 and 1998. Drawn into focus is a minority population that has claimed cultural, ethnic, and religious affiliation with the northwest region of modern day Xinjiang province, where the practice of Islamic religion and participation in government are taboo in and amongst an ethnically dominant Han Chinese population and predominantly atheist society.

Although political and religious persecution is not a new problem in China, recent events within Xinjiang (also known as the Xinjiang Uighur Autonomous Region) have compounded the problem. These include the identification of potential links between the Uighur population and Al Qaeda; the declaration and international recognition of the East Turkestan Liberation Organisation (ETLO) as a terrorist organisation by China and the United States and the linking of Uighur participation in international events, including reported training of Uighur fighters in Pakistani terrorist camps, and the capture of Uighur fighters in Afghanistan and Iraq; and vicious engagements between Uighurs and Chinese military and police in urban Xinjiang.

The current problem in the Xinjiang Uighur Autonomous Region of China is very real from the perspectives of the Chinese government and the populations that inhabit it. However, this is the only point of agreement between them, as the genesis and nature of the problem is viewed from radically divergent viewpoints. On one side of the argument is the Chinese government whose primary concern is regional stability. It is modernising its economy and the society that it supports in order to control terrorism and the expansion of radical Islamic extremism within its borders. Accordingly, the Chinese government regulates Islamic religious activity within its borders and closely monitors the activity of Uighurs and external Islamic influences within Xinjiang.

On the other side of the argument the Uighurs perception of the problem is the failure of the Chinese government to recognize their right to autonomy and independence. Also, the Uighurs accuse Beijing of supporting and proliferating religious and ethnic bigotry with the intent to subdue or eliminate Uighur ethnicity. In short, the Uighurs demand the right to self-determination.

The Uighur Region

Political and religious divergence between the Han Chinese and the Uighur populations has created conditions of extreme volatility. Between the ninth and twelfth centuries Xinjiang was divided into separate regions, each with its own ruler, religion and culture, producing a dispersion of Uighurs along three separate branches. The first branch consisting of approximately thirteen tribes moved southeast beyond the current "Great Wall" and subsequently disappeared from historical record. The second branch moved to modern-day Gannan Yugur Autonomous County and was predominantly assimilated into Chinese culture. The third branch fled towards the oases in the Taklamakan desert. It was this tribal separation and subsequent crystallisation of cultural practice within the region that the impetus for Islam to influence eastern culture was produced.

Cultural and religious influence within the region has been a product of unique geography, as it has created a situation where each of Xinjiang's oases feels particular cultural influences emanating from its closest cross border neighbours. As a result, areas in Xinjiang's northeast, such as Urumchi, Turpan, and Hami, have historically had close ties with China proper, but the rest of the region has not. Instead, in Xinjiang's west and south, cultural influences have mostly flowed back and forth between Xinjiang and Muslim regions that lie beyond the borders of the People's Republic of China in what is today Pakistan, Afghanistan, and the former Soviet republics of Central Asia.

The challenges present in modern day Xinjiang are many. Most notable is its wide diversity of geographic and geologic features, as it is one of the most geographically isolated regions of the world. For centuries, the unique geography of Xinjiang has provided natural barriers to, and in many instances assistance for, cultural, social, economic, religious and political influence in the region. Prior to expansion of inter-continental trade and establishment of the Silk Road trans-continental trade route, Xinjiang provided limited intra-regional influence within Central Asia but served as the intersection at which all of these elements interacted, producing a dynamic of inter- and intra-cultural engagement.

Located in the northwest outreaches of China, today's Xinjiang Uighur Autonomous Region, the largest of China's political units, covers an area of 1.6 million square kilometres, one-sixth of China's total area and three times the size of France. Xinjiang is bounded on the northeast by Mongolia, on the north by Russia, on the west by Kazakhstan, Kyrgyzstan, and Tajikistan, and on the south by Afghanistan, Pakistan, and India. To the east and south, Xinjiang abuts the Chinese regions and provinces of Tibet, Qinghai, and Gansu. Geographically, Xinjiang is a basin. Within its borders are three separate basins bounded by mountain ranges: First, the Tarim Basin in southern Xinjiang is bordered by the Quruq Mountains on the east. Within this basin lies the Taklamakan Desert, a 327,000-square-kilometre, mostly uninhabitable and impassable arid waste of shifting sand dunes—now of interest for its oil deposits. Second, the Turpan Basin, also referred to as the "Depression," which contains the world's second lowest elevation at 154 metres below sea-level. East of Turpan, the flat, cobbly desert continues past Hami and southeast between the slopes of the Tian, Shan and Altun Shan ranges, defining what is known as the Gansu or Hexi Corridor; this in turn runs into the Gobi Desert. The Turpan basin is linked with northern Xinjiang via a break in the Tian Shan range where the city of Urumchi is located. Third, the Zungharian basin in northern Xinjiang which also contains a desert that is less harsh than that of the Tarim basin. Its steppes and mountain slopes have traditionally supported nomadic herdsmen and permanent camps of nomad empires.

Historically, access to Xinjiang has been, and currently remains, relatively limited. Given the extreme elevations of the mountain ranges that encompass all but the eastern boundary of modern-day Xinjiang, intra-regional travel is predominantly limited to six roads that connect Xinjiang to international border countries as well as China proper. In the Zungharian Basin, one single road connects Kyrgyzstan to Xinjiang west of the town of Qoqek; in the southeast portion of the Tarim Basin, access to China is available via a single road or railroad through the town of Kumul; to the south, a highway connects Xinjiang to China, as does a highway to Pakistan through the town of Pidakkesh; to the west of the Tarim Basin in the Ili region of Xinjiang. Access to Kazakhstan is achieved west of the town of Ili Kazak, as is access to Kyrgyzstan via another highway.

Inter-state travel is limited to the ring-roads which follow the contours of the basins in which each is encompassed; thus travel beyond the current transportation infrastructure is predominantly non-existent unless on foot. As such, inter- and intra-state interactions have been historically limited given the great distances and extreme terrain one must traverse in order to gain access to specific locations within the region. This is not to imply that Xinjiang, whether pre- or post-modern, has been without rule or influence from internal and external actors, nor does it signify cultural, political, or economic isolation. It does however illustrate the unique nature of the challenges that geography has presented and the influence it has had on regional actors and the means each have utilised for multilateral engagement.

Over the centuries, the Uighur language has remained relatively unchanged, with only minor dialectic changes. In addition to the spoken language, written Uighur utilizes Arabic script. Yet, this sedentary, predominantly agrarian society has drastically struggled for recognition of an identity.

History of Uprisings

In order to understand the current cultural and political disposition of the Uighurs, it is necessary to analyze the historical foundations upon which they base their argument for autonomy and, within some Uighur circles, aspirations of secession.

After a series of bloody rebellions against the Qing Dynasty in the late 19th Century, which were fuelled by the Qing policy of cultural division and ethnic separation designed to prevent the development of alliances within the northwest region of China, Chinese military intervention under the leadership of General Zuo Zongtang effectively defeated the Turkic rebels. In 1884, the Chinese Empire incorporated the province and renamed it Xinjiang. Nevertheless, in order to effectively manage social unrest and balance the influence of Russian intervention and heated Sino-Russian rivalry in the region, the Qing appointed a Chinese military governor to adminster this sensitive, yet strategic region. In addition, the Qing established military outposts within Xinjiang and Gansu in order to afford the military governor the requisite power for controlling the region and its diverse assemblage of culture, religion, and ethnicity.

However, due to the geographic isolation and long distances for travel and direct intervention within the region, the provincial governors of the Qing Dynasty often exercised power over the province as matters of preference and personal gain, thus providing the impetus for rebellion and revolution; a cause from which the people of Xinjiang have not deviated. In 1928, the governor of Xinjiang, Yang Cengxin, was assassinated, thus bringing his deputy, Jin Shuren, into power. Recognising that there was now a void in the provincial leadership within Xinjiang, General Sheng Shicai departed Chiang Kai-Shek's staff in Nanjing and headed to Xinjiang to serve as Jin's deputy. However, Jin did not possess the same ability to control the province as completely as Yang, further driving a wedge between the government and the population. Under Jin's rule, corruption worsened and the economy further degraded. Jin had increased military presence within the province, added to the ranks of the secret police, and appointed many members of his immediate family to prominent positions of government yet could not subdue the will of the populace. The results of these actions were a series of insurrections that culminated in the establishment of the first East Turkestan Republic (ETR) in 1933.

Jin's deputy, Shicai was charged for quelling these insurrections and regaining control over Xinjiang. In direct response to the reinstitution of Qing-mandated Sinicisation, levying hefty taxes upon non-Han Chinese and conversely providing a two-year tax hiatus for migrant Hans, provision of land, seed and farmland to Han-Chinese at the expense of Uighur farmers; compensation that included government provision of non-arable land on the outer edges of the desert, and strict regulation of religious activity within the province, Moslems in the town of Hami, Kazaks in particular but accompanied by Uighurs, Tungans, and other Turkic ethnicities, initiated a violent struggle to retain their cultural and religious independence. Sheng, understanding the gravity of the situation and the strategic implications associated with failure to control this volatile region was assisted by military forces from the Soviet Union and the Chinese nationalist forces to quell the insurrection. From 1931 to 1933, Sheng, with assistance from Soviet forces, continued to hold off Uighur and Tungan besiegers, arrested, and executed thousands of people in order to establish complete control over the province. On 12 April 1933, in response to waning confidence in his abilities, Jin was deposed in a coup organised by repatriated north-eastern Chinese and White Russians who named Sheng as his successor.

Although Sheng had made partial alliances with small pockets of Uighur resistance factions throughout the region, rebellions were being generated within other portions of Xinjiang. In the latter half of 1932, Tungans and Uighurs joined forces and marched on the city of Kashgar. Approximately eight months later, in July 1933, Uighurs, Tungans, and Kyrgyz peoples alike fought to claim control of the government. After many bloody encounters and multiple attempts to lay siege on Kashgar, Sabit Damolla officially announced the foundation of the Eastern Turkestan Republic on 12 November 1933. Included in this announcement was the outlining of a constitution that would provide for governance in accordance with shari'a law, yet accommodate modern education, libraries, public health, tax reform, debt relief, economic growth and a form of democratic republic. The newly established government even minted its own coins, yet immediately began to spiral downward towards failure as rampant inflation plagued the fledgling government, and disunity among competing factions and lack of international recognition undermined its resolve.

Understanding that Xinjiang was an important partner for the Soviet Union and the threat of Japanese influence or annexation of Xinjiang would threaten Soviet security, Stalin in January 1934, deployed two brigades of Soviet troops with air support and chemical bombs, thus crushing the resistance in the town of Urumchi and driving the rebels southeast. Congruently, the Tungan Army, under control of the Guomindang, sacked old Kashgar and slaughtered as many as 4,500 Uighur civilians. Although doomed for failure from its inception, the establishment of the ETR represented a significant change in the socio-political aspirations of a historically repressed culture within China that stood together for a better future. It was the bold actions of a few brave men driven by the desire for a better life and fuelled by a long history of Han-Chinese repression that united a people to stand against the injustices of Chinese rule over Xinjiang.

From 1934 to 1942, Sheng and the Soviet Union established a mutually supporting alliance that enabled Sheng to further consolidate power and exert control over Xinjiang while providing the Soviets the requisite security to buffer Japanese expansion Central Asia. In 1941, when Nazi Germany invaded the Soviet Union, Sheng took the opportunity to loosen the Soviet grip on Xinjiang and re-establish Chinese control over the province. Thus, the Soviet Union lost access to the vast resources it required and the people of Xinjiang were dealt a terrible blow, losing both supply of manufactured goods and demand for Xinjiang's agricultural, pastoral, and extractive products. China could not fill the gap. This provided the catalyst for the Ili rebellion of 1944.

Having re-aligned with the Chinese Nationalist government Sheng's rule over Xinjiang became increasingly oppressive sparking small-scale rebellions throughout the province. In October 1944, having understood the conspiratorial nature of Sheng's position and his lust for unbridled power within the region, Chiang Kai-shek offered him a position in the GMD government that he simply could not refuse and subsequently named Wu Zhongxin as his successor.

Upon assumption of duties as the newly appointed governor of Xinjiang, Wu continued the string of violence and oppression Sheng had been known for. He also further expanded the Xinjiang colonisation programme designed to re-settle an additional one million Hans in the province. Additionally, all Turkic peoples were replaced by ethnic Chinese in all positions of administration and heavy taxes were levied against non-Han Chinese in order to finance the 100,000-man standing army now stationed throughout the province. Wu then took his policy one-step further by publicly announcing in his first public speech, that all non-Han peoples throughout the former territory of the Qing Empire were originally racially Chinese and those categories like "Uighur," "Kazak," and "Kyrgyz" did not exist.

As a means to finalize the transition from Soviet to Chinese control and revamp the poor performing economic system within the province, the GMD attempted to replace the existing Xinjiang monetary system with newly minted Xinjiang dollars. However, being focused on a rapid transition to this new currency it failed to monitor closely the quantity being produced, thereby grossly increasing inflation and temporarily crippling an already fragile and failing economic system. Further, now that non-Han money was virtually worthless and greater taxes were being levied against the Uighur masses, tradesmen and entrepreneurs wishing to maintain their livelihood were forced to pay exorbitant fees for foreign travel and trade permits in order to conduct business with long-time trading partners in the Soviet Union. To this point, the Uighurs had faced cultural extinction through forced Sinicisation of the region from the Qing Empire to the GMD regime, endured brutal political, cultural, and religious oppression, had their livelihoods removed, and were forced to pay exorbitant taxes and fees in order to survive; this would be the final straw.

As Wu began to bring in GMD military forces into the region, small bands of Kazak rebels continued to conduct raids against an unorganised and improperly prepared military system. From 1943 to mid-1944, military forces under Sheng totalled approximately 34,000, most of which were garrisoned in the towns of Hotan, Kashi, Aksu, and Kuqa along Xinjiang's southern border; and were focused on fighting the Kazak rebels near Ashan. By October 1944, Kazak, Uighur, and White Russian rebel forces had facilitated uprisings in the districts of Ili, Altay and Tarbagatay, and along the Xinjiang's border regions with the Soviet Union, Mongolia, and China. Having gained momentum through increased recruitment and steady Soviet support, the time had come to make a second attempt at establishing the East Turkestan Republic.

On 7 November 1944, about 500 Kazak, Uighur, and White Russian rebels initiated an attack on the Nationalist Air Force Headquarters located in Yining; supporting them were an additional 4,500 rebels who were focused on isolating and destroying GMD military and para-military resistance throughout the town. At the time of the attack, GMD military forces garrisoned in Yining totalled approximately 10,000, most of which were dispersed on checkpoints along the border and on the outskirts of towns. Intense fighting between the rebels and GMD defence forces ensued. By 12 November 1944, exactly 11 years after the establishment of the First East Turkestan Republic, a regionally renowned Islamic scholar and teacher named Ali Khan Tore stepped forth as its leader and officially announced the establishment of the East Turkestan Republic.

Command and control issues continued to plague the ETR as it once had during the establishment of the first ETR, and maintaining integrity across the ranks of Kazak, Uighur, Mongol, and White Russians that manned the ranks was near impossible. Compounding this difficult situation was the fact that very few, if any, of these warriors had any sort of tactical training or strategic education, and no amount of courage and determination could mitigate it. Had it not been for the direct assistance, or intervention by the Soviet Union the Ili Rebellion would have failed as quickly and as miserably as the first attempt had in 1934. Yet, till September 1945, rebel and GMD forces brutally fought throughout the province. During this time, ETR forces totalling approximately 500,000 controlled over ten separate districts in Xinjiang and had effectively defeated the GMD and seized control of the towns of Yining, Huiyuan, Sungshukou, Santai, and Jinghe, killing approximately 30,000 GMD nationalist troops. Having expanded its control of the region, the ETR fought south-eastward towards Urumqi. Upon reaching the Manas River in late September 1945, ETR and GMD forces faced each other across the river in anticipation of the next bloody battle. Having appealed to the international community for quick resolution of the Ili affair, Chiang-kai-shek ordered an immediate diplomatic assessment conducted of the situation. In the diplomatic solution, at Chiang's disgust, was the Soviet Union who would serve as the international spokesman of the ETR. In their message they stated that the people of the three districts (Ili, Altay and Tarbagtay) had no desire to separate from China, that they desired autonomy for the districts where the rebel regimes had been set up and that the reason for the revolt had been past oppression.

Over the course of the next 16 months, ETR and GMD leaders reached officially recognised agreements regarding the legitimacy and relevancy of the ETR demands; a point which fuelled desires for Uighur autonomy long after the Second ETR was dissolved in 1949 by the CCP.

The next period of active rebellion began in the town of Baren on 5 April 1990. Having been concerned with the expansion of Islam and radical extremism in Xinjiang since the beginning of the Soviet-Afghanistan war in 1979, China used this event to expand its "Strike Hard, Maximum Pressure" policy in order to tighten its political and military grip on the expansion of Islam and drive active Islamic rebellions from the province. Although reports of the incident vary greatly, the uprising was initiated and led by the Free Turkestan Movement under the leadership of Abdul Kasim. Using the oppressive and brutal nature of Chinese politics and its relentless pursuit of Islam as fuel for the rebellion, Kasim assembled a force of approximately 200 men armed with advanced weaponry and initiated attacks against para-military forces throughout the city.

Supporting Kasim's efforts were reportedly Afghan-trained Islamists who had set up loudspeakers in mosques in the villages of Baren and Turand that were broadcasting speeches praising jihad to encourage local Moslems to rise up against Chinese oppression and work towards establishing a free and independent Islamic state. In response, Chinese military and para-military forces quickly unleashed a storm of unprecedented brutality over the course of three days that resulted in the deaths of approximately 3,000 Uighurs.

In the Uighur perspective, the incident at Baren began as a peaceful protest by a small assembly of Uighur students at a mosque focusing on Chinese religious persecution. Which of the accounts is accurate is difficult to determine, however, according to a report published by the US State Department in August 2002, the Baren incident was the genesis of the global ideological influence upon Xinjiang's Uighur population.

The report explains that, upon direct observation of the unrelenting brutality and uncompromising Chinese desire to quickly deal with Uighur resistance in Xinjiang, the instigators of the Baren uprising fled Xinjiang into Pakistan and founded the East Turkestan Islamic Movement (ETIM); an organisation whose primary intent was to conduct 'holy war' in Central Asia against Chinese invaders. Included in the State Department report was evidence of potential links to Al Qaeda, which was identified as a primary weapons supplier for Islamic extremism in Xinjiang.

From 1990 to until September 2001 the Chinese government claims the Uighur resistance has totalled over 200 separate attacks resulting in the deaths of approximately 160 people and injuring over 440. Included in its estimate, over 10,000 Uighurs have travelled to Pakistan for religious schooling and "military training," including over 1,000 having trained at Taliban camps with the intent of returning to Xinjiang to participate in the separatist movement.

With a significant chunk of the populace in Xinjiang adhering to Islam, the region has witnessed widespread ethnic rioting in Urumqi in 2009 and in Hotan and Kashgar in 2011, leaving scores of people dead. In a bid to tighten its grip on the restive region, China has reportedly installed nearly 40,000 surveillance cameras in the capital city of Urumqi. By sentencing 20 people to rigorous imprisonment ranging from 18 months to 15 years in August 2012 on grounds of advocating violence and perpetrating separatism in the Xinjiang region, the Chinese government again issued a stern warning against any activity of dissent, thus slapping further restrictions on religious practices. According to the Xinjiang Daily, a state-controlled local newspaper, the judicial courts in Aksu, Kashgar and Urumqi heard five separate cases and concluded that the guilty had organised and participated in terrorist group activities including making illegal explosives.

The official mouthpiece of the Chinese Communist Party, People's Daily stated that "the forces published books and videos containing violence to incite ethnic hatred and provoke a so-called holy war against the nation... Among these radicals, four people illegally made bombs and trained others to prepare for a terrorist attack under the name of protecting them from Han nationalities." What appears strange is that no further details of any related incidents of bombings or other acts involving violence related to the trial were provided. A statement released by the exiled World Uighur Congress stated that the terrorist charges and verdicts on the "accused" were politically motivated.

According to a latest report released by the Amnesty International in July 2012, Beijing continues to intimidate families seeking information on missing relatives who have revealed human rights abuses during and after the July 2009 protests. The director of Amnesty International for the Asia-Pacific further stated that the general trend toward repression that we see all over China is particularly pronounced in Xinjiang. Moreover, it has been reported that dozens of families have come out publicly with stories of family members disappearing since July 2009.

China's Current Policy in Xinjiang

China does not distinguish between separatism, terrorism, and religious extremism, and furthermore, has a long history if intolerance to any of the above. As such, Chinese law states that that any activity associated with separatism, terrorism, or religious extremism are direct violations of national law, whereby, perpetrators of politically motivated violence have usually been caught quickly and dealt with summarily.

Remarkably though, freedom of religion is protected by Chinese constitution. There are many mosques throughout the region and Uighurs and other Muslims participate in pilgrimages to Mecca. Yet, the Chinese government routinely rounds-up "suspected" Uighur terrorist or secessionist sympathizers under the premise of being "too religious." As an added measure, through the Shanghai Cooperation Organisation and its participating members, China has also enlisted the assistance of the international community to assist in quelling the Uighur separatist activity.

Although the idea of establishing a Muslim state has not held much popularity among the majority of the Uighurs, interest in the idea has only increased with recent Chinese policies that serve to regulate the practice of Islam in the region. In addition to close religious regulation, China closely monitors migrant, immigrant and foreign residents within its borders as a means to control the potential for political or religious dissidence and continues to encourage, and in some cases, subsidize Han migration into Xinjiang: a point of contention that that is not likely to be resolved in the near future.

Analysis

The primary cause for Uighur rebellion has been Chinese misrule over Xinjiang. However, many underlying causes have incited rebellion. These are:

China's Misrule. The Uighurs have endured repeated oppression and unrelenting brutality from the Chinese government. Although very little documentation exists regarding a divergent viewpoint of Uighur intentions in Xinjiang, Chinese authorities remain firm in their belief that Uighur separatism is the primary impetus for terrorism within the province, not Chinese policy. Congruently, increased Chinese subsidized Han-Chinese migration and degraded Uighur political and social status has further aggravated an already fragile environment. Although Chinese policy has enabled expansion of Xinjiang's economy, its failure to invest and develop diverse education and carry out social support programmes has degraded living conditions of the Uighurs. As such, modern-day Uighurs do indeed have a cause for development of an insurgency.

Weakness of the counter-insurgent. The Chinese government is well known for its ability to control/contain insurgencies. The primary focus of Chinese authorities is stability. The political and military will of the government is supported by a large percentage of the populace. Governmental administrative bureaucracy outside of Xinjiang is sound, and the political infrastructure generally supports the population that it serves. Weakness is not something that the Chinese government is willing to exude, nor is it willing to allow terrorist activities to occur on its soil without extreme repercussions by its political, military and para-military wings. Therefore, insurgency within Xinjiang will not precipitate beyond a regional phenomenon.

Geography. The physical geography of Xinjiang provides a multiplicity of challenges for the Uighur people and Chinese government alike. The rugged terrain and vast distances shape a socio-political environment historically aligned with influences external to Chinese authority. Its vast deserts and widely dispersed population centres provide great challenges for effective central governmental control, and a failing regional economy provides an environment ripe for insurgent influence. Combined with large international borders with countries with known or suspected ties to terrorism and mostly isolated from the rest of Central Asia, Xinjiang's geography is a textbook example of insurgent-ready terrain. However, China understands the strategic importance of Xinjiang and has instituted governmental and militaristic control measures to mitigate the impact geography has on its ability to quell potential insurgency within its borders.

External Support. Receipt of external support in Xinjiang has usually been a component of its history. Prior to the establishment of the First and Second East Turkestan Republics, economic and military support from the Soviet Union sustained the Uighur people. Moral, political, technical, and financial support for Uighur jihadists and separatists is coming from sources outside of China. Terrorist attacks conducted by Uighurs, although relatively rare, smack of the sophistication and precision of Al Qaeda-like groups and indicate an upward trend in its influence within the region.

Political Environment. The political environment present in Xinjiang is relatively volatile. The Chinese government continues to propagate Han migration and historical religious persecution. Although normally protected by the constitution, freedom of religion in China remains in the shadow of political control.

Conclusion

From the Chinese perspective, Xinjiang has always been one of China's strategic assets as it has provided security to greater China from the influences and potential security threats from the multitude of nation-states that border Xinjiang. Given its vast expanse and diverse geographic extremes, Xinjiang naturally provides the Chinese government the ability to conduct an economy of force mission within this region. What this produces, however, is an unchecked political license for governmental representatives to rule unjustly over the province that drives the populace to seek refuge in the social, political, and economic security as provided by actors and organisations beyond China's influence.

Historically, Chinese policy has focused on cultural purity; the results of which are illustrated by Sinisisation policies implemented during the Qing dynasty. Sinisisation is still a very real aspect of everyday life in Xinjiang as Chinese sponsored Han-Chinese migration continues to decimate the Uighur ethnic majority in the province. However, coupled with the complexity of global ideological influence within the disenfranchised youth and Chinese exploitation of provincial wealth without reparation, the environment within Xinjiang becomes increasingly more volatile as China presses forward with its current policies. The relative wealth of natural resources present in the deserts and mountains of Xinjiang has led the Chinese government to realize that one solution towards relieving its increasing deficit of energy and raw materials lies within this strategic province. Therefore, what is emerging from this complex situation is an environment of social and political extremes that tears at the fibres of Uighur existence; a struggle that becomes increasingly more difficult to maintain as Chinese aggression becomes increasingly more commonplace.

The broader implications of the Xinjiang problem revolve predominantly around religion. As the plight of Uighurs continues to escalate under the oppressive hand of the Chinese government and as the direct influence of the US-led global war on terrorism efforts subside, radical extremism will become increasingly more influential amongst the secessionist and jihadist Uighur conglomerate. This will embolden radical extremist organisations to seek increasing levels of influence in Central Asia and expand the logistical and ideological footprint from which to operate. What the Chinese have failed to realize is the relative power religion wields within a population and the unifying effect that globalisation has provided towards fulfilling global ideological aspirations. As Chinese military and para-military wings escalate counter-insurgency efforts within the region, radical extremists will move towards the periphery of Chinese influence.

How the situation in Xinjiang will play out in the future is yet to be determined. Yet, even as links to the global jihad, material and ideational, have been formed by Xinjiang's insurgency, it has remained at core an indigenous phenomenon. Xinjiang remains very critical to the economic and strategic ambitions of China, being the largest gas-producing region which also possesses abundant oil and mineral reserves. As many as 122 minerals have been discovered in the province, several of them being the largest reserves nationwide. Besides, Xinjiang is China's gateway to Central Asia, given that it shares a 5,600-kilometre frontier with Mongolia in the northeast, Russia, Kazakhstan, Kyrgyzstan and Tajikistan in the west, and Afghanistan, Pakistan and India in the southwest. The exploitation of mineral resources and the opening up of the region for cotton production brought an influx of the ethnic Han Chinese to the region, thus dramatically altering the province's demography and ethnic balance and resultantly reducing the Uighurs to a minority. The resentment of and resistance to government-sponsored migration of the Han Chinese population, restrictions on the religious and cultural practices, and loss of land have intermittently caused violence to erupt in the region.

The issue of terrorism should not be misconstrued with the contentious issues of human rights violations, ethnic cleansing and suppression of the right to religious and cultural freedom. The fight against terror must never be an excuse to persecute minorities. On the contrary, the ethnic minorities need to be assured that their rights would be safeguarded at all costs by the state apparatus, or else the Muslim Uighurs will continue its chafe against Beijing's rule.

THE ROHINGYA PROBLEM

The Rohingya of Myanmar are among the world's most persecuted and vulnerable ethnic minorities. Due to their racial and religious differences with the Buddhist-majority, they have been officially declared by Myanmar's ruling military regime as non-citizens, making them legally stateless people.

Geography

Arakan (also known as Rakhine) is a state of the Union of Myanmar. Situated on the western coast, it is bordered by Chin State to the north, Magway, Bago, and Ayeyarwady Divisions to the east, the Bay of Bengal to the west, and the Chittagong Division of Bangladesh to the north-west. The Arakan Yoma mountain range, which reaches to 3,063 metres at Victoria Peak, separates Arakan (Rakhine) State from Myanmar proper. Its area is 36,762 square kilometres and its capital is Sittwe (formerly Akyab). Arakan (Rakhine) State consists of four districts: Sittwe, Maungdaw, Kyaukphyu and Thandwe. Combined, these districts contain a total of 17 townships and 1,164 village-tracts.

The official population of Arakan, in 2010, was estimated to be 3.83 million. The state is inhabited primarily by two major ethnic groups, Rakhines and Rohingyas. The majority of the people of the state are Buddhists, with the second-largest group being Muslims. The Muslim Rohingya constitute around 30% of the total population of the State and speak a dialect distinct from Burmese and Bengali. The Rohingya primarily live in the northern part of Arakan.

The state's area is sparsely populated, with very few large urban centres. Sittwe is the largest city in the state and also the centre of trade. Other towns include Maungdaw, Buthidaung, Rathedaung, Mrauk-U, Kyaukpru, Thandwe, and Tounggok. The population is primarily rural, living in the lowland valleys, hills, and forests, or along the seacoast and coastal islands of the Bay of Bengal. Arakan is the country's richest region in terms of oil and natural gas deposits.

Arakan lies at the crossroads of South Asia and Southeast Asia, between Muslim-Hindu Asia and Buddhist Asia, and amidst the Indo-Aryan and Mongoloid races. The Rohingya reflect this geographic reality and are an ethnic mix of Bengalis, Persians, Moghuls, Turks and Pathans and have developed a culture and language which is absolutely unique to the region. During its days as an independent kingdom until 1784, Arakan encompassed at times the Chittagong region of today's Bangladesh. This state survived for 350 years, until the Myanmar Buddhists put an end to Muslim rule by conquering Arakan in 1784.

The Rohingya's dilemma

The name "Rohingya" derives from Rohang/ Roshang, an earlier name for Arakan. Myanmar's military regime, the State Peace and Development Council (SPDC) rejected the status of Rohingya as a native ethnic group in Myanmar. The Buddhist Rakhine people also reject them as an ethnic group indigenous to Arakan. This unmerited view has greatly influenced even the opinions of many of the leaders of Myanmar's democracy movement and other ethnic peoples. Nearly all of them are reluctant to accommodate the Rohingya on democratic principles in their numerous alliances, thus excluding them from the country's political and democratic process.

The Rohingya are not tolerated by the majority in Myanmar because of their minority ethnicity and religion, and also because of their dark skin and South Asian-appearance. Immediately after the Muslims lost political power in 1784, the Buddhists embarked on a policy of oppressing and even physically eliminating them. The country was colonized by the British towards the end of the 1824. The anti-Muslim campaign waged by the Buddhists gained momentum in the twentieth century, culminating in a terrible massacre in Arakan in 1942, which resulted in the deaths of 100,000 Rohingya Muslims. Hundreds of thousands of others were either crippled or forced to flee their land.

Amidst rampant human rights abuses, the Rohingya have for decades borne the brunt of one of the most inhumane policies and campaigns by the Myanmar military government, which denies them citizenship, rendering the majority of Rohingya stateless. The military government has launched several "ethnic cleansing" campaigns, particularly in 1978 and 1991, killing many in the process of expelling Rohingya to Bangladesh. Many also died from starvation and disease.

In Myanmar, the Rohingya face religious repression, extrajudicial killings, forced labour, and expropriation of property, and are often denied employment opportunities and access to education, trade, and restrictions on movement, all exacerbated by the draconian "Myanmar Citizenship Law 1982" that leaves the Rohingya stateless. The government campaign of displacement, denial of culture and identity, restrictions on the right to marry and form a family, killings, rape, torture, and denial of food are a slow-burning genocide.

Almost 14 years have passed since the UN General Assembly recognised the suffering of the Rohingya at the hands of Myanmar's military regime under Resolution 47/144 of 1992. Yet the Rohingya and other Muslims in Myanmar continue to be subjected to a widespread and systematic campaign of persecution and discrimination at home, and the denial of basic protection and fundamental rights in neighbouring countries.

Rakhine state is one of the most backward regions in Myanmar and in terms of human development it is way behind the national average. There is acutely limited access to education, healthcare and public services like electricity. These factors create fierce competition over scarce resources which often lead to conflict along ethnic lines.

Like many other minorities in Myanmar, the Rohingya community of the Rakhine state suffered from persecution by other communities, which the state often failed to address. State policies have often led to widespread destabilisation of the country and given rise to militant ethno-nationalist movements, some of which have been utilised by transnational terrorist networks. Such movements were often ruthlessly crushed, indiscriminately, by the state. Consequently a large number of innocent civilians became victims of separatist movements and law enforcement operations.

Abuses against the Rohingya

Denial of the right to citizenship. Under the 1982 citizenship law, the Rohingya have been denied citizenship in Myanmar, with the authorities classifying them as "Bengali Muslims", effectively leaving them stateless. Some argue that the law, replacing the 1948 Act, was written with the specific intention of removing any Rohingya claim to citizenship that the previous law allowed.

Restrictions on freedom of movement. The Rohingya are subject to strict restrictions of movement. They are virtually confined to their village tracts and need to apply for travel passes, which they must pay for, even to visit a neighbouring village. Since February 2001, Sittwe has remained off-limits for the Rohingya of northern Arakan State. Their lack of mobility has had devastating consequences, limiting their access to markets, employment opportunities, health facilities, and higher education. The travel pass system is also used to prevent those who have overstayed their validity from returning to their village as their names are subsequently deleted from their family list. Rohingya families are required to keep "family lists", issued and maintained by the authorities. If a family member is not present during random population checks by government authorities, they can be deleted from their family's list or fined.

Control of the economy through a monopoly system. Business monopolies are granted in exchange for licences obtained with high bribes. All economic sectors are controlled through a monopoly system based on licences, which totally forbids any free enterprise initiatives. Anyone engaging in an economic activity must either sell his product to the licence holder below market price, or pay him a tax.

As soon as a new income-generating endeavour appears, a new monopoly is installed. The authorities grant or revoke licences annually and always guarantee the monopoly to the highest bidder.

Construction of model villages. The establishment of "model (or '*Natala*') villages" to resettle Buddhists on Muslim land has been ongoing since the 1950s. Such demographic engineering is designed to alter the ethnic composition of the region. The building of model villages reportedly intensified after the formation of the *Nasaka* (Myanmar Border Security Forces) in 1992. There are currently more than 40 such model villages of about 100 houses each in northern Arakan State. These model villages are built largely with the forced labour of Rohingya people. In addition, the villagers have to provide money, rations, generators, cattle, and construction materials for the newcomers. In addition to land confiscation and forced labour, these programmes contribute to the exacerbation of inter-communal tension.

Extortion and arbitrary taxation. Taxes and bribes such as 'paddy taxes', based on land surface quotas rather than yields, sales and trade licenses, fees for the observance of cultural and religious festivals and ceremonies, fees for participation in sporting activities, and extortion for corporate and military infrastructure are particularly prevalent and more diligently extracted in Arakan State, in particular in border areas controlled by the *Nasaka* border authorities. Those not able or willing to pay bribes face arrest and imprisonment. Arbitrary arrest is often employed to extract bribes from Rohingya and other Muslims. Additional extortions unique to the experience of Rohingya and Muslims relate to fees required for travelling and forming a family.

Access to employment. Requirements to apply and pay for travel permits seriously limit abilities to trade or seek employment outside a person's village. Not holding citizenship excludes Rohingyas from public service positions. Arbitrary extortion, taxes, and seizures of land and property stifle entrepreneurship and overwhelm small businesses. Forced labour takes people away from their regular employment, destroying businesses and ruining crops when harvests are impacted.

Forced labour. The Rohingya are employed on forced labour in large infrastructure projects in northern Arakan State. Most work involves the maintenance, security, building, and supplying of military camps and infrastructure projects linked to state-enterprise projects and their international partners. Because it is possible to pay a bribe to authorities for exemption, those most affected are those most at need of earning a regular income. The army continues to be guilty of imposing forced labour on Rohingya villagers and children. Since October 2009, Myanmar's Border Security Force (the *Nasaka*) has been using forced labour of Rohingya villagers in Maungdaw Township to build a Buddhist pagoda in the Baggona Village Tract of *Nasaka* area No. 7.

Confiscation of land and property. Land owned by Rohingya families is confiscated by *Nasaka* personnel, and much formerly arable land has reverted to jungle. There are also settlement programmes moving non-Rohingya peoples onto lands confiscated from Rohingya into "model villages" for retired SPDC officers and their families (built with labour extracted from the Rohingya population). Forced labourers and their communities are often required to provide their own construction materials to the projects where they are compelled to work. The growing presence of the *Nasaka* since its formation in 1992 has increased the amount of confiscations—whether for military camps, or for unique projects such as the leasing back to the original owners. In 2002 the Nasaka began to implement land use policies that expel families living "residentially" on areas previously allocated as agricultural.

Food Security. Myanmar's historical importance as a producer of rice is well-known. While this importance has faded, the country still manages to produce a net surplus of rice. Despite this, those living in northern Arakan State experience food insecurity, with 60% suffering from malnutrition because the regime confiscates, forcibly sells, or prevents rice and other essential commodities from being traded. Villagers are obliged to provide food to supply military troops. Additionally, forced labour prohibits villagers from taking care of their crops, and harvest periods are compromised.

Access to Education. Most Rohingya children do not speak the Burmese language in which public education is taught. Most village tracts have one primary school (initial 4 years), but in remote areas monsoon rains prevent children from attending even this basic level. Rohingya, not allowed to hold citizenship, cannot be employed as teachers. There are considerable gaps in the number and quality of teachers available. Additionally, extreme poverty means that many children need to work to support their families.

Persecution of Political and Community Leaders. Leaders in exile are deeply divided on the solutions to the current situation. Rohingya and other non-Rakhine organisations are excluded from membership in the umbrella organisation, the Arakan

National Council (AN). The actions and policies of the government in Arakan State have successfully pitted the two oppressed communities against each other. Tensions between ethnic Rakhine and Rohingya run high. Religious riots occur sporadically between Buddhist and Muslim, Rohingya and Rakhine groups, with reports often blaming authorities for working to stir up community unrest.

Torture and Physical Extermination. Military operations are carried out in the name of census check almost every year since the 1970s. Serious crimes like arbitrary arrest, torture, summary execution, and mass punishment to entire villagers if some undesirable incident takes place, severe beatings to the point of physical exhaustion, kidnapping and releasing on payment of huge sum of ransom, extortion of different kinds, bribe taking in different ways, forced labour with degrading inhuman treatment, gang-rape and molestation of women have been carried out by security personnel, local Rakhines and goons from *Natala* villages. The military operations also carried out forcible evictions, internal relocations and other human rights abuses are freely carried out in Rohingyas areas. In 1978, Operation *King Dragon* was launched triggering exodus of more than 300,000 Rohingyas from Arakan. Again in 1991-92 in the wake of Operation *Pyithaya* more than 250,000 Rohingas left Arakan. But more awful is the fact that rape of Rohingya women in detention camps or training centres, is an official military strategy to depopulate Rohingyas from their ancestral homes. Arbitrary arrest is used to extract bribes, particularly through falsely accusing and arresting Rohingya in border areas.

Religious and Cultural Freedom. Although Myanmar has no official state religion; the military authorities have since their inception promoted Theravada Buddhism, and marginalised other religions including Islam, the religion of Muslim Rohingyas. Islam is widely practiced mainly in Western parts of Myanmar, and particularly in Arakan State, where it is the main religion of the Rohingya ethnic minority. Successive military regimes have used Buddhism as a political weapon and as a tool to suppress its non-Buddhist opponents. Muslims, including Rohingya, living in Northern Arakan State are forced to pay "fees" to conduct Eid-ul-Adha and Eid-ul-Fitr. Traditions such as praying in open prayer grounds are restricted. Friday sermons are restricted. Times of pilgrimage coincide with further tightening of restrictions and the extraction of maximum bribes.

The right to marry and have a family. Since 1988, the *Nasaka* has imposed marriage restrictions on the Rohingyas. A series of measures has been imposed to control birth and to limit expansion of the Rohingya population. Unlike other peoples of Myanmar, the Rohingya must apply for permission to get married, which is only granted in exchange for high bribes and can take one or two years to obtain. Polygamy has been prohibited, and widows must wait at least three years to remarry. To register their children's birth, parents are charged fees that have significantly increased over the past year. In several areas, women's dignity is greatly offended, as they have to declare their pregnancy to the *Nasaka*. Moreover, building a new house, extending existing dwellings, and even maintenance and repairs also require authorisation, resulting in overcrowded and precarious living conditions. Marriage restriction is also an attempt to reduce and control Rohingya birth rates. All households require a family list, and any changes—births, deaths, marriages, addresses, even cattle acquisitions and sales—must be reported with a required fee. The charge for a birth or death can vary in cost from 1,000 to 8,000 kyat, must be declared within a week, and can also vary in the local authority's arbitrary requirements. Sometimes a scarce item such as fuel is required to be paid in place of the usual fee. The report of a birth to be delivered in person by the recovering mother within one week has also been required.

Genocide of the Rohingya. Since 1992, torture and arbitrary execution, continued detention of a large number of persons for political reasons, the existence of important restrictions on the exercise of fundamental freedoms, and the imposition of oppressive measures have continued, forcing new movements of people and waves of refugees that place a burden on the limited resources of Bangladesh and Myanmar's other neighbours. The campaign of displacement, denial of culture and identity, restrictions on the right to marry and form a family, killings, rape, torture, and denial of food are a slow-burning genocide deliberately inflicted on the Rohingya and Arakan Muslims, conditions of life calculated to bring about its physical destruction in whole or in part.

Solution to the Rohingya Problem

The long-standing Rohingya problem is an issue of religious, ethnic and political persecution. The Rohingya are denied citizenship and have become actual or potential victims of massive atrocities and crimes against humanity. Even though the Rohingya were allowed to exercise their right of franchise and elect their representatives to the Constituent

Assembly, Parliament/*Hluttaw*, and different levels of Councils in all elections held in Myanmar from 1936 to 2010 including the November 2010 elections, the military regime has declared them non-nationals, rendering them "de facto stateless".

The Rohingya are an integral part of Myanmar society. Their problem is a man-made tragedy with political and humanitarian ramifications. It is imperative that the democratic and political process in the country be "all-inclusive" and that the Rohingya be a part of it. They should be able to co-exist as equal residents of Arakan State, and as an ethnic group their rights and privileges should be ensured on par with other national groups of the Union of Myanmar.

Until the military-led government stops committing human rights violations such as land confiscations, discriminatory restrictions on employment and education, access to forest resources and arable land, together with tighter controls of local economies, and arbitrary taxes, the problems of poverty, food insecurity, and crimes against humanity will continue.

Impact on Bangladesh

The effect of the ethnic violence in Myanmar's Rakhine state has created a complex situation for its neighbour Bangladesh which continues to face a mass influx of the displaced Rohingyas from Myanmar. In spite of repeated requests from the UNHCR, several countries and human rights groups, the Bangladesh government remains firm in its stance to curb the new inflow of Myanmar refugees, while reaffirming its commitment to deal with the asylum seekers humanely.

Though the Bangladeshi authority is providing emergency relief like food, water and medicine to the Rohingyas it has refused to give them shelter within its territory. The Bangladesh government's current policy stance stems from the new domestic complexity created by demographic pressure, resource scarcity, and concern for internal security.

For Bangladesh the Rohingya refugee influx is not a new phenomenon, having started in 1978 after a military operation in Rakhine state named *Nagamin Dragon* aimed at suppressing a Rohingya ethnic uprising. Thousands of Rohingyas were killed in the operation and more than 200,000 Rohingyas fled their homes to become refugees in Bangladesh. Another major influx was recorded in 1991, when over 250,800 Rohingyas from Rakhine state took refuge in Bangladesh.

Through UN support and bilateral agreements between Bangladesh and Myanmar some Rohingyas went back to Myanmar, but many more chose to stay in Bangladesh. Two major factors might explain this trend. Firstly, the facilities provided by the UNHCR camps were a pull factor that attracted marginalised Rohingyas. Therefore, even in the absence of state persecution or physical violence, Rohingyas chose to become refugees in Bangladesh. Besides, Bangladesh being a Muslim-majority country made many Rohingyas feel secure from communal violence.

On the other hand structural reasons, such as the lack of opportunities and basic freedoms for the Rohingya community in the Rakhine state, were a push factor that to some extent compelled Rohingyas to get out of Myanmar. While allowing Rohingya refugees to enter, Bangladesh continued to pursue both bilateral and multilateral diplomacy to persuade Myanmar to take the Rohingyas back.

The Rohingya refugees and illegal migrants have changed the demographic profile of southeast Bangladesh. Currently more than 29,000 Rohingya refugees registered with the UNHCR are living in Bangladesh. Another 200,000 Rohingyas are in Bangladesh as illegal migrants. Itself one of the least developed countries, with a population density of more than 900 per square kilometre the refugees add to the mounting pressure on Bangladesh's scarce resources like land and water.

Bangladesh shares a 271-kilometre long border with Myanmar, which cuts through hills, forests, rivers, canals and sea, which make border management difficult. The porous border is rapidly becoming a conduit of transnational crime such as smuggling of arms and drugs and human trafficking.

The Bangladesh-Myanmar border region has been identified by the Bangladesh Department of Narcotics Control as an important point in the infamous Eastern route. There are at least 10 factories in the border area inside Myanmar which produces illegal drugs that are being smuggled into Bangladesh. The Rohingyas are recruited as carriers, intermediaries or traffickers.

The Rohingya militant groups are major security concerns for Bangladesh. Among the groups the Arakan Rohingya Islamic Front (ARIF), Rohingya Solidarity Organisation (RSO), Rohingya National Alliance (RNA) and Arakan Rohingya National Organisation (ARNO) are considered to be the major groups posing a threat to Bangladesh's internal security. The groups have members, supporters and sympathisers within the Rohingya refugees and illegal migrants in Bangladesh. They have evidently collaborated with the Bangladeshi militant groups such as the Harkat ul Jihad al Islami Bangladesh (HuJI-B).

Even though the Bangladesh army has almost totally disarmed the RSO by 2005, other Islamist, ethno-nationalist and narco-terrorist groups, such as the ARNO, RNA, the separatist Democratic Party of Arakan (DPA) and the narco-terrorist Arakan Liberation Party (ALP) are reportedly still operating. The ALP often coerces Bangladeshi local communities into growing poppy in the interior of Chittagong Hill Tracts. The RSO and RNA are in league with the DPA and beyond the control of any government.

'Involuntary' repatriation of the Rohingya was sometimes alleged to be 'forcible' repatriation as well. Even the UNHCR at one point of time had complained that such 'forcible' repatriation were initiated and directed by the government of Bangladesh. The Rohingya suffered no less from the Bangladeshi state even when the host country was providing them refuge. Although welcomed by the local population in the beginning, the Rohingya refugees were quickly brought under the governmental control and policy measures, mainly with the intention of policing them. Such policing is as follows:

- **The policy of encampment.** Officially, there is a total restriction on movement of the camp refugees. No refugee can go out of the camp without the prior approval of camp officials, which is seldom entertained in writing. Anyone caught leaving the camp illegally or more particularly without the unspoken 'unofficial blessing' faces harsh treatment, which includes beating from the police.
- **The policy of unburdening responsibility.** Bangladesh would be interested to see the continued presence of the UNHCR and the refugees, not for any humanitarian reason but for the sake of making profit from their presence. Despite Dhaka's claim that caring for the Rohingya is an economic burden, Bangladesh has borne little of the cost of caring for the refugees. With the exception of $2.5million that Bangladesh spent on relief prior to the UNHCR involvement, UNHCR, donor governments, and NGOs have paid for almost all of the relief operation. If anything, the UNHCR relief operation has led to a net financial gain for the Bangladesh government and its citizens, as it has increased employment.
- **The policy of repatriation.** Despite the unwillingness on the part of the majority of the refugees to return home for reasons of insecurity or lack of improvement in the situation in Myanmar, the UNHCR, with the direct consent of the Bangla Desh authorities, repatriated all but 21,117 refugees by April 1997. Since then, however, repatriation has been put on hold following the failure of Bangla Desh to clear the re-entry of 13,582 refugees out of the remaining total of 21,117. Only 7,535 got permission but those refused re-entry blocked their repatriation. Bangla Desh has declared that no refugees would be allowed to settle in Bangladesh permanently and this position has been renewed time and again, and is still the current policy of the government.

Economic and trade relations between Bangladesh and Myanmar are hampered due to the Rohingya crisis in their border areas. Bilateral trade between Bangladesh and Myanmar is only $ 100 million with Bangladesh exporting only $ 3-4 million. This needs to be definitely enhanced with Bangladesh introducing new items like pharmaceuticals, jute, cosmetics, consumer ware especially white goods, leather products, computer and IT ware into Myanmar. In return the government should consider importing food grains, agro products, timber, gas into Bangladesh. It is expected that the bilateral trade will increase to $ 1 billion by 2013. The statelessness of the Rohingya has come to define the Bangladesh-Myanmar relations and led to the increase of non-traditional security threats to their border areas.

A Sustainable Solution

A sustainable solution of the Rohingya refugee problem depends on how effectively the human development programmes are carried out in the Rakhine state. Years of underdevelopment has turned this scenic border region into a simmering conflict zone which is creating multifaceted security concerns for neighbouring Bangladesh. As Myanmar moves forward in its transition to democracy it is time to help the country develop social cohesion through promoting human development programs and enhancing its capacity for community engagement for building durable peace. This will strengthen Myanmar's democracy from within and create a cohesive and integrated society.

The Rohingya people rarely draw any attention of the local and global policy makers as the most neglected Muslim minority in Myanmar, who subsequently were forced by the military junta to become illegal migrants taking refuge mainly in

Bangladesh since 1978. As a result, bilateral relations between Bangladesh and Myanmar are contentious and continue to seesaw. Current efforts to overcome points of tension and strengthen ties are focusing on a bilateral agreements signed by both the governments.

Although during the Burmese post-independence period, the Rohingya's claim of separate ethnic identity was recognised by the democratic government of Premier U Nu (1948-1958) they became stateless without a legal nationality in 1962 when the new military rule denied citizenship, and many of them have been forced to migrate to Bangladesh, Thailand, India, Pakistan, Saudi Arabia and Malaysia. Even though they were able to migrate to the preferred destinations, their sufferings have not ended upon reaching new shores.

Challenges Ahead

The stateless Rohingya are bound to become more desperate and militant to safeguard their interests. The militancy of the Rohingya Solidarity Organisation and increasing involvement of the stateless and jobless Rohingya in many different criminal activities, including murder, racketeering, bootlegging, prostitution and narcotics is well known. Previously their activities were restricted to Myanmar but with no respite by way of seeking refuge in Bangladesh, it is quite likely that they would expand their operations well beyond the Arakan region and into Bangladesh. In fact, much of the militancy and crimes in refugee camps have been blamed on them. The list of prospective (militant) supporters mainly includes the so-called Islamic political groups, namely the Rabita Al Alam Islami and the Jaamat-e-Islam etc. In the wake of such support for militancy, it is not difficult to see that the state-to-state relationship has entered into a new dimension of transnational forces, not all of which is restricted to the state itself. Two outcomes are particularly worrisome in this connection.

The proliferation of small arms. Just to provide one example, when the Mong Tai Army of Golden Triangle drug lord Khun Sa surrendered to the Yangon authorities it handed over assault rifles, machine guns, rocket launchers, and even SA-7surface-to-air missiles. More worrisome is the fact that despite repeated denials by the Government of Myanmar, accusations of chemical and biological weapons used by the Myanmar military against 'ethnic' insurgents have surfaced from time to time. There is no guarantee that such weapons, small or exotic, would not be used to promote or contain militancy in the Bangladesh-Myanmar border areas

Drug Trade. Myanmar has already earned a reputation of being a 'narco-state.' There has been a sharp increase in illicit drug trafficking, particularly to neighbouring countries and beyond, with frustrated groups acting as 'intermediaries' or traffickers in this super profitable business. There are reports that drug addiction has increased sharply in the Myanmar-Bangladesh border regions, predictably in collusion with the Rohingyas. The growth of a nexus between arms, drugs and frustrated groups is ominous. More importantly the Rohinya as refugees live in deplorable conditions (especially in the refugee camps in Cox's Bazaar, Bangladesh), which in turn could possibly make them easy targets for recruitment by Islamic fundamentalists groups and other criminal networks.

The maritime boundary dispute between Bangladesh and Myanmar has been resolved peacefully by international arbitration on 14 March 2012 with the victory of Bangladesh to stake its claim over the resource-rich Bay of Bengal. This is essentially a precedent for other disputes in resolving crisis between Bangladesh and Myanmar including the Rohingya problem.

Conclusion

Because of the existence of uncertainties and statelessness in Rohingya, the problem has been neglected by the local and international communities for a durable solution though a coercive humanitarian intervention. It is partly due to the pitfalls of local and global governance agendas in the era of globalisation. The Rohingya crisis entails non-traditional security concerns more in line with human security issues, which should be addressed by the local, regional and international communities. The UN, and other key players must, in keeping with their own responsibility to protect, put pressure on Myanmar to stop mass atrocities in the country. International and regional communities can urge the military regime to restore Rohingya's citizenship rights along with their ethnic rights by lifting restrictions on marriage, movement, and education. Myanamar's government should have strong political will to find a permanent solution on the Rohingya refugee problems with Bangladesh.

ECONOMIC DEVELOPMENT STATISTICS

Growth Rate of GDP (% per year)

	2007	*2008*	*2009*	*2010*	*2011*
Afghanistan	13.7	3.6	21.0	8.4	5.7
Bangladesh	6.4	6.2	5.7	6.1	6.7
Bhutan	12.6	10.8	5.7	9.3	8.3
India	9.3	6.7	8.4	8.4	6.9
Maldives	10.6	12.2	-4.7	5.7	7.5
Nepal	2.8	5.8	3.8	4.0	3.5
Pakistan	6.8	3.7	1.7	3.8	2.4
Sri Lanka	6.8	6.0	3.5	8.0	8.3
China	14.2	9.6	9.2	10.4	9.2
Indonesia	6.3	6.0	4.6	6.2	6.5
Malaysia	6.5	4.8	-1.6	7.2	5.1
Myanmar	5.5	3.6	5.1	5.3	5.5
Singapore	8.9	1.7	-1.0	14.8	4.9
Thailand	5.0	2.5	-2.3	7.8	0.1

Growth Rate of Value Added in Agriculture (% per year)

	2007	*2008*	*2009*	*2010*	*2011*
Afghanistan	14.7	-14.9	44.6	-6.4	-15.8
Bangladesh	4.6	3.2	4.1	5.2	5.0
Bhutan	1.7	0.8	1.7	1.5	0.6
India	5.8	0.1	1.0	7.0	2.5
Maldives	-11.9	-3.4	-7.4	-6.9	-1.1
Nepal	1.0	5.8	3.0	1.3	4.1
Pakistan	4.1	1.0	4.0	0.6	1.2
Sri Lanka	3.4	7.5	3.2	7.0	2.5
China	3.7	5.4	4.2	4.3	4.5
Indonesia	3.5	4.8	4.0	3.0	3.0
Malaysia	1.3	4.3	0.6	2.1	5.6
Myanmar	-	-	-	-	-
Singapore	0.6	-4.3	-1.8	-3.1	3.0
Thailand	1.2	4.2	1.3	-2.3	3.8

Growth Rate of per Capita GDP (% per year)

	2007	*2008*	*2009*	*2010*	*2011*
Afghanistan	11.9	1.5	18.6	6.3	3.7
Bangladesh	5.1	4.8	4.4	4.7	5.4
Bhutan	10.5	8.7	3.8	7.4	6.3
India	7.8	5.2	6.9	6.9	5.5
Maldives	9.0	10.5	-6.2	4.0	5.7
Nepal	0.8	3.4	1.5	1.4	1.3
Pakistan	4.9	1.9	0.0	-2.0	0.3
Sri Lanka	6.1	4.9	2.4	6.9	7.2
China	13.6	9.0	8.6	9.9	8.7
Indonesia	5.0	4.7	3.3	3.4	3.6
Malaysia	5.1	3.5	-2.9	5.9	3.9
Myanmar	3.4	1.6	3.0	3.2	3.4
Singapore	4.4	-3.6	-3.9	12.7	2.7
Thailand	4.3	1.6	-3.1	7.2	-0.4

Growth Rate of Value Added in Industry (% per year)

	2007	*2008*	*2009*	*2010*	*2011*
Afghanistan	7.6	5.7	6.1	6.3	6.6
Bangladesh	8.4	6.8	6.5	6.5	8.2
Bhutan	25.4	20.4	4.8	8.2	8.4
India	9.7	4.4	8.4	7.2	3.9
Maldives	22.5	9.5	-26.2	5.2	5.9
Nepal	3.9	1.7	-1.4	3.3	1.4
Pakistan	8.8	1.4	-0.1	8.3	-0.1
Sri Lanka	7.6	5.9	4.2	8.4	9.6
China	15.1	9.9	9.9	12.3	10.6
Indonesia	4.7	3.7	3.6	4.9	5.3
Malaysia	3.0	0.7	-7.6	8.6	2.5
Myanmar	-	-	-	-	-
Singapore	6.8	-1.5	-1.4	24.8	6.8
Thailand	5.8	3.2	-5.0	12.8	-3.9

Inflation (% per year)

	2007	*2008*	*2009*	*2010*	*2011*
Afghanistan	13.0	26.8	-12.2	7.7	10.5
Bangladesh	7.2	9.9	6.7	7.3	8.8
Bhutan	5.2	6.4	7.1	4.8	8.6
India	4.7	8.1	3.8	9.6	9.0
Maldives	7.4	12.3	4.0	4.7	9.7
Nepal	6.4	7.7	12.6	9.6	9.6
Pakistan	7.8	12.0	17.0	10.1	13.7
Sri Lanka	15.8	-20.8	3.5	6.2	6.7
China	4.8	5.9	-0.7	3.3	5.4
Indonesia	6.4	9.8	4.8	5.1	5.4
Malaysia	2.0	5.4	0.6	1.7	3.2
Myanmar	32.9	22.5	8.2	7.3	4.2
Singapore	2.1	6.6	0.6	2.8	5.2
Thailand	2.2	5.4	-0.9	3.3	3.8

Growth Rate of Value Added in Services (% per year)

	2007	*2008*	*2009*	*2010*	*2011*
Afghanistan	19.3	13.8	17.2	18.1	15.0
Bangladesh	6.9	6.5	6.3	6.5	6.6
Bhutan	7.1	5.3	9.1	12.7	9.4
India	10.3	10.0	10.5	9.3	9.4
Maldives	9.2	13.5	0.5	6.3	8.0
Nepal	4.5	7.3	6.0	6.0	3.6
Pakistan	7.0	6.0	1.7	2.9	4.1
Sri Lanka	7.1	5.6	3.3	8.0	8.8
China	16.0	10.4	9.6	9.8	8.9
Indonesia	9.0	8.7	5.8	8.4	8.5
Malaysia	10.2	7.6	3.1	6.8	6.8
Myanmar	-	-	-	-	-
Singapore	9.1	4.4	-1.0	10.7	4.3
Thailand	5.0	1.3	-0.2	4.6	3.8

Source: Asian Development Bank; Asian Development Outlook, 2012; "Confronting Rising Inequality in Asia".

Sector Share 2010, %

	Agriculture	*Industry*	*Services*	*Per capita GNP, US$,*
Afghanistan	23.3	26.0	50.7	410
Bangladesh	20.3	29.9	49.8	700
Bhutan	15.6	45.7	38.8	1,870
India	14.5	27.8	57.7	1,330
Maldives	3.2	14.8	82.0	5,750
Nepal	34.7	15.3	50.0	440
Pakistan	21.2	26.4	52.4	1,050
Sri Lanka	11.9	28.7	59.3	2,240
China	8.2	59.5	32.3	4,270
Indonesia	13.2	41.1	45.7	2,500
Malaysia	7.1	36.9	56.0	7,760
Myanmar	-	-	-	-
Singapore	0.0	32.9	67.0	40,070
Thailand	8.3	48.7	43.0	4,150

External Debt Outstanding (US$ million)

	2007	*2008*	*2009*	*2010*	*2011*
Afghanistan	2,001	2,069	1,150	1,272	1,454
Bangladesh	19,355	20,266	20,859	20,336	21,451
Bhutan	725	820	795	874	1,312
India	172,360	224,500	261,014	306,438	326,601
Maldives	828	879	934	963	-
Nepal	3,341	3,197	3,495	3,442	3,655
Pakistan	40,322	46,161	52,331	57,363	61,844
Sri Lanka	14,252	15,077	-	-	-
China	373,773	378,245	428,442	548,900	560,000
Indonesia	141,180	155,080	172,871	202,413	224,757
Malaysia	56,681	66,936	68,316	73,652	80,968
Myanmar	7,567	8,103	8,602	11,240	11,841
Singapore	340,996	420,461	412,504	498,749	641,445
Thailand	74,415	76,102	75,306	100,561	115,605

Gross International Reserves (US$ million)

	2007	*2008*	*2009*	*2010*	*2011*
Afghanistan	2,784	3,591	4,209	5,321	6,121
Bangladesh	5,077	6,149	7,471	10,750	10,912
Bhutan	608	589	704	792	906
India	299,230	251,985	278,193	301,838	295,140
Maldives	308	241	261	350	335
Nepal	1,999	2,477	2,872	2,759	3,003
Pakistan	13,393	8,731	9,529	13,112	15,662
Sri Lanka	3,508	1,753	5,097	6,610	5,958
China	1,530,280	1,949,260	2,416,040	2,866,080	3,200,000
Indonesia	56,920	51,639	66,105	96,207	110,123
Malaysia	101,532	91,648	96,744	106,590	138,408
Myanmar	3,638	4,042	5,233	6,070	7,903
Singapore	162,957	174,196	187,809	225,754	237,737
Thailand	87,455	111,008	138,418	172,129	175,124

Current Account Balance (% of GDP)

	2007	*2008*	*2009*	*2010*	*2011*
Afghanistan	1.3	0.9	-2.8	1.7	0.1
Bangladesh	1.4	0.9	2.7	3.7	0.9
Bhutan	14.2	-2.2	-1.1	-9.9	-20.6
India	-1.3	-2.4	-2.8	-2.7	-3.6
Maldives	-28.4	-34.2	-21.6	-22.3	-31.9
Nepal	-0.1	2.9	4.2	-2.7	-0.9
Pakistan	-4.8	-8.5	-5.7	-2.2	0.1
Sri Lanka	-4.3	-9.5	-0.5	-2.2	-7.3
China	10.1	9.1	5.2	5.2	2.8
Indonesia	2.4	0.0	2.0	0.7	0.2
Malaysia	15.9	17.7	16.5	11.5	11.5
Myanmar	0.6	-2.2	-1.3	-0.9	-2.7
Singapore	25.8	13.9	16.2	24.4	21.9
Thailand	6.3	0.5	8.3	4.2	3.4

Trade Balance (US$ million)

	2007	*2008*	*2009*	*2010*	*2011*
Afghanistan	-5,968	-6,480	-6,355	-6,303	-6,266
Bangladesh	-3,458	-5,330	-4,710	-5,155	-7,328
Bhutan	47	-72	-90	-299	-519
India	-91,467	-119,519	-118,202	-130,593	-169,449
Maldives	-737	-890	-682	-798	-976
Nepal	-1,837	-2,410	-2,733	-4,139	-4,422
Pakistan	-9,711	-14,970	-12,627	-11,536	-10,516
Sri Lanka	-3,656	-5,980	-3,122	-4,881	-9,743
China	315,400	360,700	249,500	254,200	243,800
Indonesia	32,754	22,906	30,932	30,627	35,347
Malaysia	37,669	51,540	40,216	41,826	48,831
Myanmar	924	507	703	363	-238
Singapore	57,062	41,666	47,270	63,097	67,446
Thailand	26,640	17,348	32,620	31,759	23,502

Growth Rate of Merchandise Exports (% per year)

	2007	*2008*	*2009*	*2010*	*2011*
Afghanistan	1.3	34.4	2.1	12.7	2.5
Bangladesh	15.8	17.4	10.1	4.2	41.7
Bhutan	83.7	4.4	-13.8	5.5	22.2
India	28.9	13.7	-3.5	37.3	21.0
Maldives	1.2	45.2	-49.0	6.5	-4.3
Nepal	2.6	9.3	-4.7	-6.3	11.7
Pakistan	4.4	18.2	-6.4	2.9	28.9
Sri Lanka	11.0	6.2	-12.7	21.0	22.4
China	25.8	17.6	-16.1	31.4	20.4
Indonesia	14.0	18.3	-14.3	32.1	27.5
Malaysia	9.5	13.1	-21.1	26.4	14.5
Myanmar	23.9	12.3	-1.4	25.8	10.1
Singapore	11.2	13.5	-18.7	28.7	15.7
Thailand	18.2	15.9	-13.9	28.4	16.4

Growth Rate of Merchandise Imports (% per year)

	2007	*2008*	*2009*	*2010*	*2011*
Afghanistan	15.7	14.7	-0.8	3.0	0.4
Bangladesh	16.6	25.6	4.2	5.4	41.8
Bhutan	21.1	27.4	-9.6	39.0	40.5
India	35.1	19.8	-2.6	26.7	24.0
Maldives	18.3	26.6	-30.3	14.9	17.4
Nepal	13.9	24.1	8.3	37.0	7.7
Pakistan	8.0	31.2	-10.3	-1.7	14.9
Sri Lanka	10.2	24.7	-27.6	31.8	50.4
China	20.3	18.7	-11.1	39.1	25.1
Indonesia	15.4	36.9	-24.0	43.7	30.3
Malaysia	12.1	6.7	-20.8	34.1	13.9
Myanmar	88.0	25.6	1.9	15.8	23.8
Singapore	10.6	22.5	-23.0	27.7	17.5
Thailand	9.1	26.7	-25.1	37.0	24.7

DEFENCE STATISTICS

Gross Domestic Product

	GDP ($bn)				Rank	
	1990	2000	2011	2011 annual growth (%)	1990	2011
United States	5,750.8	9,898.8	15,094.0	4.5%	1	1
China	356.9	1,198.5	7,298.1	23.0%	5	2
Japan	3,103.7	4,731.2	5,867.2	6.9%	2	3
Russia	516.8	259.7	1,857.0	24.8%	4	4
India	326.6	474.7	1,847.9	9.7%	6	5
Canada	582.7	724.9	1,736.0	10.0%	3	6
Australia	314.0	416.9	1,371.7	21.2%	7	7
South Korea	263.8	553.4	1,116.0	10.0%	8	8
Taiwan	150.8	386.0	885.3	7.7%	9	9
Indonesia	114.4	165.0	846.8	19.6%	10	10
Thailand	85.3	122.7	345.6	8.4%	11	11
Malaysia	44.0	93.8	278.6	17.1%	14	12
Hong Kong	76.9	169.1	243.6	8.5%	12	13
Singapore	36.1	95.9	239.7	12.4%	15	14
Philippines	44.3	81.0	224.7	12.6%	13	15
World	21,976.0	32,329.0	69,971.0	10.8%	N/A	N/A

Source: World Bank, "World Development Indicators," various years.

GDP Growth and Inflation Rates

	Average real GDP growth (%)			Average inflation rate (%)		
	2001–5	2006–10	2011	2001–5	2006–10	2011
United States	2.8%	1.2%	1.5%	2.4%	2.1%	3.0%
China	8.7%	10.2%	9.2%	1.8%	3.6%	5.4%
Japan	1.5%	0.4%	-0.5%	-0.4%	-0.1%	0.4%
Russia	6.0%	3.2%	4.3%	14.3%	10.3%	8.9%
India	6.1%	8.1%	7.8%	4.5%	8.6%	6.8%
Canada	2.4%	1.3%	2.2%	2.4%	1.7%	2.8%
Australia	2.9%	2.8%	1.8%	3.0%	3.0%	3.4%
South Korea	4.2%	3.7%	3.6%	3.4%	3.0%	4.0%
Taiwan	2.9%	3.3%	5.2%	0.8%	1.7%	1.6%
Indonesia	4.3%	5.7%	6.4%	9.4%	7.9%	5.7%
Thailand	4.7%	5.5%	0.1%	2.3%	3.0%	3.8%
Malaysia	4.4%	4.4%	5.2%	1.8%	2.7%	3.2%
Hong Kong	3.0%	3.5%	5.0%	-0.1%	2.1%	5.3%
Singapore	3.1%	5.8%	4.9%	0.9%	2.6%	5.2%
Philippines	4.6%	4.9%	3.7%	5.1%	5.1%	5.3%

Source: CIA, The World Factbook, 1990–2012.

Flow of Foreign Direct Investment

	FDI inflows ($bn)			*FDI outflows ($bn)*		
	2000–2010 annual avg.	*2010*	*2009–10 growth (%)*	*2000–2010 annual avg.*	*2010*	*2009–10 growth (%)*
United States	173.5	228.2	49.3%	199.2	328.9	16.3%
China	72.0	105.7	11.3%	22.3	68.0	20.2%
Hong Kong	41.9	68.9	31.5%	42.1	76.1	18.8%
Russia	25.6	41.2	12.8%	24.1	51.7	18.3%
Singapore	18.2	38.6	152.9%	12.0	19.7	6.9%
Australia	21.9	32.5	26.3%	12.7	26.4	63.5%
India	15.9	24.6	-30.9%	8.1	14.6	-5.8%
Canada	38.9	23.4	9.4%	42.6	38.6	-7.3%
Indonesia	3.6	13.3	172.8%	2.3	2.7	18.4%
Kazakhstan	6.4	10.0	-27.7%	1.3	7.8	150.3%
Malaysia	4.6	9.1	536.6%	5.8	13.4	68.5%
South Korea	5.8	6.9	-8.4%	10.2	19.2	11.8%
Thailand	5.4	5.8	16.8%	1.7	5.1	24.4%
Pakistan	2.3	2.0	-13.8%	0.0	0.0	-35.2%
New Zealand	2.2	0.6	143.4%	0.4	0.6	201.2%
World	1,156.8	1,243.7	4.9%	1,163.7	1,323.3	13%

Source: UN Conference on Trade and Development, World Investment Report, 2011.

Energy Consumption

	Energy consumption (quadrillion Btu)				*Rank*	
	1990	*2000*	*2011*	*2010–11 growth (%)*	*1990*	*2011*
China	27.2	38.4	103.7	7.4%	2	1
United States	78.0	91.7	90.1	-0.7%	1	2
Russia	–	25.2	27.2	-0.7%	–	3
India	7.7	12.7	22.2	6.7%	5	4
Japan	17.2	20.4	17.8	-10.6%	3	5
Canada	9.8	11.5	13.1	4.0%	4	6
South Korea	3.6	7.6	10.4	3.0%	6	7
Indonesia	2.1	3.8	5.9	5.4%	8	8
Australia	3.5	4.4	4.9	4.3%	7	9
Taiwan	2.0	3.8	4.4	0.0%	9	10
Thailand	1.2	2.4	4.2	-2.3%	10	11
Malaysia	1.0	1.8	2.7	8.0%	12	12
Pakistan	1.1	1.6	2.7	0.0%	11	13
Uzbekistan	–	2.0	2.1	5.0%	–	14
Kazakhstan	–	1.6	2.0	-31.0%	–	15
World	322.7	369.4	487.1	2.2%	N/A	N/A

Note: Dash indicates that no data is available.
Source: BP plc, "BP Statistical Review of World Energy," 2012.

Energy Consumption by Fuel Type

	2011 energy consumption by fuel type (%)					
	Oil (%)	*Gas (%)*	*Coal (%)*	*Nuclear (%)*	*Hydro (%)*	*Renewables (%)*
China	17.7	4.5	70.4	0.7	6.0	0.7
United States	36.7	27.6	22.2	8.3	3.3	2.0
Russia	19.8	55.7	13.3	5.7	5.4	0.1
India	29.0	9.4	52.9	1.3	5.3	1.7
Japan	42.2	19.9	24.6	7.7	4.0	1.6
Canada	31.2	28.6	6.6	6.5	25.8	1.3
South Korea	40.3	15.9	30.2	12.9	0.5	0.2
Indonesia	43.5	23.0	29.7	–	2.4	1.4
Australia	37.2	18.7	40.4	–	2.0	1.8
Taiwan	38.9	12.7	37.9	8.6	0.8	1.1
Thailand	44.2	39.5	13.1	–	1.7	1.5
Kazakhstan	20.2	16.4	59.8	–	3.6	<
Pakistan	30.2	52.1	6.2	1.2	10.2	<
Malaysia	38.9	37.1	21.7	–	2.5	<
Uzbekistan	8.4	84.7	2.5	–	4.4	–

Note: Due to rounding, some totals may not add up to exactly 100%. Dash indicates that no data is available. Angle bracket indicates that value is less than 0.05%.

Source: BP plc, "BP Statistical Review of World Energy," 2012.

Total Defence Expenditure

	Expenditure ($bn)				*Rank*	
	1990	*2000*	*2010*	*2009–10 growth (%)*	*1990*	*2010*
United States	293.0	300.5	693.6	4.9%	1	1
China	11.3	42.0	178.0	7.1%	3	2
Russia	–	7.3	65.2	14.0%	–	3
Japan	28.7	45.6	54.4	6.1%	2	4
India	10.1	14.7	30.9	-23.9%	6	5
South Korea	10.6	12.8	25.1	10.7%	4	6
Australia	7.3	7.1	23.6	17.3%	8	7
Canada	10.3	11.5	20.2	3.0%	5	8
Taiwan	8.7	8.9	9.0	-5.7%	7	9
Singapore	1.7	4.8	8.1	3.7%	11	10
Indonesia	1.6	1.5	7.2	33.1%	12	11
Malaysia	1.7	2.8	3.7	-6.8%	10	12
Pakistan	2.9	3.7	5.6	32.1%	9	13
Vietnam	–	1.0	2.6	18.2%	–	14
Myanmar	0.9	2.1	–	–	13	–
World	954.0	811.4	1,514.6	4.3%	N/A	N/A

Note: Estimates for China vary widely. Dash indicates that no data is available.

Source: International Institute for Strategic Studies, The Military Balance, various editions; SASI Group and Mark Newman, "Military Spending 1990," 2007; and data for China is based on various sources.

Armed Forces

	Armed forces (th)				*Rank*	
	1990	*2000*	*2012*	*2011–12 change (th)*	*1990*	*2011*
China	3,030	2,470	2,285	0	2	1
United States	2,118	1,366	1,325	5	3	2
India	1,262	1,303	1,190	0	4	3
North Korea	1,111	1,082	1,159	0	5	4
Russia	3,988	1,004	956	-90	1	5
South Korea	750	683	655	0	7	6
Pakistan	550	612	642	25	8	7
Vietnam	1,052	484	482	27	6	8
Myanmar	230	344	406	0	13	9
Thailand	283	301	306	0	10	10
Indonesia	283	297	302	0	10	11
Taiwan	370	370	290	0	9	12
Japan	249	237	248	0	12	13
Sri Lanka	65	–	161	0	14	14
Bangladesh	103	137	157	0	15	15
World	26,605	22,237	20,268	-1,969	N/A	N/A

Note: Active duty and military personnel only. Data value for Russia in 1990 includes all territories of the Soviet Union. Dash indicates that no data is available.
Source: International Institute of Strategic Studies, The Military Balance, various editions.

Nuclear Weapons

	Nuclear weapons possession				*Total inventory*	
	1990	*1995*	*2000*	*2012*	*2011*	*2012*
Russia	v	v	v	v	11,000	10,492
United States	v	v	v	v	8,500	8,613
China	v	v	v	v	240	240
India	v	v	v	v	80–100	<100
Pakistan	–	–	v	v	90–110	90–110
North Korea	?	?	?	v	<10	<12

Note: Table shows confirmed (v) and unknown (?) possession of nuclear weapons. Dash indicates that no data is available. Total inventory includes both active and stockpiled arms.
Source: "Status of World Nuclear Forces," Federation of American Scientists, 2011–12.

India successfully tested its Agni-5 long-range ballistic missile in April 2012, extending its nuclear deterrent reach to 3,100 miles. The test marked India's entry into the small club of nations with such a capability and brings Beijing within range of India's nuclear forces.

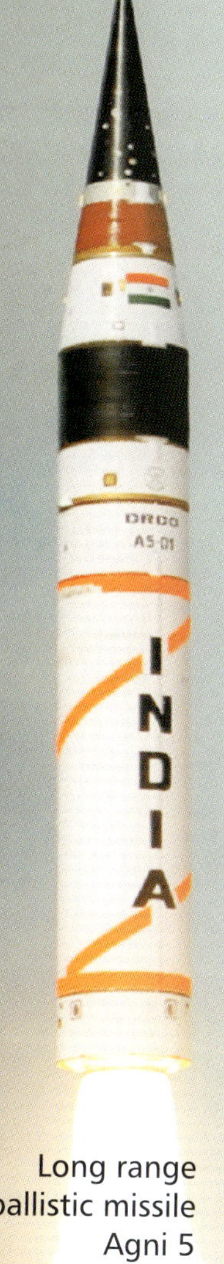

Long range ballistic missile Agni 5

DRDO

Driving Self Reliance and Innovation

The maiden flight of Agni 5, India's own long range ballistic missile took India to the elite club of five top nations in the world. Developed by the Defence Research & Development Organisation (DRDO), the R&D wing of Ministry of Defence that strives to enhance self-reliance in Defence Systems, was a major milestone in the journey of technological advancements of a young nation with glorious past of military and technological might. (End of the era of Tipu Sultans innovative rockets that gave British commanders sleepless nights, was followed by nearly 150 years of dark period during which Indian industry as well as innovativeness, creativity and industrial skill of natives were either mercilessly crushed, or in some cases, were exploited solely to the advantage of colonial rulers to fulfil their commercial and strategic interests.) Today, world-class weapon systems and equipment are designed, developed and led to production by DRDO in accordance with expressed needs and the qualitative requirements of the three services. DRDO's pursuit of self reliance has led to India's present proud position among the elite nations in the world, with India being:

- **One of the 4 countries to have multi-level Strategic Deterrence capabilities**
- **One of the 5 countries to have its own Ballistic Missile Defence (BMD) program**
- **One of the 6 countries to have developed its own Main Battle Tank**
- **One of the 7 countries to have an indigenous 4th gen Combat Aircraft**
- **One of select few countries to have its own Electronic Warfare & multi-range Radar program**

The DRDO is a one-of-its-kind organisation with its fifty two laboratories providing technology solutions to make India self-reliant in defence preparedness. The areas of research and development (R&D) cover the entire spectrum of essential specifics of a modern armed force: strategic systems, tactical battlefield systems, advanced sensors, materials, with special emphasis on the human, physiological and psychological needs of soldiers, the "men behind the machines". DRDO works in various areas of military

Light Combat Aircraft (LCA) Tejas, in flight with weapon systems

technology which include aeronautics, armaments, combat vehicles, electronics & instrumentation, advanced computing, cyber security, missiles, materials, naval systems, simulation and soldier support systems. DRDO strives to meet the cutting edge weapons technology requirements of our armed forces. It also uses the spin-offs from such technologies to provide benefits to civilian society.

In terms of tangible output, the production value of major DRDO systems for which services has placed orders during the last decade alone stands at over ₹1,50,000 crores. Its approximately 7,700 scientists, 10,400 technical personnel and 10,000 other employees have led to the production of an exhaustive range of world-class weapon systems and equipment that covers every aspect of modern warfare; as well as the well-being and combat worthiness of Armed Forces personnel.

The production value of the DRDO products is certainly not the only measure of the impact of these developments on the nation's defence capabilities. Many of these systems could not be imported or developed jointly with any other country in the era of embargoes and technology denials. The developed countries, with advanced military technologies, often offer licensed production of those systems that are obsolete for them, with barely any technology transfer. Successful indigenous development and production of strategic systems and platforms such as Agni and Prithvi series of missiles, Surface to Air Missile Akash, nuclear powered submarine–Arihant, light combat aircraft–Tejas, Unmanned Aerial Vehicles, main battle tank Arjun, state-of-the-art sonar systems, Radars and Electronic Warfare systems, etc. have given a quantum jump to India's military might. This has generated effective deterrence and has mark India's entry into the elite club of technology savvy countries. Other benefits are the growing capabilities in a wide range of militarily critical and advanced technologies, efforts in ensuring continuity of supply of components, spares in the face of changing international scenarios, developing a self-reliant Defence R&D base with spin-offs into the civil industry. In the processes of development of cutting edge defence technologies, weapon systems and equipment by DRDO, especially in an environment of technology denial regimes and inadequate industrial infrastructure, an echo system conducive to indigenous design and development of advanced military systems has been created.

Most infrastructural facilities created by DRDO are one of their kind in the country and are national assets. They include Integrated Instrumented Flight Test Ranges, Structural Dynamics and Vibration Test Facilities, Propulsion and Ballistics Test

AEW&C (Airborne Early Warning and Control System

Main Battle Tank Arjun Mk-II in action undergoing trials in desert.

facilities, EMI/EMC Test rigs, Lightning Test Facilities, Antennae Test Range, Instrumentation and Acoustics Research Ship, Underwater Weapon Test Ranges, Test Tracks for land systems for varied wheeled and tracked vehicles.

"*Balasya Mulam Vigyanam*", i.e., "The Source of Strength is Science" is the tag line of DRDO. It is science that drives the nation in peace and war. The DRDO has a firm determination to make the nation resilient and self-reliant in terms of science and technology, especially in the military sphere.

DRDO's Vision and Mission

Make India prosperous by establishing a world-class science and technology base to provide our Defence Services a decisive edge by equipping them with internationally competitive systems and solutions.

- Design, develop to produce state-of-the-art sensors, weapon systems, platforms and allied equipment for our Defence Services.
- Provide technological solutions to the Defence Services to optimise combat effectiveness to promote well-being of the troops.
- Develop infrastructure and committed quality manpower by building a strong technology base.

Heavy weight torpedo 'Varunastra' undergoing trials

CHINA AT WAR
Xiaobing Li

978-81-8274-611-4 • Rs. 1900

CHINA'S MILITARY AND INDIA
Srikanth Kondapalli

978-81-8274-689-3 • Rs. 795

CHINA RESTORED
Eric C. Anderson

978-81-8274-621-3 • Rs. 995

CHINA'S DISCURSIVE NATIONALISM
Bhavna Singh

978-81-8274-651-0 • Rs. 995

AFGHANISTAN IN TRANSITION
Beyond 2014?
Dr. Shanthie Mariet D'Souza

978-81-8274-674-9 • Rs. 795

GLOBAL SECURITY WATCH PAKISTAN
Syed Farooq Hasnat

978-81-8274-616-9 • Rs. 695

MILITANCY IN PAKISTAN & AFGHANISTAN
A Brief History of Causes and Effects
S.V. Salahuddin

978-81-8274-654-1 • Rs. 795

INDIA'S NEIGHBOURHOOD
Rumel Dahiya, Askok K Behuria

978-81-8274-687-9 • Rs. 995

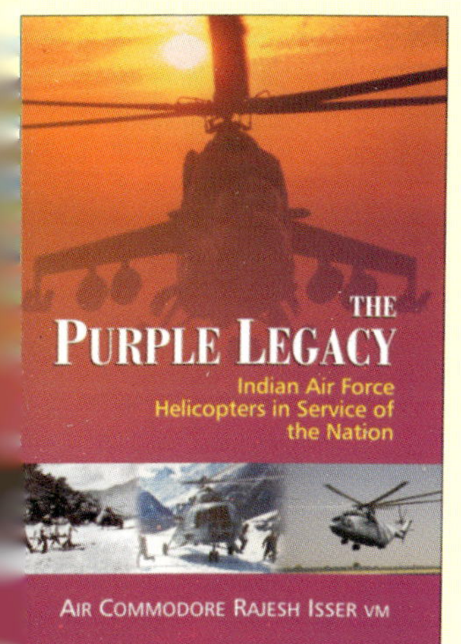

THE PURPLE LEGACY
ndian Air Force Helicopters
n Service of the Nation
ir Commodore Rajesh Isser VM

78-81-8274-688-6 • Rs. 795

LIVING WITH INSURGENCY
Dilip Banerjee, Antara Mitra

978-81-8274-505-0 • Rs. 3500

GRAND STRATEGY FOR INDIA
Krishnappa Venkatshamy
Princy George

978-81-8274-657-2 • Rs. 995

BRAHMAND WORLD UPDATE 2013

978-81-8274-518-6 • Rs. 4500